HARDPRESS.NET
HOME OF HARD-TO-FIND BOOKS

The Calcutta Review
by Unknown

Per. gen. d. 12

4.

THE

CALCUTTA REVIEW.

VOL. IV.

JULY—DECEMBER, 1845.

" No man, who hath tasted learning, but will confess the many ways of profiting by those, who not contented with stale receipts, are able to manage and set forth new positions to the world : and were they but as the dust and cinders of our feet, so long, as in that notion, they may yet serve to polish and brighten the armoury of truth: even for that respect they were not utterly to be cast away."—MILTON.

CALCUTTA :

PRINTED FOR THE PROPRIETOR, BY SANDERS AND CONES, No. 4, TANK-SQUARE, AND SOLD BY ALL THE BOOKSELLERS.

1845.

Art. VII.—THE MAHRATTA HISTORY AND EMPIRE.—RECENT OPERATIONS IN THE KOLAPOOR AND SAWUNT-WAREE COUNTRIES.

Miscellaneous Critical Notices.

CONTENTS.

CONTENTS

OF

No. VIII.—Vol. IV.

ART. II.—THE CAPE OF GOOD HOPE.

ART. III.—THE URDU LANGUAGE AND LITERATURE.

MISCELLANEOUS NOTICES.

Journal of a Residence in Great Britain, by Jehungeer Nowrajee and Hirjeebhoy Merwanjee, of Bombay, Naval Architects. London, 1841.

The main object in the establishment of our journal was, as our readers have been often reminded, the examination of works having more immediate reference to India, and of measures designed to elevate the condition of its numerous inhabitants. But though these are the avowed limits within which we proposed to confine the authority of our literary tribunal, we still reserved to ourselves the privilege of exercising, whenever such a step appeared expedient, a control over cases situate beyond the sphere of our regulated jurisdiction. Our proceedings, in the present instance, may therefore fairly be considered as an exercise of this prerogative. The volume before us, though the conjoint production of two natives of India, cannot, as of right, demand admittance to our file for the adjudication of its merits. Its character, if we may use the expression, is European rather than Oriental. Its pages are not dedicated to Indian topics: Neither can they lay claim, however partial we may be disposed to be in our judgment, to originality of thought, profound or curious speculation, graphic or animated descriptions of external nature, or forcibly drawn delineations of the peculiarities that distinguish us as a nation. Such perfections, which belong to the regular tourist, the most enthusiastic educationist could scarcely expect in the present journal. It contains simply the observations, dressed in homely language, of two intelligent gentlemen belonging to a class of our subjects who have earned celebrity for their liberality and mercantile enterprize, on some of the principal institutions, naval arsenals, edifices, scientific improvements, and amusements, more especially those that are to be seen in, and about, the vicinity of the great metropolis. As a pure emanation, however, of the native mind amid scenes to which it was a stranger, and as an earnest of that abundant literary harvest which the surrounding educational movements, and the progressive intelligence of the age fully warrant us in expecting, the work under review, on account of these circumstances, no less than from novelty and its intrinsic merit, is entitled to every attention. We are not aware that its contents are generally known by those for whom the publication was more immediately intended. We shall therefore, by means of a few extracts, endeavour to give a wider circulation to the " impressions" of our authors. But in doing so we must candidly own that we are not catering for our more advanced and intelligent readers, who, if they derive any pleasure, cannot reasonably expect instruction from such impressions which, it may be well to remark, were composed during intervals snatched from more serious avocations, and were intended, not for the purpose of establishing a literary reputation, but for the information of their countrymen, and of the natives of India generally, who may, now that steam has made the

b

attempt comparatively easy, be disposed from motives of curiosity, or other causes, to visit the great island of western civilization.

It is not our intention, though such is generally our practice, to offer any positive opinion on the literary merits of the journal, because we consider it by no means fair to subject a writer who expresses his sentiments in a foreign tongue to all those rigid tests which abound in the canons of our critical code, and which at times are unsparingly, but not improperly applied, by English critics to the compositions of their own countrymen. We would not wish it to be inferred from this avowal, that our journalists cannot arrogate to themselves any literary pretension ; on the contrary our authors, for foreigners, possess a tolerably free, copious and idiomatic style, and, moreover, exhibit, in spite of a few errors into which high wrought zeal has doubtless hurried them, occasionally a range of illustration, coupled with historical research, which shews that, to natural sagacity, they add by no means a meagre acquaintance with western literature : in short their journal, " unpretending" as they declare it to be in their dedication to Sir Charles Forbes, may be reckoned more than an average specimen of what European civilization and intercourse have effected on the natural capacity of the native intellect. We may, without being chargeable with exaggeration, go a step beyond this, and assert that, if impartially analysed, the journal before us, in so far as its aim is concerned, will, notwithstanding the absence of all studied regularity, for pertinence of remark and general accuracy of description and information, be found to bear a comparison with many of the insipid attempts at book making with which European tourists, in this prolific age of authorship, are wont to deluge the press.

It is matter of history that, since their expulsion from Persia by the Mahomedans, a considerable number of the followers of Zerdosht or Zoroaster, domesticated at Bombay and Surat. By their general demeanour and due obedience to the laws of the country, they soon gained the favor of the superior authorities, and by their intelligence, industry and activity they contributed, in no small degree, towards augmenting the prosperity of these two places. The progenitors of our journalists it seems settled at Surat. Lowjee Nasserwaujee, the founder of the Bombay dock-yard, which of late perhaps more than any thing else has tended to raise the commercial reputation of the little island, and to make it, as it were, the Liverpool of India, is the individual from whom the " Lowjee Family" takes its name. By the skill and ingenuity he displayed in constructing at Surat a vessel for the Bombay Government, he was invited by a Mr. Dudley, deputed there to watch her proper construction, to come to the Presidency in order to select a proper site for the formation of a dock yard. Lowjee being then a mere superintendent, and having before him very undefined prospects of advancement in life accepted the offer and proceeded to Bombay with twelve or fourteen shipwrights. The result was the establishment of the present docks which, in consequence of the height to which the tides rise ; the facility with which timber, of prime quality, is supplied from the teak forests to the north and east of Bassein by means of navigable streams; and the regular and superior description of shipwrights which the Parsee population invariably supply, are considered the most complete and efficient in India.

The extensive support that Lowjee received from the Bombay Government, and the wide field of useful employment that lay temptingly before him, induced him to educate his two sons in the noble profession which he had adopted. From the date of the establishment the descendants of the founder have supplied a succession of master builders to the Bombay docks: in fact, till very recently, the Parsees have had almost an entire monopoly of all the departments appertaining to it. Remarkable as is this fact, being contrary to the principle that has regulated the management of other departments of the State, we are not aware of any instance in which they have abused the almost unlimited confidence reposed in them. The opportunities to do so, have been ample; for in an extensive dock-yard, where large sums of money, from the mercantile nature of its multifarious duties are in a continual state of transition, numerous avenues must lie open for the surreptitious accumulation of wealth. But the integrity of the Parsee, whether from a scrupulous desire to adhere rigidly to the moral and excellent maxims laid down in the Zendavasta, the great work of Zoroaster,* or from some other causes, has, in a land rife, we regret to say, with peculation and dishonesty, remained unsullied. This feature so characteristic of high moral principle, no less than the peculiar one, how that without European assistance, the Ghebirs have continued to maintain their superiority as naval artchitects over every other class of natives in India, is a phenomenon not unworthy of examination, but one to which we cannot at this moment give a satisfactory solution.

So far back as 1810, when European intercourse with this country was, comparatively speaking, restricted; and when the stores of Western knowledge and improvements in the exact and physical sciences, were naturally not so open to the natives as they are now, Jamsetjee the grandson of the founder, built the "Minden," a seventy-four, without European assistance. This was the first instance, we believe, in which a ship of the line was built in the British dominions out of Europe. Naval Commanders, and others capable of giving an opinion, applauded the skill with which the task was executed, and numerous were the marks of approbation Jamsetjee received from the Board of Admiralty, and the Hon'ble the East India Company. The reputation of the dock-yard was, by this event, greatly increased, and up to the present time some twenty ships of war have been constructed there; but the spirit of competition and the irresistable force of circumstances that led to the formation, in greater numbers, of docks on this side of India, coupled by the fact of the recent purchase, at a very large cost, by the government of the extensive premises belonging to the Docking Company, at Kidderpore, have, we think, diminished, though not materially, this important branch of Bombay Commerce. Nevertheless it will be admitted that

* Vide Malcolm's History of Persia, in which this distinguished Officer pronounces an opinion on the morality inculcated in this work of the ancient Philosopher.

the numerous merchant and other vessels, which have been built there by Parsee architects will, for beauty of construction, finish of workmanship, and durability, vie with any class of merchant ships in the world. Calcutta, it is true, now has its supplies of teak from the adjoining province of Tenasserim, and European agency is, moreover, at work in the Kidderpore docks; but as the quality of the timber, it is admitted, is not equal to the Malabar, and the cost of import from the latter forests being great, unless at a particular season of the year, the Bombay architects will still have the one great advantage of durability on their side to say nothing of the superiority of artizans or subordinate agents.

The late Master-Builder, Nowrojee Jamsetjee, who, in consequence of growing infirmities, has, since the publication of the journal before us, retired from the public service, was perhaps the most distinguished naval architect of the " Lowjee Family." He built three line of battle ships of eighty-four guns each, the ' Asia' the ' Bombay' and ' Calcutta.' But though he had earned for himself the highest distinction in his profession, he was not one of those conservatives who are glad to rest contented with what they have gained, and never think of looking around them in order to watch and take advantage of the changes and improvements that science is every day making visible to the world. He was of a different mould. He saw that steam, like the giant energy of intellect was making rapid strides, and that, independently of its being employed, in small packets, for the conveyance of our Indian mails, it was extensively used as a propelling power to vessels of all dimensions. Hitherto his best energies had been devoted to the construction of vessels propelled by wind, and though it was too late in life for him to commence a new course of study, he was determined that no impediment that he could remove, should prevent his descendants from mastering a science, which it was physically impossible for him successfully to accomplish. With this laudable intention, he solicited, at the suggestion of Mr. Seppings, the late master-builder at Calcutta, and Rear-admiral Sir Charles Malcolm, the Bombay Government for permission to send two young men of his tribe to England, in order that they might have an opportunity of studying all the modern systems of naval architecture. The proposition, judicious as it was well timed, was approved; and our journalists, the former the son, the other the nephew of the Master-builder were the two that were selected.

On the 29th March 1838, they, with their "preceptor Dorabjee Muncherjee and two servants of their own caste," embarked for England on board the *Buckinghamshire*, Captain Hopkins. From religious scruples, for the Parsees like Jews and Mahomedans refuse to eat with persons of a different persuasion from themselves, a separate caboose as it is termed on board ship for the preparation of their victuals was furnished them. The voyage, from the numerous places the vessel touched at, was unusually tedious. They had, however, what in such cases is necessary a commander that consulted their comforts, and fellow passengers that were determined to make themselves agreeable. With the exception of our Parsee travellers most of the passengers were, it seems, at starting sea sick, and this circumstance affords our journalists an opportunity of propounding a preservative against this disgusting malady. It runs counter to the dicta of Lord Byron and Dr. Kitchener, the former of whom in his well known lines in Don Juan, asserts that

" The best of remedies is a beefsteak
Against sea sickness : try it, Sir"

the latter, in commenting on the poet's remedy, advises salted fish and *devils*, with *quant. suff.* of hock or brandy in soda-water. For our part we consider, from experience, the recipe of the poet efficacious, and the advice of the Dr. decidedly agreeable from its Epicurean tendency ; but as abstinence or teetotalism, in the opinion of many, is a virtue, such as think so are fully entitled to the benefit of our journalists' prescription : " we suggest, say they, to all those, who wish to escape the unpleasant effects of sea sickness, to refrain from taking wine and spirits and to be moderate in the meals for the first few days."

Previous to making the Cape of Good Hope, the vessel encountered a severe gale between the Fish Bay and the Cape Lagullas on the southern coasts of Africa. The discomforts they experienced, so long as the gale lasted, induces them to recommend to all parties the overland route as the one affording the best accommodation to passengers. The recommendation is open to question ; but if we may venture on an opinion from the number of passengers that still undertake the long sea voyage, we should say that some time will elapse before our magnificent steamers supercede altogether our first class passenger ships.

On the 20th August, the vessel reached Dover and the feelings experienced by our journalists on the occasion are described in the following terms :—

" Here we were greatly surprized to see the amazing number of ships going out and pouring into the Thames, and steamers every now and then running backwards and forwards ; we cannot convey to our countrymen any idea of this immense number of vessels, and the beauty of the sight. You will see colliers, timber ships, merchantmen, steamers and many other crafts, from all parts of the world, hastening, as it were, to seek refuge in a river, which is but a stream compared to the Ganges and the Indus, or the still larger rivers of America. We thought it a great wonder that such a small and insignificant a speck as England appears on the Map of the world, can thus attract so many nations of the world towards her ; and we asked ourselves, why should not those mighty rivers and countries, which have naturally much better accommodations for commerce than England, be not frequented as much. But a moment's reflection satisfied us on this point— the answer presented itself—and we will tell our countrymen that it is the persevering habits of the English, it is the labour and skill of that people, that is the cause of such attraction. They are never satisfied with any one thing, unless it is brought to perfection, it does not matter at what sacrifice. They are ever ready to receive improvements, and thus they have attained that celebrity in their manufactures that countries which grow materials bring them here to be converted into useful things, which are distributed all over the world ; and while other countries were satisfied with what they had, England was eager to augment her resources. And how has she effected

this? What has been the principal means of her doing it? Why, by knowledge or science put in practice, because knowledge is power; and it is by the
power of knowledge *alone*, and not by the power of arms, that she has so
many means of attracting the world to her, and extending the spread of her
manufactures; however, this is a digression—we will speak of it another time
and now return to our voyage. Another steamer arrived the next day, and
we were taken to Gravesend by their joint efforts. Thus ended our voyage,
and we returned thanks to our Creator in thus conducting us safely through
the numerous perils of the ocean."

From Gravesend our travellers proceeded to London in a steamer,
quite delighted with the first trip they ever made in such a vessel, and
quite the "observed of all observers." In fact wherever they went,
their oriental costume attracted notice, and in no place more so than at
Glasgow. The "douse folks" at the Broomilaw, crowded round them
in thousands. Nor was this disposition to gaze and follow, confined to
the commonality. Royalty herself, no mean distinction, condescended
when promenading on the terrace at Windsor, to remark the dress of
the orientals, and on their making, with the characteristic politeness of
the higher order of natives, Her Majesty a salutation, she, whether struck
by the novelty of the manner in which the homage was paid, or the peculiarity of the costume, sent, says the journal "one of her attendants
to enquire who we were and "from what country we came, which we
"informed him, but he returned again to say that Her Majesty was
"pleased to know our names, and as we knew the difficulty an English-
"man has to pronounce our names, we gave our cards to him which he
"handed to Lord Melbourne."
For a few days after their arrival in London, Sir Charles Forbes, the
staunch friend of the Parsees, was their guide. With him they visited
the Diorama and the Geological Gardens. At the latter "the mild blue
eyes and very sweet expression of countenance" of the ladies made
quite an impression, for our journalists assert that they "saw here more
female beauty in a few hours than they had ever beheld in all their
lives." But admiration for every thing British appears with them to
have been a predominent feeling. The only instance that we can
discover in the volume before us, where their opinions do not harmonize
with that of a large class of the leaders of fashion, and with by no
means an indifferent section of the public at large, and where they
venture to condemn, in gentle terms, the degeneracy of the national
taste in patronizing an amusement capable of affording neither mental
nor moral instruction is on the occasion of their visiting the opera house.
It was the last night of Taglioni's appearance in England with Majesty
as a spectator. The gentleman who accompanied them, and who seems
to have been an ardent admirer of the celebrated *danseuse*, was anxious
for their opinion which our readers will perhaps admire more for its
manly good sense than novelty.

"We were very much surprized to hear that for every night that she had
appeared upon the stage she had been paid one hundred and fifty guineas!!!
Only think,—one hundred and fifty guineas every night to be paid in
England to a woman to stand for a long time like a goose upon one leg

straight out, twirl round three or four times with the leg thus extended, to curtsey so low as to nearly seat herself on the ground, to spring occasionally from one side of the stage to another; and to get more money for *that* hour every evening, than six weavers in Spitalfields (who produce beautiful silk for dresses) could earn all of them, working fourteen hours every day in twelve months! It does appear so absurd that a dancing woman should thus take out of English pockets every night, for an hour's jumping, more than would keep six weavers of silk, their wives and families for a whole year. Had we not seen instances that convinced us the English were clever people, we should have thought them very foolish indeed thus to pay a dancing puppet."

Our journalists on two occasions visited the House of Commons, and once the House of Lords where they heard Lord Brougham briefly address their Lordships. Their first visit to the former was without interest, in consequence of no one accompanying them who could point out the different members : on the second they were more fortunate and had a good opportunity of forming an estimate of the senatorial capacity of the leaders of the Government, and the opposition, as the bill to be discussed was Lord Morpeth's relative to the Irish Parliamentary voters. Sir Robert Peel they thought a great speaker, but his " actions were odd, as he kept thrusting one of his hands out between the flaps of his coat and swinging himself round." This peculiarity, if we mistake not, is prominently noticed by the author of " Random Recollections." Of Lord John Russell they give no opinion beyond that he "was a pale looking man with a tolerable loud voice, but not harmonious, and his action, although energetic was not altogether pleasing." But the great Irish agitator seems to have attracted their attention most from the energy of his manner and the forcible appeals he made, during his oration, in behalf of his country. There is nothing singular in this; for Mr. O'Connell's powers as a speaker are admitted, though there is more of self complacency, or rather an assumption of importance, in the following than we find in any other part of the journal :

" We fancied," say our Journalists, " once when Mr. O'C. was speaking that he observed and alluded to us. He was looking toward us, and at that time in his most forcible manner he said : Mind what you are doing, the eyes of the whole world are upon you, or words to that effect. It might be fancy but such was the impression at the time."

From the days of Blackstone, who is admitted to be the greatest defender of every thing, he found established in English jurisprudence, we have been accustomed to hear the highest eulogiums passed upon those safeguards which the genius of the British Constitution has devised for the protection as well of the accused as of the society which arraigns him. With such powerful advocacy in favor of our laws, we were anxious to read the impressions which a visit to our Criminal Courts produced on our Parsee travellers. Though the cases investigated were of an unimportant character, the " quality of justice" suffered nothing by the circumstance, if any thing its superiority was augmented. The cross questioning and badgering of witnesses by the " gentlemen of the long robe," however, amused our journalists much, and led them to the not unnatural supposition that " the object of the court was to inquire into the respectability of the witness under examination, and whether he was to be believed upon his oath rather than to ascertain whether the prisoner at the bar was guilty or not guilty."

We shall pass over our journalist's minute observations on Chatham, Sheerness, Portsmouth, Plymouth, and other dock yards,—their visit to Windsor Castle and Frogmore Lodge, at which latter place they had the honor of being introduced to Her late Royal Highness the Princess Augusta, and come at once to what we conceive will prove more interesting to our native readers, to wit, the sentiments entertained by our authors of that body to whom is delegated the high and responsible duty of directing the Government of our vast possessions in the East. The reception they received was of a nature to unbend, in some degree, a disposition, however prone to be captious. It was flattering in the extreme. The Chairman and Deputy Chairman tendered every assistance which could, in any way, lead to the consummation of the objects for which the journey to England was undertaken. Sir James Rivett Carnac, the late Governor of Bombay, to whom they had letters of introduction from a native friend, was marked in his attention ; and it was through his instrumentality that our authors were brought to the notice of the Earl of Minto, Lord Glenelg, and other distinguished gentlemen of rank and influence. Gratitude, for so much kindness, was a natural feeling ; but we very much fear that under the excess of its influence discrimination ceases, in a majority of cases, to exercise its legitimate control. This is a general admission, and the following extract, we are of opinion, will not be found an exception to the rule :—

" Before taking leave of the India House, we must endeavour to remove an erroneous impression under which many of our fellow-brethren in India labour ; we think we should be doing great injustice to our own feelings, and fail in duty to our country, did we not touch upon this subject. It is thought in India, that there is a disinclination on the part of the Government to give offices of trust and emolument to the natives. We are quite prepared to say, that this is a great mistake, and we could by our own experience as well as what has passed in England before our own eyes, prove that no such feeling is in existence among the Court of Directors, or, we may venture to say, among the members of the several local Governments in India ; we have been in England a sufficient time to form an opinion on this point ; we studied under the patronage and protection of the Hon'ble Company, and during the whole time we have been in England, have received from the Hon'ble Court of Directors, individually and collectively, uniform encouragement, kindness, and facility, towards accomplishing our object, and we can assert that there is every disposition to encourage native talent and genius, to give our countrymen situations of honour and trust, and to promote in every way the welfare of the natives— to prove it, we would point out our cousin Ardaseer Cursetjee, whom the Hon'ble Court appointed chief engineer and inspector of the steam foundry at Bombay, in August last ; we think every native ought to rejoice at this, it will convince them that talent alone is *recognized*, without any regard to dress, colour or religion."

The Imperial Legislature, with a liberality that must have confounded the disciples of the Cornwallis School, removed by Sec. 87 Will. IV. 3 and 4 Cap. 85, the restrictions which had hitherto prevented persons other than British born from holding offices of trust and responsibility in India. In accordance with the letter of this Section, and with the privilege that belongs to the President of the Board of Control, Sir John Cam Hobhouse appointed the adopted son of the late Rajah Ram Mohun Roy, a writer in the East India Company's Civil Service. We know not the reasons which led to this selection, but the appointment at all events pre-supposed the existence, in the nominee of the necessary qualifications. The opponents to the liberal principles inculcated in the section may here join issue ; but it appears to us, that an independent minister of the Crown is as competent, if not more so, to decide on the qualifications requisite in a candidate for civil employ in India as a Director in Leadenhall Street. Be that as it may, the very body eulogized by our Parsee journalists, in such unqualified terms, opposed the nomination on grounds which left no doubt of their illiberality. Before this Conservative opposition the liberal principles of the President of the Board of Control easily gave way. The appointment was cancelled, and the unfortunate youth thus lost an opportunity of surmounting a barrier which a close borough system had so long erected, but which the generosity of the English Legislature intended utterly to demolish. The section remains to this day in the statute book unrepealed ; but we have yet to learn that, so far as the natives are concerned, the Directors in Leadenhall Street have made any effort to give it universal application. The ready apology for their *sectarianism* is that the qualification of the native is both morally and intellectually below the requisite standard. But supposing this, from the adverse circumstances in which the natives are placed, were true to a greater extent than we are willing to allow, it ought only to furnish a stronger argument for the employment of more effective means towards the removal of the causes of such disqualification. To upbraid a man when he will not take advantage of the door of preferment that is open to him is a proceeding that is both intelligible and just ; but to close the door with something like a determination, be his recommendations and qualifications what they may, to exclude him, and then upbraid him with incompetency is neither kind nor just. This seems to be the system still too much pursued. Beyond a few offices in the judicial and fiscal branches of the uncovenanted service with comparatively small emoluments, but with ample opportunities for the practice of extortion upon a race notorious for their moral cowardice, there is little to stimulate the ambition of the really respectable native and induce him to take part in the glorious endeavour to augment the prosperity of his country. But let the system undergo a slight modification. Let there be infused into the present circumscribed mode of dispensing India-house patronage, less of what is calculated to draw a palpable line of distinction between the conquerors and the conquered, and more of the spirit that pervades the Charter Act, and then some estimate may be formed of the effects which a prospect of superior employment will produce on our native gentry. It must stir up their ambition. It must encourage them to send their sons to Europe, where alone they can be indoctrinated in all those enlarged principles of political wisdom, and be imbued with all those high toned feelings which pre-eminently qualify men for the discharge of responsible functions, and where, as well from the wide field that lies before them, as the force of example, they will be trained, to use the language of the President of the Council of Education, in his recent address, "to apply on their return to their native country the great and beneficial principles of law and jurisprudence to the complicated affairs of a busy and improving community." If the liberality of Leadenhall Street does not produce such, or even approximate, results, then let the charge, which has so often been brought against the natives, rest in the right quarter. Under the present constitution of things it remains with the Home authorities; and it has surprized us not a little to find parties, who are proscribed from all superior offices in the different services of the state, thus deliberately eulogizing, as our journalists have done, those who have placed them under so tremendous an interdict.

We have ventured to offer these few remarks, not from a feeling of hostility to the Government of the Court of Directors, which we would be sorry to see transferred to the Crown, but from a desire to point out to our native readers the danger of taking for granted general assertions which, like the present, have, we fear, been propounded more from a sense of gratitude for past unexpected favors than from a careful and impartial examination of facts. The Court of Directors, notwithstanding all that Burke, and other political opponents have urged to the contrary, have, unquestionably by their general administration, effected much good to the country; but that they are entitled to eulogy, for any manifestations of liberality they have as yet exhibited in the dispensation of their patronage, is what we are not prepared to admit. One fact is worth more than a thousand magnificent conjectures, and general assertions, and this one fact is still wanting to make good the truthfulness of the decision at which our journalists have arrived.

We shall offer but one extract more which is of a suggestive character. It is on a subject which has hitherto, from religious prejudices, been much neglected by the natives, but which of late has demanded, from a few philanthropists, an attention by no means commensurate with its importance. We allude to the Cimmerian ignorance with which the native female mind, is enveloped. After giving a faithful picture of the manner in which a family in the middling classes of society in England educate their children our authors proceed :

" We have thus given the particulars of the acquirements and education of young females in England, in order to induce mothers in India, the 'wives of natives, to establish some such system to educate their children. Why should they not have boarding-schools conducted as the English ones, always of course having female teachers therein instead of males. For oh ? if they could but know the host of amusements and recreations that by education are afforded to females. They can read in two languages generally, and how many hours does not this pass happily away. It teaches them to think rightly and well upon most subjects. And then, drawing; how delightful is it, if you see a place, that you are enabled to sketch it upon paper, and to copy flowers and trees, and even people. Music, too, how soothing? how cheering? how enlivening? how pleasant? for a wife to be enabled to play to her husband, to her children, and to sing to solace them. And then to write to those when circumstances call them far away; to express to them at a distance the feelings which those at home bear to them, and to be able, though thousands of miles distant, to write to tell of the manners and customs of those among whom you are journeying. Oh? our dear countrymen, let us urge you, let us implore you to add to the happiness of your daughters by giving all of them education."

From these extracts, and others of an equally interesting nature which want of space precludes our noticing, our readers will be able to calculate the advantages which our journalists gained by a brief residence in England, and of the estimation in which they were held by all classes with whom they became acquainted. The uncertainty of a favorable reception, more perhaps than religious prejudices, it is alleged has deterred the more respectable of the natives of India from undertaking a visit to the dominant country, which, whatever their speculation regarding her may be, can alone give them an adequate conception of the dignity, wealth and importance of the great English nation. But if such apprehensions have had more than usual currency, they must, in a great measure, have been dispelled by the experience of Dwarkanath Tagore, who, during his sojourn in Great Britain, had honors conferred on him which nobility itself considers a distinction, and who, as a proof that his reception exceeded his most sanguine expectations, has once more left his native shore, as the bearer of an address of thanks from the inhabitants of this city to Her Majesty the Queen for her condescension in presenting them with the portraits of herself and Royal Consort, which now decorate the walls of our Town Hall. But the instance of Dwarkanath Tagore, it may be urged, is a rare one and must not be taken as a precedent for general adoption. There is truth in the allegation. The worthy Baboo unquestionably possessed advantages which do not belong to the generality, or even to a tithe of his fellow-countrymen. He courted, more perhaps than any other native, European society, and endeavoured to emulate the virtues that belong to the European character. The change to him was a change, not of kind, but degree. He proceeded, moreover, to Europe under the guardianship if we may so express ourselves of an influential official, the late Chief Justice of Bengal, and was in the possession of a fortune, which enabled him to obtain popularity by the exhibition of that oriental splendour, which is so captivating to the denizen of the west. A happy combination of these circumstances, no doubt helped to pave the way to that more than common honor with which he was greeted. But such glittering appendages belonged not to our journalists. Their aims were different, but the gratification they derived from their visit was no less complete. They proceeded to England under no powerful patronage ; neither, if they possessed the means, had they any intention to create a sensation by the lavish expenditure of wealth,—their object being the study of a profession which the creative force of western intelligence had made a mystery to the oriental naval architect. In the absence therefore of extrinsic advantages, they possessed acquirements which cannot fail to command respect. Their deportment throughout was modest ; their disposition to receive instruction was great ; and above all their devotion to their professional pursuits was so enthusiastic, that, by the exhibition of these qualities, they soon became objects of attraction. Persons moving in an exalted sphere extended towards them the " hand of good fellowship,"—proving thereby, incontestibly, that wealth is not the only surest passport to distinction. The friend-ships which such qualities engender are sincere since they spring not from interested motives. Some such friendships our journalists made which they tell us " will only terminate with their lives." Their parting ad-monition, which we gladly echo, to their brethren in the East, especially to those " who have leisure and money is by all means pay a visit to England. Amply, most amply, will you be repaid for the expenditure of your time and a portion of your fortune." If this admonition, coming as it does from those who can have no motive for deception, produce but the slightest effect, we shall not regret having devoted a few of our pages to the examination of the " unpretending" journal of Jehangeer Nowrojee and Hurjeebhoy Merwanjee.

On the Study of the Native Languages, Hindi and Hindus-tani. Selections—Asiatic Lith. Comp., Press 2nd Ed. 1830, Gulistan.

For many years after the British obtained a footing in India, the Native languages were not made a subject of study by the Civil or Military Servants of Government in general. Both branches were deficient in this important qualification for the effective discharge of their official functions. Some few indeed in the early times obtained no inconsiderable acquaintance with the Oriental languages, but they were the exceptions. Among the earliest perhaps of those who turned their attention in that direction was Governor Hollwell, whose valuable collection of curious Hindu Manuscripts, including two copies of the Shastras in Hindi and his own translation of a great portion of them were lost in the capture of Calcutta in 1756. The establish-ment of the Asiatic Society in 1784, formed a centre of attraction which drew together and preserved what oriental knowledge was afloat in society and has handed down to us many names eminent in eastern literature, among whom those of Wilkins, Balfour, Wilford, Hastings, Shore, Kirkpatrick, Gladwin and Gilchrist* are well

---

* In the Oriental Annual Register of 1801, is a poem in which the memories of the most distinguished members of the institution are embalmed—of the value of this production much cannot be said—the following may suffice :—

    " Merit's gold medal is to Gladwin due,
    Who gave Imperial Ucbar to our view ;
    His prudent laws—his sentiments on things :
    This living portrait of the first of kings,
    Persia thy lore was early Gladwin's care,
    The graces saw and bade him persevere.
    Gilchrist with odes conveying tender truth
    Smooths the rough paths of science for our youth.

known. Hastings was well aware of the value of this knowledge, but he was too fully occupied with the Herculean labor of systematising the chaotic government he found, when the pressure of external and internal difficulties was removed, to find leisure for devising any project for the education of the government servants on this important head. We know not what acquaintance he had himself with the higher walks of oriental literature, but there is no doubt that he had acquired a competent knowledge of the Persian and Urdu.

Many of the military, as in later days, attained to a very considerable colloquial knowledge of the common dialects ; the intercourse of the European officer with the Sepahi was more intimate than at present, when rules and regulations have fine-drawn duty almost to a mechanical operation : and the connections too so often formed with native women tended to create a familiarity with Hindustani as a spoken language among a good many—but very few studied the oriental dialects grammatically. The absence of Grammars and Dictionaries was an insuperable obstacle.

It was not until Lord Mornington became Governor-General that any qualifications either in a knowledge of the laws or languages of the people whose differences they were to adjust, whose crimes they were to judge and whose contributions to the revenue they were to collect, were required from the civil servants. With him however a new era opened. At the end of '98 he published an order in Council declaring that the due administration of the internal Government and affairs of the Company in Bengal required that no civil servant should be nominated to certain offices judicial and revenue until it had been ascertained that he was sufficiently acquainted with the laws and regulations enacted by Government and the several languages, a knowledge of which is requisite for the due discharge of their respective functions.

No civil servant after 1st January 1801 was to be appointed to any Judicial or Revenue office until he had passed an examination in the laws and languages which was to be fixed by the Governor-General in Council.

There was a distinction however in the examination for the judicial and revenue departments : for, while the former were required to have a competent knowledge of Hindustani and Persian, the latter were only expected to be acquainted with the Bengali or Urdu according to the province they were employed in.

But while demanding these acquirements from the public civil officers the Government was not backward in providing the means : that excellent institution the College of Fort William was established ; and Professors appointed for the different branches of study. Gilchrist was

India to him much commendation owes,
As on her Johnson England now bestows ;
While he in Asian learning dives so deep,
Ye Scribblers o'er your mourish jargon sleep;
Long since your treatises neglected lie,
And ere yourselves are dead your Grammars die.
 *   *   *   *   *
Hardwicke to thee we owe a double crown,
Who made the little meloé our own.

installed in the chair of Persian and Hindustani, and a selection of works in the native languages was compiled for the use of the students. In the next year we find the Governor-General expressing his sense of the merits of Mr. Gilchrist in having formed a valuable Hindustani Grammar and Dictionary, and thereby facilitated the acquisition of the language most generally used throughout this presidency, and for the zeal ability and diligence with which he had discharged the duty committed to him of instructing the junior civil servants who were directed to attend him for the purpose of acquiring the Hindustani and Persian.

Among the books prepared for the use of the College by Gilchrist, were two volumes of selections in the Persian and Devanagari character, the former in the Urdu and the latter in the Hindi languages. These works have formed the standard school classics of early students and with the Anwar-i-Joheili and Gulistan are generally known by the designation of the " black classics."

The path having been thus rendered accessible, it is surprising that the Court of Directors did not immediately follow up the act of the Governor-General by rendering a competent knowledge of the languages imperative on all their servants, at least before entrusting them with situations of responsibility and emolument. The College of Fort William however was not looked upon with an eye of affection by the Court, and the scale on which it was established was absolutely disapproved : it may not therefore have been thought politic to shew the soundness of the Governor-General's judgment, by adverting to the advantages which would naturally have followed the institution on the scale proposed. Whatever the case may have been we do not find the acquisition of the native languages insisted on among military officers until 1823, and then interpreters of regiments were called on to shew their qualifications for the appointments they held by passing an examination in the languages current in the provinces of the Bengal presidency and the order even then emanated from the Commander-in-Chief.

Interpreters were placed on a better footing than they had previously been. They were to be considered staff officers and exempt from Battalion duty except in cases of emergency. House allowance, hitherto only allowed when marching or in the field, was granted them in all situations. They were required to pass an examination in Hindustani before a committee of competent officers assembled by order of His Excellency the Commander-in-Chief, who were to forward a detailed report of the examination, with a certificate specifying the nature of the officer's proficiency, and their opinion of his competency to conduct the duties of an Interpreter to a general court martial.

The favorable certificate and opinion of the committee was to be sufficient authority in the first instance to hold the situation, but before being confirmed in it, he was required to undergo a further examination by the public examiners of the College of Fort William and obtain from them a favorable certificate and opinion of his qualification. Officers at that time holding the situation were required to pass the prescribed examination within twelve months.

This order was followed in a few months by another laying down the scale of qualifications expected from officers, candidates for the appointment of interpreter. They were as follows :

1st. A well-grounded knowledge of the general principles of Grammar ; to be ascertained by well selected questions, not of the niceties, but of the general leading principles.

2d. The ability to read and write with facility the modified Persian character of the Urdu and the Devanagari of the Khuri bholi, to be ascertained by written translations into Hindustani in both characters of selected orders, rules or regulations, and by reading and translating the Bagh-o-bahar, the Prem Sagur and Gulistan or Anwar-i-Joheili.

3rd. A colloquial knowledge of the Urdu and Hindui, sufficient to enable him to explain with facility and at the moment any orders in those dialects or to transpose reports, letters, &c. from them into English. This was to be tested by vivâ voce conversation.

In the course of the few next following years the Interpreterships of Regiments were filled by passed men and a spur was given to the young lads to spend a portion of their long daily leisure in an occupation which not only lessened the tedium of the day's confinement within doors, but rendered them more fitted for their duties and also opened a road to honorable and lucrative employment as regimental staff officers.

From about this time (say 1826) we may consider that none but men who had passed the Mofussil or College examinations have been interpreters, and it has been often a subject of discussion whether the old or modern interpreters were the best. This, we believe, is generally allowed that as a medium of verbal communication between the officer and sipahi, the old ones were superior, many of them being very good colloquists (though ignorant of the character and grammar of the languages) from constant intercourse with the natives, but that on the other hand the Modern Interpreters are deficient in an intimate practical acquaintance with the language which nothing but intercourse with the natives can give.

This is what might be expected when we consider that young lads just from school, with their minds accustomed to the study of languages are the ones who pass the examinations and become Interpreters—indifferent perhaps at first but with every chance of their becoming daily more competent—and we must also bear in mind in considering the amount of good done by enforcing the study, that though the prize of the regimental appointment can fall but to one, yet it incites many to qualify themselves to hold it, and thus the actual amount of knowledge of the languages diffused through each regiment is great.

While on this point we may briefly notice the slight comparative encouragement which is held out to one branch of the service, and that, one which from its long list of Subalterns and consequent slow promotion (not to mention that commissions in it are held out as the prize of superior acquirements) ought certainly not to be placed in a worse position than the rest of the army. We need scarcely say that we refer to the Artillery.   At present it consists of a body of officers equal to those of 10 Infantry Regiments on the scale of 1824 (when all branches were equalized in this particular) but instead of having ten Interpreter-ships there are only two.   The Brigades and European Battalions of Artillery have no such appointment, although allowed in every other branch of the army, and consequently the chances of an Artillery Officer holding an Interpretership are as one 1 to 75, while of an Infantry Officer they are as 1 to 15.

The first step of an examination for Interpreters having been got over, this was soon followed up by insisting on an examination for adjutant, and commissariat officers in Hindustani, and at a later period (1837) all staff officers were required to pass the Interpreter's examination.

Some modifications have from time to time been made in the rules regarding the examinations.   Some committees insisted on examining candidates in both the Gulistan and Anwar-i-Joheili, while others considered it optional with the candidate which book he would take up.   Until a few years ago, too, the candidate had to pass in all the three languages at once, a failure in one involving a re-examination in all. This was altered and one language at a time was permitted.   It was proposed too, but negatived in the Adjutant-General's Office we believe, to substitute the kayti for the Devanagari character : the former being the one in common use over nearly the whole country, while the latter is the character of printed books alone.   It is also the character in use in all correspondence of the Hindu sipahis, and as any one who can read it can also read the Devanagari (though the reverse is not the case) we think the change would have been a judicious one.

The climax has lately been reached, a colloquial examination is now to be passed by every subaltern officer before he is entitled to the emoluments arising from the charge of a troop or company.   The test we believe is not a very severe one, but still it will answer the purpose of ensuring a certain minimum acquaintance with the language on the part of all officers.

The symbolic marks and letters prefixed to the passed are rather puzzling in the Bengal army list. P, P C, P H, P C H, + are a little formidable, but when we turn to a court army list, and find C, H, M, Mm, O, P, T, Te, in all the blushing honors of red letters, and H, H, A, a, h, in the sombre majesty of black, we give up all hope of un-riddling the mysterious attainments of their possessors, and contenting ourselves with simply allowing that they are certainly men of *letters*.

We have hastily glanced over the steps taken to ensure among government servants (and the military in particular) that most desi-rable and necessary knowledge, a competent acquaintance with the languages in use among the men under their command, and from the numbers who have attained to the prescribed standard, we may fairly conclude that the amount of the knowledge of the Eastern languages among the officers of the army is very considerable.   These Mofussil examinations, it is true, differ very much from one another in strictness, as must be expected when it is considered that the members, however competent as to knowledge, may and are not always habituated to the process of examining—but let the examination be as light as it can be made consistent with the tests established and the form of report laid down, it cannot be passed without a certain amount of study.   It must be under a very extraordinary combination of circumstances that an utterly incompetent person passes—such indeed as we may resolve into *fate*, and then if it is a man's destiny to pass, why pass he must, for as Saadi says,

> " Opposing fate in vain you toil
> In Tigris stream the fish to snare ;
> If fate ordains the finny spoil
> Will live unharmed on deserts bare."

But this examination not being final, each Interpreter is forced to keep up and continue acquiring knowledge with a view to present himself before the examiners of the College of Fort William, either voluntarily or on his regiment arriving in tour of duty at Barrackpore. In one respect however, the Mofussil is severer than the College examination.   Written urzees are always given in the former to be read, while in the latter, *print* only is used ; and if a person can read a moderately well written urzee without much stammering, he must have a fair acquaintance with the character, and a *copia verborum*, which, with practice, will soon ripen into competent knowledge.

But, we must now make a few remarks on the books which form the studies of the aspirant for the P or PC before his name in the Adjutant General's army list.   We have said that certain volumes of selections from the native classics were compiled by Gilchrist, and printed under the auspices of the College about 1801.   This edition in the course of five and twenty years had been worn out, and when the study became fashionable, copies were only procurable with great difficulty and at a high charge.   The demand however, soon produced a supply.   A fresh edition was prepared and published by the Asiatic Lithographic Company in 1830, which placed the volumes within the reach of all who wished for them ; and to render them more accessible, depots of them were formed at some of the principal army stations. A copy of the Gulistan was at the same time or shortly afterwards added, which completed the series of books chiefly wanted.

These volumes contain a Grammar, the Prem Sagur, and selections from the most popular Hindustani works in Hindi and Urdu, such as the Bagh-o-bahar—Groli Bukowlee Beetal-pucheelee, with dialogues, lists of festivals and castes, and popular songs.

The second volume as containing the Prem Sagur is chiefly in request, and its pages are well thumbed by the time half-a-dozen men have prepared themselves for the examination from it.   Hour after hour have we seen a man reading and spelling and yawning over its pages with a pandit as sleepy as himself.   We have heard of men studying for ten or twelve hours a day : though that dandling fashion of poring over a work and translating it vivâ voce into English can hardly be called study.   A few hours really given to translating *into*

d

Hindustani is worth double the time so spent.   We never hear a man speak of his reading for twelve hours a day with a munshi, without feeling tempted to quote, as applicable to his case, Saadi's tale of the " devotee who ate ten muns of food in the evening and passed the night in prayer!" and the wise man's remark on hearing it, that " had he eaten half-a-loaf and slept he would have done better."

When a certain degree of knowledge of the language and character is attained, we strongly recommend the practice of translating from English into Hindustani as one likely to give a student a far better knowledge of the idioms of the language than the usual practice of *reading*.   The knowledge thus gained is in general far more deeply impressed on the mind.   Translations of such works as the Gulistan, Bagh-o-Bahar, and Prem Sagur are very useful auxiliaries in this way. They should not be referred to as dictionaries to ascertain the meaning of each word—their value is in helping a student to understand the general drift of a passage and to form a lesson in re-translating.   For the first purpose the part intended to form the day's task should be read over in the English translation, which should then be put aside ; in the latter it will form the text book.   The Gulistan has a translation attached in the printed edition, and we believe that the Bagh-o-bahar has been translated and published.   An edition of the Prem Sagur, we observe, is now in the press by Captain Hollings, and we are sure that in giving it to the world, he is conferring a valuable boon on the young officers of the army.   Indeed many people will be glad to avail themselves of its English form to become acquainted with the history of the incarnations of Krishna and the traits and traditions of the holy land of Hindu mythology.   We remember, in our younger days, when deep in the mysteries of the black classics, making a rough translation, nearly literal, as we read on through the " Ocean of Love," and achieving some twenty or thirty chapters, but we never revised or put them into a readable form : and (although we write a P before our name) as we never reached the " other side of that boundless ocean of thought," we shall not be sorry to have an opportunity in the forthcoming translation of ascertaining what " its dark unfathomed caves" really do contain.   While writing these pages we cast our eyes over a portfolio of old papers and stumbled on a sort of free and loose versification of the 23d Chapter, and as it may amuse our readers, although at the expense of our poetical talent, we annex it : we remember at the time being much struck with many of the poetical and pastoral images of the original in spite of the ludicrous figure the Gopis make—

> The maidens of Brij have left their home,
> O'er Jumna's flowery banks to roam,
> To the bughat ghat have they ta'en their way
> To pass in pleasure the life-long day,
> And their fervent limbs at noon to lave
> In the winding Jumna's glassy wave.

These maidens fair are tripping along
To the sound of the lute and sprigthly song,
The constant love and exceeding praise
Of the beauteous Krishna fill their lays,
They sing of his power and wondrous might,
Who slew the dæmons in single fight.

They seek for a spot enclosed by trees,
Where nought is heard but the cooling breeze,
Or the coo of the dove as amidst the grove
She warbles her plaintive tale of love ;
They seek for a spot where the footseps rude,
Of prying man can never intrude.

Such a spot on the river's banks they've found,
Where the Kuddum's shady trees abound,
Where the voice of man is never heard,
Or the sky e'er cloven by wing of bird,
Where all is still, save the echo sweet
Of the musical tread of their fairy feet.

Chudder, Doputtee and Ungeeah chaste,
Are thrown from their reeking limbs in haste,
Smiling and blushing their bodies they view,
Striped with love's own roseate hue,
And seek in the Jumna's envious tide,
From mortal sight their charms to hide.

But who is he of the Lotus eye
Who sits concealed in the kuddum nigh ?
In garments of yellow which loosely float
And a necklace of pearl around his throat,
With a crowned head and flute in hand,
Watching the sports of this lovely band.

As all unrob'd and devoid of fear,
They gambol and play in the waters clear,
Half hid in the streams their beauties lie,
With the lotus flowers which are floating bye.
Ah ! little they think that their bodies bright,
Are exposed to the amorous Krishna's sight.

He leaves the tree and his footsteps press
The spot where the maidens left their dress ;
He has seized their clothes and with stealthy pace,
Again repaired to his hiding place,
And waits to enjoy the maids' dismay,
When they find their garments are ta'en away.

Their gambols and sports and pastimes o'er
The maidens of Brij regain the shore,
And seek in the folds of their garments wide
Their naked limbs from view to hide ;
They search the bank in deep distress,
But find no trace of the stolen dress.

As startled deer these maidens shy
To the waters friendly cover fly,
And try to find what mortal feet
Have dared intrude on their loved retreat,
When the notes of a flute from a Kuddum high,
Proclaim that Krishna is seated nigh.

" Oh stealer of hearts," the maidens say,
" It is thou that hast ta'en our clothes away,
Let our modest blushes your pity claim
And bring us our garments back again,
Else here immersed in the waves we'll stay,
Till night has effaced the light of day." .

" When one by one," thus Krishna, replies,
" With joined hands and upraised eyes,
From the Jumna's covering waves you flee,
And stand unrobed in front of me,
And beg for your dress with suppliant air,
Then will I grant your humble prayer."

Oh Suryah, Brahma, great Maha Deb
The Maidens of Brij implore thy aid,
Oh haste to our help and to Krishna's heart
Some sense of pity for us impart,
Pity, oh pity, or else a stain
Will cleave to the Gopis' spotless name.

But all in vain is the Gopis' prayer,
It either is lost in empty air,
Or Narayan sleeps in his milky lake,
Nor will rouse himself for the Gopis' sake,
For resolved is Krishna that e'er she goes,
Each maid shall her naked charms disclose.

Then with down-cast eyes and joined hands,
Each maiden of Brij before him stands,
Her rounded limbs untrammelled by dress,
Are bright in their own loveliness,
Their bosoms fair (young love's own dwelling,)
With wounded pride and shame are swelling.

Restoring their garments he sweetly smiles,
And with honeyed words the maids beguiles,
He soothes their pride with a winning grace,
And steals their hearts by his beauteous face,
Till turning home they think no more,
Of what has passed on the Jumna's shore.

Such is one of the most celebrated feats of Krishna, the favourite
and most popular deity of Eastern India! If such be the character
of the divinity worshipped by millions, what can we expect the
character of the worshipping millions to be !

In its references to the manners and habits of the people, the Prem Sagur shews how unchanging they have been amidst the numberless revolutions which have passed over the nation. The herdsmen still " drive their flocks a field ; " the children still tend them as they did of yore when Krishna gamboled with the enamoured Gopis on the sacred buns. To be sure, poetic fiction has clothed them with attributes which cannot now be found, for we should scarcely now recognize the descendants of the beauteous Radha and Jasuda in the dirty ragged maidens we meet belaboring thick skinned buffaloes with respectable cudgels ; but still, there they are, and the village cattle in their charge going to graze ; their habits as unchanged as the course of the Jumna, along whose banks they roam. In spite of the iron grasp of conquerors, the Brahmans have retained the sway over their deluded votaries; and their customs, unlike those of every conquered nation (the Jews alone excepted) have undergone little or no change by the admixture of the habits of their conquerors.

This immutability, however, in the metropolis appears to be giving way ; the bulwarks of Hinduism are tottering under the assaults of science ; and there is little doubt but that ere many generations have passed away, Hinduism will be numbered among by-gone superstitions. A spirit of enquiry and infidelity has been raised by education, which cannot be repressed; and the endeavours of the Orthodox, by establishing a College of their own, in which European sciences and Brahmanical tenets are to be inculcated, will only assist the forward movement. A sad phase, however, appears to be in prospect for the educated class thus produced : their old faith and restraints will be removed and no other check substituted. We know how slow the growth of practical personal Christianity is with ourselves under all the advantages of early tuition and the restraints of a Christian country. What then can we expect from a race emancipated from Hinduism, as this class is fast becoming, and restrained by no moral or superstitious checks, their natural bad dispositions inflamed by new and exciting food, and their minds puffed up by the vanity of learning !

Such, however, appears to be a natural step in the history of the Hindus : yet must we not believe that in time (and that perhaps less distant than we imagine) Brahmanism, like the " elegant mythology" of the Greeks, must quail before the brighter lights of the Christian faith ? The spirit of enquiry which is now abroad, must do its work ; through its means Christianity will find its way into the villages and hamlets ; paganism will recoil before it, and hereafter we may see the word restored to its original meaning. Time doubtless must elapse before this consummation can be effected ; but in the end the caves of Elora, the temples of Muttra, and all the host of Hindu fanes will share the fate of Diana's temple at Ephesus, or Apollo's shrine at Delphi.

The age in which the Prem Sagur was written is not well ascertained. Ward considers the Hindu literature to have attained its height about two hundred years before the Christain era; the Prem Sagur would most probably be included in the writings of the classic

era; but there are many points in it that appear to have originated
in traditions derived from the Christian scriptures, which would point
out a later date for its origin. We may instance the murder of the
tribe of Gud by Kun's order, in the hope of destroying the child by whom
(before its birth) it was prophesied that he should fall, and the flight of
Bisdeo and the child to Gokul, as in all probability owing their origin
to the massacre of the innocents at Bethlehem and our Saviour's flight
into Egypt. Krishna's contest with the nag (snake) in the Jumna, his
victory over him, and his dancing on his head and leaving the foot
mark conspicuous there may appear to point to that most ancient of all
prophecies, "He shall bruise his head," as its source; but we content
ourselves with throwing out the suggestion for the consideration of
others who have more leisure to pursue the task.

The Sakontala or fatal ring has been introduced in an English garb
by Sir W. Jones, but the Urdu translation (as far as we recollect, and
we are writing from memory not having perused either for many years)
differs considerably from it. It occupies a considerable space in the
selections—its simplicity and natural descriptions are similar to those
in the Prem Sagur—the picture of Draputtee among her maidens
tending the shrubs and flowers and playing with the deer—her form
pliant as the "willow of Mujnoon"—is exceedingly poetical and pretty ;
but the story, as it may have been the standard, partakes of the uniformity
of Hindu tales. In most, a Prince rides out to hunt, and, in the ardour
of the chase outstripping his followers, finds himself involved in a thick
forest, ignorant of the way to extricate himself; he wanders on till he
meets some beauteous maiden, ward or daughter of some holy man
dwelling in the deepest shades of the forest—mutual love at first sight,
a too yielding fair one and a faithless swain form the next scenes :
desertion, shame, flight from home and adventures in her wanderings
fill up the next act ; and the story generally concludes by a re-union
and happiness to all parties.

Their stories are in general puerile, the events improbable and the
catastrophes lamely brought about ; and in perusing them we feel much
as a person does on reading the Arabian Nights in after life. There
is a feeling of utter disappointment in the stories and a wonder how
they could possibly have delighted us in childhood—but if the story is
put out of mind, and they are read for instruction in the manners of the
people, in their tastes and habits of life—then they are full of interesting matter. Songs and tales generally give a more faithful picture of
the every-day philosophy and habits of a people than the most elaborate
description. As the idioms of a language are more visible in the un-
studied conversation of the inhabitants than in the writings of the
learned, so the habits of thinking and acting peculiar to any people
come out more strongly in the easy form of songs and stories than in
the formal restraint of a set dissertation.

Our article would run to too great a length were we to add any
remarks on the Uclak-i-Hindi, the wars of the birds of the earth and
of the waters, or of the Beetal Pucheelee and other extracts contained
in these volumes; they will be found amusing and good practice in

reading when fluency has been obtained—the eye gets familiarised with the character by reading aloud pages of such stories, and it forms a relaxation from the more laborious process of translating into a foreign language, which we recommend as the main portion of study. We shall conclude the desultory remarks we have made, and which perhaps are already thought too long, with expressing our conviction that the study of the languages introduced by the Government Orders has been of incalculable value to the officers of the army, not only by greatly increasing the amount of knowledge of that kind extant in the profession; but as giving an object of employment to the younger men which has effected a great change in their habits. The habit of application induced by this study has been carried into other branches of knowledge; for a man accustomed to a number of hours and regular employment daily, becomes miserable under prolonged idleness. For his own comfort, therefore he seeks for other studies when he has passed the examination, or perhaps if his fancy takes that turn, pushes on his studies into a familiar acquaintance with more recondite branches of oriental literature. Often it leads him to re-commence his own education, and the long confinement of an Indian day is profitably spent in obtaining an acquaintance with our own standard authors, of whose works he might probably from idleness have lived in ignorance, had it not been for the stimulus given by the study of the Native languages; and thus to many the " black classics " have proved the source of introduction to their western brethren of a fairer hue.

The Romanizing and Hellenizing systems :—

1. *Suggestions for the preparation of a Glossary of Indian Techanical terms, &c., by M. Crow, uncovenanted Deputy Collector, &c. Calcutta,* 1845.

2. *The Bengal Hurkaru, in which are embodied the Bengal Herald and Calcutta Literary Gazette, May, June, July, and August,* 1845.

In the 6th No. of this work, p. 287, we were led, in a note, to remark on the mode of representing oriental terms in Roman letters, as follows :—" About ten or eleven years ago, an immense discussion was raised in our local press on this very subject. Some of the more elaborate papers, with others on kindred topics, were collected and published in a distinct volume at Serampore. With a few slight modifications the system of Sir W. Jones was all but unanimously adopted in preference to all others; and the few and unimportant differences which subsequently arose in practice have since been satisfactorily settled, as may be seen, by referring to the *Calcutta Christian Observer* for August 1842 ; so that, on this side of India, the question, with *most* disputants, has been conclusively determined."

Little did we dream, when these sentences were penned, that a disturber of the general peace of ten or eleven years was crouching at the very door. But so it turned out to be. A pamphlet from the pen of Mr. Crow suddenly and unexpectedly made its appearance. In its tone it was altogether belligerent. It bade defiance to all previously existing systems of Romanizing ; it resolved, *vi et armis*, as it were, to sweep them all away, and substitute itself in their room. A Herculean task this, beyond all debate ; and were the execution equal to the intention, long ere now would Mr. Crow's system be standing " alone in its glory" on the evacuated battle field. But this is not the only instance in which the result has proved that blustering is not the same with valour, and that big words are very different from heavy blows. After the fuss and noise of a valorous championship, the author has amply succeeded in proving that *innovation* is not *reform* in the sense of improvement—amply succeeded too, by the contrast which he has furnished, in satisfying the advocates of the old system, of the vast superiority of their own over that now proposed to be substituted in its place.

It is not our purpose, on the present occasion, to enter into a detailed comparison of the merits of any of the Romanizing systems. Our sole object is to record historically the leading facts connected with Mr. Crow's recent movement.

In the *Bengal Hurkaru* of Tuesday, 27th May, appeared a letter, republished from the *Catholic Herald*, which Mr. Crow had addressed to the Head of his church in Bengal. The letter is well written as to style, and contains many sensible and important remarks. It is however greatly disfigured by being interlarded with sundry inanities and tinctures of Romanism. The whole letter is too long for extraction. The following will suffice as a specimen :—

To His Grace the Most Reverend the Archbishop, Vicar Apostolic of Bengal, &c., &c., &c.

MY LORD,—Permit me the honour and the pleasure of presenting your Grace with four copies of a pamphlet which contains the substance of some Official Reports submitted by me to the Supreme Government of India, and approved by that high authority for transmission to the Honourable the Court of Directors. Those reports contained certain remarks on the manner of expressing Indian languages in Roman characters—a theme which has engaged the attention of many eminent Orientalists, no less than it has been worked upon by some of the worthy Missionaries employed under the jurisdiction of your Grace. It is therefore a subject in which your Grace cannot but feel a lively interest. But there are other considerations of a more important character and more intimately connected with the sacred ministry of your Grace which must heighten the interest likely to be created by the consideration of this subject.

The great mass of Catholics spread throughout India, to which body numbers are being daily added, is composed principally of people and of nations who understand not the European languages, and to whom religious instruction must necessarily be conveyed in the Vernacular tongue of each Province. The Missionaries employed among these people, although acquainted with the colloquial language of the place, are for the most part unable to read and write with facility in the various Vernacular characters used throughout India. Whilst this is the case with regard to the vernacular characters of India, there is one character, viz. the Roman, no less than one language, viz. the Latin, which is well understood by every Catholic Missionary, be he of whatever nation or located in whatever part of the world. Hence it is evident that the printing of Vernacular Catechisms and other standard rudimental works of Catholic Theology in one universal character must be attended with those great advantages of unity, uniformity, &c., which result from the preservation of our liturgy in one universal language. Most of the arguments used in support of the use of the Latin tongue in the Catholic Church, appear to me to apply with equal force in support of the use of the Roman character for the expression not only of all the Indian languages, but also of every language in the world. This view of the subject is no less extensive than the attempt to reduce it to practice is worthy of the exalted dignity, the influence, the persevering zeal, and the universal desire of doing good, with which Providence has so pentifully blessed your Grace.

The Roman character is now the universal character in which all the languages of Europe, of America, and of all the colonies throughout the world, are expressed. It is, in fact, the grand depository of all modern learning, as well as of Christian Theology. Why then should not the Asiatic languages as well as all other languages pay their tribute to this universal emporium of all modern theology, science, and religion. The work, at least so far as India is concerned, is not impracticable when placed in the hands of the Supreme Government of the country on the one side, and of the head of the Catholic Church of the leading presidency of that Government on the other. The Supreme Government of India has already taken up the cause, and, as it will be seen by Mr. Secretary Davidson's letter, inserted in the introduction of my pamphlet, intends to address the Honorable the Court of Directors on the subject. I have also sent copies of the pamphlet with letters to Mr. Mangles, M. P., to whom I am well known, as well as to several other authorities, who will no doubt cordially support the views it advocates. But in a catholic matter like this, the influence of the Government of India and of some of the authorities in England, must rank as much below the influence of the head of the Catholic Church of Bengal as the efforts of the British Government must fall short of the influence of the Supreme Head of the whole Catholic Church. It is therefore that I solicit the continuance and support of your Grace to the gigantic effort of ultimately diffusing the use of the Roman characters for the expression of all Asiatic languages to the same extent as those characters are now used for the expression of all European languages. The character of all Europe being now the same, how easy it is to translate information from any one of the European languages to another; and were the same Roman characters to be used by the Asiatic nations, would it not be equally easy to remove many of the deep-rooted prejudices which these nations entertain against the Christian Religion and its Ministers? The Roman character having once become familiar to these people as the vehicle of their Vernacular literature, the reading, if not the knowledge of the Latin tongue, the legitimate language of the Catholic Church diffused throughout the world, would naturally follow and command their respect and veneration. This would certainly be a great step in the advancement of these people towards Catholic Faith. It is a circumstance worthy of consideration that, whilst the Roman Religion is the only religion which can lay claim to Catholicity, the Roman character should already be the universal character of at least three-fourths of the civilized world. It is also remarkable that this Roman Catholic character should receive the suffrages of a Sir William Jones, a Dr. Gilchrist, a Trevelyan, a Dr. Duff, and a host of other men of learning, many of whom are most violently opposed to the propagation of the Roman Catholic Faith. In the unsearchable ways of Providence these inveterate enemies of the Roman Catholic faith have become the most zealous advocates of that *Roman Catholic* character which does and must ever continue to be the companion of the Roman language and the Roman name, which is the distinctive birthright—the polar star of our Holy Religion. Such are the thoughts, my Lord, which this subject inspires in me, and it is under their influence that I solicit the co-operation of your Grace for the attainment of the end to which they so clearly point."

The Editorial comments of the *Hurkaru* on this letter are so candid and judicious, and contain so many excellent reflections of a general character, that we cannot refrain from quoting them entire :—

" Many of our readers doubtless recollect the active part taken by this journal, in common with some of our contemporaries, in supporting Mr. Trevelyan's scheme for substituting the Roman Alphabet for the numerous native characters employed in expressing the language of India. The persevering exertions of this gentleman aided by the journals which agreed with him on this subject, were so far successful, that a great many books in the vernacular languages were printed in the Roman character and brought into use all over Bengal. More than ten years have elapsed since the period we are referring to, and during that time, the new system came to be neglected, and was, as we thought, consigned to oblivion. We have heard the scheme, and its enthusiastic advocate spoken of, indeed, with supreme contempt; but we could never bring ourselves to believe that an idea originated in such a mind as that of Sir William Jones, and by him reduced to practice, could be so utterly worthless as some of those who have taken upon themselves to ridicule it, profess to deem the Romanizing system. Be that as it may, however, after Mr. Trevelyan left the country, we heard little more of his method of writing the native languages, and for some years past, in all books printed in the vernacular tongues, the Oriental characters only have been used.

Under these circumstances, we had taken it for granted, that the Romanising system had, so to speak, gone out, never to be revived. In this, we find ourselves mistaken. We republish from the *Catholic Herald* a long and well-written letter from Mr. M. Crow, to the Roman Catholic Archbishop, from which we learn, that in the person of the former, we have a new and apparently able and zealous advocate for the substitution of the Roman for the native Alphabets, to express the native languages. We have not seen the pamphlet Mr. Crow alludes to, but he tells us, that his system is new and superior to those hitherto proposed, and that most of its advantages arise from his close adherence to the simple and consistent orthography of the Latin and Italian languages. As no specimens are before us of his mode of expressing native sounds, we can, of course, offer no opinion on the merit of his new method of writing the Asiatic languages; but if he has really improved on Mr. Trevelyan's scheme—which was, on the whole, very good, and has been found to answer very well, when it has been fairly tried—we hope to see the new system adopted. That such a result is not at all improbable, may be inferred from the fact which Mr. Crow communicates, that his remarks and suggestions as to the manner of employing the Roman character for the purpose in question, have engaged the attention of Government, which is about to address the Court of Directors on the subject.

If this experiment is to be tried, however, we would suggest to Mr. Crow, that he cannot do better than follow in the footsteps of Mr. Trevelyan, so far as to combine with his Romanized vernacular, English translations, the comprehension of which will be rendered so much more easy to the student from the use of that character.

We are surprised to find so intelligent a writer as Mr. Crow, talking of the mere capacity to read Latin words without understanding them, as calculated to command respect and veneration. Lest we should misrepresent him, however, we give his own words. He says ;—" The Roman character having once become familiar to these people as the vehicle of their vernacular literature, the *reading, if not the knowledge*, of the Latin tongue, the legitimate language of the Catholic Church, diffused throughout the world, would naturally follow and command their respect and veneration." The Italics are ours. Can Mr. Crow really believe that the *reading*, without the *knowledge*, can or ought to command respect and veneration? If he means merely that becoming familiar with the Roman character, would enable the natives more easily to acquire the Latin language, we agree with him. If, again, he thinks the acquisition of that language indispensable to the spread of the Roman Catholic religion, he is quite right, in addressing his Archbishop, to refer to that as an argument in favour of his system; but, altogether, as regards the public at large and the success of his scheme, we think it would have been better if he had separated the discussion of it from his religious opinions, and let it stand or fall by its own merits, without any reference to those of the Roman Catholic Church. Letting that pass, however, we must say that, for our own parts, one of the greatest advantages we looked to in the use of the Roman character was the facility it would give to the study of the English language, and we should have liked to see Mr. Crow dwelling on that point, instead of altogether losing sight of it, as he has done.

We shall take an opportunity of returning to this subject, when we have gone through Mr. Crow's pamphlet and considered his system. In the meantime, we will merely express our hope, that if the Government does patronise the use of the Roman character for the vernacular languages, English translations may be introduced into every vernacular book so printed; for if we were too English at one time, we are, certainly, getting far too Oriental now, when we consider the many important advantages that would result from the diffusion of our mother-tongue throughout this benighted land."

The Saturday evening edition of the *Bengal Hurkaru* or *Bengal Herald* and *Calcutta Literary Gazette*, for the 7th June contains the following explanatory statement from Mr. Crow, respecting the origin and object of his pamphlet :—

" I beg leave briefly to state the circumstances under which the pamphlet you allude to, was printed. The Honorable the Court of Directors having projected a Glossary of Indian Technical Terms, forwarded to their servants locally employed, proofs of the work, and desired to be furnished with their opinions. Among others, I had the honor of receiving a set, and offered a few suggestions for its improvement. These were so far approved by my superiors in office, as to induce them to submit my communications with commendatory remarks. The Government was kindly pleased to express its approbation of my humble labours, and to express the wish to forward my letter for the consideration of the Honorable the Court of Directors. Having experienced so much kindness and encouragement from my official superiors, and the Supreme Government, I considered it expedient for the convenience of those who may have to peruse and to refer to my remarks, to revise and condense them, and to have them printed in a pamphlet of convenient size ;

having done this, I submitted a certain number of copies for the use of Government and of some of the other authorities. I also sent some copies to those of my friends, who, I considered, felt an interest in the subject. It will therefore be seen that although the pamphlet has been printed, it was not printed for publication. The following extract from the concluding part of the introductory remarks of my pamphlet clearly indicates my views in regard to this question:—'These are the circumstances which have led to the printing of the following sheets, and they are, therefore, intended and adapted for the use of those who may feel an interest in the furtherance of the work projected by the Honorable the Court of Directors, and not for the public at large.'

The foregoing statements will, I trust, satisfactorily account for my having omitted to present you, and the other conductors of the press, with copies of the pamphlet in question. But as it has now, without my concurrence, been placed before the public, and that with remarks, from our most Respected Archbishop, commendatory of my exertions, I believe the only course now left for me is to submit the pamphlet to the criticism and comments of the liberal press of this presidency, soliciting its kind indulgence in behalf of the work. I beg accordingly to present you with two copies of the pamphlet, and to express my thanks for the liberal and friendly tone of the comments with which you have already been pleased to favor my communication to His Grace the Archbishop."

In the same paper, the Editor of the *Hurkaru*, after perusal of Mr. Crow's pamphlet, offers the following remarks which are pre-eminently characterized by fairness, practicality, and sober sound sense :—

" We are not sorry, that the little indiscretion of the *Bengal Catholic Herald* has brought Mr. Crow's production to the notice of the public, as this affords us an opportunity of offering a few remarks on the system of orthography he proposes.

Mr. Crow quotes from the *Christian Observer* the following passage, in which some important principles for the formation of an alphabet are laid down:—

'Without specifying the whole' (of the requisites for a perfect alphabet), ' I may remark, that by the common consent of the soundest philologists, the following are of the number. As every separate elementary sound ought to have a separate character to express it ; so none but separate elementary sounds ought to have separate characters. Elementary sounds radically the same, but differing somewhat in tone, time, or mode of enunciation, ought *not* to have representative characters wholly different in form.'

We quite agree with Mr. Crow in the value he attaches to what is here propounded, and admit that he could not have done better than take these principles for his guide in the construction of his new system of clothing oriental languages in the Roman character. We have seen several parts of the Glossary he refers to, and observed, that the orthography of many words in it, is such as would convey a most erroneous idea of their true pronunciation to any one who did not know what that was.

Certainly, it is absurd to write the word *Khálasá* as Mr. Trevelyan, in our opinion correctly, expresses it, *Calsa*, as it is written in the Glossary; but we cannot agree with Mr. Crow as to the word *Chokee* or *Choky*: an Italian might be in danger of pronouncing this *Koky*, but we do not think an Englishman would; for he would naturally infer that as in one part of the word, the hard sound of k is represented by k, it could never be intended to express it by ch in the beginning of the word. As a general rule, indeed, in our language, ch, where it begins a word and is immediately followed by a vowel, is soft; the exceptions are chiefly, if not entirely, Greek derivatives, as in " choral, chord, chorepiscopal, chorist, chorographer" &c.; but in the greater number of words beginning with ch, even when immediately followed by o, the sound of this compound consonant is soft as in the verb "to choke," and the adjective "choky," which last is pronounced precisely like the native word generally so expressed in the Roman character. With respect to the word "*chuprasee*," the case is still stronger, for, surely, no Englishman would be in danger of pronouncing the syllable chu, ku, for we do not believe there is a single word in our language in which the letters ch, immediately followed by the vowel u, have the hard sound of k. In what Mr. Crow says of the terminations ee and y to represent the same sound, we think he is right. With regard to the two Bengali letters which Mr. Trevelyan represents by ch and chh we do not think that Mr. Crow has succeeded in improving on that mode of expressing them, and we are sorry that we cannot give our readers an opportunity of judging for themselves, as the types necessary to illustrate our remark are not obtainable.

We do not think that much is gained by dropping letters and multiplying diacritical marks. On the contrary, though there may be a saving of space by the use of these, they rather complicate than simplify a system of orthography. Mr. Crow, it is true, expresses the word by four letters only, but he uses two diacritical marks to one of these, which is any thing but an improvement.

We pass on to a specimen given of a whole paragraph in Bengali, written according to Mr. Trevelyan's and Mr. Crow's systems, preceded by the English version of the text: we regret we cannot give the specimen.

It seems to us that both the modes of writing the language might be improved upon, but of the two, we prefer Mr. Trevelyan's. It occupies more space, but appears to us less complicated for the very reason that it has fewer of those diacritical marks of which Mr. Crow is so fond, and which are, in our opinion, so liable to be mistaken and to create confusion. In the word which Mr. Trevelyan writes *byaktir*, and Mr. Crow *beáktir*, neither comes quite close to the mark; but if the former had used for the letter a the accented *é*, we think he would have been nearer. We prefer Mr. Crow's *putro*, however, to *putra*, and his *cilo* might be better than *chhila*, (understanding that the c in the former has, as in Italian before the vowels e and i, the soft sound of our ch), but we think that the chh better expresses the compound Bengali consonant in the word, which we would write *chhilo*. Again; in the word *tahar*, Mr. Crow uses two diacritical marks for the second vowel, which is far from being an improvement. The word which Mr. Trevelyan writes *bishayer*, and Mr. Crow *bisoer* with two marks to the letter e, would be much better expressed, we think, thus—"bishoyér." These specimens may suffice to show that both systems are susceptible of improvement, but we repeat that Mr. Trevelyan's, as they now stand, appears to us the better of the two. To enable our readers to judge, however, they must first read Mr. Crow's explanation of his system, which we quote among our selections, and we must do him the justice to say that his pamphlet proves that he has given great attention to the subject, and furnished satisfactory evidence of his qualifications for the task he has undertaken. We would not have his system condemned, therefore, by our remarks on a few isolated specimens of his scheme, which he has illustrated by an "Alphabetical table, showing the application of Roman to all the Indian characters in a simple, concise, yet comprehensive plan, illustrated by 16 Indian Alphabets." We regret that we cannot conveniently give this table, but it is a proof of Mr. Crow's industry and research, which we are bound to notice. He has also given another table in which he has exhibited the Romanizing systems of Sir W. Jones, Dr. Gilchrist, Mr. Shakespeare, Mr. Trevelyan, and his own.

There are, we doubt not, many orientalists who laugh to scorn the idea of expressing the native languages in one character, and that the Roman ; but even they will scarcely deny the importance of establishing some uniform system of expressing native names and words, when in books addressed to English readers for example, it is absolutely indispensible so to express them. It cannot have escaped the attention of any man who has read works on subjects connected with India, that the most glaring inconsistencies arise from the want of such a system. Not only are the names of native places, persons, and things never expressed by the same letters in any two books, but even in the same volume we continually find them, in different parts of it, differently written ; and often so absurdly as to the real pronunciation, as to excite the ridicule of those who know anything of the matter. Surely, then, when we consider, how many there are who do read books on this country, how many more there are who ought to read them, we must admit, that, even on account of such readers only, such a system as we have referred to, is a desideratum. Even in this more limited point of view, then, the subject we have been discussing is important and worthy of the attention of orientalists, however averse they may be to the proposal to print books in the native languages in the Roman character."

On the 21st June, a letter appeared in the *Hurkaru* disclosing facts which tended to throw new light on the history of the Romanizing system now generally employed by most *practical* Romanizers, throughout the country. It is as follows :—

" To the Editor of the Bengal Hurkaru.

MR. EDITOR,—As Mr. Crow has again returned to the discussion of the Romanizing System, I hope you will favour me by inserting a few remarks on the subject. It is not my intention, *at present*, to treat of the merits or demerits of Mr. Crow's proposed scheme ; this I may do hereafter, when his letters have been brought to a close. My immediate object is simply to correct one or two erroneous statements of fact.

1st. The scheme which Mr. Crow and others are in the habit of referring to as " Mr. Trevelyan's," is that gentleman's only in a restricted sense : it is his, *not by paternity, as its author,* but *by adoption, as its patron.* When, early in 1834, Mr. Trevelyan, publicly threw out the idea of printing all Oriental works in Roman characters, he had no Romanizing scheme of his own. The learned Orientalists, with Dr. Tytler at their head, being, at that time, a powerful body, Mr. Trevelyan's idea was scouted, and publicly laughed to scorn. It so happened, that, at that very time, the subject had been seriously occupying the attention of another gentleman, in connection with various plans for the amelioration of the people of India; that gentleman was the Rev. Mr. (now Dr.) Duff. Accordingly, under the signature of " ALPHA," he published a paper " On the Possibility, the Practicability, and the Expediency of substituting the Roman, in place of the Indian, Alphabets." It is from this paper that Mr. Crow has quoted certain passages with approbation. The publication of this paper led to an immediate correspondence between Mr. Trevelyan and its author. Mr. Trevelyan, with his wonted enthusiasm, was in raptures at the " backing" which he now met with. Having no scheme of his own, he only urged " ALPHA" to presevere, pledging himself to bear any pecuniary expense which might be entailed in the prosecution of the attempt. The article now alluded to appeared in the *Calcutta Christian Observer* for April 1834, and was, at the time, highly commended by the *Hurkaru* and *India Gazette.* It was followed up by another article, by the

same author, in the May No. of the *Observer*. In this paper was developed
" the Scheme for representing the *Dévá Nágári* and Persian alphabets in
Roman characters," which Mr. Trevelyan was pleased to adopt, patronize,
and zealously propagate. In the June No. of the *Observer*, the author
completed his scheme by a third and elaborate article, containing " a representation in Roman character of the principal alphabets in Eastern India,
with Notices of Dialectic peculiarities, specimens of the mode of applying the
letters in practice, and answers to objections." It was from his adoption,
patronage, and zealous propagation of the scheme thus propounded and
vindicated by " ALPHA," *alias* Dr. Duff, that Mr. Trevelyan's name came to
be associated with it, as if he were its author. With the authorship, he had
nothing to do. The only gentlemen to whom the real author felt under
any obligation for suggestions, were Dr. Yates and the late Rev. Mr.
Pearce, as may be seen in the *Observer* for May 1834, page 241. The
scheme thus recommended to public notice was only that of Sir W. Jones,
slightly modified and improved. It is, *substantially*, the scheme which has
uniformly been pursued by the Asiatic Society of Bengal, the Royal Asiatic
Society of London, and other learned bodies, together with the overwhelming majority of learned Orientalists in Great Britain, America, and the
continent of Europe. Such a scheme, therefore, ought not to be lightly
intermeddled with ; and I cannot but sincerely regret that Mr. Crow, with
the very best intentions, should have suddenly appeared on the stage as an
innovator, rather than an *upholder*, of what promised, ere long, to become
a fixed and universally-established system. Such fresh innovations are
calculated only to disturb and unsettle the minds of men, without any
countervailing advantages, on the score of any obvious or readily-admitted
improvement. They only tend to retard, instead of hastening on, the
consummation so devoutly to be wished for, viz., unanimity in the adoption
of some one system of generally recognized aptitude and authority.

2d. It is by no means correct to say that, " apparently, the Romanizing
system had, so to speak, gone out, never to be revived." *The direct contrary
is the fact*. The Romanizing system has *never gone out*, except as *a subject
of newspaper discussion; it has been in actual operation up to this hour*, and
does not, therefore, stand in need of being "revived," in the sense of
bringing to life that which has become extinct. Fresh zeal in its behalf may
be enkindled, advocates may be multiplied, and the sphere of its usefulness
may be enlarged ; but the system itself has never been extinguished ; it has
lived on, quietly and unobtrusively diffusing the benefits of sound knowledge
among thousands of the people of this land. In *practice* it has been found
better adapted for the Urdú or Hindústáni and other dialects from the
Arabic or Persian, than for Bengali and other offshoots from the Sanskrit.
Accordingly, it has been in the North Western Provinces, that the system
has been extensively pursued. There, in Romanized Urdú, various school
books have been prepared and widely employed in the education of youth.
In Romanized Urdú, a native newspaper has, for years, been published at
the Mirzapore Press. In Romanized Urdú, two different versions of the
New Testament have been prepared and printed. At Allahabad, the American Missionaries have published various works in this character ; and
amongst others an Urdú translation of the Qurán (Koran) with notes.
From the Baptist Press, Calcutta, various works have issued in the same
character. And *lastly* the greatest work, which has appeared for years, a
translation, for the first time, of the *entire* Bible, Old and New Testament,
into Urdú or Hindústáni, has been published in Roman characters by the
Calcutta Bible Society. This great work (of which, Mr. Editor, I beg
your acceptance of a copy) is in *one* large 8vo. volume. In the Persian or

Hindústání character, the same work extends to *three* large 8vo. volumes. The system of Romanizing pursued in *all* these works is that which was propounded by the ALPHA of the *Christian Observer, eleven* years ago. About three years since, sundry rumours began to float about, that differences had arisen among the friends of the system. The subject was promptly investigated by the Committee of the Bible Society. It was soon found that these respected only the practical mode of representing *two* Persian letters, and that, on an explanation mutually given and received, even this slight difference disappeared: so that, *all practical* Romanizers have ever since been unanimous in the scheme which they have approved, adopted, and pursued.

Yours very truly,
INDOPHILUS REDIVIVUS."

This letter called forth the following remarks from the Editor :—

"It appears from the letter of INDOPHILUS REDIVIVUS, that we were mistaken in attributing to Mr. Trevelyan the authorship of the Romanizing system, which is generally ascribed to him. The scheme which is a modification of that of Sir William Jones originated, it seems, with Dr. Duff, who was the ALPHA of the *Calcutta Christian Observer*, when, in 1834, that useful periodical was so much occupied in the discussion of this subject. We also learn from our Correspondent, that, we were equally in error in supposing that until Mr. Crow's letter appeared, the system had been consigned to oblivion, and was no longer employed in printing books in the native languages. So far is this from being the case, that the Romanizing plan has never been discontinued, but is still up to this day extensively and successfully used in books printed for the instruction of the rising generation, and particularly in the North West Provinces, where it is more resorted to, because better adapted, as our Correspondent informs us, to languages derived from Persian and Arabic, than to those which are off-shoots from Sanskrit. He states that various works have been published in the Roman character by the American Missionaries at Allahabad, and besides this, that the Calcutta Bible Society have published the entire Bible, the Old and New Testament, in Hindustani in Roman letters, of which he has sent us a copy. This appears to us a splendid triumph of the system, one immense advantage of which may be gathered from this fact, that the book so printed is comprised in *one* thick octavo volume, whereas had the Persian character been used, it would have occupied *three* of the same size. This Hindustani Bible, which is now before us, and confirms us in the favorable opinion we expressed more than ten years ago, of the system, we must now call Dr. Duff's.

Under the mistaken impression that the system had ceased to be applied in the printing of books in the native languages, we were pleased to see Mr. Crow coming forward again to direct public attention to the subject. Our Correspondent may have observed, however, that we stated that we could not perceive the advantages of Mr. Crow's modifications of the system in use (which we called Mr. Trevelyan's) judging from the specimens then before us. Now, however, that we know that the Romanizing system referred to above, has been steadily pursued for years, and is still employed in printing books in the native languages, and has been found to answer every expectation formed of it, we cannot but agree with INDOPHILUS REDIVIVUS in the opinion that Mr. Crow's interference is wholly uncalled for, and that, however well intended, it cannot fail to prove mischievous if continued, by dividing public attention between two schemes, and weakening public confidence in one which has succeeded so well.

We think that it is much to be regretted that Government, before they agreed to recommend Mr. Crow's new scheme to the Court of Directors, did not inquire how far that in which so many books had already been printed, had succeeded. As it is, we trust that some enquiry will still be made into this point, before any further encouragement is given to the new mode of expressing the native languages in Roman letters. We believe, that Dr. Duff's, in spite of some anomalies inseparable from every scheme of the kind, is, on the whole, admirably adapted to convey native sounds; it has the advantage of having been tested by an experience of 11 years, and is not likely to be improved by an attempt, however ingenious at simplifying, by means of the multiplication of diacritical points, which forms such a conspicuous feature of Mr. Crow's system. We give him credit for the best intentions, for much ingenuity, and for considerable knowledge of the subject discussed in his Pamphlet, but we hope that when he learns from the letter of INDOPHILUS REDIVIVUS, that the Romanizing system instead of being extinct has been, and is still, peacefully pursuing the even tenor of its way, he will be content to leave it in the able hands of those under whose guidance it has so long gone on and prospered."

This was the signal for a series of letters in which Mr. Crow attempted to expound and vindicate his own system, while he exhibited no superfluity of fairness or ceremony towards what he now regarded as its principal antagonist. His letters were let off, somewhat after the fashion of sky rockets which obtrude themselves on public notice with hissing noise and flaming combustion, that seem to threaten havoc and ruin all around. But, like these aerial visitants, which, after a brief but fiery passage into the regions of upper space, explode harmlessly there, to the no small amusement of idling spectators, the letters have discharged their contents innocuously into the great void of profitless wrangling and quibbling controversy.

On the appearance of the second or third of the series, the Editor of the *Hurkaru* remarked as follows, on the 12th July :—

"We publish to-day another letter of Mr. Crow's on the manner of expressing Indian terms by Roman characters. Of course, he considers his system superior to every other, and in any remarks we may make on the subject, we shall, certainly, not be influenced by the vain hope of changing his opinion on this point. We will take the trouble, however, of indicating a fallacy into which he falls that vitiates much of the reasoning which he deems so triumphant. ALPHA has laid down a general rule, and applied it admirably, making only such exceptions to its application as were necessary for the sake of simplification, but never hesitating to make them where they were calculated to secure the attainment of that important object. Of this mode of proceeding, Mr. Crow has no idea. A general rule, with him, is a regular bed of Procrustes, which those who were to occupy it were made to fit, by having their limbs lopped off. For fear of departing from his adopted rule, he lops away letters, in defiance of usage and association, and thinks he has simplified a great deal by giving to the letter c, for instance, the soft sound of ch, which it invariably has in Italian, before the vowels e and i; but when the vowel that follows it is o or u, he is obliged to have recourse to a mark, which he may consider a simplifying process, but which we think quite the reverse. Do any of our readers, except Mr. Crow, think, for example, that any thing is gained by writing the word *chokee, coki*, according to his system? To be sure he has told us that c is to have invariably the soft sound of ch, as it has in the Italian before the vowels e and i; but then, is it not certain that every Englishman, and especially if he happens to

f

know Italian, would be liable to give it the hard sound of k whenever it was followed by o or u, and to pronounce Mr. Crow's *coki, koki,* instead of *chokee,* as he intends? He will answer, of course—" Oh, but you forget, I put one clear mark to denote the aspirate sound." No, we do not forget : but we think the recognised mode of expressing that sound by the aid of another letter, infinitely less liable to mistake than Mr. Crow's mark, and, consequently, that his proposed improvement is really injurious, instead of being advantageous. It is needless to pursue the subject, as, to him,

> " The man convinced against his will
> Is of the same opinion still."

Mr. Crow's grand mistake is that of confounding a sound general rule, to be applied with judicious exceptions whenever required, with a fixed law admitting of no deviation whatever. Acting upon this mistake, Mr. Crow has endeavoured to apply ALPHA's excellent general rule, and, of course, he has failed, and complicated what he intended to simplify. It is probable that ALPHA will undertake the defence of his system ; and if so, we shall gladly leave the discussion in hands so much more skilful than our own. We must beg of Mr. Crow, however, to study condensation as much as possible in his future letters, for we shall not be able to find space for them, if they are all to spread out to the length of that which we to-day insert."

On the 19th July appeared a letter from an intelligent correspondent " B," from which we quote a few remarks very much to the point, relative to Mr. Crow's application of the Italian sound of the letter *c :—*

" Mr. Crow claims for the letter C, the same sound which it has in Italian before *e* and *i ;* that is, the same as the English *ch ;* and assumes it to be the *natural* sound. But facts go to show that it is *not* the natural sound, (if there be such a thing as " natural" sounds, applying the term in this way) ; and, consequently, his whole reasoning goes for nothing. The Italian is derived from the Latin, in which language the *c,* does not seem to have been pronounced as *ch ;* and, therefore, I should be disposed to regard it as a corruption, if I held the opinion that particular letters had *natural* sounds. It is so evidently a local pronunciation that even in Italy and Sicily you have, in different States, all varieties of pronunciation, from *s* on the one side, to *k* on the other, and, of course, embracing the *ch.* It is well known that the Tuscans speak the purest idiom of the Italian, and yet their traditional pronunciation of the C before *a* and *o* is not like *k,* but is exactly the guttural German *g,* or Spanish *x ;* which fact I mention merely as a proof that no general inference can be drawn from local peculiarities.

In Spain, too, where the language is principally derived from the Latin, the letter *c* is invariably pronounced, by all who pretend to speak the language properly, as the English *th,* when it precedes *e* and *i.*

The classical pronunciation of the letter *c* before these vowels, in the modern Italian language, is, no doubt, precisely what Mr. Crow states it to be ; and had he shown any great advantage to be obtained by adopting the Italian in preference to the English pronunciation, there would have been some rational ground for discussing the matter. But I am disposed to contend that even if the English pronunciation were more open to cavil than it is, *still* it would be the proper pronunciation to adopt in the proposed Romanizing system. The Italian language is not likely to be cultivated beyond the limits of Europe, whilst the English is not only the language of the—almost universal—*governing power* in India, but the language of her numerous colonies in every part of the world, and of the whole of North America ; and seems destined by Providence to become the universal language of the world. Surely, therefore, it is most desirable to facilitate the acquisition of this medium of spreading the light of civilization and knowledge by adopting letters which convey similar elemental sounds in English and in the languages of India, instead of letters which are pronounced in a particular manner in a language foreign to both."

Mr. Crow still went on with a perseverance and energy worthy of a better cause than his new fangled scheme of Romanizing. Every one except the author himself was heartily wearied of his seemingly endless, and, in many respects, inane and inept lucubrations. At length on the 9th August, the Editor of the *Hurkaru* put forth the following emphatic announcement :—

"We decline the insertion of VERITAS. He sets out with complaining of the slowness, with which the discussion on Mr. Crow's Romanizing system is progressing, a point on which we fully agree with him, and then very *consistently* proceeds to spin out in defence of that system, nearly a column which is a mere echo of what has been better said before on the same side. We think it is quite enough that we have given ample space to Mr. Crow's own explanation and vindication of his scheme of Romanizing, and that we are not called on to occupy our columns with the communications of any of those who may fancy that he needs their assistance. It is time, in short, to put a stop to this discussion, and we beg to intimate to Mr. Crow, therefore, that his letter, which we insert to-day, must be the last on the subject. But we mean no unkindness or disrespect towards him. We hinted some time ago, that it was probable that ALPHA would take up the cudgels against this new system, but we now beg he will not do so, in our paper, at least, for if he does, he will bring out Mr. Crow again ; and many of our readers have complained of the space we have already devoted to this long discussion, and we wish to be rid of it at once."

On the 16th August, ALPHA, without entering into details which were now forbidden or unnecessary, deemed it due to himself, and the friends who had for the last ten years been acting on his system, to obtain insertion for the following letter in the columns of the Saturday evening's *Hurkaru*, or *Calcutta Literary Gazette* : —

"FAREWELL TO MR. CROW AND HIS ROMANIZING SYSTEM.

To the Editor of the Calcutta Literary Gazette.

MR. EDITOR,—Having already shut the door against any farther lucubrations on the Romanizing system, it is not my intention, by word or deed, to say or do any thing to induce you to re-open it.

It never was my purpose to enter, at length, into an examination of MR. CROW's system, or to rebut his varied charges in detail. But, after the virtual invitation at one time held out to me in your editorial columns, it was my design to wait patiently till MR. CROW's remarks, which were so heavily "dragging their slow length along," came to an end, and then, by reference to a few select examples, briefly to point out how unfairly he had dealt with the system of ALPHA, and how little occasion he had for glorying so boastfully in his own. Even this, however, after your authorative monition of last Saturday evening, I shall not venture to attempt now.

MR. CROW is a man of talents and research, and no one can know better than he does, how very easy it is for such a man—by sundry additions, omissions, and partial representations, by the jingling jugglery of words, and artful collocation of syllogistic phrases that have in them the *semblance* of solid reasoning,—how very easy it is, by these and such like means, for any one versed in the little arts and tricks of controversy, at any time and on any subject, to " to make the worse, appear the better reason." Not that I charge MR. CROW with wilfully or intentionally acting any such part. No such thing. He is so intensely prepossessed in favour of his own system, that any little merits which may rightfully belong to it, are magnified, in his eye, into surpassing excellencies that wholly over-shadow and shut out of view its greatest defects. And this over-weening prepossession in favour of the imaginary or exaggerated excellencies of his own system very natu- rally impels him to fix his gaze on the real or supposed deficiencies of that which he regards as its most formidable rival—to see these through an im- mensely magnifying medium—and, at last, to swell them into such undue proportions as utterly to cast all counter-vailing merits and advantages into the darksome shadows of the back-ground. In short, with the doating fond- ness of parental affection, the offspring of his own brain seems all beauty and perfection, while the offspring of the brains of others seem little else than all blemish and imperfection. The former seems almost or altogether right ; the latter almost or altogether wrong.

ALPHA has no occasion to feel any jealousy or rivalry towards MR. CROW and his system ; neither does he entertain any. His (*i. e.* ALPHA'S) has, long ere now, commended itself to the judgment of all on this side of India, who resolved to employ the Romanizing scheme as an instrument of practical utility—to the agents and representatives of all our great religious societies, whether British or American, between Calcutta and Ludianah. For the sake of unity and uniformity in embracing a system which, on the whole, appeared to hit on the " *media ria*," many of these magnanimously surren- dered sundry little partialities and predilections of their own on particular points. And the happy consequence has been, that, while MR. CROW's system, as yet, exists only in the dead letter of official documents or the wordy ovations of newspaper discussion, the other has, for the last ten years, been employed in imparting the seeds and principles of quickening know- ledge, sacred and prophane, to thousands and tens of thousands of our juve- nile and adult population, throughout the whole extent of the Gangetic valley.

Had MR. CROW been able to point to such a practical triumph of his system, there might be some excuse for the self-gratulations and self-glory- ings in which he has allowed himself so freely to indulge. But without pretending to aught like the gift of vaticination, I may venture to predict that such triumph it is never destined to realize. Even were the Government, in an inauspicious hour, to adopt it for official purposes, such adoption of it might tend to some confusion and mischief, but could do nothing to alter or modify the deliberately-formed views of the great mass of practical Romani- zers. However plausible it may appear in theory I have no hesitation in declaring, that, in the widest and most comprehensive sense, it will be found, in practice, utterly impracticable. Of the system, as a whole, it may truly be predicated, that *whatever is good in it is not new, and whatever is new is not good.*

ALPHA is not aware of having ever made a boastful parade of his own system. Having, once for all, fairly and fully propounded it in the *Calcutta Christian Observer* for the months of April, May, and June, 1834, he left it to stand or fall entirely on its own merits or demerits. Even when assailed by ignorance, or prejudice, of malice, he never stepped forward in its vindi- cation or defence—assured that the tree which could not outbrave the ordi- nary cross gusts and breezes of heaven, had little life or strength in it, and did not deserve to stand.   As time rolled on, his feelings were those of deep and unfeigned thankfulness to the God of Providence, who had so overruled events as to secure for the system so favourable a reception, and render it so extensive an instrument of usefulness.

Sincerely hoping that, should MR. CROW ever again appear before the Indian Public as an advocate or expounder of his own Romanizing system, he may see the propriety of dropping somewhat of the pugnacious spirit and purely controversial form which have, unhappily, characterized his recent letters.

I remain, yours, &c.,

ALPHA."

To this letter Mr. Crow, by special permission of the Editor, was allowed briefly to reply, on condition that " no new matter should be gone into, and the letter should be of such a nature as not to call for a re-opening of the question regarding the merits of different systems of Romanization."   The reply itself, like most of Mr. C.'s other productions, is more adroit than ingenuous—indicating a better acquaintance with the stratagems of controversy than with the argu- ments of a manly straight-forward logic.   What, for example, can be more preposterous than his interpretation of the heading of ALPHA's letter ?   " By the heading," says he, " which ALPHA has affixed to his letter in the last Saturday's evening *Hurkaru, he no doubt means to imply that he will* NEVER MORE *interfere with my Romanizing system.*" He then goes on to " conclude that by his farewell, ALPHA in a manner binds himself to keep the peace towards his (Mr. C.'s) Romanizing system, whether it be in public or in private, &c."   This is a fair specimen of what we have characterized as more adroit than inge- nuous ; for it is scarcely possible that the writer himself could have been deluded by his own wretched sophism, or give any thing like honest credence to the propriety of his own far-fetched conclusion.   No one ought to know better than the writer that the term "farewell," did not originally, does not now necessarily, and often does not at all include the notion or idea of " for ever."   The first lines of a popular poem in the mouth of every school boy, might have taught him the contrary :—

" Fare thee well, and, if for ever,
Still for ever, fare thee well."

Here the hypothetical *if* essentially implies that there is A *"farewell"* which is NOT *for ever.*   How often do friends, when parting only for a short season, bid each other " farewell !"   How often in concluding a letter, does the writer close with a " farewell," without the remotest suspicion that he is thereby " binding himself !" never to write any more !   But to dwell any more on such silly nibbling at one of the possible uses of a word, is worse than superfluous.   Leaving all such over-strainings of the imaginable meaning of a word, plain unso- phisticated common sense may at once expound the meaning of the heading of ALPHA's letter.   It can mean nothing more than a fare- well to Mr. Crow and his system *for the present,* and with a special reference to the *present channel of discussion,* viz. the *Hurkaru, from whose columns any farther discussion of the subject has, in the mean-while, been excluded.*

Again, in quoting these words of ALPHA, "It never was my purpose to enter at length, into an examination of Mr. Crow's system, or to rebut his varied charges in detail," Mr. C. by adroitly skipping over the significant terms " at length" and " in detail," applies the passage as if it meant that ALPHA never intended to examine his (Mr. C.'s) system at all, either in whole or in part;—though, in the *very next* sentence, ALPHA goes on to make the following emphatic declaration, " It *was my design* to wait patiently, till Mr. Crow's remarks, which were so heavily dragging their slow length along, came to an end, and THEN, *by reference to a few select examples, briefly to* point out how unfairly he had dealt *with the system of* ALPHA, *and how little occasion he had for glorying so boastfully in his own. Even this, however, after your authoritative monition of last Saturday evening, I shall not venture to attempt now.*" And yet, in the face of all this, Mr. Crow would throw dust in the eyes of his readers, —leading them first to believe that ALPHA had resolved or declined to examine or expose his (Mr. C.'s) system at all, and then insinuating that this was because he (ALPHA) could not do so with any advantage to himself or his cause ! Can unfairness or disingenuousness in controversy well proceed much farther than this ? Heedless alike of the provocative insinuations or the idle self-gloryings of any antagonist, ALPHA, we presume, will take his own way and time for defending his own system, should he ever have reason to conclude that it stands in need of any defence.

Meanwhile, let not Mr. Crow so hastily and eagerly " count without his host." Silence may arise from other causes than those which he is pleased to insinuate or allege. It may proceed quite as much from indifference or contempt. Or, it may arise from a thorough conviction that the position occupied is too firm to be shaken by such attacks as those of the present controversialist—and that to step forward formally to repel them, would be a sheer waste of precious time. Be all this as it may, we cannot but sincerely regret the course which Mr. Crow has deemed it proper to adopt. Instead of a gentle *reform* of the existing system which has been found to work so well for many years past he at once proposes a radical destruction— a perfect *revolution.* He has headed his own revolution in a way that is calculated, not to conciliate or convince, but to irritate, repel, and dissuade. For this we are really very sorry, for the sake of Mr. Crow himself, and the credit of Romanizing generally. There is much in Mr. Crow's talents and character which fairly entitles him to respect. And we cannot but regret that the former should be so misapplied, and the latter so damaged,—the former, by the devising of sophisms, and the latter by the suspicion of disingenuousness. Apart from the unhappy peculiarities of his own system, we must do Mr. Crow the justice to say, that many of his remarks on the general subject of Romanizing, and the advantages and necessity of *some uniform* system being adopted, are admirable and even masterly.

From the *Romanizing* system it may not be an unpleasing or unin-structive variety to glance at what may be termed the *Hellenizing* scheme. To a sprightly and ingenious correspondent we are indebted for the following fragment or brief notice of—

The mode of writing ancient Oriental names in Greek characters, and the inferences therefrom deducible as to the pronunciation of the Greek letters in the flourishing age of Greek literature.

The Septuagint translation of the Old Testament is supposed to have been made about two hundred and eighty years before Christ,* and could not have been made later than the year 246, B. C. if it be cor-rectly attributed to the reign of Ptolemy Philadelphus. The translators, says Horne, from the introduction of Coptic words, are clearly proved to have been natives of Egypt, and we may add that they were probably the learned descendants of Jews settled at Alexandria. At the period in question, the Greek Empire and language were in their utmost splendour and perfection. From Magna Græcia to the banks of the Oxus [50° of longitude,] and from the Pyramids to Tomi† the farthest outpost of civilization in the north of the world [nearly 15° of latitude,] the works of Demosthenes, Euripides, Plato, Aristotle, Homer, and Euclid, directed the taste, morals, politics, religion and science of civilized men. The power of the successors of Alexander was mainly founded on the superior science and civilization of the Greeks, compared with those of the nations they subjected. The little Greeks, " Græculi," as the haughty Romans called them, were no great heroes, except by their own false account,

> " Quicquid Græcia mendax
> Audet in historia."—JUVENAL.

Their dominion was upheld by wise policy and embellished by the arts, useful and ornamental. It was during this period that the Old

---

* Communis veterum sententia, versionis hujus auspicia, ad Ptolomæum Philadelphum Ægypti Regem, structuram vero et compositionem ad lxxii. delegatos ex Palæstina Judæos vel juxta Talmudican traditionem ad V. solum magistros, &c. &c. &c." the preface to the Septuagint by D. J. Gottlob goes on to state that it is better ascertained to have been effected by the private piety and industry of certain Alexandrine Jews. It is clear that closely connected as the Jews have been with the Ægyptians, neither could have been ignorant of the other's history ; and the Pyramids may yet possibly contain an Ægyptian history contemporaneous to that of Moses. We mean not, of course, history in its ordinary form, but history in hierogly-phical representations, Of this description a good deal has already been elicited from the tombs and catacombs by recent researches. Josephus would be a good author from whom to ascertain the pronunciation of Greek letters, by comparison with oriental proper names, were not the purity of his Greek questionable.

† Tomi, a Milesian Colony, where Ovid was banished, near the mouth of the Danube.

> " Hic quoque sunt igitur Graiæ [quis crederet] urbes,
> Inter inhumanæ nomina barbariæ,
> Sauromatæ cingunt fera gens, Bessique, Getæque,
> Quam non ingenio nomina digna meo !
> Sæpe sonant moti glacie pendente capilli
> Et nitet inducto candida barba gelu."—OVID TRIST.

Testament was translated into Greek, at a time when the savans of the Greek Empire had had abundant opportunity, nearly fifty years, to acquire the pronunciation of the Arabic, Persian, and Syriac languages, while a sufficient period had not elapsed for the corruption of the the language of Thucydides.* The Coptic or Alexandrine Jews, who translated the Old Testament into Greek, did so for the perusal and benefit of the learned men of the East and West; the universal language of literary men being Greek, and Alexandria being the source and centre of the literature, as well as the great emporium of the trade, of the world. The work of the Coptic Jewish transla- tors was therefore subjected to the criticism of scholars and professors from Cyrene and Syracuse, Athens and Halicarnassus, Damascus and Gaza, Babylon and Persepolis. Amongst these scholars, those who came from Syria, Mesopotamia, and Persia to study at Alexandria, allured by the patronage of the Royal Fratricide, would most likely often consist of the offspring of Greek Colonists by Persian ladies of rank,— such intermarriages being a part of the policy of Alexander, the greatest scholar of the greatest tutor. These young men would have learned to pronounce Syriac and Persian from their lady mothers, and their Oriental friends and attendants; while they learned to pro- nounce perfect Iambics from their fathers.† It must be recollected that all the free Greeks were men of great taste, correctness and elegance, both in speaking and writing. The humblest Athenian or Syracusan Citizen could detect a false quantity in a verse, a false proportion in a statue, or a false light in a painting. We poor emigrants, unlike the Colonists conducted by Alexander, have com- paratively little taste for such pursuits, and deface our language, already sufficiently sibilant and mixed, by engrafting strange words un- known to Milton, Pope, Addison or Gibbon. But the dainty Greeks were singularly jealous of the purity of their language, and it is not

---

* During the reign of Seleucus Nicator the closest correspondence and inter- course took place between the Greeks on one side and the Syrians, Persians, and Bactrians on the other. Many Greek Colonies were settled in Asia. During his reign, which ended about the same time that the Septuagint translation was written, the most favourable opportunity was given to the Greeks and Orientals to become acquainted with their respective languages, idioms, pronunciations, and literatures. It is to this period therefore from 310 to 280 B. C. that we must look to find Oriental names given correctly in Greek letters. The succeeding Greek monarchs of Asia were gradually driven to the West and confined to Syria by the Parthians, and literary communication between the East and West continually diminished, and Greeks ceased to talk Persian, or to hear it talked.

† It is impossible that the numerous Colonies of Greeks, settled by Alexander and Seleucus Nicator through Asia, in a period of fifty years, should not have learn- ed the Persian language. The Persians had possessed Asia for upwards of two cen- turies from 538 to 331 B. C. During this time their language was spread and their customs established from Palibothra to Ephesus. The Sanskrit and ancient Persian languages have many words in common. A language thus established through the most populous regions of the world by the use of two centuries could not be abolished soon by the Greeks, but must have been adopted and learned by them as Urdu, Persian, Bengali, &c. are by us. The Greeks subdued nominally or effectually Parthia or Khorasan, in 329 B. C. The Parthians rebelled against the second Antiochus about 250 B. C., and drove the Greeks out of Persia after a pos- session of eighty years,—the only occasion on which Persia in the history of the world has been possessed by Europeans.

to be supposed that in forty years the Grecian Colonies of Alexander would have forgot the first language for eloquence and rhetoric that has ever existed. The sons of the Greek Colonists, therefore, who came to study at Alexandria under its renowned philosophers, may be allowed to have been pretty perfect both in Greek and Oriental pronunciation. These young noblemen no doubt like the rest of the world might thoroughly despise the Jews,

" Quorum cophinus fœnumque supellex."—JUVENAL.

much in the same way as the sons of some of our great men here, when sent for education to England, may despise those whom they regard as poor, fanatical, and ranting Methodists. But this is no reason why the Jewish Coptic authors of the Septuagint version should not have been desirous to get credit for learning by accurately rendering Oriental proper names in Greek letters : otherwise the translation would have had no chance of being read by men acquainted with both languages, and Ptolemy II. himself from his connexion with Antiochus probably understood Syriac.

It being granted therefore that the Jewish Coptic translators of the Old Testament were either descendants of the Jewish prisoners transported by the first Ptolemy to Alexandria, or at least were Jews long settled in Egypt, where the Greek tongue was spoken by all the savans; we may, from our knowledge of the pronunciation of Persian words at the present day, attain an approximation to what was the pronunciation of Greek letters in the times of pure and classical Greek literature, from the works of Arrian who saw the writings of the cotemporaneous Historians of Alexander, from those of Herodotus and other Greek Authors on Oriental history, and especially from the Septuagint.

Alif with a medda آ [See Sir W. Jones' Grammar,] is merely a double Alif and is represented, in Greek, by alpha with the soft aspirate as ـ in 'Αδὰμ, آدم, Adam. Hence perhaps alpha with the soft aspirate in the beginning of a word was pronounced as a long or double A.

Simple Alif with fatha in the beginning of a word is rendered by Alpha with a hard accent as 'Αβραὰμ ابراهيم Abraham. Hence initial Alpha with a hard aspirate was probably pronounced like the English short a in habit.

The Alif with medda in the middle of a word appears to be represented by Alpha with an acute accent, ά, as χαρ´ρ´άν خرآن Charran or Haran. Hence alpha with an acute accent in the middle of a word was pronounced as long or double A. See Genesis XI. V. 31. and Acts of Apostles. VII. 2.

Simple Alif at the end of a word is often represented by alpha either with an acute or circumflex accent thus Σινά in the Septuagint and Σινᾶ in the Acts are سينا the Mountain Sina or Sinai. Simple ‎ا Alif, in the middle of a word, is rendered by two, or more generally one alpha, as إسحاق Ισαὰκ Isaac, and دارا Δαρεῖος Darius.

As a general rule Alif is rendered by Alpha, the broad or long or short sounds being represented by the accents or aspirates.

Alif is however sometimes represented by the Greek Epsilon ; as باعورا is rendered Βεωρ Baöor, Baour, or Beör. Alif also represents (O) Omicron.

ب	be is rendered by β beta	د	dāl by δ delta
ت	te and	ز	zāl by ζ zeta
ث	se } by θ theta	ر	re by ρ rho
ح	he and	ذ	ze by ζ zeta and σ sigma
خ	khe } by χ chi		

It must be recollected that the question has nothing to do with Hebrew which was then and had long been a dead language. The question is what were the sounds and letters representing these names in the year 280 B. C. in the Arabic, Persian and Greek languages respectively. If we know the pronunciation of the former letters which we presume not to have changed up to the present time, we also know the sound or pronunciation of the Greek letters of that time,—the latter, with the exceptions of the terminations in ος and ας, being presumed to represent *the former* correctly, or at least nearly so.

س sīn and ش shīn represent indifferently σ sigma and σσ.

ص swād is also rendered by σ sigma; ط toe by τ tau ; ع ain by ɩ α, and εε.

ف	fe by θ phi	ل	lām by λ lambda
ق	kāf by κ kappa	م	mim by μ mu
ك	kaf by χ chi	ن	nun by ν nu

و wao is rendered by βι, ω, ου,

ى ye, by η, ɩ, εε, &c.

صى	by ά	}	
هو	by ου, ω,	} Occasionally.	
ها	by αά	}	

These few and imperfect hints and notices, we must here cut short. The subject is in itself a curious and an interesting one, and, in a literary point of view, not without its utility. From its very nature, however, it must always partake more or less of the assumptive and the conjectural. Of the significance and truth of this assertion, some of the foregoing fragmentary hypotheses and inferences may be viewed as a specimen. They must, therefore, be taken simply at what they are worth by those who are competent to form a judgment in such matters. Philology, temperately, wisely and judiciously 'cultivated, is capable of affording most useful results ; though no branch of learning has more frequently, in the hands of fanciful and ingenious men, been pushed into the regions of the extravagant and the ridiculous. Hence, has it hitherto been its fate, in alternate succession, to be unduly exalted and unjustly depreciated.

Recollections of Ceylon, after a residence of nearly thirteen years ; with an account of the Church Missionary Society's Operations in the island: and extracts from a journal, by the Rev. J. Selkirk, 1844, 8vo.

THE author begins by giving a geographical description of Ceylon—its four large rivers.—*Galle*, with its spacious harbour, sheltered by high lands from every wind that blows.—*Kandy*, with its " most sacred relic of Buddha's tooth."—*Nuware Eliya* (the city of Light) with its beautiful plain,—*Anuradhpura*, with its Dagobas, 270 feet high and spacious temple containing 1600 pillars. He then notices the productions of the island,—the fine roads traversed by mail coaches—the coffee plantations and land clearances—the Jack, Bread Fruit, Talipat and Gamboge trees, the bo or God tree, sacred to Buddha, with its leaves always in motion, and the cinnamon tree, the duty on which yields government an annual revenue of five lakhs. " The better educated among the Singhalese have learnt the English language and mix among English society, they are Buddhists and have caste, but it is a *civil* distinction. The Tamulians come from India and are more enterprising people than the Singhalese." The Portuguese rule ceased in Ceylon in 1656, and was succeeded by the Dutch which continued until 1796. " Those who are now called the Portuguese are the descendants of Portuguese by native women, of all classes and descriptions ; they pass their time in *idleness, filth and sin*. The Dutch speak the Portuguese language in their families ; the dress of an old Dutch lady approaches to that of English ladies in the middle of last century, and high-heeled shoes are still in vogue among them ; they do not mix much with English society. The Moormen are travelling merchants." The Mussulmans of Ceylon seem to be as much averse to receiving education as those of Bengal. " The Vedas sleep in the trees or at the foot of them, or in caves of the ground ; they were probably Singhalese who were banished into the jungles."

Mr. Selkirk gives a short history of Gautams' life, his mortification, preaching at Benares and itinerances,—he falls into the common error that Buddhism is *atheistic*. Buddhism was introduced, according to Mr.

S. into Ceylon B. C. 306, from Babar, after various changes and successive decays and revivals : it received fresh vigour in consequence of a deputation of chiefs who were sent to Siam, and who brought over with them six Buddhist priests. He next notices the Viharas or Buddhist monasteries, the priests with their sermonisings and district visitings— the Tamul " one of the most difficult of the eastern languages"—the Singhalese of Sanskrit origin, with its inverted order of sentences and want of the relative pronoun,—the Pali which differs chiefly from the Sanskrit by casting out aspirated and rough consonants—the Ceylon Portuguese, which adopts a number of Singhalese and Tamul words.

Mr. Selkirk gives a brief account of the commencement, progress and present state of the Church Mission in Ceylon. It began in 1817. Mr. Lambrick opened the first school at *Kandy*, in 1818, in the centre of the heathen population. When Sir R. Brownrigg, the governor, was about to leave Ceylon, the Church Missionaries attended his levee and presented an address to him. Mr. Lambrick paid much attention to the instruction of the Singhalese prisoners confined in Kandy jail. In 1827 some of the sons of the Kandian chiefs, who attended the school to learn English, came of their own accord to purchase the Singhalese and English New Testament, to read and compare them at their own houses. In 1829 a plan was adopted of paying the masters their monthly salary according to the actual improvement of the children, ascertained by an examination of them under the inspection of the missionary. In 1831 Bishop Turner visited the station, and after examining the schools, said there was enough to encourage and nothing to elate : the same year a Sunday school was established, which was the means of increasing the congregation. Mr. Selkirk remarks of the schools, " they are the means by which we have met ready access to the natives, and may most justly be considered as the means to do them real and lasting good." In 1832 all the masters were Christians. In 1839 there were 13 schools and 369 children ; of whom 56 were girls. The influence of the priests in this quarter is on the wane. Mr. Oakley when appointed to the station, paid considerable attention to visiting the native hospital, villages, monasteries of the priests, and Protestant families of Kandy. In six families of the town occasional meetings are held for prayer and exposition of the Scriptures. Christian schools are flourishing in Kandy, the stronghold of Buddhism.

Mr. Selkirk next mentions Baddagamey, a station of the C. M. S. 12 miles north of Galle, begun in 1818. Mr. Mayor was the first person stationed there. He remarked concerning it in 1818, " The natives are relinquishing the worship of Buddha for the worship of devils ; temples of the devils are in almost every village and the Kapuwas or devil priests are quite as numerous as the Buddhist priests." Seven hundred pounds of gunpowder were required to blast the rocks in order to lay the foundation of a church. In 1822 the missionaries undertook the charge of superintending the *government* schools in the southern district of the island. Devil worship is extensively practised. Bishop Turner in examining the children observed, " They are as sharp as needles, I do anticipate great things from the rising generation."

Nellore, two miles from Jafna, is the next station, begun in 1818 : a printing press was established there in 1821, from which a great number of tracts issued : the plan of distributing them was, " to get a company together to listen to the reading of a tract and to the comments made upon it, and then to give one to each person that could read : several who could not read begged for tracts for their children or relatives who could." The instruction of girls was attempted at the time, but " on account of the missionary being a single man, and on that account, having no personal communication with the mothers of the children at their houses, little progress was made." In 1823 a boarding school was commenced, having on an average 30 boys, *selected* from the day schools, " the greatest part of those who have been admitted into this seminary were *heathens* at the time of their admission, and few if any have left it heathens. The festival days amounting to 75 in the year have a strong tendency to drive serious thoughts from the minds of the people. In 4 years from 1835 to 1838, over one million of tracts have been distributed in this district. In 1839 the station had 2 missionaries, 17 schools, with 761 children and 30 seminary youths.

Cotta station near Colombo was entered on in 1823 : the neighbourhood was then one mass of jungle, which had to be cleared away ere a house could be erected ; an English school and a printing press formed the first branch of labour. In 1831 Bishop Turner confirmed 17 youths. Poverty which makes the parents frequently detain their sons at home after they pass the age of twelve, has been a great hinderance to the efficiency of the schools. A great desire for a knowledge of *English* has sprung up. In 1840 the station had 40 schools and 1700 children. In 1827 the Cotta Head Seminary was established for training, as school-masters and catechists, young men selected from the inferior schools ; they were to be instructed in English, and their native *classical* tongues. In 1829 there were 10 students. In 1830 they commenced the study of Pali. In December 1831 an examination of the pupils, in Geometry, Latin, Greek and Scripture took place in the presence of the Governor of Ceylon and a number of the civil and military authorities, who all breakfasted with the missionaries. Nearly 100 students have been trained up in this institution, and the best catechists and school-masters in the island have come from it. In the Cotta schools there are 1629 pupils.

The latter part of this book is occupied with extracts from Mr. S.'s journal throwing light on the manners, superstitions, &c., of the Singhalese, and the nature of Buddhism. The island of Ceylon is assuming a position of increasing importance in the eyes of the Anglo Indians of continental India, now that the lovely sanatarium of Nuware Eliya* is becoming a place of resort from the parched plains of Hindustan—while steam is binding as with an electric chain Ceylon to India and to the remote isles which cluster in the eastern Archipelago.

* Usually contracted, Newrelia.

Journal of a Visitation in the Provinces of Travancore and Tinnevelly, 1840-41, by the Right Revd. G. Spencer, Bishop of Madras.

THE Bishop of Madras states in this Journal that Dr. Buchanan formed too favourable a view of the Syrian Churches of Travancore; " he was deceived by appearances, by the outward visible sign of Christianity presented by numerous Churches, each provided with a canonically ordained clergy, into the fond belief that the inward spiritual grace of pure Christain doctrine, and a life adorning the Christian profession, were there also; the beams of the sun are sometimes so glowingly painted upon a glacier, that we can scarcely persuade ourselves they have not left there some portion of their softening heat." He is of opinion that this Church is in a low state, " we can make next to nothing of the *adults ;* but I unhesitatingly believe that very much may be done among the children." We heartily respond to the sentiment of the Bishop that the Indian branch of the Anglican Church should not labor merely for the benefit " of a few thousand Englishmen," but should be a MISSIONARY Church. This Journal shows the Bishop to be a lover of nature; a man of simple habits; and one who feels a warm sympathy with evangelistic labours in India and with all efforts formed to ameliorate the condition of the natives ; he writes in a friendly tone of the labours of the London and American Missionaries; and is a decided advocate for education. " Such being the character of the *adults*, the Christian Missionary must turn to the children, and trust, under God's grace and guidance, to do that by *education* which he too evidently *cannot* do by *argument*." At Paulghat is " a noble range of mountains, their base in deep shade, and their tops bathed in sun light." A temple to the goddess of the small pox is erected near. His travelling over mountains suggests to the Bishop several reflections on the subject of steam communication, " a great step will be taken towards the moral cultivation of the Native character by the introduction among them of that great second harbinger, under Divine Providence, of civilization, steam; under its influence the natives cannot fail of becoming gradually more European and less Asiatic in their habits of thinking; and thinking leads to emulation and to acting." He came to Cottyam, " this Christian oasis in the vast heathen desert of Travancore." The Church Missionary Society have a College there, and particular attention is paid to the education of the Syrian Priests. In the district of Allepee there are 100,000 slaves. On his visit to Quilon the Bishop expresses the following excellent sentiments :—" I have not the slightest desire that the Church of England in India should interfere with the mission of others, who are come hither to assist us to teach his gospel to the heathen." Travancore coffee is superior to that of Ceylon. " I paid a visit of ceremony to the Rajah of Travancore, who is about twenty-six years of age, he speaks English with perfect fluency, is an accomplished Persian and Arabic scholar, and could he escape from the swaddling bands of the Brahmans, it is supposed that he would shew himself a really enlightened ruler. The puppet of royalty is moved according to their will and pleasure by the Brahmanical string. The Rajah has erected an observatory, and an astronomer has been sent to England to purchase the best instruments at his expense; he also supports a large and excellent school under the management of an English master." On the subject of palankin travelling the Bishop remarks, " I fully enter into Bishop Heber's dislike to this purblind mode of traversing the country, seeing nothing and yet enjoying no repose."

The Bishop visited Mr. Mault's station of the L. M. S. at Nager-coil, he remarks, " Mr. M. has done wonders here ; in the girl's school they make what appeared to me very fine lace. The boys being instructed in English, I undertook their examination myself, they read to me a few verses of the Iliad and also of the Greek Testament, and their knowledge of the Greek Testament is really very respectable. The Nagercoil Missionaries have fifteen thousand Native Christians under instruction, who would not wish them good speed in this labour of love in the name of our common master? I do most cordially." He came next to Tinnevelly : and observes on the Native character, " until India becomes thoroughly Europeanized by education, our acquaintance with their real character must continue very superficial." He remarks of Tinnevelly that " the parochial system is in active operation :" " excommunication, as a most efficacious means of chasten-ing, correcting, and amending those who are hardened against public exhortation, and will not be brought back by private rebuke, has been exercised here on several occasions with the best effect. Not only individuals but whole congregations have been separated by their minister from the means of grace, who are now among the faithful." " Near Tinnevelly Fort is the tomb of the truly pious learned and devoted Rhenius. Tinnevelly is a large and flourishing town and boasts a of splendid pagoda. I was much amused with the bazar, where trade seemed to possess something of European activity, instead of the oriental drowsiness and indifference generally observed in *India*." While staying at Palamcottah, he makes the following observations on Church Music, " The ordination on Sunday was more than usually *solemn* and *impressive* from the beautiful music. Several of the Tinne-velly clergy are excellent musicians. I think we too often throw away a most *valuable* accessory to devotion by our strange neglect of psalmody. The New Version of the Psalms of David, usually bound up with our Prayer Book, is *cold and lifeless*." He visited Madura, with " its ruins, the finest in Southern Indie," once the capital of the Pandion Kingdom. The Propagation Society have a Church and School there : the American Missionaries have also an English School.

A charge is appended to this Journal from which we make the fol-lowing extracts, " Before we can reasonably expect to see a really trustworthy body of native clergy, we must train up a body of native catechists, more highly and more professionally educated than those we at present possess." He recommends strongly the establishment of Christian villages in which the native Christians may be removed from the evils and temptations of Heathen associations, and which may be models for the Hindus. He says, "I am proud to bear the title of a Missionary Bishop. As long as I have a tongue to speak, and a hand to write, they shall be employed in advocating the education of the Natives of India." The Bishop has established a theological institution at Vepery, which renders it unnecessary to send students to Bishop's College at Calcutta; he lays down one important principle in the management of such an institution, " were I desirous of gaining a firm hold on the mind of a pupil, I should prefer an hour's unshackled *talk* with him to a day's lecturing." " English must be the language of light and truth, as well as of knowledge to the native pupils; same knowledge of the rudiments of medicine, with its concomitant studies of anatomy, chemistry and botany, which seems to me almost indispensable to a Missionary, might be rendered a delightful relaxation; why should he not know enough of rural economy to give a little useful advice in sowing and cropping, the management of cattle, or the improvement of a plough." We strongly recommend this Journal as conveying valuable information on various points and written in a truly mild Christian Spirit.

The Dorjeeling Guide ; including a description of the country, and of its climate, soil, and productions ; with travelling directions, and various maps, also tables of routes by land and water &c. &c. Calcutta: Samuel Smith and Co., Bengal Hurkaru Press, 1845.

As it is our purpose, by and bye, to discuss the subject of Indian Sanataria generally, we shall not at present expatiate on the characteristics of Dorjeeling. Our sole immediate object is to introduce " the Dorjeeling Guide" to the notice of our readers, and earnestly to recommend it to them, as worthy of their most favourable regard. To those who have any prospect of visiting Dorjeeling, or " the holy spot," as that term signifies, the Guide must become an indispensable companion. Even to those who have no such prospect in view the Guide will prove one of the richest and most valuable accessions to their topographical knowledge which recent years have supplied. It is not possible in few words to convey any adequate impression of the richly varied contents of the work. But sure we are that whoever possesses it, and has carefully perused it, will be ready to say that in it he enjoys a treasure, worth vastly more than its pecuniary equivalent.

The Guide not only contains all that is requisite to meet the necessary wants of the traveller, but much that is adapted to the tastes and pursuits of the man of science and the Philanthropist. It contains accurate and well-executed maps of the Dorjeeling tract, and adjacent parts, with road from Titalya on the plains ; of the dawk and river routes respectively, from Berhampore ; and of the station itself with its roads and locations. It furnishes all imaginable details respecting the time and cost of travelling by the different routes, with all particulars relative to the accommodation and expense of living at the station itself—its public buildings, hotels, and private houses. It amply unfolds its resources and supplies—its animal and vegetable productions—its meteorological, geological, and topographical characteristics. It pourtrays the various wild hill tribes that tenant " the bright spot," and the surrounding districts—the Mechis, the Lepchas, the Limbus, Haius, the Murmis, &c.,—with notices of their religion and language, their manners, habits, and customs. It re-publishes, from the *Bengal Hurkaru*, the notes of various excursions, which originally appeared under the quaint but expressive signature of " Ranald of the Mist"— notes which simply but graphically bring to view many of the singularly picturesque and sublime features of the surrounding scenery. Altogether, the Editor and Compiler has earned to himself a title to the best thanks of the Indian public for embodying, within so manageable a compass, such a vast mass of deeply interesting and important information.

We trust that the effect of publishing such a Guide will be to extend far and wide a knowledge of that peculiarly favoured locality, Dorjeeling—that the effect of such extended knowledge will be to create an irrepressible desire, coupled with the earnest determination, if possible, to visit it—that the effect of such multiplied visitation will be to accelerate improvements of all kinds in the ways and modes of conveyance and general cost of travelling and residence—and that the conjoint effect of the whole will be, to open up, for the metropolis of India and all the lower Bengal provinces, an easily and speedily accessible refuge of health, which may diffuse fresh joy and gladness over the whole face of a sickly and suffering community.

Some of the most important papers in the compilation are supplied by Mr. Hogdson, Dr. Campbell, Dr. Hutchinson, D. Liston, Esq. and J. H. Batten, Esq.

We have little room for extracts ; nor are they needed. The Guide itself we hope will, in due time, be in the hands of most of our readers. All that our space will allow us to do, is to quote the compendious summary furnished by the Editor in his Introductory Remarks. It is as follows :—

"The Editor of the following compilation having collected a variety of maps and documents relating to Dorjeeling, has been induced to put a portion of them into the form of a Guide to that station, in the hope that, from the increasing number of parties daily resorting to it, such a work will prove both acceptable and useful. This work it is intended shall be published annually, with corrections and additions.

The establishment of a Sanatarium within a short distance of Calcutta, and accessible to all the districts of the Lower Provinces, has long been regarded as an object of peculiar interest. It has been deemed of such general importance and utility, that it has received the ready attention of the local Authorities, and also the favorable notice of the Court of Directors, whenever the subject has been prominently brought under discussion.

Dorjeeling, which is situated at the distance of 371 miles from Calcutta,

h

on a ridge of the Sikim range of the Himalayas, the snowy heights of which seem to overhang the station, was first brought to the notice of the then Governor-General, Lord William Bentinck in 1829, by Mr. J. W. Grant, and Colonel Lloyd, as combining all the requisites for a convalescent depôt.

About the month of February, in the year 1828, Mr. J. W. Grant, at that time resident at Malda, and Captain (now Colonel) G. W. A. Lloyd, then employed in the Political Department in settling the boundary between the Nipal and Sikim frontier, made an excursion from Titalya into the Sikim mountains and explored as far as Rinchinpoon. When at Chongtong, their attention was attracted to the position of Dorjeeling, appearing at a distance of a few miles to the eastward of the spot on which they stood, and it struck them as one admirably calculated for a Sanatarium. It was this occurrence that led to Mr. Grant's communication to Lord William Bentinck. Colonel Lloyd, in a letter addressed by him to his Lordship's Military Secretary, Captain (now Colonel) Benson, dated the 18th June 1829, states, that he visited Dorjeeling in February in that year, and adds, that he was the only European who had ever visited it. The extreme earnestness of these gentlemen in recommending it as fit station for a Sanatarium, attracted his Lordship's attention, who was induced, by the representations thus made to him, to direct Major Herbert, Deputy Surveyor General, to explore the Sikim Hills, and that officer carried his orders into execution in company with Mr. Grant: their reports were submitted to Government in the year 1830.

His Lordship never lost sight of the expediency of establishing, on this tract of the Sikim Hills, a station for the resort of those whose health demanded relief from the heat of the Bengal plains; looking upon it, as admitted on all hands, that a Sanatarium was much wanted on our North Eastern Frontier, he considered that Dorjeeling, with reference to facilities of approach, position, climate and resources, held out a better prospect of supplying this *desideratum* than any other spot on the high lands above Silhet.

The reports of Major Herbert and Mr. Grant were perused by the Court of Directors with much interest, and they expressed their sense of Mr. Grant's zeal and intelligence in bringing to the notice of Government a position apparently so well adapted as Dorjeeling for the site of a convalescent depôt, and also highly approved of Major Herbert's having undertaken a journey to it with a view further to develope its capabilities. The Court also expressed a hope that Government would find it practicable and advisable to establish a Sanatarium at that station, which they conceived might also prove valuable as a depôt for the temporary reception of European recruits; and even as a permanent cantonment for an European Regiment.

The value of a Sanatarium so near to the metropolis of India did not fail to present itself to Lord Auckland, very shortly after his arrival in India; and from the year 1836 to the termination of his Government, his Lordship continued to take the liveliest interest in the establishment of this station, until at length, under his fostering care, it has assumed a character of such importance, as a place of general resort, that it has become the rival Sanatarium of Simla and Mussourie, especially from its being of much easier access than either of those places from all parts of the Lower Provinces.

Its perfect success has been looked upon as likely to carry with it far greater consequences than might generally be ascribed to a facility of refuge from the oppressive heats of the climate of the plains. The precariousness of health in India would make this an object of no light importance; but in looking onward to ultimate results it has been considered that such a settlement, in these hills, will tend more than any other circumstance to attach

English families and English capital to the soil of India, and to give a more general character, than has yet existed, of permanence and consistency to undertakings and establishments resting on the wealth and enterprise of Europe. The advantages to Government of this position in the mountains are also considerable, situated as it is in the centre of Sikim and within 30 miles of the Nipal frontier, on the west, and little more from that of Bootan on the east; it gives the power of effectually checking any union of these two states on the south of the snows; while the example of a just, and tolerant government in the territory adjoining them, cannot fail to have the most beneficial influence on the condition of the population of the neighbouring states, at the same time that it affords to the unsettled tribes of mountaineers the opportunity, hitherto wanting, of judging of the power, resources and moderation of the rulers of India.

The establishment of such a Sanatarium might, throughout Bengal, and more particularly amongst the residents in the capital of India, frequently prevent the long and distant separation of husband and wife, and of parent and child, and will have a much wider influence than may at first be imagined upon the public service, and yet more upon the mercantile and general European community.

The healthiness, to Europeans, of the climate of Dorjeeling may be taken to be fully established. It has now been put to the test for more than six years, under the disadvantages of difficult supplies, scanty population, uncleared jungle, and imperfect habitations, and all who have tried it speak most favorably of its influence.

All the difficulties which at first presented themselves have been overcome; roads have been made; hotels and houses have been built; bazars are in activity; and many speculations have been projected.

It is well known with what deep interest this new settlement has been regarded at Calcutta and that an Association was formed, which proved to Government that the public fully responded to their views. When the Dorjeeling committee applied for an improvement of the communications leading to the station, and shewed that the Association, which they represented, had spent nearly 50,000 rupees upon the place,* and upon the roads leading to it, it was admitted that their wishes were fair and moderate, and a readiness was expressed to give effect to them at once, as far as could reasonably be done. It was considered indeed, that by compliance, little more would in fact be granted than that a main line of communication would be made practicable, at a small expense, in a country where roads are greatly wanted, and that the works proposed, on the footing on which they would be placed in the first instance, were little more than ought at all events to be undertaken in a well regulated district.

Orders were accordingly issued for the repair of district roads, on the route to Dorjeeling; the erection of bungalows at stated intervals, and the construction of more substantial boats, than those in general use, at the various ferries that intersect the roads.

It was also considered, that as Dorjeeling increased in importance, and greater public interests became connected with it, these works might be carried further and put into a more complete form; and that if the road should become one of considerable traffic and resort, all the expense proposed could not properly be laid to the account of Dorjeeling alone, as the ferries, at least, and bungalows might be looked to for a direct return upon the money laid out; and it might be fairly speculated upon, that great,

* The estimated amount of Capital, laid out by European Settlers, up to the 31st Dec. 1844, is six lakhs of Rupees—Co.'s Rs. 6,00,000.—(£60,000)

though less direct, advantages would be derived to the intervening country, from these new channels of intercourse.

Besides, it may be excepted that Dorjeeling will, very soon, be made a depôt for Military Invalids from the Lower Provinces, and although doubts were in the first instance entertained upon the fitness of the climate for this purpose, its salubrity is now most fully established; and as Calcutta is more than 1,000 miles from Landour, and only 371 from Dorjeeling it is to be hoped a trial may be made of it as a convalescent station, and eventually it will doubtless become a cantonment for European troops.

In the meanwhile, under the civil administration of Dr. Campbell, the Superintendent, who is also in charge of the political relations with Sikim, excellent roads are being extended around the station, and generally throughout the appended territory, and every assistance is afforded by the Government to settlers and others visiting the Sanatarium.

There is a resident Medical Officer, and an Officer in command of the local Corps of Sappers and Miners, who also acts as Executive Officer in the Department of Public Works.

These officers with their families, and several individual residents, with the numerous casual visitors occupying the two hotels and the various buildings erected at the station, now form a considerable society who are enjoying throughout the year an invigorating climate within a short distance of Calcutta, and where the average range of the thermometer is about that of England and the north of France, or a mean temperature of about 55°, with occasional falls of snow in the months of January, February, and March.

The station commands the most magnificent prospect of the Snowy Range visible from any place in India, and in which appears eminently conspicuous the lofty peak of Kunchin Jinga, said to be 27,000 feet above the level of the sea; the elevation of Dorjeeling itself being 7,218 feet.

The surrounding country, in respect to natural scenery, is superior to Landour and Mussourie; and its productions, such as oaks, birches and chesnuts, are of greater variety and larger size. It has a northern aspect, which is wanting at Landour and Mussourie, and which counterbalances any supposed advantage possessed by either of those places.

The general opinion of persons who have visited Simla and Dorjeeling is in favor of the latter, as regards the natural advantages of scenery and magnificence of the forest. As to the prospect of the Snowy Range there is no variation of opinion; Dorjeeling is unrivalled in this particular: the clearances, and small settlements of the mountaineers, are much more numerous around Simla, and this gives *greater variety* to the scene; but the more bare and precipitious character of the Simla mountain is surpassed in grandeur and beauty by those of Dorjeeling. The atmosphere of Dorjeeling is drier than that of Landour and Mossourie; this it owes to its greater distance from the plains and the position of the loftier Sinchal which obstructs the passage of the ascending vapours of the terai, while at Mussourie, which overhangs the Deyra Dhoon, the atmosphere, during the warm season, is charged with the damp of the lowlands.

Simla, according to Dr. Webb,* is often visited with a typhoid fever and epidemic sore throats of a virulent character, while at Dorjeeling such diseases have hitherto been unknown, and with the exception of small pox, the scourge of all countries and climes, it may be said to be without any disease whatever peculiar to it, and to be beneficial in the recovery from all ailments.

* See Transactions of the Medical and Physical Society of Calcutta.

The comparative elevations of the Bengal Sanataria are as follow :—

Simla, ...feet	7486
Dorjeeling,.............................	7218
Landour, ...	7200
Mussourie,..............................	6800
Almorah,..............................	5520
Cheera Poonjee,........................	4200

In conclusion ; all, without exception, who have visited Dorjeeling, concur in describing it as possessing a climate superior to that of Landour or Mussourie ; and thus at length is supplied the *derideratum* the want of which has, hitherto, been so seriously felt by the inhabitants of the metropolis of India and of the Lower Provinces, and a Sanatarium is secured to them equal to any in India, and within the reach of all, at a moderate expense.

Transactions of the Medical and Physical Society of Calcutta.— Vol. IX.—Part I.—Calcutta, 1845.

A VALUABLE volume of a truly valuable series. Besides papers, more or less elaborate, on divers important subjects, it contains the proceedings of the regular monthly meetings of the society, held at the Asiatic Society's apartments. From the very nature of the subjects treated of, and the copious use of scientific technical terms, the work cannot be generally popular, in the ordinary sense of that word ; though it does abound with particular statements of fact, which, if segregated from the surrounding mass, and somewhat divested of their technical garb, could not fail to prove generally, if not universally, interesting. To members of the medical profession, more especially in India, such a volume, recording in an authentic form the researches and experiences of so many able and acute observers, must possess a value that cannot easily be over-estimated. Indeed, apart altogether from the consideration of its being a repository of useful facts, experiments, and verified conclusions, the periodical publication of such a work is well calculated to generate the very excellence of which it is designed to become the permanent memorial. When men are habitually taught to feel that their peculiar experiences, or successful operations, or happy discoveries, whether of latent causes or of apposite remedies, are, through the medium of such an established channel, to be made available for the enlightenment, guidance, or encouragement of others, without limitation of clime or colour,—such an ever-present conviction cannot but stimulate the powers of inquiry, sharpen the faculty of observation, and beget a habit of minute accuracy in noting and recording phenomena which otherwise might be unattainable. Accordingly, when we turn to the papers of which the volume now before us is composed—whether we regard the style in which one is written, the power of condensation exhibited in a second, the erudition of a third, the dexterity of professional skill and the fertility of professional resource displayed by others,—we cannot but conclude that the work is one which would reflect credit on any Body or Society of men, even in the most favoured abodes of science and civilization.

The authors of the larger and more elaborate papers are by Doctors Finch, Sprenger, Webb, O'Shaugnessy, Goodeve, Wise, Kirk, and Batson. If we were to notice any of these in detail, the two that would fall most legitimately within our more appropriate sphere, are the first by Dr. Finch, " On the effect of change of climate on the health of the Native Army ;" and the second, by Dr. Sprenger, on the " Arabic terms of Materia Medica." The more immediate object of the former being, " the health of the Native Army," it developes principles and establishes facts which admit of a vastly more extended application. The introduction to the latter contains some useful information respecting the principal Arabic works on Materia Medica. The author is evidently an enthusiast in oriental pursuits. He reminds of the palmy days of the Tytlers, and Prinseps, and Wilsons. Like them he appears to regard Orientalism as a mine, which needs only to be explored, to give forth treasures that may strip the laurel from the brow of modern pretensions. And if, unlike them, he succeed in realizing his gorgeous visions, sure we are that there is enough of Baconian philosophy in his profession, to treat with candour and receive with thankfulness any genuine revelations of hitherto hidden or lost knowledge which he may bring to view. In the blaze of his zeal for the wondrous and recondite verities, supposed to be buried beneath the mountain load of antiquated rubbish, he seems occasionally to lose sight of the consecutiveness of his reasoning. " I know," says he, " most of my colleagues, look down upon Arabic medicine, but I do think it would be better, to look first, into it. I am sure that there is no man in Asia, nor in Europe, neither a native nor a white man, who has a sufficiently profound knowledge of Arabic medicine, to justify him in passing any opinion at all upon it. " Here is a negative universal—no exception—none whatsoever ;—" no man in Asia, nor in Europe, neither a native nor a white man." Here is certainty—certainty absolute ;—" I am sure that there is no man. " Here is ignorance—and as regards the object, ignorance total ;—" no man " possesses sufficient knowledge—not, to warrant him in passing a comprehensive, enlightened, authoritative opinion on the subject of Arabic medicine—but not sufficient knowledge, " to justify him in passing *any opinion at all upon it.*" What! does the worthy doctor include himself too in this category of ignorance? He does, formally and expressly he does:—" I cannot, " says he, " boast myself of knowing more about it than other people. " Very good. But, as regards other people, they were *all* pronounced ignorant: hence the Doctor was led to draw the legitimate logical conclusion, that, in consequence of such ignorance, they were not " justified in passing any opinion at all on the subject." Himself he formally places in the same category as *all* the other ignorant people. Of course, his own logical conclusion must apply with equally valid and intensive force to himself; so that, by his own demonstration, he himself is not " justified in passing any opinion at all upon it?" But no!

the ignorance of all others justly precludes them from passing an opinion ; but the asserted or confessed ignorance of the author himself does not preclude him! Notwithstanding his own acknowledged ignorance, he feels himself quite justified in passing a very strong and decided opinion on the subject—an opinion so strong and decided that he bravely hazards the assertion, that " the present state of *medical* practice, is *not much superior* to that of former ages," among the Arabs—that " they *cured as many patients,* and *killed less,* than we do, notwithstanding our superiority in anatomy and other preparatory studies "—that " much that was in those times familiarly known and acted upon, would *greatly improve our own knowledge and practice, even at the present day.*" When Dr. Sprenger has once succeeded in bringing to light those hitherto recondite and undiscovered stores of Arabic medical science, we shall be ready to believe in the reality of their existence, even as we are ready to believe in the real existence of the Philosopher's stone, when once its discovery is put beyond the pale of rational dubiety. Meanwhile we shall take his dogmatic assertion at what it is worth—viz. as the assertion of one who declares, that " no man in Asia nor in Europe, neither a native, nor a white man " knows enough of the subject to " justify him in passing any opinion at all upon it "—and that he himself " cannot boast himself of knowing more about it than other people."

Respecting his brethren in the medical profession, Dr. Sprenger appears to us to indulge in incautious and unwarranted language. His words are, " The majority of the members of our profession are now much more defective in all literary education, than they have been at any time before." Now, our own impression is a clear and decided one—viz., that, at no previous period, did the profession possess a greater number of men endowed with high literary accomplishments. But here lurks the fallacy, and, consequently, the source of the Doctor's hallucination. Though, in words, he speaks of " *all* literary education," it is palpable, from the context, that his " all " of literary education, is, to a great extent, if not almost exclusively, restricted to a learned orientalism, and more especially the crabbed philological asperities of an antiquated and obsolete Arabic lore. There was a time when the classical enthusiast in Europe could not allow any thing to be deemed worthy of the name of Literature, save that of Greece and Rome. So now, the comparatively ignorant and consummately conceited Maulavi or Pandit can allow nothing to be worthy of the name of Literature or learning, except that of Arabic or Sanskrit. That such persons, in their inflated self-complacency, could, and can still, think and speak after this fashion, is nothing strange, though it is at the expense of their credit as men of learning, judgment, and good sense. They know only one species of Literature, and that is their own; what they do know, they extol, perhaps idolize ; what they do not know, they, with the usual presumption of ignorance, profess to despise, perhaps abhor. Now, the plain dictate of sound reason, in all such cases, is, to admit that to be fact which is fact ;—to confess that the domain of literature is not one invariable homogeneous surface, but a richly and endlessly diversified mosaic —that it consists, not of one, but of many compartments, with their destinctive configurations and characteristic constituent elements. There is such a thing as occidental literature ; there is a Greek and a Roman literature ; there are also such things as English litera- ture, German literature, French literature, Italian literature, with many more. To these let us freely and ungrudgingly add those other things, entities, or realities, known under the names of Arabic, Sanskrit, Tibetian, Chinese, Burmese, Singhalese or any other oriental literatures. All of these have their own distinguishing features— their own peculiar national idiosyncracies—their own distinctive merits and demerits. How far the merits or demerits of each may prepon- derate is not now the question. All that we plead for, is, that whatever merits may be truly alleged as belonging to any, we should, in fairness and in candour, freely concede to it the credit of possessing them. Amongst the different genera and species of literature, there may be a good, a better, and a best. But let no man who has devoted his time, talents and energies to the exclusive study of one, presume to declare that it is the only one worth studying, or venture to exalt it to a despot's throne. To Dr. Sprenger, we wish all possible success in exploring the caverns and labyrinths of Arabic literature ; and would rejoice exceedingly to see him return to the light of day, laden with spoils worthy of such heroic devotedness. But, for the sake of his credit, and the success of his own cause, let him carefully abstain from a style of writing which is sure to produce a damaging reaction against both. Let him not claim for his favourite study a monopoly of excellence, which, until it is fairly seen, others will be apt to reckon as the spontaneous growth of his own fervent and fertile imagination. Let him not set up for it the yet unverified plea of possessing exclusive un- rivalled prerogatives, which must be at once and disdainfully repudiated by ten thousand reclaiming voices from the wide and ever-extending republic of letters.

The Anglo-Indian Passage ; homeward and outward ; or a card for the overland Traveller from Southampton to Bom- bay, Madras, and Calcutta, &c., by David Lester Richardson, Author of Literary Leaves, &c.

THIS is quite a gem among guide-books. Having seen various favourable notices of it, we were predisposed to think well of it. But, having now perused the work itself, we feel justified in saying that it has considerably surpassed our expectations. Not that we were not prepared for a superior production from the pen of an author who has so distinguished himself in the world of letters ; but that we did not expect him to lavish much of his literary powers on such a work of mere utilitarianism. The present publication, however, only adds another to the many proofs which go to shew, that, in the hands of a master, the most intractable and unpromising materials may be divested of their roughness and grossness, and made to exhibit symmetry of form and beauty of expression.

The whole work is got up in a style of superior taste and elegance. The binding, the paper, the printing—all are excellent. The illustrations, numerous and well executed, embracing as they do most of the principal objects and views along the route, constitute one of the most charming features of the work. It contains all needful directions to travellers,—conveyed in language, at once sprightly, chaste, and classical. Fuller delineations of remarkable persons, objects, and scenes, it very judiciously throws into a well stored Appendix, original and selected. And, what forms a new characteristic of such a work, the scenery of the ocean finds its due share of pencilling therein. This part of his task, from its novelty, the author deems it necessary to introduce with something like an apology. But we fain hope that no such apology is really needed; as it certainly cannot be by any reader of ordinary taste or intellectual accomplishment. The " ocean sketches" constitute, in our judgment, a very precious accession to an already well replenished repository of valuable information. Facts, in their proper place, are of indispensable utility. But man is endowed with other faculties than those that meet with their full gratification in bare naked facts, which are but the dry bones of knowledge, with little or nothing of the glow and warmth that ever effloresce in the gorgeous forms of life and beauty. There are in the human mind susceptibilities of a nobler, more generous and etherial kind—susceptibilities of sentiment and emotion which, properly cultivated and directed, tend to honour and adorn humanity, while they cannot fail to elevate their happy possessor into regions of purest and serenest joy. Of this no one is more conscious than our author. When afloat on the main ocean, with nought around him but sky and water, he did not, like the idealess emotionless throng, fold his arms, and close his eyes, and sink down into a state of morbid, listless, unreflecting apathy. No; with eyes open, and mind awake, and sensibilities quickened, and imagination winged for flight, he " experienced an inexpressible delight in watching the ever-varying aspects of the wide round ocean and the shadowy dome of air—the vast and glorious canopy of that solitary world of which their little vessel seemed the centre." Hence the origin of the " ocean sketches." And what gave such exquisite pleasure to his own mind he has wisely judged may give pleasure to others. Hence, again, the publication, of these " studies of sea and sky"—these " records of air and water."

No overland traveller should leave Calcutta, in any of our magnificent steamers, without first procuring a copy of this delightful volume; and no one, who has once got it, will ever have reason to regret or begrudge the very moderate price he has paid for it.

Observations on the Nosological arrangement of the Bengal Medical Returns, with a few cursory remarks on Medical Topography and Military Hygiene, by Fred. J. Mouat, M. D., &c. &c. Calcutta, 1845.

IF, as has been remarked, "there is no subject in the whole range of Medical Science and Literature, that is beset with so many difficulties, as the classification of diseases," there can be, at the same time, but few subjects of deeper interest or more vital importance to the medical practitioner. Dr. Mouat, therefore, has done well thus pointedly to direct general attention towards it. The pamphlet itself bears all the marks of that spirit of reflection and research and indefatigable industry for which the author is so distinguished. We can only afford space for one brief extract from his own explanatory preface :—

"The first part of this brochure was written at the suggestion and request of the late Dr. Murray, Inspector-general of H. M. Hospitals in India.

"My present object in publishing detached remarks, which cannot lay claim to any originality or profoundness, is again to direct attention to subjects which have long occupied the very limited leisure at my disposal for professional or extra official pursuits.

"It is well known that orders have been received from England to report upon the existing system of returns adopted in the medical departments of the three presidencies, with a view to assimilate them, as nearly as practicable, to those adopted in the royal service.

"Every medical officer who has the slightest regard for the interests of his profession and service, must hail this onward movement as the harbinger of much future benefit to both, if fully and fairly carried out ; and is, therefore, bound to afford all the information in his possession however small it may be, to those who are engaged in the laborious and responsible task of remodelling the reports and returns from an army and country which present unrivalled opportunities for professional research, and of which the medical department now labours under the disgrace, of having during the greater part of a century, furnished no data sufficiently accurate for the compilation of the statistical records required by the War Office.

"That this is the fault of the system in use, and not of the men appointed to carry it out, it would be easy to prove.

"It is my apology for the present publication."

The pamphlet, though of a strictly professional character, contains much that is fitted to interest and edify the non-professional reader. The concluding remarks, relative to the immense importance as well as the means of collecting topographical information, are especially valuable. Something in this respect has already been done by members of the Medical Service ; and we hope that their meritorious example may suffice to stimulate others to tread still more successfully in their footsteps.

SANDERS AND CONES, TYPS., NO. 4. TANK-SQUARE, CALCUTTA.

MISCELLANEOUS NOTICES.

Miscellaneous Writings in Prose and Verse, comprising Dramatic Charades, Poems, Songs, Tales, Translations, Travels, &c. &c. by A. H. E. Boileau, Captain, Bengal Engineers. Calcutta,

ERRATA.

The following should have appeared in our last Number :—

In No. IV., Article "Sir P. Francis," page 569, for "Messrs. Vansittart, *Grafton* and Forde," read "Messrs. Vansittart, *Scrafton*, and Forde."

At page 571, for "nineteen guns" read "seventeen guns."

In No. V., Article "The Sick Room in India"—p. 72, line 2, for "sad realities life," read "sad realities *of* life."

Same article, page 96, line 1, for "it is a great thing to *commence* with external nature," read "it is a great thing to *commune* with external nature."

Same article, page 101, line 12, for "certainty—*on* what is nearly a certainty," read "certainty—*or* what is nearly a certainty."

sense and peculiarities of the ...
died ; rational principles of reform, opposed to any thing like extensive and sudden innovation, were advocated ; impartial, and as often virulent, strictures on public men and measures were made ; class interests were defended and reprobated ; the occupations of the field and water, which afford so much amusement to the thorough-going sportsman, were liberally canvassed : in short, every stimulant that could excite was resorted to—but in vain. Readers admired, but did nothing more. There was no such thing as emulation, and a desire to co-operate and excel. The energy of the leaders of public taste, under the action of so much indifference and so little sympathy, gradually waxed fainter and feebler. It lapsed into listless inactivity. It died away ; and thus the few shoots

* Dr John Grant, H. M. Parker, R. Rattray, H. Torrens, Captains Macnaghten and Richardson were the most strenuous supporters in the service of periodical literature.

that were the harbingers of an abundant literary harvest by degrees shrunk up and withered.

It would, doubtless, be an agreeable and profitable task, to such as have the ability and leisure, to trace the cause of this indifference to literary pursuits in India, the successful cultivation of which, more perhaps than aught else, has, both by its original destination, as well as by the power which it has ever exercised, contributed to the worth and glory of all civilized nations. Some speculators have attributed this indifference to the despotic character of the government, which, independently of conducting its affairs with secrecy, discourages, to a certain extent, among its servants the free interchange of opinion on questions of public importance; others, to the oligarchical and exclusive constitution of the services, which, from the liberal manner in which the members are remunerated and the certain prospect they have, without dread or fear of competition, of attaining a comfortable eminence, unless they commit some flagrant offence, has the effect of removing from them all incentive to mental exertion, beyond that required for the exercise of their official functions; others, to the little encouragement that is held out by the dispensers of patronage to those whose inclinations lead them to be aspirants for literary fame;—and not a few attribute the indifference to the base motive of fear, which compels many to oppose their natural propensities, in case their exercises in the higher domains of pure reason and intellect, should act as a bar to their advancement in life, on the often urged plea, we apprehend, that a man of erudition and fancy lives so much in the region of his own thoughts as to be quite unsuited for those employments which more properly belong to the every day working world. Whether one, or all of these causes combine to fetter the exercise of the mental powers, and keep our men of education the drudges, as it were, of a heavy and complicated routine, we will not stop to enquire. The fact nevertheless stands out in all the nakedness of metaphysical abstraction, that the dignity of literature, if not contemned, is viewed with indifference in India, and that literary pretensions are seldom or ever a passport to preferment.

In spite of these chilling influences which are sufficient to nip the blossoms of genius, and check the free unbosoming of the soul, a few "choice spirits" have nevertheless ventured, with commendable boldness, to present their "imaginings" to the public in a form more durable and compact than they could possibly have received from our transient periodical press. The first of these, for be it remembered our retrospect goes no further back than twenty years, was the author of the "Draught of Immortality and other poems," Henry Meredith Parker, whose versatile genius, it is said, woke the admiration of that great utilitarian, Lord William Bentinck, and induced him to admit, what he had hitherto considered impossible, that literary attainments and excellence in dry official routine, were qualifications which admitted of a happy combination. Parker's writings must be familiar to most of our readers. They would have shown to advantage, and commanded attention, had they appeared in any of our English periodicals. The immediate impression on perusing them, is that they are the outpourings of a man of quick sensibility, vivid imagination, and exquisite refinement,—one who to vigour and felicity of language added an exuberance of wit and elasticity of spirits, the ready and agreeable accompaniments of natural genius.

After Parker came Captain D. L. Richardson, author of "Literary Leaves in Prose and Verse," and almost, we regret to say, the only one that is left to us of the small band who, in days gone by, struggled manfully to impress the public mind in Calcutta with the importance of having a periodical literature. Perhaps of all our Indian literati, Richardson can alone claim the proud distinction of having, through good report and evil report, clung to literary avocations with the greatest tenacity. His productions, possessing as they do great elegance of diction, condensation of thought, and a succession of delicate images "sicklied o'er" perhaps too much with the feeling of despondency, have, as it is well known, elicited the applause, in England, of men who are fully alive to the genuine breathings of genius, and who are not liable to be deceived and dazzled by insipidity and fictitious glitter.

The next literary competitor was Dr. Hutchinson, Secretary to the Medical Board, and author of the "Sunyasse," a poem, which, independently of its possessing a few happy touches of feeling and fancy, was, on its appearance, assailed by the daily press, with all the virulence of offended criticism. Its merits were not, in our opinion, fairly tested. A lurking animosity towards the author had, in some measure, sharpened the edge of the critical knife; and with the existence of such feelings nothing was to be expected but an unsparing attack, which, while it would expose the poet to the derision of multitudes, would at the same time have the effect of wounding his feelings. Had the "Sunyasse" been less disfigured by pedantry and conceit, it might have attained a transient, though not permanent, celebrity; but with such blemishes the vast majority were too much disposed to join in the merriment which the raillery of the literary censors had raised. The work soon sank into contempt; and before many weeks had elapsed became the sole property of the pastry cook, and the itinerant vendors of old books.

With the exception of the three whom we have incidentally mentioned, and whose productions, may be reckoned the property of the past, no one save Mr. Robinson and Captain Boileau have, since the commencement of our career, afforded us an opportunity of testing their "epical pretensions to the laurel." Whatever may be the difficulties against which we have to contend, we cannot, though the field for poetry in the East is extensive, conscientiously complain, like our brethren of modern Athens, that poets "swarm here like the spawn of the cod fish, with a vicious fecundity that invites and requires destruction." We have, it is true, had a few of the description of authors here complained of, but their destruction was rendered unnecessary, as their publications, in every instance, fell "still born" from the press. But to proceed with Captain Boileau.

Most of the miscellaneous pieces which compose the volume before us have before been wedded to immortal type, so that the attentive reader of our journals, metropolitan and mofussil, will not fail to discover among the " great variety," which Captain Boileau has here crowded together, many familiar faces. As the volume (which we may here mention is a disgrace to typography in this country) contains no preface, we cannot precisely divine the motives which induced the publication. Nor is it at all necessary, that we should. Our author's researches in the field of science, as his lectures on Iron Suspension Bridges, and his labors in the Great Trigonometrical Survey abundantly testify, have been eminently successful; and it was perhaps this very success in one great department of human knowledge, propelled no doubt by that love for fame and restlessness inherent in many natures, which induced him to collect together his soarings in the wide expanse of poetry and song. The attempt, under any circumstances, was a hazardous one : for a mind constituted as our author's is, and accustomed to scientific investigation, subtle analysis, and classification, can scarcely be one which we would pronounce best suited to

> Give to airy nothing
> A local habitation and a name.

Captain Boileau first introduces his readers to a journal of operations against Bhurtpore. As a dry piece of journalism, written to wile away the tedious hours of a campaign, it is a very clear and creditable performance; but that he should publish it, after so long an interval, without subjecting it to a revision, by the rejection of all such matter as was useless and uninteresting, is a proceeding the propriety of which we consider somewhat questionable. Let us not be misunderstood. There are for instance recorded in the " Journal of Operations" many incidents which can afford no interest to the general reader, and many rumours noted which have been either confirmed or falsified by time ; such as that—" On the 25th March 1826, Colonel Auburey gave a dinner to Major Lockett, the Political Agent, Captain Williamson, Assistant Surgeon Steart, and ourselves ;" and again, " On the 29th January heard sundry reports not much to our credit, concerning the manner in which Doorjun Sall was treated upon being made prisoner. He was plundered of every article of his dress except the bare *lungootee*, and remained thus naked, until an officer gave him a table cloth as a wrapper, which was the only clothing that he possessed during the two days that he remained in camp. Can this be true ? " Now Captain Boileau has had ample opportunity for ascertaining whether this question, so innocently asked, be true or not. If true, it has detracted, in no small degree, from the reputation which the British have ever maintained for treating their enemies with consideration and humanity,—if false, he assuredly ought not to have allowed such a stigma to go uncontradicted.

From the two elaborate journals of a " Tour through Shekhawutee and of a " Mission to Beekaneer," the former of which was published in the *Gleanings in Science* in 1831, and the latter in the *Delhi Gazette*, and which are fair samples of Captain Boileau's industry, inquisitive disposition, and masculine understanding, we shall turn to those compositions, on which his fame, as a successful cultivator of the muses, depends. The first in the list of precedence and by far the most comprehensive, is an offering to Calliope, in five cantos, entitled the siege of Bhurtpore.

It was said of Alexander the Great, that on viewing the earthen tumuli which tradition pointed out as the graves of Achilles and Patroclus, he wept, mourning the fate of the hero who had not a Homer to hand down his achievements to posterity. The feeling was a natural one, and, whatever the cold blooded sons of sobriety and prudence may say, is one which has been shared in by many a hero from Macedonia's madman to the Swede. But unfortunately poets are not so plentiful as heroes, and many a successful leader, who has experienced all the delights arising from the " earthquake shock of victory," has, for the want of a bard, gone down to the grave "unknelled, uncoffined, and unknown." To rescue the chief of Bhurtpore, Lord Combermere, from so dire a calamity our author, with a feeling of enthusiasm, for he was an actor in the seige, comes to the rescue, and endeavours to narrate in rhyme the glories of his hero, and the incidents of that eventful campaign.

It would be a waste of time to enter on the oft debated question whether the Iliad, the Æneid, and the Jerusalem of Tasso are the only poems deserving of the title of epic, or whether others may not be reckoned in the category. It is sufficient for our present purpose that we here quote the dictum of a celebrated modern critic who asserts " that, the epic poem is universally allowed to be, of all poetical works, the most dignified, and, at the same time, the most difficult in execution ;" and then follow it up, by pointing out briefly a few of the requisites which, we conceive, ought to be possessed by those who aspire to commemorate, in song, great and heroic enterprizes.

And first of all the event which is to be pourtrayed, in a poetical form, ought to be great and interesting, and one, if possible over which antiquity has thrown its hoar. This latter consideration is material, for a poet cannot, with contemporary and well authenticated history, safely avail himself of all those collateral and fictitious aids, the judicious employment of which have materially contributed to raise the writings of our celebrated epic poets to so sublime a pitch. In so far Captain Boileau has been unfortunate in the selection of his subject. The " Siege of Bhurtpore" however signal the victory achieved by the British, and no one ever anticipated any other result, does not, to our apprehension, contain materials for the formation of an epic poem. There is little or no story connected with it, no plot, no incident sufficiently striking to inspire, which could not be infinitely better told in " humble prose." But admitting that both plot and incident did exist, our author, we fear, lacks the creative power, " the vision and the faculty divine" to do them justice. He is deficient in sublimity, in description, which is the true touchstone of warmth of imagination, and above all in force of expression—three distinct qualities but which ought to be harmoniously blended in an epic poet. But for fear we should be supposed to deal too severely with Captain Boileau, we shall lay before our readers a few extracts taken at random from his poem.

The first is a description of an Indian line of march :—

> Thus marched the assembled hosts, enclosed between
> Whose living walls a motly crowd is seen,
> Where, sheltered from the foe, in cumbrous throng
> The Baggage of the army moves along.
> Here, first and mightiest of the burthened crowd,
> The lordly Elephant sustains his load ;
> In state he walks, majestically slow,
> And towers above the busy crowd below.
> Not his the load that meaner beasts may bear
> Of brittle furniture, and household gear;
> On him the spreading tent alone is laid
> That yields in summer's heat a grateful shade,
> Or that, when autumn inundates the fields,
> Wards off the flood, and friendly shelter yields.
> Such is his load who ruled the forests o'er
> And bid their inmates tremble at his roar;
> Who once roved free and fearless o'er the plain
> Nor knew mankind, nor felt his galling chain ;
> But now enslaved his strength gigantic lends
> To those who tamed him, and submissive bends.
>
> Next him the Camel comes, with pace sedate
> Uncouth in form and clumsy in his gait ;
> Yet search the Indian world, and none may find
> A drudge more useful to the human kind.
> Patient and strong, enduring of fatigue,
> He plods his weary way for many a league ;
> And prosecutes for days his weary toil,
> Nor seeks for water in the barren soil.
> Not so the rest who follow in his train
> And pant and labour on the sandy plain ;
> Yoked to their cars the Oxen, from afar,
> By tedious marches creep to join the war ;
> And still unwilling as they tread the road,
> Scarce bend their stubborn necks beneath the load ;
> Unmoved they hear their driver's frequent cry,
> Or sullen to the sounding lash reply.

The next is a description of the preparations for filling the depôt, in which the practical engineer shows to greater advantage than the poet :—

> Here swarthy Blacksmiths ply their busy trade
> And point the Crow, or shape the massy blade
> That helps the soldiers hand, unwonted toil,
> To trench the surface of the hardened soil.
> With ceaseless din the groaning bellows sound,
> Vast hammers ring, and anvils clank around;
> While, mingled with the rest, the various cries
> Of passing groups in loud confusion rise.
> Here labouring hinds apply the hatchet wide
> Or jarring bill-hook to the grindstone's side ;—
> By skilful workmen lofty steps are made
> To assist our columns in the escalade,

> While other hands the ready mattocks spread
> And fix each handle to its proper head.
> Others, with force united, lift with ease
> The weighty Maulet, and Chevaux de Frise,
> Arrange the stores, and, piled in long array
> The fresh-wrought Gabions and Fascines display.

The bombardment of the fort is in our author's best style, though the action is not described with sufficient fire and impetuosity :—

> Nor less within the City's verge they pour
> Of deadly shells an overwhelming shower
> That hurls its dreadful conflagration down
> Among the streets of that devoted town,
> And furious as it rushes on its way
> Spares age nor sex, does nought but burn and slay.
> Ah 'tis a splendid though an awful sight,
> Amid the stillness of the deep dark night,
> To see the fiery shells ascend on high,
> Like some wild meteor blazing in the sky,
> Then swift descending, glance like lightning down
> From the vast height of their aerial throne,
> And, bursting sudden, as they reach the ground
> Spread desolation and dismay around.

Though pathos is not one of the prime ingredients in epic poetry, it has sometimes been employed with great effect. Its language is never bedecked with tawdry ornaments, but is bold, ardent, and unaffected. The following lamentation for those who fell during the siege can scarcely be said to contain these qualities :—

> The battle strife is o'er, yet in mine ear
> The sound of war is ringing loud and clear,
> In lengthened peal the cannon-shots resound
> And wake the echoes in the woods around ;
> They sound a requiem for the soul that's fled,
> They ring the death-knell for the gallant dead,
> They tell the world that Edwards is no more,
> His course is finished, and his glories o'er !
> Nor thee alone, brave Edwards, may they mourn,
> From friends, from family and kindred torn,
> Let Armstrong's widow for her husband weep,
> And Brown's, now buried in eternal sleep ;
> The Pitmans too have drawn their latest breath
> Nor part the brother-comrades even in death,
> And Candy's spirit, gently lingering, flies
> To seek a happier mansion in the skies.

To our thinking this is as bad a specimen of the pathetic as we ever in the course of our reading remember perusing. If Captain Boileau's genius, like Robert Montgomery's, to use the language of Macaulay " be not far too free and aspiring to be shackled by the rules of syntax," we will venture to say that no " cannon shots," from the day they were first fired, ever performed such feats as they are made to do in these few lines. In the first place, they are a made to " resound' which is natural enough, then to " sound", like Roman Catholic priests

" a requiem for the soul that's fled ;" after this they ring the death knell
for the gallant dead ;" then again " tell the world that Edwards is no
more," that " his course is finished and his glories o'er ;"—rather
tautological pieces of intelligence by the way,—and last of all " they
may mourn" if they choose, for the said Edwards and others. This truly
is making the most of a simile. Nor is this all. Some fastidious
reader may likewise object to the introduction of so plebeian a name,
in an epic, as " Brown ;" but our author has a good precedent for
this departure from poetical propriety in Lord Byron, who asserts
that, in the celebrated siege of Schmacksmith, there fought, along with
the Strongenoffs and Strokenoffs, " sixteen called Thompson and nineteen named Smith, and that the elder Jack Smith " fell immortal in a
bulletin."

We like our author's " translations" from the French the best, and
his charades, lyrics, &c. the least. Did space permit, we would make
room for some of these translations ; but as their merits would not be appreciated, without lengthened extracts, we must rest contented with merely bestowing on them a general meed of approbation. They possess,
with few exceptions, liveliness, an indefinite license of caricature, and
above all, an easy flow of versification, which we look for in vain in
Captain Boileau's other productions,—a tacit proof, some people might
be disposed to say, that he is more at ease when in the saddle of another's
Pegasus than his own.

Not being at present in a mood for oriental criticism, we need pronounce no positive opinion on Captain Boileau's translations, into the
Hindustani language, of some of our national ballads. Of the few
specimens which we find in his volume the following, on Moore's well
known Venetian air, will perhaps be considered the best. The sentiments and euphony of the original, in our judgment, appear to be preserved with great fidelity. ;—

NO. II.
FROM MOORE'S NATIONAL AIRS.

Row gently here, my Gondolier ; so softly wake the tide,
That not an ear on earth may hear, but her's to whom we glide.
Had heaven but tongues to speak, as well as starry eyes to see,
Oh ! think what tales 'twould have to tell of wand'ring youths like me.

Now rest thee here, my Gondolier ; Hush, hush, for up I go,
To climb yon light balcony's height, while thou keep'st watch below.
Ah ! did we take for Heaven above but half such pains as we
Take day and night for woman's love what angels we should be !

HINDUSTANI TRANSLATION OF NO. II.

Ho ! Manjhee, ho ! suhuz se keo, dand hulkee hath se tan ;
Kih kisee ka nu soonega siwae *Oos* ke kan.
Asman ke ankh Sitara hue, uor oos ka jeebh bhee ho,
Tho kaisee bat nu kahta hue ham juwan-logon ko !

Ho ! Manjhee, ho ! ub choop ruho, kinare chul, Sook-das,
Burunde men hum chur jaen, toom ruho nao ke pas.
Istree ke jitna din o rat soch hue hum logon ko,
Gosain ke ootne howe bat, tho kaisa poon nu ho !

The practice which has, of late, been pursued by Jeffrey, Macaulay, Sydney Smith, and others, of reprinting, with their names, the most celebrated of the miscellaneous papers which they had, from time to time, contributed to the periodical press is one which, however justifiable in their individual cases, is likely to be attended with dangerous consequences to literature, if too closely followed by a class of writers, who, with mediocre pretensions, are too often prone, we fear, to estimate their productions, rather by the effects they have produced on themselves, than by the satisfaction they have afforded, or are likely to afford, the public. If the truth must be told, we apprehend that it is to this unfortunate propensity we are indebted for the volume now before us. If Captain Boileau has received, and we doubt not he has received, his meed for most of these fugitive pieces, which were published anonymously, he ought, in all justice, to have remained satisfied instead of seeking, by a republication in his own person, for a reconsideration of their merits. Compositions of an ephemeral character, unless bearing the strong impress of genius, seldom show to advantage after they have had their day ; and when they are exhibited afresh they often have the effect of removing from their author a portion of that favorable opinion which the public were once wont to entertain, at least, of his judgment.

Here we must conclude. If, in estimating Captain Boileau's powers of poetical composition, we have said aught offensive, we are sorry for it, because we entertain for his scientific and classical attainments the highest respect. With many prepossessions in his favour, it has yet been our endeavour, in the exercise of an unpleasant vocation, to hold the scales of criticism with the strictest impartiality.

Voyage dans L'Inde, par Victor Jacquemont, pendant les annees 1828 a 1832. Publie sous les auspices de M. Guizot, ministre de l'instruction publique. Paris. 1841. 6 tomes.

Travels in India by V. Jacquemont from 1828 to 1832. Published under the patronage of Monsieur Guizot, Minister of Public Instruction. Paris 1841, six volumes quarto.

In France, the Government patronizes Oriental Literature to a far higher degree than the English Government does—in fact literary men hold a much nobler status in society there. The ablest men in the government have been elevated by their literary or scientific acquirements. In England, we have the aristocracy of birth or of money—in France, we have nature's aristocracy—the aristocracy of talent. The execution of the present work is an honour to France : it embodies a large mass of valuable information, given by a foreigner who looked with an impartial view on English Society in India. Victor Jacquemont was sent out on a scientific mission to India in 1828 by the Paris Society of Natural History ; he proceeded from Calcutta to Agra and the Himalayas and as far as Chinese Tartary. Prohibited by the inhabitants of Ladak from going farther, he travelled to Kashmir, then to Central India,

k

and was about to proceed along the Malabar Coast, when death cut him off in December 1832. Three of these volumes contain his Journal; two have drawings in Zoology, Botany and Conchology; and one a series of articles on Indian Natural History.

He embarked from France in a French Corvette, much inferior in discipline to the English vessels : he touched at Teneriffe, a basaltic island, the inhabitants of which are intelligent and imitate English customs ; " the half castes, through their idleness, worse than that of the Spaniards, are engaged in the most wretched occupations." Teneriffe, like all countries colonized by the Spaniards, is retrograding in civilization. He remained a short time at Rio Janeiro, with its black population, abject and indecent—its French milliners—the Portuguese aristocracy " pompous abroad, poor within their houses, with the negro type in their features,"—and its licentious court pandered to by the mercantile class. Jacquemont contrasts the South American with the North American States, and thinks the former are no better now than when colonies of Spain. " What use is the liberty of thinking and acting to those who neither think nor act." He next proceeded to Brazil ; he gives a description of its present political and commercial condition, " free before being worthy of freedom." He afterwards visited the Mauritius.

Jacquemont landed at Calcutta in June 1829. The following are some of the observations he makes on North India : they deserve attentive consideration as coming from an intelligent Frenchman and one who viewed generally with a dispassionate eye " the English in India :"—"*Calcutta* is the *commercial* capital of India, Benares the capital of the Hindus, and Delhi of the Mussulmans; an English capital situated in the North West Provinces would have a greater moral influence, associated with the prestige of past times.—Conversation languishes at English dinner parties, as the English do not understand the art of conversation.—Long prayers are bad in India where the climate disposes one to sleep." Jacquemont visited *Chandernagur* with its thirty sipahis ; he found no pleasure in it owing to the entire want of society ; through its elevation it is cooler and healthier than Calcutta, " the silence which reigns in places whose prosperity is stationary or decreasing, has something gloomy but affecting in it."—The *Asiatic Society of Calcutta* is " composed of a small number of men skilful but of little influence in society, and of men of high rank but ignorant." Jacquemont attended what was called " a crowded" meeting of the society,—it numbered 20 ! " The museum is kept without order and taste, the objects are the prey of rust and insects.* The Asiatic Society as a body is a mere cypher, there are no researches made in common, no association among the members for labouring towards a common end."—The Europeans in India give little of their leisure time to study, their night dinners dispose them to sleep, and their hours of leisure are devoted to idleness and bodily indulgences.—The English of the middle class are not satisfied, like the French, with money sufficient to support them, but they are anxious to become wealthy capitalists.—The military are the only

* We are glad to say that, in this respect, things appear to be on a different footing now.

persons to whom there is much leisure; a few of them are distinguished in literary pursuits, the rest sleep and smoke all day.—The huka is used at all dinner parties in Calcutta, with the exception of the Governor General's.—The English ladies follow strictly the London fashions, notwithstanding the difference of climate.—Persons whom they have never seen are written to as—Dear Sir.—The Europeans of Calcutta have little curiosity to know the country."

" Rivalries or ridiculous jealousies often produce alienation between the families at a Mofussil station: every family lives a retired life, and with the exception of occasional dinners where almost all meet, they pass the greater part of their evenings alone.—The Raja of *Burdwan* has built a suspension bridge between Hugli and Perua over a stream which is considered to have been the ancient bed of the Dammuda. which now flows into the Hugli at Diamond Harbour. Lord Amherst at the time of the Burmese war asked the Raja for a loan of a certain sum of money, promising to repay it at the end of 25 years, the Raja declined saying he did not know whether 25 years hence the Company would possess the country.—Burdwan is healthy owing to the elevation of the soil and its freedom from jungle.—Kankar is seen first at Dignagur where are many sugar manufactories.—*Hazirabag* is the residence of the political agent for the ceded territories; he has 1,000 men under his command, placed in detachments through the district which is almost one vast forest. It has a civil surgeon who is engaged extensively in the lac trade. Twelve miles south of Hazirabag 200 maunds of iron are manufactured daily by natives. Oranges and grapes are produced in abundance, tigers are very numerous. At a short distance from it there are quicksands placed over subterranean currents.—Passed one mile on the sands of the Soane before seeing a drop of water, it takes 4 hours to cross.—*Sasseram* is a city of Mahommedan tombs; the dwellings of the living occupy less space than those of the dead; the country between Sasseram and Benares is free from jungle and better peopled. —At *Benares*—attended two dinner parties where even the Champagne that was drunk in abundance could not melt the ice of etiquette which prevails at those reunions; every one the next day complained of the dulness of the preceding evening; happy are we French who are unacquainted with this horrible slavery to coteries, who know nothing of this plague of English life but its name—fashion. There is one man however who compensates for the antisocial disposition of his fellow countrymen—James Prinsep; he devotes his mornings to architectural plans and drawings, his days to assaying at the mint, and his evenings to musical concerts.—If there be any place in India where Europeans ought to associate on friendly terms with the Hindus, it is assuredly Benares; a great number of the natives possess what the English value so high— birth and fortune—and here all the knowledge of Asia is concentrated— yet there is no acquaintance kept up between the Hindus of the city and the Europeans of the cantonment: the English have so few conversational powers that they cannot carry on a conversation without a supper; this resource they are deprived of in the case of the Hindus.—At *Mirzapur* the English unsociableness is more conspicuous by their houses being 2 or 3 miles miles distant from one another.   The trade in salt at Mirzapur has diminished very much owing to commercial monopolies. —The Roman Catholic Bishop of Agra lives in a truly apostolic style; his dinner was served up in the commonest pottery on a table without a cloth, no silver, his knives of iron, his spoons of tin,—a sight disagreeable to an Englishman, but effaced here by the dignity of poverty."

Jacquemont's remarks on Central India are very valuable, as also on the North West Provinces; he makes observations on the geology and botany of the different places he visits.   Since the publication of Heber's Journal, no work has issued from the press better calculated to afford accurate information on India.   The execution of the work is very creditable to the French Government.   The price is high—250 rupees—but we trust some public library in Calcutta will purchase it.

A Charge delivered to the Grand Jury of Bombay, September 25th, 1845.   By the Honorable Mr. Justice Perry.   Bombay: American Mission Press, 1845.

THE practice of addressing charges to Grand Juries has often proved exceedingly beneficial to the community.   Sometimes in England political prejudices have constituted the most distinguishing feature of such charges, and then the office of Judge has been prostituted and the tribunals of Justice have been degraded.   But when Judges of experience, after observing, in various circuits, the increase or decrease of particular kinds of crime, the causes of such increase and decrease, the effect of social customs, the delusions of criminals and witnesses, and the manner in which the influence of resident justices and others can be more effectually brought to bear on the course of national improvement,—when such Judges have availed themselves of such observations, and have imparted to Grand Juries their wise suggestions and impartial counsel, they have raised the character of their office and enlarged its usefulness.

Such charges have seldom been delivered in India, but why this is so, we know not.   We hail Sir Erskine Perry's brief address now before us, as a sign that some among our present Indian Judges are willing to exhibit a new example.   We believe that several of them are men who might very usefully enlarge their charges, and that the respect of the community for them is so great, that their advice and remarks would be received with cordial pleasure.   Mr. Justice Burton at Madras, we notice, although he is the youngest of our Judges, has not hesitated to point out to a Grand Jury whom he was addressing, the influence of a sound education on sound morals; and Sir Erskine Perry in the charge before us admirably avails himself of an allusion to the progress of commercial enterprize, to point out the superior importance of moral improvement.   He says :—

" It is impossible for any bystander to watch the progress which India is now making in material improvement without the liveliest satisfaction.   The great social discovery of modern times, of the admirable results to be obtained by the association of numbers in one common enterprize, is beginning to be fully appreciated in this country, and native enterprize and capital may be seen quite ready to enter upon any path, which the superior experience of their British fellow subjects has pointed out as safe and practicable. I trust, if I may be allowed to express a wish, that this new agent of civilization may be kept within its proper bounds, that the same good sense which has hitherto prevailed in Bombay to prevent any improper application of it, may still continue to be exercised, and that due commercial enterprize may never here at least degenerate into wild speculation. But however gratifying it may be to witness what is going on in India for the material improvement of the country, no thinking man can be satisfied with this alone, nor fail to admit that the moral progress of a country is far more important in its bearings on human happiness, and all that is really great in the character of a nation, than the mere accumulation of worldly wealth."

We are glad also to notice the manner in which he calls attention to the relation of Justices to the Superintendent of Police. We have reason to fear, that in Calcutta, the arrangement of this relationship is not sufficiently distinct, and that considerable embarrassment and some extra official proceedings on the one side or the other, must often necessarily follow.

The only two cases in the Calendar before him, on which Mr. Justice Perry remarks in this charge, are, one of murder, in which the body of the murdered person was not found, and one of endeavouring to extort money by threatening to accuse of a felony. Some circumstances in the former case led him to make the following important observations on the value of confessional evidence :—

"The point on which I wish to say a few words is as to the value of confessional evidence. At first sight, nothing appears so satisfactory and trustworthy as the confession of a prisoner who has been apprehended under suspicious circumstances. The love of life and self-preservation being so deeply implanted in our nature, it may be reasonably supposed that where a party accuses himself of a crime which calls down upon the offender the punishment of the law, his statement may be received with implicit credit. A wider experience and a more intimate analysis of the motives by which human conduct is governed, demonstrate that such conclusion is by no means universally true. Instances are upon record beyond number, where prisoners to avoid some immediate evil, have accused themselves of crimes of which they were not only not guilty, but of which they could not by any possibility be guilty, such as witchcraft for instance

To avoid the pains of torture, to gain the favor of the authorities, to explain any suspicious circumstances by inventing others charging a more heinous offence, all these are motives likely to produce, and which have over and over again produced, a confession of crimes altogether fictitious. And as the English law had perceived that such motives are likely occasionally to operate to produce a simulated confession, it has been laid down as a general rule, that whenever any influence is held out to a prisoner to confess by those in authority, the confession made under such circumstances should not be receivable at all. The principle on which this goes undoubtedly proceeds on an accurate observation of human nature, but possibly in practice it may be extended too far, by excluding the confession altogether, instead of subjecting it to the closest examination. One would conceive that the true rule should be in all such cases to admit the confession, not as conclusive evidence, but for that which it is worth, and that it should be the duty of the

Judge to point out and dwell upon the motives which might lead to the confession being false, and should compare it with the rest of any corroboration from the surrounding circumstances.

I have dwelt upon this point because, in nearly all the cases which come up from the Mofussil, a confession of the prisoner is obtained, whereas with prisoners taken in Bombay a confession is very rarely forthcoming. As no effect is produced without a cause, and as undoubtedly no confession is made without a motive, and a motive having the supposed interest of the party more or less remotely in view, it is quite obvious that some general cause must be at work to produce the difference between the two systems. On no one point, perhaps, connected with criminal jurisprudence, do the ideas of Asiatics and Europeans differ more widely than in the mode in which prisoners should be treated with respect to confessions. Very few inhabitants of the East, I apprehend, and perhaps not many even amongst our own countrymen, who have been long domiciled here, would object to a prisoner who has been apprehended under suspicious circumstances being taken up and flogged until he made disclosures. I have no doubt that in a great many instances, this practise succeeds in eliciting the truth, and that without it, in very many cases, the truth would go undiscovered. Yet the system is attended with such evils, it necessarily admits of such occasional tyranny, it enables such large irresponsible powers to be vested in parties wholly unfit to possess them, and the consequences and results which ensue on feigned confessions being produced are so dreadful to contemplate, that after an experience of many hundred years, the whole of civilized Europe has tacitly abandoned the practise. The putting to the *question*, as it was mildly called in the language of ancient Rome, once found a place in all European codes, not excluding the English, but I am not aware that it exists now in any country of the western world except perhaps in Russia. It is clear however to me, that the theory which once prevailed so extensively in the West, and which it has required a large experience and a refined jurisprudence to extirpate, still prevails very extensively in the eastern world, and this is quite sufficient to account for the very great number of confessions which make their appearence in Mofussil cases.

With respect to the admissibility in evidence of confessions obtained under such circumstances, the point would probably be a matter of discussion by counsel at the bar. The English law has probably gone too far in its anxiety to exclude any confessions that might possibly have been extorted, and I have already stated, that in my opinion the true and expedient rule should to be to admit and examine the confession, and to contrast it with all the circumstances of the case, the influences by which it might have been extorted, and especially by the confirmation or denial which it might meet with from the statements of the prisoner at the trial. A judge, however, of course cannot act on his own, possibly crude, notions of what is expedient, but bows implicitly to the rule of law. That rule is neatly and concisely summed up in a celebrated work on evidence as follows:—" It has been considered necessary in all cases, previous to receiving a confession in evidence, to inquire whether it has been voluntary. The usual questions are whether the prisoner has been told that it would be better for him to confess, or worse for him if he did not confess, or whether any language to that effect has been used. The presumption of the truth of the statement is supposed to cease, when there is ground to apprehend that it may have been wrung from a timid and apprehensive mind, deluded by promises of safety, or subdued by threats of violence or punishment. This, as was before observed, is an observation not wholly unconfirmed by experience. But perhaps the cases are rare, in which such unfounded self-accusations occur, or at least where a Jury would be misled by them; and certainly the rule occasions, in a multitude of instances, the escape of the guilty. There is a general feeling which seems to be well founded, that, the rule has been extended much too far, and been applied in some cases where there could be no reasonable ground for supposing that the inducement offered to the prisoner was sufficient to overcome the strong and universal motive of self-preservation."[*]

These remarks are worthy of much attention in this country. We knew a case in which a man was sentenced to imprisonment for life, in Alipore jail on the evidence of his own confession; some subsequent confessions of other parties, which were completely corroborated by other evidence, made it clear that this prisoner could not have had any share in the offence for which he was condemned; and so after some years he obtained his liberty. His confession had in fact been extorted by torture; and thus, first torture, and then false imprisonment, had been the result of a loose system of encouraging the native police in obtaining confessional evidence. There cannot, we fear, be a doubt, that wherever it is necessary to assume an appearance of great activity and zeal in detecting offences, the native police will not scruple, if it can be done without discovery and punishment, to compel prisoners whose main offence is the inability to bribe them, to accuse themselves of offences of which perhaps none know so well that they are innocent, as the very police officers who maltreat them. And, therefore, if confessional evidence be received cautiously in England, it is still more justly liable to suspicion here.

In an appendix to his charge Sir Erskine Perry prints some interesting statistical tables. We find by these that the average yearly number of prisoners in the Bombay House of Correction for the 5 years from January 1, 1840, till December 31st, 1844, was 744. The average of sick persons yearly in the same period amounted to 236, and the average number of deaths yearly was 12. This gives a better return than any English house of correction, but the period for which the prisoners were confined is not specified. The *daily* average for the same period of five years was 119; the average of the sick 11; the per centage of deaths was 1.63; and the per centage of deaths to sick was 5,27. And yet it appears that there have been great complaints of the unhealthiness of this place of punishment.

We thank Sir Erskine Perry for his little tract, and heartily do we hope that he may apply the powers of his mind, during his residence in India, to her moral improvement. Little indeed has been done in this way by the Impeys, and many more who have sat on the English Bench. Few are the British Judges who have exerted their great influence assiduously and wisely, for great and noble ends. But some there are who have been of another mind; although there has been but one Sir Henry Blossett. There are now, however, on the Indian bench some men of great ability and of true philanthrophy; and to these we hope that we shall not look in vain for earnest efforts to adorn their elevated station, as well by acts of public benevolence as by the exercise of impartial justice.

[*] Phillips on Evidence.

The Education of the People of India ; its political importance and advantages: pp. 26. Calcutta ; published by Ostell and Lepage, 1845.

THIS small pamphlet has been published anonymously—why; we know not. For sure we are that there is nothing either in its style or substance of which the author need be ashamed. If it enounces no new, striking, or original views, it at least propounds some important old ones, in language that is lucid and for the most part elegant. Such seasonable reiteration of fundamental principles, neither generally acknowledged in theory, or energetically acted on in practice, is what the peculiarity of *present* circumstances urgently demands, and what must prove vastly more beneficial than any unverified speculations, however ingenious, or any novel suggestions, however brilliant or profound.

If our space admitted of it, we would gladly quote large passages from this sober, judicious, and will timed pamphlet. But we can only find room for the author's own summary of its contents :—

" In these considerations, our object has been to point out, by investigation the state of society, its past history, and the character and condition of the population, the true nature of those obstacles, which must be overcome, ere justice can be properly administered, and the welfare of the community secured. Institutions and laws may bridle the outbreaks and disorders of society,—encourage and assist its progress in improvement, but they will not change the character of a nation, or give a stirring impulse to that improvement;—they will not create it, where it does not already exist. Climate will invigorate the body and give tone to the mind, or impart weakness and listlessness; the nature of the country will materially affect the character of its inhabitants; war and oppression will disorganize society, and make the people abject slaves. But what except education, will give them a new character, new desires, new hopes, and new impulses ? What save education will awake among them a spirit of improvement ? "

Undoubtedly, a *sound* education, widely diffused throughout the native community of all classes and grades, must be regarded as one of the primary instruments of its effectual amelioration. Of the partial good which has already resulted, amid many disappointments and drawbacks, from the educational measures hitherto adopted, our own pages furnish demonstrative testimony ; see vol. II. p. 31.

And when, in the spirit of the remarks there made, we simply state that the article in the present number, on *Rammohun Roy*, is the *bona-fide* production of an educated Hindu, we think we have furnished a fresh argument to the friends of sound education to persevere more earnestly than ever in their philanthrophic labours.

SANDERS AND CONES, TYPS., NO. 4, TANK-SQUARE, CALCUTTA.

NOTE TO THE MAHRATTA ARTICLE IN No. VII.

It has been pointed out to us that in the following expression, used in No. VII. of this Review, we have done injustice to Colonel Wallace:—" He (Col. Outram,) arrived at Samangurh,—the fortress was carried forthwith." These words, *taken by themselves*, certainly are open to misapprehension; but we may refer to our other notices of Col. Outram to shew that we never supposed him to have been the Military Commander at Samangurh; that, previous to the 14th January, we referred to his official duties as purely political; and up to that date only gave him the credit due to a Diplomatic Agent and Military Volunteer, who had counselled wisely and had acted boldly. Our words, at page 227, were, " Col. Outram had joined General Delamotte's camp the day before the storm, in a political capacity, and henceforward, &c."

We willingly, however, allow that, when writing the Mahratta article, we were ignorant of the extent to which, as we are now informed, General Delamotte had devolved the conduct of operations at Samangurh on Col. Wallace; as also of the fact, that *before* Colonel Outram's arrival in camp, Colonel Wallace had made his arrangements for the storm. Nor were we aware that it was under Col. W.'s immediate orders that Capt. Græme of the 5th M. L. C., accompained by Mr. Reeves and Col. Outram, routed the covering party of the Kolapoor rebels.

Writers on contemporary history must reckon on being accused of malignity, one-sidedness, &c.: we may however, once for all, say that we are of no party, but, to the best of our ability, are the advocates of truth. We may err from deficient or wrong information, but hardly from either malevolence or partiality. In the present instance, our assertion may be the more readily credited, in that we have *no personal acquaintance with any of the Officers, employed in the S. M. Country, on whose conduct we have remarked. By their official acts, and by these alone, we have judged them.*

Art. I.—1. *The East India College, Haileybury.*

2. *The East India Register for* 1845.

About twenty-one miles from the Metropolis of England, in the rich and well-cultivated county of Hertford, is situated the College in which, according to Act of Parliament, young men are educated, who are destined to fill employments in the Civil Service of India. The locality and surrounding scenery, though of a kind not comparable with the romantic beauty of Devonshire, or the still wilder views of the west of England, may yet challenge competition with any of our midland or even southern counties. The country for some miles around, of a description truly English, exhibiting in a series of undulations, the shades of the forest, the well watered pasture land, and the rich waving of corn fields, may at times be termed almost picturesque. The college itself stands at the foot of a heath, and on a gentle declivity almost encircled with umbrageous woods! As a building it has nothing which can admit of a moment's comparison with the glance at any one college in the vista of High Street, Oxford, or with the great square in Trinity College, Cambridge,—nothing which can attempt to vie with those associations that crowd on us as we gaze on the distant towers of Granta, or on the Panorama which meets our view when standing on the heights of Shotover, or those of Bagley wood; but yet the scenery round Haileybury is of that kind to which either of the Universities, with all their proud and cherished recollections, must infallibly yield. On the heath above the college bloom in the early Spring months the varied flowers whose sweetness no "heart that loves the Spring" can well refuse: in the glades of its woods, and in the very gardens attached to the institution, may be heard on a Summer's evening the cuckoo's "wandering voice," and the ceaseless melody of the nightingale has cheered the labours of the student throughout the livelong night: the country for several miles is studded with gentlemen's seats: even the associations which History and noted characters alone can supply, though sought for in vain in the college, are not wanting to heighten the quiet beauty of the neighbourhood. The Rye House, notorious for the well known plot of that name, but now harmless as the resort of peaceful anglers, lies at the distance of a short two miles from Haileybury: an evening stroll, almost insufficient for a good constitutional walk, will conduct the hard-reading student to Amwell—the Amwell of Cowper, immortalized in his verse. The very highway on which his prince of roadsters, undying John Gilpin, must have ridden his famous race, forms the boundary of the well known Hailey Lane. Ware, the goal of his travels, is considerably less than "full ten miles off," and in the valley which forms the separation of the counties of Essex and Hertford, hallowed by that name so dear to every brother of the gentle craft, the Lea of Isaac Walton pursues its meandering course. This peculiarity cannot have escaped the observation of any who have ever had the opportunity of visiting either of our Universities, and who are acquainted with the character of Oxfordshire, or the wide, dull, flats, extending round Cambridge. Most of our public schools have been in like manner but little favoured by the natural advantages of site, although the taste and liberality of their founders may have built the edifices themselves in a style severe and dignified. In expanse of park-like ground, and clusters of noble trees, they have the advantage over Haileybury, but in rustic scenery the latter place may fairly bear away the palm. The Etonian, it is true, may well be proud of the distant view of his Windsor, or of the swiftly running stream of his Thames, and may adore in his 'Shooting fields' the shades of many noble characters as holy as his Henry's. The Rugbœan may view with admiration the magnificent elm trees which overlook the "school close," or the leafy group which centres on the gentle ascent of "the Island." The Wykehamist may extol the distant view of the grey College as seen from the chalk downs of Hants, and the Harrovian look from Harrow Hill over a wide extent of plain till he almost descries the rival towers of Eton in the distance;—but when once we quit the immediate ground on which any one of these places stands, poetry and its attendant train vanish at once from our thought. Rugby with the "trim hedge rows" of Warwickshire—'the dullest of our midland counties'—unvaried by scarce a single small spinney: Harrow with its equally uninteresting succession of plain and field: Winchester with its hot and glaring table land, where hardly a tree relieves the tired eye : even Eton, though more favoured by the hand of nature—cannot hope to supply the pleasing effects produced by a ramble through Herts. For a county so near London we know of none so captivating, and many old Haileybury men, we are sure, must recall with pleasure endless strolls through the glades of Lord Salisbury's woods, or the no less pleasing walk towards the splendid park of Pansanger.

It was amidst such scenery that, at a period of more than thirty years ago, were laid 'broad and deep' the foundations of the East India College. Those who, for that period, have been amongst the ruling influences of India, there received all their primary training; and, with but a few exceptions, the Civil Service of India have issued forth from its walls. Those only whose almost antediluvian existence carries them back to a period when Haileybury was not, and those—some seventy or eighty in number—who passed at the India house when civilians were in great request, can have no immediate personal sympathy with our subject; but the place where their relations or friends, or at any rate where their fellow workers received their education, cannot be supposed to be totally devoid of interest; and it is the attention of the Civil Service, indeed of every friend to India, whatever be his profession, which we would endeavour to excite whilst treating of the system, with its merits and demerits, therein pursued. The appointments to Haileybury, like other Indian ones, are vested uncontrollably in the hands of the Directors, of whom each member has generally two a year to dispose of, and on some occasions even more. The nominee is referred to the India house examiners in order that his qualifications may be tested previous to entrance. Of the test he undergoes there, we may have to speak anon; if rejected on trial he is thrown back for another period of six months, if pronounced duly qualified he enters college the very next term. We would wish that those of our Readers who spent many days at Haileybury would return with us and spend one more day in its precincts, that those who are mainly ignorant of the internal working of the institution would take one glance at its component elements—at the motley crew who form the brotherhood of the college. We will take the opening day of term, the fourteenth of September or the twenty-third of January, and what a varied crowd shall we there see assembled! It is true that the beginning of an Oxford or Cambridge term collects almost every species of youth, from the head of the acknowledged aristocracy of a public school to the unobtrusive *freshman* just emancipated from the thrall of a private tutor, and amalgamates the somewhat incongruous materials into one consistent republic; but of these many have been looking forward to the universities as that which shall put the coping stone on the education of their earlier years: they have foreseen this termination for a long time previous, and in most cases the change is only from a smaller to a greater world,—one composed of nearly similar materials, but cast in a deeper and more comprehensive mould. The men from public schools meet there the friends of their early school days, they again associate with their cotemporaries, or find themselves on an equality with those who had been the heroes and giants of a preceding generation. The less prominent characters, who have nevertheless been looking forward to this situation for some time back, are soon borne along by the common stream, and mingle insensibly with the great mass: all have gone to the university in order to attain the passport to real life, and to be stamped with that which shall give them currency in whatever profession they choose. Not so with the world of Haileybury. The golden shower of the Directors' patronage often enriches places where it is least expected, and a large variety of characters, whose early career was far removed from the thought of India, are there brought together under one denomination. Look in at Haileybury on the first day of term, and trace the previous fortunes of the *freshmen* there assembled. The man of some six or eight terms spent at Oxford or Cambridge, who has evaded the Proctor's vigilance in the contests between gown and town, or daringly driven a tandem down the forbidden precints of Trumpington, who could boast that he had passed through the ordeal of the " little go," and was looking forward to high honors at the finale of his degree: the *alumnus* of the public school, fresh from his early triumphs at Eton or Rugby ; the less marked individual from the private academy ; the student who has only succeeded in passing at the India house, by the continued exertions of the regular Haileybury " crammer ;" the incipient soldier transferred from the warlike atmosphere of Sandhurst, or Addiscombe, or Woolwich, to exchange the sword and shield for the pen and the toga ; the midshipman quitting the lee side of the quarter-deck for the more congenial, though less romantic, regions of civilized life ; the Highland youth blooming as the very heather of his native hills, and betraying by his silvery accents the land of his birth—all these, varying in age from the schoolboy of sixteen to the full grown citizen of twenty-one, thrown promiscuously into one and the same term, are the elements from which must be drawn the future utility not only of the college itself, but of the executive government of the three presidencies of India. We have drawn attention to this feature of Haileybury life, because it forms one of the most fertile sources of abuse, and is the door at which most of the anomalies which prevail there, can be laid with the greatest confidence. With materials as heterogeneous as the above, with a considerable degree of freedom and unrestraint, and with no self-denial imposed, with all the sources of evil which prevail in a large public school— the same opposition to authority, the same proneness to follow the lowered standard of expediency established by the majority, with the outward and visible forms and regulations of a college, and with none of its internal dignity or self-respect on the part of its members, Haileybury was expected to present the same goodly appearance as Trinity, or Balliol, or Christchurch, and it fell far short of the reality of Rugby or Eton, or Winchester. Fatally, indeed, were the expectations formed of Haileybury disappointed. For years the East India College carried on its surface an unhappy prestige of notoriety: the eyes of the world only marked it on the occasion of some internal revolution, fraught with ruin to the perpetrators. Men were unacquainted with the temptations to which the embryo civilian was there exposed, and knew it but as a place of bad repute, whose chief characteristics were extreme laxity of morals, and periodical volcanic eruptions. Of the apologies which might be made for the delinquents, of the defects co-eval with the establishment of the institution, and of those which grew out of its progressive structure, many even of those whose sons were educated within its walls, remained entirely ignorant. For years it dragged on a tedious existence, now threatened with dissolution, now evading publicity by its unobtrusive character, but always unknown, or at least misunderstood; and even with the brightening prospect of better days, we feel that Haileybury, as the *officina* of the Civil Service of India—with facts and realities instead of doubts and suppositions,—requires to be laid bare before the eye of the public. We intend reviewing both the course of education there pursued, and also the whole internal economy of the college. And first, the line of study, extending over a period of two years, must claim our attention; we shall then see how far that training may be expected to fit the student for the stage on which he is to appear.

Many may not be aware, that, after a fluctuation of opinions regarding the time which should be spent at Haileybury, it was ultimately decided that four terms, or a space of two years, should alone entitle a student to go forth from its walls. The wisdom of such a decision is apparent at a glance. Under the previous law, by which a certain high standard of proficiency obtained in two terms or one year, emancipated a student from thraldom, Haileybury was perpetually being denuded of all the hard working and steady men, who might reasonably be expected to effect some change for the better in public opinion; and those left behind were, as might be conceived, the idle, the thoughtless, and the refractory. At the same time the course of study underwent modification, and at present it stands somewhat as follows. In his first term the student continues his early studies in mathematics and classics, the former extending over six books of Euclid, and the latter embracing some congenial and not unfamiliar subject taken from the range of Roman and Grecian literature.   An English theme, for the composing in his own language, which is rightly deemed an essential qualification for a future public servant, is also imposed as a weekly tax on his exertions ; and considering that his presence is required only for *two hours* a day in the lecture room, he would seem to have no cause to complain of being overworked. But the tendency of his education must also be decidedly oriental, or nothing would be done towards his especial training for India; and a language, the acquisition of which has been termed the labour of a life time, and whose first appearance is invested with the power of a Medusa, has been selected as the one on which he shall make his first essay as a linguist.   The merits of the Sanskrit as a language, and the reward which may be reasonably expected from its literary stores, we have endeavoured to set forth in a previous number without undue partiality or depreciation.   But the question before us now is not how far the history of mankind may be illustrated, or philology enriched, by further researches into that ponderous dialect of old.   We are to educate a large number of students for a wide-extended service, and the doubt naturally arises, is Sanskrit to be deemed an absolutely requisite element, a *sine quâ non*, in an education which has other views before it besides mere disquisitions into learned oriental tongues? We acquiesce in the justice of many of Mr. Wilson's arguments in behalf of his favourite study : we allow that a knowledge of the literary remains of a nation on which so many of their customs and modes of thinking are based, gives its possessor a firmer hold on the affections of a people than otherwise he might have been enable to attain.   It is highly desirable that the repository of all that the conquered hold dear, should be regarded with a favourable, but also a discriminating eye, by the conqueror; and the more we combine a knowledge of manners as gained from books with that acquired in free intercourse with the natives of every order, the better for ourselves and for those we have to deal with.   But is it just, is it even expedient to force the acquisition of such cumbrous knowledge on one and all promiscuously?   Shall all, without regard to their peculiar qualifications as linguists, be compelled to toil at one language, which, while it gives them at first no reward worthy of their labour, cannot fail to inspire them with a dislike for every other.   It is remarkable how few make any progress in Sanskrit beyond a knowledge of the merest rudiments, sufficient to enable them to pass muster at the examination. There seems to be no medium in this study, no place reserved for him who attains a moderate degree of proficiency. The Sanskrit scholars are divided into two sets, between whom there is no break, or gradual succession of steps : one or two hasten onward, and give promise of future excellence, but the greater part are unconscious of the slightest effort to advance. The unwilling labourer, forced to toil for two years at a language which he is told will not enable him to exchange a single word with any native of any part of India, 'drags his slow length along' for a period of four terms, happy if Sanskrit does not prove the indirect means of an additional six months' residence in college, and of a corresponding degradation in the ranks of his cotemporaries. It must, however, be added, that in the event of the abolition of Sanskrit, there would be an inevitable increase in the number of subjects studied; and we are bound to state what appears to us the only valid argument for its retention. A fair knowledge of that parent language places the Uriya, the Bengali, the Hindi and Mahratta dialects at the absolute disposal of the student. He has but to extend his arm in order to obtain a complete victory over any or all of these ; whilst if destitute of the substratum of Sanskrit, the future Bombay Civilian would commence Mahratta unaided, and the Bengali apply himself to Hindi or to the current vernacular of Bengal without the slightest previous smoothing of the way.* Apart from all considerations of the intrinsic value of the language as the great storehouse of the Hindu's religious ceremonies, and the mainspring of his daily avocations, we must allow that Sanskrit bestows on its votary a commanding influence over very many of the Indian dialects, such as it is utterly vain to expect any where else. Arabic, it is true, gives an easy access to Persian ; Persian in its turn, when combined with a slight knowledge of Arabic, places the most polished form of Urdu within a single day's march. But there are very few of the vernacular tongues in which Sanskrit is not largely mixed up. Even in the Deccan languages, which present many distinct and original features, a considerable proportion of Sanskrit vocables have been inserted, and the Sanskrit scholar seems to stand on an eminence overlooking the mighty peninsula of India, from whence far as he may cast his eyes, from the Panjab to Cape Comorin, he beholds a confusion of varied tongues, (thirty-two is the number enumerated by orientalists), from all of which, like a feudal sovereign from his vassals, he may fairly be said to have some

* Are those civilians who came out before Mr. Wilson's reign, hampered by an ignorance of Sanskrit in mastering the vernacular ? Let our readers decide. We leave the question open.

claim to obedience.   It is but just that we should state clearly
this one great argument by which the study of Sanskrit finds
supporters in England.   Its premises are unquestionable, but
on the other hand we very much doubt if such a knowledge as
would really assist in mastering the derivatives of Sanskrit, is
ever acquired by any save one or two students out of the whole
body.   A glance at the way in which the examination test
is generally got up will best serve to illustrate our meaning.
The portion absolutely exacted from all amounts to about
300 lines !   The indolent student on his attendance at lectures
has not contrived to retain much of what is going on: if
called upon to translate, he has managed by some means
to come off, not exactly with credit, but not absolutely with
dishonor.   At the final examination, however, he begins to
entertain fears of his reaching the mark, and he accordingly
sets to without delay to make up in a couple of nights for
the idly spent hours of a whole term.   The process by which
he accomplishes this desired end is curious.   A verbal
analysis of the whole—such a one as contains the translation of
the minutest and constantly recurring particles—is procured
from some partner in trouble, and by assiduously poring
ever this some half dozen times, he at last becomes enabled to
recognise most of the words in the original.   Not that he would
know them again if met with in a different book, or even if
transposed from the order he has been accustomed to ; but by
a judicious series of pencil marks and other equally legitimate
hieroglyphics, he is enabled to pass muster when *translating
from his own book*, and shuts his hated volume with a degree
of satisfaction, rejoicing that for one more term he has escaped
being numbered with the victims of rejection.   We were
amused a short time ago in reading the report of the Muhammadan College at Hooghly, to see that few of the Arabic or
Persian Scholars could read a word out of any book except their
own.   It would seem that the idle and the careless present the
same features in every quarter of the world, and resort to the
same devices in order to hide their ignorance on the banks of
the Lea as on the banks of the Hooghly.   Of the general
tone of the place in which such despicable subterfuges are upheld
we leave our readers to form their own opinion without comment from us.   It may perhaps not be generally known that
the Sanskrit system at Haileybury is the offspring of Mr.
Wilson.   We have ere this given his reasons for the same, but
on a fair and calm survey of the whole we cannot conscientiously
subscribe to his undisguised preference for that over all other
languages.   We would encourage by all means the true Sanskrit

scholar, we would reward him for his drudgery and enrich him with prizes, but the toil and the reward should be left for such eager spirits as would voluntarily undertake any thing however arduous which shall render them more efficient members of the profession. Many students who have been discouraged by the grim aspect of Sanskrit have shown themselves above the average in Persian, Urdu or Bengali, and although the test required in the former is by no means outrageous, it has often proved the means of disheartening a workman otherwise ready to put his shoulder to the wheel. We grieve that we should have to differ from so high an authority as Mr. Wilson: we would urge all who feel conscious of the will to dare and the power to execute, to acquire a fair proficiency in that language, after which the resistance of others, though determined, shall seem tame and spiritless by comparison; but with all our consciousness of the fund of utility which may be extracted from its stores, or the vantage ground which is gained by ascending its slippery heights, with all our strong desire to see its study more general and its worth more accurately known, we dare not advocate its being forced on all who enter the East India College. We have shown on what footing we could wish to see it placed: let it but have a fair trial after our fashion: the result will hardly produce fewer decent scholars than have as yet appeared under Mr. Wilson's plan.

If any of our readers are disposed to think that too little is required in the first term, they will have no cause for complaint when told of the array of subjects which start up into life at the beginning of the second, and only terminate with the final emancipation from College. It is true that at first the range of subjects—old and new—does not seem to impose too heavy a burden on the collegian—that his days and nights may be consecrated to ease unrestrained—but the edifice is suddenly extended and based on much broader foundations. A variety of pursuits, some altogether strange, others not utterly foreign, but all tending to render the British youth worthy of the great *Mission* he is to fulfil, suddenly unfold their manifold stores. The weekly theme is discarded, the classics languidly exist, as before, the mathematical course progresses into Algebra and Equations, the Sanskrit is retained—wrongly as we think—but a new oriental language, the captivating Persian, now appears on the stage, and the science of political economy, with the gigantic study of the Law, raise their vast forms aloft to engage the attention of the student. Of these we will first discuss the claims of the Persian to be an element in the course of education. Several years ago, when that language was still used in

c

all our courts, and was employed everywhere in official transactions, the Court deemed its acquisition to be an object of such high importance that they appointed a native Persian—a gentleman of high rank and extensive acquirements—to be Professor of Arabic and Persian at Haileybury.   His place, lately vacated, was filled by a most worthy successor, Major J. R. Ouseley, who for a considerable time held the equally responsible post of examiner in the College of Fort William.   In the present day, although Persian is no longer recognised as the language of our courts, yet, as might be expected, many of its peculiar terms inundate every document.   Numerous Latin expressions still survive from the old law Latin of our courts at home, and seem likely to last as long as the English language itself, and Persian in the same manner maintains its ground with sturdy indifference to Act or Regulation.   This, according to our way of thinking, is exactly as it should be, and though, if reconstructing our courts, we could not well recommend such a union of two jarring elements, such a reconciliation of oil and vinegar, as has actually taken place in the mixture of Persian and pure Sanskrit derivatives, still, as the fusion has been made, we view it as a really fortunate circumstance.*   Law terms, like those of every science, must be somewhat recondite; and those of the Persian are as expressive and manageable as any set of their kind.   It follows then that a moderate acquaintance with this language is absolutely incumbent on the Haileybury youth. With Persian he gains an easy access to the polished Urdu, he finds it recurring at every step when learning the routine of his business, and his ear may readily detect its clear and ringing tones amidst the fainter echoes of the dull sounding but no less comprehensive Bengali.   The time devoted to Persian, and the quantity read during each term, is exactly sufficient to give the necessary amount of knowledge, without encroaching on studies of equal or even higher importance; and a further insight into this lively language may be gained with less distraction and with additional opportunities in the College of Fort William.

We next come to the study of political economy, and it may not perhaps at first appear why this should be a regular component in the Haileybury course.   A glance will make it evident. The causes of wealth and poverty, the social condition of the cultivator, the nature of land tenures, the changes in a large

* This of course is only applicable to the Lower Provinces.   The transition in the North West from Persian to Urdu must have been easier of accomplishment. Owing to the spread of Bengali, Persian is being more and more confined to the actual legal phrases. and the state of things in which Mr. C. Trevelyan could say that *ddhesh* for *Hukm* would not be intelligible, is now passing away.

body of population, the modes in which national prosperity may be increased, will all at some future time form matter for the speculation, if not for the actual employment of the civilian. The Revenue officer will have ample opportunities for tracing the various windings of political economy, and will recognize the truth or falsity of many of its systems. Cause and effect will be to him equally familiar, and if a slight discrepancy in theory and practice does at times occur, he will acknowledge in the visible working of many great truths, the necessity of some acquaintance with the principles of the science. But in order to examine with certainty the condition of the Asiatic, he must first cast his eye over that of the European. He must be shown the causes of English wealth and prosperity before he can fully comprehend those of oriental degradation. Accordingly the series of lectures explain to him the position of the tenantry, churl and freedman, villain and serf, throughout most European states: he learns why the Irish cottier is poor, vilified, and degraded; why the French *metayer*, though contented and in seeming affluence, must yet in his best aspect be far removed from the genuine hearty content of an English peasant: he illustrates and compares what at first seem the discordant institutions of the East and the West, and traces with delight a resemblance between the middleman of Ireland and the Talukdar of Bengal. This is hardly the place for a disquisition on the land tenures of India, or on the science of political economy from its rise to the present day; but it may not be irrelevant to show something of the real character of a science whose most valuable discoveries may yet be far in the distant future. Some may be old enough to recollect the time when political economy was but in her cradle. Her giant truths had indeed ever been stalking over the field of history, but their importance was disowned or at least unacknowledged by the many. From the days of Munn and Malines to the dawn of the science under Adam Smith, its maxims had however been gradually stealing a faint assent from speculators more clear sighted than their neighbours. At length the clouds were rolled away and men began to run into the opposite extreme. The wildest and most unhealthy doctrines were promulgated and caught up. Unholy devices were upheld as the sole means by which the national evils resulting from a rapid increase in the population could be warded off. The public, at first thirsting for the new draught of knowledge, turned away in horror from the poison it contained. The maxims of the few were set down as those of the science itself, and the tendency of Political Economy was again hid in darkness. But under the fostering hand of those whose views are sound and healthy, the inquirer receives no shock to his old established belief—is not startled by the propounding of audacious theories—does not meet with a horrid vision at every turn of the road. In a calm and philosophic spirit he learns the real value of the science. Its importance to society is demonstrated by an appeal to facts. Its truths stand out in relief when made the test of great commercial questions. And at Haileybury, avoiding with care the miry paths into which so many visionaries have wandered, or only showing them in order to deter the unwary follower, the Professor leads his hearers through a succession of green fields and pleasant places, whose produce is a rich and teeming crop, and where rank luxuriance is unknown. At one time throwing a light on the fabric of Oriental Government—the want of fixed institutions—only relieved by the occasional happy accident of such characters as Akbar—at another rapidly surveying the courses of monied distress at different periods in the History of Greece and of England, of France and of Rome—now rising to discuss the events from which sprung our national debt—now descending to the details connected with the gradual improvement of the science of agriculture—here drawing a picture of that primitive state where flocks and herds alone constitute wealth—there happily discursive on the technicalities of cultivation—now giving a slight sketch of the causes which affect the general credit of a nation—now pausing to see how the earth may be made still more fruitful, and replenished still further in obedience to the great command—amalgamating all these topics into one continuous series, the Lecturer aims at making his subject popular, and uniformly succeeds. If the value of the study is to be estimated by the ardour with which it is followed, we may safely pronounce Political Economy to be a gem of the first water. The Lectures of the present able Professor are attended with less reluctance by the students than those of any other branch, and it is here that we generally see at the close of every term the fairest average of merit distributed amongst the greatest number. It is true however that frequent opportunities of practically employing the axioms of this science do not occur to the great body of civil servants. A secretary may possibly find it aid him in his notes, or a Member of Council in his minute : a collector may be indebted to his early reminiscences whilst endeavouring to thread his way through the tangled labyrinth of Revenue questions, which men of high ability have professed themselves unable to comprehend after a thirty years study. But any daily application of its principles in a direct point of view is frustrated by the position of the Indian official.

A lord of many acres, uniting a sound knowledge of the science with an equally sound uprightness of purpose, may every day give a practical illustration of it on his estate. A landed proprietor in Ireland might find it direct his endeavours to raise from their prostrate condition the wronged and neglected children of Erin. But no such outlet for a beneficent philosophy is placed at the disposal of the English resident in India. We read of constant appeals to our native Babus and Zemindars in behalf of the ryot; let them study philanthropy and Political Economy combined, and the result will be highly beneficial to the interests of both master and man.*

We shall revert to this branch in connection with the study of History; for the present, *Law* must cause us to diverge for a few pages. When we consider that many civilians are destined to fill at some time the important situation of an English judge, and that not in a country whose inhabitants have been known to him since his childhood, but in one where everything from first to last is strange and uncongenial—that he is to present the spectacle of a man, calm and dignified, holding the even balance of the scales of punishment, and deciding on cases where life and death are at stake, it would not seem too much to require that one-half of the time spent at College should be devoted to the acquirement of a regular legal education. But, as usual when legislating for a body whose future destinations are uncertain, we should fall into a grievous error did we advocate the claims of law to the exclusion of other knowledge. Of the many who leave Haileybury, but one-half, or even less, are called upon to fill the responsibility of the judicial chair. Some become political secretaries, or agents, others are sheltered in the customs, or preside over the salt or the opium department, and some remain devoted to revenue matters, and turn away from the dark side of human nature, crime and its attendant punishment. Hence any thing like educating men for a particular line whilst in England is rendered nugatory, and the course of law resolves itself into a general exposition of the principles on which it is based. Strong meat is withheld by a judicious hand; and in order that the tyro may not be dismayed by the iron toughness of the subject, or wearied with its technicalities, a course of moral philosophy and the great unwritten laws of nature is selected as affording the fairest opening for all. Accordingly the Collegian is led at first to the break of that broad gulf which must ever separate the confines of morals and of law. He sees how near they approach and again how far diverge. Why the

* We might also include the maligned class of Indigo Planters in this appeal.

law from its hard character "never speaking but to command, and never commanding but to compel," is forced to leave many provinces entirely untouched, and to extend its rigid sceptre only over the trespasses which cause a positive injury to society or to individuals regarded as integral parts of society. These are the first views selected from the mighty landscape. We proceed a little further, and equally interesting scenes are displayed. The *quæstio vexata* of the origin of property, our duties to ourselves, to each other and to society, the *jura belli et pacis*, international law, the varying principles of inheritance, primogeniture and equal partition, the laws of sale and contract, all the numerous cases which can reasonably be supposed to arise in a highly civilized state of society, set forth in language at once energetic and clear, are selected as the course of law which naturally follows from the moral philosophy of Paley. It may be imagined that such a great and comprehensive view, drawn with a graphic pencil, and evidently bearing directly on the duties of a public servant, must allure the greater number, and lead them fearlessly to grapple with the more detailed and intricate portions of the science. And when we tell our readers that, reluctant to enter on the duller and drearier paths, and imbued with an enlightened spirit of philosophic enquiry, the Professor often dared to branch out into several parts on which the law seems hardly as yet decided, that he would discuss in the spirit of Montesquieu the systems of law best suited to societies in their different phases, and would enquire whether some points hitherto abandoned to the moral code might not with safety be brought within the grasp of the legal, when he would contrive to invest his seemingly dry and barren subject with interest and freshness, and almost with fascination—when we assert that law on its first stages at Haileybury seems to carry on its face much that is calculated to allure and little to deter, shall it not be thought strange if we say that of all the branches taught, law, with the exception of Sanskrit, is decidedly the most unpopular! Such however is the stern reality of the case. A few, conscious of the parts they may be called on to sustain, endeavour to make themselves masters of the first great principles : the greater part are hopelessly ignorant of the very nature of what they hear weekly discussed. They are not told that in India they will occupy the stations of barristers, that they will be forced to plead in the courts, and that the measure of their legal knowledge is to be the measure of their success in life. Many are aware, in spite of the Cimmerian darkness which hangs over the future of their Indian life that a legal examination does not form one of the criteria of fitness for the public service, or a subject of anxiety to the authorities of Fort William College. They know that ignorance of the principles of jurisprudence will not be brought against them as an absolute disqualification for office ; and they turn away from the law lecture, not to pursue other studies perhaps of equal importance, but to revel in the hey day of unrestrained idleness. Yet the youth of sixteen is not altogether without excuse. It must be conceded that the subject, loaded from its very nature with numerous heavy *impedimenta*, and appealing to the manifold authorities who stand as the beacon lights of the science, presents such a succession of appalling objects, hill mounting over hill, and Alp arising upon Alp, that many, trembling notwithout reason at the growing labours of the path they have chosen, retire with precipitancy altogether from the field.

After the primary course, which however must leave much unsaid, some one particular region is selected. The collegian enters on the department of criminal law, crimes and punishments, with the objects of the latter according to the system of Bentham,—on a slight sketch of the proceedings of the Court of Chancery—and on an excellent exposition of the great rules of evidence. We may be excused for digressing still further on this latter part, as the weighing and digesting evidence forms perhaps the most difficult part in the duty of the English *Hakim*. It has been well observed that in England little or no difficulty is ever experienced in deciding on the actual evidence, however intricate may be the law, whilst in India the resolving of such double-tied knots as are often woven by two opposite parties, forms matter of serious perplexity to the bench. At home the separation of law and fact—the point where one terminates and the other begins—may often prove a question to try the powers of the clearest sighted : the two join issue on a kind of debateable land, and the boundaries of either cannot be clearly ascertained. But suppose the doubt removed, and the weighing of mere evidence is comparatively easy. Truth, or at least the germ of truth, when brought into court by almost every witness, under the fire of a searching cross-examination, expands into a full blown flower. The principles of evidence are easily tested on so smooth a surface. But in India the very contrary is the case. Tossed about in the stormy and opposing tides of native evidence, who has not felt the want of a guiding hand, when, even in a common case of affray, the testimony of two opponent Zemindars and their clans have been so totally irreconcileable, and yet so ingeniously supported, as to baffle the most penetrating glance ? Something, it is true, beyond a mere set of rules is needed to unravel the tangled web, and it is only a thorough acquaintance with native character which makes one man to catch at some parts whereby all is made clear, whilst another less gifted wanders about in darkness inextricable. Well indeed may each magistrate in our Indian courts pray for the discerning wisdom of Solomon, for the intuitive perception of human nature which conveys the power of extracting the small kernel of truth from the vast shell of falsehood which enshrouds it. But the στοιχεία of law must not be neglected for this knowledge so justly prized; and of the whole course at Hailey-bury, we know no branch more eminently useful than the series of lectures devoted to the subject of evidence.

In spite of what we have written, a conviction forces itself on our mind that the advice said to have been given by Lord Eldon to a young barrister proceeding as judge to the colonies would be best fitted for all young civilians, even those who have learnt as much law as came within their reach: " Give your decisions concisely," he said, " without attempting the law of the case, and your own good sense will probably conduct you to a just determination: if you attempt to give your reasons, ten to one you go wrong." Those of our readers whose especial vocation is the law, and who can therefore speak *ex cathedra*, may possibly agree with us. But no one will pretend that a little is not better than nothing. Even were the present course enforced with strictness on one and all, we should have fewer complaints of the deficiency of legal training in the Company's servants. The elementary course, followed by a rapid sketch of criminal law and of equity, and rounded off by a series of lectures on evidence, are as much as can be expected in a place where so many trades are taught, and it is perhaps more desirable that the broad principles, and not the minutiæ, should be the object of study during the contracted space of a year and a half. We would rather see the student imbibe a moderate draught at the great fountain of abstract law, than drink deep at the lesser spring whence flow the Regulations, Criminal and Revenue, on which the executive Government of India is based. Such were the sound views of Sir James Macintosh, to whose clear and vigorous exposition of enlarged truths many of our readers must have listened with attention. We quote the following from his life :*

" His course of lectures extended to four terms of four ' months each. It was not his practice to commit any part to ' writing, but he trusted to notes of his plan which he filled up ' at the moment of speaking. He began with a rapid review of

---

* Sir James Macintosh succeeded Mr. Christian, on that gentlemen's death in 1818, and continued to lecture until 1824, when he resigned.

' English history, the great events of which he described chiefly
' with an eye to the progress of civilization and refinement, and
' the gradual rise of the liberties and judicial establishments of
' the country. He afterwards explained the foundations of the
' English constitution, attempting as much as possible to make
' his remarks the means of opening the minds of the young
' students to questions of general policy and constitutional
' jurisprudence. He examined in a popular way most of the
' leading questions which present themselves to all who are
' called upon to take a part in public life in this country, and
' the deeper and more enlarged principles which regulate
' legislative wisdom in countries remote from England and from
' European communities, and where a fundamental difference of
' laws, usages, and religion requires the exercise of that tolera-
' tion in judgment and that freedom from prejudice which only
' minds of the higher class, when patiently exercised, can fully
' attain. His aim was to impart on these subjects, and on English
' law, in which Blackstone was his text book, as much as
' possible of that information which every English gentleman
' ought to possess, and to lead to an impartial and unprejudiced
' view of those forms of society and government which his
' hearers were to witness in the distant country where they
' were to exercise their knowledge."

And such or nearly such is the course now pursued by the
present able law Professor at Haileybury. Orientals and law
are decidedly the two most practically important subjects in the
whole College course. A knowledge of the first is indispensable
as the vehicle for diffusing the second, and the latter is what one-
half the service may have cause to deem the staple business of
life. We have been led into a longer digression than we
originally intended; but the subject is frequently canvassed here
and at home, and it seemed essential that we should clearly
define how far the law studies in reality reach.

But we have got our student into his second term, let us
carry him in safety through his third and fourth. In the next
six months there is a comparatively small addition to the daily
task. The mathematics appear in the form of statics and
dynamics as set forth in a small book of Professor Whewell's,
now published as part of the general standard for degrees at the
University of Cambridge. The classics remain. The political
economy disappears and is succeeded by history: not the history
of great revolutions or stirring events, studded with anecdote
and embellished with the biographies of noble characters, but
history as exemplifying the gradual progression of national
wealth and the diffusion of the sciences and arts of civilization.

D

One term however is invariably devoted to the history of the
Indian empire, from its earliest period under the priestly
dominion of the Brahmans, to the latest victories of Hastings
and Lake in our own immediate times.   And we can affirm
with confidence that very few collegians ever set sail for India
without a tolerable acquaintance with the spirit of Manu's laws
and his state of society, with the ever shifting dynasties of the
Muhammadan sovereigns, and the gradual but steady advance
of English dominion throughout the land.   In this term another
oriental language—the last and perhaps the most useful—
appears on the scene.   The medium, as all know, of communication between natives of all parts of India, in one district
rugged, in another polished to an extreme, but ever comprehensive and capable of indefinite improvement, the first thing of
which the want is most felt in landing, the language in which
the first imperfect attempts at conversation with the natives are
made, a passport over India as French is on the continent, and the
correct speaking of which is considered the characteristic of a
gentleman—who would not regret that the Hindustani, or more
correctly, that *Urdu*, should be excluded from the walls of
Haileybury?   And this suggests to us the consideration of a
point which it is only with extreme diffidence that we
can venture to approach.   The propriety of leaving orientals altogether out of the Haileybury course, and reserving them
untouched for their natural soil, has been discussed by high and
very competent authorities, and it is only because we have
theoretically and practically gone over the subject in all its
bearings, that we can venture to set ourselves even for a
moment on the opposite side.   It has been remarked, and with
some reason, that as Law, History and other branches are
equally as essential to the training of the civilian as the native
languages themselves, it would be more equitable to teach as
much of the former as possible where they can be got at, and
to leave orientals for the time when the fountains of European
knowledge shall entirely fail.   The progress of two months at
Fort William is that of a year at Haileybury, and even the sum
total acquired at the latter place is with most students little
beyond the mere rudiments of the language.   Now admitting that
the acquirements of the majority are but moderate, still it is a
great victory to have surmounted the first principles in any
way whatever ere reaching India.   The native Pandit or
Munshi, with but a few solitary exceptions, furnishes a painful
living instance of the truism, that some men however erudite,
are utterly incapable of imparting their knowledge.   They
never for a moment dream of aiding, superintending or directing

into proper channels the labour of the *Sahib*, and the latter is forced by a continual cross fire of questions to extort from the obsequious native the fact of his moving in the right or wrong path; happy if the mistaken oriental notion of politeness does not leave him in the bliss of that ignorance, which is discovered only in the hour of trial. Imagine then the drudgery of Sanskrit, Arabic, or even Persian and Urdu acquired by a large body of young men with the assistance of such an unanimated Dictionary as we have described. Even supposing that a longer period was granted for College studies than at present, very few would ever gain a deeper insight into the languages of the east, than was absolutely incumbent. If every thing had to be begun afresh in India, little would be done in a period of a year and half towards gaining a mastery over the Literature of the East. We grant that many of our best Orientalists knew nothing of the Eastern tongues before their arrival in India; but the peculiar facilities allotted to Leyden and to Wilson are not to be looked for as every day occurrences. To few is the ring granted whose commanding spell the genii of language obey, and we should shudder at the thought of a large number of young men set down in India without the least preliminary instruction in any one dialect of the East. The stock of the majority at present is certainly slender, although several good exceptions might be drawn from the College reports of the last three years, but India and its climate seem strangely opposed to wearisome drudgery at rudiments which all must surmount, and it is with these views that we should vote for the maintenance of the present system, if only subjected to a few salutary modifications.

After the third term the car of learning is considered to have received the heaviest load it can bear, and it progresses towards the *denouement* with a staid and regular motion. A change in the Mathematical course, where Astronomy succeeds to Dynamics, an increased energy visible on the part of the already energetic, and a brushing up of the dimmed and neglected faculties by the idle and the careless, together with a more direct and earnest appeal from the Professors, are the only changes visible in the fourth and last term. The final examination approaches, and the goal is already in sight. This one differs in no material respect from those already undergone. Its length is the same reary period of three weeks. Its hours of intense study pass as tediously as they did a year ago. But it may be asked how are those who have neglected the call during the period of preparation, enabled to meet the day of trial? The answer is, that except for certain allowances made, they would appear utterly

at a discount.   On a certain date, however, lectures cease, and
the days for examination in each peculiar subject, are duly noti-
fied to the public.   Then the struggle commences.   Note books,
analyses, references, all that can give strength to the weak,
or veil the naked position of the defenceless, are sought for and
read up with the force of desperation.   The midnight oil is
burnt by both the reading and the fast man; by the former as
a matter of habit, by the latter as a short and momentary
concentration of his powers.   The race is commenced in earnest,
and after days spent in answering questions on paper, and nights
in hard reading, the final day arrives.   A detachment of Directors
proceeds to visit the institution.   We pass over the joy and the
grief, the congratulations and the heart burning, the discontent
of the ambitious who have fallen short of their high hopes, the
satisfaction of the idle who have *passed* when they least expected
it—the prizes are distributed, a speech is made by the chairman
to exhort those leaving College to re-doubled energy in India,
and the railroad conveys the emancipated students from the
precincts of Haileybury perhaps for ever!

   It will no doubt be asked by several of our readers what
kind of test the examinations are, and how far they prove fit
coping stones for the course we have endeavoured to describe?
The subjects, at least the European ones, are only tested by an
inquisition on paper: the questions are diffuse, and comprise the
whole range of the lectures : ample time is given for answering
them, and while he, whose mind is literally running over with
his subject, can hardly find a full opportunity to deliver himself of
all his varied stores, it would be singular if out of the same wide
range of questions, the dullest could not select some three or four
of which he knows something.   For a mere pass the standard is
exceedingly moderate, and the aid of a *well-kept note book* for
three nights before the history or the law examination, generally
enables the hindmost to meet the call made.   In the language
of the Turf, a short and vigorous rush brings up those who have
lagged behind in the early part of the race, and if they do not
contend in the first rank, they yet manage to save their distance.
While on the subject of the examination we would fain call
attention to a most pernicious custom, the bane of the scholar in
every age, but more deeply rooted and more dangerous in its ultimate consequences at Haileybury than elsewhere.   We allude to
the excessive and continuous hard reading, the wear and tear
system of intense fagging, which prevails year after year within
its walls.   We do not speak to afford an excuse to the indolent,
or to deter those who make a boast of their fortnight's assumed study, but we raise a warning voice to him who for

months extends his labours throughout the dreary night, until as he throws his wearied frame on his couch, he hears the song of the early lark, and sees the first bold streaks of the summer dawn illuminate his room, who rises unrefreshed from a shortened period of rest to resume the ceaseless round, and whose exertions, as they commence with his entrance and only cease at his departure from college, must certainly have a lasting effect on his system and constitution. There is no service in the world, no climate under the sun, in which the union of moral and intellectual with physical superiority, should be an object of more earnest prayer than in the civil service of India: no profession where the "mens sana" in the "sano corpore" should be the point which all education should ever keep in view, yet with numerous examples ringing in their ears, and with a foreknowledge that all their vigour will be required to meet the encroaches of a burning clime, this detestable custom is persisted in by the students of almost every generation. Such warnings have often been held out, and as often disregarded. Even in the climate of England the effects of hard reading for a first class have ruined the prospects of many a gifted individual : many a noble heart has cracked under the pressure of preparation for an approaching degree. What then shall we say of such an expenditure of faculties on the part of those whose frame is to be exposed to the damps of Bengal, or the hot winds of Hindustan, to the scorching of Guzerat, or the noxious breath of the Concan: who may have to brave, if required, the fatigues of a journey in the glaring months of May and June, or may be destined to imbibe a slow and secret poison from the leaden gusts of the Sunderbunds? Yet with a full and even an exaggerated account of the climate of India, this system is allowed, lauded, encouraged. We say encouraged, because it seems an acknowledged axiom at Haileybury, that the more a victim is inclined to work, the more he shall be required to perform. If the soil has returned a bountiful crop in one season and gives promise of yielding still more abundantly in the next, a further return is demanded with greater avidity. The mental field is taxed to the utmost extent of its bearing. Every source of fertility is unnaturally forced into action. Every means employed to increase the value of the harvest. There is no medium, no seeking to lessen the wide difference between the advanced few and the retarded many. The former are hurried on, and the latter suffered to lag behind unnoticed. It is one of the greatest faults in the whole system that the standard for mere passing is so despicably low. A certain and a very limited proficiency in two European branches only is compulsory, and even they lie at the option of the student.* If he has the slightest turn for mathematics he can gain his point without an effort. If he has paid the commonest attention to history his aim is reached with the most moderate exertions. It would be remarkable if from the expanse before him he could not single out one vulnerable point, on which a breach is easily effected. Out of *four* European branches he devotes himself to *two*, and from the claims of his creditors he receives a quittance in full. In the three orientals the test is of an equally moderate kind, although these afford us on the whole, a better criterion ; but the aspirant for prize and place sees no limit to his labours. If he is deemed to be possessed of any ability, seven arms as it were are extended to arrest his suffrages, and he turns half bewildered from one subject to the other. Perhaps the struggle is prolonged by a severe contest with one or two rivals equally zealous and able. Others look calmly on, while these maintain the friendly strife. The spectator is cool and unembarassed, while the combatants strain every nerve. The former satisfies the examiner, who is aware he has got all that he can fairly expect ; the latter is required to devote himself to each separate subject as if there were no other calls on his leisure equally loud and importunate : to the one, Haileybury shall teem with reminiscences of the toils and troubles of Hercules, to the other, it shall recall nothing but the down beds and the ease of Sardanapalus.

So much for the European part of the system. We have shown in discussing the Sanskrit question, the devices by which the desired end is reached, but it would be unfair to imply that the other Oriental languages fare no better. The standard attained by the best men in Persian and Urdu is decidedly beyond the respectable ; in several instances it has been positively meritorious ; and even the attainments of the majority are deserving of commendation. The innate dislike to a new language which prevails in the case of the Sanskrit, is disarmed by the recognized utility of the Urdu : Persian has a considerable number of votaries, and a fair general tableau is generally presented at the closing scene in these two departments. *A vivâ voce* examination, on which signs of the system *by rote* occasionally appear, and a translation on paper from the original into English, and *vice versâ*, are demanded from, and performed with a gre at

* We have been given to understand that the very moderate test, required in two branches, has been *lately lowered still more*, and demanded in *all the four* European subjects ! ! !

or less degree of accuracy by, every individual.* Under Mr. Wilson's searching eye the axe is now laid at the root of the old pernicious method : *cramming* and its inefficient results are rapidly passing away. A few more vigorous strokes and it will entirely disappear, and a fair standard of acquirements be substituted in its stead. It has often occurred to us that a set of subordinate native teachers—the Munshi and Pandit—might be productive of considerable advantage to the by-reading at Haileybury. They might attend on the hard working student when out of the lecture room, and lighten the task of surmounting the first principles. In these enlightened days, when ancient prejudices are fast fading away before the light of reason, and Hindus are found to cross the dark ocean in order to perfect their medical science, a judicious remuneration might induce some of the respectable and well educated natives to undertake such an office. Care would be required in the selection of individuals, and superintendance by the authorities when fairly set down to their work. A few difficulties perhaps would at first be encountered, but the plan is fraught with advantage to both native and European. Amidst the crowd who swarm at the College of Fort William, there are some three or four who might be capable of such an undertaking.

Such is a sketch of the educational course of the College. To all thinking minds it will afford scope for the most serious meditation. On the acquirements there made may greatly depend the future efficiency of the man, and the happiness of thousands. The utility of any subject few will wish to deny, but the impossibility of all or even of any considerable number attaining to a very high proficiency in each department, will be equally recognized. Were we asked which should give place to the others, we should find it hard to decide where all are so eminently useful. Cicero fixed it as the grand qualification for an orator that he should be " nullâ non arte perfectus,"—that acute natural powers, and deep erudition, the art of combination and the art of unfolding, acquaintance not only with the first principles, but a thorough insight into the heights and depths of all useful sciences, should be united in him who aspired to sway the feelings of multitudes by the mere magic of his voice. And such, however ideal the vision may be deemed, would we wish to be the aggregate of faculties in him who is in any way to influence the destinies of countless human beings in the territories of the Company. Of no species of learning can it be predicated, that its possessor will thence derive no

* Mr. Wilson's reform in the Persian and Urdu is deserving of all praise—alas ! that we should have to dissent from his views on Sanskrit.

advantage to himself, or be able to import no benefits to others. No talents, however diversified, will be suffered to remain idle in the land of the East. The civilian will find in the path which he is to tread, numberless opportunities for the exercise of his acquired strength, and every healthy and exalting pursuit may there be indulged with peculiar facilities. Is he of a dry, mathematical, and reasoning turn of mind? Does he aim at reducing to practise long cherished theories of law and jurisprudence? The duties he will perform when seated on the bench, are the basis of that which has been his earliest and most favourite pursuit. Has he been endowed with the gift of tongues, and would he add fresh strings to his bow by the addition of new dialects? Oriental Languages, with all their highly coloured charms, the flexible Sanskrit, the ever copious Arabic, the sweetly modulated Persian, the polished Urdu, are seen to unroll their endless varieties, and attract him to the regions of poetry and romance. Has antiquarianism imbued him with a desire to grope amidst ruined monuments raised in bygone generations, and the reliques of great names now past? The wonders of Salsette, the architecture of Muhammadan sovereigns, shall occupy all the leisure he can spare from graver duties. The Taj Mahal and the Kutb Minar, Ellora and Ajunta seem to call on him with a loud voice to explore their secret recesses. Does he still dwell with fondness on the early studies of his youth, and sigh amidst the somewhat discordant tones of Eastern song for one echo from the melodies beloved of old? His leisure hours may be devoted to the 'perusal of favourite authors: the admired characters of antiquity may yet form a daily means of relaxation. Is he a naturalist? India spreads her vast jungles around him, and teems with every strange variety of bird, beast, and reptile. A botanist? the trees of the forest are for him clothed with their gorgeous apparel: the plain is variegated by grass and herb, whose properties and classification are yet half unknown. Is he an artist? A new series of landscapes and human beings shall crowd on his canvass: the tall and manly Rajput, the graceful Bengali, the grim looking Sannyasi, and the venerable Sheikh, variations of feature and dress, of hill and river, of temple and tower, the palmy groves of Bengal, and the rushing cascades of the Himalayas, the tomb hallowed by superstition, and the palace raised by ambitious hearts, transferred to his paper, shall glow with even more than the brightness of their originals. Has he no cunning of any sort?—Would he choose rather to study the living page of nature, and draw his conclusions from the world of men and things? Character in all its Protean shapes, now calculated to deter by its extreme ugliness, now giving evidences of a better spirit and a hope of future promise, preserving the same grand outline unchanged, but shaded on the detail to a countless variety of hues, spreads out a picture before him on which he may gaze without fatigue.

It would be hard to curtail the number of branches of the Haileybury course, but equally hard to sit down in silence on the subject. The root of the evil—so many trades taught and so few mastered—lies in one or two simple causes. Classics and mathematics, though appointed by universal consent, as the standard of education in England, do not bear directly, it is said, on the after life in India. They should yield to such pursuits as have a more direct influence on the fitness for civil employ. At best they are but kept up, not perfected or even advanced, even by their most devoted followers, at Haileybury. It is a gain if the motion is not a retrograde one. Abolish them and more time will be left for the useful branches of law and history and the wide field of orientals. Now if the standard for admission at the India House was what it ought to be, none would enter Haileybury without having established the fact of their possessing a fair classical education; but the criterion is of a kind so perfectly childish as to afford no security of the sort. Not a forward boy on the fourth form at any public school, but would positively laugh it to scorn. If the standard were raised, and proof of positive merit in either *the classical or mathematical line* demanded before a single student could set foot in the College, it might then be assumed that the foundation had been duly laid: we might proceed to rear the superstructure by means of the studies more peculiarly applicable to India. The genius presiding over classics would then depart, satisfied that his just claims— to educate for India as well as for the church or for any other profession—had been openly acknowledged, and the student expatiate freely on the new field opened to him for the first time. But with the present miserable qualifications demanded in Leadenhall-street, and the early age at which admittance is possible, this consummation cannot as yet be looked for. It is however one of the reforms we would most strongly advocate, although our aim is rather to point out abuses than to suggest remedies, against which objections are certain to be raised. The suddenness with which appointments are bestowed, the unexpected transfer of youths from any thing but classical atmospheres, would be given as reasons against this desirable change. About two years ago the propriety of admittance at the early age of sixteen, was questioned at head-quarters, and the result showed itself in an order not to admit under seventeen. Even this act

E

of grace is but a half measure.   Men who have come out early
to India, and departed as soon as their period of service was
ended, may perhaps rejoice on receiving the rod of dismissal
from the arena of public life very shortly after entering
on the years of their prime.   Many of those who landed
at eighteen were magistrates at twenty-four and collectors
at thirty.   But few will presume to say that their efficiency would have been lessened had they only landed on the
attainment of their majority, or even at a later period.   From
the age of seventeen to that of twenty, a great and vigorous
shoot is often made in the intellectual tree.   The stripling is ex-
changed for the man, the faculties receive a mighty impulse, the
character is formed, and its strength and weakness prominently
brought out.   Even physically the period is one of no less
importance.   The frame is more strongly knit, and the muscles are
hardened.   Hereditary strength and hereditary tendency to
disease are often developed in the limits we have mentioned.   A
chest seemingly weak expands into healthiness and breadth ;
a constitution apparently strong betrays signs of some internal
malady.   The transition from a temperate to a torrid clime
at so critical a moment may prove highly detrimental where the
change is going on.   How many of the youngest civilians have
been prostrated by sickness, while those two or three years older
have stood the trial manfully !   Even suppose that neither escape,
the man of settled constitution is surely more calculated to repel
the deadly attack, than he whose physical powers are yet undergoing the process of transmutation.   Physically, intellectually,
morally, the delay of those three years would prove an invaluable blessing.   Increased opportunities of learning, and a more
eager desire to use them, increased power of resistance against
evil, a more free intercourse with men of maturer age and more
powerful calibre, a more extended acquaintance with the resources of England and the interesting questions there daily
agitated, above all a judgment more capable of comprehending
the vast responsibility of the service on which he is about to
enter—these are a few of the advantages opened to the civilian
by a residence in England for those three or four years which
mark the transformation from youth to manhood.   Some whose
good fortune entered them at Haileybury as late as was possible,
may occasionally lament that they are young in the service and
old in years; they may feel a passing twinge at seeing others at
the goal of their labours, whilst they themselves are at some
distance from the desired haven ; but a calm retrospective glance
will convince them of the inutility of such regrets, and supply a
fund of inward satisfaction in the consciousness that the addi-

tional time spent in England has rendered them more equal to appreciate their liabilities, and more competent to discharge them.

We have hitherto attempted little beyond a sketch of the studies pursued at Haileybury: the picture would be incomplete without some description of its internal economy and regulations. It is here that the dreariest portion of our task commences, and that truths must be written which will give pain to ourselves and our readers. The whole internal discipline is now lodged in the hands of the Principal. He can rusticate, dismiss, and assess all minor penalties without calling in the aid of any other individual. A short time ago this power was vested in a council of Professors, of whom the Principal was the chief member, and where his vote carried a preponderating influence. Before this awful synod delinquents when summoned were allowed to plead their causes in person, and it was not a little startling to hear them put in practice before such a court, the knowledge they had derived in the course of their law lectures. They had learnt something of the technicalities of prosecution, of the modes of weighing evidence, and of the rights of a prisoner at the bar, and the Law Professor might well be startled at the magic power he had evoked and was unable to quell, when students were heard cross questioning witnesses for the prosecution after the most approved rules, objecting to all hearsay or secondary evidence when evidence of a better kind remained unheard, and arguing on the minutest points in their own favour with a volubility which might have raised them to eminence amongst the gentlemen of the long robe. All opportunity for this idle display has been very properly taken away. The Principal now represents the whole council, and walks, untrammeled by any colleague's advice, to put down abuses as they arise. Of abuses indeed there are a plentiful crop, perhaps not of that kind which attract general attention and demand the strong hand, but those which creep on slowly and infect multitudes with contagion. The Principal, —consul without a colleague, and dictator without a master of the horse—can but launch his arrows where the target visibly appears. Absence at chapel, lateness of hours in returning to college, constant inattendance at lectures, and other such palpable violations of rules, may call forth the exercise of that authority with which he has been so properly clothed: these irregularities appear like half-sunken reefs in the tide of student nature, and the searching eye of authority can single them out at once. But the under current which sweeps round them, silent and apparently gentle, but in reality deep and headstrong, who shall hope to controul and direct into a safe channel?

Subordinate to the supreme authority we have "the Dean," whose range comprehends all minor and daily recurring improprieties that are not of magnitude sufficient to attract the notice of the Principal. His place is by no means a sinecure even with the steadiest college set ; but the remaining Professors, under no obligation to attend to the internal discipline, lead a life undisturbed by any college revolutions. Without intending to cast the least slur on the character of any of the College dons, or to impugn their efforts for the branch they immediately superintend, we must state that the absence of constant intercourse between them and the collegians, forms a most fertile source of evil to the institution. The Professor appears for two days in the week at the hours of his lecture, and then vanishes as suddenly as he had appeared. A veil conceals him from the public. An unpenetrated mystery hangs over his daily avocations. Content with a regular attendance at his lectures, he can have little desire, as he has no power, to controul the thoughts and deeds of the mass, with few of whom he is personally acquainted. Should those to whom he is known apply themselves earnestly to his peculiar department, he can sit down satisfied. But he cares not how his votaries thrive in their other studies. Law can have no connexion with or interest in Sanskrit : orientals no desire to promote the study of history. It is rather a rivalry between the two who shall attract the largest crowd, who shall gain the greater number of votes, not a generous contention who shall send forth the recruits armed at all points, accoutred with every weapon both for attack and defence. Besides this, Professor and student are alike profoundly ignorant of the kind of after life in India, of the duties to be performed, and the stations to be filled. Vague and undefined notions of magisterial functions and political appointments, are reiterated without a clear idea of the duties attached, and those who have never visited our Indian empire, like most other Englishmen, entertaining no vivid picture of the reality, but at best only competent to call up a few dim and indistinct hues of the Indian landscape, are unable even if they desired it, to shape the course of education with certainty to its end. Let us not be misunderstood. The Professors of the East India College are individually men of first-rate abilities. Few more competent could be found in the kingdom. Lectures on political economy at Cambridge were held before empty benches, and the Haileybury law course, if delivered at Oxford, would, we are sure, be frequented by an eager and numerous assemblage. But our Haileybury dons have no idea of acting in concert, or of holding up for inspection any wares but their own. A directing power, weighing the proportions which each branch according to its utility should bear with the other, repressing undue excess in one field, and preventing listlessness in another, embracing in a wide fold the whole course of education, would be the best and shortest road to a complete reform.

The liberty enjoyed and often abused by the collegians is of an ample kind, equal indeed to that allowed at either of our Universities. Two or at most three hours spent in the lecture room, attendance at both morning and evening chapel—and the remaining hours of the twenty-four are placed at their own disposal. But how is such a space of time employed? To what pursuits do the non-reading part of the community devote themselves? Some are content literally to smoke away their existence in and about the precincts of the College. Others wander down to Hertford or Ware, and there fritter away the day in discontented idleness, unprofitable follies, or even far worse.* It was a common argument with the majority, that, in the absence of all the most healthful and approved recreations of youth and manhood, they were compelled, in spite of their better nature, to seek relaxation from forbidden enjoyments. Such excuses, it must be allowed, were not without justice. Human nature stood forth, and with a good deal of sophistry but with some foundation of truth, vindicated herself from the imputation of ready indulgence in a wilful and a wanton spirit. It was evident that ere proceeding to condemn, a reasonable chance of amendment, and a return to a better state, should have been held out to those against whom the accusation was brought.. This could only be by presenting opportunities for healthy and rational amusements, and in a happy hour the old Fives Court was repaired, and a new cricket ground laid within a minute's walk of the College. We have before spoken of the bodily training, which in our opinion, is full as necessary as the mental, and we here repeat our firm conviction that both respectively should be attended to by those who must encounter the heat and damp of an India climate. Fives, cricket, and the no less generous recreation of boating, are now maintained, with only the fluctuation incident to such sports, by each successive generation; and those who, for want of other employment, would formerly have been seen in the low haunts of Hertford and Ware, now find more congenial attractions in the best and manliest of exercises. Perhaps it does occasionally happen that an ardent votary of

* We have here been describing the peculiarities of more than one generation. The characteristics of either may be met with any day at Haileybury, but the partial reform wrought by the renovation of cricket and other manly sports, is of more recent date, and its consequences are but partially visible.

cricket is "plucked" at the examination: that one renowned for his skill at the oar, loses an extra term: but these are solitary instances, and only to be lamented for their result to the individual, not to be taken as indications of a spirit prevalent with the majority. The College to a certain degree has been purified. Liberty is enjoyed by many with considerable discretion, and even the proximity of a railway, which contracts the journey to Town to the space of an hour or little more, does not seem to have called for more severe restrictions. We dare hope that a new era has commenced in the College History, and it will not perhaps be thought trivial if we date the starting point at the new impulse given to healthful bodily exercise.

But in spite of this dawning of better days, which we would fain see expanding into a clear and diffused light, we are forced to confess that the tide of Haileybury morality is at a very low ebb. We grant that some of its glaring vices have totally disappeared or are in a rapid decline: that emeutes against the authorities are becoming of rare occurrence: that reckless extravagance, rioting and drunkenness are—when taken as characteristics of the body—almost numbered with the things that have been. The Professors may rest in their beds without fear of being awoke by the blowing up of the college gates: the fifth of November is no longer celebrated for a period of three weeks or a month, but confined to the almost legitimate limit of a night: we do not often hear of daring spirits raised by their exploits to a notoriously bad eminence: the outward appearance presents fewer of those astounding defects which at once attract and repel: but the heedlessness, the hard impassive character, which no charmer can arouse,—the absence of all moral thoughtfulness, or anything like a steady resistance of evil,—the proneness to sink in the stream without one single struggle to rise—the hours vainly squandered which should have been spent in improvement,—the idle senseless mirth that soon passes into folly,—the laugh of the careless which is raised not against, but at or with, sin,—these are the dark shadings which excite our deep and poignant regret, and which call with an almost despairing voice for the hand of some vigorous Reformer.

It was a maxim of the late Dr. Arnold's—one which formed the basis of all his reforms, and by which he solved the hitherto hidden problem of public school education—that whenever a boy failed to show evidence of some positive good, and by his contagious example of evil seemed likely to injure others, he should immediately be removed from the chance of either giving or receiving infection. It was to this, coupled with his own noble example, that he owed his great success in education. Signs of good, active and progressing, were expected as a positive right and title to remain at Rugby. The combination of evil was put down not by one mighty and gigantic effort, but by a well directed series of attacks, which sapped and undermined the strong foundations on which it was based. We may feel a slight reluctance to advocate the application of a rule so rigid and unbending : not that we are doubtful even for a moment of its ultimate success, but its working would require exquisite judgment, coupled with unshrinking firmness, and the stage where it would be tested differs, in many wide respects, from that where its efficiency was practically tried. A boy removed from Rugby was still unblemished in the eyes of the world. No mark of infamy was set upon his brow : no profession in life closed its avenues against his entrance. But the appointment to Haileybury is the very bread of existence. Ejected thence, the outcast would find all doors shut against him. The army would refuse its shield. The church would turn away her countenance : the universities draw back from all communication with the branded one. It is for this reason that removal from Haileybury, except for the grossest irregularities, is almost unknown. Occasionally the thunderbolt is launched by the college authorities ; or a director, exasperated by the recurrence of the same offences, and the same hopeless admonitions, removes his nominee from the college and transfers him to " the cavalry." But even such cases are rare, and are only put in force with the most impracticable subjects. The majority, well aware that nothing short of the most glaring offences will affect their position, and that mere unproductiveness can form no plea for their removal, run to the utmost length of their tether. They are fully sensible of the reluctance which prevails amongst the higher powers to inflict a punishment which effectually darkens all their prospects in life : that they would pause ere consigning by a single word or a dash of the pen the unfortunate victim of bad example to an irrevocable doom. Indeed it would be little short of a miracle if compassion for one reduced to such extremities were not the feeling uppermost in the mind. Pity withholds the hand upraised to strike, or intercepts the descending blow ; and the student, warned in vain for the twentieth time, returns to pursue his old courses with the like profitless termination. A few salutary examples would soon open the eyes of the many: the judicious application of such a maxim as we have described—startling though it may seem—would effectually sweep away the barriers to improvement which are now firmly maintained by the spirit

of carelessness and sloth.   But the reluctance to enforce it, to
select one out of a set, or even to remove a set entirely, would
prove the main check to its utility, and reduce it to an idle
theory or a vain and unmeaning threat.   In the absence of such
a decisive measure we see little chance of a *permanent* improvement at Haileybury.   Its very constitution is one of the greatest
anomalies known.   A college without its dignity, a school
without its restraint, how could it be other than the most anomalous of institutions? Most persons are aware of the funda-
damental principles on which a great public school is based.
It being impossible that any set of masters can keep in view the
movements of five hundred boys, a large portion of the internal
discipline is delegated to the sixth form.*   Authority is vested in
their hands with safety, while the acts of one member are
controlled by the opinion of the rest, and while an ultimate
appeal lies to the supreme government.   The sixth are the
quellers of disturbances, the opponents of petty tyranny, the
adversaries of physical force.   With such a body, moulded
indeed after his own unrivalled model—forming a link between
the lower boys and the masters themselves, and holding out a
practical illustration of the aristocracy of mind—Arnold carried
out his noble designs.   There was no great gulf between those
who commanded and those who obeyed, alike impassable by
either party.   A succession of steps broke the fall, and a link
was established between every gradation from the highest to the
lowest.   It would be foreign to our purpose to go further into
the dangers or the capabilities of a great public School.   We
have slightly digressed in order to shew that Haileybury is
replete with all the temptations of such an institution, without a
single one of its salutary checks.   Wide is the breach there
betwixt master and man.   A few perhaps may be personally
acquainted with the Professors, but the greater part have little
or no connection with them, and are therefore still less influenced
by the example of those whom they only see in the lecture
room.   Failing such a beneficial intercourse, we look in vain for
a constituted authority in the social fabric itself.   The more
common evils of all schools—tyranny and the law of the
strong—are of course not in the catalogue of Haileybury sins;
but with almost every other the cup is filled to the brim.   Where
there is no directing breeze, the vessel floats about at random
wherever the current may set.   There is the same league against
authority, which is the peculiar property of the dull in spirit,

* We take the sixth form as being the highest power next to the masters, and as
existing in *every one of the large public schools*.   It would be out of place here to
discuss the different positions of the *fifth form* at Eton, Harrow and Rugby.

and the quick in body: the carelessness, the disregard of the proprieties of life, the lowered standard after which actions and words are tested, the easy accommodating conscience, the ridicule, not the hatred, which aids the besetting sin. These are to be found more or less at every large public school, and they exist in none more flourishing, or more unchecked than in the so-called East India *College*.

Nor on the other hand has Haileybury any of the characteristics of a good College. We should say that of all the influences which tend to make our Universities what they are, the raised tone of public opinion and the consciousness of self-respect on the part of its members are among the most prominent for good. Where a higher motive is perhaps wanting, this secondary feeling fills the vacuum; but its importance, in the absence of the " pearl of great price," must not be unduly depreciated. A member of one of the finest institutions in the world, surrounded by the most ennobling historical associations, and by venerable piles whose aspect cannot fail to inspire feelings of reverence, how could the Oxonian present other than a fair and seeming exterior? Bulwer has well observed that it is at College where men first find out that a good cricketer or a good boon companion is not equal to one invested with hereditary advantages or personal qualities of a high and commanding order. In the primitive state of society which exists in a school, the attributes of personal strength and activity are looked upon as the most desirable of qualities. Like the Ethiopian tribe mentioned by Herodotus, who always selected the strongest and tallest for their king, the popular voice in a school invariably exalts the hero of games in which courage and dexterity are indispensable, into a prominent station amongst his compeers. A steady, hard-working boy is thought nothing of, a clever, idle one may be admired by a few, but the fortunate youth who combines a moderate portion of ability with fearless energy of head and hand is sure to take by storm all hearts and suffrages. At College these temporary distinctions cease; and talent united with exterior gentlemanly address upsets the basis on which a juvenile Sampson had previously risen to eminence. A quiet but irresistible tone of high feeling is the mainspring by which the best part of the University are moved. Ancestral titles and wealth, though at times attracting a few to bow down before an idol whose influence is so widely felt,* join with learning and talent in raising the public standard of opinion, and based on the solid foundations of the transmitted worth of

---

* " Tuft hunting" is we think, more characteristic of Oxford than Cambridge.

F

aristocracy, and the no less acknowledged power of mental pre-eminence, the edifice without and within may challenge comparison with any in the world. At Haileybury nothing of this kind can as yet be expected. We have shown it to be devoid of the internal discipline of a public school, and it is as wanting in the raised criterion of public opinion which is the chief element for good at our Universities. We also mentioned the influences of time and place, which are certainly not without their effect; and we heard it remarked by one, whose long experience gave him a title to speak authoritatively, that little good could be expected from a set of young men thrown together in a building so unacademic as Haileybury. We would fain attempt some description of that venerable edifice to those unacquainted with it. The south view indeed, bearing some faint resemblance to a College, may hope to escape, though it cannot defy criticism; but the interior is singular and unique of its kind. No comparison with any other Academic building can be instituted, for it resembles none whatever; but any one who has visited the Queen's barracks at Weedon may be able to form a tolerable notion of the imposing interior of Haileybury Quadrangle. We have there no mouldering turrets; no pillars, simple and severe, grown grey under the hand of time: nothing even of that quiet and yet chaste style of architecture which forms a characteristic of the modern Colleges at Oxford. An inelegant row of yellow-brick building is displayed on three sides of a capacious square, and on the fourth, to which in virtue of its position grey stone has been allowed, we view a couple of long edifices of exactly the same make and dimensions, between which not the slightest distinguishing mark can be perceived. One of these, we are told, is the dining hall, the other is the College Chapel! Little of reverential feeling can ever be called forth at the sight of such a house of prayer: no visible sign of the sacred character of the place can be discerned by the most attentive observer: no hymns of thanksgiving, commingling with the deep-toned voice of the organ, float at evening time round the walls of the College: no echoes answer to the mellowed sounds which should pour forth from the precincts of the house of God: no variegated light is reflected from the panes on which all an artist's skill has been expended. Without and within the hand of man has contributed no one single aid to devotion. We are no advocates of that religion which needs for it's exercise the extrinsic aids of swelling domes and stately piles. We have no sympathy with the man whose meditations only find vent in the long aisles of a Minster; whose prayers refuse to come forth in the unpretending quiet of a country Church. But allowance should be made for the position of a large body of young men, and we ought not surely to neglect any lawful means by which their feelings may be led into a train suitable to devotion. All Oxonians will remember the impressions first conveyed when entering on the dim religious light which half shades, the cloisters of Magdalen College, or is mellowed into softness in the interior of its Chapel: or how they walked with a feeling somewhat approaching to awe down the magnificent hall of Christ Church. The only impression which could be conveyed to the mind of a visitor at Haileybury, is one of disappointment or regret. Associations of time in a building of modern date, cannot of course be expected, but the assistance of Art should not surely have been disdained. A sum comparatively trifling would have given to the Chapel the form we could most desire, and a second story added to the walls of the College would not have increased beyond measure the outlay of the whole.* It may be thought strained to ascribe a part of the faults of the institution to the shape and fashion of its walls: to say that the gross and earthy materials of bricks and mortar should have so powerful a connection with the finer elements of the mind: but until the experiment has been fairly tried, we shall set down its unlucky shape and appearance as one amongst the obstacles to Reform in the East India College.

It it worth while again to take a glance at the Educational part of the institution, in order to see how far it may affect the personal fortunes of individuals. The first thing which strikes us when searching for practical results is the impossibility of predicting the future success of the man from the Collegiate course of the student. We may look down the roll for a series of years, and our eye be attracted by names sufficiently familiar from their after career, but distinguished at College by no one single addition from the common herd. Again we may see others, apparently " marked, quoted, and signed," but whose after career has not answered to the promise of the early start. Some few shining spirits, conscious of ability, and competent at once to appreciate the line opening to them, have taken the lead from the first and maintained it to the last. The same energy which carried off a series of prizes at College has pushed its possessor onwards from the lowest to the highest step in the ladder. The talents but partially exercised in the miniature field of Haileybury, found a free vent in the clear open of Indian business. The favourite study was followed in a larger sphere;

* Said to have originally cost the enormous sum of £200,000 !

the weapons, tried and confided in, were exercised against more powerful enemies.   The embryo Orientalist, Lawgiver, Economist pursued their chosen line, and each met their due reward. But there would be several who, in spite of a strong natural good sense, and an inherent manliness of disposition, might shrink from entering in the race where so many of the strong and swift were contending.   The atmosphere of thoughtlessness which surrounded them, perhaps the consciousness that their minds, though healthy, were not exactly fitted to become storehouses of learning, stifled any rising energy and rendered them content to pass on unobserved.   Many of this class may now be lamenting that they did not take a deeper draught of knowledge, when the spring was within their reach: but we feel confident that the clear-sightedness which was barely remarked in the character of the youth, is now playing its part manfully in the ranks of our Judges of Sessions and our Revenue officers.   Ready comprehension of truth, and a sound judgment, unfettered by prejudice or narrowness of views, is the greatest boon which the official can dispense to those who actually live or die according to his capacity: but these are qualities, which if not united with some honorary distinction, pass almost unnoticed in the crowd.   The clever and idle form another class whose prospects it is equally difficult to foresee. The character which refuses to undergo the toil of competition, or shrinks from casting its stake where the game is doubtful, and the reward small, may yet cast off its fetters when transplanted to a wider scene.   At the moment of departure for India the whole fabric undergoes a change.   Dormant energies begin to awake, capacity long hidden under a careless exterior, rises for the first time to the surface, and those who began to press on at an earlier period, are astonished to see themselves passed by others whose ability or whose will they had always doubted.   It is not intended to urge that men are better for thus stifling their talents: that the intellectual garden if overrun with weeds, is invariably certain of producing a finer crop than if it had undergone a continuous process of cultivation. We merely wish to point out that under the present non-compulsory system of work at Haileybury, faculties are constantly suffered to rust and opportunities to pass away unused.   Meanwhile the early fruit is prized, because it appears in the absence of competitors: the later, whose growth was repressed by chilling frosts and biting winds, is generally of a finer and more perfect kind.   The one has been sooner exposed to the genial influence of the sun, and has quickly reached the furthest point of perfection of which it was capable.   The other, on whom

light and heat fell more unevenly, was slower in arriving at
maturity, but that maturity was more valuable from the very
absence of early promise.   Hence it was difficult to foresee in
England what characters would rise to eminence in India.
Once there, and the mist of uncertainty soon cleared away,
a few years showed whose peculiar turn of mind had fitted him
for India, and how far he was likely to ascend.   We would
submit our rule for the corroboration of the Civil Service generally.   Many can doubtless select from the ranks of their
cotemporaries a living example of its truth.   We have not here
taken into account the varying chances of fortune.   Many have
enjoyed her favouring breezes from the first.   A perpetual
trade wind would seem to fill their sails wherever they shaped
their course ; but—setting apart all adjuncts of luck or connexion, or patronage—we contend that the Haileybury career is
a very unsafe criterion to test the chances of future pre-eminence or even of common efficiency.   We make an exception in
favour of the conspicuous man of talent, about whom there can
be no mistake, and we would draw the same line in the case of
the slenderly endowed youth whom no stirring occasion can ever
excite ; but without these two extremes our rule will hold good.
When steady and continued exertion shall be made a necessary
title to Haileybury degrees, and when the whole course shall
have been modified, we then may hope to define from the
beginning what shall be the height to which each man shall
ascend, and how at every step he will be able to acquit himself.
    Our great objection to Haileybury is not on account of its
active influence for evil, but for its negative power for good.   It
is not there that the veil is first torn from the face of inno-
cence, and the pure and spotless character first tarnished by the
contact of pollution.   The knowledge of good and evil has been
imparted in all cases before the entrance into College.   That
dread period in which the daily change is only one of deep and
deeper debasement has been surmounted, and the promise of
better things may be looked for with something more than
hope.   But just at the epoch when the example for good is most
desirable, when the soft clay might be ready to receive and
retain a lasting impression, it is shaped in a mould of no better
kind than what we are compelled to term the moral degradation
of Haileybury.   Some few perhaps have already gone further
than this.   The change with them is almost complete.   They
have emerged from the slough : they have passed through the
worst portion of the fiery ordeal, and are resting on the metal
which has been tried, and stood the test, not on the one which
has shrunk from encountering a power so scorching.   But even

they are unable to stem the torrent, which, without apparent violence, irresistibly carries along all who come within its attraction.
Alive themselves to the evils with which they are surrounded,
they are powerless to oppose any adequate check to their advance.
They are themselves hardly clean from the universal taint, and we
believe that few, however matured their character, have ever
passed through Haileybury without feeling that their keen sense
of evil has been blunted, and the edge of their sensibilities dulled.
A choice of two courses is left to Haileybury Reformers, to
reduce the misnamed College into a public School, or to raise it
a step higher, and render it a College in deed as well as in word.
The latter is the plan we would advocate. Haileybury gives the
finishing stroke to English education, and beyond that nothing
additional can be expected.   Let it then be made a fit rehearsal
for the great drama of life.   There are able men set over the
Institution, who might be capable of doing something towards a
change so desirable : we do not doubt their earnest aspirations,
but on considering the difficulty of inspiring all with a genuine
spirit of co-operation, and the unequal fight which must be
maintained so long ere any good effects be visible, we are at
times tempted to lower our weapons in despair. Like the gallant
Highlander whose heart, swelling at the torpor of his leader, burst
forth into an appeal to the well-remembered name of Dundee, so
whilst gazing on the equally fatal torpor of Haileybury, we are
fain to cry out in the same hopeless accents for, "one single hour
of Arnold."

It will, no doubt, be said, is this a true representation of the
place where the character of so many civilians receives a lasting
impression? Are those who should present the spectacle of Christian Judges—Christian not in word alone, but in spirit and in
reality amongst an unbounded population of the heathen, who
are to be the salt which is to impregnate the mighty mass in
which it is known—are they subjected to the tainting influence
of an atmosphere where so little of a truly healthful character is
to be found? On the scene where the first act of their lives is
concluded, shall we seek in vain for any higher incentive than an
eager thirst for College honours, and that only in a few cases?
Our task would have been more congenial, could we in all
conscience have described it otherwise.   But it were indeed a
wonder if a place so constituted did not abound largely with the
spirit of Ahriman.   We have indicated the early age at
which entrance is permitted, as one of the most fertile sources of
harm.   Liberty which is turned to lawful ends at the age of
nineteen or twenty, is certain to be abused at that of sixteen : at
the former epoch it is an equitable privilege granted in virtue of

the power to enjoy without excess : at the latter, it is a concession which is presumed on to the uttermost limit. The man views it as a right incidental to his position: the boy is bewildered by the novelty, or dazzled by the glare. The consequences of this and other incidental evils are what, with unfeigned regret, we have felt it a duty to describe ; idle, careless habits, hatred of application, dull hardness of character, conventional morality, selfish extravagance, and at times worse. The body of the professors do not seem to be sufficiently aware of this state of things, and make no efforts to counteract it. If their co-operation were unanimous, earnest and uninterrupted, the danger might be mitigated, if not entirely removed. We exhort them to turn their attention to this neglected point, one of far more importance than mere attendance at lectures, or mere rank at the examination.

Meanwhile we would hope that the Court will not be backward in availing themselves of the best stamp of material at hand. We have forborne touching on the subject of private patronage, and but for one circumstance would have refrained from it altogether. An admirable example was set a short time ago, by one whose long residence in India well qualified him to judge what kind of ability was there most required. We allude to the Haileybury nomination presented to Eton, by the late Deputy Chairman of the Court. It was to be tried for by all, without partiality or favour, whose acquirements gave them the least title to hope for success. Why should not this plan be followed in respect of other large public schools ? The result could hardly be other than an infusion of ability, and even of talent, genuine, diversified and sound. A certain number of appointments might be reserved for this especial purpose, and private patronage still be no loser. To require that all nominations to friends and connections should give way to this truly patriotic object, would be to demand far more than human nature could bear. Whilst the power is so close at hand, men will ever provide for their sons and relations, but this regard for natural ties might still be joined to a due provision for those places where a fair proportion of good metal may reasonably be supposed to lie. We do not, however, wish to discourage the practice of giving appointments to the sons of Indian residents. Those bestowed on men whose forefathers have toiled away their existence in the East, are, in our opinion, judicious and equitable. Such is the case with those immediately, or even remotely, connected with members of the Court. Their sympathies are in a certain measure transplanted to the East. They look on India, where their fathers or friends spent the better part of their lives, if not exactly as a second home, still not as the hated land of exile. They feel a natural inclination for the soil in which they have an hereditary title to labour, and they start with a healthy determination to welcome all toil in a service where few can say that their sphere is too contracted, or their means of doing good too small.

Let it not, however, be supposed that Haileybury is a concentration of all the powers of evil, unmixed with even the least partial good. In the course of study, there is ample room for amendment, but even as it stands, no one will deny its great practical utility. Many of the subjects are unattainable elsewhere. Oxford itself cannot promise such facilities for useful knowledge as the lectures on law and political economy. Those studies which attracted the speculative mind of a Malthus, and those to which the matured experience of a Macintosh was devoted, apart from all consideration of the great masters themselves, have a claim on the attention of all those who would carry the book learning of College into the visible realities of life. The whole field of education wants but a judicious reform to make it one of the best and most perfect conceivable. To raise the Haileybury standard of morality will be a harder task. We do not cry out against gross and unsightly forms of vice. Drunkenness and debauchery, which once were of daily occurrence, have almost passed away before the dawnings of a better spirit. The Augean stable would seem to have been partially cleansed; and but the lesser, though unceasing labour of Tantalus to remain. The fight against evil must however be unremitting in order to hold out any hopes of victory; by ceaseless vigilance alone can the conquest be achieved, and the enemy will only retreat when continually assailed by all parties united in one great common cause. Court, professors, studenthood, we would invite them one and all to combine their endeavours, and be divided no longer. The question of the abolition of Haileybury has been canvassed at different times, and but lately the prevalent feeling of the Directors leant visibly towards such an extreme measure. Its great expense, and the non-fulfilment of cherished hopes, were dwelt on as the reasons for such a vote of condemnation. Of the various schemes which rose up in its place, an *Indian* education at either university, or a searching examination at the India House preparatory to departure, we here say nothing. They are all open to endless objections, and are inferior to what may, and, we will add, *will* be made of Haileybury. We leave it to others when carried forward to the hopeful future, to picture to themselves their fairest vision of a College, liberally endowed, and cordially supported, under the guidance of men whose heart and soul is in their work, containing nearly a hundred young men, in the prime of opening manhood, one and all grasping with avidity at the knowledge within their reach, contending for the meed of praise with a generous spirit of rivalry and above all worldly incentives impressed with a deep and unfading sense of the moral obligation they had entered on, of the exalted character of the service they were fated to perform.

But even as the case now stands it is no slight advantage to have some connecting link between the members of an extensive service. Such a bond of union is not inadequately supplied by Haileybury, and the ties formed there are rarely severed during the longest period of residence in the East. Even with different college generations the charm is of little less effect. To have loitered, or to have laboured in the same four walls, to have looked forth from the same chamber on the same quadrangle, though at an interval of years, to have pursued the same favorite studies with the same acknowledged success, to have extorted the sweet tones of praise from the same approving voice, and to have toiled under the same watchful eye,—these are amongst the influences which all have felt and which few can disregard. And apart from all these considerations we would appeal to the members of the service, whether occasional opportunities for good were not to be found in the daily routine. The seeds of a better fruit though smothered for a while, must at times have burst forth into something like life. The spirit of Ormuzd every now and then proved the stronger and defied the chains and the upraised arm of the oppressor. Many will doubtless remember some adviser whose words, then slighted, are treasured with gratitude now. And many, very many, must remember with feelings, to whose expression we hardly dare trust ourselves, the pure and exalting character of one, who for an unexampled length of time was amongst the heads of the establishment. They will recall his form, the fire of whose eyes time has failed to dim, who for more than thirty years saw depart in gradual succession those who now form the Civil Service of India. The ear must frequently re-echo with the deep measured tones of that voice which was never wanting in earnest and manly exhortation, and at a distance of time and place his noble simplicity of character must recur with tenfold force to the mind, perhaps not unmingled with regret that the example held out was not more assiduously followed. Above all they will remember the chapel, not the least important scene of his labours, where with eloquence well suited to the purpose, he would wage war against evil in all its protean shapes, where he would delight to cheer on the way-farer in the only true path, or would rouse in starting accents the sleeper from the fatal calm of his lethargy, and this in language some times quaint and antiquated, but ever glowing and energetic, proceeding straight from and going at once to the heart!

On such a green and refreshing oasis we would wish to take the last look of our subject. Haileybury in spite of the dark side of the picture which is too often uppermost, cannot fail here and there to inspire more wholesome recollections. And such will undoubtedly pour forth most readily at the mention of him, whose earnest hope, as it was his undoubted privilege, could shape no aspirations more heartfelt than "not to be entirely unremembered in the great body of the Civil Service of India." Unremembered indeed he can never be. Spite of years and of engrossing cares the example of that moral and intellectual greatness may now and then touch some secret spring long disused, and one earnest thought inspired by his remembrance, one echo from the eloquence so often dwelt on of old, may bring back in a flowing tide all the deeper feelings of our nature, as fresh, as pure, and as warm as ever.

☞ When the foregoing article had been not only projected, but well nigh completed by one of the regular contributors to this work, a somewhat elaborate and able paper on the same subject, embracing also that of Fort William College, reached us. The communication was altogether anonymous. The short note which accompanied it, was simply signed "A Subscriber," without date, or name of residence, or any sign or mark, internal or external, by which the author might be identified. Had it been otherwise, we would, at once, have entered into communication with the author. And now, we trust, since he is "A Subscriber," that, when his eye catches this notice, he will at once furnish us with the means of so doing. If his object be privacy, he has only to say so, and his name will be as safe in our keeping as in his own. A letter addressed to the care of our Publishers, will at any time reach us.

Before dismissing this topic, we may advert to the subject of anonymous communications generally. Of this description, many have already been forwarded to us. But, except in a single instance, in which the author treated of his subject in a way which commended itself to our own judgment, we have not availed ourselves of any of them. Surrounded as we happily are by a staff of as able and willing auxiliaries as India can supply, we are wholly independent of any such contributions. And surely it is always more pleasant to have to deal with substances rather than with shadows—with actual personalities than with empty names.

While we have to thank all anonymous friends for the good-will evinced towards us, and their hearty sympathy with our great object, we must entreat of them henceforward to disclose their names, *in confidence*, to the Editor, if they really desire their proffered services to become practically available.

ART. II.—1. *The Vedánta Chandrika;—an Apology for the present system of Hindu worship. Written in the Bengali language and accompanied by an English translation. Calcutta,* 1817.

2. *Translations of several principal books, passages, and texts of the Veds, and of some controversial works on Brahmanical Theology. By Rajah Rammohun Roy. London,* 1832. *(Partly reprinted, in Calcutta,* 1845.)

3. *The Philosophy of the Hindús ;— The Uttara-mímánsá or Vedánta. By H. T. Colebrooke, Esq., New Edition, London,* 1837.

WERE we disposed to take our departure, for a season, from the domain of the inductive Philosophy altogether, with all the glorious monuments of its triumph, we could not do so more effectually than by plunging at once into the bottomless abyss of Hindú metaphysics. Such, however, is not our present intention. Our sole design is one of plain, sober, practical utilitarianism.

It is now pretty generally known that, in this country, under the common appellation of Hindúism, there are two great generic systems of religion, with their respective divisions and sub-divisions endlessly multiplied. There is the system of Polytheism, with its idolatrous rites and ceremonies, followed from time immemorial by the great masses of the people. There is the system of Monotheism, running through all gradations between the opposite extremes of Spiritual and Materialistic Pantheism, professed in theory at least by the more learned classes of the native community. Of all the modifications of nominal monotheism, that which is commonly known under the name of "*Vedantism,*" has always been accounted the most orthodox, that is, the most accordant with the Vedas, the great, primordial sources of Hindú theology. Now, since of late years, very great efforts have been made in Calcutta and elsewhere to revive and re-invigorate, by a fresh infusion of life and energy, this system which had gradually become in a manner superannuated and effete, the curiosity of individuals has been considerably excited, and the question has on all hands been raised, "*What is Vedantism ?*" To answer this question, in as compendious, plain, and intelligible a form as possible, is our sole immediate object.

The works placed at the head of this article, with Wilkins' Bhagavat Gíta, would furnish all the needful information. But as these cannot be accessible to most readers, nor, if they were,

could they, in their own original native forms, prove acceptable or even tolerable reading, our purpose is to spare their time
and patience, by attempting to extract the pith and marrow out
of them. Of the works of Wilkins, Colebrooke, and Rammohun Roy, we need say little. They have been too long and too
well known to every Oriental scholar to require the aid of any
fresh criticisms at our hands. Of this only need we remind the
less experienced of our readers, that of all the men who have
ever written on the Indian Philosophy, Colebrooke is at once the
most profound and the most trustworthy. The translations of
Rammohun Roy often do not faithfully represent the original:
by the adoption of certain words and phrases, which in the
English language, are the vehicle of true and pure ideas, he
often contrives to throw a colouring of verisimilitude and refinement over the sentiments of his author, which really does not
belong to them. The general fidelity of Wilkins as a translator
has never been impeached; but his important services, in this
respect, have been limited in a great measure to the Bhagavat
Gíta. Colebrooke, on the other hand, has gone over the whole
range of Indian Philosophy, beginning with the Vedas themselves.
Of the standard works on the different systems he has supplied,
partly analyses and party translations; and never were analyses
or translations furnished by any one who more signally manifested his possession at once of the ability and the will to be
rigidly precise—drily, scrupulously, systematically accurate.
Of the first work at the head of this article, less is known;
indeed, very few appear to have ever heard even of its existence.
As the original production of a native of our own day, on a very
abstruse and metaphysical subject, it is at once curious and
important. It was published, in 1817, anonymously; and
the following are the only scanty particulars which we have
been enabled to glean concerning the author and his
work. His name was Mrityunjaya Vidyalankara. He was head
Pandit of the College of Fort William; and afterwards
Pandit of the Supreme Court under Sir Francis Macnaghten.
He died, about 1820, at Moorshedabad, on his return from
Benaras; bearing universally the character of a very learned
man in all the Darsans or systems of Sanskrit learning and
philosophy. He was himself wholly unacquainted with the
English language. His son, who succeeded to his station at
the Supreme Court, has been known to ascribe the credit of
having aided his father with the English translation to the late
Sir W. H. Macnaghten. Of the work itself only two hundred
and fifty copies were originally struck off; and as there has
been no second edition, it has long been difficult if not impos-

sible to obtain a copy ; indeed, we have never seen one except that which has fallen into our own possession.

With these few prelimimary remarks, we proceed at once to answer the general question, *What is Vedantism* ? This, for the sake of distinctness, we shall do, under various leading heads—

I. The History of the Vedant System.

The *founder* of the system is universally acknowledged to be Vyása ; which *name* by its derivation seems to allude to the peculiarities of his birth, like many names in Hebrew. To this another term is sometimes added or prefixed as Vyása-deva, from his being one of the divine sages ; and Veda-vyása from his having collected together the Vedas.—He is also, from the name of his father, called Paráshara ; and from the name of his mother Satyavati-suta.—Beside which he is also called Dwai-páyana and Krishna-dwaipáyna from his having been born on an island or rather a dark sand bank in the river Jumna : and Vádaváyna from the name of the place to which he most frequently went on pilgrimage. There are other names, but these are the principal.

He was by birth an illegitimate child in high life, being the son of Paráshara, a brahman by Satya-vatí, the wife of king Shántanu. Hence he was the reputed brother of king Vichitra-vírga and grandson of the great sage Vashishta. After the death of his reputed brother, he, from a custom similar to that among the Jews, married his brother's wives, and had by Ambá or Ambiká, Dhaita-rashtra ; by Ambáliká, Pándu ; and by a female slave, Vidura : all of whom particularly the first two became greatly celebrated in the pages of history.

As an author he is the greatest in the Sanskrit language, and may be regarded as the father of Hindú literature. He spent his time chiefly in writing and teaching. He had five distinguished disciples to whom he taught the Vedas and Puránas. To Paila he taught chiefly the Rig-veda ; to Viashampayna, the Yajar-veda ; to Jaimani the Sáma-veda ; to Sumanta the Utharva-veda ; and to Suta chiefly the Puránas. His principal works were the collection of the Vedas, the Vedant Darsan, the Mahábhárata and Shri-Bhagavat and other Purans.

The Vedant appears to have been the last but one of the six Darsans, or leading systems of Hindú Theological Philosophy ; so that the author of it had an opportunity of improving on those who had gone before him in studying the philosophy or metaphysics of Theology. The first Darsan was the Sánkhya written by Kapila ; the second, the Nyáya by Gautama ; the

third, the Vaishéshika, by Kanáda ; the fourth, the Pátanjalí,
by Patanjala ; the fifth the Vedant by Vyása ; and the sixth
the Mímánsá, by Jaimani.

The *antiquity* of the Vedant system cannot be determined
with exactness, though we may ascertain enough for every useful purpose.   According to the Hindú accounts, Pándu was the
son of Vyása—the son of Pándu was Judhisthira, whose reign
is reckoned at 36 years; that of his successor Parakshit at 60 ;
that of Janamejaya at 84 ; that of Shátaníka at 82.   Then
follow twenty-five successors, whose reigns make 625 years.
Then follow 14 other reigns said to be 500 years. Again,
fifteen others said to be 400 years.   After these are eight reigns
not defined, which we put down at the rate of the last 200 years.
Then comes the reign of Vikramaditya, which is acknowledged
by scholars to be 57 years before the Christian æra. Thus, even
by the account of the Hindús themselves, the Vedant system
was only about two thousand and forty-four years before the
Christian æra.

But as the Hindús are known to exaggerate in their numbers,
it may be safer to take the reign of their kings—supposing the
number of these to be accurately recorded, a point which may
well be doubted—at the mean rate of kings among the Jews,
and in our own nation. 66 reigns by the Hindús give 2,000
years, which is about 30 years to each reign on the average.
21 Jewish reigns give 505 years, making 24 years to each. 55
English reigns give 1000 years, which is an average of 18 years
to each.   By the Hindú standard, then, the antiquity of the
Vedant system would be about 2,000 years before Christ ; by the
Jewish standard about 1600 ; and by the English about 1,200.
As the lives of men might be longer at the time alluded to than at
present, we should not object to the Jewish standard : and we
shall certainly not be going to excess if we take a middle number between the Jewish and English, and say 1500 before the
Christian æra.   This, which is by far the most favourable supposition that can be made for Hindúism, brings the subject
within the first authentic dates of History.

The *evidences* on which the *antiquity* of the system rests are internal and external.   Internal evidence is found in the existing
works of the author the Vedanta Sára—the Mahábhárata and
the Shri-Bhagavat.   In an episode of the Mahábhárata called the
Gíta, Vyása gives a minute account how the system was taught
by Krishna to his disciple Arjuna ; so that in addition to its
being sanctioned in part by the Vedas and other Darsans, he
professes to have received it from the deity incarnate.

External evidence is found in the universal consent of all

scholars that the Vedant system embodies the sentiments of Vyása, and in the frequent allusions made to it as his system by writers since his time. The work which exhibits the system in its most striking colours is a dramatic one, called Prabodh-Chandrodaya, which, by personifying all the powers and passions of the mind, and bringing them to engage in a war of extermination with each other, shews the dreadful effects which the system produces in the territories of the soul.

II. The Doctrines of the Vedant System.

Of the *nature* and *attributes* of the Divine Being. The Vedant teaches the simplicity and rationalistic unity of the Divine Being (átmá adwaitiya) in his own original, proper, and abstract nature. It teaches that God is light, but in what precise sense, physical or metaphysical, it is not very easy to determine : the word used to express this is jyóti and not diptí. It teaches that he is eternal, self-existent, immutable, perfect, incomprehensible, omniscient, infinitely happy, and the sustainer of all. These are stated in the first lines of the Vedánta Sára :

> Akanda sachchidánandam abáng mánasa gócharang
> Atmánam akhiládharam.

It never speaks of God as possessing power except when connected with matter; but this may be to shew that the power of spirit cannot be known except by its influence over matter. It teaches in a peculiar manner the ubiquity of God, maintaining that he is within every thing and without every thing. The existence of God in every thing is called vyasti ; and the existence of every thing in God is called samasti. This may be regarded as the most knotty point of the system : and it must be confessed that it is exceedingly difficult to make the natives understand how God can be in all and through all, and yet not an essential part of all. The Sánkhya system makes God a *witness* of all but not in all and through all ; the Vedant virtually and actually makes God every thing and every thing God, and is in reality only one of the many forms of pantheism. On this subject, so frequently and so ignorantly controverted by modern innovators, the statements of the reputedly Divine Vyása himself, the original author of the system, in his own *sútras* or aphorisms, are thoroughly explicit. Abstractly he asserts that the Supreme Being is "the material, as well as the efficient, cause of the universe"—and that "an effect is not other than its cause." And as if this were not explicit enough, illustrations of every sort are adduced to prevent the possibility of mistake. "Hair and nails," says Vyása, in vindicating his assertion that the Supreme Brahm is at once cause and effect, or the material and efficient cause of the universe, " hair and nails which are insensible, grow from a sensible animal body; and sentient vermin (scorpions, &c.) spring from inanimate sources (cow-dung, &c.") " The sea is one and not other than its waters ; yet waves, foam, spray, drops, froth, and other modifications of it, differ from each other :" similar is said to be " the singleness and identity of Brahm as cause and effect." " The same earth exhibits diamonds, rock, crystals, red orpiment, &c. ; the same soil produces a diversity of plants ; the same food is converted into various excrescences, hair, nails, &c. As milk changes to curd, and water to ice, so is Brahm variously transformed and diversified." " In like manner, the spider spins his web out of his own substance ; spirits assume various shapes, &c. &c."

The work of *creation.* On this subject, loosely and improperly styled " creation" in connection with Vedantism, the Vedant stands opposed to the Sánkhya system. The latter maintains that God, shining on matter, communicated to it certain properties, and then left those properties to their own operation ; he remained only a witness : whereas the Vedant teaches that God himself is in some way essentially connected with the matter, and that it is the union of the deity with matter which gives to all its properties their specific influence ; or rather, to speak more accurately still, it is the fact that every portion of matter is in reality but a modification of the substance of Brahm, that makes it to be what it is. To form a correct idea of the subject of creation it is necessary to consider the agents employed in it —its nature and extent ; and the influence to which it is subject.

The first cause of all is Brahm. He is represented as inhabiting his own eternity, or in figurative language, since the coiled serpent is the emblem of eternity, as resting upon this emblem. Brahmá is represented as the first of created beings, and as springing immediately from the navel or centre of the deity. The raw materials of the creation are represented as formed or rather *drawn out,* or *educed* by Brahm *from himself* in the same way as the spider's web is formed, *drawn out,* or *educed* by it, from itself. These materials, i. e. *prakriti* and three *gunas* are put into the hands of Brahmá, and he is ordered to exert himself in the work of creation, or rather, the work of *formation, collocation* or *composition.* He did so for some time but not with success, on which account he betook himself to severe meditation on Brahm and penance, after which he succeeded better, and finally committed his work to successors called Prajapatís. The term Swayambhú applies to both Brahm and Brahmá, but most commonly to the latter.

The description given of the creature man as the chief work of God is remarkable. The Vedánt teaches that man consists of three parts—one spirit which is included in two cases or bodies. The spirit of man is regarded as immaterial, and as *an essential part of the Supreme Being.* The corporeal part of man is supposed to consist of two bodies called the Sthúl Sharír and the Sukshma or Linga Sharír. The Sthúl Sharír is the material gross body consisting of flesh, blood, bones, &c. The Linga Sharír is the sublimated body which is said to consist of three parts called Pránamaya-kosh, Vigyanamaya-kosh and Manomaya-kosh. This is regarded as the exact counterpart of the gross body, and as the vehicle of the spirit when the gross body dies. By it the consciousness of identity is preserved, and the person recognized after death as before. If the spirit becomes absorbed in Brahm or immured in vile flesh, this body is supposed to vanish; otherwise through every stage of being, it is supposed to be immortal.

The extent of the creation or universe is also remarkable. The universe is divided into three parts—including all on earth, and all in heaven, and all under the earth. Beginning with the earth they reckon seven parts above and seven below. The worlds or regions of worlds above, beginning with the earth, are Bhúr-lok, Bhúvar-lok, Swar-lok, Mohar-lok, Jana-lok, Tapo-lok, and Brahmá or Satya-lok. The first three are supposed to exist one day of Brahmá or 2,160 millions of years; the second three, one hundred of his years; while the last one is eternal. In the last or highest heaven are supposed to be four kinds of blessedness—the first is called Sálokya, *i. e.* co-habitation with God; the second, Sárúpya, likeness to God; the third, Sáyujya, union with God; and the fourth, Nirvana, absorption in God. The worlds or regions of worlds under the earth are Atal, Vital, Sutal, Talátal, Mahátal, Rasá-tal, and Pátal. It is the last of these which is regarded as hell. It is divided by some into twenty-one, and by others into twenty-eight, compartments—and the name of each corresponds with the kind of punishment which is there inflicted, or the kind of vice which has produced the punishment.

The influence to which every creature and to which all things are subject is called Máyá. This Máyá may be regarded as the influence of spirit on spirit, and time on matter, or of the supreme spirit on the qualities of matter, and the influence of time upon the matter itself. By the former, the deity works or operates in all; and by the other, matter, as unsubstantial, is destined to perpetual vicissitude and change. The Vedant theory is that the presence of the deity in the three qualities of truth or reality, passion, and darkness, gives to them all their influence over the soul, and that this influence is invariably according to the quantity of each of these qualities in the constitution of the creature. If the Satya-guna or truth or reality preponderates, then the creature will be powerfully influenced to subdue his passions, and to seek after God as the chief good and only reality. If the Raja-guna or passion preponderates, the man will be inclined to gratify his passions and to become inordinate in his desires and attachments to the creature. If the Tamaguna or darkness preponderates, he will be urged on from sin to sin and from one miserable condition to another. While under the influence of these qualities men think they do just what they please, but are ignorant at the time that they are doing nothing more than unconsciously yielding to, or obeying the impulses of, a blind and uncontrollable necessity, often mistakenly designated " God," in all the good and evil they practise, and in all the good and evil they enjoy or suffer from their deeds. This is the Máyá or universal influence of the deity, by which he constrains all beings good and bad to do, suffer, and enjoy just what he pleases. This influence in the Vedant system is, in its nature and operation, just what attraction is in the natural world ; and the consistent Vedantist recognizes it in all that he sees and in all that he feels, in all that he does, enjoys or suffers. All is Máyú.

Again, the whole world is destined, at the expiration of one day of Brahmá, to return to its primœval chaotic state. So that a period will soon come when all that now appears will vanish away. The world, with all its busy scenes, and all its various actors, will have gone—have passed away as a dream, a shadow, an illusion. The Vedantist, seeing that all is so soon to vanish away, professes to regard the whole as a mere appearance, unsubstantial and unreal, or, in his own words, all Máyá. And to such an extent do some carry this notion that they profess not to believe in the reality of an external world at all, or in the reality of their own existence, or any thing that they do, or suffer, or enjoy !

The nature of *sin* and *holiness*. There are no rules laid down like those of the moral law to define what sin and holiness are. What is consistent with truth, or rather, simple *reality*, is thought to be holiness ; what has a mixture of truth or reality and error or unreality, imperfection— and what is full of darkness or error, sin—hence all characters are considered of three kinds, good, bad, and middling, called uttam, and addham and madhyam. In the different incarnations which are all acknowledged in the Vedant system, sin and holiness seem to be determined by the object for which the incarnation took place. *The end is always supposed to sanctify the means.* So that if Krishna becomes incarnate to destroy Konsa, and a washerman stands in his way, it is no sin to kill the washerman and run away with all his clothes! The present Vedantists may discard these incarnations; but if so, what becomes of their system professedly received from an incarnation? In the case of those who aspire after final emancipation from the flesh or matter, perfect indifference to the world, and the things of the world is reckoned the highest holiness; and strong attachment to the world, and the things of the world, is considered as the greatest sin. In the Christian system, virtue consists in purifying and regulating the affections in regard to things below, and elevating them to things above; but in the Vedant system, in extirpating them altogether.

There is one point in which the Vedant system strangely degrades the Deity. It supposes and affirms, that, when connected with matter or incarnate, he cannot be free from the effects or influence, which matter invariably produces upon mind; and hence he is frequently represented in these circumstances, as infatuated and bewildered with the operation of those qualities in matter which he himself had communicated.

The *method* or methods of *obtaining deliverance* from sin. There are two methods sanctioned by the Vedant; or rather, one is recommended and the other is allowed. The knowledge of God is the one, and the practice of works is the other; the former is designed for philosophers or superior minds, and the latter for the common people. The persons who pursue the first are called Brahmagyání, and those who pursue the other Karmagyání. There are prescribed rules laid down for each of these. The former is taught to look with contempt on all the common gods and goddesses, and by profound meditation, constant abstraction of thought and severe mortifications, to aspire after absorption in the Supreme Being or virtual annihilation; the latter is taught to respect the common gods, to follow the rules laid down in the shastras, and to expect a reward of longer or shorter duration, proportioned to his works.

Of a *future state.* In this the Vedant differs little from the commonly received opinions of the people. To the man who obtains a knowledge of God final emancipation is awarded. Being absorbed in the deity he is supposed to attain to the highest bliss, which consists in the total loss of personal identity and self-consciousness, to be freed for ever from all connection with matter, and to remain through eternal ages a small but essential part of the deity, just as a drop of water falling into

the sea becomes a small but essential part of the ocean. They
suppose this state to be attained by some at once and by others
gradually.

On those who seek salvation by their works a reward is bestowed equal to those works. All such rewards are sensual in their
nature and limited in their duration. They allow the aspirant
to gain what he wishes, but after he has enjoyed it for a limited
period, and, by the enjoyment, exhausted his stock of merit, he
must again go through the process of acquiring more. And this
process goes on from generation to generation, to the end of the
world or destruction of the universe, when all such will return
to a state of non-existence—to be reproduced at the pleasure
of the Supreme Being. Those who neither obtain the knowledge of God, nor attend to the duties of their religion, are
doomed to one of the 28 hells, and to be degraded by being
born in the shape of insects or brutes, and suffering through
these successive births, till they have expiated their crimes
and return again to human beings, or till they are involved in
the general destruction of the universe.

III. Some of the principal deficiencies and faults of the
Vedant system.

Its great and striking deficiency in regard to God, is, that
it represents him as destitute of love and other moral perfections. "God is love," but the Védant says, no, that is a thing
which enters not into his nature at all—He loves no one, he
hates no one, and no one can be like him till he ceases entirely
both to love and to hate. How desolate to us does the character of God become when we take away his boundless love !
Compassion to the guilty, is also unknown in the Vedant.

The want of a moral standard by which actions are to
be weighed. When there is no law there is no transgression.
Scattered precepts may be referred to in the shastras, but there
is no royal law like the ten commandments by which the
sinner can be speedily tried and convicted. This want of a moral
standard has doubtless contributed much to that total want of
compunction for sin which we observe even in those who
have committed the most flagrant offences.

The want of a suitable atonement by which sin may be
forgiven. The great atonement proposed by this system is
abstraction (yog), which is to be promoted by penance or bodily
suffering, as if a man could by application of thought raise himself to God, and by the sufferings of his body make an
atonement for the sin of his soul. The body is a sinful body
and all it can suffer is not more than it deserves, so that there can

be no merit in such sufferings.   It is said, as is the sin so should be the sacrifice, but no such sacrifice does this system propose to appease the forebodings of a guilty conscience.

The positive tendency of the system to fill the mind with the greatest degree of arrogance.   It teaches every man to say, I am God, it is God that is in me and does all, apart from him what am I ? When a man is thus taught to identify himself, in a literal and physical sense, with God, how is it possible to convince him of the evil of his nature and his sinfulness in the sight of a holy God? Hence we see no repentance for sin, as sin, against God.

Want of religious motives to action.   It presents no God to be glorified, no motive to make us love our neighbour as ourselves, for we are to become perfectly indifferent to self and to all, and learn neither to love nor to hate.   There is no motive of gratitude to compel to action.   All that is seen is the misery of being connected with matter and a desire of emancipation from it.   No grace to be hoped for or imparted—no motive arising from the recompence of reward, for if any thing is done with a desire of reward the whole reward is lost.   Every act must proceed from a motive of super-attenuated, undefinable, unattainable, metaphysical disinterestedness.   Now where there are neither love to God or man, gratitude, grace, nor future rewards to influence, what motive can there be for religious obedience ? In this respect it may be said that the Vedant is the coldest, or, if we were allowed to coin a word, the most *icyfying*, of all systems ever proposed to the attention of man.

Want of religious consolation in trouble.   The sufferings of all are punishments, and not chastisements.   The idea of moral training by discipline and suffering is unknown. God is not seen as sanctifying any trouble to good.   There are no promises of support in sufferings and of happy deliverance out of them. Not one ray of comfort does this system offer to the man involved in trouble.   It presents no examples of patience in suffering and of the happy termination of suffering under the gracious care of a wise and gracious God and Father. Communion of saints, as involving sympathy and love, is a doctrine unknown to the Vedant. It acknowledges no connection between suffering in this life and glory in the next—no momentary lightness of affliction to produce an eternal weight of glory.

Total want of animating prospects for the future. The resurrection of the body and the life everlasting are doctrines unknown to Vedantism. Life and immortality are brought to light only by the gospel. The state of absorption, at which the Vedantist aspires, is too high and too repulsive both in its means and its end for any mortal ; and the state of happiness by works which it allows is too low both in its means and its end to be worthy of the acceptance of a rational creature.   Hence Prithu the first king, when requested to make his choice, said, give me neither the one nor the other, but a place where I may hear and learn the glories of the deity.   But a life after death and a blessed immortality in the presence of the ever blessed God is unknown in the Vedant system ; and what is there to animate the mind of a thinking being where this glorious prospect is taken away ?

Its hard and unbearable restraints for the present.   Its requirements are so severe that it needs the brightest prospects for the future to enable the mind to endure them.   And yet without any prospect of an individual, eternal and happy exis-tence, it requires the most severe self-denial.   It requires the body to be entirely subdued and its passions to be extirpated. Desire and anger are to be utterly expelled—pleasure and pain are to become equally indifferent—the body is to be tormented in every possible way by hunger and thirst, by heat and cold, and nakedness, to weaken its influence over the spirit.   The spirit is to be exercised with the severest mental discipline. The language to it is, tapa, tapa, tapa. The spirit is to be puri-fied only in the fires of penance, therefore exercise penance. All friends and the comforts of society are to be abandoned. A man has little chance of gaining absorption except by an entire renunciation of the world and a literal retirement from all its concerns to some sacred forest.   And all this for what ?   Anni-hilation at the best—and after all, if the sun is south of the equator when he dies, it may all be lost labour.

IV.   The arguments by which it is defended.

By an appeal to the Vedas.   These are regarded as the word of God and of divine authority.   One text from the Vedas in confirmation of any doctrine is equivalent to a mathematical demonstration .   And after such text has been adduced the Vedantist professes to be more certain of the thing confirmed than he is of his own existence.

By tradition.   The purans, their traditional scriptures are very numerous, and though in general held in low esteem by the Vedantist, and considered to belong to those who seek the inferior kind of salvation, yet they are quoted as authority when they contain passages in favour of the system.

By human reasoning.   Some of this reasoning is of the most subtile kind as may be seen in the six Darsans ; and the Vedantist thinks himself at liberty to take from any of these

Darsans whatever may suit his purpose. And as there are a number of points in which they all agree, they are made to confirm one another.

By similitudes. They are very fond of an apt similitude, and it has often more weight with them than the strongest argument. Thus they say, God is like fire, not defiled by contact with corruption—like atmosphere without all and within all. They say the world is all an illusion, whereas people think it is a reality ; just as a man seeing some thing at a distance thinks it is a snake, a living thing, but on approaching finds it a rope, a senseless thing.

V.   Some of the doctrines of Vedantism which offer *special* obstacles to the progress of Christianity.

The system itself being of great antiquity and more suitable to the corrupt reasonings of man will be an obstacle. Looking at the New Testament alone, and forgetting that Christianity, in its original germ and first announcement, is as old as the fall of man in paradise, the adherents of Vedantism say, we have a system older than yours, and one which provides for all, high and low, according to their wishes. We therefore need nothing more. As the philosophic part of the system was invented by those who despised idols, it is peculiarly suited to entrap those of the present day who are throwing off idolatry.

The doctrine of the Divine Unity, as plausibly but erroneously taught in the Vedant, offers a special obstacle to the doctrine of the Divine Unity, in a tri-personal distinction, as inculcated in the Sacred Scriptures. In this it stands opposed to Christianity just like Muhammadanism. It is more mild in allowing the deluded to worship their idols without persecution ; but at the same time affects a great contempt for them. Its adherents are very firm in the belief that God is *adwaitiya,* without a second, in a sense more peculiar than true—and hence the difficulty, by any argumentation addressed to the unaided reason and the unsanctified heart of man, to convince them that there are three persons in the one undivided Godhead, the same in substance and equal in power and glory—the Father, Son, and Holy Spirit.

The view taken by the Vedantists of all incarnations militates against their getting correct views of the incarnation of Christ as prophet, priest and king to his church. They regard them as for a special object, which object they suppose to have been realized in their life time ; and they think they have nothing to do with them except as they choose to profit by their example or any of their precepts. In this only the present system differs chiefly as containing more illustrations.

Their belief that there is nothing amiss in the spirit itself; that all that is wrong is its connection with flesh; that knowledge and devotion only are necessary to its liberation ; and that these are to be obtained by the use of merely human means, militates strongly against the doctrine of the soul's depravity, the need of regeneration, and of the aid of the divine spirit to effect it. These essential doctrines of Christianity will be long resisted, and it will be after long and painful 'struggles, and not without the application of an energy that is more than human, that the Vedantist will be brought to confess his sinfulness and helplessness, and to implore the mercy of God to pardon, and the influence of the Spirit to sanctify.

The doctrine that the soul of man, is not the work or creature of God, but an essential part of himself, stands in strong opposition to the Scripture doctrine of creation and of Christian humility. Here are the *ipsissima verba* of Vyása himself ;— " *The soul is a portion of the supreme ruler, as a spark is of fire. The relation is not as that of master and servant, ruler and ruled, but as that of whole and part.*" If a man believes himself to be an essential part of God, where is the ground for humility ? No ; he rises up and determines to conquer the body or matter that separates him from his original source, and thus to mingle again and be lost in the ocean of Being. How opposed is this to confessing himself a creature of God, and a guilty sinner, deserving of everlasting punishment !

The doctrine of pantheism taught by the Vedant militates strongly against the Christian doctrine of repentance and reformation. If God is in every thing, or, more strictly, is every thing, moving all that is moving and fixing all that is fixed ; if he impels us to all we do as the gáyatrí teaches ;—then, where is the ground for repentance ? As creatures we are bound to acquiesce in the divine will ; but if not creatures, but parts of himself, how shall the parts find fault with the whole, and repent of what he does ? And what motive is there for reformation in any case, when it is believed that every one, good and bad, acts only as God acts in him ?

The doctrine of salvation by knowledge through works forms a strong barrier against the doctrine of salvation by grace through faith. The Vedant like every other false system teaches that man can save himself,—that if he attains a knowledge of God, that will be his liberation—and that this knowledge he can acquire by the use of certain means. How sad to be told that knowledge is all in vain, that he must be saved by another and not by himself, and that salvation is not of works lest any man should boast. In this, however, Vedantism is opposed to Christianity only in the same way as Muhammadanism, Popery and Puseyism are.

The severe austerities required by the Vedant system make its adherents look with contempt on the mild system of the gospel. To make the soul fit to receive emancipation, according to the genuine unadulterated doctrines of Vedantism, the body must be reduced, the world must be literally abandoned, and the soul must struggle its way upwards towards the deity. But the gospel teaches a man to use the world and not to abuse it, to live in it and yet prepare for heaven better than those who live in the woods. This to the Vedantist, ignorant as he is of the power of Divine grace, appears more impossible than if you were to tell him that he could constantly remain immersed in the water and yet live and breathe.

The evil effects of the system, if overcome by the reception of the gospel in some cases, will yet, being only partially eradicated, be long left as evils to the Christian Church. We must not think that all the work is done when Vedantism is abandoned in favour of Christianity ; but must recollect that the notions so long imbibed will be practically overcome only by degrees. The idea that God is in all or is all, will still cling to the mind and lead it to form many an excuse for sin, for neglect of duty, and the want of vigorous exertion. There will always be danger of these men corrupting the gospel. Such are some of the special obstacles which Vedantism offers to Christianity as far as they have come under our observation.

VL How to combat Vedantism and to convince its adherents of the truth of Christianity. A few brief hints on this copious theme is all that we can aim at supplying.

We cannot undertake to state what is the *best* method of combating Vedantism, but it appears to us that it may be fairly objected to, on the following, amongst other grounds.

On the ground of its time. This is nothing to us but much to the Hindús. It was the production of the Káli-yog. Now as the Jews said, can any good thing come out of Nazareth, so the Hindús say, can any good come out of the Káli-yog. If this argument answers no other purpose, it will at least be turning one of their sharpest weapons against themselves, and shew how vainly they argue against Christianity as the product of the iron age.

On the ground of its object. The immediate object of this system, according to one of its principal standards, the Bhagavat Gíta, was the encouragement of the most bloody war that was

I

known ; a hundred times more bloody than the battle of Waterloo. Arjun the hero looked with horror on the scene, and begged the incarnate God to allow him to desist, but in order to urge him on in it, as the means of fulfilling the Divine Will, Krishna made to him a full discovery of this Vedant system.

On the ground of its statements. The Vedant system, in its original authorities, has its singular theories in physics as well as metaphysics. The former, however, being of a more palpable character, may be brought more summarily to some recognized test. Here, then, is the theory of the great Vyása himself, on a subject intimately connected with physiology :— " When nourishment is received into the corporeal frame, it undergoes a threefold distribution, according to its fineness or coarseness: corn and other terrene food becomes flesh; but the coarser particles are rejected, and the finer nourishes *the mind!* Water is converted into blood; the coarser particles are rejected as urine ; the former supports *the breath !* Oil or other combustible substance, deemed igneous, becomes marrow ; the coarser part is deposited as bone, and the finer supplies the faculty of speech !" Again, the same author declares that " a hundred and one arteries issue from the heart, one of which passes to the crown of the head." It is along this artery that the liberated soul, whose " proper abode is the heart," makes its escape. From the crown of the head it passes along a sunbeam, through various regions to the sun. Thence it proceeds to the moon, which, according to Vyása, is far beyond the sun ! If it is to be rewarded with final absorption, it advances from the moon to " the region of lightning," which is far beyond the moon. Thence again to " the realm of Varuna, the region of water, for lightning and thunder are beneath the rain-cloud, and aqueous region"—and all of these far beyond the moon, which itself again is as far beyond the sun ! " At length it arrives by the realm of Indra—at the abode of Prajápati or Brahm." But if the soul has not merit enough to earn final absorption, it must stop short, subject to transmigration, at one or other of the intermediate regions, generally that of the moon. There, " clothed with an aqueous form, it experiences the recompense of its works ; and thence it returns to occupy a new body with resulting influence of its former deeds. The returning soul quits its watery frame in the lunar orb, and passes successively and rapidly through ether, air, vapour, mist and cloud, into rain ; and thus finds its way into a vegetating plant, and thence, through the medium of nourishment, into an animal embryo !" Once more, the system itself sets forth, that a man by attending to the rules of abstraction and penance, will obtain final emancipation; then, some of its authorities assert, that, if the sun be on the south side of the equator when he dies, he will not. All the explanation we have been able to get from the Pandits of this, is, that it is impossible for such a man to die when the sun is on the south side of the equator!

On the ground of its duplicity. It theoretically pours the utmost contempt on idols—on works—and on the heaven they secure; and yet gives practical rules, for the worship of these idols, the performance of these works, and the securing of this heaven, to those who have no heart to seek after any thing better.

On the ground of want of evidence of its inspiration or Divine authority. Of such evidence there is not a single shred, or any thing that bears the remotest semblance of a shred, in existence.

On the ground of its changeableness. Its author appears first to have been an idolator; then a deist and absorptionist; and finally, as appears from the Bhagavat which contains the sentiments of his old age, he appears to have renounced the doctrine of absorption in the deity and to have formed the opinion that it was infinitely better, in the society of Yogis, to dwell near to God and enjoy his favour. As its author, so its adherents are continually changing and making alterations in their system, both by way of addition and subtraction, so as to reduce the whole to a mass of fluctuating, heterogeneous, and self-contradictory materials.

On the ground of its peculiar dogmas. Of these the leading ones have already been noticed; and it is needless to repeat how repugnant they are to reason and conscience—how derogatory to the character of God—and how subversive of the best interests and hopes of man.

The following are some of the arguments which might be used to convince its adherents of the truth of Christianity:—

On the ground of mere reason, the External Evidences of Christianity may be urged on all *really educated* Vedantists, with resistless, or, at any rate, unanswerable effect.

Having pointed out their desolate view of the divine character, next show how beautiful God appears in the Scriptures, as a God of Love, and of compassion to the guilty. Perhaps there is no attribute of the Divine Being, more likely to touch the heart than that of his love.

Having shewn their want of a moral standard by which actions are to be tried, shew the excellency of the Decalogue, particularly as explained by our Lord. Ram Mohun Roy felt that in this at least Christianity was superior to Vedantism. If willing to take this, shew them that they must take the whole.

After having shewn that man is a sinner, and that the Vedant system furnishes no adequate atonement for sin, shew that the Christian system furnishes one as great as our sins, and as extensive as our wants ;—an atonement by which God can consistently with his holiness, justice and righteous government, forgive the sins of the greatest offender, and grant him grace to walk in newness of life. How superior to imperfect works !

After pointing out in what way their system fills the mind with pride and arrogance, shew how the Christian system promotes the deepest humility, by leading us to consider ourselves not as gods, but as creatures—insignificant creatures, sinful, helpless and miserable creatures ; and by presenting to us the bright example of him who, though he thought it not robbery to be equal with God, yet made himself of no reputation.

After having shewn how devoid their system is of motives, point out the powerful motives of the Gospel ;—a God to glorify, a soul to save, a Saviour to honor, a neighbour to profit, a hell to avoid, a heaven to obtain, and grace promised for the accomplishment of all these great objects.

After proving how destitute their system leaves the soul of comfort in trouble and in death, point out the great consolations of the Gospel. Here all things work for good, and fit for a far more exceeding and eternal weight of glory.

Having shown how absurd the notion is of being absorbed, and losing the consciousness of existence, even if it could be attained, point out the superior state of immortality and eternal life in the presence of that God in whose presence there is life, and at whose right hand there are pleasures for ever more.

Having directed them to their unsocial and cruel mode of seeking absorption, shew them that the yoke of Christ is easy, and His burden is light. The end is glorious and the way plain and easy. Not that the Gospel exempts from self-denial, mortification of the flesh, and deadness to the world ; but teaches how to attend to these without literally abandoning the world, and, while attending to them, to look forward to the recompense of reward.

Such are some of the arguments by which a Vedantist may be encountered, and if they are urged with calmness and affection, there is reason to believe they will not be entirely without effect.

Why should subjects—subjects, fraught with such tremendous importance for weal or for woe—ever be taken up in the spirit of *mere partizanship,* or *narrow-minded sectarianism ?* It is not surely of the nature of a game, which one may take up for sport, or exercise, or the display of dexterity. The arguments of particular men, on the one side or on the other, may be feeble and futile, and yet this may indicate nothing as to the inherent goodness or badness of their cause ;—it may only prove the ignorance, the presumption, or the unskilfulness of the champion. How often is the detection of a fallacy mistaken for the discovery of a truth! How often is an honest but intemperate zeal the prolific source of all manner of fallacies! It is not by the logic of the schools—the subtile hair-splitting dialectics, whether of Aristotle or of Gautama— that great moral and religious questions are ever to be settled. The real seat of all opposition to conviction, in the higher departments of moral and religious truth, is not the *head* but the *heart.* Once conquer, restrain, or regulate the biasses, predilections, and impetuous desires of the latter, and the former will cheerfully follow in the train of rational evidence, wherever it is to be found, and to whatever goal it may legitimately lead.

☞ There are some, to whose judgment, on many points, we would implicitly defer, who may be disposed to regard the insertion of the foregoing article as *out of place* in the pages of the *Calcutta Review*. On this point, however, we cannot surrender our own deliberately formed judgment and resolve. We must, therefore, in the true spirit of liberal candour and mutual forbearance, make up our minds to agree to differ. Our original, and still unaltered, design, was not a limited or circumscribed one—but wide and all-comprehensive. Our projected work was not to be exclusively or mainly political or religious, literary or scientific, civil or military, topographical or statistical, judicial or commercial, entertaining or grave:—it was, on suitable occasions and in due proportions, to be *all of these together.* It was intended to embrace the discussion and elucidation of every subject, which, directly or indirectly would tend to excite, increase, or perpetuate an interest in Indian affairs, and, thereby, in any way, help to accelerate the progress of Indian amelioration. In the present circumstances of India, it is plainly impossible to secure the desiderated *variety* of articles for *every* number; but what is wanting in one, will be supplied in another ; so that overspreading a series of numbers will be found a diversity of papers fairly embracing topics in every leading department of interest or utility. Such was the conception of the general plan which we originally formed to ourselves; and such is the plan we are determined to pursue still. The steady increase, alike in the number of our regular subscribers and regular contributors, is an unmistakeable proof that the plan has sufficiently commended itself to the judgment of an intelligent and reflecting community. Those friends, therefore,—constituting we doubt not a very small minority,—who, in their zeal for our welfare and success, suggest the propriety of omitting a certain class of articles altogether, must excuse us for being better acquainted with our own original plans and intentions than they can possibly be—and for resolving stedfastly to cherish these intentions, and unwaveringly to prosecute these plans, in the time to come. Jokes and jibes and jeers, together with the application of any epithets which may readily be drawn from the hacknied vocabulary of illiberal cant, are alike lost upon us. We can well afford complacently to smile at these and such-like. As Calcutta Reviewers we stand on our own footing—quite independent of every existing branch of the local press. We know no envies; we feel no jealousies; we cherish no rivalries. Our earnest wish is to contribute our humble share towards upholding the respectability, the decency, and the dignity of the Indian press—a press, which, whatever be its faults and shortcomings, has heretofore rendered essential service to the country, and is destined hereafter to render increasingly still more—a press, too, which has double claims on the generous and the just, from the mere circumstance of its having been treated, in high places and by high personages, with so much of undeserved obloquy and reproach. Should any of our labours meet with the approbation of our cotemporaries, we shall rejoice in their expressions of friendly feeling and good will; if the contrary should be the case, we shall endeavour meekly to profit by any admonition or reproof which may have any thing real or valid for its foundation. Every genuine friend of India we shall hail as our friend ; and we shall know no enemies, except those who may be the enemies of truth, purity, and righteousness.

ART. III.—1. *Traité de Géodésie, ou exposition des Méthodes trigonométriques et astronomiques, applicable soit à la mesure de la terre, soit à la confection des canevas des cartes et des plans topographiques ; par L. Puissant, Chevalier de l' ordre Royal et Militaire de St. Louis, &c.—Paris* 1819.

2. *Méthodes Analytiques pour la détermination d' un arc du Meridien ; par J. B. J. Delambre, Membre de l' Institut National et du bureau des Longitudes, &c. &c., précédées d' un Mémoire sur le même sujet, par A. M. Legendre, membre de la Commission des poids et mesures de l' Institut National.—Paris, An. VII.*

3. *An account of the measurement of an arc of the Meridian between the parallels of* 18° 3' *and* 24° 7', *being a continuation of the grand meridional Arc of India, as detailed by the late Lieutenant-Colonel Lambton, in the volumes of the Asiatic Society of Calcutta; by Captain George Everest, of the Bengal Artillery, F. R. S., &c.—London* 1830.

4. *Geometrical Theorems and Analytical formulæ, with their application to the solution of certain geodetical problems, by William Wallace, L. L. D. Emeritus Professor of Mathematics in the University of Edinburgh, &c. &c.—Edinburgh* 1839.

THERE is much of truth in a common proverbial saying, that one half of mankind is unacquainted with the other half. This is not more true regarding those portions of the human family that are farthest separated from each other in local habitation, than in respect of those who, though dwelling side by side, are separated and disjoined from each other by differences of rank and station, differences of opinion and motive, or differences of intellectual habits. We have heard of a Princess of the blood royal, who, on being told that many people, during a period of scarcity, were dying of starvation, declared that she thought them very foolish to permit themselves to die from such a cause ; for her own part, rather than die of hunger, she would even live on bread and cheese ! We have heard too of a man, who being asked how he thought Astronomers could predict eclipses, declared that nothing could be more simple—they had only to look in the Almanac ! These are extreme cases, and may, perhaps, be referred to extreme thoughtlessness, rather than to extreme ignorance ; but it cannot possibly be questioned that there does exist, in every class of every community, a great amount of ignorance regarding the habits and pursuits of all the other classes. To break down the barriers that thus dissever the different sections of the human family, and to excite in the breast of each a kindly and generous sympathy with the hopes and fears, the joys and sorrows, the successes and disappoint-ments of all, is one of the blessed effects that may be expected from that general diffusion of sound knowledge by which the present age is so distinguished. Unquestionably it is the will of Him " who has made of one blood all generations of men to dwell in all places on the earth," and who has linked the various classes of Society together by mutual interests and obligations and dependencies,—that such a generous and intel-ligent sympathy should exist among those whom he has thus made brothers in the same family, and fellow-workers in the same service.

Perhaps there are no two classes of men who are less acquainted with each other, who know less of each other's ends and objects, difficulties and perplexities, hopes, fears and feelings, than the mathematical and the non-mathematical portion of the commu-nity. Speak to the generality of men about a mathematician, and immediately there rises up before them the image of a wretched parchment-skinned old man, in the world but not of it, dissociated from all the concerns that interest his fellow-mortals, and spending his days and nights in vain attempts to trisect an angle and to square the circle, to do that in one par-ticular way which every carpenter does a hundred times in a day without any difficulty in another, looking with an eye of scorn on all the pursuits of the working world, and despising the finest productions of human intellect and taste, because he does not see what they are meant to demonstrate! It is ever thus, that men will ply the pencil of the carica-turist in sketching those whom they do not know. Thus the merchant will be described as a man whose whole soul is in his ledger, whose affections are all concentred in " another and another lakh ;" the lawyer is pictured as a compound of prece-dents, and *rules nisi*, and *certiorari ;* and every class is conceived of by every other with reference only to those singular excep-tions in whom the peculiarities of the class are ridiculously prominent. There have undoubtedly been triflers in mathe-matics, as well as in other pursuits ; but it is a grievous mistake to suppose that mathematical studies, even of the most abstract kind, are necessarily destitute of a direct bearing upon the ordinary interests and concerns of man. Lord Bacon, who did more than any other man to render the sciences practical, seems fully to have understood the important connexion that subsists between the cultivation of abstract mathematical science and the progress of mankind in practical science. Not to mention the multitudes of passages in his philosophical writings, we may quote a letter to the Marquess of Buckingham, in which he states his conviction that the foundation of the Savilian and Sandisian Professorships of Geometry was of more importance than the foundation of Dulwich Hospital. The letter is as follows :

" *To the Marquess of Buckingham.*

" My very good Lord. I thank your Lordship for your last loving letter. I now write to give the king an account of a patent I have stayed at the office. It is of license to give in mortmain eight hundred pound land, though it be tenure in chief, to Allen, that was the player, for an hospital. I like well that Allen playeth the last act of his life so well ; but if his majesty give way thus to amortize his tenures, his courts of wards will decay : which I had well hoped should improve.

" But that which moved me chiefly is, that his majesty now lately did absolutely deny Sir Henry Savile for 200*l.*, and Sir Edward Sandys for 100*l.* to the perpetuation of two lectures, the one in Oxford, the other in Cambridge ; foundations of singular honour to his majesty, the best learned of kings, and of which there is great want ; whereas hospitals abound and beggars abound never a whit the less.

" If his majesty do like to pass the book at all ; yet if he would be pleased to abridge the 800*l.* to 500*l.* and then give way to the other two books for the university, it were a princely work. And I would make an humble suit to the king and desire your Lordship to join in it that it might be so. God ever preserve and prosper you.

" Your Lordship's most obliged friend and faithful servant,

" FR. VERULAM, *Canc.*

York House, August 18, 1618.

" I have written to my Lord Chamberlain, being Chancellor of Oxford, to help in the business."

We find also in his will that Lord Bacon designed the endowment of two professorships on the model of the Savilian Professorship. The following is an extract from his will :—

" And because I conceive there will be upon the moneys, raised by sale of my lands, leases, goods and chattels, a good round surplusage, over and above that which may serve to satisfy my debts and legacies and perform my will ; I do desire and declare that my executors shall employ the said surplusage in manner and form following ; that is to say that they purchase therewith so much land of inheritance as may create and endow two lectures in either the Universities, one of which lectures shall be of natural philosophy and the sciences in general thereunto belonging ; hoping that the stipend or salaries of the lecturers may amount to two hundred pounds a year for either of them ; and for the ordering of the said lectures, and the election of lecturers from time to time, I leave it to the care of my Executors to be established by the advice of the Lords Bishops of Lincoln, and Coventry and Litchfield.

Nevertheless thus much I do direct, that none shall be lecturer, if he be English, except he be master of Arts of seven years' standing, and that he be not professed in divinity, law or physic, as long as he remains lecturer; and that it be without difference, whether he be a stranger or English; and I wish my Executors to consider of the precedent of Sir Henry Savil's lectures for their better instruction."

We regard these extracts, (especially the former) from the incidental writings of the great father of practical utilitarian philosophy, as most valuable testimonies to the importance of the study of pure demonstrative science, and as furnishing a rebuke to those multitudes who believe that they are treading in the footsteps of Bacon when they decry the study of pure mathematics as a remnant of scholastic trifling.

To the enlightened advocates of practical philosophy it is not difficult to shew that a science which brings man into contact with the eternal relations of things, which brings us back to the principles on which the universe is constructed, and which must ever be the director of observation in regard to the actually existing universe, cannot be a useless study if judiciously cultivated. Neither should it be difficult to convince the man who is accustomed to observe and analyse the workings of the mind, that so far from dissociating their devotee from the rest of the world, mathematical studies are best of all fitted for cultivating those talents and accomplishments which enable a man to attract and please and instruct his fellows. It may seem a somewhat startling affirmation, but we are persuaded it is true, that the imagination is the faculty which the mathematician is called chiefly to exercise. We speak not of course of the mere *learner of mathematics,* who can merely make himself master, by an effort, of a proposition of which the demonstration is put before him. We do not regard *him* as a mathematician at all. At the best he stands in the same relation towards the true mathematician in which the brick-layer stands towards the architect. He may doubtless discharge all his functions without a particle of imagination. But mathematical invention is effected by forming in the mind new combinations, by so tracing relations and connexions as to be able intuitively to detect the bearings of a demonstrated truth upon other subjects than those regarding which it is demonstrated; and this we suppose is just as much an exercise of the imagination as is that put forth by the poet or the painter.

But we despair of being able to convince the generality

K

of readers, by taking them into the study of the mathematician, that he is or can be any thing but a being poring over diagrams and tables, and puzzling his brains over imaginary difficulties. We therefore propose not to enter into the study of the recluse, but rather to bring him out into the wide world, and shew him engaged in one of those works which he only is able to accomplish, in order that our readers may see that he is capable of entering with effect into the business which men regard as useful and important to them. Of all the practical works that are accomplished by the *direct* application of mathematical studies, the two greatest are astronomical and geographical. The latter, or rather one great department of the latter work, is that which is now to occupy our attention; and it is our purpose to give a very rapid view of the object to be accomplished in a trigonometrical survey, and then to make some remarks on the great trigonometrical survey that has for a long time been going on in British India.

The idea of a great Trigonometrical Survey of a country, to be undertaken by the Government of that country, was first conceived by General Watson, at the suppression of the "rising" in Scotland in 1745. The execution of it was committed to General Roy, and was originally intended to extend no farther than the disaffected districts of the Highlands. The design however was subsequently enlarged, and the grand Trigonometrical Survey of Great Britain and Ireland was projected—a Survey that has cost the country an enormous sum of money, which, albeit it has not been paid ungrudgingly, it is yet very creditable to the country to have paid. This Survey, begun just a hundred years ago, has been frequently suspended, but never wholly abandoned; and it is now, we believe, brought within a little of its termination.

This survey has effected much for science in various ways. It was in the course of conducting it, that the real difficulties of the accomplishment were evolved, and the most scientific men in Europe were set to work to overcome them. The extreme accuracy that was required, gave an impulse to the efforts of our instrument-makers, and may be regarded as having given a beginning to the process of improvement in this department, which has advanced so stedfastly ever since, that now we have probably attained almost as near perfection as it is permitted to man to reach. It was in this Survey too, that the great accuracy of the instruments first brought into notice an element that had never been taken account of before, and whose treatment gave occasion to the discovery of some of the most elegant propositions in spherical trigonometry. As this element is a very important one, we shall endeavour to explain its nature in a popular way, so that all may be able to apprehend its nature, and so to form some estimate of the extreme accuracy required, and happily attained, in such works as those in question. Every one knows that the three angles of every plain triangle are equal to two right angles. But this is not so in regard to spherical triangles. If, for example, we look at a common globe, and observe a spherical triangle formed by any arc of the equator, and by two quadrants of meridians, we at once see that the angles at the base of this isosceles spherical triangle are each of them right angles. Their sum therefore is two right angles, and the sum of the three angles of the triangle exceeds two right angles by the whole amount of the vertical angle, or the angle formed by the meridians with each other at the pole. A moment's thought will shew any one that this angle is the same part of four right angles that the portion of the globe's surface, included within the triangle, is of the hemisphere, or bears the same proportion to eight right angles, that the area of the triangle bears to the area of the sphere. Now this, which is evidently true of the particular triangle that we have selected as the simplest for illustration, is true of every spherical triangle. The angles of every such triangle are always together greater than two right angles, and the excess of their sum over two right angles will always be to four right angles, as the area of the triangle to the area of the hemisphere; and this is what geometers call the 'spherical excess.' Now when it is considered how very small a proportion the area of any triangle actually measured on the earth's surface bears to the whole of that surface, it must be evident that the spherical excess must, in all cases, be very small. In the English survey it seldom, or we believe never, exceeds four seconds; and it would, of course, be ridiculous to take such a quantity into account, were the observations not made with a degree of accuracy unknown before.

Perhaps a more important survey in some respects than the British one was that undertaken by the French nation at the period of the Revolution. The reasons which led to the undertaking are highly interesting, and are so germane to our subject that it can hardly be deemed a digression if we briefly state them.

In all ages and in all countries during which and in which a moderate degree of civilization has obtained, it has been felt to be a matter of great importance, as well as of considerable difficulty, to ascertain a uniform standard of measure, which may be easily verified and tested when necessary. The breadth of the human thumb, and that of the human hand, the length of the human foot, of the fore-arm, of the arm, and of the distance to which a man can stretch with his extended arms, have been adopted, probably in every country, as rudimental standards; and have given rise to measures corresponding to the *inch*, the *hand*, the *cubit*, the *yard* and the *fathom*. Then in larger measures we have the distance that a camel can travel in a day, and, as a measure of surface, the quantity of land that a yoke of oxen can plough. Now it is with these measures as it is with human language. *Plerumque ex captu vulgi induntur, atque per lineas, vulgari intellectui maxime conspicuas, res secant. Quum autem intellectus acutior, aut observatio diligentior, eas lineas transferre velit, ut illæ sint magis secundum naturam, verba obstrepunt.** As the stature of man and the developement of the several members of his body vary very considerably, it is evident that the measures thus ascertained cannot be regarded otherwise than as rude approximations, which may serve well enough for the ordinary purposes of half-civilized life, but are quite unfit for accurate, and especially for philosophical purposes. Accordingly we find that, just as the meanings of words are fixed down from time to time by definitions of encreasing accuracy, so the standards of measure have been attempted to be reduced to greater accuracy from time to time. For example the *inch* having been found to be about equal in length to three grains of barley, this came to be fixed upon as its standard length. This of course is but a clumsy correction, and some might suppose that it was rather a retrogression than an advance in the march of accuracy. As there is a principle involved in the matter which will perhaps be of some use to us in the sequel, we shall take the liberty of devoting a sentence or two to the exposition of the rationale of it. The length of a barley-corn is doubtless as variable as the breadth of a man's thumb or the length of his foot. Indeed it may be expected to be much more so, inasmuch as the developement of the human body takes place during a long period, and consequently the influences that affect it, being extended over many years, are more likely to give a uniform average result than those that affect the growth of a crop of corn, which is perfected in a single season, and the size of whose grains must be modified by countless varieties of soil, climate and exposure. How then can it be said that the length of three barley-corns is more likely to be

* "Words are generally imposed according to vulgar conceptions, and divide things by lines that are most apparent to the understanding of the multitude; and when a more acute understanding, or a more careful observation, would remove these lines, to place them according to nature, words cry out and forbid it."—*Bacon's Novum Organum, Aph.* 59.

uniform than the breadth of a man's thumb? Simply because the average of *three* is more likely to be uniform than any *one*, however selected. Accordingly we believe it will be found that if thirty-six grains of barley be taken at random from a well-winnowed heap, and extended end to end in a straight line, and then thirty-six others be taken and extended in the same way along-side of the former line, the difference of length of the two lines will be very small indeed. We have heard that some of the Arab tribes have improved upon this method of correcting their measures, by greatly diminishing the length of the standard, and consequently encreasing the number of times that the standard must be taken in order to measure any considerable length. It is said that their standard is tested by laying a certain number of hairs taken from a horse's tail alongside of each other. Now although we do not doubt that the thickness of a horse's hair varies quite as much in proportion as the length of a grain of barley or the breadth of a man's thumb, yet it is probable that the united breadth of any thousand of such hairs, especially if taken from the tails of several horses, will differ very little indeed from the united breadth of any other thousand hairs similarly selected. This method we suppose must have been handed down from the days when the mathematical sciences flourished in Arabia.

But it is very evident that none of these methods would at all suffice for the construction of measures sufficiently accurate for the purposes of advanced science. In every country where science has made any considerable progress, there must be a standard measure, made with consummate exactness, and preserved with the greatest possible care, by which those measures made for ordinary use may be tested. Now if we possessed any material which was perfectly indestructible and unalterable by the progress of time, the friction of use and the variations of temperature, the actual length of this standard would be a matter of perfect indifference. Any one length would be quite as good as any other. All that would be necessary, would be arbitrarily to assume a particular length, and to give to it a particular name, to divide it in the most convenient manner, and to adhere fixedly to its length as a standard. But as all the materials within our reach are variable and perishable, it becomes necessary to have some mode of verifying the standard itself, in order that it may be with perfect confidence relied on as the instrument of verification for all the other measures. Such verification of the grand standard must evidently be derived from some great natural element, which may be assumed as invariaable.* Two such elements have been suggested by mathematicians as the basis of a standard of length. It was proposed, we believe by Huyghens, that the length of the pendulum which vibrates seconds in any particular latitude, as for example in the latitude of 45°, or half way between the equator and the pole, should be adopted as the standard unit of measure.† The other standard proposed is that of the length of some of the great lines that might be drawn through the earth's centre, or of one of the great curves that might be drawn over its surface; as the equatoreal or polar radius, or any other radius of the earth, or the equatoreal circumference of the earth, which may be regarded as a circle, or any of the meridians on the globe, which approach very nearly to ellipses.

It is evident that the adoption of a new standard of measurement cannot be effected without considerable inconvenience; the conservative principle is so very strong in the minds of the multitude in regard to those things that have to do with their daily and hourly habits. However certain classes of politicians may tell us that change in itself is neither good nor bad, but that change from a better to a worse is evil, while change from evil to better is good, the multitude will generally declare, in regard to those things, that change is always in itself an evil, or at least is always attended with various evils. Accordingly it is only in periods when men are in the spirit of change, when the stability of things is broken up for a time, that even improvements can be easily introduced. Such a period was that of the French Revolution, when the foundations of all things seemed to totter as with a fearful earthquake, when all social and civil institutions were overturned, and men's minds were so unhinged that they preferred adopting any thing that was recommended by novelty, rather than remaining satisfied with the things that had the sanction of usage. We presume our readers are aware that at an early stage of that fearful period, the philosophers of France undertook to introduce a great reformation in regard to

---

* We are not entitled to conclude that any of the grand elements of our system are absolutely invariable. It is very possible that the radius and circumference of the earth for example may be subject either to fluctuations or to permanent changes. But if such changes do take place, their period must be so long, as to set us free from any danger of their discomposing our standard during any moderately long period.

† This may be the proper place to remark, in case any of our readers should be ignorant of the fact, that it is quite sufficient to ascertain a fixed standard of lineal measure, all the other standards being made dependent on it. The unit of superficial measure is of course a square, whose side is the ascertained unit of lineal measures, that of solid content or measure of capacity, a cube whose edge is the said lineal unit; while the unit of weight may be fixed at the weight of such a quantity of pure or distilled water at a given temperature, as shall just fill the unit of solid content.

all those habits and usages of men which have reference to numbers. Every thing was to be numbered by tens, hundreds, thousands, &c. Lengths, areas, moneys, weights, periods of times, arcs of circles, every thing that was numerable, was to be numbered by tens. We may here remark by the way, as has been remarked before in substance by Professor Playfair, that if they had carried their spirit of reform a step farther, and had abandoned the decimal notation altogether, and adopted in its stead the duodecimal, they would probably have succeeded in gaining a footing for the innovation much better than they have actually succeeded. We know no reason why we should count by *tens*, except that we have been endowed by our Creator with ten fingers; and although this might be a very good reason for the original adoption of the decimal notation when men used their fingers as account books, it seems a very insufficient reason for retaining it in these times, when every man and woman is in every civilized country taught the elements of accounts. But there is a very obvious reason why a duodecimal notation should be preferred to the decimal. It is simply this, that the number *twelve* is divisible without a remainder by no less than four other numbers, whereas *ten* is so divisible only by two. It is somewhat remarkable that this consideration did not weigh with the revolutionary philosophers to adopt the duodecimal notation and division: and we are afraid we must conclude, though the conclusion be little to the credit of science, that they were led to decline this system by the very consideration that ought to have induced them to adopt it—to wit that its preferableness had led the common sense of mankind to adopt it in a great number of instances in the division of their standards, (as among the English the shilling consists of 12 pence, the pound of 12 ounces, the year of 12 months, and the circle of the Zodiac of 12 signs, the average day and night of 12 hours each,) notwithstanding the obstacles that were thrown in the way by the decimal scale of numbers. But be this as it may, it formed part of the meditated reform to introduce a new standard of measure, whose basis should be some grand unalterable line, and which should be divided and multiplied according to the powers and reciprocal powers of 10. The question then came to be, what should be adopted as the basis of this standard, which was designed not only for France, but for the world. "The fixing on a national and universal standard of measure, (says Professor Playfair,) and the abolition of the present diversity of weights and measures, was an object that very early drew the attention of the Constituent Assembly. It was proposed in that assembly by M. de Talleyrand, and decreed accordingly, that the

King should be entreated to write to his Britannic Majesty, to engage the Parliament of England to concur with the National Assembly in fixing a natural unit of weights and measures; that under the auspices of the two nations, an equal number of Commissioners from the Academy of Sciences and the Royal Society of London might unite in order to determine the length of the pendulum in the latitude of 45°, or in any other latitude that might be thought preferable, and to deduce from them an invariable standard of measures and of weights. This decree passed in August 1790. The Academy named a Commission, composed of Borda, Lagrange, Laplace, Monge and Condorcet; and their report is printed in the Memoirs of the Academy for 1788, (Published 1791). Three different units fell under the consideration of these Philosophers; to wit, the length of the pendulum, the quadrant of the Meridian, and the quadrant of the Equator. If the first of these was to be adopted, the Commissioners were of opinion that the pendulum vibrating seconds in the parallel of 45°, deserved the preference, because it is the arithmetical mean between the like pendulums in all other latitudes. They observed however that the pendulum involves an element which is heterogeneous, to wit *time*, and another which is arbitrary, to wit, the division of the day into 86,400 seconds. It seemed to be better that the unit of length should not depend on a quantity, of a kind different from itself, nor on any thing that was arbitrarily assumed."* These reasons for rejecting the length of the pendulum, and preferring the length of a quadrant of the meridian, are certainly quite insufficient. It must have been a matter of utter indifference to the man who bought a *metre* of tape for shoe-ties, whether the length with which he was served were equal to that of a pendulum that at a certain place would vibrate 3,600 *times* in an hour, or whether it were a 40-millionth part of a line that would stretch all round the earth, passing through both poles! For the purpose in view, the pendulum would questionably have been a far better standard; it could have been verified at any time, with a moderate amount of labor; and a verification could even have been made at any place, the length of the seconds pendulum in any latitude being easily deduced from its ascertained length in any other latitude. It is impossible that these and many other considerations should not have occurred to the French mathematicians as favoring the adoption of the pendulum for the standard, rather than the quadrant of the meridian; we are therefore very

* Edinburgh Review, vol. IX., and Playfair's Works, vol. IV.

strongly inclined to suspect that they made this ascertainment of a metrical standard a mere pretext for procuring the means of accomplishing a most desirable object, the measurement of an arc of the meridian. If they had told the people that this measurement would enable them to determine with greater accuracy the size and figure of the earth, and to ascertain with greater precision the latitudes and longitudes of places on its surface, they would probably have been met with the question, *cui bono ?* But when they gave out that they were to regulate the length of a yard of ribbon, and the size of a pint of wine, every man saw that the object was a good one, and gave it his hearty suffrage. If we be right in this conjecture, it is certainly very humiliating to think that one of the most important admeasurements of a great arc of the Meridian should have been achieved by means of what might have been called in the dark ages "a pious fraud;" humiliating that the projectors of it should have been willing to resort to such an expedient, and humiliating that such an expedient should have been necessary in order to attain the object desired.

Be these things as they may, the French Commissioners proceeded with vigour to the execution of their task, which, though laborious, was to them doubtless a labour of love. The arc selected was more than nine and a half degrees in length, extending from Dunkirk to Barcelona. The measurement of this arc was committed to MM. Mechain and De Lambre. They began their labours in 1792, and prosecuted them with the greatest assiduity and success, notwithstanding that they met with much opposition from the ignorant and excited peasantry, who, like all uncivilized men, put the worst possible construction on what they could not understand. It was indeed a "pursuit of knowledge under difficulties," and De Lambre was many times in imminent danger of his life.

It is not consistent with our plan, or with the exclusive orientalism prescribed for all the articles that appear in these pages, to give any detailed account of this Survey. We only note a few of the particulars in which the mode of operation, and some of the results deduced from the measurement, differed from those of the great Indian Survey, which is the main object of our present dissertation.

We may state, however, that the instruments employed, both for measuring the altitudes of stars for the purpose of ascertaining the positions of the stations, and for measuring the angles of the terrestrial triangles, were four Borda's repeating circles, made by Lenoir, an instrument-maker of great celebrity, and whose work seems to have done full justice to his reputation.

L

Two bases were measured, one at Melun by De Lambre, and the other at Perpigan by Mechain. They were each about 7 miles long, and it is one proof of the accuracy of the whole survey, that though they were 436 miles apart, yet the lengths of each, as estimated by triangulation from the other, did not differ from its measured length by more than 10 or 12 feet.

The result of the measurement gave the compression of the earth's poles $\frac{1}{334}$ part, or in other words, the earth's polar diameter was found to be to the equatoreal as 333 : 334.

It is, after all, the determination of the figure and size of the earth that is the great object to be attained by the measurement of an arc of the meridian, which always forms the main part of a Trigonometrical Survey. If the earth were a sphere, or a spheroid, or any regular figure, it would be sufficient to measure one long arc, and to ascertain the latitudes of various stations throughout its length; but it is found that the earth, though nearly an oblate spheroid, is not accurately so. Its figure is not regular; and therefore, in order to get a knowledge of its size and figure, it is necessary to know the lengths of degrees of latitude in all parts of its surface. The more such arcs are measured therefore, and the farther they are distant from one another, the more nearly will our knowledge of this important geographical element approach to accuracy. Accordingly, ever since the perfect accuracy of geographical knowledge began to be appreciated, it has been a grand object with scientific geographers to have as many arcs measured, and in as distant places, as possible. A clear - summary of all that has been done in this matter is presented by Professor Airy, in his report on astronomy presented to the British Association in 1832. This gives such a clear statement of the whole matter that we shall take the liberty to lay it entire before our readers:

" The materials upon which a knowledge of the earth's figure was grounded, at the beginning of the century, were the following : The arc measured in Peru by Bouguer, Lacondamine, &c.; that measured in Lapland by Clairaut, Maupertuis, &c. ; that in America by Mason and Dixon, &c. ; that, from Rome to Rimini by Boscovich ; and that from Barcelona to Dunkirk measured by Delambre and Mechain. Besides these there were some others, as one in Piedmont by Beccaria, one in Austria by Liesganig, and one in India by Reuben Burrows, to which little credit was given ; and there was Lacaille's measure at the Cape of Good Hope, which could not be reconciled with the others. One arc of parallel had also been measured in France : and one of much greater value in England. The pendulum experiments (serving, with the help of Clairaut's theorem, to determine the proportion of the earth's axes,) were principally scattered observations by De la Croyère, Campbell, Mairan, Bouguer, Godin, Maupertuis, Lacaille, Legentil, Phipps, Malaspina, and Borda. The last of these (confined to Paris,) were the only ones from which great accuracy could be expected ; of the others, the only set in which a series of considerable geographical extent were observed by the same persons and with the same instrument, was Malaspina's. The observations of the attraction of Schehallien, and Cavendish's experiments with leaden balls, had given a pretty good knowledge of the earth's mean density.

In the years 1801, 1802, 1803, the arc measured in Lapland (which, according to the calculations of Clairaut and Maupertuis, seemed to present a strange anomaly,) was remeasured and extended by Ofverbom, Svanberg, and others, so as to embrace an amplitude exceeding $1\frac{1}{2}$ degree. For the geodesic part, as well as for the astronomical determinations, the new repeating-circle was used. The conclusions at which they arrived differed from those of Maupertuis, and are more in accordance with those given by other measures. But they did not succeed in pointing out the cause of their difference; and, as far as their measures admitted of comparison, they confirmed greatly the accuracy of the former measure. The former measure has lately been much discussed, especially by M. Rosenberger in various numbers of the *Ast. Nachr.*; and the general opinion I think is now, that the first measure was the best, and that its anomaly depended only on the ruggedness of the country. In the *Phil. Trans.* 1803, is an account of the English measure of an arc from the south-eastern part of the Isle of Wight to Clifton in Yorkshire. The bases were measured with Ramsden's steel chain, and the horizontal angles with a large theodolite: the astronomical observations were made with Ramsden's zenith-sector. There is no doubt that, for its length, this was the most accurate arc that had been measured. Yet a point near the middle of this arc presented an anomaly in regard to the direction of gravity. The measure was afterwards extended to Burleigh Moor: and it thus comprehends an arc of nearly four degrees. Two arcs (of which the details are to be found in the *Asiatic Researches*,) were measured by Colonel Lambton in India. The first of these, near Madras, was of $1\frac{1}{2}$ degree: the other, beginning near Cape Comorin, nearly 10 degrees. The latter has lately been extended by Captain Everest, to nearly 16 degrees. The methods adopted in these measures differ in no respect from those of the English measure: and this arc is undoubtedly the best that has ever been surveyed. The French arc from Dunkirk to Barcelona has been extended by Biot and Arago to the little island Formentera in the Mediterranean (near Iviza), and its whole length is now nearly $12\frac{1}{2}$ degrees. Of the excellence of the geodetic part of this there is no doubt; but there seems some reason to doubt the goodness of the astronomical determinations, though no labour was spared by the observers. The account of this forms a conclusion to the *Base du Système Métrique*. The Piedmontese arc of Beccaria has been remeasured with much care by Plana and Carlini: and the account is published in the *Operations Géodésiques et Astronomiques en Piémont et Savoie*. It is clearly proved that the astronomical part of Beccaria's measure was erroneous: but the result of MM. Plana and Carlini's measure is still anomalous; perhaps not more so than the form of the country would lead us to expect. I may mention here that Zach, in the *Monatliche Correspondenz* and in the *Correspondence Astronomique*, has shown clearly that Leisganig's measure is worth nothing. An arc has been measured by Gauss from Gottingen to Altona, of 2 degrees; the astronomical observations being made with Ramsden's zenith-sector; some accounts of it will be found in the *Ast. Nachr.*, and in a small work entitled *Bestimmung des Breitenunterscheides*, &c. An arc of $3\frac{1}{2}$ degrees has been measured by Struve, the northern extremity being on an island in the Gulf of Finland. In many parts of this operation, new instruments and new methods have been used: in particular, for the determination of the latitudes, great reliance was placed on the method of observing stars with a transit instrument whose motion is confined to the prime vertical : accounts of the measure are in the *Astronomische Nachrichten*. The distance on the arc of parallel between Dover and Falmouth having been ascertained in the course of the English survey, and difference of longitude between them being determined, by Dr. Tiarks, by the transportation of chronometers, the length of an arc of parallel for one degree in a definite latitude is found, and this determination assists much in the determining the earth's figure. But a far longer arc of parallel has been measured on the Continent, from Marennes (near Bordeaux) to Padua. The geodesic part of this measure had been nearly completed by the French Government, while the country was in their possession ; all that was wanting was to connect the surveys on opposite sides of the Alps. This was effected (though not without difficulty,) by Austrian and Sardinian officers. It was then necessary to determine the difference of longitude of the extremities. This was done by dividing the arc into six portions, in each of which a point could be found visible at both its extremities, and observing at each extremity the absolute time at which small quantities of gunpowder were fired at the middle point. The French part was undertaken by M M. Nicollet and Brousseau ; the rest by M M. Plana and Carlini. The result thus obtained is perhaps liable to considerable doubt, as the errors of all the different observations are accumulated. It is unfortunate that the difference of longitude of the extremities has not been determined without any intermediate determination.

The above, as far as I am aware, are all the measures that have actually been made within the present century. But there are others to which we may look as not far distant. The survey of Ireland that has lately been and is now going forward, is, I suppose, in accuracy and in excellence of arrangement, (I am not speaking of the minutiæ of the map, but of the principal triangles, by which the great distances north and south, or east and west are to be measured,) superior to every preceding survey. Little is now wanting for the measure of an arc of meridian but the observation of zenith-distances of stars at its extremities. The country is also favorable for the measuring an arc of parallel of considerable extent : and a new method of producing intense light, introduced into practice by one of the gentlemen employed on the survey, will probably give the means of determining the differences of longitude on a long arc without the errors produced by intermediate stations. It is also understood that our Government have long contemplated the repetition or extension of Lacaille's measure at the Cape of Good Hope : and several circumstances lead me to hope that this undertaking, which would perhaps contribute more than any other to our knowledge of the earth's figure, will ere long be seriously taken up. The extension of Struve's arc is in contemplation."

We have searched in vain for any information regarding the arc said to have been measured by Mr. Reuben Burrows, and are almost driven to suppose, although it is exceedingly unlikely that Professor Airy should have made a mistake on the subject, that he had been misinformed. Mr. Burrows did make many observations of latitudes and longitudes of places in Bengal, and these he says were more accurate than any others previously determined. A list of them is published in the Asiatic Researches, and various articles by Mr. Burrows himself, are contained in that noble collection. This makes it likely that if ever he had attempted such a work as the measurement of an arc of the Meridian, we should have found there the details of the operations. But neither there, nor in the Gleanings of Science, nor in the Asiatic Society's Journal, have we been able to find the slightest allusion to any such work. Besides, we do not believe that there were in all India at that time any instruments with which one could have thought of attempting an operation of so great difficulty and delicacy. In the absence then of any information on the subject, we think it most probable that Mr. Burrows had made a proposal that an arc should be measured in India, and that Mr. Airy, through inadvertence, supposed that it had actually been accomplished.

We must, therefore, in the present state of our information, regard Col. (then Brigade Major) Lambton, as the actual originator of the grand Trigonometrical Survey of India. The manner of its origination was not unlike that in which the Scottish survey was begun. It was at the conclusion of the war with Tippoo Sahib, that Lambton proposed to survey part of the territory that had been conquered; and especially to throw a series of triangles across from Madras to the opposite coast, and so to determine the latitudes and longitudes of many important places, which were understood to be very erroneously determined in the survey executed by the laborious Colonel MacKenzie. Lambton's plan was first submitted to Colonel Wellesley, in whose regiment he had formerly served; and he, as every one would expect, at once caught hold of the benefits to be gained, and the difficulties that would have to be encountered, and seems to have resolved to leave no stone unturned, but to get the work accomplished. He sent up the proposal to Government, with his earnest recommendation that it should be acceded to, and most probably he had also privately used his influence with his brother, the Governor-General; for we find him in correspondence with Lord Clive, the Governor of Madras, on the subject.

The history of the proceedings, in regard to the commencement of the Survey, is not quite accurately given by Colonel Everest in his work now under review; and it will be necessary for us first to quote a passage from the work, and then to make a few remarks regarding it:

"In the commencement of the great Trigonometrical Survey in 1799, under my predecessor, one steel chain by Ramsden was the only measuring apparatus, (Vide As. Res., Vol. VII. p. 321.) The history of this was rather singular. It had been sent with Lord Macartney's embassy as a present to the Emperor of China, and having been refused by that potentate, it was made over by his Lordship to the Astronomer, Dr. Dinwiddie, who brought it to Calcutta for sale, together with the Zenith Sector, (a beautiful instrument *for that time* by Ramsden). The purchase of both was made by Lord Clive, the Governor of Madras, at the instance of the Earl of Mornington,

Governor-General of India; and by the recommendation of Sir Arthur Wellesley, who commanded the 33d Regiment of Foot, Lieutenant William Lambton, then a subaltern in that Regiment, was first drawn from obscurity, and placed in the situation for which he was so eminently qualified. Amidst the blaze of glory which has since encircled the brow of his Grace the Duke of Wellington, the small but steady light which is emitted from so trifling a gem can hardly be deemed deserving of notice; but the time may yet come, when it will add in some wise even to the renown of the hero of Waterloo, to have been the patron of one of the most illustrious geodists that ever lived, and of one of the most important meridional measurements that have ever been undertaken."

With the sentiment expressed in the concluding sentence of this extract we do most heartily concur; but as we have stated, the account of the facts is not quite correctly given by our author. Lambton was not at this period a subaltern in the 33rd Regiment. He had previously to this been appointed Brigade Major to the King's troops under the presidency of Fort St. George. In fact he seems never to have done duty with his Regiment in India at all. He had been barrack-master in the province of New Brunswick, and during his absence his regiment had come to India; almost immediately after joining it in Calcutta, Lambton was appointed by Sir Alured Clarke to the office just mentioned. It does not seem that he ever knew Col. Wellesley until he was his fellow-passenger from Calcutta to Madras: and it is said that, during the voyage and after their arrival at Madras, Lambton was sadly chagrined by the inattention which he supposed that he suffered at the hands of the future duke. But it would have been strange if a man of such merit as Lambton could have been so long, (for the voyage was long and stormy) a shipmate of the Duke of Wellington, without his discovering his talents, and being ready when occasion offered to do what he could to render them available to the service of his country. It appears moreover that the instruments were not purchased from Dr. Dinwiddie by Lord Clive at Madras, but that they were bought at Calcutta, probably by Lord Mornington himself, and sent down to Madras.

When they reached Lambton, he found that they were in a wretched state. The telescope of the zenith sector was so rusted that it was impossible to move the tubes for the adjustment of the focus. Far away from all means of procuring the assistance of professional instrument-makers, most other men would have been daunted by such an initial mishap; but Lambton had that genius which seems almost to rejoice in difficulties, for the very pleasure of braving and overcoming them. It is a maxim that we have often heard from the lips of the venerable author of one of the works whose titles stand at the head of this article, (the late Professor Wallace), that *no man can ever be a practical philosopher unless he can bore with a saw, and saw with a gimlet.* If this power of adaptation to circumstances, and fertility of resources, be needful in England, where intelligent professional men are every where at hand, and where the only barrier that the philosopher finds to the employment of their services consists in the difficulty of paying them, how much more necessary must it have been in India, (and in the days when the wealth of Crœsus could not have purchased the services of a workman superior to a common *Mistry*,) where the perpetual *bangs, bangs* (bamboo) must be made to do duty on all occasions. With what kind of saw Lambton bored his holes, and with what kind of gimlet he sawed his bamboos, we do not know, but he succeeded in putting the instrument into working order.

Now here we are going to indulge in a little political reflection, which we suppose will not be reckoned either very original or very profound. When we took occasion a few pages back to discuss the question of the thickness of horses' hairs, we had to refer to the mathematical doctrine of chances, or as it would perhaps be more accurately called, the doctrine of averages. Now it is this doctrine which is, we suppose, at the foundation of the popular political creed, that the government of many is better than the government of one. If we could always get the best and the wisest man in the community for our ruler, then we might expect his rule to be more salutary than that of a multitude composed of men, many of whom are neither good nor wise. Were this possible, then we suppose the sound political creed would be that of the old poet:

Ουκ αγαθον πολυκοιρανιη, εις κοιρανος ιστω,
Εις βασιλευς.

But in practice it would be altogether impossible always to select the wisest and best man as Governor, and the doctrine of averages has been had recourse to, and men have found that the system of πολυκοιρανιη, or the rule of many, although it may not be so good as would be the rule of the one best and wisest man of the many, or of any one above the *average* of wisdom and goodness, is so much better than that of any one man below that average, as to afford the best *chance* or the fairest expectation, of the adoption of salutary measures. Now to the application of this doctrine. If Lord Mornington or Lord Clive, or Colonel Wellesley had been supreme and despotic in the government of India, then the survey would have been accomplished at once ; but if a certain member of the Finance Committee of the Madras Government had been so supreme, then it would never have been accomplished at all.   This sage expressed the sentiment of but too many of his colleagues in office, when he stated that such a survey was utterly unnecessary. On being told that many important places were wrongly laid down in all the existing maps, his answer was, " If I wish to proceed to Seringapatam, I have only to tell the palankeen bearers, and they will find their way to it just as well as if it were ever so accurately placed in the maps." It would perhaps have been too much to expect that a member of a Finance Committee should have been able to understand that a map might be of other uses than to direct a set of palanquin bearers ; but such things as these are very apt to make us feel how little valuable is money in the regard of the all-glorious Governor of the Universe, when He permits it so often to be under the control of such men. " *Buy the truth and sell it not,*" is the counsel of the wise man, but if all traders in this commodity were of the spirit of this man, it would soon become, in mercantile phrase, a *drug* in the market.

All these difficulties were, however, at last surmounted ; and Brigade Major Lambton had full permission granted him by the Court of Directors to proceed to action.   He seems, as soon as he obtained the consent of the Governor-General, to have ordered from home some instruments in addition to those purchased from Dr. Dinwiddie ; but in regard to the early operations there is a confusion in the published accounts, which we have not been able to remove.   This is due to the total absence of dates in Lambton's accounts as published in the Asiatic Researches.   In other respects, we may mention once for all, they are as clear and definite as possible, and afford all the information that could be desired regarding the mode of conducting the Survey.   But the absence of dates is inexcusable in a professedly historical article.   It is quite true the measurements are not in the slightest degree affected by the times at which they were made, but to those, who, like us, seek for information as to the *history* of the work, it is just about as provoking to be unable to assign the *times* at which the work was accomplished, as it would be if, in studying the results of the measurements, we were unable to assign the *places* where the measurements were made ; for what *place* is to geography, that *time* is to history.

We presume our readers are generally acquainted with the great principle of the method adopted in conducting a trigonometrical survey.   For the sake, however, of such as may be very nearly ignorant of the subject, we shall give a very brief sketch of the principles, treating the subject with a view to its being understood by the least learned of our readers. If we have two triangles which have the angles of the one equal severally to those of the other, then we know that whatever proportion any one side of the one triangle bears to the corresponding side of the other, the same proportion does each of the other sides of the one bear to the corresponding side of the other. If then we know all the three sides of one triangle, and if we know one side of another triangle whose angles are severally equal to the angles of the former, we can at once find its other two sides, by a mere question of the rule of three. Now we might have tables to show us the sides of triangles whose angles are of all possible values, and whose one side is of a given length; and such tables we virtually have; for from the tables of sines, tangents and secants, we can at once calculate the sides of a triangle of which we know one side and the angles. If then the earth were a plain surface, a trigonometrical survey would be effected simply thus. We should have to measure with great accuracy as long a line as possible on its surface, and from the extremities of this line we should have to view a station visible from them both, and to observe the angles formed by the measured line with straight lines—(rays of light proceed in straight lines)—joining its extremities with the observed station, and then to calculate the lengths of the sides of the triangle. Thus two other lines would be determined, which we should again make use of as bases; and observing the angles subtended by lines joining their extremities with other stations, we should spread a triangular net-work over the whole country.

Such in very deed a trigonometrical survey is; only as the earth is not a plain surface, but nearly a spherical figure, we have to consider our measured base, not as a straight line, but as an arc of a great circle of the sphere. The lines, however, in which light proceeds to us from the station under observation to the extremities of our base, are straight lines, and therefore we have to reduce them to the curvature of the earth. The sum of the angles of a plane triangle is always equal to two right angles, but this, as we have incidentally stated before, is not the case with the angles of a spherical triangle; and therefore it is not enough that we know *two* angles of such a triangle, as would be sufficient were it a plain triangle, but it is necessary to measure all the three. We might indeed deduce the value of the third angle, by means of the proposition formerly alluded to, regarding the constant proportion that subsists between the area of the triangle, as compared with the whole surface of the sphere, and the excess of the angles over

two right angles ; but it is found much better to measure all
the angles, and to use this theorem as a test or means
of verification ; and this the rather because we do not know
with perfect accuracy the whole area of the surface of the
earth, neither can we know with perfect accuracy the area
of any particular triangle on that surface until we have
actually made the measurements and calculations in question?
But suppose a country actually surveyed according to this
method, a map could not be made from it unless we knew
very accurately the direction of some one line in it with
reference to the points of the heavens.   Thus an astronomical
element is necessarily introduced into a trigonometrical survey ;
—and accordingly in every survey it is of the greatest moment
to determine with extreme precision the direction of one line,
from the ascertainment of which all the other lines are known
at once.   In other words, it is a necessary part of a survey to
draw an accurate meridian line, that is a line which shall
stretch due north and south, or which shall coincide with a great
circle passing through the poles of the earth.   This is effected
by determining exactly the difference of *longitude* of two stations
differing as much as possible in their latitude from each other ;
and this difference of longitude again is determined by the
difference of *time* between the two stations, or in other words,
the arc through which the earth must revolve round her axis
before a heavenly body which is now on the meridian of the
one shall be on the meridian of the other.   Thus we see that
the French academicians, in rejecting the pendulum as the
standard of their measures on account of its involving the heterogeneous element of *time*, really outwitted themselves, since the
very line which they chose could not be even ascertained
without reference to this very element.   But we have a shrewd
suspicion, of which we have given a hint before, that the
adjustment of the metrical standard was a mere cloak under
which these philosophers deemed it necessary to cover a good
design.

But there is still another matter to be taken into consideration, and that one of the most important of all.   We have
already seen how simple a matter would be a trigonometrical
survey were the earth a plane surface, and have shewn how the
difficulty is enhanced when we view it not as a plane but as a
sphere.   But then it is not a sphere, or any other regular
geometrical figure ; and the difficulty in passing from a sphere
to a figure that cannot be described by exact geometrical
methods, is, as may be easily supposed, much greater than that
of passing from a plane to a sphere.   Moreover it is not even

accurately known what is the figure of the earth; and it is one of the main objects of a survey to determine this point. And for this purpose the determination not merely of the *direction* of the meridian line, but also of the *lengths* of various portions of it, becomes of the greatest importance, and forms a main part of the work in every great trigonometrical survey. For this purpose the latitudes of various stations along the meridian line must be ascertained with most consummate precision, and the actual distances between these stations calculated with the utmost accuracy, and thus the actual length in miles, yards or feet, corresponding to a degree of latitude in different parts of the world, ascertained.

Suppose then we had to commence a trigonometrical survey of a country, our first object would be to measure a baseline. For this purpose we should select a piece of ground as level as possible, and completely free from all jungle, forest or human structures. We should then have to measure with the most accurate scale that we could find or construct, its exact length;—and here the question arises what kind of rule we should adopt for so important a purpose; for this is truly the base or foundation of the whole operation, and its inaccuracy must be multiplied indefinitely thoughout every portion of the work. Various plans have been recommended. Some have thought that good deal rods, very carefully selected, well coated with varnish, and with varnish also injected into the pores of the wood under a heavy pressure, would sufficiently answer the purpose. This has not however been found to be the case. The French philosophers during some part of their survey used glass rods, but they also from obvious causes were found to be inconvenient. The English surveyors, after testing the various methods, thought a good steel chain sufficiently accurate, and such a chain made by Ramsden was used in the English survey. Precisely similar to their chain was that to which allusion has been made, as having been bought from Dr. Dinwiddie, and used in the Indian survey. We confess that this has always appeared to us the least satisfactory part, or rather almost the only part that is not quite satisfactory, of the whole proceeding. We have not hardihood enough to put our judgment in competition with the judgments and great experience of the distinguished men who conducted the English and the Indian Survey; but we gather courage enough at least to state our own opinion when we reflect that the English surveyors might perhaps not have used the chain, or at least not have trusted exclusively to it, in a country where the changes of temperature are so much more sudden and so much wider in their range than in England.

Moreover we find that the chain, though unquestionably the easiest instrument in use, and possessing great advantages from its great portability, has been abandoned in the Irish Survey. The instrument there made use of is composed of two rods of metal of different degrees of expansibility, joined together in such a way that the distance between two particular points remains fixed and invariable. In fact it is precisely the same in principle with the gridiron pendulum, with which many of our readers are doubtless familiar.*

This must be said however of Col. Lambton, that nothing could exceed the pains he took to gain from his chain the best result that it was capable of affording. As soon as possible, he got a new chain from England, and this he very wisely never allowed to be taken to the field at all, but reserved as a test, whereby that actually used was constantly verified. Dr. Dinwiddie's chain, which was used in the field, seems to have been an excellent one; it was constantly used with what we may almost be permitted to call religious care. When it was to be moved, one man held a link with each hand: a whole troop being thus stationed along the length of the chain, it was on a signal given instantly lifted up throughout its whole length, and its bearers, with measured steps, and without the slightest jerking or shaking, proceeded to move it along. Mean time the supports on which it lay were moved, and as soon as they were properly placed, it was deposited with the same care with which it had been lifted. Its one end being fixed to the precise point that had been the termination of its former resting place, a certain amount of weight was suspended at its other end, so as to give it a definite amount of tension; and thus stretched, its temperature throughout its whole length was accurately observed. These particulars were registered, and thus one length of the chain was measured.

The mode in which the chain was tested from time to time, by the reserve chain and by a brass scale, we shall describe in Col. Everest's own words. It will be observed that he does not quite approve of the method adopted by his predecessor, but continued it for want of a better :—

"At the time of the receipt of the new chain, the standard brass scale three feet in length, by Cary, referred to by Captain Kater in the Philosophical Transactions for 1821, arrived also in India, and the late Lieutenant-Colonel resolved to use this in his future comparisons. But the difficulty of transferring a multiple of one hundred feet to a wall from

* Since the above was in type we have learned that rods precisely similar to those used in the Irish survey have latterly been employed here, and have of course superseded the use of the chain.

this scale, in successive portions, was almost insurmountable ; and though great credit is doubtless due to the ingenuity of the projector, yet I must in candour avow, that the results of the different trials never agreed sufficiently well with each other to satisfy my mind as to the fitness of the contrivance for so delicate a purpose. I will describe the process then in my own way, that others may judge as well as myself.

A wall of brick and mortar, about two and a half or three feet high, two feet thick, and a hundred and six feet long, was built up, well levelled and plastered with the finest lime stucco, in which it is known that the natives of India excel. The drawing and weight apparatus were placed at its extremities. The base transit telescope was adjusted in the rear, and by means of it a fine pencil line traced right through the middle of the upper surface from one end to the other. The two microscopes of the eighteen-inch theodolite were fixed upon small iron tripods with adjusting screws, and the runs of the micrometer of one of them determined when in focal distance with respect to the standard scale. Over the whole a sufficient number of tents were pitched.

A bar of teak strengthened with iron, and capable of holding the points of the beam compasses at a distance of ten feet asunder, was provided ; as also a sufficient number of brass buttons well polished, with the shanks sunk into small masses of lead, of which the two that were used at the commencement and termination were rectangular, and the intermediate ones round.

The first five buttons were built into the masonry to a level with the surface of the wall at two and a half feet asunder ; all the rest at ten feet. The buttons having been placed approximately, the operation commenced by taking off two and a half feet from the standard scale, and transferring it in successive portions till the first ten feet were completed ; then the points of the beam compasses were transferred from the deal rod to the teak bar, and this new distance was similarly set off on the wall by portions until the whole hundred feet had been attained.

Each chain was alternately stretched along the pencil line of the wall by means of the drawing and weight apparatus, and the arrow-head in the rear having been accurately brought to coincide with the mark on the first button, a mark was drawn at the advanced arrow-head on the last button, and the distances between the standard scale mark and those of each of the chains was measured by the micrometer, whose runs had been previously determined.

I have said that I am not altogether satisfied as to the adequacy of this method ; but circumstanced as we were, without instrument-makers, I could not then see what better could have been substituted. It is so much easier to find fault than to remedy defects, that we naturally revert to the former in preference to the latter ; and I must avow that, when left to myself at Kullianpoor, I pursued the very same principle in making my comparisons, with the exception that instead of a wall of masonry, I used large slabs of sand-stone, of ten feet long, supported on stone pillars, under the idea that they might be less liable than the masonry to be affected by the changes of temperature which took place during the measurement."

We have dwelt somewhat long on this branch of the operation, because it is best of all suited to our purpose of making our unmathematical readers know what are the difficulties with which mathematicians have to contend. Every one thinks he can measure a straight line ; and yet there is no one who cannot see that it were both a tedious and a difficult process to measure a line of five or six miles in length, were he obliged to observe by a microscope that the end of his foot-rule was each time placed in precisely the same point that the other end occupied before, and were he obliged moreover to observe the temperature of his foot-rule each time; yet it is not difficult to see that such scrupulous accuracy is absolutely indispensable if our work is to be worth any thing.   The chain was 100 feet in length; well, let us just suppose for a moment that either from inattention to change of temperature, or from carelessness in changing or shifting the chain, an error of an inch on each chain's length had occurred—this would give in each mile an error of 52.8 inches, or 4.4 feet, and on a base of seven miles in length the error would amount to no less than 30.8 feet. But it is not only with lines of seven miles in length that we have to do; we have to estimate from the measured base the whole circumference of the earth, and whatever error be in our base, it will pervade our determination of every line. Allowing therefore $69\frac{1}{2}$ English miles as the mean length of a degree of latitude, and supposing for simplicity's sake the earth to be a sphere, an error of an inch in a hundred feet of our base line would give an error in the amount of the earth's circumference of about twenty-one miles.   This, it will be admitted, is not a trifling error, and yet we will venture to say that if any one will measure a line of 100 feet in length by any of the ordinary methods, and will repeat the measurement a dozen times over, he will not get any two of the results to agree within several inches of one another.*

The next part of our process will be to discover the longitudes of various places visible from one another, and the first of them visible from the extremities of our measured base.   As it is chiefly the *difference* of longitude of the several places that we want, and not the absolute longitude of any of them as measured from any given meridian, as that of Greenwich, our object will be effected by suddenly extinguishing or veiling bright lights at the one station, carefully noting the *time* at which the extinction takes place, and also noting with great accuracy the time at the other station at which the extinction is observed.   As we may assume that the passage of light between stations so little removed from each other is instantaneous, this method

---

* Professor Wallace states that on one occasion, Sir John Herschell and Professor Babbage being present, 100 feet of a base line in the Irish survey were measured six times over, and that the extreme difference of result as seen through a powerful microscope, did not exceed half the breadth of a dot made by a sharp steel po'nt on a plate of metal!   This is an amount of accuracy almost incredible; yet in this way 700 feet could be measured in a day.

may be carried to any degree of accuracy. All that is wanted is to have at each station two or three clever observers with good stop-watches; every time that a light is veiled at either station the time must be marked on the watches, and then by astronomical means the time at each of the stations must be ascertained. Such observations must of course be repeated many times at each station, and the mean results taken. Of course the parties at the different stations acting in concert, will fix the times at which they are to give the signals. It is fixed for example that a light which is burning at a station A is to be veiled at the instant at which a certain star comes on the meridian of that place; an observer looking through a carefully placed transit instrument gives the signal; the light is veiled by an assistant, the time is instantly noted by an observer at that station, and also at the station B to the westward of A. Then when the star reaches the meridian of B, a light is veiled there, and the time noted as before at both the stations. This may be repeated many times throughout the same night, when various stars previously named come on the meridians of the two stations. The differences of times will then be compared, and the longitude determined by the simple rule of three, for since the earth rotates uniformly on her axis, completing her rotation in 24 sidereal hours, the difference of longitude between two stations will be to 360° as the time between their passing under the same star is to 24 sidereal hours.

The longitudes of a sufficient number of places being thus ascertained, we shall be able to calculate with precision the direction of a meridian line passing amongst them.

The strictly trigonometrical part of the business now begins. We proceed to one extremity of our measured base-line; and having a large and accurate theodolite, we fix its centre just over the terminal point of our base. Having a light fixed over the other terminus, we direct the telescope of our theodolite towards that light, and then we turn the instrument round, and elevate or depress it, until we bring it to bear in the same way on a light fixed at one of the stations as A. We then read off from the graduated circle of the theodolite how far the telescope has been turned round, and this reading gives us the angle contained by our base line and a line joining its extremity with the station A. We take the same observations for the station B, and then proceed to the other extremity of our base and repeat the process, registering of course the results. Then we proceed to the station A, and direct the telescope of the theodolite to the two extremities of the base line, to the station B, and to another station C. Thus we proceed at all the stations, and thus get a series of triangles, all whose angles are known, and whose sides can be calculated from the tables.

Of course each of these angles is measured many times, and the mean result taken; for it is certain that the best instrument in the hands of the best observer will never give precisely the same value of the same angle in two different observations of it. And here we must express our dissent from a principle adopted by Col. Everest, and invariably adhered to throughout the survey, never to reject an observation, but to take the mean of all, although one of the set should be manifestly a bad observation. This, we think, an unsound rule. Suppose, for example, that nine observations of an angle should agree with one another within a fraction of a second, but that a tenth observation should differ from all the other by twenty seconds, it would seem to us quite clear that this tenth observation was a bad one, and should be rejected altogether; but Col. Everest, by taking the mean result of the whole observations would have allowed such an observation to alter the result to the amount of two seconds from that indicated by the nine concurring observations. This is an extreme case, but the principle is that uniformly adhered to in this course of the Indian survey.

As some of the sides of these triangles, and the production of others, will cut the meridian line, we will get another series of triangles of which the various parts of that line will be sides, and as other sides and angles of these triangles have been calculated, we shall be able to deduce from them the precise lengths of the various portions of the meridian line.

We have next to ascertain with great precision the latitudes of the extremities of our meridian line, and of various stations throughout its length; and this is perhaps the most delicate part of the whole process. The method used is just the same in principle with that which is put in practice every day by thousands of sailor-boys every where over the wide ocean; the difficulty therefore consists wholly in obtaining the amount of accuracy that is necessary for our present purpose. The instrument used for the purpose in the English and Indian surveys was the Zenith sector, an instrument which we need not describe at length, but which is in effect an instrument that enables us to measure the distance from our Zenith of any heavenly body at the moment of its crossing our meridian. At each station therefore various fixed stars are observed, whose declination, or distance from the equinoctial, has been previously ascertained; then the sum or difference, as the case may be, of the Zenith distance and the declination of a star will give the latitude of the place. It will give some idea of the extreme accuracy that it is deemed necessary to attain in the ascertainment of the latitudes of the extremities of the arc, when we state that that of Formentara was derived from the mean of no less than 3900 observations! This is a portion of the work, an error in which must always vitiate and render nugatory the whole proceeding from beginning to end.

Having thus obtained the length of an arc in degrees by observation of the latitudes of its extremities, and having previously ascertained its length in feet by calculation of the sides of our triangles, the work is complete. We can deduce the precise length of a degree of latitude, and from this we can calculate the magnitude and figure of the earth.

From this short sketch our readers will be able to form some general idea of the methods adopted, and also of the difficulties to be surmounted; but we have not attempted to give any idea of the corrections to be made, which after all constitute the main difficulty. The lines that have been measured by the theodolite, have not, for example, been lines on the earth's surface, but straight lines described by the rays of light passing between two stations considerably elevated above the earth's surface. The arc measured, being necessarily on elevated ground, is too long, and from it must be deduced by calculation the true length of an arc at the level of the sea. For this purpose barometrical observations of the elevation of its several parts are required. We have moreover said little or nothing of the necessary tests for verification, or the necessary allowances that must be made for possible errors. As an instance of the latter we may just mention that certain anomalies in the English arc, and a great anomaly in Lacaille's arc at the Cape of Good Hope, are accounted for by errors in the determination of the latitude, occasioned by the plummet which indicates the Zenith having been deflected by the attraction of neighboring mountains. This latter arc is now being remeasured with every likelihood of the anomaly being removed.

When an arc of the meridian has been thus measured, the survey of the country is comparatively an easy matter. All that is required is to spread a net-work of triangles over the country, and so ascertain the distances and bearings of a vast number of stations from one another. They will then fall accurately into their places on the map. The Indian survey has now been going on without interruption for a period of forty-six years. The longest arc ever measured has been determined with all possible accuracy by Col. Lambton and Col. Everest. The whole of what is called the peninsula of India,

N

has been minutely surveyed and mapped, and now the operations are in active progress for the survey of Bengal. Already seven series of triangles stretch north and south from the Himalaya down to the southern parts of Bengal, and ere very many years (that is, not many in proportion to so great a work), Heaven continuing to favor the enterprise, we shall have the whole of this noble country surveyed and mapped with a degree of precision, which we may safely say that human means cannot enable us to exceed.

And now, if we be asked what is the great benefit to be derived from all this expenditure of money and labor, we might answer by asking our querist to tell us how the money and labor could have been better bestowed. If a man should choose to become stoic, and tell us that pain is just as good as pleasure, that the bitterest and most nauseous viands are just as good as the sweetest and most delicate, we have no means of demonstrating to him that he is in error. All that we can say is that by the constitution which we have received from our Creator, we are naturally and irresistibly led to prefer enjoyment to suffering, beauty to deformity, knowledge to ignorance. Now there are certain men who think that knowledge is as valuable a commodity as any of those on which money is generally spent; and we do not think it will be easy to refute their opinion. We have, for example, two Irish peers, both young and both rich, and both, as we understand, largely endowed with the frank honesty and enthusiasm of their country, the one of whom, if reports be true, spends his fortune and his labor, his days and nights in the formation and execution of designs for wrenching off knockers from the doors of his fellow-citizens, and various other similar ingenious feats. The other also is addicted to untimely hours, but his vigils are occupied in gazing on a polished plate from which various specks of light are reflected. Now we cannot for our part see that the noble earl is a whit worse employed than the most noble marquess. To the *one* it is probably just as pleasant to separate the stars of a nebula as to the *other* it doubtless is to separate a knocker from a door. The *former* may take as much pleasure in witnessing the eruption of the lunar volcanoes, as the *latter* doubtless takes in smashing a watchman's lantern. The *one* may have as much enjoyment in gazing quietly on Charles's wain as the *other* doubtless has in driving his own tandem car. The *one* may delight as much in the contemplation of the brilliancy of the dog-star as the *other* doubtless does in listening to the yelp of his own fox-hounds. But if there be few that can sympathise with the *odd* tastes of the earl, in comparison with the multitudes who enter into the feelings of the marquess, then we must just entreat that he be allowed to take refuge under shelter of the time-honored maxim, *De gustibus non est disputandum.* And so if the Honorable East India Company choose to employ their officers in surveying the country, we cannot for the life of us see that they are employing them to worse purpose than when they send them to put Kings on the throne of Cabul, or to drive Ameers out of Scinde.

But independently of the direct advantages derivable from the survey of a country, there are various secondary advantages which perhaps are equal to the direct benefits. It is very common to talk of the discoveries that were made by the alchemists and astrologers, of other kinds than those that they wished to make. Although we cannot help thinking that these have been considerably over-rated, yet it is unquestionably in accordance with all we know of the history of science, that the direction of the minds of philosophers intensely to any subject will always be followed by the production of important discoveries ; and accordingly we find that many very important inventions and discoveries do in effect trace their origin to the trigonometrical survey. We may just mention one or two that occur to us, although we know that there are many more. The Drummond light is one of the most important. It was invented by Lieut. Drummond, who was employed in the British survey, and who would never have sought for such a light but for the necessity that arose for a means of brighter illumination than any previously known, in the course of surveying in the murky atmosphere of the northern part of our native island. When we consider the multitude of precious human lives that may have been saved by means of this light since it has been applied to the purposes of light-houses, we are filled with admiration of the goodness of the great Controller of the affairs of men, who thus links up the power of doing good with the faithful and vigorous discharge of our duties, although these duties should seem to be of a kind the least likely to yield practical benefit.

It is probably in great part also to our great trigonometrical surveys that we are indebted for the amazing accuracy that has been recently introduced into the manufacture of our philosophical instruments ; an accuracy whose benefit extends to all departments of practical science. It is only the resources of a nation that can afford a sufficient inducement to men of first-rate talents to devote their labors to the perfecting of philosophical instruments; but the skill acquired in the prosecution of this object is available for all other purposes as well as those that originally lead to its acquisition. Perhaps it is not too much to say that instruments have now been put within the reach of all who can have occasion for them, which but for the trigonometrical survey should have been beyond the grasp of all but the most opulent. As an example we may instance the beautiful sextants that are now to be found on board of every ship. Not many years ago there were ships of considerable tonnage, undertaking long voyages, whose Captains would bluster if you talked about a sextant or a chronometer; would tell you that nothing is to be depended on but the *log*, the *lead* and the *look-out:* and would tauntingly ask you what your chronometers would do for you in the Swin in a dirty night! On board ships of the same class now we should probably find two or three excellent sextants, such as would formerly have cost £30 or £40 a piece, (but which have not cost more than £6 or £7,) besides three or four very tolerable quadrants, the property of the boys. We believe that this amazing improvement in the quality, and diminution of the price, of instruments, is directly traceable to the skill that was acquired, and the zeal called forth, by the requirements of the trigonometrical survey.

It is also a matter of no little moment to have a body of scientific men perambulating a country, and having their attention necessarily attracted to its geological and other features. We have lately met with a case in point in connection with the Indian survey, which ought to have gone far to reconcile the members of the Madras Finance Committee to it; we allude to the discovery of gold ore in the Mysore country by Lieut. Warren, (now Col. Warren) the first assistant of Col. Lambton in the survey. To the surveyors also we are indebted for many incidental notices of the topography, climate and geology, of the countries through which they carried on their operations.

To our estimation one of the greatest benefits that have accrued from the trigonometrical surveying of countries is the attention that it has led men to bestow upon geometry. This, as might have been expected, has been productive of many very beautiful and elegant, and if this be reckoned of more consequence,—useful propositions. Of these the finest examples are contained in the work of Professor Wallace—whom by the way men in the last days of his life began to call Dr. Wallace, as if it were an honor to such a man to be called by a title which is

conferred upon every man who can administer a dose of jalap !
As in the case of Francis Bacon with the viscountship of
St. Albans, the scientific community have refused to recognize the title, and Professor Wallace is Professor Wallace
still. This work contains some of the finest exhibitions of
pure geometrical skill that are to be met with in our language.
We do not know whether the work has met with a reception at all equal to its merits. It is not improbable that the
title may repel some who have given but little attention to
geodesy, but who are capable of appreciating a work on pure
geometry. To such we would cordially recommend Professor
Wallace's "Theorems and Formulæ."

Col. Everest's book is one that must be of much importance
to professional men, while the detail of the operations is
interesting also and entertaining to ordinary readers. As we
have long detained our readers with what must, we fear,
have proved to many of them a somewhat wearisome article,
we shall attempt to make our peace with them by offering
them a specimen of the gallant Colonel's racy manner of
describing his adventures :

"There is a stream near Hyderabad, called the Moosee, which falls into
the Kistna below the ferry of Wadapullee, by which I had intended to
pass to the station of Sarangapullee above alluded to ; for the Kistna, being
a considerable stream, has at its principal ferries a regular set of round
boats formed of the hides of oxen, which are large enough to carry horses
and even float camels across ; whereas the Moosee, being at ordinary times
barely ankle-deep, has no such provision.

Calculating on the fordability of the Moosee, I had ordered the supplies
for my camp to be prepared at a village on the southern bank ; but when, in
my march from the station of Nealamurree towards Wadapullee, I reached the
crossing, I found this rivulet, so insignificant at Hyderabad, now filled to overflowing, carrying away trees and other floating objects in its foaming current.

Thus cut off from all communication with the provisions which had been
prepared for my followers, and obstructed in my progress, it is easy to imagine the blank looks and long visages which met me on every side. But
crosses of this kind are seldom without a remedy ; and I learned, on enquiry,
that there was, about fifteen miles distant, a place called Kompullee, below
the confluence of the Moosee and Kistna, where there used to be a ferry-boat,
and that a sufficient supply of rice to meet the wants of my party could be
procured at a hamlet near my camp, provided they would consent to thresh
it themselves.

The milk of buffaloes, too, was procurable ; but g'hee (oil of butter), that
prime ingredient in Indian cookery, rivalling our old North-Wiltshire cheese
in its rancid smell and pungent taste, and turmeric, to which the savoury
curry owes its peculiar flavour and colour, and d'hal (a small vetch) on
which Juwans and others "love to feed," and cloves, cardamums, and cinnamon, and other spices, together with betel-leaf, and areca-nut, and tobac-
co, of which such plenteous stores had been amassed on the opposite bank
of the envious Moosee, were not to be had at any price.

Matters were, however, arranged for present necessities, and by the following evening the camp was transferred to Kompullee, where we once again had abundance to eat; aud having turned the flank of the Moosee, had at last attained the north bank of the Kistna, which pouring down over a bed of rocks shelving and dipping at all angles, was really a formidable obstacle. As it was of great importance that my carriage-cattle should be conveyed to the opposite side, I had my elephants brought to the water's edge; but neither caresses nor menaces could induce them to try the passage. Probably it was fortunate that they did not make the attempt; for these powerful animals, though more at home in the water, perhaps, than any other quadrupeds, are, from the size of their limbs, proportionably more in need of what sailors term sea-room, and in a river which, like the Kistna, abounds with rocks and inequalities, were very liable to receive some serious injury, of which their natural sagacity rendered them peculiarly apprehensive.

The boat which was to convey me and my party across this roaring and angry flood, was put into the hands of the *Coblers* to be duly patched and undergo the necessary repairs, for it was an old, and crazy, and leaky vessel, which had for some time been laid up high and dry; but now, when no alternative was left, but either to await the subsidence of the flood, or trust ourselves to this frail craft, I found that there was no sort of reluctance on the part of my people to risk their persons; and even the Juwans, who had been so restive and unruly at the outset, now seemed to vie with each other in volunteering their services.

It was a spirt of exceedingly fine weather, such as does take place at intervals in the rainy season in India, when the atmosphere is so perfectly clear and transparent that all idea of comparative distance is confused : the power of vision is then almost unlimited, and the proximity of objects can only be judged of by their apparent magnitudes. I have since observed some approach to this species of limpidness in the Appenines and Southern Italy, but there is nothing like it in England; and as it is rare even in India, it became an object to avail myself of the opportunity.

The boat or leathern basket contained about six persons, with a proportion of dead weight; so having reduced the baggage and followers to the smallest possible quantity sufficient to carry the instrument (an eighteen-inch theodolite). my little party embarked, and in three journeys, which, as it required to undergo repairs after each, occupied it till night-fall, the vessel had conveyed to the south bank all whom I intended should accompany me.

Previous to embarking I left the camp, with tents, cattle, &c. under charge of Mr. Voysey, with directions to proceed onwards to Polichintah along the north bank, and await my arrival there; and as the station-flag of Sarangapullee was in sight about twelve miles off, and in appearance hardly two, I proceeded, attended by one of the sub-Assistants, and after some hours toiling over rocks and through jungle, I reached it just as the setting sun was shedding its last rays on the horizon.

Thus separated from my baggage, and without a shelter against the inclemencies of the weather, I learned to know what an Indian climate must be to the houseless European.

The sky had during the day been bright and cloudless beyond compare; but shortly before sun-set black threatening clouds began to grow together into a frowning mass; and at last, when all their batteries were in order, a tremendous crash of thunder burst forth, and as if all heaven was converted into one vast shower-bath, the vertical rain poured down in large round drops upon the devoted spot of Sarangapullee.

I had procured a charpaee (a rude bedstead or litter) from a village about five miles off, and having bent down the branches of a young tree and covered them with rice straw, I had hoped by the assistance of an umbrella to protect myself against the effects of the storm : but on awaking in the morning, I found that I had been lying all night with my clothes soaked through ; and yet so sound had been my sleep from fatigue, that I had been totally unconscious of the circumstance.

The observations were all finished to the south of the Kistna in five days of very hard and laborious work, and I then recrossed at one of the established ferries near Polichintah, and proceeded with my operations as before.

It would be monotonous and tiresome to proceed with such a detail as this ; for I have selected one instance amongst many, only to shew what the hardships and severities are which a person engaged in the great trigonometrical survey of India then had to encounter."

We should like to extend this extract, but we must have done. We therefore conclude by expressing our high sense of the credit that is due to the Honorable East India Company for the liberal spirit that they seem to have shewn throughout the whole conduct of this noble undertaking. We are not, as may be inferred from much of what has gone before, professional surveyors, and have never been personally employed in this or any other great survey, but so far as a mere theorist can judge from published documents, we should conceive that all the arrangements have been made on the most liberal scale and in the most ungrudging manner.* And their liberality seems to have met with a generous return on the part of their servants employed in the operation. Lambton and Everest seem to have permitted no difficulty to shake them, no danger to appal them, no sickness, short of the strongest burning fever, to lay them aside from their chosen work ; and while India occupies its place on the terrestrial globe, their names will be remembered as the great promoters of our knowledge of its geography.

* It will perhaps surprise our readers to learn that independently of the charge of a large establishment, the measuring of each angle in the low country of Bengal costs the Government on an average about Rs 900. This is chiefly expended on the purchase of trees to be cut down for the purpose of opening a free passage for a ray of light between the stations. This expenditure is of course unnecessary in the hilly parts of the country.

ART. IV.—1. *The Women of England, &c. by Mrs. Ellis. Fifteenth Edition.*

2. *Memoir of Mrs. Ann H. Judson, &c.   London*, 1830.

" WE have many valuable dissertations upon female character, as exhibited on the broad scale of virtue ; but no direct definition of those minor parts of domestic and social intercourse which strengthen into habit, and consequently form the basis of moral character."

*   *   *   *   *   *   *

" Had I not known before the commencement of this work, its progress would soon have convinced me, that in order to perform my task with candour and faithfulness, I must renounce all idea of what is called fine writing ; because the very nature of the duty I have undertaken, restricts me to the consideration of subjects, too minute in themselves to admit of their being expatiated upon with eloquence by the writer—too familiar to produce upon the reader any startling effect."

We would adopt these words from Mrs. Ellis as prefatory to our own remarks on the same subject.   A book that, within a few years, has gone through fifteen editions, stands in no need of our commendations.   With many defects of style, Mrs. Ellis is a valuable observer on what she aptly terms " the minor morals of domestic life."   To us, she appears to lay undue stress on that golden time, the date of which it is difficult to ascertain, when people were infinitely wiser, better and happier than they now are.   There is likewise something ornate and ambitious in her style, which leaves the impression that she had rejected a great many simple words and phrases, without, after all, hitting upon a very happy mode of expression.   Nor do we assent to the exclusive nationality of the characteristics, good or bad, which she attributes to English women.   Having noticed, as in critical duty bound, these defects in the book before us, we proceed to the pleasanter work of recommending it to our country-women.   It abounds in practical and practicable hints on relative duty ; in accurate sketches of domestic life, and in warm appeals to what is best and most loveable in the feminine character.   Take as a sample the following passage, answering the question, " For what is woman most valued, admired, and beloved ?"

" In answer to this, I have little hesitation in saying,—For her disinterested kindness.   Look at all the heroines, whether of romance or reality—at all the female characters that are held up to universal admiration—at all who have gone down to honoured graves, amongst the tears and the lamentations of their survivors. Have these been the learned, the accomplished women; the women who could speak many languages, who could solve problems, and elucidate systems of philosophy? No: or if they have, they have also been women who were dignified with the majesty of moral greatness—women who regarded not themselves, their own feebleness, or their own susceptibility of pain, but who, endued with an almost superhuman energy, could trample under-foot every impediment that intervened between them and the accomplishment of some great object upon which their hopes were fixed, while that object was wholly unconnected with their own personal exaltation or enjoyment, and related only to some beloved object, whose suffering was their sorrow, whose good, their gain.

"Woman, with all her accumulation of minute disquietudes, her weakness, and her sensibility, is but a meagre item in the catalogue of humanity; but, roused by a sufficient motive to forget all these, or, rather, continually forgetting them because she has other and nobler thoughts to occupy her mind, woman is truly and majestically great.

"Never yet, however, was woman great, because she had great acquirements; nor can she ever be great in herself—personally, and without instrumentality—as an object, not an agent."

These doctrines will bear transplantation into any climate; the details of duty vary, but the principles are steadfast. We have selected the above passage, as a fair specimen of what we have blamed as well as what we have praised in Mrs. Ellis' style. The first paragraph is clear and unmistakeable; the second is rather superfine. If, however, we rightly understand her meaning, we entirely agree with her; a woman makes an admirable *adjective*, enhancing the value of the *noun* to which she is joined, but is of comparatively little value when standing alone.

It may appear rather an abrupt transition from domestic life in England, to the biography of an American Missionary in Burmah; but we feel that there is no incongruity between the two subjects. Mrs. Judson's narrative exhibits the practical working of the principles Mrs. Ellis enforces. And, though few who read these pages, have exactly the same field of duty that lay before the wife of a Christian Missionary, yet we believe no woman desirous of doing right can read Mrs. Judson's memoir without benefit.

It would be a pleasant task to study and sketch the characters of those women who, within the last thirty years, have landed on these shores as the wives of Missionaries. From a like number, in any other position, it would be difficult to select so many who have done honor to their sex and religion, and we have never heard of one who brought disgrace on either. In our Mofussil stations, Missionaries, especially if they be not the accredited agents of the Established Church, are exceedingly little known to those among whom they reside. There is often a lamentably exclusive spirit on one side, particularly among the clergy, which we are bound to say does not exist on the other. A chaplain will rarely, if ever, listen to the sermon or prayer of a dissenter; but we never met a dissenter who objected to join in the worship or receive the instructions of a churchman. Let us not quarrel with light, because it does not come through our own windows. If 'we see one casting out devils,'—exorcising the evil spirits of ignorance and idolatry,— in the Saviour's name, are we to 'forbid him, because he fol- loweth not with us?' He, by whose name we call ourselves, has answered that question.

Often, on reaching some place which we knew to be a Mis- sionary station, have we felt grieved and surprised at the apathy and ignorance shewn by the lay inhabitants of a cantonment when the Misionaries were mentioned. Frequently, they seem hardly aware of the existence in their immediate neighbourhood of people whose business it is 'to proclaim the glad tidings;' or they speak disparagingly of them and their labours. We have afterwards visited the little Apostolic colony, and there we have seen, as at Agra, children who have been rescued from starva- tion, crime or slavery, taught the word of God, instructed in the arts of civilized life, and habituated to its comforts: a little leaven working in the inert mass around. Or, as at Futtygur, we have found not only mental and religious instruction going forward, but an important manufacture established, sufficient, if we mistake not, to cover the expences of the orphan school and mission; or as at Loodiana, we have seen the scriptures, and other books, translated, printed, and circulated in a variety of languages. And, what is still more important, we have, at each establishment seen a little community diffusing divine truth, not merely by direct preaching, but by the mute elo- quence of example. Those who have never visited these Mis- sionary locations, would probably be surprised to find their do- mestic skill, mechanical dexterity, intellectual culture, and even refined taste. The Mission premises are generally beyond the limits of the cantonment, and form a little world in itself: an orphan school, a printing press, a workshop, a garden, a chapel and a burying-ground, are all frequently to be seen within the enclosure, where every thing breathes the air of quiet activity, habitual cheerfulness, and exquisite order. The burial-ground conveys to an old Indian, home feelings that are rarely aroused in this country. With scarcely an exception, we all cherish the hope of ending our days at home, and almost every European grave in India is the record of an untimely death. Even, among those who have relinquished the prospect of returning to Europe, few can guess where their bodies will be laid; very few can look at the grave of a wife, a child, or a brother, and anticipate being buried in the same spot. A Missionary family however have not only renounced their native land, to live and die among the heathen, but have usually restricted themselves to a given field of labour. One after another of their slender band is removed; now an infant, now a mother; perhaps the patriarch of the enterprize, or, it may be, one in the vigor and prime of life, who had just devoted himself to the work. Each is laid in the quiet enclosure on which his eyes had daily rested; and of the survivors, each reckons on being sooner or later buried there too.

Among the pioneers of Missionary enterprize in Asia, the Judsons shine conspicuously. They were natives of Massachusetts, in the United States; he had resolved on a Missionary life before he became acquainted with Miss Hasseltine, and she counted her cost when she married Mr. Judson. It is pleasant to observe the spirit in which this couple undertook their work, and to watch this steady operation of the same principles throughout their career. Mr. Judson, when asking Mr. Hasseltine's consent to the marriage, writes thus—

"I have now to ask you whether you can consent to part with your daughter, early next spring, to see her no more in this world; whether you can consent to her departure for a heathen land, and her subjection to the hardships and sufferings of a Missionary life; whether you can consent to her exposure to the dangers of the ocean, to the fatal influence of the southern climate of India; to every kind of want and distress; to degradation, persecution, insult, and perhaps a violent death. Can you consent to all this, for the sake of Him who left his heavenly home, and died for her and you; for the sake of perishing, immortal souls; for the sake of Zion, and the glory of God?"—(Page 52).

In a similar strain writes his betrothed to a female friend.* " I feel willing, and expect, if nothing in Providence prevent, to spend my days in this world in heathen lands. * * * My deter-

* Mrs. H. Tighe.

minations are not hasty, or formed without viewing the dangers, trials and hardships attendant on a Missionary life.   Nor were my determinations formed in consequence of an attachment to an earthly object; but, with a sense of my obligations to God, and with a full conviction of its being a call in providence, and consequently my duty.   My feelings have been *exquisite* in regard to this subject.   Now, my mind is settled and composed, and is willing to leave the event with God,—none can support me under trials and afflictions but him.   In him alone, I feel a disposition to confide."—(Page 54).

These may appear only the glowing expressions of youthful enthusiasm, for the writer had scarcely passed her twentieth year, and her affections had just been given to the man with whom she was "to spend her days in this world in a heathen land;" but the event proved that there was no self-deception. These words were written, on the 8th of September, 1810, and it was on the 23d October, 1826, that Mrs. Judson closed her career.   During the sixteen intervening years, her confidence in God was assailed by many a tempest, but 'it fell not, because it was founded upon a rock.'

When the Judsons, accompanied by some other Missionaries, landed at Calcutta in February 1812, they received a welcome not unlike that which awaited certain other individuals, who once arrived at Thessalonica on a similar errand, "These that have turned the world upside down, are come hither also." The admission into India of any one not in the Company's Service, was in those days deemed objectionable by the local Government; and those who came to preach Christianity to the heathen, were considered doubly formidable.   Our business, however is not at present to criticise our rulers, but to trace the outline of an exemplary female character,—we will, therefore, only remark, that being deported from the Company's territories, and finding no eligible opening for their labours in the Isle of France, the Judsons embarked for Rangoon.

The work before us is chiefly composed of Mrs. Judson's letters and extracts from her private diaries.   These are exceedingly interesting, and exhibit in simple, unambitious language, the good sense, piety, and fortitude that characterized her life.   It strikes us as one great beauty in her character that she wholly merged her own tastes and pursuits in those of her husband.   She was willing, not only to labour for the good of others, but to study exactly what kind of work devolved properly on the wife of a Christian Missionary.   In every case, a wife is useful and happy just in proportion as she can thus identify herself with her husband.   He may have a thousand calls on his time and attention, exclusive of domestic affairs. He has a profession as well as a family ; her profession is that of being a wife. This one relation is the pivot on which every duty turns.

We pass rapidly over the unostentatious sketches that Mrs. Judson almost unconsciously gives of her own and her husband's labours, to direct the reader's attention to those scenes of unexampled suffering in which the Christian virtues of her character were so fully developed. She had been obliged to seek the restoration of her health in her native land. With partially recruited strength, she returned to her husband in December, 1823, just at the commencement of those differences that led us into a war with Burmah. The American Missionaries, whom the Burmese Government identified with Britons, had previously removed to Ava, where Mr. Judson and his fellow-labourers were thrown into prison. His wife describes the events of this period with a touching simplicity, and a noble firmness, worthy of that Christian heroine, Lady Rachel Russell. We follow her to " the inner room," where she retired with her four little Burmah girls, (orphans, whom she had adopted, and was educating as Christians) when her husband was dragged " to the death prison." We accompany her " to the governor of the city, who had the entire direction of the prison affairs," and from whom she obtained permission to see her husband, who " crawled to the door of the prison to meet her, for she was never allowed to enter," and then we can somewhat estimate the value of her expressions. "My prevailing opinion was, that my husband would suffer a violent death, and that I should, of course, become a slave, and languish out a miserable, though short, existence in the tyrannic hands of some unfeeling master. But the consolations of religion, in these trying circumstances, were neither few nor small. It taught me to look beyond this world, to that rest, that peaceful, happy rest, where Jesus reigns and oppression never enters."—(P. 296.)

Greater trials awaited her.* She had obtained permission to make a little bamboo room in the prison enclosure, and felt happy, indeed, when allowed to move her sick husband into the hovel, " so low that neither of them could stand upright, but a palace in comparison with the place he had left." Once more, she became a mother ; of her own trials and sufferings she makes little mention, and it is hardly possible for readers who have

---

* We refer our readers to " Crawfurd's British Embassy to Ava" for some particulars of the sufferings endured by the American Missionaries. Crawfurd's account shews that Mrs. Judson's narrative is far from exaggerating the perils and hardships of their situation.

never seen or felt the like, to understand their intensity. Exposure to the elements is, of itself enough in a tropical climate, to wear out a European woman, and here we see a delicate young mother, traversing the streets of Ava between the jail where her husband lay, panting with fever, and the palace, where she presented her fruitless petitions for his release, or the mitigation of his sufferings. At the same time, she was nursing her own new-born babe, and taking care of her Burmah orphans. One of these little girls caught the small-pox. We cannot resist the temptation of extracting a few sentences from this part of Mrs. Judson's narrative :

"She," (that is Mary, the little Burmese,) " now required all the time I could spare from Mr. Judson, whose fever still continued in prison, and whose feet were so dreadfully mangled that, for several days, he was unable to move. I knew not what to do, for I could procure no assistance from the neighbours, or medicine for the sufferers, and was all day long going backwards and forwards from the house" (i. e. the bamboo hovel, already mentioned,) " to the prison, with little Maria in my arms." We next find her using her needle to inoculate her own infant, her other protegees and the jailer's children, all of whom took the disease favourably, except her own little girl. Before the child recovered, the mother was herself prostrated by the same disease, but not until the fame of her successful inoculation of the jailer's children had brought the inhabitants of the neighbourhood to her. "I inoculated them all with a needle, and told them to take care of their diet, which was all the instruction I could give them." As to herself, though she recovered from the small-pox, she says, " My watchings and fatigues, together with my miserable food and more miserable lodgings, brought on one of the diseases of the country, almost always fatal to foreigners." It was in this condition, in the middle of the rainy season, " when the mud almost buries the oxen," that she set out in a bullock cart for Ava, where she had left her medicine chest, when the prisoners had been moved to another town, Oung-pen-la. Her strength barely sufficed to bring her back to the prison, but we must give her own words : " Our dear little Maria was the greatest sufferer at this time, my illness depriving her of her usual nourishment, and neither a nurse, nor a drop of milk, could be procured in the village. By making presents to the jailers, I obtained leave for Mr. Judson to come out of the prison, and take the little emaciated creature round the village, to beg a little nourishment from those mothers who had young children. Her cries in the night were heart-rending, when it was impossible to supply her wants. I now began to think that the very afflictions of Job had come upon me." * * * "Had it not been for the consolations of religion, and an assured conviction that every additional trial was ordered by infinite love and mercy, I must have sunk under my accumulated sufferings."—P. 310.

The parents and their child were marvellously sustained through two years of unremitting trials, until the success of our arms in Burmah obtained their release, and Mrs. Judson could write that " no persons on earth were ever happier than we were during the fortnight we passed at the English camp." But, her " warfare was accomplished; " she had returned to her Missionary labours at Amherst, and wrote to her husband, (who had accompanied the Bristish Embassy to Ava,) " I have this day moved into the new house, and, for the first time since we were broken up at Ava, feel myself at home." She wrote thus, on the 14th September, 1826, and on the 24th of the following month she was a corpse. Fever attacked her, and her worn out frame could not rally from its exhaustion. " She died in a strange place and surrounded by strangers," uncheered by the presence of him to whom she had been a faithful helpmate, and leaving her little Maria to the care of strangers. When the bereaved husband returned from Ava, " he almost expected to see his love coming out to meet him as usual; but he saw only in the arms of Mrs. Wade, a poor little puny child, who could not recognize her weeping father, and from whose infant mind had long been erased all recollections of the mother who loved her so much." Six months afterwards, the little Maria was laid beside her mother. These are melancholy details, and as they stand, in the work before us, are inexpressibly affecting. But, " Why seek we the living among the dead ? "

We have thus glanced at Mrs. Judson's life, from the conviction that, although so long published, her biography is less known than it ought to be. What is technically termed Missionary labour may be the duty of few who read this Review, but every one who has received the light of Christianity is to a certain degree responsible for those within his reach. Each one may assist in spreading that " diffused sense of right which *a few who intensely feel it*, shed around them."*

While reading the journal before us, we were struck by the aptness of a remark of Walter Scott, on "the Pilgrim's Progress." He says, " to express that species of inspired heroism by which women are supported in the path of duty, notwithstanding the natural feebleness and timidity of their nature,

* Isaac Taylor.

Christiana and Mercy obtained from the Interpreter a Guide, called Great-heart, by whose strength and valour their lack of both is supplied and the dangers and distresses of the way repelled and overcome." A great heart indeed had the gentle Ann Judson, one striking feature of which was self-denial; perhaps we might more properly call it the absence of selfishness; for hers seems to have been one of those rare dispositions, "the precious porcelain of human clay,"* in which there is scarcely any *self* to be denied. This happy temperament was in her ennobled by the highest religious devotion.

Selfishness, in its thousand insidious forms, is indeed the very taint of our nature, ever ready to break forth in every climate; but the position of *Europeans in India* peculiarly favours the development of this evil. We allude not to extreme and offensive instances, but to that quiet respectable self-pleasing that rather gains credit in the world; instances like those which the inspired writer had in view when he declared, "as long as thou doest good to thy self, men will speak well of thee." A man may forego his own gratifications, that he may supply the wants of his parents and sisters at home. A woman may count no trouble too much for her child's benefit, nor any sacrifice too painful, if she can but remain with her husband and contribute to his comfort. To such be all honour, and happily there are few who can read these words without spontaneously reverting to living instances of such conduct within their own knowledge. But something higher seems to be required, and we venture to affirm that in India, the heart becomes narrowed and the feelings blunted. How very few of us, for instance, can look upon the heathen around as responsible and immortal, like ourselves! Even those who, in their own persons desire to live as candidates for eternity, and who take a lively interest in the temporal and spiritual well-being of others, who are of the same speech and colour with themselves, are often startled at discovering their own indifference towards the surrounding heathen. In England, a vast proportion of the details of active charity are carried out by women; not indeed without errors and abuses, but still, in a way that, on the whole, keeps the kindly sympathies healthily active. The Clergyman's daughters, who teach in the Sunday School,—the mistress of a family who visits her housemaid's sick-bed, there to administer relief and consolation,—even the little girl who with her collecting card, levies sixpences for some favorite charity,—all these are

---

* We trust to memory for this quotation from a note to one of "Miller's Bampton Lectures," a work not easily forgotten by any who have once read it.

actively engaged in behalf of others who have no claim on them, except as fellow-beings. In England, any one whose heart awakens to a desire of usefulness, has but to hold out a hand to the objects that every day presents. Here, on the contrary, we hardly know how to exert any kindness, beyond that of giving money. Our servants are ill,—they go to their own houses ; we may stop at the door as we pass, in the evening or morning, and ask how they are, but our entrance would be unwelcome, and often impossible ; and, if admitted, we should find no reception for the comforts we desire to administer. If we bring refreshment for the body, our touch has polluted it ; if we would speak peace to the soul, there is no common ground on which we can stand. These circumstances produce a deadening influence on the heart, and tend to extinguish its best desires.

On more than one occasion, we have adverted in this Review to our social position as sojourners in a strange land ; and it appears particularly desirable at the present period to record our actual condition, for it is one of transition, and the next ten years will probably effect a greater change in the position of both foreigners and natives in India, than the last fifty have done. Before, therefore, rail-roads have brought the extremes of the empire within easy visiting distance, and the expiration of the Charter has thrown India more generally open to Europeans, we would fain store our portfolio with faithful sketches of Anglo-Indians as they are. The notice we have taken of Mrs. Judson's life, naturally leads us on this occasion to consider the position of our fellow-countrywomen in this land, and to note its peculiar advantages and disadvantages.

Rapid and frequent communication with Europe has already rubbed off so many of the old ' qui-hye' characteristics at the Presidency, that we must turn to the Mofussil for almost all that remains peculiarly and exclusively Indian in society. In the small and remote stations, there may still be found folk who do not own allegiance to those two most exacting of task masters, *Everybody* and *Nobody* ; gentlemen who venture to wear white jackets when *Everybody* is perspiring in broad-cloth ; and ladies, who during the hot weather, pay visits in the evening instead of the morning, though *Nobody* will be equally rational. Few positions in life afford better touchstones of character than the ' unchartered freedom' we speak of ; people are then relieved from the social pressure which, in more crowded society, keeps us all more or less, in our right, or our wrong, places. There are many, especially women, who, on finding no conven-

P

tional standard of morals and manners to appeal to, are almost as helpless in their liberty, as a Chinese lady would be, if her feet were unbandaged. Minds must be at once firm and tender, that can continually 'be a law unto themselves.'

In the remote corners of this land, on its barren plains, or by its mighty rivers, some solitary Christian pitches his tent, far from any being with whom he can exchange a word in his own language, or to whom he can make his thoughts intelligible. From day to day he follows the routine of business or pleasure. No Sabbath bell announces the hour of prayer. No happy holiday faces bespeak the day of rest ; nothing external, in short denotes the march of time, or distinguishes one day from another. Piety that can grow, or even exist, under these circumstances, must be of a genuine and hardy kind. In England the temptations are of a different kind ; religion there has excitement, bustle, party-spirit, watchwords, a language, and almost a dress, of its own. These externals may be termed the *paper currency* of Christianity ; they may or may not represent what is sterling, but there is great temptation to pass them off *on ourselves* for solid gold. We speak now especially of local influences in their bearing upon woman's character, and we must not forget the large numbers of ladies at home who are without any fixed place in society, while here, where we seldom see an unmarried woman of five and twenty, the domestic feelings early find their natural sphere of action. Interest, painful or pleasurable, of the deepest kind, is not wanting in our domestic life, but we might vainly search for the classes from which the most popular living writers have taken their best sketches. The milliner's apprentice, deprived of her natural rest, that ladies may have their dresses to wear at some particular gala—the shivering mother who, by plying her needle all day long, barely earns six-pence for her hungry children—the single woman, living on a scanty annuity and endeavouring to relieve the solitude of her lodgings by the society of a cat, a canary bird, and a box of mignionette—the governess, to whom the bread earned by honourable labour is rendered more bitter than if it were that of abject indolence—all these classes are as rare as are the wealthy dowager with her jointure and establishment; the rich and independent spinster, with tastes more akin to those of a country gentleman ; and the dear old grandmother or great grandmother, who occupies her own snug arm-chair, by so many a fireside at home.

European life in India sadly lacks the evening and morning tints. With very few exceptions, we are all bearing the burden and heat of the day, passing the active portion of our lives as exiles, and hoping that our sun will set, where it rose, in our own country. At the same time, the climate debars us from watching the growth of our children, whom we are compelled to send away from us, just at the age when intimate sympathy and confidence would be a priceless blessing to parent and child. This blessing is, indeed, too often over-looked or scorned by those who have it within their reach.   There is not a more disgraceful barbarism lingering among us than the current phrases that designate as troublesome and uninteresting the very period of life that ought to be most highly prized by parents.   From the time that a child is no longer a plaything, till the boy is ' to choose a profession,' or the girl is 'to be introduced into society,' that is to say, during the seed-time of existence, parents are too often contented to relinquish to strangers the culture of the soil. Indian parents, however, have rarely a choice in the matter ; even if qualified to be their children's teachers, the paramount consideration of health decides the question of sending them away.

The precarious tenure of domestic life is the very canker of domestic happiness in India.   Not only are the children often sent to England, while yet mere infants, but sickness frequently compels the wife to seek health either in Europe, or our own hill stations. - Besides these trials, which press pretty equally on all classes, we must not overlook the hardships which in this climate are specially experienced by people of small income. To the wealthy, whether civil, mercantile or military, climate is a matter of secondary importance.   A large airy house, well ventilated, carefully closed and opened at the proper hours, with a good equipage and good servants will make the damp of Calcutta or the hot winds of Delhi endurable, if not almost enjoyable. It is the adventurer struggling with pecuniary difficulties, who feels the full misery of a tropical climate. We allude to the man whose avocations expose him to the sun, and the woman whose dwelling does not keep out the dust, glare and rain, and the scanty dimensions of whose habitation give only the choice of suffocation from hot air impregnated with dust, or of a similar fate from the entire stagnation of that element.   Most sojourners in the East must, of course, come at first under this class ; but as the majority of the Company's servants are Military, we limit ourselves, on the present occasion, to a notice of the inconveniences which the wife of a Regimental Officer, when she first ' buckles on the knapsack,' must calculate on, and the hopeless, endless evils that beset women in the Barracks.

A woman when she marries a soldier, ought to recollect that his profession entails on her a definite and often a very arduous

duty.   Not that she is to become that most offensive hybrid, a
soldierly woman. She may easily lay aside all that is becoming and
delicate in her own sex, but she cannot in exchange assume any
masculine qualities higher than those of slang and indifference.
Her ' highest glory and best praise' are of another kind.   She
has to bear as best she may, the privations peculiar to her lot,
and to watch against its natural fruits, irritability, frivolity,
slovenliness, procrastination.   She has to encounter the ' sudden
partings, such as press the life out from young hearts;' to incur
responsibility alone ; to suffer sorrow by herself.   Let us suppose
an every day case, when a corps has just reached a new station.
Here is a Captain or Subaltern with a wife and family.   At
first they must remain in tents, while they look at the several
available houses in Cantonments, in search of one that will
dovetail into the very unequal dimensions of their means and
their wishes.   Having curtailed the latter, and perhaps a little
exceeded the former, they are housed by the time the hot winds
set in, and congratulate themselves on being at length settled for
two or three years at least.   Being a quiet, domestic pair, who
have always managed to keep out of debt, they do not launch
forth like many of their neighbours ; but, then, they like to
have every thing nice and neat about them; and are very
accessible to the temptation of cheap bargains.   One of the first
discoveries they make is, that a bow-room at one end of the
house can be built for the merest trifle ; in fact, that it would
be such an improvement as to ensure the sale of the Bungalow
any day, for more than it cost.   Just then, there is a capital
opportunity of buying cheap furniture; and, as our friends
are bent on remaining where they are, for two years at
least, they may as well make themselves comfortable.
The bills for workmen and auction purchases turn out rather
heavier than was expected ; and are the harder to meet
because the eldest child's drooping health makes it imperative that she should be sent home in the cold weather ; and
there are certain other inevitable expences anticipated a few
months hence.   The husband and wife discourse of these matters, rather uneasily, but console themselves that they can save
a good deal before the cold season.
    At length, the rains break up ; the mornings become cool and
bracing ; the *tatees* are consigned to the godowns, and even the
punkahs are taken down.   Little Missie's cheeks lose somewhat
of their chalky tint, and her mother tries to persuade herself that
they are becoming rosy, and that there can be no necessity for
sending her home this year ; but the father, more rationally, recollects the effects of the last hot weather, and resolves to make any

sacrifice rather than expose his darling child's health to such another ordeal. The sad, sad day arrives, when the parents consign their little one to a friend who is on her way home, and promises to take care of the child ; the mother feels like one 'whose occupation's gone' until a newly arrived little one opens a fresh source of interest. But now a new care arises. The annual relief of the army is published. "The relief is out," and their regiment is ordered to the North-West frontier, a march of some two months from their present station. The tents and camp equipage which had been sold a few months before, for a mere trifle, must now be replaced at a ruinous expence ; there is a report that the number of troops at the station they are leaving will be much reduced, so that houses and furniture are a mere drug in the market. Then, every body who has changed his abode, knows how unaccountably demands for money start, as it seems, absolutely out of the ground, on the eve of his departure. Some servants are to be paid up and discharged; others are to be hired and cannot proceed without an advance of wages. Hackeries and camels have also to be engaged, and half the hire must be paid in advance. Numberless are the petty expences which arise after the last rupee of ready money has been spent.

It is well when scenes like these do not produce recrimination, petulance, and alienation, but we are supposing a really attached couple, who have good sense and good temper sufficient to keep down these altercations. A loan from the Agra Bank relieves their present difficulties, and they hope that, before the first instalment becomes due, an Adjutancy or a Brigade-Majorship, or " *something or other*," that sheet-anchor of the sanguine, will come in their way.

The regiment at last *moves*, and those who have marched with one can alone know the comprehensive meaning of that expression. On the first march, the cook, who had received an advance of pay, runs away ; the khidmutgar declares he knows nothing of kitchen work ; the ayah strikes for higher wages, and worst of all, the dhaee is seized with a fever. The baby is hungry and peevish, the elder children catch cold, and the poor mother is almost at her wit's end. She finds too, that the two huge camel trunks, in which she had stowed away the hot weather clothing to be left behind, have somehow been brought with them, instead of the pair containing the flannels and warm dresses for the camp. But she tries to laugh down the lump that she feels rising in her throat, and to make the best of whatever is within her reach. We will not follow out the annoyances of the march, the lame camels, and recusant hackery-drivers ;

the smashed crockery, and grumbling servants; the swarms of flies that light on the table whenever the skreen is lifted, and the two stirring boys, who cannot be kept from running in the sun and among the cattle.   Nor need we describe the sudden storm that fills the tents with blinding, stifling dust, or the heavy rain that soaks them, so that they defy all efforts at pitching, while the lady sits forlorn in the palkee-gharee into which she has huddled all the children and women servants, to keep them dry.   All these are common grievances, and, with health and good humour, may be borne without much difficulty.   After the first week's march, matters some how jolt into their right places, while the delightful clear, cold weather that succeeds the Christmas rain, braces up the system; the corps continues its route in good spirits, and count on the day when it is to reach its new destination.   They arrive, and find orders awaiting them to proceed on foreign service, to some hostile region, to which no man of common sense would take his family.   Then does the wife begin to number the days that remain to her before she sees her husband depart for a place whence so few have ever returned; then do the couple feel the grinding pressure of pecuniary distress.   Remittances must be made for the child that is gone home; fresh expences must be incurred, to fit out the husband for his campaign, and the wife must be provided with a suitable residence in our own territories.

These are times when the blessing of our Hill Stations can be really appreciated.   Loneliness is indeed lonely to a woman of narrow income, living by herself in the Plains.   The long, hot day is spent with darkened doors, while none but dusky faces and foreign tones are around her.   The breathing-time of evening comes, but brings not the delightful snug drive in the buggy, in lieu of which she is fein to satisfy herself with a chair on the east side of the Veranda, whence she may regale herself with a view of the scorched compound, and its dreary enclosure of sun-dried clay wall.   The children are ill, but there is no father to share their mother's fatigues and anxieties.   The woman, in short, who was accustomed to look for guidance at every step, now finds she must walk alone, over a rough and dreary path.   The Hills, however, offer a mitigation to many of the trials we have named.   There is a ' refreshment' which none but Indians can estimate, in being able to keep the windows open all day, and in always having something fresh and green without to rest the eyes on.   There is society in the blazing and crackling of the pine-wood fire of an evening; there is luxury in breathing the mountain air and watching its salutary effects on the children.   These sweets are infused by a Father's hand in the bitter cup that he sees it good for many of his creatures to taste and drink deep of; it is with pain we observe how often the blessing is abused.

We need not here dwell on the squabbles and jealousies that render it so difficult for ladies to live comfortably together, and to which we may attribute the fact that *chum* is almost exclusively a noun masculine. Men can live in the same house, share the expences of house-keeping, and see as much or as little of each other as they like. Thus they can go on, month after month, without any misunderstanding. How it comes, let others tell; we only state the fact that ladies are rarely gifted with the like power, and that their taking a house together in the Hills generally proves a failure. These petty bickerings and childish peckings at each other are bad enough, but they are thrown into the shade by more glaring evils.

In the case we have been supposing—which is nevertheless, far from imaginary,—what are the wife's specific duties? Obviously, in the first place, that her husband should suffer no one gratuitous anxiety on her account and should feel no one care that she can avert. Now is the time to shew that her affection for him is something higher than selfish tenderness. A woman will sometimes, in her passionate fondness, urge her husband not to leave her, or not to expose himself to danger, though he could not, in honor and duty, hold back. She will seek some loophole through which he may creep, to avoid the hardships of the service on which his fellow soldiers are going, and if he has accompanied them she will weary him with importunities to seize the first pretext for returning,—in plain English, for deserting his post. If these importunities find a confederate in the husband's own heart, he will probably make them an excuse to himself, for doing what he is already well inclined to do; but if he be made of the stuff of which a true soldier is composed, he will only feel mortified that his wife is of so different a stamp so incapable of appreciating his duty. Her lamentations will at length appear to him but the wailings of a peevish child, deprived of some favorite toy, and her opinion, or even feelings, may proportionately weigh little with him. A true wife feels that her husband's honor is in her keeping; that it is her privilege to urge and cheer him forward, in the straight path of duty, not to allure him away from it. She recollects that he has plighted his word, not only as her husband, but as a public servant, and that it is base and cowardly to 'eat the salt' of Government in time of peace, and hang back in the day of need. Looking no further than the motives to be gathered from reason and affection, she may learn not only that safety depends very little on place, but that there are considerations higher than personal safety. So common-place a view of the case is open to all: but the heart that has learned to look beyond what is visible and transitory, will have a yet more unfaltering confidence, while pursuing the course of duty.

Deeper anxieties, however, than any we have spoken of, may corrode the mind of an absent husband, when he thinks of a young, pretty and inexperienced wife left with no guide but her own discretion. This is delicate ground, which we would not explore in search of personal gossip. We would only entreat our country women to consider the poisonous fruits which they have seen of imprudence, and to enquire whether they are not fostering within themselves the very seed that would, when occasion served, bring forth a similar harvest of bitterness. —" *Our Kabool disasters.*"—The present, and even the rising generation must be gathered to their father before these words lose their fearful import, or the ideas they convey can pass into the chamber of mental petrefactions. Yet is there one disastrous result of the Affghan war that has rarely been adverted to—the domestic infelicities that arose from the domestic separation of the campaign.

Any one who observed the current of military life in our Upper Provinces during the season when the army of the Indus was assembled, must remember the dismal crash of family comfort on every hand which accompanied that event. No force on so large a scale had been assembled for many a day. Young ladies had perhaps heard from the elder matrons of India legends about former campaigns, about a soldier's dangers, and a wife's anxieties. All these however belonged to past times, as much as the wars of York and Lancaster, and were listened to as having been shocking enough for the sufferers, but not as likely to affect the present generation. A treasure escort, or a change of station was about the severest service that many of our officers had seen, when the anticipated campaign beyond the Indus set the whole military world astir. The rendezvous of the force at Ferozepore, in 1838, was a grand spectacle :—war in its holiday garb, with its hideous features concealed. The troops left Hindustan, as the newspaper correspondents averred, ' in the best possible order, and the highest spirits imaginable ;' ' may be they did, may be they did'nt,' as Bailie Nicol Jarvie would say. Our present enquiries respect those who were left behind. Of these, the Officer's wife of whom we have drawn a faint sketch may be taken as a sample ; perhaps we have selected a peculiarly favourable case, for we have assumed on both sides more than an average share of affection, good sense, and rectitude. It would be easy to find instances where a husband's extravagance or neglect demanded tenfold circumspection and prudence on that part of his wife. But, without adverting to extreme cases, either favorable or unfavorable, let us estimate the position in which the majority of these ladies were left. Young in years, still younger in experience, the mothers of childern, either pressing on their hourly attention in this country, or demanding yet deeper solicitude at home. They were the wives of soldiers, who might at any moment be called to scenes of peril, of anguish, and of death itself: they were the partners of men whose incomes had barely sufficed for the exigencies of a peaceful cantonment life, and the greater part of whom were involved in debt by the contingent expenses of taking the field, and keeping up a double, or, if there were children at home, a triple establishment. These are trials that neither a soldier nor his wife, if worthy of the name, will shrink from. The conduct they elicit tests the character. It is then that we find in ourselves and in others, depths and shallows that we dreamed not of until fathomed by the sounding-line of sorrow.

Many a feeling of womanly heroism was called forth and ripened during the years that saw our troops beyond the Indus; but these were the exceptions, and we are bound to say that the general aspect of conjugal life, during that period was not remarkably creditable to the ladies of the land. We are not about to notice those cases of flagrant misconduct, which incurred reprobation in every society; and which have received the brand of public censure. The misfortune is, that condemnation, and, what is more important, *compunction*, usually slumbers till the evil has become irremediable. Might it not be wiser to try in time the preventive system?

Next to genuine religious principle, there is no guarantee so safe for a wife's discretion as that furnished by strong attachment towards her husband. Instinctively, almost unconsciously, she says and does nothing in his absence that she would not in his presence. Were she to make the effort, she could not act otherwise. The existence of this feeling we are not so romantic as always to take for granted. Let us borrow the definition of it, as given by one who combined the skill of an anatomist with the touch of a painter. Coleridge says that enduring personal attachment, " in addition to a depth and constancy of character of no every day occurrence, supposes a peculiar sensibility and tenderness of nature, a constitutional communicativeness and utterancy of heart and soul; a delight in the detail of sympathy in the outward and visible signs of the sacrament within—to count, as it were, the pulses of the life of love. But, above

Q

all, it supposes a soul which, even in the pride and summer time of life ; even in the lustihood of health and strength, had felt oftenest and prized highest, that which age cannot take away, and that which in all our lovings is *the* love, I mean, that willing sense of the unsufficingness of the self to itself which predisposes a generous nature to see in the total being of another the supplement and completion of its own."

This describes affection in its full and glorious perfection, and we venture to say that the heart which recognizes within itself even a faint likeness of the feeling above described will need no rules to keep it within the circle of wedded duty.   While setting before us a high standard, we must, however, take the the world as it is, remembering that

> " The tenderest and the wisest pair
> Find something, every day they live,
> To pity—and perhaps forgive." *

The wrecks of domestic peace which were so fatally numerous among the divided couples we advert to, occurred just among the common-place characters, who, as Meta Klopstock says in her sweet broken English, " Marry as people marry, and are happy as people are happy."   They were not the victims of strong passion or urgent temptation, so much as of personal vanity, and the restless idleness of a vacant mind.

Society at our Hill Stations partakes a good deal of the characteristics of a watering-place, or a garrison town in England ; it consists for the most part of people who studiously leave behind them their habitual cares and employments, or of those who say they have nothing to do.   Like causes produce similar results in all latitudes.   Men who have several hours of every day to get rid of, naturally seek the society of any tolerably pretty and pleasant young woman, especially if her attractions are backed by a good tiffin on the table at two o'clock. Their attentions are agreeable, and gradually create a craving for this kind of stimulus ; love of admiration involves petty jealousies, extravagant dress, paltry shifts, and a thousand other evils, equally deteriorating to a woman's domestic character. " The Dalrymples " of " Charles O'Malley," and the Bennet family in " Pride and Prejudice," convey a fair notion of the results of this sort of life ; the one, a clever caricature ; the other, a Wilkie-like picture, such as none but a woman, (and few women except Jane Austen,) could have drawn.   The colouring need be but slightly changed to stand for a portrait of many of our large military stations, as well as of life in the

* Cowper.

Hills. If the effect of this flutter and frivolity is pernicious to the unmarried girl, it is still more so to the married woman. A man comes home perhaps from business that has kept him for many hours amidst clamour, heat and bustle. Weary and disinclined for any thing but rest, he may appear but dull company to his lady, compared to the "nice creature" who has been making himself agreeble all the morning, retailing the freshest gossip, mending pens, or copying music. On the other hand, *monsieur l'epoux* on entering the house, is hot, dusty, blinded by the glare outside, harldy able at first to distinguish objects in the dim cool drawing-room, and, when his vision has adapted itself to the twilight, does not perhaps altogether relish finding that the "jackanapes" whom he had left there soon after breakfast, has not yet concluded his visit. The dissatisfaction he feels oozes out in his manner, and the wife thinks—if she does not say—what a cross man he is. Perhaps they both recover their good humour before evening; but the continual recurrence of scenes like these takes the bloom off affection, or effectually prevents its growth.

If our partiality for what appertains to ourselves is proverbial, this partiality is by no means incompatible with a peculiar sharpness in detecting the faults of those with whom we come in closest contact, and with a propensity to draw unfair comparisons between our own and our neighbours ' belongings '— "his wife, his man-servant, his maid-servant, his ox, his ass, or any thing that is his." We quote not irreverently the words of the commandment; the temper we speak of is not far removed from coveting. Could we but scrutinize other people's families as closely as we do our own, the comparative estimate might be very different. Women are more addicted than men to confidential chat, to unbosoming their grievances, real or supposed, to each other, though by the way it is a most dangerous luxury for wives to indulge in. We appeal to those who have compared notes upon domestic concerns whether the disclosures made on both sides have not elicited remarks like these; "Really, now! I always thought your husband was so "*very* considerate!" Or, "well! I *am* surpised! I often wished *my* husband was as liberal as yours," and thus the comments run on through every member of the establishment, until both parties *might* learn that they are, at any rate, no worse off than their neighbours. But a very different estimate of her own condition rises to the mind of a wife whose vanity has just been thwarted by her husband.

The present observations do not, we repeat, allude to flagrant and irretrievable misconduct. Our object is to urge our countrywomen to rouse the powers and employ the blessings meted out to them, in such a manner as shall quench the smouldering, habitual imprudence, which though it may never burst into a flame, yet consumes the heart of domestic happiness. Personal vanity is, we are persuaded, the prevailing root of bitterness, and it flourishes most in an uncultivated soil. Literary and domestic tastes have the immense advantage of supplying a woman's mind with that habitual nourishment which renders her independent of stimulants, whether gossip or flattery. The evils indeed that we describe as prevalent in Anglo-Indian society may be traced in a great measure to the low tone of intellect which generally prevails, except at the Presidencies. People who have lived for years in the remote parts of our Upper Provinces have become so mentally acclimated, that they are hardly aware how far they lag behind civilized lands; but those who arrive fresh from "the fine full flow of London talk," or even from the enjoyment of some of its branch streams, feel sorely the insipid, contracted, monotonous character of Mofussil conversation. The gentlemen are perhaps, as much addicted as the ladies to *talking shop*, (we know no classical equivalent for this barbarous expression;) but then the former have to handle subjects of intrinsic interest, which redeem their discourse from absolute inanity. For their fair partners, we cannot say as much; they too often come within the Apostolic category of those women who were "idle, wandering about from house to house; and not only idle, but tattlers also and busy-bodies." Indeed, what we remarked some pages back respecting piety, may be applied to literature in the far off corners of society; it is either pursued for its own sake, or it is neglected. There is no fashion or competition in the matter; very little credit is to be gained or lost by mental polish or rust.

In absolute seclusion, the temptation is to slovenliness, and an indecorous neglect of the amenites of life; but where there is a society large enough to admit of competition, yet small enough for every body to know every body, the temptation is to excel in matters that are level to every understanding; table, dress, furniture and equipage. Writers on English life declaim against the spirit that prevails at home, especially among the mercantile and professional ranks, of striving to seem what they are not; and condemn the struggles and evasions practised by people who wish to pass for richer, younger, or, as the phrase goes, *more respectable*, than they really are. One would think there was no temptation to this infatuated folly among the Company's servants. The salary of every man from the Governor-General down to the drummer boy is as well known as that twelve pence make a shilling; the age of each individual may

be ascertained within a year or two from the date of his entering the service, and it only required a very slight calculation to
fix the age of a lady almost as accurately as that of the moon,
even before Mr. Curnin's ungallant proposition to the Military
Fund, placed on record the birth-day of most of the Bengal
officer's wives. Then, as to employment, we all stand on a
level, as serving the same master. Thus *ticketed*, as it were,
and set forth at our proper value, we all might, if we liked, fall
into our proper places like the pieces of a dissected map.
But, in steps the demon of rivalry instigating many a mischievous prank. The Commissioner had such and such things at his
table, and how can the Collector ask him in return without
giving him an equally good dinner? The Colonel's lady gets her
millinery overland from Europe; how then can the Major's
wife appear in " country made attire." Pity it is that people
cannot estimate the beauty of *fitness*. Moreover, in this service,
we are all sure to take our turn on the upper steps of the ladder,
if we only live long enough, and if we do not, still wilder is
the folly of squandering the money that might provide for our
families, not to speak of the unalienable claims of charity.
After all, the most reckless expenditure can never gain a man
even the paltry reward of being supposed richer than he really
is; vanity, therefore, sometimes takes a different turn, and we
hear an unblushing avowal, if not an actual boasting, of debt
from people who go on without a single effort at retrenchment.

A *griff* might estimate a man's wealth by the profusion of his
establishment,—an old Indian knows better; and, when he sees
the expenditure of people obviously exceeding their salary, he
takes it as the criterion not of the money they have to draw
upon, but of the debts they have contracted. Poverty is a sore
evil; debt a still sorer one; and, where either the one or other
has been inevitably incurred, and honest struggles are made to
get out of the net, every hand should be stretched forth to help
the sufferer. But it is difficult to express the indignation we
feel towards people who see in debt no paramount obligation to
self-denial; who go on living on other men's property, and then
call themselves ladies and gentlemen, perhaps *Christians !**

---

* Let us not be understood to affirm that the majority of our service, or even
of the military branch of it are in debt; on the contrary, within the last twenty
years, a much more healthy tune has arisen on pecuniary as well as on other moral
questions. The error, indeed, in some quarters, takes another turn   In India, as
elsewhere reformed spendthrifts make the most determined misers.   Still, inordinate expence on one side, and inconceivable softness on the other, have created
in India a system of relationship between debtor and creditor extensive and peculiar
enough to be noted as one of the characteristics of Indian Society.   We have read
many duns and replies to duns that would be quite invaluable to " *Punch*," but
which are disgraceful to the society that countenances the evil.

Doubtless, the chief blame in every such case must rest with the husband, in whose power it always lies to limit household expenditure, in military phrase, "to stop the supplies." The wife however is seldom exempt from censure ; it is too frequently her vanity which prompts the outlay, or her recklessness that asks ' what is the use of denying myself *this*, when *he* will lay out twice as much on *that?*' Is this the part of a faithful helpmate? And may we not trace to these feminine habits of extravagance, (for every thing is extravagant that exceeds our income,) the financial imprudence which too commonly prevailed among the ladies who remained in India, when our army took the field in 1838 ?

A stranger, fresh from home, accustomed to go into a shop, ask the price of an article, and either at once agree to the purchase, or if he thought it too dear, pass on to something else—such an one might think our ladies the most thrifty and economical of human beings, if he saw a committee of them assembled to examine the contents of a native merchant's pack, a cloth-dealer, a shawl merchant, a jeweller or haberdasher. Great is the strife of tongues; close the huckstering on both sides. Each lady boasts how cheap she got satin from Gopee-nath, or ribbon from Ramjee-mull. But bargaining is not economy, either of time or cash. There is a struggle, almost like jockeyship, between buyer and seller. The scene perhaps ends in the dealer packing up his goods, without having sold a pice worth, the ladies coolly observing that they did not want to buy any thing—they merely wished to see what sort of goods the man had. More frequently, there is no resisting the insinuating pedlar's "very new fassun," combined with his assurance, "Ready money not want. Note of hand Mem Sahib (the lady) give," and he leaves behind a good share of his property, carrying away in exchange more than one I. O. U. Perhaps he knows the value of little spicy morsels of gossip, to exhibit at the next house where he stops. Every body disclaims personality and inveighs against scandal; practically, however, very few turn away from the bait.

> "Each thinks his neighbour makes too free,
> Yet likes a slice as well as he." *

When General Pollock's army were on their way back to Hindustan, a *Kapra-wala*—cloth dealer—at a large station was exhibiting a sheaf of the aforesaid notes of hand, some of a very old date and for large sums. "How can you venture to

* Cowper.

give so much credit?" said a gentleman who was present. "Dekho (see) Sahib," replied the dealer, "officer all full-batta get—they come back Hindustan, all very khūsh (happy) to see Mem Sahib look pretty—then she say, there is one little bill,—Sahib pay money." Probably some accounts were thus adjusted; but, to a quiet spectator, there is something very humiliating in observing the address with which native tradesmen play off the weak or unamiable feelings of their fair customers against one another, as well as the waste of time and temper caused by these bargaining scenes. We are inclined to believe that, in every respect, a lady loses more than she gains by such "keen encounter of wits" between her and a pedlar.

While on the subject of unbecoming expenditure, we are tempted to say that we have often looked on a bride's *trousseau* as a very Pandora's box. "Weddings, mournings and christenings," as the milliner's advertisements class the three most solemn events of human life, have a prescriptive right to a peculiar costume, and really there is a tempting variety of garb for each occasion, that a lady must sometimes, when reading the catalogues, be almost puzzled to know which she would most like to have occasion for. Personal neatness, purity and good taste, we love—indeed we could hardly love a woman destitute of them; but these graces do not require her to commit the absurdity of purchasing for *one* occasion, what is quite incongruous with her ordinary habits. Suppose a wedding-dress ordered from Calcutta; *the* important day must be fixed with reference to the probable rate of *Dawk banghy.*—At length the local postmaster receives "an advice chelán (notice)," announcing that on a certain day, a parcel of a certain weight was despatched from Calcutta. Need we say how its arrival is watched? The "bánghywála" (postman) at last makes his appearance

> "True to his charge, the close packed load behind,
> Yet careless what he brings, his one concern,
> Is, to conduct it to the destined *Chouk.*
> But Oh! the important budget!" *

What examination it undergoes, especially if it arrive during the rains, as to whether the corners of the box have been bruised! what quick tearing away of the yellow wax-cloth wrapper, and what impatience till the 'bearer' brings the hammer and chisel to open the shining tin case! "Beautiful! lovely! elegant! so becoming!" exclaim the select committee of friends

* Cowper.

who are assembled to examine the interesting arrival. " Very expensive, of course," adds the mother, " but then *It is only for once.*" And if it *be* " only for once," is there no bad taste in making a short lived exhibition which cannot be kept up? The chances, however, are that one expence will usher in another. The lady who has a becoming morning dress will not like to appear less advantageously in the evening. If she looks well in the delicate bridal array she wore during the hot weather, she " really must have something nice," for the cold season. Perhaps her husband's approbation may suffice during the honey moon, and possibly she may then come to her senses sufficiently to wonder how she could have been so absurd as to buy such an exprensive dress; and wish that she had the money they cost, to pay the merchant's bill. But in a very large number of cases, the *trousseau* is only the first of a long train of expences.

These are homely and undignified details we grant, and we shall be judged misanthropic if we predict the ruin of a family from a bunch of wedding favours. But, " trifles make the sum of human things." A tolerably long and extensive acquaintance with Indian society has taught us that love of dress and show dries up the springs of charity in many a woman's heart, baffling every appeal to her liberality with the ever-ready, " I cannot afford it." Perhaps the propensity may not originally be stronger here than at home ; but, in our Mofussil at least, it cannot be gratified without a larger outlay not only of money, but of time and thought than it demands in a highly civilized country.

This was one of the points we had in view when, at the beginning of this article, we said that India fostered selfishness and inanity. Both of these evils are more easily supplanted than uprooted. Direct resolutions, or even struggles against a wrong habit, may be ineffectual, but the practice of an opposite good one can hardly fail to slacken the enemy's grasp. When a new channel is cut there is hope of turning off the stream from its old course. A woman who will resolutely devote a certain time daily to reading a book that exercises her powers of attention, finds both her leisure and appetite abridged for frivolous occupation. If she will appropriate a certain portion of her money to charitable purposes, and observe the good that it effects, she will thus learn somewhat of the true value of silver and gold, and will grudge the needless outlay on ' things which perish in the using,' of money that might bring on her ' the blessing of him that was ready to perish, and make the widow's heart to sing for joy.' A certain amount of attention directed to the ignorant and distressed, will open her eyes to her own blessings and responsibilities. The grand point is, to decide on some specific, practicable plan, and then hold to it. Be it but half an hour daily for reading, or a Rupee a week for charity, let it be regularly appropriated, and the collective result will soon surprise the gatherer.

We have ventured, in no unfriendly spirit, to comment on the faults and foibles of our country-women in India, hoping that some among them may be roused to their own higher destinies, to the happy possibilities within their reach. Among them, we know there are many who will feel that *they* at least have not sat for any of our portraits; and many more, who are willing to exert themselves in the pursuit of higher aims, if they only knew how to begin. We have adverted to some of the peculiarities which limit and paralyze benevolent exertion towards the natives, but there is scarcely a station in India that does not contain women and children, perhaps of purely European blood, and bearing the name of Christian, who require to be " excavated from the mass of heathenism in which they lie embedded," as much as any Hindu.

Among these, it strikes us, lies the legitimate, the imperative field of duty, to every Christian lady in India, especially the wives of officers. Personal kindly interest, opportune help, countenance of the deserving, sympathy, and above all, example, would do much for these neglected females; but whoever attempts the work must be prepared to meet with much discouragement, perchance disgust. The popular literature of the day headed by that noble fellow, Punch, is doing much towards bringing the poor, face to face with the rich. We fear, however, that the interest thereby excited turns too much on the picturesque accessories of poverty.

One class of exaggerations is gone out of fashion; the love-in-a-cottage, and brown-bread-and-milk school, has vanished before the stern realities of homeless starvation. Fictitious poverty is now more frequently invested with *moral* interest—the highest of all interests, if correctly employed, but too frequently used to impart embellishments for which we look in vain among the poor and ignorant. Real life contains very few " Oliver Twists" and " Little Nellys." Perhaps we are prepared to sympathize with a youthful, heart-broken widow, in her decent, mourning garb, refusing to be comforted. Help may, however, be as much needed, by a poor uncouth looking girl, in a dirty white bed gown, resembling one whose appearance and words now rise vividly to our remembrance, as she mingled her lamentations for " the poor fellow she had just buried," with most business-like consideration respecting the next husband she should take, " when decency would permit." " My mother," said the poor girl we speak of, who, be it observed was herself a

R

mother, though not quite fourteen years old, " My mother is thinking of a *poticary* for me, but I would rather take another man out of the Artillery." " You had a good husband, then ?" said we, " Indeed I had, my mother thought he was not kind to me because he used to beat me ; but I deserved it well, for I was a great scamp." " A great scamp !" we repeated, in some dismay. " How ?" " I used to be playing marbles with the boys, when he wanted his supper ready." Pity must put on her walking-shoes, when she steps forth to help cases like this, or when she is not chilled, while listening to some narrative of sudden bereavement, by some such parenthetic remark of the speaker's as this : " At that time I was in the light Company, the next husband I got was the Canteen Sergeant, and the man I have now, is only a Lance Corporal." And this reminds us of a woman who, after listening respectfully to some remarks about the ignorance in which her daughter was growing up, replied : " Yes, but people are just as bad at home, when I married my first husband, poor ignorant creature that I was, I did not know a Sergeant's stripe from a Corporal's."

When a European Regiment was taking the field, our commiseration for the cares and sorrows of the women who are left behind, has ere now been rudely disturbed by observing the anxiety of parents that their daughters should be married before the Corps marches, " Why," we have asked, " should you allow such a mere child to marry, when her husband will leave her next week." " Because she can then draw wife's pay while he's away : and if any thing should happen to him, she will get her six months' widow's pension." On these, and many other points, perhaps the women of the barracks merely *say*, what some of their more refined sisters *think*. At any rate, there is wisdom in training ourselves to remember that people *can feel*, who do not feel in precisely the same way that we should ourselves on a like occasion.

Even a marching regiment, however, is not without its scenes of tender home interest, of which one instance recurs to our recollection. It contains no incident which has not frequently occurred to others ; but we know it to be true, and, indeed in these remarks on Barrack life, we give no one illustration beyond the pale of fact.

It is now many years ago since H. M.'s 44th Regiment embarked on the Ganges in a fleet of country boats. Among them, at that time, were two sisters, the eldest of whom was not above sixteen years old : Mary and Eliza were great favorites in the regiment, and were both married to kind and respectable men. The husbands, desirous of securing more comfortable accommodation than could be found in the boats provided for the privates, arranged that their wives, each of whom had a young infant, should proceed in the boat with the Sergeant-Major and his wife, while they themselves were with their Company. Near Dinapore, the fleet encountered a violent gale, and was dispersed, and many boats were swamped. Towards night, the tempest lulled, and the shattered remnant of the fleet, "cast anchors out of the stern, and wished for day." They missed the Sergeant-Major's budgerow, which had been driven across the river, while the other boats had sought refuge on the Dinapore bank. Next morning, as soon as it was light, a small party of the 44th, including the two husbands we speak of, went across in a *Dinghi*, to see what had become of the budgerow. They found it aground, close to the shore, the after part under water and only the bow visible. The Sergeant-Major and his wife, with the crew were sitting on the bank, cold, dripping and hungry. Having been on the roof when the vessel struck, they had managed to scramble ashore; but Mary and Eliza were in the cabin, and no one had ascertained their fate. All was now calm; the river had subsided sufficiently to admit of the men breaking open the roof with hatchets, and making their way into the cabin. There lay the two young mothers, each with her infant; the water appeared to have rushed in so suddenly as to suffocate them, before they could even make a struggle. Some of the men immediately returned to Dinapore, to carry the sad news and to bring back some women to dress and lay out the bodies. About sunset that evening a mournful group were assembled, some standing on the bank; others crowding the sterns of those boats that had escaped the storm; all eagerly watching the course of a black speck that was seen approaching from the other side. Just below its confluence with the Soane, the Ganges takes a bend, expanding into a vast lake-like sheet of water, and this broad, shining surface now reflected the boat, as it neared its destination. In it stood the boatmen, nearly naked, plying their huge, unwieldy oars, and apparently unconscious what freight they carried. There were the grey-headed Sergeant-Major and his wife, pale, exhausted, death-like: beside them sat two young men, who neither spoke nor moved, but whose eyes were fixed on a white sheet, spread over part of the deck of the boat. There also were the women who had crossed the river in the morning; they were loud in their wailings and lamentation as they neared their comrades, and lifting up the sheet, showed the corpses of poor Mary and Eliza, each dressed in grave-clothes and each with her infant resting on her arm. They were buried at Dinapore that same evening.

Interest of another and more harrowing kind, attaches to the interior of a barrack, especially in reference to its influence on woman. Wisely do those interested for Hindustan aver that its inhabitants can make no general advance in improvement, while the female part of its population are uninstructed. But will any intelligent Hindu or Mussulman believe that these are more than high-sounding speeches, when they look at European female life in India—when they see the condition of mothers and daughters in our barracks—living and growing up without any instruction, principle, or restraint, that might stand them instead of those motives to self-respect which even native women may feel? "Perishing for lack of knowledge;" their bodies perishing by scores,* because their understandings have not been exercised regarding the simplest physical laws—and their souls passing away into the presence of Him, who alone can estimate the cruel temptations amidst which these poor creatures lived and died; but who assuredly will not hold guiltless those women who, with more knowledge, leisure, and money at command, saw their sisters perishing and passed by on the other side.

There is not an Ensign's wife who might not effect some good, however small, to some one portion of the classes we allude to. There is not a native regiment that does not reckon, besides its non-commissioned officers, a number of drummers, who with their families, bear the Christian name, but are distinguished from the surrounding heathen by little except their indiscriminate diet, and by coming to the Padree Sahib, the commanding Officer or the Magistrate to be '*Shadi-kur'd*' or '*Christian-kur'd.*'—married or christened——We have seen many a couple come to be married who could not even make the responses to the service in English; and mothers bringing their children to baptism without an idea that to '*Christian-kur*' meant any thing beyond to '*nam lagao,*' (affix a name.)

We protest against the 'tu quoque' answer, that like heathenism may be found at home. One evil is no palliation for another, and at present we are not haranguing about the moral destitution of other countries, but trying to grapple with an evil at our own door. Men and women are equally skilful in diluting down duty to their own taste; there is 'a lying spirit' ever at our ear whispering that what demands self-denial is impracticable. And,

---

* No returns are published of the deaths among the children of our European soldiery, but the mortality is frightful. We can at this moment recollect not less than half a dozen women, sober and well conducted, who, out of families of five, six, seven or nine, have reared respectively one two or three children, or are now entirely childless. Even this sweeping away by death is scarcely so serious an evil as the languid, feeble frames, which we see in those who reach maturity.

truly, when we look at the wall of ignorance and misery that encompasses our European regiments, to hope for a breach in it by any human means appears about as reasonable as it would be 'to compass about for seven days' an enemy's fortress, and expect the walls to fall down 'at the sound of the trumpet.' Some-times, however, a bolder or more clear-sighted champion discerns in the citadel of vice and ignorance a *practicable* spot against which an assault may be hopefully directed. Experience proves that this assailable point is to be found among the young.

Calcutta contains several institutions both public and private for imparting instruction to the young; within the immediate circuit of our Presidency there may perhaps be an adequate supply of educational machinery; but Calcutta is not India, nor is the Bengal presidency limited to Bengal. The events of the last seven years have drawn an unusually large proportion of our European troops to the North-West Provinces; too remote from Calcutta to admit of any but a very small number of the children of these regiments benefitting by schools at the Presidency. Indeed it would be madness to transport them thither, while loca-lities with a much better climate are close at hand.

The Upper and Lower Orphan Schools are among the best known of our Calcutta educational institutions. The former, few of whose inmates are of purely European blood, is probably more eligibly situated in the plains than in a colder climate. The Lower School contains a majority of unmixed European parent-age, and for such there can be no question that they would be better located in the Hills. In both establishments the system of training for the girls might be greatly improved by being rendered more homely and practical; more a preparation for the stations they are likely to fill. A soldier or clerk would probably rather that his wife knew how to cut the largest possible number of shirts out of a piece of long-cloth, than that she could work the most beautiful bead-purses in the world. Not many weeks have passed since we were conversing with a respectable woman who came to India about twenty years ago as a soldier's wife. We asked her about the characteristics of the Eurasian women in the barracks, whether they were not better suited for that life as constitutionally acclimated, and as less accessible to the tempta-tions of drink than our poor European women. Her reply was, 'They care less for liquor, but more for clothes. One of them would do any thing for a pair of gold-ear-rings;' 'and do you,' we inquired, find no better habits among those from the Orphan school?' 'Indeed,' replied our informant, 'I see very little they have learned there. They like to be lolling on the bed all day, reading a story-book, or talking Hindustani with one of their own sort.'

There is another, and in most respects an excellent establishment in Calcutta, the European Female Orphan Asylum. It was established some thirty years ago by Sir Jasper Nicolls and the late Reverend Mr. Thomason. A friend, well qualified to judge, assured us lately that he could name at least thirty of the girls brought up there, who are now the heads of families, and whose lives are an honour to their sex and faith. Great, then, must be the good this institution has effected, but its benefits would be incalculably extended, were it transferred to Chirra-Poonjee or Darjeling. Nature never intended that English girls should be brought up in Bengal : had those our friend spoke of been reared among the Hills, they *and their children* would have possessed far better constitutions physically, and we cannot help thinking that they would have been morally improved. Mental energy, we are aware, does not always accompany bodily strength ; but the former is very rarely found when the latter is wanting.

Within the last twelve months our Indian newspapers contained a proposition for establishing schools on the same principles as the European Orphan Asylum of Calcutta, but on a more extended plan, embracing boys as well as girls ; not limited to Orphans, but admitting full blood European children, whether Catholic or Protestant, both of her Majesty's and the Company's service. The projector contemplated that the new schools should be located in the Hills, in a climate where our efforts to train the heart and intellect, should not be neutralized by the relaxation, the listlessness, and the irritability that are almost inseparable from the European frame, born and brought up in the plains of India. It is mortifying that the plan we allude to appears to have excited small interest in the army. Some money subscriptions and donations have been registered in the provincial newspapers, and, so far, the materials for the work are accumulating. But money alone will not suffice ; before any such scheme is realized, a lively and persevering interest must be aroused, especially among our ladies, on whom it peculiarly devolves to support a plan designed in the first place to benefit the soldier's daughters.

The pressing need for such a refuge can only be estimated by those who have lived among our troops, whose duties have presented to their view European women in the barrack, on the march, in boats, and in camp ; who have seen young girls and married women, in the midst of drunken, half-naked men, hearing little but blasphemy and ribaldry, exposed to the extremes of heat and cold, surrounded by influences that render decency nearly impossible, and make devotion seem almost a mockery. Well might we despair of finding even 'ten righteous' in such a scene of degradation. But let us remember that, when a man gifted even with prophetic discernment, believed that his nation contained not one worshipper of the true God, Omniscience saw therein 'seven thousand men who had not bowed the knee to Baal.' Neither is the moral desolation of our barracks uncheered by some bright spots. Throughout the present article, we have had reference peculiarly to our countrywomen; and therefore, while we duly appreciate well conducted soldiers, we now speak only of their wives. Among this class there are some, towards whom we feel a reverence that we want words to express. Sober and industrious in their habits, humane to the sufferers around them, holding on their unostentatious, upright demeanour, we have known them actually succeed in training their daughters to better habits than are sometimes found among 'finished young ladies.' Compared to worth like this, what are the sheltered, cultivated, applauded merits of women in a happier class? Those we now have in view, live their life of hardship, and when they die they are buried,

> " No marble tells us where, and with their names,
> No bard embalms and sanctified his song,"

But 'their record is on high,' and the last great day shall declare it.

To prevent mistake, we may as well state in explicit terms that, in the foregoing remarks, we have had more particularly in view the extreme desireableness of establishing institutions of *various grades*—suited to the wants of *different classes* of society—and offering something like a *reasonable guarantee* for their *permanence* not less than their *efficiency*. We are fully aware of the vigorous and praiseworthy efforts, which, in this respect, have already been made in different quarters by private individuals—such as the Mackinnons of Mussourie, and the spirited founders of the magnificent establishment of Manor House in that highly favoured locality. All such initial efforts ought to meet with the commendation and encouragement which they so eminently deserve; while a sketch of the rise and progress of these and similar institutions, with notices of the causes of their failure or success, would be specially serviceable as paving the way for the ultimate realization of stabler and more extended designs.

ART. V.—*History of Europe from the commencement of the French Revolution, in* 1789. *By Archibald Alison, F. R. S. E. Advocate—Vol.* 7, *(Chapter LI—LII; the British Empire in India,) Third Edition: Edinburgh,* 1843.

WHATEVER proceeds from Mr. Alison's pen is entitled to respectful attention. Whether we cordially sympathise with the historian in the sentiments he has expressed, or utterly dissent from his opinions, it is impossible, without an entire and most reprehensible abandonment of all the candour and impartiality, which ought to distinguish the proceedings of the literary judge, to withhold from the work, which we have named at the head of this article, a full, if not an over-running measure, of liberal, well-merited praise. Mr. Alison has written a standard work, which has narrowly escaped being a great one. We cannot add that we make this qualification more in sorrow than in anger. Mr. Alison's short-comings are the results not of any unavoidable intellectual deficiencies, but of a certain—apparently stubborn—not wilfulness, which has caused him, as though in very wantonness, to mar the excellence of a performance, which the presence of a little more care and a little more self-denial—care in the correction of small facts and the perfection of a style always animated and often eloquent; self-denial in the non-obtrusion of his own political prejudices and far-fetched philosophical deductions—would have left the reader of the present and of future generations very little to desire.

If we have ever any reason to regret the limited sphere of our labors, in this journal, it is when we rise from the perusal of such a work, as Mr. Alison's History of Europe. We read, but as regards the work in its integrity, it is permitted to us to do no more. It is only in the incidental character of an historian of India that this writer comes in any way before the literary tribunal, which we have erected, and the prerogatives of which we have clearly defined. Mr. Alison has devoted a portion of the seventh volume of his history to a narrative of the Rise and Progress of British Power in the East. It is not only our privilege, but our duty, as Indian reviewers, to notice these chapters of Indian history. We perused them with no ordinary interest. Our expectations were raised to a height, perhaps more complimentary than just to the historian. We thought that Mr. Alison's genius was of a character the most likely of all others to do justice to so magnificent a theme— we thought that we should find in the Indian chapters of his voluminous work, an animated, graphic, picturesque, narrative of our military career in the East, and, though not without a tinge of prejudice, a philosophical review of the causes of our extraordinary success. But we have been greatly disappointed. With something more than the ordinary measure of prejudice and one-sidedness which characterises Mr. Alison's historical writings, is united, in these chapters, considerably less of the accuracy of the narrator, and the depth and sagacity of the philosophical historian, whilst, at the same time, the language is even more defective than in any other portion of the work. We repeat that these errors of mere wilfulness no critic can readily forgive. Mr. Alison's many and great merits can not be pleaded in extenuation of such offences as these ; for when a writer can do better if he will, we have a right to expect that he should do so ; and the greater the pretensions of the work, the more inexcusable the small vices, which disfigure it.

It is not our intention to point out all the errors into which Mr. Alison has fallen. We shall content ourselves with noticing a few. At page 25, the Historian asserts that—

In India, notwithstanding the long period that some districts have been in British possession, and the universal peace which reigns from Cape Comorin to the Himalaya Mountains, the natives are still ineligible to offices of trust both in the civil and military departments.

Had Mr. Alison perused the existing charter of the Indian Government, he would have perceived that natives of India are not " ineligible" to offices of trust. Had he made any enquiries relative to the practice of the Indian Government, he would have ascertained that natives of India are, every week, appointed to offices of trust. Whether they are yet admitted to a fair share in the administration of the country is a question, which may properly be discussed ; but if full justice is not done to them, it is not because they are " ineligible ;" nor is it to be inferred that they have no participation in the Government of the country because they have not as much as is justly their due.

Mr. Alison's views of the religious creeds of the inhabitants of India and the neighbouring countries appears to be somewhat obscure. At page 26, he says—

The mild and pacific followers of Bramah have in different ages been obliged to bow the neck to the fierce *idolaters of Kabul.*

Why the Affghans should be called idolaters we are at a loss to determine. Mr. Alison's knowledge of these matters appears to be about on a par with that of a recent Governor-General, sent out to India on account of his consummate knowledge of Indian affairs, who asked an officer, lately returned from a residence of many years in Persia and Affghanistan, whether in those countries he had ever been brought into contact with Mahomedans. Mr. Alison does not seem to be aware that the people of Kabul are Mahomedans.

Again, after enumerating all the different varying creeds of the people of India, " rigid followers of Shiva, savage pagans of Tartary, impetuous fire-worshippers of Persia," &c. &c. Mr. Alison says—

Heathens and Cannibals are found in great numbers in the hilly regions of the North Eastern frontier.

It would seem from this that Mr. Alison does not consider that the Hindus are generally heathens. As regards cannibals, we believe that there are a few in the hilly regions skirting Assam—but we are a little startled to find them classed with " heathens" in such a manner as to lead the reader to suppose that the one species of humanity is as numerous, in the hilly regions, as the other.

At page 28, with reference to the diversity of classes in the Indian army, Mr. Alison observes :

When the regimental parade is dismissed, the soldiers break into separate knots: the gradation of caste is destroyed, the distinctions of faith return; the Sudra sergeant makes his salaam to the Brahman or the Rajput private; the Mussulman avoids the Christian, the Shiah the Súní ; the Hindu all : and an almost impassable barrier of mutual distrust and jealousy obstructs all amalgamation of opinion or unity of action, even upon those national objects which separately interest the whole body.

Now we can assure Mr. Alison that very much of this is fabulous. There is little or none of the segregation off parade, which he attributes to the different classes composing a native regiment. They mingle familiarly in camp or in lines ; and recent events have not shewn that the mixture of creeds has presented any obstacle to mutinous combination. That men of different faiths, or different castes do not cook and eat together is true ; but beyond this, there is little or nothing to indicate the religious creed or religious rank of the sepoy. In some regiments, indeed, there is such an entire absence of all class feeling, that the Mussulman sepoys subscribe their quota towards the celebration of Hindu festivals and the Hindu towards the due outward observance of the ceremonials of the Mahomedan.

Speaking of the sepoy army, Mr. Alison observes that,

The first mention of them (the sepoys) in history is when a corps of 100 natives from Bombay, and 400 from Tellicherry assisted the army at Madras, in 1747.— *P. p.* 31-32.

Mr. Alison should not have written " the first mention in history," but the first mention in such histories as he had taken the trouble to consult.   There were sepoy levies in Bengal forty years before this date.   We could help the historian to authentic notices of native troops as early as 1707.

Mr. Alison entertains a most exalted opinion of the magnificent state of the Indian sepoys.   He says,

Each private sepoy is attended by two servants ; in the field there are, at an average, nine followers to every two fighting men.. . . . . .when the pay given to a private soldier is so considerable as to admit of his keeping two servants in the camp and a still greater number in the field, no want of recruits will ever be experienced.—*P. p.* 33-34.

The historian, in the above passage, has betrayed an entire mis-comprehension of the real state of the case.   He has apparently been led astray, by some statements, which he has read— probably, correct enough in themselves, but not sufficiently explanatory for the guidance of those, who have no local experience or information to assist them to a right understanding of the facts so succinctly stated.   It may be true that the number of camp-followers with an army in the field exceeds the number of fighting men, in the ratio set down by Mr. Alison, though we are inclined to think that the estimate* is somewhat overdrawn —but we certainly were not before aware that this prodigious mass of suttlers consists of the personal attendants of the sepoys. The camp-followers of an Indian army are perhaps the most motley crew which is ever set in motion by a word : but these multifarious components of the great living mass are wholly, or were chiefly the salaried servants of the native soldiery no more than the varied ingredients of the *magna caterva* of tag-rag and bobtail which may be seen moving down the slopes of Epsom downs, at the close of the Derby day, are the personal attendants of the gentry who have just before quitted the course.   These camp-followers are ghomastas, shroffs, buneahs, butchers, tradesmen of every possible description—thieves, beggars, camel and horse-dealers, officers, servants, &c. &c.—a vast number of each denomination being attended by their relatives and dependents. Nor, must we omit to specify a fact, perhaps unknown to Mr. Alison, a vague reference to which has not improbably led him into the error now under notice—that every *horse* with the army, be it ridden by an officer or a trooper, is attended by two men—a syce (or groom) and a grass-cutter : and that every camel has also its personal attendants.   That every soldier in the mounted branch of the service has two servants to wait upon his *horse* is undeniably true ; but these servants are entertained

* The usual calculation is that the camp-followers are triple the number of the fighting men.   But, as respects the mounted branches of the service, this estimate is somewhat under-drawn.   With the latter the number of camp-followers is, probably, as five to one.   But the great bulk of an army consists of foot-men.

and paid not by the trooper, but by the Government which he serves. The soldiers themselves, both in cantonment, and in the field, have generally a share in a personal servant, paid by themselves—whilst a native officer has a servant of his own, if a subadar perhaps more than one—but Mr. Alison will find upon enquiry that this is the full extent of the sepoy's suite. That the native soldier is liberally paid we admit. But his personal expenditure is not heavy. If he indulged himself to any great extent, he would be unable to save, as with few exceptions he ever does, so large a portion of his monthly income, to be remitted, or carried home to his family. This saving propensity is one of the most striking and the most honorable characteristics of the native soldier,—one, which contrasts, most favorably with the selfish, and often brutal prodigality of his European brethren in arms. "They never take their wives or children with them 'to their regiments, or to the places where their regiments are 'stationed. They leave them with their fathers or elder bro-'thers, and enjoy their society only when they return to fur-'lough. Three-fourths of their income are sent home to 'provide for their comfort and subsistence, and to embellish 'that home in which they hope to spend the *winter* of their days. 'The knowledge that any neglect of the duty they owe their dis-'tant families will be immediately visited by the odium of their 'native officers and brother soldiers, and ultimately communi-'cated to the heads of these families, acts as a salutary check on 'their conduct ; and I believe that there is hardly a native 'regiment in the Bengal Army, in which the twenty drummers, 'who are Christians, and have their families with the regiment, 'do not cause more trouble to the officers than the whole eight 'hundred sepahis."*—As the sepoys send home to their families three-fourths of their salaries, they must pay their two servants out of the residue, which is to supply all their personal wants. This residue is something less than five shillings a month.

We feel some disposition to question the accuracy of Mr. Alison's characterisation (at page 35) of the native cavalry; but the theme is an ungrateful one, and we willingly let the panegyric of the historian pass—the more especially as the cloud, which at one time overshadowed that branch of the service, has more recently been well nigh dispersed. But there is a confusedness in his account of the manner, in which the Indian army is officered, that calls for more distinct notice. At page 361, Mr. Alison says :

The immense host is entirely under the direction of British officers, nearly five thousand of whom are employed in this important service ; but

* Sleeman's *Rambles and Recollections of an Indian* official.

the non-commissioned officers and subalterns always were natives, and the avenue to more elevated promotion is now open to the most deserving of the number.

We do not quite know what meaning Mr. Alison may have intended the above passage to convey, but we are certain that the meaning which it does convey is something very remote from the truth. *Some* of the "non-commissioned officers and subalterns" of the sepoy regiments are, it is true, natives; but in both capacities the natives are ridden over by Europeans, and their real authority reduced to *nil*. What "more elevated promotion is now open" to the native soldier we have not yet discovered.

Before passing on to one or two more important points, which we purpose to notice at greater length, we may briefly allude to a few minor inaccuracies, which certainly ought not to be found in such a work as Mr. Alison's history :—

Such a treaty was immediately concluded with the Hindu potentate, on terms highly favorable to the English ; and shortly after hostilities commenced, by Colonel Clive marching with two thousand men against the French fort of *Chandernagore, on the Hooghly, eighty miles above Calcutta.*— *Page* 53.

Mr. Alison will, doubtless, be surprised to learn that Chandernagore is little more than *twenty* miles from Calcutta.*

For the first and the last time in his life, Clive called a council of war : the proverb held good and the council declined to fight ; but the English general consulted only his own heroic character, and led his troops against the enemy.—*P. p.* 55-56.

Mr. Alison appears to be ignorant of the fact, that Clive himself voted against fighting ; and that, too, not in the ordinary course of things, confirming the judgment of his inferior officers, for contrary to all custom—all propriety—he was the first to give his opinion. The historian in a note adds this comment. " The shelter of numbers is never sought but by those ' who have not the moral courage to act on their own convic- ' tion ; true intrepidity of mind never seeks to divide respon- ' sibility ;"—a bitter, though unintended censure on the conduct of Clive, who not only sought the opinion of others, in an emergency, but apparently endeavoured to bias their opinion, by most irregularly declaring his own. It is true that the " heroic character" of the heaven-born general was but for a brief season extinct—his courage and constancy soon re-asserted them-

---

* As Admiral Watson with his ships of war, the Kent, Tiger, &c. sailed up to Chandernagore and attacked the fort from the river, this mistake is rather curious. The sight of a British fleet eighty miles above Calcutta would, indeed, be an astonishing one. For a very animated description of the capture of Chandernagore, we may refer our readers to Mr. Macfarlane's " Indian Empire."

selves, and regardless of his own previous decision and that of the eight officers, who voted with him,* he resolved, on the very same night, to advance ; but Mr. Alison's account of the affair, which contrasts the heroic character of Clive with the pusillanimity of the council, is obviously calculated to mislead. No one, relying on his authority, would believe that the transaction occurred as we have stated it.

Again, at page 73, we are told, that,

The death of his (Hasting's) rival, the *Maharajah* Nuncomar, left him without a rival in civil administration, &c. &c.

As Francis was in India, and Clavering alive, at the time of Nuncomar's execution, Hastings, by no possible figure of speech can be said to have been without a rival.

Of the vices of Mr. Alison's style we may give the following examples :—

The British were sheltered, in the early part of the day, by a high bank from the cannon-shot of the enemy ; treachery and disaffection reigned in their ranks ; and before Clive led his troops in their turn to the attack the victory was already gained.—*Page* 54.

Mr. Alison here says that treachery and disaffection reigned in the ranks of the British. He means to say that they reigned in the ranks of the enemy.

Lord Clive was one of the greatest generals and bravest *men recorded in history.*—*Page* 61.

One more example will suffice. Mr. Alison appears to be strangely neglectful of the rules of relative and antecedent—

In order, however, to carry into execution the pacific views of ministers at home, a nobleman of high rank and character, *Lord Cornwallis, was sent out by Mr. Pitt, who united in his person the two offices of Governor-General and Commander-in-Chief.*— *Page* 96.

It is here not Lord Cornwallis, but Mr. Pitt, who is said to have " united in his person the two offices of Governor-General and Commander-in-Chief."

These, it may be said, are small matters ; but we repeat that it is because they are small matters we consider them all the more amenable to censure. A work of such high pretensions ought not to be disfigured by such ignoble errors. We have no toleration for the slatternly habits of the woman, who flaunts it in velvet and diamonds, whilst there are holes in her gloves and darns in her stockings.

But we willingly pass on to the consideration of more important matters.

---

* Capt. Coote (afterwards Sir Eyre Coote) and five others voted for the advance.

At page 39, Mr. Alison, with reference to the tried fidelity of the Sepoy Army, observes :—

At the mutiny of Vellore, which shook the Indian empire to its foundation, and *was brought on by an absurd interference with the religious feelings of the troops*, the sabres of the native *dragoons* were dyed as deep as those of the British, in the blood of their unhappy countrymen.

It is probable, we think, that if a Wellesley, and not a Bentinck, had presided over the Government of Madras in 1806, Mr. Alison would have given a somewhat different account of the causes of the Vellore mutiny; because he would, in that case, have taken greater pains to arrive at a knowlege of the truth. There was no "absurd interference with the religious feelings of the troops." There were certain alterations introduced into the uniform of a portion of the Native Army—alterations, which the sepoys, prompted thereto by designing parties, construed into an *intention* to "interfere" with their "religious feelings :" but it is no more in accordance with strict historical truth to affirm that the Madras authorities "interfered with the religious feelings of the troops," because an act, bearing no reference whatever to these feelings was thus designedly and maliciously misconstrued, than it would be, to impute to them a similar gross and culpable indiscretion, because an attempt was made, and not altogether unsuccessfully, to impose upon the ignorance and superstition of the natives, by alleging that the benevolent efforts, instituted at that time to introduce *Vaccination* into India, had for their end the inoculation of Hindus and Mahomedans with the *views* of Christianity. No Government is, in such cases, fairly chargeable with the evils arising from the gross ignorance of one part of its subjects and the malicious machinations of another part,—teaching the more imbecile to "believe a lie" and stirring them up to the resistance of never-contemplated aggressions. No sagacity—no fore-sight can be proof against the malignant misrepresentations of designing men, who make a harvest of the credulity of their weaker brethren. If the causes of the Vellore mutiny did lie in an alteration of the head-dress of the sepoys and certain other less important equipments, the charge now preferred against the Madras Government would, for these reasons, be essentially unjust ;—but the truth is that the new head-dress produced the mutiny only as the last straw, is said, in the proverb, to break the camel's back. If the sepoys had not been induced to believe that they were about to be converted into *topiwallahs*, some other leperous distilment would have been poured into their ears—some other offensive innovation would have been attributed to Government—and the last straw would still have been found.   The immediate cause of the mutiny lay in the wilful misrepresentations of the adherents of the old Mysore dynasty ; the pre-disposing cause is to be found in the culpable indifference of the European officers of the Army to the welfare of their men, and the arrogance with which they were wont, with rare exceptions, to treat them.   Under a long course of systematic repulsion the attachment of the sepoys to their officers had gradually died away.   They felt that they were wronged ; and were in a frame of mind, well prepared for the credulous reception of any stories, however, preposterous, illustrative of the contumely of their masters.   They were ready to believe that the habitual disregard to their feelings, widened by the conduct of their officers, was about to manifest itself in more overt acts of outrage ; they felt that the iron heel was upon them, and found it easy to believe that they were soon to be crushed out-right. Thus prepared, they fell a willing prey to the wiles of the adherents of the Mysore family—crafty agents, who were ready to seize upon every circumstance of a remotely suspicious character to convert it, by some forced construction, into an evidence of the hostile designs of the British Government in the East.   The real culprits were those, who, by their contumacious and arrogant behaviour and their habitual disregard of the claims of the sepoys, had raised the spirit of mutiny in their breasts—a spirit which required, but the veriest trifle to call it forth into heavy and destructive operation.

We are the more desirous to insist upon this point, since we have lately perceived, with feelings of poignant regret, that other highly respectable writers are still inclined to keep alive the error, some forty years ago so industriously circulated both in India and in England, which assigned to apprehensions on the score of religion the sanguinary outbreak at Vellore. There is never wanting an inclination to attribute to religion, when any the slightest pretext for doing so exists, the authorship of whatever mischief, social or political, is manifested in the progress of affairs.   When many possible causes exist, the most unpopular agent is sure to be selected, by almost universal consent, as the one on which the opprobrium shall rest, and a possibility becomes a reality in the mouths of those, who are too glad of such an opportunity to do an injury to that which they detest.   Religion is the most common of all scape-goats. The mutiny at Vellore was eagerly seized upon, at the time of its occurrence, by men who uttered an incredible quantity of nonsense to prove that a few itinerant preachers, scattered over the immense continent of India, and a few copies of tracts or fragmentary portions of scripture in the native languages, circulated among a hundred millions of Asiatics, would infallibly lead to the overthrow of the British power in the East—eagerly seized upon by others, who wrote bulky volumes of inconceivable trash in praise of the beauties of Hinduism, and contended, with a plentiful lack of sense, that the introduction of Christianity would corrupt the moral purity of the immaculate followers of Brahma and Shiva—as a proof that the Natives of India were ready to resent, to the death, every symptom of a design to convert them to the religion of the stranger.   This fallacy was ably exposed and fully refuted at the time, when it was first launched into circulation, but it was too congenial to the feelings of men to be suffered very readily to slide into nothingness, and we are not therefore surprised to find it again put forward—and that, too, with a show of dispassionate candour, calculated to delude the unwary reader into a belief that the sifting of two score years had tended only to exhibit its unmistakeable truth.   Among others, Mr. H. H. Wilson, in the first volume of his recently published continuation of Mill's History of India,* has declared that "there can be no reason to seek for any other origin of the mutiny than dread of religious change inspired by the military orders."   He asserts,

The causes of this alarming occurrence necessarily engaged the attention of the public both in India and in Europe, and an acrimonious controversy ensued, which can scarcely be said even yet to be at rest.   Not that there was any sufficient reason for difference of opinion.   To an impartial judgment the real cause was liable to no misconception; but its admission involved inferences which were pressed by one party, beyond their due limits, and of which the grounds were therefore denied altogether by the other.   The question of converting the natives of India to the Christian religion was supposed to depend for its solution upon the origin of the massacre at Vellore.   By those who were unfriendly to missionary efforts as well as those who were apprehensive of these efforts upon native feeling, the transaction was appealed to as decisive of the reasonableness of their fears, and as justifying their opposition.   No better reply could be desired, by the friends and supporters of Missions than a denial that the Vellore mutiny had any connexion with the propagation of Christianity,—a denial in which they were undoubtedly wide of the truth.† The essential and main-

---

* We have great respect for Mr. Wilson's abilities ; though we have often occasion to dissent from his opinions.   It is a   source to us of deep regret that so much talent should be so often employed upon the wrong side.

† The Rev. Dr. Buchanan thus writes to the Government of Bengal :   "I understand that the massacre of Vellore has been unaccountably adduced, as some sanction to the principle of opposing the progress of the Christian religion in Bengal. I had opportunities of judging of the causes of that event, which were peculiar.   I was in the vicinity of the place at the time.   I travelled for two months immediately afterwards in the province adjacent, with the sanction of Government, and I heard the evidence of Christians, Mohammedans, and Hindus, on the subject.   That the

spring of the mutiny was religious principle, although its occurrence was influenced in the manner and season of its development by incidental and local excitement.

And again, making a faint show of candour and impartiality, he observes :—

Here however in fairness to the question of the conversion of the natives of India to Christianity, the nature of the panic which spread among the Sipahis requires to be candidly appreciated. It is a great error to suppose that the people of India are so sensitive upon the subject of their religion, either Hindu or Mahommedan, as to suffer no approach of controversy, or to encounter adverse opinions with no other arguments than insurrection or murder. On the contrary great latitude of belief and practice has always prevailed amongst them, and especially amongst the troops in whose ranks will be found seceders of various denominations from the orthodox systems. It was not therefore the dissemination of Christian doctrines that excited the angry apprehensions of the Sipahis, on the melancholy occasion which has called for these observations ; nor does it appear that any unusual activity in the propagation of those doctrines was exercised by Christian Missionaries at the period of its occurrence. It was not conversion which the troops dreaded but compulsion, it was not the reasoning or the persuasion of the Missionary which they feared, but the arbitrary interposition of authority. They believed of course erroneously that the Government was about to compel them to become Christians, and they resisted compulsory conversion by violence and bloodshed.* The lesson is one of great seriousness, and should never be lost sight of as long as the relative position of the British government and its Indian subjects remains unaltered. It is not enough that the authority of the ruling power should never interpose in matters of religious belief, it should carefully avoid furnishing grounds of suspicion that it intends to interfere.

We must go a little out of our way to make a few remarks

insurrection at Vellore had no connexion with the Christian religion directly or indirectly. immediately or remotely, is a truth which is capable of demonstration."— Letter from the Rev. C. Buchanan to the Governor-General, 7th Nov. 1807 ; Parliamentary Papers relating to Missionaries, &c., 14th April 1813. Dr. Buchanan undoubtedly believed in what he asserted so roundly, but he was strangely mis-informed. The most zealous and able defenders of the cause, Lord Teignmouth, in his considerations on the duty of diffusing Christianity in India, and Mr. Wilberforce in his speeches in 1813, afterwards published by himself, do not go to the same length : they only deny that the Vellore mutiny was connected with any unusual extension or activity of Missionary proceedings.

* The opinion that the Government had some such project in view was not confined to the Sipahis. Mir Alim, the veteran minister of the Nizam, and as has been seen, the staunch friend of the English, expressed his surprise that the British government should think it just or safe, to compel the troops to wear the semblance of Christians ; and a like astonishment was manifested by the ministers of Nagpur.— Letters from the Residents ; M. S. Records. Of the universality of the feeling, there is also published an impartial testimony. Purnia, the Dewan of Mysore, gave it as his opinion that the Hindus were more alarmed and dissatisfied than the Mahommedans.—Lord William Bentinck's Memorial, 45. And Sir Thomas Munroe writes : "however strange it may appear to Europeans, I know that the general opinion of the most intelligent natives in this part of the country is, that it was intended to make the sepoys Christians."—Letter to Lord William Bentinck, 11th August, 1806. This letter also shows, that, in a part of the Peninsula where the adherents of the family of Hyder were most numerous, there were no reasons for believing that any intrigues had been at work in their favour.—Life of Sir J. Munroe, I.—363.

on these passages. We give Professor Wilson all possible credit for a desire to treat this question fairly and ingenuously; but he deceives himself, if he thinks that he has succeeded in bringing to the task an amount of historical impartiality sufficient for the candid consideration of such a question. He has not, in truth, divested himself of those oriental prejudices and partialities, which led him to deliver a strong testimony against the propriety of abolishing the beautiful system of Suttee. The lapse of twenty years would seem to have detracted nothing from the conservative tendency of Mr. Wilson's opinions. He appears to be as little of a reformer in 1845, as in 1825. His mind has seemingly made no progress, during the interval, although had he been open to such influences, every year must have afforded him a fresh proof of the little danger arising from a judicious interference with the so-called religious feelings of the natives of India—every year must have presented him with a new catalogue of reasons for mistrusting his own judgment, for acknowledging the utter causelessness of the apprehensions, which he has so long entertained. The concluding sentence of the last extract, which we have made from Mr. Wilson's history is eminently characteristic of the writer. How far it serves to establish his claims to be considered as a fit person to undertake the continuation of Mill's history we leave it to the admirers of that eminent writer to determine. It has been said that in India all politicians are, more or less, reformers—a truth undeniable, we believe, when uttered with reference to those who read the book of the world with open eyes and clear faculties, looking abroad on men, studying the national character by means of intercourse with all classes of the community; watching closely the effects of legislative interferences, and duly considering the inevitable tendency of every new reform to prepare the soil for the introduction of still more extensive innovations. No Indian statesman, indeed, can be other than a Reformer. But there has existed a band of dry students, looking through the dusty spectacles of orientalism on ornate manuscripts, instead of on the wide country; conversing with bigoted *pundits,* who live upon the ignorance and superstition of their fellows, instead of deducing the opinions and probing the feelings of all classes of the population—a crew of hard, disputatious book-men, enamoured of eastern learning and thence of eastern customs and eastern errors—almost we may say of eastern *filth*—who were wont to raise a voice against every benevolent effort made by a Christian government to purge this immense stye of its dense layers of impurity ; who were wont to cry out against "dangerous innovations," to predict indeed the overthrow of our Anglo-Indian empire, whenever a Christian statesman bethought himself of rescuing the widow from the flames of the funeral pile, or the infant from the strangling fingers of her mother. This class of *obstructives* is now nearly extinct. No man can now-a-days, without incurring abundant ridicule, defend the amenities of the Hindu system of cruelty and idolatry any more than he can dilate on the treasures of wisdom and wit contained in the venerable volumes of Eastern literature, once said to be depositories of " science and poetry and thought," of the highest order, and the most inestimable value ; and they, who have, during the last quarter of a century, lived a waking life, are apt to suspect the men, who, in the year 1845, talk so freely about the danger of innovation, of having passed *their* time, like Rip Van Wynkle, in Sleepy Hollow, utterly oblivious of all that has been going on in the sentient, stirring world around them.   The Hindu mind, at the present time, so far from being in a state, from which anything of violent opposition may be apprehended to menace the benign efforts of a Christian legislature to introduce wise reforms, based upon principles of reason and humanity, is, we believe, well prepared not only for the reception but for the origination of great moral and religious changes.   To discourage and to check these yearnings after better things would be an act of as wicked and insane folly,

> ————— as though a mother should strive
> To stay the lusty manhood of the child
> Once weak upon her knees.

It appears to be Mr. Wilson's doctrine that the Government of India should exert itself not to avoid the appearance of evil ; but to avoid the appearance of good.   They ought, according to this authority, not only to abstain from doing good, but to be careful lest any one should suspect them of wishing to do good. It is not without a feeling of lively gratitude that we consider how very few participate in Mr. Wilson's sentiments—that the *obstructives* of which he is the *facile princeps* are fast ceasing to exist ; and that the stream of Reform, to which we may well apply the fine descriptive line of the Roman poet,

> Labitur, et labetur in omne volubilis ævum,

is rolling on, in a strong, voluminous, irresistible tide.

We are no advocates for the exercise of blind unregulated zeal in the obtrusion upon the people of India of legislative reforms or in private interference with their religious prejudices or social customs.   We have sometimes seen reason to deplore the want of judgment exhibited in the well-intended efforts of men, the purity of whose motives and the sincerity of whose conduct, are, in spite of the sneers and the questionings of those, who ridicule failures in which they rejoice, and are sceptical of a piety which they do not understand, entitled to the sympathy and admiration of all good men. It is a subject of deep regret that the most enthusiastic and the most devoted are not always the most prudent—the most judicious. It is necessary that every reformer should not only feel strongly but think deeply—that he should not only desire to do good, but that he should patiently study *how* to do it. The errors of devoted men, whose impulses are always in the right direction—whose souls are animated with the most earnest aspirations after the happiness of their fellow creatures—who pursue the grand objects of their lives, with toil and tribulation utterly regardless of self—are indeed most painful to contemplate; for, whilst we love such laborers for their zeal and self-devotion, we can not but be sensible that their labors are not mere labors in vain, since every failure in the right direction, resulting from a want of wisdom in the agent, becomes, in the hands of its enemies, a reproach to the cause itself. And that the cause suffers greatly by such failures no reasonable man can deny. Constituted as is the great majority of mankind we can not expect that a due distinction should be drawn between the excellence of the thing to be done and the wisdom of the agent attempting to do it. It is one of the tritest of trite common-places, that the short-comings of the latter are no indications of the unworthines of the former; but, obvious as is this truth, there is nothing so often overlooked, in heedlessness or in wilfulness, by the world. Fortunate, indeed, is it that there are men amongst us, in whom untiring energy, devoted zeal, and the most ardent philanthropy are united with brilliant talents, sound judgment, and an abundant fertility of resource—conspicuous in their successful employment of varied legitimate means of working towards the same great end. It is gratifying indeed to reflect that such men exist among us, for never was there a period in the history of British connexion with the east, in which a greater amount of good can be achieved by laborers of this class. The season is most propitious. The signs of the times are most encouraging. A great Reformation is developing itself; and at such an epoch, the skilful handling of dexterous men—men neither rash nor timid—may rapidly bring it to perfection. The danger of such interference exists, but in the imaginations of the Obstructives, who conjure up difficulties which they would fain see in real, insurmountable existence. This is not the place to demonstrate, by a reference to detailed facts—facts with which the daily life around us is everywhere gravid—the utter groundlessness of the fears which have been expressed by the enemies of the progress of Christianity in the east; but something has already been done elsewhere in this journal, and much more will we hope be done, to prove by the array of a magnificent phalanx of stubborn truths that the alarm entertained by such sophists as Professor Wilson is the ricketty child of ignorance and prejudice.

At the close of his sketch of the administration of the Marquis of Wellesley, Mr. Alison, in the second edition of his history, appends the following note :—

As the author is now to bid a final adieu to Marquis Wellesley's administration in the East, he trusts that he will not be accused of unbecoming feeling, but rather of a regard for historic truth, when he quotes in corroboration of the facts stated in the preceding chapters, the following passage in a letter with which after perusing this work, that great man honored him.—" Lord Wellesley had not the interview with Fouché of which you speak [this is now corrected]. But in all other respects he is ready to bear full testimony to the accuracy of your history and to the impartial and beautiful spirit in which it is conceived and written."—*Marquis Wellesley to Mr. Alison :* 20th November, 1840.* The imprimatur of such a man is indeed a testimony in relation to his own transactions, of which an historian may justly feel proud.

Now, assuredly, we do not charge Mr. Alison with the entertainment of any "unbecoming feeling," but on the other hand, we are considerably at a loss to decide whether the greater measure of beautiful simplicity is evinced by the historian or by the statesman. As Mr. Alison's account of the Wellesley administration abounds in high-flown panegyrics of the noble ruler and his illustrious brother—as the Marquis is every where pronounced to be the greatest man to whom the destinies of India have ever been entrusted—a statesman of gigantic calibre, beside whom Clive, Hastings and Cornwallis, are very pigmies—as his history is rife with such delicate compliments as the following, we can be at no loss to comprehend the secret of the noble Marquis' complacent admiration :†

Vigor and resolution are not alone capable of achieving success, though they are generally essential towards it; wisdom in combination, forethought in Council, prudence in preparation are also indispensable; and it was in the union of these invaluable qualities with the courage of the hero and the heart of the patriot that Lord Wellesley was unrivalled.—*Page* 126.

In vigour of resolution, moral courage, diplomatic ability and military

* From the phraseology of this letter it would appear to have been written by a secretary (probably Montgomery Martin) and not by the noble Marquis himself

† It may not be wholly irrelevant to add that Montgomery Martin is the chief authority, on whom Mr. Alison in the preparation of his chapters of Indian history. appears to have relied.

combination, he was the first of British statesmen even in the days of Pitt and Fox.—*Ibid*.

and held

—— The very highest rank as a scholar in the age of Porson and Parr.—*Page* 124.

This great statesman was relieved from the cares of sovereignty, and embarked at Calcutta, on his return to England, amid the deep regrets of all classes of the people, leaving a name imperishable in the rolls alike of European and Asiatic fame.—*Page* 219.

The administration of Marquis Wellesley exceeds, in the brilliancy and importance of the events by which it was distinguished, any recorded in British history.—*Page* 222.

Other passages of a similar tendency might be quoted. That the octogenarian statesman should have been enraptured with the "impartial and beautiful spirit" in which the history, containing such passages as these, is "conceived and written," is something extremely natural; but that Mr. Alison should, in sober seriousness, have published the letter expressive of the Marquis' delight, as a triumphant testimony in favor of the impartiality and beauty of his work, is we confess something surprising. It would have astonished us greatly if the Marquis of Wellesley had not thought so ardent an admirer of his character, an impartial and beautiful writer.

We do not quarrel with Mr. Alison for freely expressing the high opinion of the Wellesley administration, which he appears so sincerely to entertain. He has every possible right to express such opinions, and we have none to question the honesty of the historian. Viewed through a certain medium—and that, too, the one through which such exploits, as those distinguishing the government of the Marquis of Wellesley are commonly regarded, it is unquestionable that his Lordship's policy was a "vigorous" policy—that his administration was a most "brilliant" administration, and that he himself was eminently "successful." But we confess that there are still clinging to us certain antiquated notions, which lead us very greatly to question the success of the governor, who systematically violates the instructions he has received from his employers, and sets at naught the provisions of the legislature, under which he holds his appointment. We do not now purpose to consider the character of the Marquis of Wellesley, for which indeed we entertain very high respect, nor the individual acts of his government, which may have been in themselves necessary acts most meritoriously executed—we merely say, and in justice to others it behoves us to say this much, that in estimating the success of a governor, it is incumbent on the historian to consider well the nature of the office entrusted to him, and the objects, which he was commissioned to fulfil. Lord Wellesley was appointed Governor-General of India under a charter, which expressly prohibited the prosecution of measures, such as those which he delighted to carry out; and he proceeded to the East, with instructions framed in accordance with the spirit of that charter-act. His government—however able, however vigorous, however brilliant—was, from first to last, a long violation of that charter, of those instructions; and we, who are not easily dazzled by glitter, nor stunned by noise, are apt to consider the merits of his administration, nor merely with reference to the deeds which were accomplished, but to their consonance with the clearly prescribed duties which he was commissioned to perform. The clause in the charter-act may have been a monument of the folly of the legislature—the instructions of the home authorities may have been characterised by the most glaring inaptitude; still the Governor-General was bound to shape his measures in accordance with the spirit which they breathed; and we can not readily concede that a systematic disregard of the course of policy prescribed by the legislature of Great Britain and enforced by the Court of Directors can be viewed in the light of *success*. Lord Wellesley succeeded in doing precisely what he was commissioned not to do. It matters not whether the events, by which his administration was distinguished " exceeded in brilliancy and importance any recorded in British history"—it matters not whether he himself evinced the most consummate sagacity, the most unshaken resolution, and the most extraordinary vigour of execution—we hold that these points, in estimating the merits of the Wellesley administration, are not entitled to the regard which it has been the custom of historians to bestow upon them—in most instances to the exclusion of all other considerations. Not very dissimilar to this was the verdict of Lord Wellesley's cotemporaries in England. In spite of the great victories achieved and the vast extent of territory acquired, during the reign of the noble Marquis, the successes of his administration were viewed with very little complacency at home. The Court of Directors had written a very stringent letter to the Governor-General, when in India, censuring his Lordship's warlike policy; but the Board of Control, having taken alarm, intercepted the letter. The correspondence was printed after the return of the Marquis to England, and at a General Meeting, the Court of Proprietors passed a resolution approving of the conduct of the Directors in endeavouring "to restrain a profuse expenditure of the public money and to prevent all schemes of conquest and extension of dominion, measures which the legislature had declared to be repugnant to the wish, the honor, and the policy of the nation." This resolution was carried by a majority of 928 to 195.

We have made these observations with no desire to detract from the reputation of one of the ablest—we may add, one of the most honest, men, who have ever visited the land of the East: but it appears to us that the question, which we are now discussing, involves a principle of the utmost importance— a principle, which is too often lost sight of altogether in these days of unscrupulous aggression. The world is already much too prone to admire the splendid achievments of ambitious statesmen, who on touching the shores of India not seldom consider themselves free from all trammels either of superior authority or of Christian morality; and who equally disregard the mandates of their employers and the commands of God. It is because there is vastly too much of this independence in high places, and too great a propensity in lower places to admire and to extol this independence, that we have felt ourselves under an obligation, to do as much as lies in our power, to strip the truth of all the meretricious adornments of pride and pomp, which at present encumber it, and to consider not so much whether the statesmen, who have successively grasped the sceptre of India, have carried out their measures with ability and success, as whether those measures, were, with relation not only to eternal rules of right but to peculiar circumstances, in strict accordance with the duties which they were called upon to observe towards those, who were set in authority over them, as well as towards the great family of mankind. We are well aware that the opinions we have expressed, in this as well as in other articles, on what we conceive to be the duties of Christian statesmen, are opposed to those, which are current not only among men who think not at all, but among those who, we are bound to believe, think long and deeply upon such subjects; but this admitted fact only tends to impress us still more profoundly with the conviction that it is our duty to endeavour to bring about a more healthy state of feeling than that which seems everywhere to exist—to lead man's minds towards a more sober, a more serene investigation of the true character, estimated by right Christian principles, of great political events. It is not without sorrow —it is not without alarm that we perceive the strong propensity of historical writers to over-estimate the "brilliant" achievments of statesmen and warriors of the "vigorous" class, and to treat with scorn and contempt, the forbearance

U

of rulers, who abstain from earning a glorious reputation at the sacrifice of Christian principle, and consent to be accounted weak rather than bring themselves to *be* wicked. The historians, who are so enraptured with the brilliant achievments of a Clive and a Wellesley, do not fail to speak scorn of such rulers as Cornwallis, Shore, and Bentinck ; and thus not only hold out a premium upon political immorality, but crown the mischief by perpetuating among the masses of mankind the delusive casuistry, by which alone this immortality can be nourished and supported.   If it be true that an immense deal of mischief is done in the world by the early familiarity of our Christian youth with the writings of Homer and Virgil—writings, in which warlike exploits, though often a mixture of treachery and barbarity, are painted in the most attractive colors, and the characters of warriors, though often a base compound of selfishness and ferocity, extolled in the most glowing language,—how true must it also be that the historian, who rivets in after life the chains of false sentiment and low feeling which in early youth have been imposed by the Heathen poet, is the parent in his turn of a vast amount of social evil.   In his pages, martial achievments are not merely described in language that attracts—and great men extolled in language that inspires —in his pages, it is not alone the description and the praise which animate with ambition and impel to emulation, but he stands forth openly and avowedly in the character of a teacher ; he appeals to the reason more than to the imagination; he deliberately brings all his powers of ratiocination to bear upon the task of persuading men, through the medium of their understandings, to set a higher value upon achievments of a dazzling and astounding character, convulsing nations and perpetuating anarchy and confusion, than upon peaceful acts of beneficence, which make no noise, but quietly fertilize the soil of humanity and industriously scatter abroad the good seed, which in time springs up, a rich and abundant harvest of Civilization and Christianity.   However feeble the arms which we oppose against this giant of error, we feel well assured that we shall not lift them up altogether in vain ; they who " polish and brighten the armory of truth " do something, and, in the noble language of our motto, " were they but as the dust and cinders of our feet, they were not to be cast away."

We make one more extract from Mr. Alison's history—a passage, which, though belonging to the exordium of his narrative of the Rise and Progress of British power in India, we have reserved to the last, because it demands from us more detailed and elaborate consideration than the extracts on which we have hitherto commented :—

Mr. Burke has said that if the English were to be expelled from India, they would leave no better traces of their dominion than the hyena or the tiger. Even at the period when this celebrated expression was used, it savored more of the fire of the orator than the sober judgment of the statesman ; but had that great man survived to these times, he would have gratefully retracted the sarcasm and admitted that of all the marvels attending the British sway in the East, the most wonderful is the extraordinary blessings which it has conferred upon the inhabitants . . . . Brilliant as has been the career of England in the European world during the last half century, there are several circumstances in its internal situation, which can not be contemplated without painful feelings. Among these, the constant and uninterrupted increase of crime through all the vicissitudes of peace and war, unchecked by penal vigilance, undiminished by intellectual cultivation, is one of the most alarming. But under the British empire in the East, a very different and much more satisfactory progress has taken place. Rapid as has been the *growth* of crime in the European dominions of England during the last half century, its *decrease* in her Eastern possessions has been still more striking ; and the steady powerful rule of a central government has done as much for the inhabitants of Hindustan as the vices consequent on a corrupted manufacturing population have undone for the people of Great Britain. From the returns of commitments and crimes in many different provinces of India for the last thirty years, it distinctly appears that crime has, during that period, diminished one-half, in many places sunk to a sixth in the end ; whilst it has in the same time more than quadrupled in the British Islands, and in Ireland multiplied nine-fold. Nor is it difficult to perceive to what cause this remarkable difference is owing. Robbery and plunder, the crimes of violence, were those chiefly prevalent in India, growing out of the lawless habits which ages of mis-rule had diffused through a large portion of the population. These savage and dangerous crimes have been everywhere severely repressed, in some districts totally extirpated, by the strong and steady arm of the British Government. The long-established hordes of robbers have been in most places dissolved; the Pindarees who so long spread ruin and desolation through Central India rooted out ; the gangs of Dakoits and Sooties, who levied a frightful tax on honest industry, transported or broken up. But if this unwonted feeling of security against hostile spoliation, is so generally perceptible even in the provinces, which have enjoyed the benefit of European protection for the longest period, what must it be to those, which have lately been rescued from a state of anarchy, misery, and bloodshed, unparalleled in the modern history of the world. . . . . The extraordinary diminution of crime, especially of a violent kind, in all parts of the Indian peninsula of late years, and progressive amelioration of the people, is in a great measure to be ascribed to the extensive and powerful police force, which is very generally established. The discipline and organization of this civil body is admirable ; and such is its extent that in the provinces of Bengal and Behar, it numbers one hundred and sixty thousand men in its ranks. In most villages there are two or three, in many ten or twelve of this protecting force permanently established. Europeans may feel astonished at the magnitude of this establishment ; but experience has completely demonstrated that it is highly useful and indeed indispensable amidst the habits of lawless violence to which ages of license and rapine have inured the inhabitants of India. The rapid diminution of crimes of violence in Bengal under the operation of this preventive system, proves that a remedy has been discovered and applied to the prevailing causes of evil in those regions; would that human wisdom could devise an equally effectual preservative against the passion for illicit gain, sensual indulgence, and habitual intoxication. which are now, like a gangrene, overspreading the face of society in the British Islands.—*P. p.* 10-16.*

It is painful to us to be compelled to disperse with a harsh voice such pleasant visions as these, and to bid the dreamer arise and look with waking eyes, on the truth. Alas! that anything so delightful to contemplate should be other than a bright reality. Mr. Alison's comparisons appear to us to be singularly infelicitous. The vices of a corrupted manufacturing population have long been a favorite topic of discourse with writers of a particular political creed much given to the very common failing, of eager and impulsive theorists—a propensity to beg the question. A "corrupted manufacturing population" is one of the cant phrases, which form the stock-in-trade of these political hucksters. It has just so much truth in it, that a populace, whatsoever be its character, whether urban or agrarian, is ever more or less corrupted; but that there is more vice in the manufacturing than in most of the agricultural districts of Great Britain, we even at this distance take upon ourselves confidently and emphatically to deny. More than one elaborate report laid before Parliament within the last few years, containing a large mass of statistical details, has gone far to explode this fallacy—a fallacy, which, we believe, indeed, has long ere this gone the way of all such figments.†

---

* We have omitted from the pages quoted in the text, some passages relative to the rise of a middle class in India, drawn from the more industrious of the cultivators of the soil, and a little rhapsody on the subject of the wide diffusion of " a taste among them for luxuries and convenience to which their fathers were strangers." From the very bottom of our hearts do we wish that Mr. Alison's picture were a faithful one.

† A recent writer in the *Westminster Review* has well remarked;—"The antiquated notion of the superior morality of the rural population is now nearly abandoned. It received a heavy blow and a great discouragement from the publication of the first Reports of the Poor Law Commissioners in 1833, and again from the · Reports of the Factory Commissioners' in 1834, as well as from the 'Constabulary Force Report' of 1839. If any doubt remains upon the mind after reading the above documents, it will be dissipated by comparing the conduct of the mob in the agricultural riots of Kent and Sussex in 1830, with the manufacturing outbreak in Lancashire and Cheshire in 1842, and still more perhaps by a perusal of the concluding passages in the official Report made to Government last year, regarding the distress in Stockport, which was quoted in a former number of this review. In fact, this idea like some others that we have had occasion to refer to, is the mere offspring of poetical association, not of calm enquiry or reflection. We find it difficult to believe that wickedness can disfigure the sweet scenery of rural life, or that virtue can haunt and hallow the streets of the smoky city. We are apt, moreover, to condemn what is evil in proportion as it offends, not our moral judgment, but our cultivated taste—and to forget that vice is not the less hideous, though it may be less disgusting, when perpetrated in green lanes or shady forests, than in the dismal courts and alleys of Glasgow or of Liverpool."

This, however, is a point altogether foreign to the objects of the present enquiry. It is beyond our province to investigate the comparative immorality of the manufacturing and agricultural districts of Great Britain; but we may, with reference to the comparison instituted by Mr. Alison between the state of crime in England and its Indian dependencies, demur to the test, which the historian has applied to its elucidation. We do not look upon such tables as those which Mr. Alison has quoted in his appendix, as correct indices of the actual state of crime, progressive or retrogressive, in one country or the other.* They exhibit not the amount of crime; but the amount of detected crime, and may, in many instances be regarded, as valuable indications of the increasing or diminishing efficiency of police establishments. It has been well said that " the number of crimes detected forms no surer criterion of the number committed than do the fish which are caught of the fish in the sea." In England, it is unquestionable that the means of detecting crime have greatly improved within the last twenty years; but it is not so certain that the relative amount of crime has increased beyond the extent to be anticipated from so vast an increase of the population. Mr. Alison's opinions on these points appear to be widely different from our own. He sees in the " extensive and powerful Police force which is now pretty generally established," and whose " discipline and organization" he tells us are so *admirable*, the cause of the alleged diminution of crime within the provinces of India. Now we can assure Mr. Alison, that our Police force, " extensive" though it be, is so far from being admirable, that it is admitted everywhere to be a standing reproach to the British Government. The dishonesty, the rapacity, the indolence, the cowardice, the utter inefficiency of our Police are evils not asserted in a spirit of faction by the opponents of Government, but are candidly and openly admitted by the servants of that Government, who ceaselessly deplore the existence of a state of affairs, which it is indeed difficult to amend. Mr. Alison could, by no possibility, have alighted upon a more unfortunate object of admiration than the Indian Police.

* We could produce other tables, more worthy of consideration than those which Mr. Alison quotes from Montgomery Martin—We happen, at this present time, to have before us, some statistics prepared by Dr. Hutchinson, in his valuable work on *Indian Jails*, which tell a somewhat different story. This writer has shown that in 1835, there were 37,527 prisoners in the Jails of Bengal, the North West Provinces and the Straits of Malacca (our penal settlements); and in 1842, the number was 47,736. During this interval there were some years both of increase and decrease, the highest number being 56,637—but it would seem that there are more persons in our jails now, than ten years ago. As Mr. Hutchinson received these returns, as secretary to the Medical Board, their accuracy can not be questioned.

We do not mean to deny that within the British provinces crime has considerably decreased. We should not be as hopeful as we now are of the ultimate destiny of the Hindu races, if we did not believe that contact with Christianity and civilization has already done something to humanize the people. Crime has decreased in *spite* of the admirable efficiency of the Police—but we must not flatter ourselves that our direct efforts for the advancement of public justice have not hitherto fallen far short of the wishes—we might almost add the reasonable expectations of all benevolent minds. Something has been done, of late years, to render justice more accessible to the people; but much—very much has yet to be done, before the upper classes will cease to consider it more expedient to conceal, even at a considerable cost, crimes committed upon their estates, than suffer them to be investigated in our courts of justice; and the lower classes cease to think it better to suffer any wrong, and to spend their last anna in *douceurs* to the admirable Police, rather than appear as prosecutors or witnesses;—much has yet to be done before our courts will be regarded in any other light than as the *arena* on which great battles of perjury and corruption—of bribery and chicane—are to be fought,—the longest purse and the toughest conscience infallibly winning the day. Some seven or eight years have elapsed since Dwarkanath Tagore—a name almost as well known in European countries as in his own,*—delivered, before the Police committee assembled in Calcutta, the following opinion of the Indian Police, and we can assure Mr. Alison that what was truth in 1837, is truth in 1845 —" I think that from the Darogah to the lowest peon the whole ' of them are a corrupt set of people—a single case could not ' be got out of their hands without paying money—the wealthy ' always get advantage over the poor. In quarrels between ' Zemindars and Indigo Planters, large sums are expended to ' bribe these people—when any report is called for by the Magis- ' trates from the Darogah, even in a true case, that report could ' not be obtained without paying a large sum of money; and ' should the case be between two rich parties, the richest or he ' who pays the highest would get the report in his favor. If a ' Jemadar or Peon is sent to a village for any enquiry, there is ' immediately a tax levied by them on all the ryots in the ' village, through the gomastah of the Zemindars, and this mode

* And therefore, in the present instance, referred to by us. The Indian reader must bear in mind that we are replying to Mr. Alison; and that it is necessary to adduce, for the edification of the home community, much which in India must be looked upon as a very superfluous elaboration of an universally admitted truism. For him it is totally unnecessary that on such a subject as this, we should quote Dwarkanath Tagore, or any one else.

' of extortion has so long prevailed as almost to give it the
' character of a just demand.......If a dakoity takes place in any
' neighbourhood, the Darogah and all his people will go about
' the villages and indiscriminately seize the inhabitants, inno-
' cent or culpable, and it often happens, that persons so taken
' although of the most suspicious character, in the particular
' transaction, are released on some money inducement being
' given to the officers....In short nothing can be done without
' paying for it whenever they are called upon to interfere."—
And when asked by the committee, " Do you find yourself as
Zemindar on all occasions of reference to the Police obliged
to have recourse to bribes?" this distinguished native honestly
replied, " Yes, I do find myself so obliged, believing that
' unless I did so, I should not even in a right case obtain
' justice"—and many European gentlemen, resident in the
Mofussil, if called upon, would have made a similar reply. The
facts stated, indeed, are sufficiently notorious in India; but it
would appear that in England a different estimate has been
formed of the merits of this *admirable* body of men.

Should Mr. Alison still feel sceptical of the alleged deficiencies of our Indian Police we would recommend to him the
perusal of a chapter on this subject in one of the last, and
we may add one of the best works on India, which has emanated
from the London press. Colonel Sleeman is an honest and
unprejudiced writer, and no one will suspect him of over-stating
the defects of any Government establishment. In the magnificent work entitled *Rambles and Recollections of an Indian
Official,* (briefly noticed by us in a former number) this able
and excellent officer has given us a little of the experience
derived from his long and intimate connexion with the Indian
Police force: and in order that the historian of Europe may
learn in what manner the vigilance of this "admirable" body
diminishes the amount of crime throughout the country, we
may not unprofitably quote a few passages from the interesting
chapter to which we refer:—

The Police Officers employed on our borders find it very convenient to
trace the perpetrators of all murders and gang robberies into the territories
of Native chiefs, whose subjects they accuse often when they know that the
crimes have been perpetrated by our own. They are, on the one hand,
afraid to seize or accuse the real offenders, lest they should avenge themselves by some personal violence or by thefts and robberies which they often
commit, with a view to get them turned out of office as inefficient; and, on
the other, they are tempted to conceal the real offenders by a liberal share of
the spoil and a promise of not again offending within their *beat.* [And so
crime is diminished.]......When they cannot find them (the real offenders)
the native officers either seize innocent persons, and frighten them into con-

fessions ; or else they try to conceal the crime, and in this they are seconded by the sufferers in the robbery, who will always avoid if they can a prosecution in our courts, and by their neighbours, who dread being summoned to give evidence as a serious calamity. The man who has been robbed, instead of being an object of compassion among his neighbours often incurs their resentment for subjecting them to this calamity ; and they not only pay largely themselves but make him pay largely to have his losses concealed from the magistrate. [And so crime is diminished.]........Crimes multiply from the assurance the guilty are everywhere apt to feel of impunity ; and the more crimes multiply the greater is the aversion the people everywhere feel to aid the Government in the arrest and conviction of criminals ; because they see, more and more, the innocent punished by attendance on distant courts at great cost and inconvenience, to give evidence upon points which appears to them unimportant, while the guilty escape owing to technical difficulties, which they can never understand. [And so crime is diminished.]........To escape all these threatened evils they pay handsomely and depart in peace. The thannadar reports that an attempt to rob a house by persons unknown had been defeated by his exertions and the *good fortune* of the magistrate ; and sends a liberal share of spoil to those who are to read his report to that functionary. This goes on more or less in every district........Some magistrates think that they can put down crime by dismissing the thannadar ; but this tends only to prevent crimes being reported to him ; for in such cases the feelings of the people are in exact accordance with the interests of the thannadar and crimes augment by the assurance of impunity thereby given to criminals........It is a common practice among thannadars all over the country to connive at the residence within their jurisdiction of gangs of robbers, on the condition that they shall not rob within those limits, and shall give them a share of what they bring back from their distant expeditions. [And so crime is diminished.] These are things of daily occurrence in all parts of our dominions, and the thannadars are not afraid to play such ' fantastic tricks ' because all those under and all those above them share more or less in the spoil, and are bound in honor to conceal them from the European magistrate whom it is the interest of all to keep in the dark. They know that the people will hardly ever complain from the great dislike they all have to appear in our courts, particularly when it is against any of the officers of those courts, or their friends and creatures in the district police. [And *so* crime is diminished— Oh ! the *admirable* Police !]

We wish to be distinctly understood. It is of importance that, having proceeded thus far (we speak of the general tendency of this journal, and not of the particular article upon which we are now engaged) in the work, which we entered upon with doubt and hesitation, little more than a year ago, that our readers should distinctly understand the principles upon which we desire to conduct it. Our leading object is to put forth such clear and temperate expositions of existing evils and to suggest such remedies, complete or partial for these evils, as may appear to be practicable and efficacious. To accomplish this it is necessary that there should be a diversity of labor— a diversity of laborers. In a community so limited as this— one in which we are necessarily dependent on the voluntary exertions of individuals, already perhaps over taxed by official duties, it can not be expected that we should gather around us —nor indeed, would it be desirable, if possible to do so—a band of regular contributors, entertaining doctrines, wholly or even partially consonant the one with the others, upon questions which have, perhaps, not been sufficiently considered and canvassed, to induce much fixity of opinion on any side.   The political creeds of the majority are unsettled; there are many shades of opinion, but rarely, save in a few extreme cases—and these extremes it is possible may sometimes be shadowed forth in our pages—much decided antagonism.   Occasionally we may fall in with an eager theorist, with more of impulse than discrimination, who, drawing pictures of an Utopian, Paradisaical state, and seeing with his own eyes that the reality falls far short of the bright ideal, denounces, in unmeasured language, the short comings of the British Government and chafes indignantly at every mention of the benefits, which after its own bit-by-bit system of reform, it has conferred and is conferring on the people.   There are, on the other hand, a few, whose sympathies are of the narrowest dimensions, and who resent all allusion to existing evils, as though it were a direct affront to them as servants of the state.   They can not be forced into admissions even of the most obvious character; they can not concede that India has yet many wrongs to be redressed, that the British power has yet much to do before its name can be celebrated in terms of glowing panegyric in connexion with its wonderful empire in the East.   But the mass of thinking men are agreed as to the wisdom and propriety of avoiding either extreme.   They see that there is much still to be done—that there are evils, many and great, reaching across the whole length and breadth of the land; and that Government, in the due fulfilment of its obligations to its Eastern subjects, must be constantly employed in the work of perfecting great ameliorative reforms.   To be idle is to be criminal.   We can not stand still. In this country every ruler must be a reformer—every Government must be one of progress.   Now we conceive that to expose evils and to suggest remedies is not necessarily to reproach, even by inference, the Governing body.   Readily admitting that much has been done, we can not but perceive that much more remains to be done; and we are hopeful that every new year will see a diminution of the pile of unperformed duties.   It is our purpose not to reproach—not to revile— not to menace—but, strong in hope and in faith, to encourage, and as far as in us lies, to assist the beneficent endeavors of Government, whose advances in the right direction we shall ever feel more pleasure in setting forth and illustrating than in

w

commenting on its fallings short.   It is in no factious—in no
querulous spirit that we have set about our present task.   It
will please us better to work with the Government than against
it; and we are not without a hope that in the prosecution of
our duties we shall find ourselves more frequently the allies
than the opponents of legitimate authority.

We especially desire to avoid all exaggeration, in our exposition of existing evils.   We would not willingly go one inch
beyond the ascertained truth.   It is true that self-complacency,
national as individual, is more common than self-depreciation.
That the world is more prone to flatter itself with the assurance
that it has gone far enough in well-doing than to admit the
conviction that it has fallen lamentably short of the verge
of duty; and on this account, it may be less injurious to
the interests of humanity to condemn, than to extol over much;
but when we remember that there are never wanting enemies to
truth—hostile to, because fearful of, direct revelations—who
stand ready armed with minute practical details and ingenious
logical proofs, to convict the earnest exponent, who should
chance, in the plenitude of his zeal, to over-step the boundaries
of demonstrable fact, of what is ever sure to be called gross
exaggeration; and, as a little leaven leaveneth the whole lump,
to condemn, perhaps for one single error, the entire mass of truth
with which it is surrounded.   We cannot but acknowledge the
immense detriment, which the cause of humanity sustains at
the hands of the advocate, who innocently exaggerates even
in a single point.   But we desire not that caution should degenerate into timidity—that the fear of not being fully believed
should deter honest men from declaring the ascertainable,
demonstrable truth.   There is enough on record in official
documents—enough capable of immediate and irrefutable proof
—to establish every case of alleged evil without betaking ourselves to vague indefinite assertion, wanting shape and circum-
stantiality, and as such exposed to contradiction equally vague
and uncircumstantial.   It shall be our endeavor in this work,
by appealing to acknowledged—in most instances, official—
authorities; requiring the reader to take little or nothing on
our bare, unsupported testimony—to lay open the real state of
the country and to carry conviction to the hearts of our readers.
At the end of such an article as this we cannot undertake to
exhibit, as we could desire, the whole amount of error involved
in Mr. Alison's comprehensive Pœan—the triumphant shout of
complacent admiration called forth by his recognition of the
immense blessings, which have been showered upon the people
of India from the heaven of British rule—indeed, any one

article would be insufficient for the embodiment of such an array of evidence, as we should desire to lay before the British public, on affairs of such high importance; but we pledge ourselves that in this work the requisite evidence shall appear, and we are much mistaken, if, in the sequel, we shall fail to convince even Mr. Alison himself, that the picture, which he has drawn, is more beholden to the bright tints of imagination than to the grave colors of plain historical truth.

A few words in this place will suffice. It is undeniable, that under British rule, the natives of India have been secure against foreign invasion. They have not lived under the presence of alarm, which is said to have unceasingly disturbed them, when desolating inroads upon their fair provinces were made by sanguinary foes, who swept the country with the besom of destruction and manured every field with blood. But, admitting this, we do not feel equally well assured that the blessings of this kind of security may not be over-valued. Our own opinion is that the fear of invasion exercises but scant influence over the happiness of a nation. A fear of evil is but a slight evil after all. However mighty it may be in itself, it is but insignificant in the distance. Political events are the cause of a very minute fraction of the misery, which overshadows the life of every individual. It is the curse which crouches at our door, which follows us into the fields, which is beside us at our up-risings and our down-sittings,—which shuts out the sun at noon-day and darkens the blazing hearth and turns even the prattle of children into notes of woe—this is the curse, the daily, hourly, ever-present curse, which fills the cup of misery to the brim. When England dreaded the appearance on her coast of the mighty power that had disturbed all continental Europe, did men sleep less soundly in their beds—or meet each other with less cheerful faces in the streets; was there less of feasting and merry-making—of marrying and given in marriage; did the husband return, at evening-tide to his home, with a less serene heart, and bless his little ones with diminished feelings of security and hope, because the French fleet was looked for, every morning, from the white cliffs of happy England? We do not fear to assert that there was scarcely a man in Great Britain, whose happiness was not more seriously affected by the fear of a visit from landlord or tradesman—or a tax-gatherer—than the expected advent of Napoleon Bonaparte; before whom an accepted bill, or an over-due quarter's rent had not cast more terrific shadows, than the coming of the French army. The evils which embitter life are those, which are peculiar to the individual circumstances of a man—which reach him in the inner-most recesses of home, affecting all his domestic relations and clinging to him, whithersoever he goes, with all the torturing tenacity of the poisoned robe of the Centaur. Now, in India, a sweep of Mahommedan horse desolating with fearful suddenness an entire village, was doubtless a terrible thing when it happened, and families may have been cut off in a single day ; but these were not events of daily—hourly occurrence ; the curse was not ever present to wither up the sap of life and turn the garden into a drear desert.   It may, we think, be fairly questioned whether the doubtful evil of a possible Mahommedan invasion was ever capable of filling men's minds with such intense apprehension of coming ruin, as that which every day the presence of a corrupt and rapacious Police force strikes into the hearts of the abject dwellers in our native villages.   It would be difficult to conceive any condition of things more surely calculated to keep the people in a constant state of tremulous uneasiness, than the settlement among them of a gang of petty officers of police, exercising, with all the authority of law, their lawless propensities, and using the insignia of office as instruments wherewith to practise the grossest oppression without danger of resistance from the oppressed. In estimating the happiness of a people we must consider well what it is that affects their domestic happiness—what are the evils which reach them in the recesses of their homes—and are in daily and hourly operation, to terrify and depress.

We wish that we could regard, with complacency equal to Mr. Alison's, the alleged diminution in the extent of crime within the provinces of India.   That a blow has been struck at certain understood forms of criminality, and that the knowledge we have gained, after long years, of the nature of some one or two great criminal leagues has been turned to good account in the suppression of the discovered evil, in its old original aspect, we readily admit ; and in doing so we gladly seize the opportunity thus afforded us, to bestow most hearty commendations on those earnest and intelligent officers of the Company, to whom India is so much indebted for the suppression of Thuggee, the partial suppression of Female infanticide, human sacrifices, and other huge abominations, which the soul sickens to contemplate.   They have done well ; they have directed all their energies to the good work of keeping down great understood evils—they have moved forward, and with manifest success, in a specific course of duty ; what they have attempted to do they have done, and they are not without their reward.   But to cut down one form of criminality is not to destroy crime.   The disease has eaten into the whole constitution of Indian society—the subtle poison permeates the entire system—and it is not by attacking this or that symptom, that we can hope to overcome the disease.   We direct our remedies towards the suppression of certain outward and visible aspects of the internal disorder—we apply our lotions or our cerates to the symptomatic ulcers, which present themselves on the surface of the diseased flesh and betray the impurity of the life-blood which flows through its every vein—but, in doing this, we do little more than throw back the disease itself on the vitals, to appear again under a new aspect and perhaps with renewed virulence. *Sublatâ causa tollitur effectus.* We must not content ourselves with the application of external remedies, which at best can do nothing more than mitigate urgent symptoms—we must employ such agents, such subtle searching as will creep from the inmost core to the outermost tegument and purify the gross blood, of which the ulcerous blots on the surface of the body are merely visible indications.   To suppress is not to eradicate.   In many instances we fear, that in destroying an understood form of crime, we give birth to one not understood —we exchange an intelligible symptom which we are competent to reach for an unintelligible symptom which is beyond our reach ; and leave the disease itself in all its pristine malignity. Thus, Thuggee has been suppressed by the vigorous efforts of the British Government ; and men are rarely, in these days, strangled by the way-side—but they are poisoned by hundreds and thousands, and the murders, thus committed by professional gangs, as remorseless and cold-blooded as the Thugs, are rarely detected and punished.   Hear, upon this subject Colonel Sleeman—the man to whom above all others India is indebted for the suppression of Thuggee:—

The impunity with which this crime (poisoning) is everywhere perpetrated and its consequent increase in every part of India, are among the greatest evils with which the country is at this time afflicted.   These poisoners are spread all over India, and are as numerous over the Bombay and Madras Presidencies as over those of Bengal.   There is no road free from them, and throughout India there must be many hundreds who gain their subsistence by this trade alone.   They put on all manner of disguises to suit their purpose ; and as they prey chiefly on the poorer sort of travellers they require to destroy the greater number of lives to make up their incomes. .... People of all castes and callings take to this trade, some casually, others for life, and others derive it from their parents and teachers.   They assume all manner of disguises to suit their purposes; and the habit of cooking, eating and sleeping on the side of the road, and smoking with strangers of seemingly the same caste, greatly facilitate their designs upon travellers.   The small parties are unconnected with each other, and two parties never unite in the same cruise.   The members of one party may be sometimes convicted and punished, but their conviction is accidental, for the system which has enabled us to put down the Thug associations cannot be applied, with any fair prospect of success, to the suppression of these pests of society.—*Rambles and Recollections of an Indian Official, Vol. I. p. p.* 114-115.

Here Mr. Alison may see that in India there is some difference between the amount of crime committed and the amount of crime detected. It is necessary that we should be sparing of our illustrations, else we might teach the historian how much crime we have driven from the land to the water—how mightily dakoity—ay, and Thuggee too—under a sense of insecurity in the fields and on the roads—have now betaken themselves to the teeming thoroughfares of our rivers.

We are well aware that the condition of India Question is one of difficult solution—and it is therefore the very last which it would become us to approach in a spirit of dogmatism. We have recently been told that it is as possible to be too near, as too far from an object, for the formation of a correct estimate of its character and its dimensions*—an objection not unfrequently raised, by those who know nothing about a subject, to the writings of those whose circumstances and position have rendered it impossible but that they should know a great deal. And never is this assumption more frequently manifested than when the state of the colonies and dependencies of Great Britain is under consideration. It is this wonderful intuition into remote affairs which Judge Halliburton so adroitly ridicules in the last series of his " Sam Slick" papers. " Your long acquaintance
' with the provinces and familiar intercourse with the people,
' says he, (the colonial secretary to Mr. Slick) "must have made
' you quite at home on all colonial topics." " I thought so once,"
' says I, " but I don't think so now no more." " Why, how is
' that ?" says he. " Why Sir," says I, "you can hold a book
' so near your eyes as not to be able to read a word of it ;
' hold it further off and get the right focus and you can read
' beautiful. Now the right distance to see a colony and know
' all about it, is England—Three thousand miles is the right
' focus for a political spy-glass. A man born here, and who
' was never out of England knows twice as much about the
' provinces as I do." "Oh! you are joking," says he. "Not
' a bit," says, I, " I find folks here that not only knows every-
' thing about them countries, but have no doubts about the
' matter, and ask no questions ; in fact they not only know no

* Foreign Quarterly Review (October 1844) a periodical conducted with very considerable ability, which has recently contained some valuable articles relative to Indian affairs—a little marred perhaps, in some instances, by the party-spirit infused into them.

' more than me, but more than the people themselves do, what
' they want; it's curious, but its a fact." It *is* a fact; and perhaps, even more palpable with reference to India than to
what are called the "*colonial*" possessions of the crown.

If the question were one merely between those who know
something about the matter and those who know nothing, it
were one of easy adjustment. But the truth, as we have
already stated, is, that there is as wide a difference of opinion
between men, who have spent all their lives in India and who
have enjoyed good opportunities of arriving at a correct opinion
of its real condition, as between the knowing and the unknow-
ing of the world—the seers and the blind. There are some
who still contend that India was happier and more prosperous
under the Mahommedan than it now is under the Christian yoke;
whilst others, esteeming the propounders of such an opinion as
little better than madmen, delightedly expatiate on the immense
benefits which have accrued to the people from the dominion of
so benevolent and enlightened a Government as that of Great
Britain. Of these antagonist opinions we may perhaps, on a future occasion, present our readers, with some genuine specimens
gleaned from our editorial Portfolio—the writers of them
being, in all instances, we believe, men of sound ability, extensive experience, and unquestionable sincerity. We shall then
have an opportunity of exhorting Mr. Alison, whilst reconciling
these generally conflicting opinions, to observe that on one
point these two very dissimilar writers manifest the supremacy
of similar convictions—they all betray an equal measure of faith
in the merits of our *admirable* Police. We can assure the
historian that in this there is nothing remarkable, for although
reasonable men in India, as elsewhere, differ from one another,
on every other possible subject, there is no difference of
opinion regarding the characteristics of the admirable Police.
Men of the extremest shades of opinion here meet together on
common ground. No sooner is the Indian Police brought
upon the *tapis* than the voice of discord is stilled; and men, the
pronest to controversy and disputation, say *ditto* to each other.
There can be no conflict of sentiment, no jarring notes of
dissonance, when every Christian servant of Government, from
the highest to the lowest—every independent resident in the
Mofussil—every journalist—every Englishman, indeed, with
eyes to see, and ears to hear, and faculties to comprehend, points
his slowly moving finger, and looks with face of deepest sorrow,
at the same great festering sore, which eats into the sides of
this unhappy country, and resists all efforts to allay the pain
which it shoots into every nerve and fibre of the social body.

There is a remedy for this, as for all the other evils, under which the country has long been groaning; and this remedy is now, we hope, in incipient operation. The disease has existed too long—has taken too firm a hold of the constitution; the frame is too universally permeated by gross humors; there is so much impurity, so much corruption everywhere—so deep a taint, not only from the original disease, but from the destructive remedies, employed to reduce it ; that no reasonable man would ever look to see a cure speedily effected by any other than miraculous agency. The healing process to be effective must be of slow operation. The curative influences must gradually—almost insensibly, extend themselves from the innermost parts, working their way, with subtle, penetrating force, through every minute artery, purifying the life-blood, invigorating the nerves, and at length making their slow way to the surface and plainly declaring the cure they have wrought in the altered aspect of the face of Indian society. To raise the tone of moral feeling throughout the country—to elevate the sentiments of the people—to purify their hearts—to open their eyes to the true nature of the beautiful and the deformed—to train them to love what is fair and of good report ; to hate what is unseemly and disgraceful ; to respect themselves and to sympathise with their brethren ; to know rightly the dignity of man ; to duly regard his prerogatives ; to worship the holiness of truth ; and to feel, in their inmost hearts, the sublime happiness of doing and of being good ;—these are the chief remedial efforts, which we must exert to change the diseased, deformed body into one instinct with health and beauty.

To educate the people is to do all this. Education, using the word in its most extensive acceptation, supplies the only remedy whereby all morbid influences can be overcome and the disorder thoroughly eradicated. Other remedies are but for a season, this is for all time. Other remedies touch but one symptom or another ; this reaches and destroys the idiopathic disease of which all these symptoms are but secondary emanations. Still, as in a previous article* we have emphatically declared, we desire to see every possible auxiliary set at work— every remedy, or even palliative employed, to mitigate this or that local ailment, or to suppress urgent symptoms as they arise. These secondary local applications need not interfere with the progress of the great remedial agent, which alone can effect the radical cure. They will wonderfully assist each other. By

* *Calcutta Review—No. IV.—Art. I.—Indigenous Education in Bengal and Behar.*

inducing through means of external changes, a present state of ease and tranquillity, we render the native mind a fitter—a more enduring receptacle of those great truths which we desire to instil into it. Indeed whilst society is in a state of feverish unrest—whilst men's minds are disturbed and a sense of present security no where exists—it is clearly no time for the triumphs of education. At such a season— in such a posture of affairs—we must scatter our good seed amidst choaking thickets, and it were in vain to look for a harvest. All local reforms are valuable—nay indispensable auxiliaries; let them be duly estimated as such, but let no man think that by attacking symptoms, which are but secondary, he can reach the disease itself. No; this were an error of grievous magnitude—one the evil consequences of which it were difficult to over-rate—one which if universally encouraged, would be fatal to the advancement of the happiness, the prosperity, because the intellectual and moral culture of the people. Our work will not live beyond the hour until we begin to touch the *heart.*

☞ After the preceding article was not only written but sent to press, we met with a passage in a work on Government, now rather scarce, which appeared to us very briefly and felicitously to express a sentiment that cannot be too frequently and earnestly impressed on the minds of right-thinking men. And as the passage, in question, in its main scope and spirit, tends to corroborate and enforce some of our own remarks, we here quote it entire :—

"It is wonderful how forward some have been to look upon it as a kind of presumption and ingratitude, and rebellion and cruelty, and I know not what besides, not to alledge only, nor to own, but to suffer any one so much as to imagine that an old established law could in any respect be a fit subject for condemnation. Whether it has been a kind of personification that has been the cause of this, as if the law were a living creature, or whether it has been the mechanical veneration for antiquity, or what other delusion of the fancy, I shall not here inquire. For my part I know not for what good reason it is that the merit of justifying a law when right should have been thought greater, than that of censuring it when wrong. Under the Government of laws, what is the motto of a good citizen? To obey punctually, to censure freely. Thus much is certain; that a system that is never to be censured will never be improved; that if nothing is ever to be found fault with, nothing will ever be mended; and that a resolution to justify every thing at any rate, and to disapprove of nothing, is a resolution which, pursued in future, must stand as an effectual bar to all the additional happiness we can hope for; pursued hitherto, would have robbed us of that share of happiness which we enjoy already. For is a disposition to find 'every thing as it should be,' less at variance with itself than with reason and utility? The common-place arguments in which it vents itself justify not what is established in effect any more than they condemn it; since whatever now is establishment once was innovation."

ART. VI.—1. *Indian Atlas. Nos. 47-48, 65-66.*

2. *J. B. Fraser's Journal of a Tour through part of the Snowy Range of the Himalaya Mountains, aud to the Sources of the Rivers Jumna and Ganges, with Map,* 1820.

3. *Illustrations of the Botany and other Branches of the Natural History of the Himalayan Mountains,* 2 *vols. by J. Forbes Royle. M. D. V. P. R. S.,* 1839.

4. *Moorcroft's Travels in the Himalayan Provinces with Map. Edited by H. H. Wilson,* 2 *vols.* 1841.

5. *Asiatic Researches, vols. XVI. and XVII. Mr. G. W. Traill's Statistical Sketches of Kumaon aad the Bhotia Mehals.*

—*Mr. J. H. Batten's Settlement Report on Gurhwal. Printed by order of Government, N. W. P.,* 1843.

6. *McClelland's " Geology of Kumaon,* 1835."

7. *Account of Kunawur in the Himalaya Mountains, with Map, by the late Captain A. Gerrard, edited by G. Lloyd,* 1841.

—*Narrative of a Journey, &c. to the Boorondo Pass in the Himalaya Mountains, by Major Sir Wm. Lloyd, and Captain A. Gerrard, &c. &c. Edited by G. Lloyd,* 1840.

8. *Bengal and Agra Gazetteer,* 4 *vols.* 1841 *and* 1842.   *Articles " Hill Sanataria."*

9. *Notes of Wanderings in the Himalaya, &c. &c. by* ' *Pilgrim,*' *Agra.* 1844.

LET not our readers be alarmed at this catologue ; we are not going to tax their patience with any elaborate notice of these several productions, nor could we presume to dilate on the multiplicity of objects which they present to the critical eye.   The list which heads our pages, serves to indicate the regions in which we intend for a short time to expatiate. Those who accompay us in this excursion may, indeed, add largely to the number of their guides, and find much matter for amusement with something also occasionally to enlighten their understanding in the light leaves of Archer, Skinner, Mundy, Fane, Bacon, and last, not least, Jacquemont ; in the pictorial and letter press illustrations of White and Roberts; and in the profounder page of that journal, which has now for some time been the repository of all that is useful and elegant in the labours of the Bengal Asiatic Society and its correspondents.

An eminent naturalist, not long since retired from public

service in India, and the fruits of whose scientific labors have yet to appear in their complete and European form, was accustomed to speak of common journal writers and specimen collectors as *travellers*, meaning we suppose, by that term to convey, with as much urbanity as possible, his contempt for the crudities of their Reports, and the self taught and unscientific character of their knowledge. With less delicacy, and with less ground for the depreciation which they attempted, some of his occidental opponents delighted to treat the naturalist himself as '*a mere Indian observer and collector.*' Now, it is undoubtedly true, that observers and collectors ought in every way to be encouraged, and we should be the first to decry any attempt to undervalue their labours, or to cool their zeal by any disparaging remarks. But, for the sake of our Indian reputation, we earnestly beseech all ' travellers' to stick to their collections, and, in their observations, not to wander beyond the record. It is lamentable to see an amiable author plunging beyond his depth, or floundering in the mud, when he might with safety and pleasure disport himself among clear and shallow waters, and even gather precious stones and gems for philosophers on the bank.

The great defect of all Indian writers, who treat of natural history, geography, geology, and in fact of all the *ologies* which belong to the tracts they visit and describe, is, that they make a 'jumble' of their information, and do not in their written accounts distinguish what they have actually seen and known from what they heard and guessed at, or from what having seen, they do *not know.* There has been only one individual in these regions, who was entitled, by his great attainments in every branch of learning and science, to describe the country in each and all of its various relations, material or otherwise ; and if *James Prinsep* had been spared to us, there can be little doubt that the Humboldt of the east would have rivalled the fame of his western prototype. We do not ask the reader to take up a volume of Humboldt or a paper of Prinsep, and compare therewith even the clearest descriptions of our Indian writers on similar topics ; for, to expect that such a comparison could be sustained would be but a senseless conceit, and would expose our own ignorance of cause and effect. It results from the very constitution of Indian society, which is composed for the most part of public servants, that those who are alone available for the duties of scientific research, work with fettered hands and in a limited sphere,* while they are generally wanting in

* It is only very recently that the Government relieved the Superintendent of the

the advantages of a complete education and matured experience. But in addition to these inevitable disadvantages, we are, we think, justified in saying, that there exist two other far from necessary causes to which the defect alluded to as characterizing our Indian descriptive literature may be fairly attributed ; *first*, the fatal facility with which a local Indian reputation may be acquired ; *secondly*, the ignorance and apathy which prevail concerning the progress of knowledge in Europe. It is one object of our article to aid in correcting the first evil. Already we hope that people are beginning to discover that before a man can take rank with the *emeriti* of the intellectual world, he must achieve a triumph over self-opinionativeness, emptiness, and the whole brood of sciolism ; that he must eschew long windedness, and cultivate brevity ; and above all, that he must tell something worth knowing in a manner worth listening to. With all due respect to the ancients of the Service, we think we perceive in the young civilians of our day, a diminished belief in the heaven born and brahmanical intellectualism of their *caste*, and a less firm confidence in the puffs of the Indian House, and especially of those which issue from the honored lips of the old China captains who enact the orator and make valedictory addresses at Haileybury examinations. Still, there is much room for alarm at the ease with which celebrity is gained in this climate of rapid growths; and ' clever*ish*' settlement reports and heavy judicial minutes are still too certain steps in the ladder of Indian fame, although the Government have ceased to evoke any more stupendous essays on ryotwary and zemindary settlements.

The cure for the second evil which we have mentioned,— a disregard to the state of knowledge in Europe,—is of course to be found in visits to that enlightened quarter of the globe ; or, where that remedy is impossible, in study, and reflection, and intercourse with those who have enjoyed better opportunites of mental improvement. A course of novels, magazines and reviews—even the *Calcutta Review*—is rather too mild a discipline ; and yet we know of some very distinguished characters between the Himalaya and Cape Comorin who receive their whole supply of intellectual food from these store-houses. But the truth is, nevertheless, undoubted, that if a man—even in the receipt of 3,000 Rupees per mensem—once allows himself any lee way, and fails to keep his mind up to the point of

N. W. P. Botanical Gardens (to whom also, the whole tea-growing and tea-manufacturing experiment in Upper India is confided) from the duties of Accouchier to the Civilians' wives of Suharunpoor, and of Body Surgeon to the convicts at that station.

average European intelligence—a point easily ascertained in these days of quick communication and cheap books—he will soon drop irretrievably behind, and be distinguishable from the Native craft around him only by his colour ; or he will be stranded fast and immoveable on the shoal of pretending mediocrity. Without disparaging the claims to distinction of our Everests, Wilsons, Falconers, Royles and other oriental luminaries, who now enjoy the full reflected blaze of intellectual light in the west, we may be certain, from their own acknowledgment, that they underwent some slight eclipse on their first entrance into their new orbit. To use a more homely illustration, these Cocks of the School in India felt that they were only fifth form boys in England. What, then, shall be said of those, who, neither visit the fountain head in their native land, nor imbibe fresh knowledge from imported draughts,—what shall be said of the Sciolists of India through whose imperfect and confused statements, the land we live in is made known to the intelligent world ? What shall be said of those, who unprovided with the sacred fire, venture to lay their irreverent hands on the sublime altar of nature in the Himalaya ? Our object in drawing attention to the frailties, which have hitherto been spared more or less by all authors east of the Cape, is not to propound any newly discovered moral, or to illustrate a stale truism. It is to provoke even the present occupants of the field to a new and holy emulation, and to a warfare against the sins which most easily beset them. And what may we not hope when we behold such a champion, as H. M. Elliot, of Agra, entering the arena?* We need not in his case, we are sure, utter any warnings against the dangers of rapid reputation, and his own voice would be the loudest in preaching the true faith to the rising generation.

> Certare ingenio, contendere nobilitate,
> Noctes atque dies niti præstante labore,
> Ad summas emergere opes, rerumque potiri.

We might leave these noble words of Lucretius ringing in the ears of our audience, but we fear that unless something in a humbler strain is added by way of application, our Indian mediocrity will be indefinitely prolonged, and the race of *Mikronoustics* (to use a word borrowed from the banks of Camus) will still infest our literature, and—for we now come

---

* This gentleman's " Supplemental Glossary " should be in every body's hands " If he do not receive such notice from the Court of Directors " (to use the Revenue Board's words) " as will encourage him to bring the work to completion," may their Kingdom depart from them !

to the point which we have been aiming at—a full, free and catholic book, we emphatically repeat the word, *book* on the Himalaya, will fail to greet our longing vision. Can it be doubted that if the French nation or the Germans had been in possession of Affghanistan for four years, Europe would ere this have been made acquainted with the *entire* physical, external, internal, moral, intellectual, historical and statistical condition of the country? Would a few geographical notes by one, a few political essays by others, a few conjectures at the geology by some, and a few descriptions of military campaigns, and two or three versions of the tragedy of the massacre have been the sole literary and scientific result of the expedition?

If any Englishman is disposed to deny the inference which we draw, we request his careful perusal of the several works named at the head of our paper. Let him examine by way of experiment, the four maps, placed first in the list. Here he will find the very perfection of confusion, "confusion worse confounded"!—We defy any one on his mountain travels to ascertain from these maps, whether his next march will lie over the top, or along the side of a hill, or through a valley. The great chains of mountains are marked distinctly enough, but the delineation of the subordinate ranges and inferior offshoots and spurs is singularly defective; while the forest of names, chiefly those of insignificant hamlets and cowsheds, bewilders the examiner. To these maps, we suppose, must be attributed the ludicrous insertions even in the last edition of Hamilton's Gazetteer, where hill peaks, and small local shrines figure as " towns in Northern Hindustan!" We have heard that the heights given in these maps and which were for the most part barometrically determined, have been found, on the whole, correct in the course of the great Trigonometrical Survey. The geographical distances, and the latitude and longitude of the important points, as well as the extact position of the chief mountains are also accurate. The surveyors, too, to whom we owe these productions, were, speaking after the manner of India, as competent as they were zealous. But of what advantage are these merits, if, through the defects we have enumerated, and the unartistical appearance of the drawing, we cannot discover our way by the aid of the mountain maps, nor shew them to a foreigner without a blush? It is a fact that in one of our hill provinces a map of the country between the Sutlej and the Kalee rivers, compiled and printed at *Berlin*, has been preferred, not only by travellers, from Europe, but also by some of the residents in the province, to the less luminously arranged, though more minutely accurate copies of the official

Atlas. We ourselves have no hesitation in saying that the small sketch of the seat of war with Nepal, given in Mr. Toby Prinsep's "History of the Political and Military Transactions during the administration of the Marquess of Hastings," is much superior to its more ambitious successors, owing to its distinct delineation of the principal chains and rivers. Yet this work was published in 1825, and we are now in 1845, and the hills themselves have been held by the British since 1815! If thirty years of possession have failed to produce even tolerably good maps, what can we expect to see in the department of General Science?

The work by Royle, which appears the third in our list, is certainly a highly valuable one; but, we cannot help thinking that its value would have been greater if the author had attempted less, and had confined himself to the botany of the Himalaya.* The very circumstance that the writer's own knowledge of the mountain districts was but limited,—and which enhances his personal merit,—though it may not seriously affect the description of *plants*, is an essential disadvantage when information concerning other branches of natural history, especially geology, is conveyed through the language or reports of others. A specimen of *Juniper* or of *Saussuria* at once announces its birth in a highly elevated and snowy alpine region, and no one could impose on a botanist by placing in his Himalayan herbarium a leaf of bazaar *pan*. But the case is far different with rocks. A lump of quartz tells no tale by itself. A specimen of trap or granite, brought to a philosopher by a forgetful or careless traveller, may cause as much injury as would arise from the inability to discover these rocks in another ignoramus, who should attempt to describe a country without the faculty of observation, and without the necessary knowledge to qualify him for the task. These remarks, however, are only by way of illustration. When we say generally, that we wish Dr. Royle's work had been *all* equally complete with his admirable arrangement of the Himalayan and other Indian plants according to the natural system; particularly, that the botanical part had been more complete, and that his description of the Himalayan *Cupuliferæ* and *Coniferæ* especially had been fuller and better illustrated, we feel confident that he will take our slight

---

* It may interest most of our European readers, and not a few of our Indian, to become acquainted with the etymological composition of this expressive term. Let them know, then, that *Him* is a Sanskrit word for *cold* or *frost*, and *alaya* a Sanskrit word for *abode* or *residence*. So that the two together mean " *the abode or residence of cold and frost*." What appellation could be more applicable than this to the loftiest range of mountains on the globe—whose peaks are covered with everlasting snows?

criticism in good part, and not consider any of our previous
remarks as directed at him. We are sure he will himself lament
with us, that after the lapse of thirty years, we are still without
a true and catholic account of the British possessions and protected states in the Northern Hills.

As stated in our first paragraph we shall not attempt a criticism of all the remaining books and papers in our list, at least
on the present occasion. We must however except the case of
" Pilgrim and his Wanderings;" for, this piece of authorship has
been brought to light in our own days and demands some particular notice at our hands. Of the others we must be content to
say,

> Sunt bona, sunt quædam mediocria, sunt mala plura.

We cannot help lamenting the prejudices of Fraser, which
coloured his descriptions; and the veterinary education of
Moorcroft, which confined his views and narrowed his observations.* In the case of Mr. Traill, we cannot but regret that,
where so much has been told, so much has been left untold by
one, who had immense means of obtaining information, and
great personal zeal and activity. In the case of Mr. Batten we
can only hope that he knows what is expected of him from his
situation and that his settlement report on Gurhwal will not
entirely content him. Dr. McClelland in a new edition would,
we doubt not, himself make not a few corrections in his "Geology of Kumaon," and, above all, would alter its title to that
of a " Sketch of the geology of some 50 miles of the Kumaon
Province in the neighbourhood of the outposts at Lohooghat and
Petora Ghur;" while one, now so great a benefactor to the
cause of Indian science would, doubtless, extend his zoological
notes, and modify his exclusive calcareous system of Goitre, if
an opportunity were again afforded him. Gerrard's account of
Kunawur is, geographically and statistically, excellent; and the
map attached to it, though on too small a scale and deficient in
the modern effect obtained from shading and embossing, is still
a great help. But, Alexander Gerrard had only scientific
opportunities, and his acquirements were insufficient for his
position. We attach little or no value to any of the Gerrardian
dissertations on the snow line, because the observations on
which they were founded, belong not to the great belt of the
snowy range which separates the northern mountains of

---

* We always feel a little uncharitable displeasure against this Adventurer, notwithstanding his subsequent misfortunes — because, on account of a slight risk and
casual inclemency of weather, he, with the full opportunity of settling the doubt,
omitted to ascertain the real facts connected with the Affluents and Effluents of the
Manusurower and Rhawun Lakes.

Hindustan from Thibet and Tartary, but, to the western offshoot or *lower nivalic* ridge which separates West Gurhwal and Bissahr from the intermontane region of Kunawur. The Lloyds, author and editor, are hardly original luminaries; they shine chiefly by the reflected light of Gerrard. Their narrative is not uninteresting, but, we fear many of our observations on Indian sciolism would not be altogether inapplicable in their case. There is an Indian word which especially suits this kind of production, and our oriental readers will understand us when we declare that with the exception of Royle's volumes, all the fruits of travel and research which appear on our list, are decidedly *kutcha* (raw.) To amend this state of things, and elicit the appearance of something *pucka* (mature,) we must assume the monitor for a short time and offer some advice to our friend Pilgrim, and others, whose names are not in our frontispiece.

Our general admonition is merely a repetition of what has been previously urged.—Let every one who has opportunities of observation in these magnificent regions learn as much as he can, and when he begins to record his observations, let him measure the extent of his learning by the standard of European acquirements. A volume of Humboldt or Cuvier will always be a very good test. He will then know how much to state positively, and how much to furnish for the decision of others. He will know that there is nothing disgraceful in catering for the masters of science, and that as the provider of the feast, he will always hold an honourable place at the board, a far more honourable one indeed than that to which those who unworthily take the highest seat are consigned after they have been detected. Perhaps, our traveller may have acquired his knowledge of minerals in India, and, on the same principle that a Lempriere's Dictionary on his book-shelf constitutes the newest ensign of a corps a classical authority at his mess, he may have been dubbed a geologist, because he can distinguish hornblende from mica, and can perform the grand experiment of making limestone effervesce in acids. He must not however on this account, and on the strength of having Lyell's Elements in his library, declare that the fossils which he has picked up or purchased belong to the Oolitic series, nor must Old Red Sandstone be a household word in his mouth. He will allow us to read to him the following extract from the letter of an eminent English geologist (with a copy of which we have been favoured) teaching the lesson that even where previous education somewhat entitles a man to make comparisons and to assign affinities between material phenomena

Y

displayed in different countries, great caution must be observed in announcing facts : " I agree with you as to the importance of ' working out each country upon its own peculiar evidence. I ' would even recommend any young geologist to forget or keep ' in the back ground all the series of European types and only ' to bring them forward as terms of comparison, *after* he has ' reached sound definite conclusions. The contrary plan has ' done much mischief, led to rash conclusions, and prevented ' observers from sifting the evidence before them." It is not always, however, that such a lesson is required. Sometimes ignorance is avowed with delightful *naivetè*. The following words are actually printed in a " Journal of a Tour"—we will not be more particular : " We are again among granite and gneiss rocks, and the white soil of the valley is neither calcareous nor—*cretaceous !*" no indeed, and the writer might have added, it did not appear to be cream cheese ! Perhaps a wanderer may appear who has hitherto been an oracle among his assistants, one profoundly versed in horticulture, whose cabbages win an annual prize—in the ' Mufussil' we always see the same names as winners at races, flower shows, and the like—and whose gorgeous dahlias are the theme of all admirers. Let such a genius remember that flower garden botany is easily acquired and that even boarding school misses are great adepts in discovering the sexes of plants. If his foot be on the Himalaya, he must beware of talking of Scotch firs as the monarchs of the coniferous tribe,—of the English (robur) oak as the only true oak, thus bastardizing the whole race of Himalayan quercees,— of daisies being abundant on every hill—or of *British* heather clothing the cold and rugged bases of the snowy peaks.

If the visitor be a Governor-General he must not exhibit his ignorance of Political Geography. For instance, he must not say to a *Kumaon* functionary " Well, Sir, and are the *Goorkha* Chiefs becoming reconciled to our rule ?"* Gentlemen, also, who wish to be understood, must not in any paper professing to be intended for scientific readers, use the Jonesian mode of expressing native words in one-half of their discourse, and the Gilchristian mode in the other half: nor, must they permit themselves to speak of the Himalayan ranges and the Landour and Simla ranges as one and the same thing. When mentioning, too, the snowy mountains *par excellence*, it would be as well to use one term, either the Sanskrit, or the Hindi, and not to confuse the mind by the mention of the Himalaya, the Hemala, and the Himachul range within a dozen pages. Thibet Proper,

---

* A *fact* is here alluded to.

too, or the country immediately subject to Lhassa, should not be confounded with Tartary, Chinese Tartary, &c., and in mentioning the Trans-Himalayan regions, the names of the several divisions, such as Ladakh, Bultee, Heoondes, &c. should be given separately in the languages of the inhabitants themselves, the Chinese, the Nepalese, the hill people, and the English. We may here add that the latter are quite as singular in their use of the word *Thibet* (unknown to the Native tribes, at least west of Lhassa) as they are in that of the word, Yak. Above all things, great caution is necessary in the adoption of casual native names of plants, animals and even places. The coniferus trees of the Himalaya are most terribly nicknamed by some of our best authors. Chill, Kyl,—Deodar, Kelon,—Rao, Ragha, Raësulla,—Khutrow, Chibrow, Pindrow, Oonum, Moorin, Moorinda,—these and many other names represent four or at the utmost five trees of the Pinus and Abies family! As an instance of confusion arising from native names of animals, we content ourselves with the following : The 'Surrow' of the Western Hills and the 'Thar' of Nepal and of the hills even far less easterly, is one and the same deer, the " *Antelope Ther* " of zoology. But in the Western Hills the wild goat, (a regular *capra*) is indiscriminately called *Ther* and *Thar.* Hence if an Eastern gentleman talk of *Thars,* the Western gentleman goes out to shoot goats, much to the astonishment of his friend, and vice versa. In regard to places, it is ludicrous to behold the care with which, some parties of travellers note down in their tablets the number of minutes occupied in each ascent and descent, while others are exactly recording the names of the neighbouring hills and glens as set forth by different grinning mountaineers around them. These natives are very quick at catching traits of character, and as they know that no Englishman will be content without some name or other, they give him the first which occurs to them; if a mountain, generally the name of the highest village in sight; if a stream or valley, that of the uppermost or the lowest or the central hamlet, generally their own, in its course. Sometimes they give fancy names of their own manufacture just to quiet the 'Sahib.' Hence arise the multiplicity of names assigned to the several *Dandas* and *Dhars, Gudhs,* and *Garhs* of the mountain districts.

With respect to geography itself, we fear that many of our Calcutta friends have rather hazy notions concerning the locality of the several Hill Stations; but, it is still more singular to observe how few residents at the Sanataria are themselves quite aware of their local habitation. They

seem to be ignorant that Simlah and Sabathoo are situated in
the Bara Thakooraien, that Landour and Mussourie are in
Gurhwal, called in olden times from its capital Sreenugger;
that Almora, Nainee Tal, Lohooghat and Petoraghur are in
Kumaon; that the Sirmoor Battalion at Deyrah Doon, is not in
Sirmoor; that three-fourths of the western hills belong to
protected native rajahs and ranas, and not to the British
government; that Kumaon and half of Gurhwal are under
direct British rule; that the Bhootias of Bootan, of Bhote,
and again of the Kumaon Bhotia Mehals, are not one and
the same people; and that the people of Kunawur, the Thakooraien, Bissehr, Rewaien, Sirmoor, Gurhwal and Kumaon
have not all the same manners, customs, language or dress,
though they are all mountaineers. These are all great facts,
and, may be, great truisms. But, nevertheless, we know
a good many ladies and gentlemen at Simla and Mussourie
who will not be too proud to study them, and some will
even honour us so far as to read up the *Calcutta Review*
for improviso sallies at their next dinner party. Do our
Calcutta friends smile at our trivial wisdom? We challenge
the most learned of the *ditch*, if untravelled, suddenly and
without preparation to mark down the place where *Kussowlee*
ought to be in the maps!

We deem it right also to remark that it is not true that in
every valley of the hills lovely young mothers are to be seen
watering the heads of their children. The custom of putting
children to sleep by means of small spouts of water so placed
as to trickle on the head, is far from universal in the western
part of the Hills and is quite unknown except in that direction.
The gross calumnies against the Hill people of the Thakooraien
and Bissehr contained in Fraser's Work, have only a slight
foundation in the former predatory character of the inhabitants
of some few divisions, and in the immoral character of others.
He wrote under the influence of the prejudices of his lowland
servants and the sepoys of his guard, and of the slanderous
jealousy of the Gurhwalees and other hillmen. But we have
lived to see an excellent and most charitable society for the
conversion of the Hill tribes *between the Sutlej and the Kalee*,
actually founded on Fraser's descriptions and on similar libels.
The disgusting custom of polyandry is more particularly aimed
at by our Christian missionaries. Yet, it is a fact that this
practice of giving one woman five or seven husbands and these
brethren, is not common in the central and lower hills, which
form the neighbourhood of Simla, is only known in that part
of west Gurhwal called Rewaien, and so far from being even

known in east Gurhwal and Kumaon is there laughed at as a joke of the European, and is broadly contrasted by the opposite practice of a most liberal polygamy. The continuance of this vile custom in some parts of Bissehr and in Kunawur and in scattered villages of the Thakooraien, is attempted to be excused on the plea that the sale of hill women by the Goorkhas and the consequent diminution of female population has not yet been compensated by fresh births, by the return of emigrants, or by new immigrations. We shall not in this place pursue this topic farther, except by taking the opportunity to declare that the following extracts from Lieut. Bacon's " First Impressions" afford us one of the strongest proofs that he, for one, stands very much in need of the admonitions, we have given. The words which we quote form a conversation between the author and a young " mountain damsel" on the road between Rajpore and Mussourie.

" Alas, Sir ! is it for the infant to instruct its parent ? or,
' for the young kid to direct the steps of the goat ? I am but
' a child in knowledge, and do you bid me shew you what our
' wise men call their own ? Shall I tell you of my cows, or of
' the butterflies which sport over the flowers, or of the eagles
' sailing aloft yonder."

" Yes : even there you could tell me much which I do not
' know. But have you no family or home to talk to me about ?
' There I cannot enter, I can only learn by hearsay. Are you
' married ? Married ! certainly I am married, and have seven
' handsome husbands, the finest men in the village, but I can-
' not say they are such tall straight fellows as the servants who
' follow you gentlemen from the plains."

" Seven husbands, did you say ? What, all your own, or
' did I misunderstand you ?"

" Ay ! truly, seven husbands ; what else should I say ?
' We are not like the unfortunate women in the plains, who, it
' is said, have but one man, good or bad, belonging to them.
' But I am wrong to say seven ; I have only six now ; one of
' them I discharged yesterday ; he was an useless fellow with
' only one eye, and a crooked back," &c. &c. &c.

Though this dialogue is only calculated to create a smile among those at Mussourie and elsewhere who are acquainted with the habits of the people, we cannot let off Lieutenant Bacon with a laugh. We denounce it as an enormous invention, which would be inexcusable in a novel or romance, from the gross ignorance of fact it displays, but which, appearing as it does, in a narrative of a work the preface to which states that all " the facts are to be relied on," demands the severest censure

of an honest critic.   No such woman using such language and
telling such a tale could possibly have been met with at the
place mentioned.   She was driving cows to her village.   It
must therefore have been one of the villages near Mussourie.
Let any body visit Jurcepanee, Bhutta, Kyarkooly, and examine the condition of the female inhabitants; and then state
whether any damsel exists there who can turn off her seventh
husband,* or command fifty better men.   "But why break a
butterfly on the wheel?"   As a punishment to Lieutenant
Bacon—who, we believe, in England edited or joined in editing
some Oriental Annual or other instructive work on India—he
should if still alive and unrepentant, be asked to translate into
the mountain dialect of Mussourie his own version of this memorable conversation.

About the *dirtiness* of the mountaineers there can be no
mistake, but still they must not all be classed in one rank.   In
the degrees of uncleanness, the Sirmooree, we think, is "facile
princeps," among those at least who wash once or twice in
their lives.   As for the Bhootias and others nearer the snow
who never wash, they are entirely beyond our scale, the lowest
on which, that is, the least dirty, or the Kumaonees who wear
cotton dresses, are justly placed in one of Pilgrim's Chapters.
Those mountaineers who wear hempen clothes may be supposed
to occupy the middle place, for, it is the woollen garments and
blankets which appear to mark the foulest of the foul.

Nor must we omit to correct a common mistake about the
indifference of the Hill men to *caste*.   The coolies at Simla and
Mussourie are not the very cream of the brahmanical and
rajput tribes, and some amongst them do things with the view
of making themselves useful which lowlanders would foolishly
decline.   But in all the essential matters of Hinduism, the
great majority of mountaineers (not Bhootias) are scrupulous
followers of the law, whilst in superstitious observances they
beat the plainsmen hollow.†   The indifference of the Hill men
to the virtue of their wives is often mentioned.   There is some
truth in this opinion when applied to the poorer classes; but

---

* What   different customs prevail in different places!   Every traveller and
author agrees in stating that in the Hills, even among families professing to be of
high Rajput caste, the value of a daughter is fourfold that of a son; the value resulting from the practice of buying a wife from the parents.   Compare with this our
article on Infanticide and its causes in another part of India.

† Gentlemen often confound different tribes in the Hills which they would not do
in the Plains.   We have been told that one of the new settlers at Nainee Tal wanted
to kill *kine* openly, because his mountain workmen ate dead buffaloes.   These foul
feeders were all Domes of the mason and carpenter tribe, while all his coolies and
other labourers wore the Rajput string, and considered the touch of a dome to be
pollution.

death and mutilation are too often the consequences to the mountaineer, whether man or woman, who holds this opinion. Indeed, in some districts to enact the 'gallant gay Lothario' almost amounts to suicide, whilst all the Helens are *noseless* proofs of marital vengeance.

The pusillanimity and unsoldierly qualities of the Hill men, as compared with real Goorkhas, are not unfrequently descanted on. Let the Officers commanding the three hill corps in Deyrah, Jutog, and Kumaon refute this calumny. If not, why do they enlist more than half of their soldiers from amongst the common hill tribes, especially of Gurhwal and Kumaon? Poor John Conolly at Kabul, and Eldred Pottinger, could have told a different tale; and many hundred families whose sons and brothers, we can point to, exhibited the most chivalrous valour and met with an honorable grave at Charekar and in the Kohistan.

We should weary our readers if we combated any longer the ignorant and unphilosophical opinions and assertions current on Himalayan subjects. We close our present remarks therefore, by rebutting the following additional popular errors. 1. That there are no tigers in the Hills. 2. That cholera and fever do not ascend beyond a certain height. 3. That Dwalagiri, the highest peak of the Himalaya, is visible from Landour and other parts of the British districts. 4. That the atmosphere of the mountains is singularly clear. In Kumaon and Gurhwal the loss of life annually by tigers is still most deplorable. Cholera in 1823 and 1828 committed awful ravages up to the very base of the snowy Peaks. Intermittent fever is the curse of every village, high or low, during the rains, whilst according to the official and medical reports one peculiar form of fever almost vies with the plague as a mortal disease in some districts *close to the snow*, and not only in vallies. Dwalagiri is not visible—how could it be?—even from heights of 8,000 and 9,000 feet above the Kalee river, 150 miles east of Landour; and, finally, there is no part of the world where in the summer months dirty mountain haze, thick and impalpable (a totally distinct phenomenon from the clouds and mists of the rainy season) so utterly obscure the view and so disfigure the scenery, as in the Himalayan regions.

We are loath to quit our airy retreat and descend to the dull plain of every day life. We are enthusiasts about the hills, though we permit no untruths concerning them, and we feel altogether with the mountaineers when they cling to their homes, and refuse to be comforted when taken away elsewhere.

Dear is that shed to which his soul conforms,
And dear that hill which lifts him to the storms ;
And as a child when scaring sounds molest
Clings close and closer to the mother's breast,
So the loud torrent and the whirlwind's roar
But bind him to his native mountains more.

We purpose, if permitted, to return again to Himalayan subjects on some future occasion, and to treat of the following topics for which our present space is insufficient. First, the great geographical features of the northern mountains. Secondly, their geology. Thirdly, the scenery which they afford. Fourthly, the Hill Stations or Sanataria, and Cantonments of troops. Fifthly, the Resources and Real Use of the Hills. The ' utile' and the ' dulce' will be thus fairly discussed. We bring this article to a close with a few words on Pilgrim's Notes. We intend to use this Book again as a handle for our further dissertations, and shall therefore defer all extracts therefrom till that time. In the meanwhile, we place on record our general satisfaction on the perusal of this simple volume and our commendation of its good intentions and occasional ability. Pilgrim,—whose identity with a gentleman well known in Upper India for the combination of great practical usefulness with a vein of accomplishments and enthusiasm, is, we believe, no longer a secret,—must excuse us for lamenting that the first vehicle of his Notes was a newspaper, and that he has mixed up controversy with his descriptions of scenery. To the last circumstance, we are indebted for a wearisome reiteration of the beauties of the Nainee Tal station, and the merits of its supporters and founders; to the first we must attribute the repetition of epithets, partaking of exaggeration and indistinctness. *Beautiful, exquisite, immense, awful, magnificent* and the like are fine words—nay excellent words, but, to prove anything, they should be sparingly used. When too frequently used, they impair the effect of particular descriptions and throw a shade of doubt on the fidelity of all. We also cannot exactly discover why the names of official persons are sometimes mysteriously abbreviated and hinted at, and at other times openly published to the profane. Messrs. Lushington and Batten must, if they have any fun in them, laugh heartily at finding themselves sometimes designated at full length, then immediately after figuring as Mr. L. or Mr. B., or my friend B., or a high authority in Kumaon, or an official gentleman in the Province, or as Commissioner, or as Judge, Collector, and Magistrate! We can excuse this kind of careless writing in the original letters, but why, did Pilgrim republish his lucubrations in a collected form without due emendation and a regard to the " ars lini ? " We cannot help thinking, too, that he has paid an unwise courtship to the existing powers, and at all events has ventured far out of his depth, when he allowed himself to speak in the manner he has done of Mr. Traill. Visitors at Nainee Tal, who know nothing of the province of Kumaon, will, if they believe Pilgrim, form a totally erroneous opinion of Mr. Traill's motives in adopting what is styled a 'Chinese policy' in regard to European travellers. Of this more hereafter. In the meanwhile we emphatically warn Pilgrim that there must be something rotten in a work which assails Traill, the beloved* of the Hill men, and Shore, the Friend to India.

In conclusion, we again reiterate the assurance that the preceding observations have been penned in no hostile or unfriendly spirit towards any of the authors whose works have been thus briefly noticed. On the contrary, towards all of them, whether personally known to us or not, we have no reason for cherishing aught but feelings of kindliness and good will. Our grand object has been, to point out the desirableness and necessity of aiming at a higher standard, with a view to the realization of still nobler performances. At the same time, we regard it as at once our duty and our privilege to encourage and foster all efforts, however humble, that are in any way calculated to attract the attention of the British public towards this glorious but too long neglected realm—and to excite an interest in the developement of its resources and the progressive amelioration of its inhabitants. There is not one of the publications already named, from which something interesting or useful may not be gleaned. Some of them are written in a style eminently adapted to the tastes of a large class of readers, who might not enjoy the more learned researches and more scientific delineations of a Humboldt or a Prinsep. But, in proportion to their fitness to suit the popular demand, ought to be their freedom from mistakes that may generate and rivet erroneous impressions in the popular mind.

* Vide Gurhwal Settlement Report, page 7, by way of comment on pp. 151 and 152 of Pilgrim's Notes.

ART. VII.—1. *Illustrations of some Institutions of the Mahratta People, by William Henry Tone, Esq., formerly commanding a Regiment of Infantry in the service of the Peishwa. Calcutta, 1818.*

2. *Elphinstone's Report on the territories conquered from the Peishwa. Calcutta, 1821.*

3. *Jenkin's Report on the Territories of the Rajah of Nagpore. Calcutta, 1827.*

4. *History of the Mahrattas, by James Grant Duff, Esq. Captain 1st or Grenadier Regiment of Bombay Native Infantry, and late Resident at Satara. Longman, London, 1826.*

5. *The Bengal and Agra Gazetteer for 1841 and 1842.*

SCARCELY more than a twelvemonth has passed since our pages contained a brief outline of the leading events of the last few years in the Punjab, and furnished a catalogue of atrocities which to many readers, especially to those in Europe, may have appeared unduly coloured and exaggerated. It is difficult to understand how any country can escape absolute depopulation when scourged by such calamities, and we shrink with horror from the details of individual suffering involved in these wholesale butcheries. There is, however, a pertinacious vitality in *mankind*, that rallies from the most tremendous slaughter of *men*. The Sikhs are not the only people

> " Whose morning dawn was with blood o'erspread,
> Their evening-fall was a bloody red ;
> Their groans were heard on the mountain swarth ;
> There was blood in the heavens and blood on the earth."

Such is the train of thought suggested by perusing the works, the titles of which stand at the head of this article. Before using them as authorities it will be only courteous briefly to introduce the authors and our readers to each other.

We have disinterred from the back shelves of our library, the worm-eaten pages of Jenkins's and Elphinstone's valuable reports. Such state documents are too little read. They afford better lessons of Indian statesmanship than half the more pretending publications of the day. Grant Duff's volumes should be in the hands of all who desire acquaintance with the Mahrattas. He lived among them for years, understood their peculiar character, and, without any pretension to commanding talent, seems to us to have combined the chief qualifications necessary to a good Political Agent: He was industrious, impartial, and benevolent. He was not, moreover, a mere book worm.

He studied men and manners in the camp, the cabinet, and in the peasant's field, as well as in the dusty records of his office. He examined the past that he might understand the present; and such we consider to be the duty of every Indian official who would not be led by the nose by his assistants, European or Native. Research of this kind has, however, its besetting dangers : it tempts men to become mere devourers of indistinct manuscripts, and it is apt to lure them into the wide waste of speculation, where, mounted on the hobby of some favourite theory, they challenge and combat the strongest evidence that will not take the road they themselves have chosen. Grant Duff escaped these temptations : he was eminently practical. His book is written with the candour and gentlemanliness of the accomplished soldier, combined with the kindliness to be expected from a disciple of Mount Stewart Elphinstone. If the minute details of some portions of the Mahratta history in some measure fatigue the reader, he is rewarded by the fullest information on the character of a very peculiar people, too generally believed to be as the Sikhs, a modern sect, or, like the Pindarees, to have been mere bands of marauders, instead of being one of the oldest races of the Indian peninsula. The record of that portion of Mahratta history that came under Grant Duff's personal observations, appears to us to possess the rare merit of thorough impartiality. Each topic and individual is treated manfully but courteously. Truth was his grand object. He sank no point by which it might be ascertained or illustrated ; but, while doing so, he uniformly treated his opponents with unassuming candour. Elphinstone's statements both in his history and official report, agree with those of Grant Duff. Rushton's *Gazetteer* is a treasury of information to those who can separate the wheat from the chaff ; but the winnowing is rather a formidable task. We should gladly welcome another series, more leisurely compiled than those for 1841 and 1842. Our Government offices teem with records which, under moderately judicious editorship, would incalculably enrich such a work.

Besides the above authors we have gleaned information relative to the Mahrattas from other writers, who advert to them directly or indirectly. Mill's notice of them is singularly meagre and unsatisfactory, and not always accurate. Gleig evidently *means* to follow Duff, but occasionally embellishes his authority in a way that might have passed in "the Subaltern," but is unbecoming in an historian. Wilkes and Orme throw much light on those portions of Mahratta history which they treat of ; and the same may be said of " Scott's Dakhan "

" Waring's History of the Mahrattas" makes much pretension, which is very scantily fulfilled.   We have been more edified and amused by Mr. Tone's seventy-six modest pages than by Waring's quarto.   " Broughton's Mahratta Camp" is unpretending and interesting, and brings before us Mahratta manners and Sindhia's Court.   Hamilton's notices of the Mahratta country in his *Gazetteer* are extremely valuable.   Sutherland's brief sketches are excellent.   The Mahrattas and their country were little known when Rennell wrote; his notices are therefore scanty and inaccurate.

This enumeration of authorities, at the outset, will excuse us from perpetual references.   With their assistance, we now proceed to offer to our readers a brief sketch of early Mahratta History, down to the time when the several states of Poona, Berar, Baroda, Gwalior, and Indore branched of; when, following the diminished fortunes of the junior branch of the Satara family at Kolapoor, we shall hastly glance at the recent military operations in that and the Sawunt-waree country.

Maharashtra, or the country of the Mahrattas, is, according to Hindu geographers, one of the five principal divisions of the Deccan,* or, country south of the Narbadda and Mahanaddi rivers.   The limits of Maharashtra are variously given: Mahommedans seldom troubled themselves about geographical questions, and it was long after they had overrun the different provinces of India, before they enquired respecting their original divisions.   Mahrattas, indeed, are seldom mentioned by Mahommedan writers until the deeds of Shahjee, and his son Sevagee, brought their countrymen prominently to notice.   When the historian Ferishtah alludes to the Mahrattas he calls them " the Hindus," " the Bergis," meaning by the first appellation the population, generally, in contradistinction to their moslem conquerors ; by the second, designating them marauders.†

Two points of the Mahratta history have, however, been

---

* The Deccan of the Hindus comprized the whole Peninsula south of the Narbadda and Mahanaddi, but Europeans have adopted the Mahommedan definition, and limit it to Telingana, Gondwana, and that portion of Maharashtra above the Western Ghats, being generally the country between the Narbadda and Kistna rivers.

† Mr. Elphinstone states, at page 457, volume 2 of his History of India, "the word Mahrattas first occurs in Ferishta, in the transactions of the year A. D. 1485, and is not then applied in a general sense."   This is an error   It strikes us we have repeatedly seen them mentioned at earlier dates.   By a hasty reference we have now found three such references. A. D. 1342, Ferishtah, as translated by Dow, says " He at the same time conferred the Government of Doulutabad and of the country of the *Mahrattors* upon Cuttulech, his preceptor."   Page 289, volume 1.   Again, at two places, in page 320 of the same volume, " Sirvadon, Chief of the Mahrattors" is mentioned.   In Scott's translation of Ferishtah's History of the Deccan, among other inmates of " Feroze Shaw's" Zenana, in A. D. 1398, are noted, " Rajpootees, Bengalees, Guzratees, Telinganees, *Maharattine.*

recovered by the mazes of antiquity. Ptolemy tells us that, in the second century there was a large city called Tagara, one of the principal marts of the Deccan, or country of the south ; well known to the Greeks, and frequented by Egyptian merchants, 250 years before Christ. Its exact position has been the subject of controversy. Mr. Elphinstone considers that the site has yet to be ascertained, while Grant Duff places it on the Godavery, about fifty miles below Pyetan,—supposed to have been the Paithana of Ptolemy. Learned natives recognize the name of Tagara, and Grant Duff alludes to ancient deeds of grants of land engraved on copper plates, styling its monarch " the Chief of the Chiefs of Tagara." The second fact is, that a conquering sovereign, by the name Salivahan, whose æra begins A. D. 77, and is the one now ordinarily used in the Deccan, ruled in the Mahratta country. He is said to have subdued the famous Vikramaditya, king of Malwa, but this could not have been the case as there are 135 years between their eras. The capital of Salivahan is recorded to have been at Pyetan on the Godavery.

The foregoing seem to be the only facts that can be gleaned from the mass of legendary accounts regarding Maharashtra, and its many petty independent states, antecedent to the inroad of the Mahommedans under Alla-ud-deen, in the year of our Lord 1294. At this time, Jadow Ram-deo Rao was king, rajah, or mayhap only " chief of the chiefs." He was at least sovereign of an extensive country, though there were at the time several other chiefs in Maharashtra independent of his authority. Jadow Ram-deo Rao ruled at Deogurh, the modern Doulutabad. His conquerors, astonished at his wealth and power, styled him King of the Deccan. The plunder of his capital supplied Alla-ud-deen with the wealth which enabled him to usurp the throne of Delhi.

To make our subsequent historical details intelligible, it will be requisite briefly to describe the position and features of the Mahratta country. Mr. Elphinstone's History of India gives the following boundaries of Maharashtra. On the north, the Sautpoora range of hills, from Naundode, near Baroach, on the western coast, to the source of the Wurda river. On the east the Wurda river, which, taking a south easterly course, joins the Wyne Gunga, south-west of Chanda. On the south the boundary is a waving line, running past Beder and Kolapoor to Goa ; while the western limit is the line of coast from Goa to Damaun, and thence inland to Naundode.

The trapezium enclosed within this outline, covers about one hundred thousand square miles, and is estimated to contain between six and seven millions of inhabitants. Some portions of the country are thickly inhabited, but large tracts are desolate, or very thinly peopled, giving as the average of the whole, scarcely above sixty to the square mile.* The most marked feature of the country, whose boundaries we have defined, is the Syhadree range of mountains, commonly called the Ghats. They run along the western coast of India, at an average distance of thirty-seven miles from the sea: their summits are from three to five thousand feet in height, rising abruptly from the west, and supporting a table-land which averages three thousand feet above the sea, and slopes gradually towards the east. This range divides Maharashtra into three great tracts, the Concan, the Concan Ghat Mahta, and the Desh, (Des) or country to the eastward of the high lands. The Concan is that portion of the country which lies between the Syhadree mountains and the sea, and extends in a long narrow strip from the river Taptee, at Surat, to the Portuguese town of Goa. This division varies in breadth from twenty-five to fifty miles, and contains about twenty thousand square miles, or one-fifth of all Maharashtra. The Concan is a very rugged country, " interspersed with huge mountains and thick jungles; intersected by rivers and numberless rivulets." Some portions, however, especially near the coast, are remarkably fertile. Towards the Ghats the country is wild and picturesque in the extreme, the jungle verdure is there perpetual, and vegetation most luxuriant.

The table land above the passes is called the Concan-Ghat-Mahta, or Concan above the Ghats. The highest part of the Syhadree range is that which immediately faces the Concan. The breadth of this chain of mountains is about twenty or twenty-five miles, including the space from the summit of the ridge facing the Concan, to the termination of the branches on the east side ; the whole intervening space being designated Concan-Ghat Mahta.† The area will thus be equal to rather

---

* Mr. Tone, who was an officer in the service of the Peishwa, says, " I believe it may be safely asserted that through the whole country (Bengal and Behar excepted) one acre in fifty is not cultivated." He wrote in 1818, and doubtless alluded to the country around Poona where he had served; but even there, and distracted as the Peishwa's territory had been. we consider his statement to be above the mark. The Satara and Poona lands now bear a far different aspect; indeed wherever British influence extends, and common care and intelligence is exerted, the change is soon extraordinary. We have, in more than one quarter, seen cultivation doubled, nay trebled, in a single year.

† The general elevation of the Bombay Sanatarium in that portion of the Syhadree range called the Muhabaleshwur hills is 4500 feet above the sea ; the highest summit is 4700 ; the height above the subjacent country in the Concan, is 4000 feet, and above the general level of the Deccan, at its eastern base, 2300 feet. The average breadth of the table land on which the settlement has been established is eleven miles and a half, and the average length, eleven miles.

more than half that of the Concan. The whole tract from Joonere to Kolapoor, is fairly populated, and the vallies are well cultivated. The people are hardy and patient, and under Sevajee made excellent soldiers. The Mawulees (or Mahratta inhabitants of a portion of the table land and valleys called the Mawuls) were the main instruments of his rise. North of Joonere, the valleys are less cultivated, and are occupied by Bheels and Coolies who were all plunderers, but many of whom have been reclaimed. The summits of the hills are frequently crowned with huge basaltic rocks, forming natural fortresses of great strength. Many of them have been improved by art, and from the earliest times these mountain fortresses have been considered among the strongest in India. Mr. Tone says, " I have counted, in a day's march through Candeish, nearly twenty fortresses, all in sight, in different directions." Often as the majority of these places have changed hands, they have seldom been taken by main force. Many contain springs of pure water; all have reservoirs, and, in native warfare, their weak garrisons could defy powerful armies. Gold or stratagem, treachery, famine or a *coup-de-main* usually gained them; it was reserved for the British to carry by storm in open day such places as Panalla, Samungurh, and Manogurh. The third great division of Maharashtra is the Desh, or Des, being the open country eastward from the foot of the Ghat-Mahta. The Desh is by no means an unvaried level, but becomes less broken as it recedes easterly. It is intersected by four chains of mountains running east and west. The Sautpoora, Chandore, Ahmednugur, and Mahdeo hills; the first being the northern boundary of Maharashtra, the last lying to the north of Satara. The general aspect therefore of the Mahratta country, is hilly. The valleys are well watered, but indifferently cultivated. Five great rivers, the Narbadda, the Taptee, the Godavery, the Deema, and the Kistna permeate the country.

The mass of the inhabitants are Hindus* separated, as elsewhere in India, into the four great classes, but, as usual, innumerably sub-divided. The Brahmans have long almost monopolized all civil and military offices ; though while thus secularly employed, they forfeit the veneration evinced towards those who devote their lives to spiritual concerns. They com-

* " The Hindus" are too generally considered, or rather talked and written of, as one race, much as half-enlightened Indians believe all Feringhis (Franks) to be one people : their ignorance may be excused, but Englishmen should understand that between the Hindu of Tanjore, Mysore, Bengal, Oude, Maharashtra and Rajputana there is quite as much difference in language, customs, forms and features as obtains between Russians, Germans, French, Spaniards, Italians and Englishmen.

menced as servants; they now command in almost every Mahratta Durbar. The name of Mahratta is applicable to all the inhabitants, but Grant Duff states that "amongst ' themselves a Mahratta Brahman will carefully distinguish ' himself from a Mahratta. That term, though extended to ' the Koonbees, or cultivators, is, in strictness, confined to the ' military families of the country, many of whom claim a doubt- ' ful but not improbable descent from the Rajputs." He might have added that all over India the Mahratta chiefs are considered to be Soodras, of the three great divisions, husband-men, shepherds, and cowherds. Mahratta women are well treated; those of rank are generally veiled, but it is little, if any, disgrace for them to appear uncovered. Scott Waring witnessed the wife of the Peishwa, Bajee Rao, practising her horse; and Mr. Tone says, at page 9, "I can affirm having seen the daughter of a Prince making bread with her own hands, and otherwise employed in the ordinary business of domestic housewifery." Widows usually perform Sutee with the bodies of their husbands, unless when they have infant children, or are themselves called to govern, which has so often happened of late at every Mahratta court. In such cases the veil is, in a great measure, relinquished. The widow having then to counsel with men, and even to go into battle, forgets that she is a woman. Within an area of 100,000 square miles, there must doubtless be great variety of form and feature, but the Mahrattas generally may be considered small, active, well made men. For Hindus their features are coarse. They are hardy, persevering, and abstemious. The cultivators and shep-herds are frugal, patient and industrious, and possess as many good qualities as can be expected from a people whose country has for centuries been a battle field. They have the cunning incidental to their condition; to a race who have long lived on the defensive, who have been accustomed to be squeezed, and who have learnt to pay nothing that could not be enforced. The notions of Mahratta chiefs and soldiers are, for Indians, peculiar. They have none of the pride and dignity of the Rajput, Sikh, Jat or Patan, and little of their apathy or want of worldly wisdom. The Mahratta considers plunder and profit to be the object of war; for this he will undergo fatigue, privation and danger, but he has no notion of endangering or sacrificing his life on a mere punctilio. Mr. Elphinstone, after strikingly shewing the points of difference between the sentiments of Mahratta and the Rajput, affecting even the outward appearance of the two nations, remarks, " there is something noble in the carriage ' even of an ordinary Rajput; and something vulgar in that

' of the most distinguished Mahratta. The Rajput is the most
' worthy antagonist ; the Mahratta the most formidable enemy ;
' for he will not fail in boldness and enterprize when they are
' indispensable, and will always support them, or supply their
' place by stratagem, activity, and preseverance."

The village system prevailed in great purity in Maharashtra ;
all the accessible land in the country was portioned off into
villages, the boundaries of which were defined. The arable
land was divided into fields, and every field was *named* and
registered. The majority of the cultivators were hereditary
occupants, (meerasdars) who could not be ejected as long
as they regularly paid the assessment on their fields. The
Government servants in charge of circles of villages were
called Deshmukhs, and their accountants, Deshpandyas ; the
first answering to the Talukdar or Zemindar, the second to
the Canungo of Hindustan. There were also a class of farmers of the revenue called Khotes. One or other of the
above would occasionally take advantage of circumstances,
and usurp the lands over which they had been appointed mere
Collectors. During a period of anarchy, and under native
rule, such persons effected in Maharashtra what in a time
of peace, and under a British Government, was deliberately
accomplished in Bengal; shewing that hasty, though well
intentioned, legislation may affect the rights and welfare of a
people even as much as the worst tyranny. Every village was
a miniature common-wealth. Each had its establishment of
officials. The Patell, or headman, was usually a Sudra; he
held an office nearly corresponding to the Punch, Mokudum, or
Lumberdar of the N. W. Provinces. He superintended the
cultivation and managed the police. Disputes that he could
not adjust were referred to a punchayet of "the inhabitants
best acquainted with the circumstances." The Patell's clerk
was termed Koolkurnee ; he was usually a Brahman, though
occasionally as, in Hindustan, of any other caste. His office
corresponded to that of Patwaree, or record keeper.* There
was likewise the Mhar, or Dher, being the Goreit, Bolahar or
Dowaha, that is, the scout guide, and watchman of the village.
Then there were the handicraftsmen, and others, few of whom
are now found as public servants in villages under British
administration, but who are all over India recognized as remnants of the primitive village system, and used to be paid by land
assignments. Though in the Concan, as in Bengal, the Khotes,

* The Patell and Koolkurnee are terms introduced by the Mussulmans. The
original Hindu appellation of the former was Gaora, or, if the village manager,
Gramadekaree ; the Kalkarni was designated Gramlekak.

or farmers of the revenue, and the Pergunnah chiefs have generally transmitted their office to their sons, and superseded the
village maliks; in the Ghat Mahta, each village has still its
Patell and Koolkurnees.

Ten years ago Colonel Sutherland pronounced the Berar
(Nagpore,) and Satara Governments, the best native adminis-
trations in India, implying that their demands were the lightest
on the cultivator. The injunction of the Shaster, that the
Prince should only take one-sixth of the crop, is every
where disregarded ; where payments are in kind, three times
that amount, or half the crop, is more usually exacted ; it is
a lenient administration that demands only one-third from
irrigated and good lands, and one-fourth from dry and poor
soils. As elsewhere, there are other petty but vexatious
cesses, and the customs system among the Mahrattas, as in
other parts of India, is a fruitful source of annoyance to
traders, yielding little corresponding profit to the rulers. The
cultivators are divided into two great classes, Meerasdars, or
hereditary occupants, with certain proprietary rights, and Oop-
rees or tenants at will.   " All property, or shares of hereditary
' right in land, or in the district and village establishments,
' termed under the ancient Hindu Governments, *writtee*, is
' now best known throughout the Mahratta country, by the
' name of *wutun* ; and the holder of any such, enjoys what is
' considered very respectable, the appellation of **wutundar**."
Vol. I. p. 43, *Grant Duff*. So much are rural honours valued,
that the fractional portions of the office of Patell were often
sold at high prices ; each holder of a portion designating himself Patell. When the monarch of an empire, Sindhia clung
to what he called his hereditary Patellship.

Of the nine* existing Mahratta States, none, except
Suwunt-warree, a petty chiefship, can claim any antiquity.

---

* They are 1.   Gwalior or Sindhia's Country.
        2.   Indore, or Holkar's ditto.
        3.   Berar or Bhonsla of Nagpore.
        4.   Baroda or Ghaekwar.
        5.   Satara or the lineal descendants of Sivagee's son Sumbagee.
        6.   Kolapoor or the Lineal of Sivajee's second son Rajah Ram.
        7. { Dhar.
        8. } Dewas, are petty chiefships held by two of the oldest of the
                  Mahratta families " the Powars."
        9.   Sawunt-waree,—properly Waree, a small state dependant on
            Beejapore, the chiefs of which are called Desaee, Deshmukh, or
            Sawunt, *hence*, Sawunt-waree.
    There are also many Jagirdars, more or less powerful, some holding direct from
the British Government, others depending on Satara, Kolapoor, &c.
        Absorbed into the British Territory.
1.   Poona or the Peishwa's Principality.
2.   Tanjore, or the Territory of Venkajee, Brother of Sivajee.

Satara ranks from 1664. Kolapoor, from a younger branch of Sivagee's family that separated in the year 1729. The rest are formed from later acquisitions granted to Military Commanders, chiefly by the Peishwa, to be held in subordination to the Empire, but which never paid allegiance to Satara, and a very brief one to Poona. All the principalities, except Satara, Kolapoor and Sawunt-waree, are beyond the limits of Maharashtra; and except about Nagpore, where there are a few Mahrattas, the ruling classes in those countries are as much foreigners as are the Mahommedans in Oude, or the English in Calcutta.

With this brief general sketch we now proceed to our historical notice. In the year 1294 Alla-ud-deen, the governor of Oude and nephew of the Khiljee king of Delhi, Jelal-ud-deen, without asking the sanction of his uncle, moved across the mountains and forests of the Vindhya range, and, after a toilsome and dangerous march of 700 miles through hostile countries, reached the El Dorado of Deogurh. His force consisted only of 8000 men, a small army for so formidable an undertaking, but as large a one as its bold leader could have fed on such a route. Ramdeo Rao Jadow, the Mahratta prince of Deogurh, negociated terms, but his son broke the treaty, and drew on his country doubly severe terms. Large cessions of territory were made, and the victor carried back with him the accumulated treasures of centuries. Thus enriched, Alla-ud-deen returned to Delhi, only to assassinate his uncle, and seize the imperial throne. During the reign of Alla-ud-deen almost all Maharashtra was subdued, but on his death the Mahrattas recovered the greater part of their territory; and endeavoured to regain Deogurh. Its Mussulman garrison was, however, relieved by the Emperor Mubarik, who took the Mahratta leader Hirpal Deo, prisoner, and caused him to be flayed alive. Several insurrections occurred. The Emperor Mahomed Tughluk, among other wild schemes, endeavoured to remove all the inhabitants of Delhi to Deogurh, the name of which place he changed to Doulutabad, intending to make it the seat of Empire. He had partially executed his merciless design when the Deccan fell from his hands, to be recovered after nearly four hundred years by Aurungzebe, only to remain a nominal appendage of the Mogul Empire for less than the term of a single life, and then to be for ever rent from the Delhi throne.*

---

* Aurungzebe only completed the conquest of the Deccan in the year 1687, and Nizam-ul-mulk became independent in 1723. Thus the Moguls had a troubled and exhausting occupancy of thirty-six years in reward for centuries of exertion and incalculable expenditure of life and treasure.

The rebellion of the fugitive nobles,—who, in the year 1344, fearing the royal treachery, rose on their guards, slew them, fled to Doulutabad, and there, electing one of their own number, a simple commander of a thousand horse, as their king, raised the standard of rebellion,—belongs to the record of the Mahommedan empire in the South; but without a brief notice of the circumstance the Mahratta history would be unintelligible. The rebels agreed on a plan of warfare which has ever been the favourite one in the Mahratta country. A portion of the allied force under the new King, Nazir-ud-deen, defended Doulutabad, while the other chiefs acted on the communications and supplies of the besiegers. The Emperor divided his force accordingly, and himself prosecuting the siege, he sent a strong force against the field detachments.

The Delhi Empire never was at peace. It was especially troubled during Mahomed Tughluk's reign; and now, when he had nearly reduced Doulutabad, he was urgently called away by an insurrection in the North. The confederates emboldened by his departure gained courage; they were joined by many Mahratta chiefs, and, under Zuffir Khan, one of their own ablest leaders, gave the Imperial general battle, slew him and gained a great victory. Nazir-ud-deen came out from Doulutabad to meet his victorious army, but, observing the influence that Zuffir Khan had obtained, wisely resigned the throne in his favour. Zuffir Khan had originally been the slave of a Brahman, who treated him kindly and foretold his future rise. The new king changed his own name to Alla-ud-deen Husein Kangoh Brahmani, in gratitude to his old master, whom he appointed his treasurer. Thus originated the name of the Brahmani dynasty.

Alla-ud-deen commenced his reign in the year 1347. His rise was mainly caused by the succours afforded by the native (Mahratta) chiefs to whom he was not ungrateful. His dynasty lasted about 150 years. Maharashtra was, at his accession, divided into petty principalities. Every holder of an inaccessible hill or deep jungle was a polygar, literally a rebel. The new sovereign subdued the weak among those in the plains, and conciliated others by grants of lands, or by the confirmation of their possessions. By such means he made himself master of almost all Maharashtra, except part of the Concan-Ghat Mahta, which his successors did not succeed in conquering until a century later. During this period there were several insurrections, but chiefly induced by Mahommedan officers. The Mahratta chiefs were generally faithful.

In 1396 the terrible famine designated " the Durga Dewee"

commenced, and lasted for twelve years, depopulating large tracts, and leaving traces of its effects for forty years after. The inhabitants of whole districts were swept away; village land-marks were lost; their boundaries were forgotten, and, when the periodical rains returned, and endeavours were made to restore cultivation, the whole country was discovered to be in one mass of disorder. The polygars had increased in all directions; the hill forts formerly reduced by the Mahommedans, and abandoned in the great dearth, were now held by banditti, who infested the country and destroyed the returning hopes of those who had escaped nature's terrible calamity. Great efforts were made during successive years to repeople the villages and to reduce the hill forts. No rent was demanded for lands during the first year of fresh occupation, and only a tobra (horsebag) full of grain for each bigah during the second year. But little was effected until, by a systematic plan, the robber forts were reduced throughout the Syhadree range. An able commander by name Mullik-ul-tijar had great success. He subdued the whole Ghat-Mahta, and carried his arms into the still unconquered part of the Concan. He besieged and obliged a rajah, whose surname was Sirkay, to surrender, insisting on his embracing Islamism. The Mahratta consented, but deluded the Moslem into a previous expedition against the Rajah of Kondan, whom he designated his hereditary enemy. A detachment of 7000 Mahommedans started under the immediate orders of their commander, and, guided by Sirkay, as to an assured victory, were led into an ambuscade and every man massacred. The Deccanees, Hindu and Moslem, have always been noted for such wiles of wafare.

Mahommed Shah, the second Brahmani monarch, divided his kingdom into four turufs (or quarters), to each of which he appointed a Governor, or Turufdar; but as the empire extended by conquests from the rajahs of Telingana, Beejaungur, Orissa and the Concan, it was found necessary further to subdivide the management of the country, separating each of the former divisions into two. Several arrangements were also made with a view of securing the fidelity of the local governors, but they all failed. Mahommedans can conquer, they cannot retain. There seems to be something in their creed and customs opposed to permanency and to good government. The subdivision into eight governments took place in the year 1478, and only eleven years afterwards, Adil Khan, the governor of Beejapoor, the founder of the Adil Shahee dynasty, declared his independence: soon after, four other Chiefs assumed the purple. Only three* of these states, formed from the extinction of the Brahmani dynasty, were in existence when the Mahrattas rose into notice. The revolutions in the several Mahommedan states of the Deccan all aided the eventual emancipation of the original inhabitants. The majority of the forts, especially in unhealthy parts of the country, were held by Mahrattas, sometimes as hired soldiers of the Mahommedan government, but more frequently as Jaghirdars and hereditary defenders of the soil. In all times of weakness or of tumult these garrisons called Gurhkuris made their own terms: they either threw off the yoke altogether, or joined the party or pretender that offered the best terms. Deshmukhs, Dessaes, and other rural chiefs also, whether they acquired authority by birth, or as Collectors of revenue, or as military leaders holding lands in wild and secluded quarters, all made their harvest of Mahommedan dissensions and of Moslem pride and ignorance. From these Chiefs are descended the present "Mankurees," literally great men, many of whom, though reduced to poverty, claim superiority to the present mushroom monarchs of their race, and pay them very unwilling homage.

Except the Sawunt-waree family and the Powars of Dhar and Dewas, the princes of the present day are men of yesterday, descended at best from petty village officers. The Holkars were shepherds, and Mulhar Rao, the first leader of the name, for years grazed his uncle's sheep in Candeish. The Sindhias were of a higher, though broken family, so that Ranoojee, the modern head of the clan, served the second Peishwa as a common Bargir, and report says, even carried his slippers. Damajee Ghaekwar and Pursojee Bhonslay were stirring leaders who rose from the ranks and occupied and bequeathed to their descendants the countries they were sent to plunder or to manage. Ballajee Wishwannah Bhutt, the first Peishwa was hereditary Accountant of a village in the Concan and was originally employed as a common revenue Karkoon or clerk. The family of Powar were Deshmukhs of Phultun in the sixteenth century: and the Sawunts were, even earlier, Dessaees or Deshmukhs of their present country of Waree, near Goa, and rose into importance, under the kings of Beejapoor during the war with the Portuguese.† Bhonslay

---

* The Beejapoor, or Adil Shahee,
  Ahmednugur, or Nizam Shahee,
  Goleondah, or Kootub Shahee

† Hamilton erroneously dates their origin from the time of Sambajee the son of Sivajee.

was the original name not only of the Waree family, but of the respective founders of the Berar, (Nagpore,) Satara and Kolapoor houses, though only the two latter were related to each other. We will now briefly trace the history of their common ancestors.

Babjee Bhonslay was hereditary patell of several villages near Doulutabad. He had two sons, the elder named Mallojee, the younger Wittojee. Mallojee Bhonslay was an active, stirring soldier, and was employed under the banner of Lookhjee Jadow Rao, a Mahratta chief of rank in the Beejapoor service. Mallojee, having been for several years childless, engaged the services of a celebrated Mahommedan saint in his favor. A fine boy was in due time born, and, in gratitude to the Saint was called after him, "Shah," with the adjunct of respect, "jee." Thus in the year 1593 was born Shahjee the father of Sivajee. Mallojee by an act of extraordinary impudence, took advantage of a jocose speech of his leader Jadow Rao on the occasion of the Hooli saturnalia, and procured the unwilling acquiescence of that Chief to his daughter Jeejee's betrothal to his son Shahjee. Mallojee's opportune discovery of a large quantity of treasure reconciled Jadow Rao, and enabled him to purchase the rank of Commander of 5000 horse, with the titles of Rajah, from the weak and venal court of Ahmednugur, upon which the nuptials between the young couple were celebrated. Mallojee's good fortune was attributed to the auspices of the Goddess Bhowanee, who prophesied that one of Mallojee's race should become a king, re-establish Maharashtra, protect Brahmans, and the temples of the Gods; and that his posterity should reign for twenty-seven generations. With his new title, Mallojee received charge of the forts of Sewneree and Chakun, and of the Pergunnahs of Poona and Sopa.

The Deccan monarchies were at this time constantly assailed by the Moguls. The Mahratta chiefs played their own game during these contentions. As a specimen of the times and of the value that was attached to their alliance, we may mention that Shahjee's father-in-law, Jadow Rao, having deserted the Ahmednugur standard in the year 1621, was rewarded by the Emperor Jehangir with the rank and authority of Commander of 15,000 horse. He did not long enjoy his honors. Nine years afterwards he desired to return to his allegiance, was inveigled into a conference within the walls of Doulutabad, and there murdered. On this, his widow, a woman of masculine habits, with her followers and many of her connexions, for ever abandoned the cause of the Nizam-shahee monarchs.

Shahjee, who had now succeeded his father and was recognized as a bold and able leader, followed the example of his mother-in-law and received the rank of a Commander of 5000 horse with a suitable jaghir. He was, however, soon disgusted, and offered his services to the Beejapoor Government to act against the Moguls who were then effecting the conquest of the Ahmednugur state. His offer was accepted, and he soon obtained the distinction of being considered the most active and dangerous enemy of the Imperial arms. Doulutabad however fell to the Moguls; its minister became a pensioner, and its monarch a prisoner. Shahjee did not lose courage. He proclaimed another prince, assumed the management of the remaining Ahmednugur territory, and soon recovered a great portion of what had been lost. In the year 1635, Shah Jehan was at length excited by the audacity of Shahjee to make a great effort to reduce both him and his supporters. An overwhelming force, in four divisions, moved against them, and the Deccanees were beaten at all points. The Beejapoor king then agreed to pay a tribute of twenty lakhs of pagodas; and, the forts of Shahjee being captured, he petitioned for re-admittance into the Imperial service. This was refused, but he was told that he might enter that of Beejapoor.

In the year 1627 Sivajee had been born in the fort of Sewneree, close to the town of Joonere, fifty miles north of Poona. Three years afterwards, to the great displeasure of Jeejee Bye and her friends, Shahjee married a second wife, Tuka Bye Mohitey, by whom he had a son called Venkajee. He had a third son, Suntajee, whose mother was a dancing girl.

In the year 1637, the Beejapoor Government entrusted Shahjee with the post of the second in command of an expedition into the Carnatic. On his departure, he left his family, and his Poona Jaghir in charge of a Brahman named Dadajee Konedeo. The Agent was an able revenue officer and a faithful servant. He recovered the broken districts, encouraged agriculture, and, by good management, greatly increased the prosperity of his charge. Shahjee's services in the Carnatic obtained for him a grant of several of the vallies called the Mawuls of Concan-Ghat Mahta in the neighbourhood of Poona; these he likewise placed under the Brahman's care. Dadajee found their hardy and simple inhabitants in the utmost penury, scarcely clothed, and barely able to defend their wretched huts from the wild beasts of the forest which daily increased on them. He took many of the Mawulees into his service, gave advances of seed grain to others, and by demanding no rents for nine years, and then establishing very light assessments, recovered a considerable portion of country. It is pleasant to find in the dark catalogue of India Rulers an occasional Dadajee Konedeo. Would that there were more such as he among our own ranks! Men who lived for their duty, for the improvement of their respective charges, and not simply for the accumulation, (even though it be honestly,) of so many thousand Rupees to take with them to Europe.

The men of business in Maharashtra were Brahmans. It was no part of the duty of a soldier to bend to the work of a scribe. Dadajee gave his master's son a good education, according to the notions of the times and the country. Sivajee could never sign his name, but he was an excellent horseman and marks-man. He could use the matchlock as well as the bow, and was master of the different kinds of swords and dagger used in the Deccan. He was also instructed in the rules and observances of his caste and in the popular parts of Hindu mythology. He loved to hear the " Kuthas," or tales, in verse or prose, of the gods and heroes of antiquity; he delighted in martial exercises, and he hated the Mahommedans, as Hannibal hated the Romans. While a mere boy he joined some plundering bands in the Concan-Ghat-Mahta; and, taking a fancy to the rude Mawulees, was often absent for whole days with parties of them, on plundering and hunting excursions. He thus became familiar with the defiles and paths of the rugged country around Poona, and attached to himself the most daring of the wild inhabitants. He marked the positions of the strongholds in his neigbourhood, and early determined to seize one of them. As peace now existed with the Moguls, and the Beejapoor army was employed in the Carnatic, the hill forts, generally neglected, were guarded even more slenderly than usual. Sivajee took advantage of this neglect: he bribed the Killadar of Torna, near Poona, to yield the place to him, and then wrote to the Beejapoor court, offering increased rent for the surrounding district, and protesting that he had nothing in view, but his sovereign's advantage. His statement being backed by liberal bribes to the courtiers, he was allowed for several years to pursue his own schemes unmolested. Treasure was found at Torna; and its discovery of course attributed to Bhowanee, the tutelar goddess of Sivajee's family. Arms and ammunition were purchased, and within three miles of Torna he erected, on the mountain of Morbudh, the fortress of Rajgurh.

Sivajee now advanced step by step; one stronghold after another fell into his hands, and with them the command of the circumjacent territory. These continued successes at length alarmed the weak Beejapoor monarch, who could however hit upon no better expedient for reducing the rebel son, than to decoy and imprison the loyal father, then usefully employed in the Deccan. Bajee Ghorepuray, another jaghirdar, was the tool chosen for this act of treachery: he invited Shahjee to his house, and then had him seized. It was sufficiently well known that he was guiltless of any connexion with Sivajee; but it was believed that the son, whom the royal arms could not reduce, might be brought to yield, if the torture and imprisonment of his father was the alternative. Shahjee was accordingly confined in a stone dungeon, the door of which was built up, and he was informed that the single remaining aperture should be closed if his son did not submit within a certain period. For four years Shahjee remained a prisoner, and eventually owed his release to disturbances in the Carnatic and to the king's fear that Sivajee, who had opened communications with the Emperor Shah-Jehan, would offer his allegiance to the Moguls. On releasing his prisoner, the king permitted him to return to the Carnatic, first binding him not to avenge himself on Bajee Ghorepuray. Shahjee agreed to the terms. He verbally complied with all the demands made on him, but he did not forget that his brother of the faith had invited him to his house, and there seized his guest and delivered him to Moslem bonds. He was therefore no sooner clear of the toils than he wrote to Sivajee, " If you are my son, punish Bajee Ghorepuray of Moodhole." This is the only record of communication between the father and son during many years. Well did Sivajee execute the vindictive order. He watched Ghorepuray's movements until the year 1661, when, finding a fitting opportunity, he pounced upon his victim, slew him and many of his family, and plundered and burnt their village. Shahjee was loud in acknowledgment of the pious deed, and soon after, came from the Carnatic to visit his son, and thank him in person for his filial conduct.

During his father's incarceration, Sivajee had been comparatively quiet, but no sooner was Shahjee released, than his son successfully resumed his unscrupulous efforts for effecting the conquest of the entire Ghat Mahta and Concan. At this time, (1656,) Prince Aurungzebe was his father's viceroy in the Deccan, and was entering on those intrigues with the celebrated Meer Joomleh, the minister of Golcondah, which led to the direct interference of the Moguls in that state; and which ended in the entire reduction of Golcondah, and the admittance of Meer Joomleh into the Mogul service.

The Mahommedan power in the Deccan was fast approaching its close, but the wily, and occasionally sagacious Aurungzebe, little thought that, while undermining and gradually absorbing the Mussulman principalities there, he was only clearing the field for a more powerful rival,—that he was preparing the way for "a people of fierce countenance," whose banner, within thirty years of his own death, should wave over the walls of Delhi, and whose leaders should soon after be levying contributions from Lahore to Tanjore.

Beejapoor was at this juncture, in the throes of dissolution; it had lately very narrowly escaped the clutches of Aurungzebe, and was distracted by a factious and treacherous nobility, under the weak administration of an infant king. An effort was, however, now made to put down the insurrection of Sivajee; a large force was collected, and Afzool Khan, an officer of high rank, appointed to the command. He was a bold but arrogant man, and boasted, at taking leave, that he would bring back the rebel in chains to the footstool of the throne. Afzool Khan, however, knew the strength of the country in which he was employed and gladly listened to the humble messages of Sivajee, who, affecting only to desire peace, disclaimed all thought of opposing so great a personage as the Khan. The Moslem was deluded, and sent Puntojee Gopinat, a Brahman in his employ, to arrange with Sivajee the terms of the Mahratta's submission. The envoy was received with all honor, and Sivajee conducted himself during the first interview with great humility. During the ensuing night, the rebel leader secretly visited his guest's quarters, and, addressing him as his spiritual superior, appealed to him as a brahman, in favor of his own cause, which he stated to be that of the Hindus generally. Sivajee urged that he had been called on by the goddess Bhowanee, herself, to protect brahmans and kine, to punish the violators of temples and to resist the enemies of religion. These arguments were seconded by large promises, and the interview ended in Puntojee's entering into a scheme for assassinating his master. Accordingly, the brahman returned to the Mogul camp to report that Sivajee was in great alarm and ready to surrender, if he could only receive a guarantee of his personal safety from the mouth of the Beejapoor commander. The deluded Khan fell into the snare. The place appointed for the meeting was a space, cleared for the occasion, at the foot of the fort of Pertabgurh. One road through the jungle was cleared; all other avenues were closed. A force was told off to attack the Beejapoor main army, when, the death of Afzool Khan should be announced, by a signal of five guns from Pertabgurh. Parties were also so disposed as to cut off whatever escort might accompany the victim. Two persons only were let into the secret of the dark deed about to be perpetrated.

Sivajee prepared for the death grapple, as for a religious though desperate deed. Having performed his ablutions, he placed his head at his mother's feet and besought her blessing. Then, attiring himself with a steel chain cap and hauberk under his turban and cotton gown, he concealed a bichwa, or crooked dagger, under his right sleeve, and placing on the fingers of his left hand a wagnuk,* he leisurely proceeded down the hill to the interview. Fifteen hundred troops escorted Afzool Khan; but he was requested by the traitor Puntojee to halt them, when within a few hundred yards of the base of the hill, lest Sivajee should be alarmed and decline the interview. The Khan accordingly advanced armed simply with his sword, and attended only by a single soldier. Sivajee, too, was accompanied by one attendant, and as he approached the place of interview, repeatedly halted as if in alarm. To give him confidence, the traitor Brahman begged that Afzool Khan's follower might fall back. The chiefs then advanced and being introduced by Puntojee, gave each other the usual oriental embrace.† Sivajee, while his right arm was round the Khan's neck, with the left, struck the wagnuk into his bowels. Afzool Khan feeling himself wounded, pushed the assassin from him, and attacked him sword in hand. The chain armour of Sivajee resisted the blow, and, before the Khan's single attendant could step up to his support, the chief was slain, and his brave servant, refusing quarter, shared his fate. The signal was forthwith given; the ambuscades rushed out, few of the escort escaped and it was only through especial orders, sent by Sivajee, that the slaughter of the main body of the enemy ceased.

The success of this abominable scheme established Sivajee's power: the plunder of the Beejapoor army provided him with military equipments as well as with treasure; and the fame of the exploit encouraged his friends and terrified his foes. He fulfilled his promise to the traitor Puntojee Gopinat, who received the stipulated reward and afterwards rose to high rank

* A steel instrument with three crooked blades, like tiger's claws, made to fit on the fore and little finger.

† How unchanged are Asiatics. Nearly three thousand years ago "Joab said " to Amasa, ' Art thou in health my brother ? and Joab took Amasa by the beard, " with the right hand, to kiss him, but Amasa took no heed to the sword that was " in Joab's hand ; so he smote him therewith in the fifth rib, and shed out his " bowels to the ground." 2 Sam. xx. 9, 10. Joab's weapon must have been something like a wagnuk.

in the Mahratta service. A hundred years afterwards the descendant of Puntojee paid the penalty of his ancestor's perfidy
on the very spot where the traitor Brahman had betrayed the
confiding Beejapoori.

Another effort was however soon made against Sivajee. A
force, twice the strength of that lately sent under Afzool Khan,
was employed under Seedee Johur. Sivajee's light troops de-
vastated the enemy's country while he threw himself into the
fort of Panalla. The Seedee prosecuted the siege for four
months, during the worst season of the year. The post was still
tenable, but all the approaches to it were occupied, and Sivajee
felt the error he had committed in thus allowing himself to be
encaged. But, treacherous himself, he knew whom he could
trust. He asked for terms and proceeded, slightly attended, to
one of the enemy's batteries to negotiate a surrender. He thus
threw the Seedee off his guard, and during the ensuing night,
descended the hill, at the head of a chosen band of Mawulees,
passed the besieger's posts and was well on his march to the fort
of Rangna before his flight was observed. When the fact was
ascertained, he was sharply pursued, and was overtaken at a
defile within six miles of the fortress. He left a party of his
Mawuls under command of Bajee Purvoe, who had formerly
been his enemy, with orders to hold the pass until a signal
from the Fort of Rangna announced his own safety. The orders
were obeyed, the post was held, but at the cost of the life of the
generous Purvoe. Sivajee himself thus escaped, but many of
his forts were captured, and the Mahrattas would have suffered
more severely, but for the court intrigues that caused the
removal of the brave Seedee from the command of the invading
army. This was however an expiring effort on the part of the
Beejapoor Government; the revulsion expedited its own fall;
while Sivajee, bending to the storm he could not brave, quickly
recovered his temporary losses and was soon again in the field
with fresh strength.

At this time (1662), the Sawunts, or lords, of Waree offered, if supported by the Court, to reduce the rebel, but
they were soon abandoned by their weak paramount and the
whole of their own territory was subdued by Sivajee who,
however, restored their Deshmukhee rights and by his judicious treatment soon attached them warmly to his cause. He
occupied Sawunt-waree with his own troops, and drew their
infantry to fight his battles in distant quarters. Sivajee was
now master of a long line of sea coast. He built ships
and commanded an advantageous treaty from the already
degenerate Portuguese of Goa, who supplied him with guns

and naval stores.   The successful rebel had now become a powerful Prince.   Through his father's timely mediation, he was admitted to treat with the Beejapoor minister, and was recognized as master of a tract of country more than 250 miles in length, averaging 50 miles in breadth and in parts extending 100 miles eastward from the sea.   He also had at command a devoted army of not less than 50,000 foot and 7000 horse.

Being at peace with Beejapoor, Sivajee next turned his arms against the Moguls.   For a time the Mahrattas were unsuccessful; many forts fell into the hands of the enemy, who established their camp at Poona.   Sivajee was not slow to take advantage of their position, and to use his own knowledge of its localities.   Understanding that the Mogul commander, Shaisteh Khan, occupied the very house in which he had himself passed his boyhood, Sivajee determined to cut him off in the midst of his guards.   Accordingly, with twenty-five favourite Mawulees, the Mahratta Chief entered Poona at night ; passed through the Mogul troops, wounded Shaisteh Khan, slew his son and many of his personal attendants; and then leisurely retreated, lighting his torches in defiance as he ascended the hill of Singurh, in the face of his pursuers.

In the year 1664 Shahjee was killed by a fall from his horse. He died in possession of large jaghirs including the whole territory of Tanjore, to all which his younger son Venkajee, who was on the spot, succeeded ; Sivajee reserving the assertion of his own right until a favourable opportunity should offer.   In January of that year, having effected the requisite arrangements and gained perfect information as to localities, he made a feint of attacking the Portuguese settlements at Bassein and then, at the head of four thousand horse, made a dash on the rich city of Surat, systematically plundered it for six days and leisurely carried off his booty to the fort of Raigurh.   The Dutch and English factories only escaped.   Their small garrisons stood on the defensive and by their gallant bearing, created a very favourable impression on the minds of the Moguls as well as of the Mahrattas.   Shaisteh Khan had been recalled and the great Jey Sing in conjunction with Dilere Khan was now employed against Sivajee and carried on the war with unusual energy.   Sivajee incautiously threw himself into the strong fortress of Poorundhur, which was reduced to extremity and the Mahratta was induced to trust to Jey Sing's guarantee and surrender himself.   Sivajee's conduct seems unaccountable.   At no time had he been so strong, and dissention was rife in the Mogul camp.   Poorundhur might have fallen, but Sivajee would not have been himself if he could not have effected his own escape. Raja Golab Sing's conduct at the present day in the Punjab seems much akin to this; unscrupulously cutting off all who trust him, he is constantly trusting himself in his enemy's hands. Man is every where unaccountable, but he who has to deal with Asiatics can least calculate, with certainty, on the future by the past. He must be prepared for every vagary, for the violation of the plainest dictates of prudence during peace, for the neglect or breach of all the rules of strategy during war. He may reasonably expect *that* to be done which should not be done, *that* to be neglected which should be effected. No European diplomatist or soldier is so likely to be ensnared as he who, having taken the usual precautions, feels himself secure. The treaty signed, the picquets doubled, neither can be regarded as a guarantee of safety. Certain eventual destruction may await the enemy's move; he may be assured of it on *all* rational calculations, but the goddess Bhowanee or some other Deity or Demon may have promised success—the day of the Feringees may have passed, and the infatuated wretches rush on destruction. Their desperation then *is* dangerous. Rashness, nay madness, has succeeded in striking a blow where the best plans have failed. Indian officials should ever be on the alert.

Sivajee at once surrendered twenty forts, with the territories attached to them, and trusted to the fidelity of Jey Sing to be secured in possession of the remainder of his conquests as a Mogul fief, as well as for sanction to spoil the Beejapoor territory. Aurungzebe generally confirmed Jey Sing's arrangement and invited Sivajee to court. He accepted the invitation, but previously assembling his officers, gave them strict orders as to their conduct during his absence, warned them not to obey any order sent by himself, unless it was brought by certain messengers, and then at the head of 500 choice horse and 1000 Mawulees, proceeded with his son Sambajee to Delhi. Aurungzebe, though possessing considerable ability, was a very short-sighted politician. It was foreign to his character to keep his word; or even to break it in a straight forward manner. He might have at once put Sivajee to death; he preferred to degrade him, probably with the intention of eventually taking his life, or, when sufficiently humbled, of employing him like Jeswunt and Jey Sing, as a tool of his own policy. Sivajee was accordingly received contemptuously, and when his bold spirit revolted, he was placed under surveillance and made to expect the worst. He soon decided on the course he should pursue, and found an ally in Ram Sing, the son of Jey Sing, under whose charge he was placed.

Indignant that his father's engagement should have been violated, he aided the prisoner's flight.   The circumstances of Sivajee's escape concealed in a basket are not among the least romantic of his actions.   He returned to the Deccan and soon recovered all his lately ceded possessions.

The first exploit now performed was the recovery by escalade of the strong fortress of Singurh, which among others had fallen into the enemy's hands.   The fort is situated on the eastern side of the great Syhadree range, and is nearly isolated, being connected only by narrow ridges with the Poorundhur hills, while north and south it has a continued acclivity, often almost perpendicular, of half a mile.   The summit is capped by a huge black rock, forming a craggy precipice, more than forty feet high and two miles in circumference.   This rock was girdled by a stone wall, with towers at intervals, and was strongly garrisoned by a select body of Rajputs under a leader of renown.   Having ascertained that, in the confidence of their own prowess, and of the strength of their fastness, the garrison had become negligent, Sivajee consulted Tannajee Maloosray one of his bravest officers, as to the best plan of surprizing the place.   Tannajee replied that, if permitted to take his own younger brother and 1,000 selected Mawulees, he would engage to seize the fortress.   His offer was accepted.   A dark night was selected for the assault.   Having received their orders at Rajgurh, the Mawulees separated, and by different paths, known only to themselves proceeded to the rendezvous in the vicinity of Singurh.   Tannajee then divided his men into two parties, one to storm, the other to support.   He selected the most precipitous point of the rock, and by means of rope ladders, led his advanced party, one by one, up the precipice. Scarcely three hundred had ascended when the garrison were alarmed.   The challenge of the foremost sentinel was answered by an arrow, and the bowmen then plied their weapons in the direction where they perceived, by the lights, that the garrison were collecting.   A desperate conflict ensued, and the Mawulees were gaining ground, when their leader was slain.   They then fell back and were on the point of retreating by the fearful path they had ascended when Tannajee's brother, Sooryajee, with the relief, appeared, rallied the fugitives and upbraided them for deserting their Chief, saying " will you leave your father's corpse to be tossed into a pit by Mhars ?"   He added that the rope ladders were destroyed, and that now was their time to prove themselves Sivajee's Mawulees.   In an instant the tide was turned and with a deafening shout of their battle cry. " Hur Hur Mahadeo," they returned to the charge and were soon in possession of the Fort.   Of the Mawulees, nearly one-third were killed or wounded, and five hundred of the Rajputs with their commander were found dead or wounded.

Sivajee was hardly consoled for the loss of his gallant officer by the capture of the important post.   When congratulated on the success of his arms he sorrowfully replied, " The den* is taken, but the Lion is slain; we have gained a fort, but alas! I have lost Tannajee Maloosray!"   Sivajee, who as he paid his soldiers regularly, was chary of gifts, on this occasion gave every surviving Mawulee a pair of silver bangles, and rewarded the officers proportionally.

A new tide of conquest had now opened on Sivajee; again, fort after fort fell before his arms or finesses.   The city of Surat (October 1670) was again plundered; and for three days, at the head of 15,000 men, he leisurely squeezed all who had any thing to yield.   The English factory, as before, defended themselves.   Hearing of the approach of a Mogul army, Sivajee suddenly decamped, leaving behind him a letter for the inhabitants in which he demanded a tribute of 12 lakhs of Rupees as the price of exemption from future plunder.   Such was often, with the Mahrattas as with the Sikhs, the origin of their territorial acquisitions.   They plundered the weak, and gradually assumed a proprietory right in all they had the power to destroy or molest.   Their visits were commuted for *chouth*, or a fourth of the produce to be paid as protection, or rather exemption money; gradually the stronger party appointed their own collectors, and, step by step, assumed the government of the lands they had originally wasted.   This year, we first hear the word *Chouth*.   The large town of Kurinja being plundered, a regular agreement was taken from the local authorities to pay one fourth of the yearly revenue; in consideration of which they were not only to be exempted from plunder but protected.

Sivajee's attention was now turned to the sea as well as the land, and his exertions were unremitting on both elements. He sought either to expel the Portuguese from the Coast or to reduce them to the condition of tributaries.   His troops, who had hitherto rather harassed than attacked the Moguls and had been formidable chiefly in forests and fastnesses, began to meet the Emperor's troops boldly in the plain and daily with increased success.   His usual tactics were to affect retreat; to draw on the Mogul horse in their usual tumultuous disorder, and then, either to lead them into an ambuscade or, suddenly

* Singurh Lion's dwelling,

rallying his apparently broken parties, to return to the offensive, and, by repeated attacks on the broken squadrons, to
sweep all before him.   The Mahratta and also the Sikh horsemen were long famous for such manœuvres, and so prevalent is
this Parthian policy not only among the Mahrattas, but
throughout Indian warfare, that it is not unusual, as at the
battle of Assaye, for gunners, when ridden over by cavalry, to
lie quietly down till the torrent has passed, and then to rise and
turn their guns on the squadrons that have overwhelmed
them.

In 1673, Sivajee, after a siege of several months, captured
the fort of Satara.   The place had been long used as a state
prison : its captor little anticipated that it would be the dungeon
of his successors, whence they would be released and reinstated
by the English traders with whom, in their merely mercantile
character, he now first became acquainted.   Sivajee, who had
long struck coins and styled himself Maharaja, was in June of
this year formally enthroned.   He was weighed against gold,
the whole of which being then given to the Brahmans, sharpened
their wits for the discovery that the donor was of high Rajput
descent.

Aurungzebe's attention had been for some time withdrawn
from the Deccan by the disturbances arising from his revival of
the Jezia or Hindu capitation tax, a measure which transformed
the Rajputs from faithful dependants and followers into stout
rebels.   Raja Jeswunt Sing had died at Kabul, fighting the
Mogul battles.   He was rewarded by an attempt to convert
his children by force, but this outrage on his family, together
with the Jezia, drove the Rajputs into a hostile confederation
which occupied the Emperor for two years.   In the year 1676
he again felt at liberty to turn his attention towards the Deccan,
and at this time he seems to have believed that his schemes for
weakening the several kingdoms in that quarter had taken
effect.

The Mogul influence had for some time been paramount at
Golcondah : there was, what was called, a close alliance with
Rajapoor ; and even Sivajee now found it his interest to pay
temporary tribute.   Having determined to proceed to the
Carnatic and oblige his brother to yield (according to Hindu
law,) half their father's inheritance, he came to an understanding with the king of Golcondah, and took the politic step of
offering a sop to the Mogul commander to spare his possessions
during his absence ; jocosely comparing his paying tribute to
giving oil-cake to his milk cow, by which " she would produce
the more milk."   In 1676-7 he proceeded on his expedition at

the head of 30,000 horse and 40,000 foot, but Venkajee soon found the inutility of opposition, and agreed to divide the revenues of Tanjore and his other districts, on which peace was concluded between the brothers.   After an absence of eighteen months, Sivajee returned to Maharashtra and was soon again in hot hostility with the emperor.

The Moguls, having now thrown off the mask towards both Golcondah and Beejapoor, appeared before the latter place. The Regent called urgently on Sivajee for aid.   He gave it effectually, cut off the Mogul's supplies and obliged them to raise the seige.   His reward was the abrogation of the Beejapoor rights of sovereignty over all the conquests he had at different times made.   During this compaign Sivajee's son, Sambajee fled in discontent from his father to the Mogul commander Dilere Khan, who proposed to Aurungzebe to set him up as a counterpoise to Sivajee, but the Emperor declined to take a step that would virtually recognize, and thereby strengthen the predatory system.   Dilere Khan being soon after displaced, avenged himself by conniving at Sambajee's escape.   The latter returned to his father and received partial forgiveness but was detained at large in the fort of Panalla.

Scarcely were the terms of the engagement with Beejapoor concluded when Sivajee's earthly career closed.   His last illness was caused by a swelling in the knee-joint, ending in fever that carried him off on the 5th April 1680, in his 53d year.   Few conquerors have effected so much with equal means.   Long disowned by his father, and unaided by the local chiefs, until by his own stripling arm he had rendered himself independent, he died the recognized ruler of a territory fifty thousand square miles in area ; his name was dreaded from Surat to Tanjore, and in every quarter, between those remote points, his bands had levied contributions and tribute.   The Mahommedan yoke was now for ever broken in Maharashtra.   The long dormant military spirit of the people was roused, to be quelled only in the entire disruption of that system on which it had risen.   The genius of Sivajee emancipated the Mahrattas ; succeeding chiefs, by neglecting the policy which had aggrandized their founder and adopting an organization which they could never perfectly master, precipitated the state to a second downfall.

Our brief sketch will have shewn the line of tactics that Sivajee pursued.   Personally brave, he never fought when he could fly, or when stratagem or treachery could effect his object : but whatever was his design, he weighed it deliberately, gained the most accurate information on all necessary points, and then, when least expected, pounced upon his prey.   The heavy and slow moving Moguls must have been sadly puzzled at encountering such a foe. Many stories are told of the terror his very name inspired. He was feared both as a soldier, a marauder and an assassin. His own dagger, or those of his emissaries could reach where his troops could not penetrate ; no distance or precaution could keep his prey from him. The old Jaghir system under which the Mahratta chief served the Deccan kings was a good foundation for the regenerator of his country to work upon ; but it must be remembered that it was not with the chiefs that Sivajee commenced operations, but with the despised and half starving peasantry of the Ghat-Mahta and Suwunt-waree. It was when Sivajee had gained a name, and had himself become a *chief*, that chiefs joined his standard. It is ever so in India. There is always ample material abroad to feed the wildest flame of insurrection, but not until it has assumed a head, will those who have a stake in the land, join it. They will talk, they will write, they will plot, but seldom, unless in instances of great infatuation, when misled by false prophets, will the chiefs of the land join an insurrectionary move, so long as their own *izzut* has not been touched.

During Sivajee's whole career, he cannot be said to have enjoyed, or rather suffered, one single year of peace. He seems from the outset to have declared perpetual hostility against all who had any thing to lose. His pacifications or rather truces, were but breathing spaces, to enable him to recruit or collect his means, or to leave him unshackled to direct his whole force in another quarter. Aurungzebe played into Sivajee's hands by his timid and suspicious policy. The Emperor was incessantly changing his commanders, and feared to entrust any one of his sons or generals with means sufficient to quell the Deccan insurrections, lest the power so deputed should be used, as he himself had used it, to the usurpation of the throne. Thus distrusted, his children and officers managed the war with Sivajee as with Beejapoor and Golcondah, for their own aggrandizement. They fought as little as they could, while they plundered and received bribes as much as possible.

There was thus much in the times and there was still more in the condition and *feeling* of the country, favourable to Sivajee. His cause was, or appeared to be that of the people. They had long groaned beneath a Mahommedan yoke, and some openly, all secretly hailed a liberator of their own blood, caste and country. It was this strong feeling in his favor that enabled him to procure the excellent intelligence for which he was noted : his spies were in every quarter, in the very zenanas and durbars of his enemies, and always gave timely warning of all designs, and full information of the weak points against which to direct his enterprizes. With all these advantages it may seem more surprizing that Sivajee's rise was not quicker, than that it made the progress we have shewn; but it must be remembered that the Mahratta chiefs were never unanimous, that few ever joined the founder of their empire, that Sivajee's officers and soldiers were the creatures of his own genius, and that for many years the majority of his troops were infantry, excellent in their own strong country, but ill adapted for foreign conquest. Above all, there was the prestige of antiquity and of power around the Mahommedan thrones, and especially around that of the Great Mogul. In no quarter of the world does so much respectful fear attach to long established authority as in India. If there is little veneration for sovereignty, there is abundance of awe. Loyalty and patriotism we put out of the question; but in every case of insurrection the majority of chiefs and men of war, of all castes, will first offer their services to the established power to fight either for or against their own kindred and country; and it is only when refused employment that they flock to the newly displayed banner. The middle and lower classes act differently; their sympathies will be with their fellows, but they will naturally be cautious to conceal their feelings until the progress of events and the conduct of the contending parties afford some clue to the probable result of the struggle. Thus Aurungzebe might originally have commanded the services of all that were then considered the fighting classes of Maharashtra, but his suspicious temper, fearing to admit Hindus into his ranks, and even refusing the services of the Deccan Mussulmans, drove them into the ranks of his enemy. The Mahommedan Government in India had, in short, lost its tact, elasticity, and vigour: luxury had sapped the Moslem strength and deadened their one solitary virtue. Their hardihood declined, and with it their empire fell. Sivajee was the first to take advantage of the imperial decay, and his example was soon followed in every quarter of India.

Sivajee early established a strict military system. His Infantry, as already stated, were originally recruited chiefly from the Concan and Ghat Mahta. The Hetkurees of the former were good marksmen, but his chief dependence was on the Mawulees, or inhabitants of the mountain valleys. He employed the latter on all undertakings requiring cool courage and hand to hand work. They never failed him. The usual arms of both were a sword, shield and matchlock, but a bow was substituted for the matchlock of every tenth man, as being useful in ambuscades and night attacks. The cavalry were of two classes, Sillidars or men bringing their own cattle, and Bargeers who were mounted on horses of the state. A select body of the latter, forming a third and very important class were designated the Pagah or household troops. Individuals of this body were mingled with the Sillidars and ordinary Bargeers to overawe them, and act as spies on their conduct. Horse and foot of all ranks were hardy, active and abstemious. Camp equipage was unknown among them, a single blanket in addition to their light coarse vestments completed their wardrobe, and a small bag of parched grain sufficed for their commissariat supplies. Thus furnished, the infantry would for days and days thread the defiles and jungles of their wild country, and, by paths known only to themselves, appear where least expected ; while the cavalry, supplied with small saddle bags to hold such grain or plunder as they might pick up, swept the country at the rate of fifty, sixty and even eighty miles within twenty-four hours. The grand secret of Mahratta hardihood was, that chiefs and officers shared equally in the privations of their men. A picture was once taken of the Peishwa Bajee Rao by order of his enemy the great Nizam-ul-Mulk, as he chewed his dinner of parched grain, sitting on his horse with all his baggage under him, and his long Mahratta spear stuck in the ground by his side, while he thus took his repast.

Plunder and profit formed the object of all expeditions, the test, and in Mahratta eyes, the only proof of victory. During Sivajee's life, all plunder was public property. It was brought at stated periods to his durbar, where the man who had taken it was praised, rewarded or promoted.

> " Then lands were fairly portioned ;
> " Then spoils were fairly sold :
> " The *Bergees* were like brothers
> " In the brave days of old."

Sivajee had sense enough to perceive how much he should personally gain by the punctual payment of his army. The pay of the infantry varied from three to ten Rupees per month, that of Bargeers from seven to eighteen, and of Sillidars from twenty to forty. All accounts were closed annually : assignments were given for balances on Collectors, but *never* on villages. Cows, cultivators and women were exempt from plunder. Rich Mahommedans and Hindus in their service, were favorite game. Towns and villages were systematically sacked, and where money or valuables were not forthcoming, Sivajee would take promissory notes from the local authorities.

He shed no *unnecessary* blood ; he was not cruel for cruelty's sake, but on these occasions of plunder he mercilessly slaughtered and tortured all who were supposed to have concealed treasure. An Englishman, captured by Sivajee at Surat, reported that he found the marauder, surrounded by executioners, cutting off heads and limbs.

The mountain fortresses were the key-stones of his power. His treasure, plunder and family safe, he could freely move wherever an opening offered. His garrisons were under strict discipline, and were composed of mixed classes as mutual checks. All were told off to such duties as were respectively suited to their habits. Brahmans, Mahrattas, Ramoosees, Mhars and Mangs were in every Fort. The whole were called Gurhkurees, and were maintained by hereditary assignments of rent-free land in the neighbourhood. The Ramoosees, Mhars and Mangs were the scouts and intelligencers ; the Mahrattas formed the garrison. All relied for their daily bread on the charge of their post ; it was, in Grant Duff's words, " the mother that fed them."

The rainy season was usually the holiday of the Mahrattas ; the Infantry took their ease, the Cavalry horses grazed at will on the rich pasture lands,—and as often as possible on those of the enemy. This was however a busy time for Sivajee and his confidants. They now made their enquiries and spied out the land for the ensuing campaign. At the autumnal Dussera, the scattered bands were collected ; the Bhugwa Jenda, or national flag, was unfurled, and the wild marauders poured like a torrent over the country. Under penalty of death, not a woman was taken into Camp,* and, unfettered and unencumbered, Sivajee's bands struck the severest blows at points most distant from the places where they were expected.

It is only justice to state that this extraordinary man, while devastating other lands, was not unmindful of the duty he owed to his own subjects. In his conquered territory, and where the inhabitants had compounded for security, he was kind, considerate and consequently popular. He usually took two-fifths of the crop and protected the ryot in the enjoyment of the remainder. He set his face altogether against the farming and assignment system, now, as formerly, so prevalent throughout the Mahratta and other native states. In civil cases he employed Punchayets, the best if not the only resource in countries where official honesty is uncertain. Punchayets may decree

---

* In this and in some other matters the English might with advantage take a leaf out of Sivajee's book. Endless trains of cattle and camp followers constitute a very weak point in our military system.

wrongfully; but, under efficient superintendence and such checks
as are easily applied, they will administer quicker and more substantial justice, among a rude and simple people, than the most
strait-laced courts.   The truth or falsehood of nine out of ten
cases that are tried in Cutcheries, and that may long enough
puzzle the wits of strangers, is well known in the adjoining
villages.   It needs, therefore, only that interested parties be
prevented from being members of Punchayets, that such courts
be open, and as far as possible, that suits be decided by them
at a single sitting, which may be effected in ninety-nine cases
out of a hundred.

To assist in the management of affairs, Sivajee appointed
eight principal officers, the chief of whom, or Prime Minister,
he designated Peishwa, an ominous name for his descendants.
Among his countrymen and admirers, Sivajee is still spoken of
as an incarnation of the Deity, to which opinion his deeds of
blood and treachery are no drawback.   Mahrattas consider that
political assassination is wise and proper, and that necessity jus-
tifies murder.

Sivajee was small of stature and of dark complexion.   His
countenance was intelligent and animated, his eyes piercing, his
frame active rather than powerful, and, as already mentioned,
he was master of all the weapons commonly used in his country.
Scott Waring calls him a good son to a bad father, but he does
not shew that there was ever any intercourse between them;
and, as we have shewn, the only proof he gave of dutiful
regard was in the destruction of his father's enemy; unless
indeed it be considered an act of filial piety that he seized his
parent's jaghir in his absence, and by his rebellion against
Beejapoor occasioned Shahjee's long and cruel imprisonment.
On the whole, we may pronounce the founder of the Mahratta
Empire to have been *the* man of his day in India: greater
than any of the Mahratta chiefs who succeeded him, and
unrivalled since, even by Hyder Ally or Runjeet Sing.
Sivajee could not only conquer and destroy, but he could
legislate and build up.   There is the germ of civil organization
in his arrangements; and had he lived the ordinary period of
man's life, he might have left to his successors a united and well
established principality.   He died suddenly, and with him his
empire may be said to have expired.

Sivajee left immense treasure.   The amount has been variously
estimated but always in millions of pounds sterling.   Heaped
together in his coffers at Rajgurh were the dollars of Spain, the
sequins of Venice, the pagodas of the Carnatic, and all the
various goldmohurs of the different quarters of India, with

innumerable kinds of rupees of every shape and stamp. But all his spoil, the harvest of more than thirty years of crime and blood, of restless nights, of ceaseless and unseasonable marches, did not bring peace to the owner, nor save his son from a fearful death; it did not preserve his successors from the prison his own hands had prepared, nor his people from being split into factions that soon sealed their own destruction.

Sivajee had four wives; two survived him, of whom one performed Sutee; the other, having intrigued to raise her own son, Raja Ram, to the *guddee*, was put to a cruel death by her step-son, Sambajee, who executed all the parties concerned in this scheme for his supercession.

Once established in power, Sambajee shewed, indeed, a soldierly spirit in the field, but his government was lax, cruel and corrupt. His troops plundered the husbandmen with impunity; and this relaxation of discipline, though it attracted a large accession of daring and dissolute adventurers to the Mahratta standard, yet proved a bad preparation for meeting the formidable power that was coming against them. Aurungzebe was now employed in the final conquest of Golcondah and Beejapoor. When the absorption of those two kingdoms had been effected, he pushed the Mahrattas more closely, and, after some desultory operations, at length by a bold stroke, such as Sivajee had so often struck against the Moguls themselves, seized Sambajee, while in a state of intoxication, at an outpost slenderly guarded. Aurungzebe offered his captive life on condition of his becoming a Mahommedan; "Not if you give me your daughter," was the bold answer of Sambajee. Stung by the insult, the Emperor caused him to be cruelly mutilated and then beheaded.

Sambajee's *life* might have injured the cause of his people: his cruel death, in the words of Grant Duff, "aroused their vengeance without alarming their fears." Raja Ram, the surviving son of Sivajee, was now declared Regent, during the minority of his brother Sambajee's son. The boy was however soon after taken prisoner by the Moguls, and was kindly treated by the daughter of Aurungzebe, who familiarly called him Sahoo or Shao,* his name being Sivajee. For a time the tide continued against the Mahrattas, but far from being

---

* Among the elegant English misnomers of Indian words was that of Shao Raja whom the Bombay factors of his day designated "the Sow Roger." The ignorance as to all that concerns India to this day in England is great, but some light has broken on our countrymen, since, in the year 1764, Guthrie, the Maltebrun of his day, thus described the Mahrattas and their country, "Mahrattas are a kind of mercenaries inhabiting the mountains *between* India and Persia." Maltebrun following Tone is generally correct.

disheartened, their energies were rather thus drawn out.   Raja Ram, after making arrangements for Maharashtra, and for the re-assemblage of his friends around the " Bhugwa Jenda," or national flag, when fortune should be more propitious, took refuge in the Carnatic.   On the plea of his nephew's captivity, he assumed the government in his own name, was enthroned, distributed the usual presents, and made extensive grants of lands including much that was not in the actual possession of the Moguls, but more that had never belonged to his predecessors.

After a brief but eventful career, Raja Ram died of fatigue, caused by long exposure when escaping from Zoolfikar Khan, the ablest, though one of the most venal, of the Mogul officers employed in the Deccan.   He had besieged Raja Ram for seven years in the fort of Ginjee, and when *obliged* to take the place, gave the Raja due notice to escape.   On other occasions Zoolfikar acted with sufficient energy : within one period of six months he is said to have marched in pursuit of the Mahrattas 5,000 miles, and, in this space of time, to have engaged them nineteen times.   In the year 1,700, one month after Raja Ram's death, Satara was captured by Aurungzebe.   Raja Ram left two sons, Sivajee and Sambajee, the former being the elder was, though an imbecile, placed on the *guddee*.   He was only ten years old, but his mother, Tara Bye, was a woman of energy and the virtual ruler.   She moved from fort to fort, encouraging her son's adherents, while in five different directions, his troops kept the field under able officers.

Aurungzebe was now at the head of his own army ; and successively captured the principal strongholds of the Mahrattas. Torna was carried by escalade, sword in hand, during the night : all the others were won by gold.   Several were retaken within the year, and the Emperor's hold on any of them lasted only while a strong force remained in the neighbourhood.   The climate, the difficulty of bringing up convoys, the feeling of the people, all were against the Moguls.   But while the Mahratta fortresses were thus temporarily yielding and their country falling a prey to the Mogul, their own predatory bands were daily extending the influence of the Mahratta name.   For a third time they levied contributions on the city of Surat and plundered Burhanpoor, while their squadrons simultaneously ravaged Malwa, Candeish, Berar and Guzerat.

The Mogul system, with all its pageantry, was rotten at the core.   The royal presence, or the occasional effort of an able and honest officer, might gain a brief success ; but what could one old man, bowed down with the weight of ninety years, with centuries of care and crime on his brow, perform ?   One who, though he had long exceeded the usual span of life, now felt he was approaching the hour of his own long account. Nor could the empire be upheld by chiefs and generals who had never been cordially trusted, and whose success on behalf of their master, would, in his eyes, be little less than treason, entailing on the victors disgrace, if not death. Most of them therefore were in the pay of the Mahrattas. They allowed convoys to pass into the fortresses they besieged and occasionally even fed the garrisons themselves. So far from protecting the royal districts from plunder, the Mogul army connived at, if they did not aid in, their devastation; and the more farseeing chiefs, collected and husbanded their resources, and quietly awaited the struggle they perceived must follow the Emperor's death. Worn out with disease, and vexed by the ill success of his measures, Aurungzebe now allowed himself to be almost persuaded by his favourite son Kaum Buksh, to recognize Mahratta independence and to pay the Surdeshmukhee, (ten per cent.) on the revenues of the six Soobahs of the Deccan. Their insolence and daily increasing demands alone prevented the fulfilment of the compact. Feeling his end approach, Aurungzebe moved on Ahmednugur; his army was attacked and defeated on the way, and the aged and dying Emperor narrowly escaped falling into the hands of his enemies.

Aurungzebe's last march was made. He died at Ahmednugur, on the 21st February, 1707, and left the heritage of his manifold crimes to his three sons. To the measure of their respective ability, they followed his example. Two soon fell in civil conflict, and the eldest, Sultan Mauzum, succeeded to the distracted and already dismembered sovereignty, under the name of Shah Alum.

The release of Shao, the son of Sambajee, had been more than once proposed as a counterpoise to the party of Raja Ram's family; but, although as a preparatory measure, Aurungzebe had caused the youth to be united in marriage to two influential families, he had always hesitated to carry out the scheme. On the death of the Emperor, Shao fell into the hands of Prince Azim Shah, who released him when he was immediately joined by many influential persons, and early next year (1708) seized Satara. Daood Khan, the Mogul Deputy in the Deccan also supported him. Thus countenanced, Shao's cause was on the ascendant, but young Sivajee, or rather his mother, Tara Bye, had still a strong party. During the monsoon of 1709, their partizans cantoned at Kolapoor, and the next year, Sivajee determined to make that town and the neighbouring fort of Panalla, the residence of his Court. In

the year 1712, the young Prince died of small pox, when
Ramchundur Punt, the ablest supporter of the Kolapoor party,
removed Tara Bye from the administration, placed her and her
son's widow in confinement, and seated Sambajee, the son of
Rajis Bye, the younger widow of Raja Ram, on the *guddee.*
Next year, Shirzee Rao Ghatgay of Kagul, a name infamously
notorious in modern Mahratta history, joined the party of
Sambajee and henceforward acted as a partizan of Kolapoor,
or under the banner of Cheyn Kulik Khan, better known as
the great Nizam-ul-Mulk, who was now Mogul viceroy of
the Deccan, and who, wishing to weaken the Mahrattas by
internal dissension, favored the Kolapoor party.

In the year 1714, Ballajee Wishwanath, the ancestor of the
Rulers of Poona, was appointed Peishwa, and received a grant
of the Pergunnah of Poona, and the fort of Poorundhur.
Raja Shao was already a cypher and his Minister the real
ruler of the Mahrattas. The latter now took the first step
towards the dismemberment of the empire by encouraging
every Chief at the head of an army to administer the country
he occupied or commanded. The Peishwa thus gained temporary partizans, but the Satara Raja soon lost dependants.
Unlike his father and grandfather, Raja Shao acknowledged
himself a vassal of Delhi; and while in the actual receipt of
tribute from the Mogul Officers, he affected, in his transactions
with them, to consider himself merely as a head Zemindar or
Deshmukh of the Empire.

During all this time, the distractions at Delhi were clearing
the way for Mahratta aggrandizement. Ten thousand of them,
under Ballajee, accompanied Syud Hoossein Ally, the Viceroy
of the Deccan, to take part in a struggle against the Emperor.
Ferokhsere lost his life in the contest, and the Mahrattas remained at Delhi till they had obtained from his successor,
Mahommed Shah, grants of * revenue and privilege which not
only confirmed them in their own possessions, but authorized
their inquisitorial interference, in every province of the Deccan.
The minute intermixture of territory and the coparceny
system that divided districts and even villages between rival
authorities, was a sufficient curse to the people as well as loss
to the Mogul, but this legalization of the Mahratta demands

* The year of Mahommed Shah's accession, in 1720, forms an inportant era in
Mahratta history. The Imperial Grants they then obtained acknowledged their
claim, first to the *Chauth*, or fourth of the revenue of the six Soobehs. Aurungabad,
Berar, Beder, Hyderabad. Beejapoor, and Candeish. Second, to the *Surdesh-mukhee*
or tenth in excess of the Chouth ; and thirdly to the *Suraj* or sovereignty of the
sixteen districts possessed by Sivajee at the time of his death. Thus was the
Mahratta aim of years gratified.

on the reserved territory was a virtual cession of the whole. It subjected the country to the double tyranny of two sets of tax gatherers—" that which the locust left, the cankerworm devoured."

Bajee Rao succeeded his father Ballajee Wishwanath as Peishwa. As able an administrator as his father, he was a better soldier. Against the opinion and advice of more timid counsellors, he advocated extending the Mahratta conquests into Hindustan. Under his banner in Malwa in the year 1724, we first hear of Ranoojee Sindhia, Mulhar Rao Holkar, and Oodajee Powar : the two first, the founders of their families: and the last, the regenerator of his, and the founder of the Dhar principality. Already did the ambitious Peishwa look to a universal Mahratta Empire. He promised the Raja that his flag should wave from the Kistna to the Attock; and alluding to the Moguls, " let us strike," said he, " at the trunk of the withering tree, the branches must fall of themselves." All the ability and experience, however, of old Nizam-ul-mulk, now again the Mogul Viceroy in the south, were employed to baffle the Mahrattas and evade their claims. This he perceived was to be best effected by fanning the flame between the rival cousins of Kolapoor and Satara and throwing his weight into the scale of the weakest, Sambajee. In the year 1727 he stopped all payments, pending, as he said, a settlement of the Mahratta sovereignty. The usually pacific Shao was roused to action. The Nizam endeavoured to excuse himself by declaring that he only meant to relieve the Raja of his overbearing minister, the Peishwa. Shao would listen to no terms, hostilities ensued, and the Kolapoor troops were subsidized by Nizam-ul-mulk. The Satara party, whose cause was managed by the Peishwa, gained the day, which will appear the less surprizing when it is known that Sambajee and his ministers each sought to obtain the handling of the Nizam's subsidies, not to enable them to meet the enemy but to employ the cash for their own private debaucheries.

Nizam-ul-mulk was not the person to continue a losing game; he therefore patched up an arrangement and abandoned the cause of Kolapoor. Sambajee, left to his own resources, was, in the year 1729, so utterly defeated as to be obliged to yield his claim to the Mahratta Sovereignty to Shao; and to accept a Principality, comprehending, with certain reservations, the tract of country between the Warna and Kistna Rivers on the North, and the Toongbuddra on the South. The treaty now made was offensive and defensive and provided for the division between the parties of such conquests as might conjointly be made to the south of the Toongbuddra. But there never has since been any cordiality between the Kolapoor and Satara Chiefs, or rather between the former and the usurpers of the authority of the latter; for, within two years of the above mentioned compact, the Peishwa Bajee Rao completely defeated the Ghaekwar and his other rivals in a decisive battle near Baroda, which left him the virtual head of the Mahratta Sovereignty.

From this year (1729) we date the separation of the Kolapoor Principality from that of the elder and Satara branch. The lieutenants of the latter, or rather of the Peishwa, proceeded in a bright but brief career, while the Kolapoor Chiefs, holding aloof from the upstart servants of their family, proceeded in a course of piracies and petty warfare with the Dessaees of Waree and the Jaghirdars around them. The last time the armies of the Mahratta Empire acted together was in the year 1795 at Kurdla, where Nana Furnuvees, the clever but timid minister of the Peishwa, induced Sindhia and Holkar, the Ghaekwar, the Nagpoor Raja and almost all the Jaghirdars to combine against the Nizam. On this occasion the Mahrattas brought into the field 140,000 men, horse and foot.

The Peishwas had long been the Mayors of the Satara Palace. They received their Khillats (dresses) of investiture from the imprisoned descendants of Sivajee, but they were virtually monarchs of the Mahratta confederacy. The submission obtained from the founders of the several rival Principalities was certainly loose enough from the beginning; but they *did* allow, in theory, the same superiority to the Peishwa as he conceded to his puppet of Satara. A double government, an imperium in imperio, has long been the fashion of India; prejudices and old associations are thus sought to be soothed, and the fact is overlooked or forgotten that a rallying point is thereby left to their enemies by those in power. The good sense of more than one of the Peishwas led them to think of ending the farce, but a timid policy prevailed. The Ruler of Poona continued to call himself the servant of the Raja of Satara whom he kept a prisoner, and the Chiefs of Gwalior and Indore, retaliating on the former, plundered and insulted him at will, while styling themselves his Lieutenants. A decree could have been obtained from the effete King of Delhi in favor either of Sindhia or the Peishwa, and would have carried as much weight in India as did Pope Zachary's in Christendom, when the second Pepin obtained his sanction to place Childeric in a monastery, and add the title of King to his Mayorial designation.

Henceforward we follow the fortunes of Kolapoor and Sawunt-waree. In December 1760, Sumbajee the last lineal descendant of Sivajee died without issue, when his widow adopted a boy called Sivajee, and conducted the government in his name. The Kolapoorians were, at this time, not content with plundering and levying *Chouth* on shore, but they engaged in piratical expeditions along the western coast. In the year 1765, the British Government sent an expedition against them and reduced the ports of Malwan and Rairee,—the former place belonging to Kolapoor, the latter to Waree. The connexion of Kolapoor with the Nizam was generally maintained, and, in the time of the Peishwa Mudhoo Rao Bullal, caused the loss of several districts, which were however recovered by the Raja taking part with Rugonath Rao during the period of his authority.

In the year 1766, Malwan and Rairee were restored, on condition that the Kolapoor Raja should indemnify the British Government for all losses and expences, and that the Dessaee of Waree should enter into a new treaty. The piracies of these petty states were then for a few years suspended, only to break out more violently than ever. In the year 1789, fresh operations were contemplated against them, and only suspended out of consideration to the Court of Poona, whose dependant the Raja of Kolapoor was erroneously supposed to be. The Mysore war then occupied all the attention of the British, and the pirates worked their will, until the year 1792, when an armament was fitted out against them. A humble apology was however accepted, and a treaty concluded, by which permission was obtained for the establishment of factories at Malwan and Kolapoor. None of these measures, however, were of any avail to check the system of piracy, which continued until the year 1812.

The petty states at Kolapoor and Waree were at war, during nearly twenty-three years, on a foolish quarrel, regarding some royal privileges obtained for her husband, Kem Sawunt, by Luximee Bye, a neice of Mahdajee Sindhia. Lord Minto, then Governor-General, was solicited to aid Kolapoor, but he declined interfering. The Peishwa was less scrupulous, and sought to take advantage of the contest to subjugate both states. Acting under his orders, one of his officers, Appa Dessaee, obtained possession of Chickooree and Menowlee, and endeavoured to establish his own authority over Sawunt-waree. The infant Sawunt was strangled, but Phoond Sawunt the next heir, taking advantage of the temporary weakness of the Poona commander, expelled him from the country and seized the government.

During the first Mahratta war with the English, the Kolapoor troops were not found in the ranks of their countrymen, but their system of piracy and petty plunder continued. In the year 1812, therefore, when the British Government was settling the affairs of the Mahratta country, it was determined at length to put down the long permitted piracies of Kolapoor and Sawunt-waree. Stringent measures were adopted; the Raja at once yielded, consented to a new treaty, and was, in return, guaranteed against the agressions of all foreign powers. Phoond Sawunt was at the same time obliged to cede Vingorla, and engaged to suppress piracy under penalty of being also deprived of the forts of Rairee and Newtee. Some mercantile engagements were at the same time concluded.

Soon after the ratification of these arrangements, Phoond Sawunt died, and Doorga Bye became regent. Regardless of the British guarantee, she immediately attacked Kolapoor and seized the fort of Burratgurh which had formerly belonged to Waree. The old Lady would listen to no remonstrances and withdrew only on the advance of a detachment of the Madras Army. She still, however, continued refractory, and though no retaliation was permitted on the part of the Kolapoor troops, the British were at length obliged to enter the Waree territory, and in the year 1819 completely reduced it. Certain cessions were then exacted as security against future misconduct, when the British troops were withdrawn, and Sawunt-waree, in its reduced limits, left independent.

During the last Mahratta war, the Kolapoor Raja heartily espoused the British cause and was rewarded by the restoration of the two districts of Chickooree and Menowlee, already referred to, yielding an annual revenue of three lakhs of rupees. In July 1821, the Raja was murdered in his palace, by a chief whose jaghir he had resumed. During the disturbances at Kittoor in 1824, the conduct of the Kolapoor authorities, was very suspicious, and in a matter of dispute with Sawunt-waree, the young Raja infringed the treaty, and refused to abide by British arbitration. In this affair he was decidedly wrong, and he ought to have been punished. In our dealings with Native States, it is as unfair to overlook palpable breaches of engagement as it is cruel to stretch or twist dubious questions. The homely adage " get an inch and take an ell" no where better applies than among Indian rulers. The first encroachment is the precedent for succeeding ones. The smallest infraction of a treaty should be promptly noticed; timely reproof may stop a career of ruin. We are quite aware that it is from no ungenerous motive that such admonition is often withheld; but we are not the less satisfied that a little trouble at the outset, where differences arise, might often avert broils, and eventual absorption. Most Native chiefs are mere children in mind, and in the ways of the world; and as children they should be treated, with affectionate sympathy, but with systematic firmness. Grant them the most liberal construction of their respective treaties; but whatever that construction be, explain it clearly, and enforce it strictly. Slips should not pass unnoticed, but severity ought to be reserved for cases of obstinate contumacy. Such policy would convince all concerned, that their amendment and not their destruction, was the desire of the lord paramount. After a certain career of vice or contumacy, the offender should be set aside, and replaced by the nearest of kin, who gives better promise. One man should not be permitted to ruin a state; nor in any case should the paramount benefit by the error of the dependent. Were some such principles as these steadily acted on, less would be heard of the bankruptcies and distractions of tributary and subject states.

In the year 1825, the Raja was, more questionably, interfered with when desiring to resume Kaghal, the jaghir of Hindoo Rao, the son of the notorious Shirzee Rao Ghatgay. Both the father and son had long abandoned the Kolapoor service for that of Gwalior. Our right of interference referred only to *externals*, and we had no *right* to meddle, even by remonstrance, in domestic matters. Such slippery handling of engagements on our part, irritates Native princes and affords them pretext for bad faith. In December 1825, the Raja's misconduct obliged Government to march a force into his country, when a new arrangement was negotiated, stipulating for the reduction of the Kolapoor Army, *attention to the advice of the British Government*, and the non-molestation of Hindoo Rao and certain other Jaghirdars. Such a treaty could hardly have been expected to stand, nor did it. Princes do not relish unsought advice, any more than other individuals, especially if it be such as they are pledged to take. It was we believe, Colonel Sutherland, who rightly called the obligation to take counsel " a withering clause;" its very nature, indeed, is to provoke irritation and opposition, and *to entail* eventual coercion. At any rate, it is useless to provide that advice should be taken without specifically entering on the face of the engagement the penalty for neglect. The matter then becomes plain and all parties can calculate their game. The treaty

E E

under notice, was scarcely signed before the Raja broke through all its provisions. Instead of reducing his troops, he increased them, and seized the possessions of the guaranteed Jaghirdars. Twice during the year 1827, a British force was assembled for the purpose of bringing the Raja to reason. In the month of October the troops moved on Kolapoor, when that fortified town, though occupied by between 2 and 3,000 Arabs and Sindhians, immediately surrendered. New terms were then dictated, restricting the Kolapoor Army to 400 horse and 800 foot exclusive of garrisons. Chickoree and Menowlee were resumed, and certain Jaghirdars, whom the Raja had molested, received perpetual instead of life guarantees. The forts of Kolapoor and Panalla were occupied by British garrisons at the Raja's expence. He was also mulcted 1,47,948 Rupees for damage done to his neighbours; and territory yielding 50,000 Rupees was retained until the amount should be liquidated. A Minister was also nominated by the British Government, which retained to itself the power of removing him and appointing another. This last measure was as inefficacious at Kolapoor as it has been every where else.

In the year 1829, the Governor of Bombay, visited Kolapoor, and then proposed to withdraw the garrisons from that town and Panalla; but the measure was deferred, because the management of affairs had at that time fallen into the hands of an inimical Dewan. This person was removed, and his sovereign was warned, that if it should again be found necessary to send troops to Kolapoor, they would be permanently saddled on him. The Raja was a man of considerable, though misdirected, energy and ability. He quickly threw off the shackles of the British Government and systematically disregarded every provision of the treaty. His army was increased to nearly ten thousand men; and, having no funds to pay them, having lost his best districts, having no field of plunder or piracy open to him, his finances fell into the most deplorable disorder. The troops were seldom mustered more than once a year; the men lived where they liked, and, being always a twelvemonth or more in arrears, were permitted great license, and became, as might have been expected, a mere mass of marauders, dangerous only to their own Government. In the Civil department there was the same reckless improvidence as in the Military. All the ancient titles and offices were kept up, and the same state affected as when the Kolapoor family had arrogated Mahratta sovereignty. Centralization was the order of the day. Every Chief, every official of any rank resided in the city of Kolapoor. There were not less than twenty-one Mamlutdars to manage the revenue of a tract of country not exceeding 2500 square miles and scarcely yielding a clear income of five lakhs of Rupees. All these Mamlutdars constantly remained at Kolapoor and acted by deputy. The Durbar was therefore a scene of perpetual intrigue and chicanery, varied only by the lowest debauchery. Every Indian city is more or less a sink of iniquity: among them Kolapoor became a bye-word for foulness, for corruption and ill faith. Forgery and fawning were the steps to favor. Almost every Chief and Officer was, like the sovereign, loaded with debt; their estates and villages were mortgaged to money lenders, and the Raja himself subsisted from day to day only by squeezing his Officials and by anticipating the revenues of the state. We have said that the Raja had ability, we may add that his mind seems to have been tinged with insanity. In his saner moments, he was intelligent and energetic; occasionally, even just. He daily held open Durbar where all had admittance. Petitions were received, summarily discussed, and disposed of without appeal. The Mamlutdars and courtiers were thus checked and their illicit gains generally reverted to his own coffers. The highest officers were to be seen in chains, one day, and the next raised to greater honors: allowed their full swing for a time, and then, imprisoned, tortured and mulct. Strange as it may appear, such practices do not prevent scrambles for place now in India, any more than they did in olden times in Europe. Mahrattas indeed seem to enjoy such a troubled sea of politics. It offers a fair field for their peculiar abilities. They prefer even more than other Indians a mere nominal salary with the dim prospect of perquisites, to a fair and limited remuneration. It is astonishing how men become accustomed to live with their heads in their hands. It is now in India, as it was centuries ago in Greece and Rome. The Kolapoor system, however, had peculiarities of its own. So desperate had become the fortunes of the Chief, and of the court myrmidons, that the great majority were reduced to depend for their daily bread on the palace bounty; nearly a thousand of these minions fed daily at the Durbar, and were reduced to the condition of mere personal retainers. Stranger still is the fact that with such a head and such instruments, the condition of the country was not wretched. The secret lay in the Raja's vigorous despotism. An open Court, with summary cruel punishments kept down crime. While the city and the Palace were filled with iniquities, the villages flourished; few, if any, fell into disorder, and, when the Raja's career ended, little waste land was to be found within his principality. His offences thus lay

in prodigality, in personal debauchery and in expending double
or treble his income, rather than in unduly squeezing his cultivators. His last act was that of a desperate gamester. Shortly before his death in the year 1839, he affected to proceed on a
pilgrimage to Punderpoor, but the whole was a mere scheme to
plunder certain wealthy parties on the Kistna. For this purpose,
his ragged army was nearly doubled, every effort was made to
raise immediate funds, and even the family jewels were pledged
with this unholy object. Death cut short the project, and then
cannon and other munitions of war were found concealed in the
carts that were to accompany his train. On the Raja's death,
his eldest son, the present Chief, then a minor, was placed on
the *guddee*, and a Regency was formed by order of the British
Government, consisting of his mother, his maternal aunt, and
four Karbarees. The two ladies of course quarrelled. The
British political agent, on paying a hasty visit to Kolapoor
from Belgaum, finding them in warm contention, judged it politic to leave them so, considering that, he should most effectually hold the Durbar in check by contenancing both. Within
six months of the agent's departure, the aunt, who went by the
title of Dewan Sahib, being the most energetic and most
unscrupulous of the two, got the better of her kinswoman and
assumed the whole powers of government. Her supremacy,
thus acquired, was acknowledged by the British authorities,
though the step excluded the mother of the minor sovereign
from all authority.

We return to our sketch of Sawunt-waree affairs. The
measures taken in 1819 were soon found ineffectual to protect
the British frontier from plunder. The Waree Government
was unable to subdue or restrain its own turbulent Chiefs; and
the British Authorities were constantly annoyed by the distractions of this petty chiefship. In the year 1822, the Dessaee
then in his twentieth year, was ousted from all authority by
his Ranees, supported by an influential Minister. So great
at length, became the disorganization of the country that, in
the year 1836-7, the British Government was obliged to
interfere, and to send a force to occupy the forts of Mahdogurh
and Naraingurh and the town of Waree. The Dessaee, thus
relieved from his domestic persecutors, was delivered over to a
guaranteed Minister. He, of course, soon quarrelled with his
Monitor, but his complaints being attributed to the influence
of disreputable favourites, he vainly appealed to the British
Agent, (the Collector of Rutnagirry.) A formidable rebellion
ensued, which it required a British detachment to quell. In
1838, troops were again called out, being the fourth time, that

armed interference had been employed in Sawunt-waree within nine years. Phoond Sawunt, who has within the last twelve months again given so much trouble was then in arms, plundering the Waree villages and threatening the British frontier. The Dessee thwarted all the efforts of this rough-riding Minister, to put down the rebellion, and accused him of being in league with the rebels. The British Government, tired at length of fighting the Dessee's battles assumed the direct management of the country, until such time as there should be a probability of his governing it well. Mr. Spooner, a Bombay Civil Servant, was placed in charge of the territory, but had a very up-hill game to play. The country, one of the very strongest in all India and in many parts believed to be inaccessible to regular troops, teemed with malcontents. While many had real grievances, some feared the indispensible reductions incidental on the new arrangements; and others dreaded the substitution of a strong Government, for their old system of misrule. All could plot, and even fight confidently, having their friendly jungles to fly to,—a sure refuge in the sympathizing neutrality of the border State of Goa. On one occasion, the rebels acquired temporary possession of Waree; another time, they captured the fort of Humuntghar, blockaded the passes, plundered travellers, and attemped to levy the government revenue. They were not only recruited from the Goa territory, but one of the leaders at the capture of Humuntghar was a Goa Dessaee. A Suwant-waree Local Corps was, at length, raised, and a new Governor having arrived at Goa, who was less friendly to the malcontents, they were finally put down. Nine of the leaders were condemned to death, but their sentences were commuted to banishment for life. A barbarous execution of a number of prisoners also took place, under the orders of Lieutenant Gibbard, the Adjutant of the Local Corps. He pleaded the orders of the Political Agent, but was himself very properly made to answer for his iniquitous deed, before a military tribunal. Suwant-waree was thus, as the phrase runs *settled*, but the flame was only smothered, and no sooner did disturbances break out in Kolapoor, than the Waree people were again up, and the son of the Dessaee was himself in arms.

We have now brought our sketch down to the period of the late disturbances in Kolapoor and Sawunt-waree. The united area of these two states does not exceed four thousand square miles and their joint nett revenue after deducting jaghirs, and rent-free lands, scarcely amounts to seven lakhs of Rupees. But as already observed, the whole tract, especially Sawunt-waree, is a remarkably strong country, combining, within a small area all the strong points of mountain and jungle fastnesses. The inhabitants, moreover, though poor, are hardy and lawless, and still bear in mind the exploits of Sivajee's favourite Mawulees and Hetkurees.

Predatory habits formed during centuries of anarchy, are not to be changed in a day. British supremacy, has, throughout India, restricted the field of plunder and of warfare, but sufficient time has not yet elapsed materially to alter the feelings and associations of the children of marauding times. We have taken from the lawless their hunting grounds; we have prohibited their spoiling their neighbours, but we have neither given them an equivalent, nor allowed them an outlet for their energies. We have not even rendered their own homes secure. The guaranteed Princes, who can no longer array their followers for foreign raids, must turn their hungry energies against those very followers. Money they *must* have to feed their own luxurious lusts. If they cannot plunder strangers, they must harry their own people. The rule holds good throughout India. The instances among Native states where the cultivator is certain of reaping what he has sown and of being called on to pay only what has been previously agreed, are most rare. Indeed, they are to be found only in some few states of very limited extent where the reigning chief, being a man of probity as well as of ability, sees with his own eyes, hears with his own ears, and setting aside Ministers and Agents, looks after his own affairs.

The Southern Mahratta states afford a good illustration of our argument. They have experienced all the inconveniences of a strong supremacy without participating in its advantages. The British Ægis has been thrown over the Rulers and Ministers of Kolapoor and Sawunt-waree, while no effectual measures have been taken to enforce their doing their duty to the governed. It cannot, indeed, be denied that these territories have been most egregiously mismanaged. Countries that have been repeatedly in arms within a short term of years, *must* have grievances. Half armed, hungry men do not give their throats to the sword for mere amusement. Men do not, for ever, love to struggle in a hopeless cause. We may then fairly infer that there *has been* abuse, and as both Kolapoor and Sawunt-waree have, during several years been, in a manner, directly governed by British Agents, we are obliged to attribute the maladministration which has entailed so much expence of blood and treasure, to our own ill digested schemes; to the affectation of holding aloof, while, we were daily and hourly interfering in the most essential manner, through Native Agents, by placing in the hands of Native underlings, powers that no Native of the present generation has head or heart to bear. With a British Superintendent in Sawunt-waree, and a Native Agent in Kolapoor, acting as Minister, as Regent, as factotum, under the Political Agent at Belgaum, neither of the disaffected states can be considered as having been under a domestic administration ; but our Government is as distinctly responsible for their bad, as it would have been entitled to the credit of their good management.

Sawunt-waree offers a notable proof, that the sword alone cannot sustain an Anglo-Indian administration. Martial law had long prevailed, the country had been harried ; some malcontents had been justly condemned, other unfortunate men had been butchered. The Native Government was wholly suspended ; the management was entirely in our own hands, and yet, no sooner had troubles arisen in Kolapoor than it became certain that Sawunt-waree would rise. The worst expectations were realized. With scarcely an exception, every Chief in the country took up arms, and forty of them, with their personal followers, driven from their fastnesses are now in the dungeons of Goa, rather than surrender to British clemency. There is something very lamentable in all this, and it calls for no ordinary enquiry.

The circumstances of the Kolapoor outbreak are different. We have already noticed the dissensions among the members of the Regency. The supremacy of the Raja's aunt was not of long continuance, and more than one change preceded the late outbreak. At length, a few months before the insurrection commenced, Dajee Krishen Pundit, a Brahman, who had risen from a subordinate position in one of our civil offices, was placed at the head of the Regency. Within a month of his accession to power, his two co-adjutors were dismissed by the Political Agent for peculation, and the Pundit monopolized the combined powers of Minister and Regent. Dajee could not have been a notoriously bad man ; the probability is, he was both able and moderate. But unlimited power has turned wiser heads than are to be found among the underlings of an Anglo-Indian *cutchery*. We accordingly find that Dajee neither bore himself meekly, nor was content to follow those two golden maxims, to let well alone, and to endeavour to make the best of local, even though bad, materials. He seems to have forgotten that he was a foreigner among a wild and a proud people, who could only be managed peaceably by and through their own countrymen ; that if he did not employ the

Natives, they must and would oppose him; and that they could not remain neutral, and indubitably would be either his coadjutors or his enemies.   Nevertheless, Dajee *did* make many changes, and *did* provide for his Brahman kinsmen.* He, more-over, not only checked the abuses and illicit gains of the Man-kurees and other chiefs, but by touching their dignity made himself personally offensive; there can therefore be little doubt that, though few of them openly engaged in the insurrection, the majority instigated and encouraged the acts of the rebel Gurh-kurees and refractory Sebundees. The former, we have already ex-plained, were the hereditary holders of the hill forts that dot the Kolapoor country.   From father to son, they had lived and died at their posts, and were supported by certain lands dependant on their respective charges.   To interfere with arrangements which had existed since the days of Sivajee if not before his time was any thing but prudent ; nor can we perceive the policy, any more than the justice, of irritating the hereditary soldiery of this wild country.   The immediate cause of offence was the appointment of Mamlutdars (Revenue Officers) to manage the Gurhkuree lands.   Perhaps it would be more correct to say that the Gurhkurees resented the removal of their own immediate agents, and the doubling up of appointments by which the charge of their affairs was made over to Mamlutdars who managed the adjoining districts.   This measure, as they supposed, affected their honor, and placed them at the mercy of strangers.   We are far from believing that the Bombay authorities had any design to mulct the hill garrisons ; there was, therefore, the less excuse for trifling with their feelings, it may be their pre-judices, by appointing people to do for them what they pre-ferred doing themselves.   We need hardly add that no stranger Mamlutdar *could* have been appointed to whose fingers a portion of the proceeds of the Gurhkuree lands would not have ad-hered.

In July 1844 the flame broke out ; the garrisons of the strong forts of Bhoodurgurh and Samungur, refused to admit the

---

* We have no desire to run down Dajee, on the contrary we look on him as a favourable specimen of an Anglo-Native agent. Had he been *better* or *worse*, matters would have turned out differently. Had he leagued with local oppressors, had he gone hand in hand with the plunderers and tyrants he found around him, his reign would at least have been longer. Had he been a " faultless monster" he might have saved the state. But in all such cases, the difficulties in the way of a Native agent are immeasureably greater than what would face a European Officer. An ordinary Englishman may do a hundred things that the best and purest Native dare not attempt   The latter too has his peculiar advantages. Each has his fitting place ; and the grand point of skilful Anglo-Indian administration turns on the judicious blending of the double agency. Europeans and Natives may, conjointly, build up what either, acting singly, would mar.

Mamlutdar appointed to manage their lands. Dajee Pundit for a long time endeavoured to cajole the recusants, and eventually sent two of the principal officers of the state to cajole them into submission. The Gurkhurees were firm, and refused not only to admit any Mamlutdar except of their own selection, but required the guarantee of the Naiks (Chiefs) of the five Regiments of Sebundees at Kolapoor as security for their future good treatment. The very positiveness of the poor creatures seems to bear testimony to their having experienced wrong, and their fear of further injury. Dajee Pundit was desirous of granting their demands; but the Political Agent forbad any concession to men with arms in their hands; and, hearing in September, that the malcontents had levied contributions in their neighbourhood, recommended that a force should be sent against them.

It is to be regretted that before the British functionary counselled recourse to arms, he had not done something more than communicate with the malcontents through Native agents; that, in short, he had not himself visited the scene of disorder. We have little doubt that he might have entered either Samungurh or Bhoodurgurh with perfect safety, the former being only a long mornings's ride from Belgaum. Or, supposing that he could not have proceeded thither in person why not have called in a deputation from the recusants to state their grievances? This question may rouse the yells of fire-and-faggot politicians. "Visit or receive, men with arms in their hands!" they will say. We reply, yes, decidedly so, as long as no overt act of hostility has been committed, and while there is reason to believe that the disaffected are moved by real, or even supposed, wrongs. It is not the fashion we know to argue thus,—the more the pity, —and the greater the necessity that our voice, feeble though it be, should be raised in the cause of humanity and of truth. Unfortunately, British Indian history abounds with instances where the neglect of so simple an act of justice has cost us dear, both in blood and credit. Whether, we ask, is it more creditable to grant terms to men in arms, *before* or after they have used those arms? The historical reader will be familiar with cases of Civil and Military revolt, and will have observed, that in the great majority of instances, all that was at first humbly craved, and forcibly demanded only when redress had been refused, was finally conceded *after* blood had been shed. Are we always to slay, in order to prove our strength? Far better to relinquish so sanguinary a dominion! This is one view of the case,—that justice should *first* be fully done, and that we should

F F

enter on no quarrel with dirty hands. We may however meet the coercives on their own ground, and entirely deny the necessity, at the present day, of brute force to vindicate our honor. Whatever may have been the case fifty years ago, a preliminary fusilade is not now requisite to prove that our measures of mercy are voluntary. Who, in his senses, ever doubted that the British Government *could* coerce the Gurkhurees and capture their forts? Who ever denied that the Barrackpoor Division could annihilate the unhappy 47th Bengal N. I.? There *have* been instances where prompt and rigid austerity was perfectly justifiable; but, for one such emergency, a dozen have occurred where early moderation, combined with firmness, would have been the true course of policy.

Acting on the Agent's recommendation, the Bombay Government issued instructions that a Detachment, amply sufficient to effect the pacification of the disturbed districts, should move from Belgaum, the Head Quarters of the southern division of the Bombay Army. With whom the selection and strength of the field force rested, we are not exactly aware. It consisted of 1200 men, including two Companies of European Infantry, one Company of Native Rifles, a few Irregular Horse; and sixty Artillery men with four mortars, two howitzers and two nine-pounders. One hundred labourers also accompanied the Engineer Officer as Pioneers. The whole were placed under command of Lient.-Colonel Wallace, 20th Madras N. I. This small Detachment though in Division Orders on the 12th September, did not march till the 16th, and arrived opposite the Fort of Samungurh, thirty miles distant, on the 19th of the same month. The strength of the fort lay chiefly in its position on the summit of a scarped rock; its walls were found to be from twenty to sixty feet high, and between one and two miles in circuit. The hill on which the fort stands is however commanded by an adjoining rock; the place was wretchedly equipped, and garrisoned by only three hundred men, and might, probably, have been seized by a coup-de-main, the first day. It is obvious, however, that if the fort was not thus to be captured by a sudden attack, there was not much hope of the success of a detachment scarcely exceeding 1,000 bayonets and unaccompanied by battering guns. Fifty mortars might have settled the matter in a few hours: the fire of four could only have afforded amusement to the garrison of so extensive a position. On the 20th, Colonel Wallace took possession of the hill, commanding the fort, and the next day commenced shelling, but with little or no effect. On the 24th, the pettah was carried by storm, and no effort was wanting, on the part of the British Commander, to reduce the fort; but, he soon found himself helpless, and applied for reinforcements and battering guns. The distance from Belgaum does not exceed thirty miles, and yet, the guns, being impeded by heavy rain, did not arrive for more than three weeks, by which time much of the moral effect of the Military movement had been lost, and the Gurkhurees had recovered confidence and recruited their numbers.

On the 22nd September the garrison of Bhoodurgurh sallied out upon the Kolapoor troops sent against their Fort and drove them off with loss. Alarm now spread, and fears were expressed for Rutnagiry, Vingorla and even for Belgaum itself; at which last place sudden and novel precautions were taken sufficient to indicate alarm and to provoke attack. When shall we gain experience and learn to be always on the alert? In the words of Washington, "to organize all our resources, and to put them in a state of preparation for prompt action" * * * "to endeavour by unanimity, vigilance and exertion, under the blessing of providence, to hold the scales of our destiny in our own hands." Reinforcements were now ordered from various quarters towards the disturbed districts, and on the 8th October, General Delamotte, by order of the Bombay Government, assumed command of the troops in the field. On the 11th, four battering guns reached Samungurh, and were placed in position, and by the evening of the next day a practicable breach was effected. When the guns arrived, Mr. Reeves, the Commissioner, allowed the garrison the opportunity of a parley to state their grievances; but he soon found that the Gurkhurees only desired to gain time, in expectation of support from Kolapoor, where, in the interim, the Sebundees, encouraged by our supineness, had risen in open revolt, and seized and confined the Minister Dajee Pundit; and where, in fact their Leader, Babajee Thirakar had assumed the Government. Affairs were therefore allowed to take their course, and shortly before daylight on the morning of the 13th, the place was stormed and carried with little opposition. During the day, Mr. Reeves and Colonel Outram accompanied a Wing of the 5th Madras Cavalry under command of Captain Graham and cut up a large body of malcontents who had collected in the neighbourhood with a view of supporting the Garrison. Colonel Outram had joined General Delamotte's camp the day before the storm, in a political capacity, and henceforward, wherever employed, threw into all proceedings that moderation, energy and ability, which have every where so strongly marked his career.

To save further bloodshed, the Joint-Commissioners Mr. Reeves and Colonel Outram, now offered, with certain exceptions, an amnesty to all who would immediately return to their allegiance. Few, if any, accepted the terms ; a strong presumptive proof that the unfortunate men had real grievances. The day after the capture of Samungurh, Colonel Outram with Colonel Wallace and 500 men of his Brigade proceeded to Kaghal, one march from Kolapoor, with the view of procuring the release of the Minister who was imprisoned in the Fort of Panalla, as well as of supporting the Raja and well affected chiefs against the disorderly troops and their disloyal leaders. The movements of the Head Quarters under General Delamotte were more dilatory and less decided. He did not leave Samungurh until the 20th October, and then hesitated a long time whether to move on Kolapoor or Bhoodurgurh, the garrison of which last place had on the 10th October plundered the British pergunnah of Chickooree, and robbed the local treasury. Whatever was to be done, should have been done quickly ; expedition was every thing, and had a second blow, such as that at Samungurh, been speedily struck, in *any* direction, the probability is, that the insurrection would have been subbued.

There seems at this time to have been disunion in the counsels of the authorities, but their exact nature has not transpired. Government, evidently, was very ill informed as to the nature of the outbreak, or the means most likely to quell it. Like most other insurrections, it had in the first instance been mismanaged and trifled with ; its dangers were then exaggerated ; troops were poured into the country under hap-hazard commanders, and it was only at the last stage of proceedings that efficient means of tranquillization were adopted. On the 24th October, after much negotiation, and not until Colonel Wallace's detachment had been strengthened, Dajee Pundit was released and the young Raja of Kolapoor with his aunt and mother and the majority of his chiefs left the city and joined the British camp. The movement had been strongly opposed by the Kolapoor troops, about 500 of whom under Babajee Thirakar, finding their wishes defeated, absconded and joined the Bhoodurgurh malcontents. Babajee may be regarded as the leader of the rebellion. He had imprisoned the Minister, usurped the government, and instigated the raid on Chickooree. He and certain other principals were, therefore, excepted in an offer of amnesty which was held out to such as should return to their allegiance; but, strange to say, when, General Delamotte *did* at last appear before Bhoodurgurh with every means of speedily capturing the place, he admitted the garrison to a surrender; and actually allowed himself on the evening of the 10th to be detained for several hours at one gate, while Babajee Thirakar with his party escaped from another. Thus was the flame spread, rather than extinguished; for Babajee immediately moved to the still stronger fortress of Panalla, where the Kolapoorians imagined that as in olden time, a long, if not permanent, stand could be made against all comers.

On the 25th November, General Delamotte appeared before Panalla, where Colonel Ovans, the Resident at Satara, was now imprisoned. This Officer, who had lately been appointed Special Commissioner in the Southern Mahratta country to the supercession of both Mr. Reeves and Colonel Outram, had been waylaid on the 17th November, while incautiously travelling dak with a very slight escort from Satara to Kolapoor, and carried prisoner to Panalla. We pretend not to know the reason of Colonel Ovans' appointment, but after carefully comparing all we have heard on the subject, it is our belief that the Bombay Government, already in no good humour at the long continuance of hostilities, were at this time irritated by Colonel Outram's refusing to accept the permanent charge of the Kolapoor country, and therefore at once accepted the resignation, which he volunteered only on the expiration of hostilities. This must have been the real motive that actuated, perhaps unwittingly, the authorities, though they may have likewise disapproved of some particular measures he had pursued. We see at least no other mode of accounting for the act. The rumours and assertions circulated by a portion of the Press at the time must have been erroneous regarding the man who was selected to go to Kolapoor when affairs *looked black*, was offered the permanent civil management *when they looked blacker*; was then employed as a Military Commander in putting an end to the war; and has since the termination of hostilities been nominated to the charge of the Political and Military relations at Satara.

Whatever may have been the cause of Colonel Ovans' deputation, his career was, thus summarily, cut short, and the political management in the field remained in the hands of Mr. Reeves and Colonel Outram. Strenuous endeavours were made by the Commissioners to effect the release of Colonel Ovans, whom the malcontents vainly tried to make the means of ensuring their own safety. All their overtures were, however, disregarded; they were desired to release their prisoner and surrender at discretion, or stand the consequences. They did release him, hoping thereby to obtain terms of surrender, but they soon discovered their error.

On the 27th the Pettah was captured; and on the morning of the 1st December, the batteries opened. The same afternoon the breach, being reported practicable, was stormed and carried in gallant style. Some of the garrison endeavoured to escape into the adjoining Fort of Pawungurh, but were so closely followed by the British troops, that this second fortress fell into our hands the same day. Babajee Thirakar and some other ringleaders fell in the storm, and *many* prisoners were captured by the parties of troops judiciously placed in the plain around.

On the 5th December, Colonel Wallace with a Light Force proceeded against Rangna, seventy miles distant. He reached it on the 9th, the same day carried the Pettah, and the following night placed two Guns and two Mortars in position : their play, during the next day, caused the enemy after dark to evacuate the fort, and fly into the Sawunt-waree jungles. The principal fortresses of Kolapoor having thus fallen, their Gurkhurees being slain, imprisoned or dispersed, and the country being full of British troops, there was now a temporary lull; but it soon appeared that the theatre, only, of hostilities had changed, and that the war itself was as far as ever from a conclusion. Two thousand of the Waree people, under Phoond Sawunt, and Anna Sahib, the son of the Dessaee, who were at this time devastating the Concan and stopping the roads, were joined by the fugitive Kolapoorians. From the nature of the country the military operations now became more difficult. Wherever an enemy can be approached, there is little cause for alarm. The strongest fortress or best intrenched position, if relied on, renders the occupiers the more certain prey. It is but a question of time; the result is certain. In a rocky, jungle country, however, abounding in deep, damp ravines, and in forest covered hills and dells, and occupied by an acclimated people, the case is very different. In all such miasmatic localities, as long as malcontents are satisfied to fly to-day, to starve to-morrow, and altogether to live or die as the beasts around them, they may long baffle the operations of regular troops under ordinary Commanders. And thus it was that the Sawunt-warree people acted; and thereby created, even beyond their own immediate limits, more alarm than their wretched means should have been permitted to do; but the fact is, that our regulars are as little adapted for jungle fighting as were Aurungzebe's heavy Northmen to cope on their own ground, with Sivajee's light Mawulees and Hetkurees.

Troops employed in mountain and jungle warfare require something more than mere bull-dog bravery. Coolness, tact, activity and a general acquaintance, at least with similar localities are as necessary in the leader, as is some adaptation of his men to the enterprize. Soldiers that will fearlessly mount a breach, silently stand in array to be mown down by artillery, or unflinchingly hold their ranks to repel repeated charges of Cavalry, will falter under a dropping fire from unseen foes. Men must be familiar with rock, ravine and jungle, to fight well among them. It is curious how ill we generally make our selections from our ample and varied resources—employing grenadiers as bush-rangers, and keeping riflemen for garrison duty—pushing into the front of battle men who are fit only for the Invalids, and keeping the young and active soldiers of every rank, comparatively in the back ground. We generally get so well out of our scrapes that the waste of blood and treasure is too little considered; and few lessons are gained from past experience.

Fortunately for Government, the man they wanted was at hand. Colonel Outram who was now, about the end of December, at Bombay, with the intention of proceeding to Europe, at once forgot past neglect and past injuries, and came forward to rescue the Government from their difficulties. He volunteered to return to the seat of war, and there organize and lead a light corps. Nobly did he fulfil the large expectations that were now centred in him. Within a fortnight he was again in the field, the soul of all active measures; his very advanced guard driving before them, the half armed rabble that had kept three brigades at bay.

Never was the magic power of one man's presence more striking, than on Outram's return to the seat of war. It might seem invidious were we to dwell on the panic that then prevailed at Vingorla and Waree, but the slightest glance at the proceedings in those quarters will shew that the insurgents had inspired a ridiculously formidable idea of their own importance. All communications had long been cut off; the posts were brought *by long sea*, from Malwan to Vingorla, and many of the inhabitants of this latter place, nightly took refuge in boats in the harbour. The troops were harassed with patrolling duty, yet the neighbourhood was rife with murders and robberies, the perpetrators of which sent insulting messages to the authorities. On one occasion a religious meeting was dispersed by a wag suddenly calling out that the enemy were upon them. Vingorla, be it remembered, stands in an open country.

At Waree, matters were if possible still worse; there the troops remained as in blockade, not a soul venturing beyond the lines. All outposts were called in and the malcontents permitted to consider themselves masters of the field. When the garrison was reinforced by the arrival of the 10th and a part of the Bombay Native Infantry the authorities determined to occupy the gorge of the valley of Seevapoor, in which lay the villages of the insurgent Phoond Sawunt, and thus cut off this focus of rebellion from the less disturbed districts. The scheme was a good one, but failed from the manner in which its execution was attempted. A detachment of two hundred sepoys set out; they were *sniped* at from the jungle and one man was wounded, when instead of closing with the enemy, they took post in a sort of enclosure, and were soon beset by increased numbers. A reinforcement of two hundred men joined them, but the combined force, after losing twenty killed and wounded, retreated to Waree. This success, of course, increased the confidence of the insurgents whose insolence was not restrained even by the arrival soon after of Her Majesty's 2d Regiment. They gave out that they were tired of thrashing sepoys and wished to try the metal of the "*Lambs.*" They soon obtained an opportunity of proving their metal, but the sight of that fine corps was too much for their nerves. The Europeans were then kept idle, first at Waree, then at Dukhun-waree, and full scope was given to the activity of the enemy.

At this juncture, Outram landed at Vingorla, where, picking up two or three excellent Officers, he pushed on to Waree, and thence towards Seevapoor. From this date, the 14th January, matters took a turn; hitherto the three Brigades had been playing bo-peep with the enemy, and from the tops of the Ghats, examining through telescopes, the stockades below, which the Commanders did not think it prudent to attack. But now, at length, a decided movement was announced for hemming in the rebels in the valley of Seevapoor. Twelve hundred men were placed under Outram, with orders to beat up the low ground from Waree towards the forts of Munohur and Munsuntosh; Colonel Carruthers, with a Brigade, was to occupy the Seevapoor valley on the other side of the ridge on which those forts are situated ; while Colonel Wallace was on a given day, to descend the Ghats, and it was reckoned that his troops, dove-tailing with those under the immediate command of General Delamotte, would complete the encirclement of the rebels. This is not the time or place for commenting on Colonel Wallace's descent of the Elephant Rock, and premature attack on the open village of Seevapoor. That Officer probably thought that he acted for the best, but we doubt whether disobedience to orders can ever be so viewed. Without any disparagement of his personal courage, we cannot help thinking that Colonel Wallace manifested a very contradictory estimate of the enemy's strength. If they had been as formidable as he considered them, then his descent of the rock, exposed to such a foe, was absolute infatuation. Nothing but their weakness and cowardice could justify the risk. But if the foe was so contemptible, he could have easily taken the route *he was desired,* driven them from stockade to stockade, *at the time ordered,* and, thus, completing the chain of operation, have probably ensured the apprehension of every individual rebel Chief. Much have the merits of Colonel Wallace's case been debated, but we cannot perceive how he could have expected to escape a Court Martial, though he may have reckoned on ensuring an honorable acquittal from the nature of his offence. There seems however, to us, no more resemblance between his disobedience at the Elephant Rock and Nelson's at Copenhagen, than there is between the fame of the two offenders. Judgment having been already pronounced on Colonel Wallace by a military tribunal, we should have avoided referring to his case, could our narrative have been otherwise rendered intelligible.

To return to Colonel Outram. No communication was practicable between the troops above and below the Ghats, and he was left with his small band to his own resources, without definite orders, and with very scanty supplies, to carry out the most difficult operation of the campaign. Merrily and confidently he advanced through the wild sylvan scenes never before trod by European foot. The ears of his people were now daily saluted by the echo of the Artillery on the overhanging Ghats ; sounds which could only be supposed to indicate " the tug of war " above, and loss of ribbons and laurels to those below. But such fears were soon relieved by finding that the firing was only Colonel Wallace's long practice with extra charges from the summit of the Elephant Rock at the village Seevapoor, some three miles distant in the Concan below.

Each day Outram found points of his route stockaded by the enemy, but they never made a stand, the advanced guard and skirmishers being generally sufficient to disperse the wretched rabble. At length, on the 20th of January a combined movement was ordered upon the high peak to the west of Munsuntosh. The main attack was to be made by Colonel Carruthers, who, supported by a portion of Colonel Wallace's brigade, was to carry some stockades in his front, and then move up the Dukhun-waree or Seevapoor side of the ridge, while Colonel Outram was to make a diversion from the Shirsarjee or Gotia valley. This last detachment performed their part; but, on reaching the summit of the peak, from which an extensive view was commanded, no sign appeared of either brigade. They saw the stockades which Colonel Carruthers was to have attacked, but which being now taken in flank were abandoned, the enemy flying to Munsuntosh, within eight hundred yards of which fort Outram established a post. Colonel Carruthers's brigade had been prevented by the nature of the country from taking their full share in the operations of the day. The next morning another combined movement was made on the village of Gotia, immediately below the forts; again the nature of the country favoured Outram, the advanced guard of whose detachment captured the village with all its stockades, though very strongly situated.

From these brief details we may infer how easily the war might have been terminated, months sooner, by more decided measures. The enemy had only to be reached, to be routed. The troops, both Bombay and Madras, were ready for their work, but a spirit of undue caution and delay prevailed at Head Quarters.

We cannot understand how it happened, but Colonel Outram was now left, unsupported, to carry on operations against Munsuntosh. One of those accidents which no human foresight can obviate, frustrated his attempt to gain that fortress, by a coup de main. He carried three stockades, below the fort, attempted to blow open a gate, failed, and was driven back with considerable loss. He held his ground, however, high upon the ridge, retained possession of the stockades, and was on the eve of again storming the fortress when the enemy evacuated not only Munsuntosh, but the adjoining fort of Munohur. Outram had skilfully thrown out parties, to command the debouches from the south and south-west faces of the forts, leaving the remaining portions of the cordon to be filled up by the brigades. Colonel Wallace however failed on his part, and thus suffered the rebel Chiefs, who had all been encaged, to escape over the Sisadrug ridge, close to one of his posts, into the Goa territory. Outram followed hard upon their track, had several skirmishes, took many prisoners, and on one occasion, nearly captured the Chiefs. Again he scoured the wild country beneath the Ghats, encouraging the loyal, and beating up the disaffected villages. The nature and value of his services during the operations we have glanced at, are not to be measured by the actual opposition experienced or loss sustained, but by the estimate formed by other Commanders of the obstacles and enemy to be encountered, and by the fact that the rapid and skilful movements of his small detachment, terminated, in a few days, an organized opposition which had for six weeks kept at bay three brigades, differently handled. The total silence of Government, and the non-publication of any opinion regarding the Sawunt-waree operations, might at first sight, lead to the inference that Outram's management gave as little satisfaction as did that of his fellow Commanders. But, the promotion since bestowed on him, amply proves that Government took the same view of his conduct throughout the campaign as did General Delamotte, Colonels Brough and Wallace, and indeed all his comrades. Outram's is an almost isolated instance of a man receiving not only civil promotion but brevet rank, without his good fortune exciting jealousy; a remarkable exception, only to be explained by his rare qualities as a soldier, and his conciliatory demeanour as a man.

The tone of our remarks upon Colonel Outram may savour of partial panegyric, to those of our readers who have not followed out his career as we have done. No personal feelings however, can mingle in our praise of a man whom we have never seen, and whom we know only by his public acts. Those who have watched his course, will probably concur in our eulogiums; indeed any unprejudiced man, reading the despatches published during the war, the proceedings of Colonel Wallace's Court Martial, and the discussions which they elicited at the three Presidencies, must acknowledge that every affair in which Outram had a voice, was carried out with an energy and promptitude, very unlike the procrastinating indecision perceptible elsewhere. He arrived at Samungurh,—the fortress was carried forthwith; and, (what so rarely happens in Indian operations,) the success was immediately followed up, by despatching Captain Graham to disperse the enemy's covering force; a work which that officer ably accomplished. Again, in the despatch published by the Bombay Government, we see

Outram mentioned as " the man, who volunteered his services,
" and was among the foremost who entered the fort of Panal-
" la." The reader has only to contrast the whole conduct of
his detachment, from the 16th of January to the conclusion of
hostilities, with any other operations of the campaign, and he
will bear us out in the opinion that he was the soul of every
decided measure.

If our narrative has kept to Colonel Outram's detachment it
is for the simple reason that they appear to have had all the
fighting to themselves. No discredit thereby attaches to the
troops under the other Commanders who were always ready
for action, and who, when opportunity offered, as at Samungurh
and Panalla, behaved with the accustomed gallantry of the
Madras and Bombay Armies.

We must wind up this hasty, though perhaps prolix
sketch of Sawunt-waree affairs. By the capture of Munohur
and Munsuntosh the strength of the insurrection was broken.
The strongholds of the rebels were taken, their boldest leaders
slain or captured, and all others to the number, as already stated, of forty, fled for shelter to Goa. Outram was then again
called on to act the diplomatist. His parties still followed
up the remaining small marauding bands, while he himself,
proceeded to Goa, and by the union of firmness and concilia-
tion induced the Portuguese authorities to remove their
sympathizers from the frontier, and to substitute a cordon of
such troops as would prevent the Goa territory being made
the place of ambush from which the insurgents should at
discretion devastate Sawunt-waree. And now we may be
permitted to congratulate Government on their selection of
such a man as Col. Outram to the important duties of the
Satara Residency. Our satisfaction would be increased could
we persuade the authorities to give him such assistants as he
can trust at Satara and Waree and place him in authority at
the central post of Kolapoor with combined powers as Resident,
Commissioner and Military Commander.

Improved arrangements, we are aware, have already been
made. The Anglo-native Agent at Kolapoor has been replaced
by an able British Officer, and in Sawunt-waree there could
not be a better Local Superintendent than the officer lately
appointed. Captain Jacob is, like Colonel Outram, a good
soldier as well as an able and conciliating Civil Officer. Such
are the men required; men, who, personally despising danger,
are forward in the hour of action, and reckless of their own
blood, are chary of that of others. In no quarter of India are

such men more appreciated than in the Southern Mahratta country, where their names alone, are worth Regiments. They will preserve peace if it is to be preserved, and if the sword must be drawn, will carry on war, so that it shall speedily end in permanent and prosperous tranquillity.

After more than six months of military operations, and the employment of nearly ten thousand troops, in so insignificant a corner of India, peace has been secured, or, more correctly, war has ceased. Let us now by honestly and carefully looking into past abuses and errors, and by not too rigorously judging those who have been driven or reduced to misconduct, secure the future tranquillity of the country. This can be effected only by a *permanent* system of good management *consonant to the spirit of the people.* We should remember that rude tribes are not ripe for refined institutions, and that it is better to work on quietly, slowly and surely, than to risk new convulsions by sudden, even though beneficial changes. The people of Kolapoor and Sawunt-waree have, we believe, been partially disarmed and many of their fortresses have been dismantled. Both these measures should be completed. Broad military roads should also be constructed to intersect these territories in all directions and the jungle cleared at least a hundred feet on either side. Such operations will involve present expence, but they will prevent future sacrifices. No country, such as that under notice, can be reckoned secure until those responsible for its peace have facilities for quickly reaching its most remote corners at all seasons of the year.

Half a dozen good officers under such a man as Colonel Outram might, in a few years, wipe away the reproach that is now attached to our name in the South Mahratta country. Under their supervision, all real rights and immunities would be clearly defined, and speedily established, and all imaginary claims dismissed. A revenue system would be organized calculated to protect cultivator from undue exaction, and a scheme of police might be enforced that would make the rock and the bush too hot for marauders. The Mankurees, Chiefs and Jaghirdars would settle down into their places. The Raja of Kolapoor and the Sin Dessaee of Sawunt-waree, would each, also, find his level; they would respectively be the pageants that mild, meek sovereigns in the East, who have the good fortune to possess *wise and virtuous* Viziers, usually are. They would be treated with respect, and they would profit by the amelioration of their territories. The labour, the responsibility, and let us not forget, *the honor of all improvements,* would belong to the

British officials, who eschewing the fiction of a double government, putting aside all screens of Dewans, Ministers or Karbarees, would openly stand forward as the avowed managers of the country, on behalf of the ruling power.

The readers of this Journal will observe that we distinguish between the cases of these Mahratta States and that of Oude, where every measure short of superseding the King has been fruitlessly tried. Our relations with Kolapoor and Sawunt-waree stand in a different position. We have ourselves been for years the managers of these countries : the present disorganization has been matured before our own eyes, and in our own hands ; we should therefore nurture our charge until its health is thoroughly recruited and restore full sovereignty to the legitimate Princes, if we can then find among them any whose characters will justify that measure : otherwise we must continue to be the direct managers, and persevere in a course so manifestly advantageous to the hereditary Chiefs themselves. No pains should be spared to explain to them the eventual intentions of Government in their favour, and they should be as clearly informed that intrigue or treachery will, at once and for ever, forfeit their thrones. Free personal communication on the part of the European Superintendents with these Princes, and constant, though not intrusive, endeavours to enlighten their minds may gradually, effect much. But whatever be the result, the British Government will have done its duty, and the good administration of the country will have been secured, either in our own hands or in those of the hereditary rulers.

We are quite aware of the difficulties in the way of our scheme, and of the tact that will be required to carry it out, but we are not the less confident of the result, if the superintendence of affairs is entrusted to the hands we have suggested. Intrigue, nay rebellion, may at first arise ; but it will not be repeated, if summarily and decidedly dealt with. As our scheme admits of no *just* cause being given for insurrection, and provides that determined malignancy shall receive no quarter, we can perceive no likelihood of the arrangement meeting with prolonged opposition. It is the spasmodic tyranny of weak Rulers that invites continual attack. The Government that is one day oppressive, the next cowardly, and the third day frantically vengeful, may fairly calculate on insurrections on every emergency. The British administration of the present day happily acts in another spirit, and the East India Company has only, where legitimate openings offer, to carry among the Ryots of its protected Princes some portion of the benevolence that now influences its dealings towards its own subjects, and protected India will soon assume a new aspect. Blessings will, then, be poured out, in many a rich plain and fruitful valley, where curses are now plentifully showered on those who have, unwittingly, given over the husbandman, the strength and marrow of the land, bound hand and foot, to the tender mercies of his irresponsible tyrants.

Note.—The deliberate opinion we have formed of Colonel Outram, has in no respect been altered by the perusal of that florid romance, entitled " the conquest of Scinde." concocted by the Governor of Guernsey from facts and fictions furnished by the Government of Scinde. The foregoing remarks were written before the appearance of Colonel Outram's letter to General Napier; a letter that was not needed to set " the Bayard of the Indian army," (as Sir Charles Napier in an inspired moment happily designated him), right in the eyes of the Indian public. Still less do they require a further vindication of his conduct, though they will welcome every item of information that he may feel justified in giving. We fearlessly assert that every right-minded man, acquainted with the progress of events during the year 1842, not only acquits Colonel Outram of the absurd and contradictory charges alleged against him by the Napiers, but recognizes in his conduct throughout Scinde transactions both Civil and Military, the spirit of a soldier, a gentleman, and a Christian. We may hereafter have the gratification of sketching the career of this much abused man, who, with a singularly conciliatory and kindly disposition, had the fortune to incur the hatred of two first rate haters, (Lord Keane and Sir Charles Napier.) men too, who fully appreciated his good qualities, till his manliness and honesty thwarted their own views. In the year 1838, Outram carried to Affghanistan a character such as could not be paralleled by any officer of his standing in India. His services during the first Affghan campaign were second to those of no officer then and there employed. Had he remained in the Ghilzee country or at Khelat many of our disasters might have been averted.

But it is by his civil management, first, of lower Scinde, and then of both the Upper and Lower Provinces and of all Belochistan that Outram has won our highest admiration. When the European inhabitants of Calcutta trembled for our Indian empire; when, in the highest places, men grew pale at the evil tidings from Affghanistan, Outram held his frontier post with a firm hand, a brave heart, and cheerful tone that *ought* to have been contagious. Vigilant, conciliatory and courageous, he managed, with his handful of troops, not only to prevent the Ameers from taking advantage of our disasters, but to induce them to aid in furnishing supplies and carriage for the relieving, then considered the retreating, army. The merits of his exertions on that occasion are little understood. He obeyed, as was his duty; but he did not the less clearly perceive the ruinous tendency of the Government orders. He had the moral courage to sacrifice his own immediate interests by stemming the then prevalent tide of cowardly counsel. James Outram in one quarter, and George Clerk,—a kindred spirit,—in another, were the two who then stood in the breach;

who *forced* the authorities to listen to the fact against which they tried to close their ears, that the proposed abandonment of the British prisoners in Affghanistan would be as dangerous to the state as it was base towards the captives. These counsels were successfully followed : the British nation thanked our Indian rulers, while, of the two men, without whose perservering remonstrances and exertions Nott and Pollock might have led back their armies, without being permitted to make an effort to retrieve our credit—Clerk was slighted, and Outram superseded. As cheerfully as he had stepped forward did Outram now retire, and again when his services were required was he ready to act in the field, in willing subordination to the officer who had benefited by his supercession.

The Napiers accuse Outram of jeopardizing the British Army in Scinde : this is mere nonsense. His negotiations, followed up by Sir Charles Napiers's acts, were sufficient to endanger his own life. They did so, and nothing but his own brilliant gallantry and that of his small escort rescued them from the toils. The British Army was able to take care of itself. Had Outram, however, when deputed to Hydrabad, been permitted the *fair discretion* that his position demanded, had he been authorized definitely to promise any reasonable terms ; his abilities and his character would have secured an honourable peace ; but it was not in human nature that the Ameers should long continue to listen to an Envoy sent to demand every thing, and to offer nothing. This was not negotiating, it was dragooning. A British Officer escorted by a single Company was not the proper delegate for such a mission. Sir Charles Napier at the head of his Army was the fitting Ambassador.

Outram's chivalrous defence of his assistant Lieutenant Hammersly is one of the many instances in which he advocated the right at the peril of his own interests. Hammersly was as brave, as honest hearted a young soldier as ever fell a victim to his duty. We knew him well and no one who did so need be ashamed to shed a tear over his fate. He was literally sacrificed *for telling the truth*—a truth too that was of vital importance to the beleaguered Candahar army—nay to the interests of British India—Peace be to the memory of this noble fellow.

CALCUTTA REVIEW.

ART. I.—1. *The origin of Pagan Idolatry, ascertained from Historical testimony and circumstantial evidence.* By *George Stanley Faber.* 3 vols. 1816.

2. *Religions de L'Antiquite, par J. D. Guignaut.* Paris, 1825.

3. *Researches on the Tenets and Doctrines of the Jains and Buddhists, by W. Francklin.* London, 1827.

4. *Researches into the nature and affinity of Ancient and Hindu Mythology, by Vans Kennedy.* London, 1831.

5. *Fragmens Bouddiques, par M. J. Klaproth.* Paris, 1831.

6. *Budaic Sabism, or Adoration addressed to the Almighty.* Calcutta, 1817.

7. *Memoires, relatifs a l' Asia, par J. A. Klaproth.* Paris, 1828.

8. *Melanges Asiatiques, par A. Remusat.* Paris, 1825.

9. *Descriptive Catalogue of the Oriental Manuscripts of Col. Mackenzie's Collection, by H. H. Wilson.* Calcutta, 1828. 2 *vols.*

10. *Annals and Antiquities of Rajasthan, by Colonel Tod.* London, 1829.

11. *History, Antiquities, Topography and Statistics of Eastern India, by M. Martin.* London, 1833.

12. *Radjatarangini, ou histoire des rois du Kachmir, par A. Troyer.* Paris, 1840. *Deux tomes.*

13. *History of the Indian Archipelago, by Crawford.* Edinburgh, 1820.

14. *Epitome of the History of Ceylon, and the first 20 chapters of the Mahavanso, by G. Turner.* Ceylon, 1836.

15. *Foe Koue Ki ou Relation des Royaumes Bouddhiques, voyage dans la Tartarie, dans l'Afghanistan et dans l'Inde, executé a la fin du 4 me Siecle, par Chy Fa Hian, traduit du Chinois, par Messieurs Remusat, Klaproth el Lundresse.* Paris, 1836.

15. *The Sacred and Historical books of Ceylon, by E. Upham.* London, 1833. 3 *vols.*

16. *Notes on the religious, moral and political state of India, before the Mohammedan Invasion, by Colonel Sykes.* London, 1841.

17. *Illustrations of the Literature and Religion of the Buddhists, by B. Hodgson.   Serampore, 1841.*

18. *Essai sur le Pali, par E. Burnouf et Chr. Lassen.   Paris, 1826.*

19. *Transactions of the Bombay Literary Society, 1819-23.*

20. *The History and Doctrine of Buddhism in Ceylon.   London, 1829.*

21. *Introduction a l' histoire du Bouddhisme Indien, par E. Burnouf.   Paris, 1844.*

If to various subjects of physical science the term "boundless" may be applied, as denoting the wide and extensive scope they afford, the epithet is eminently appropriate to different branches of oriental research, and particularly so to investigations into Buddhism—in its *origin, doctrines* and *affiliation* with other systems of ancient mythology.   When we find such a man as the late Abel Remusat of Paris, who devoted twenty years in the prime of life to the study of Buddhism in its esoteric and exoteric forms, confessing at the end of that period, that he was still an *enquirer* into the Arcana of Buddhist lore,—it ought to make every writer who discusses the question enter on it with a feeling of modesty and in the spirit of an humble student, actuated by the cautious tone of the Baconian philosophy. We want *more light* to be shed on various points ;—when the numerous Jain MSS., which are now treasured up in the libraries of Jesselmir, Patan and Cambay, shall be thrown open to the investigation of the learned,—when analysis shall be made of the valuable MSS. in the possession of the Bombay Asiatic Society,—when the stores of Buddhist history and philosophy now scattered throughout the wide empire of China, or buried in the monasteries of Tibet and Nepal, shall be presented to the perusal of the savans of France, Germany and England—then may it be hoped that several questions now obscured by the hoar of antiquity shall be solved, and that those mists shall be dispersed, which at present hover over many investigations connected with the religion of Buddha.   As in geology, though there may be wide differences of opinion between the respective advocates of the Vulcanian and Neptunian theories, as to whether there are alternate periods of repose and convulsion, or of sudden revolutions in the globe—still all enlightened geologists coincide in their views on the principal points of the system,—so in Buddhism there are discrepancies among writers on this subject as to the *precise* year of Buddha's advent, the *particular* time when Buddhism spread to the countries bordering on India, &c. &c.

—but on the *great* historical events of Buddhism and the nature of its dogmas, there exists almost unanimity of opinion between the orientalists of the continent and those of England and India. Hence, the observation made by Whewell on the progress of physical science is applicable to Buddhism, " whatever farther advances may be made, *the past will be the stepping stone to future discoveries,* but can never be overturned by them."

Buddhism, " the fairest branch of the religion of India," called also Samaneism, DESERVES THE ATTENTIVE STUDY OF EVERY PERSON, who agrees with the sentiment of the poet "Homo sum, nil humani a me alienum puto"—whether we consider it, in its *extent,* as a religion which has spread from the Indus to the Pacific and from Ceylon to the regions of Siberia; the religion of nearly half the human race :—or in the *influence* of its doctrines, speaking of moral duty and justice to the wild conquerors that poured like a torrent over the fertile table lands of Asia. Through its agency the Nomadic tribes of Central Asia and the Tartars acquired the arts of civilization. " There are nations who owe all their intellectual culture to Buddhism from the alphabet to metaphysics." We see in the history of Buddhism the successful results of appealing to *popular* feeling in a religious creed. Buddhism opposed itself to the *exclusiveness* and *monopoly* of an hereditary hierarchy; it boldly proclaimed the grand truth of the *equality* of all men in the sight of God, and set its followers in array against the dogma of religious caste; by its adopting the cœnobite or monastic system in its propagandism, it imparted an *esprit de corps* to its missionaries and bore with immense moral force on the various regions where it was planted. Buddhism in former days united North with South India, Kashmir with Ceylon in the bonds of a common faith. Monsieur Landresse remarks—" Is it not a grand and wonderful spectacle to observe that religious doctrines, in which morals and metaphysics, cosmogony and psychology are continually blended, are established and perpetuated far from the regions where they have originated and independently of the influence of the causes which have produced them—re-uniting, by a most abstract philosophical system, people placed at the two extremities of civilisation in Asia, and less separated by a wide interval of country than by the difference in climate, manners and language? What is more surprising than to see the same ideas, on the perfectibility of the human soul and its identity of nature with the Divinity, propagated ages ago with the language which is peculiar to them and the legends which consecrate them, from India to China, from Bengal to Tibet, from the deep valleys of the Himalaya as far as to the snows of China? What is of greater importance within the domain of oriental literature than to penetrate the profound obscurity which envelopes the history of India previous to the Mussulman invasion ; to observe the social condition and political division of the kingdoms of Central Asia prior to the Mohammedan conquests ; to mark the relations which link these people to one another, whom general opinion represents as in a state of habitual isolation from one another ?" Hodgson, to whom oriental scholars owe the deepest obligations for the zeal and enthusiasm with which he devoted twenty years at Katamandu to the exploring of those treasures of Sanskrit Buddhistical literature, which had for ages been buried in the libraries of the Tibetan monasteries, makes the following observations on this point: " The Bauddha religion demands our best attention, not less on account of its having divided with Brahmanism the empire of opinion for ages, within the limits of India proper, than for its unparalleled extension beyond those limits in more recent times, and up to the present day. It is probable that during four or five centuries at least, Buddhism was as influential within the bounds of the continent of India as Brahmanism ; and it is certain that the period of its greatest influence there was synchronous with *the brightest era of the intellectual culture of that continent.* The Brahmans themselves attest, again and again, the philosophical acumen and literary abilities of their detested rivals."

In this article we do not profess to give more than an *outline* of a subject which is *vast* and *comprehensive* in its nature, and which would occupy *half a life time in its thorough investigation.* New light is being shed upon it every year ; but, however obscure certain points may be, *progress* has been made to a considerable degree. To use the language of Locke—" it is well to know the length of your plummet, though you cannot fathom with it the depths of the ocean !" In the present age the arts, sciences and belles lettres are in a state of gradual advancement, and the same impulse has been communicated to investigations into Buddhistical literature. The researches of such men as Burnouf, Lassen, Wilson, Klaproth, Prinsep, &c., have altered the views of Orientalists considerably respecting Buddhism ; as Mr. Turner, in his valuable introduction to the Mahavanso, remarks, " European scholars on entering upon their researches towards the close of last century, necessarily, by the expulsion of the Buddhists, came into communication exclusively with *Hindu Pundits ;* who were not only interested in confining the researches of Orientalists to *Sanskrit* literature ; but who, in every possible way, both by reference to their own prejudiced authorities, and their individual representations, laboured to depreciate in the estimation of Europeans, the literature of the Buddhists." Hence the quotations of oriental scholars from Sanskrit works as to the history and dogmas of Buddhism deserve the same consideration as the testimony of Livy and the Romans to the Carthaginian character and *Punica fides*. Even Hodgson's remarks on Buddhism are in various respects erroneous, as they were derived from *Sanskrit* documents principally. Remusat warns every scholar to be very cautious in admitting the testimony of the *Brahmans* on the subject of Buddhism. As Edward the Third laid his ruthless hand on the archives and literary remains of the Scottish nation, in order to extinguish all national recollections and efface the remembrance of former glory, so did the Brahmans with the MSS. of the Buddhists in India. Faber's useful work on Pagan Idolatry is of very little value as an authority on Buddhism; inasmuch as when he wrote it, *Brahmanical* testimony was almost the only light that could be procured; hence his writings teem with fine spun theories. Bryant's work may be called a philosophic dream. Bentley could have known little of Eastern literature when he pronounced Hindu civilization to be of *modern* origin. Ward's View possesses little authority on Buddhist questions. Vans Kennedy and Colebrooke have pointed out many of its errors. Georgi, in his Alphabeticum Tibetanum, a book until of late years in great repute, devoted much labour to the attempt to prove that Buddha was the founder of Manicheism! while Barthelemi, who wrote in 1791, maintained he was a Greek deity! Sir W. Jones with that philosophic caution, which characterises all great minds, has given it as his opinion, that a complete account of Buddha will only then be obtained when access shall be had to the literature of China, Scandinavia and Japan. Even Colebrooke acknowledged that his reading and research were insufficient for investigating the subject accurately.

Wilford, by relying on Sanskrit authorities exclusively, became the dupe of Brahmanical subtlety, and penned his "laborious absurdities," respecting the Holy White Island of the west, which brought on him a severe fit of illness, when he discovered the cheat imposed on him by the Brahmans who made erasures in the MSS. Of late years the study is pursued in the spirit of Mr. Erskine's remark, "It is indispensably necessary to judge of the doctrine of the Buddhists by the accounts given of them by themselves, and not by the representations of their rivals." *Facts* and historical testimony must be taken as the basis of all research; "facts and not fables, historic lights, not poetic coruscations."

THE CHIEF SOURCES OF MODERN INFORMATION ON BUDDHISM are principally derived from four quarters: 1st, *Chinese* documents, translations from Indian originals, detailing the origin and progress of Buddhism; among these are the travels of Lao Tseu and "Foe Koue Ki ou relation des Royaumes Bouddhiques," which, both by internal evidence and the testimony of contemporary writers, bear every mark of veracity.   Chinese pilgrims came at various periods to India, via Tartary and the Himalayas, in order to visit the shrines endeared to them by being associated with the rise and extension of Buddhism.   Remusat was of opinion that the Chinese, before the Christian era, took part in the commerce of western Asia, and kept up relations with the line of towns between China and Persia.   The frequent intercourse between China and India by means of embassies, gave the Chinese an excellent opportunity of judging of the state of India.   2nd, The translation of the Pali Buddhist Historical Annals of Ceylon by Mr. Turner, called the Mahavanso, which gives a systematic chronology of the Kings and events both in Ceylon and Bahar, for the space of 24 centuries.   3rd, The decyphering of coins, inscriptions, &c. by Prinsep ; Dr. Mill has shewn by them the extent and influence of Buddhism in India in former ages.   4th, The MacKenzie MSS. analysed by the Rev. Mr. Taylor of Madras, and Professor Wilson ; the Rev. Mr. Taylor draws the conclusion from them that "originally the Brahmans were most certainly foreigners to the Peninsula, and to know that is one important step in tracing their remoter origin."

The question has long been discussed by very able advocates on both sides, WHICH IS THE MORE ANCIENT, BUDDHISM OR BRAHMANISM ? In former days writers deriving their views from Sanskrit works, naturally conceded the priority to Brahmanism, but of late years the subject has taken a new form.   Writers now place the difficulty in this point of view by investigating those preliminary enquiries.   Were Brahmanism and Buddhism formed *independent* of each other ? Or is one *derived* from the other ? Or do both proceed from a *common source*, i. e. from a religion more ancient than either?   Monsieur Troyer, the able translator and commentator of the Rajatarangini, or History of the Kings of Kashmir, from his investigations into the spread of Buddhism in Kashmir, one of its primitive seats in India, draws the inference—" That Buddhism and Brahmanism sprang from a source common to both, and about the same time—that the doctrine of Brahmanical caste shows that Brahmanism could not have been before Buddhism, which recognises the primitive equality of mankind, traces of which are still preserved in the Huli festival and at Jagarnath, where all castes mingle together." When referring to Buddhism, we should remember that the Buddhism existing *now* probably differs very much from *primitive* Buddhism, as the Brahmanism of the Puranas and Tantras varies widely from the system inculcated in the Vedas and laws of Manu ; Buddhism includes within itself an esoteric or theistic system and an exoteric or allegorical polytheism.

Buddhism has local differences. In Nepal there are *married* monks, and the Buddhist system is more metaphysical and refined than that of Ceylon, and differs from that of Ceylon, which has a priesthood. The Mahavanso mentions various schisms and heresies which arose at different periods among the Buddhists—the domination however of a certain religious system at a particular era does not imply that it had previously maintained the *semper eadem;* thus it was only a short time before the Mussalman invasion of India that the linga worship, though of ancient origin, gained among the people an ascendancy. Upham, in his " History and Doctrines of Buddhism," from an examination into the history of Buddhism, arrives at the conclusion "that Buddhism, as now existing, is in fact two systems of different eras wrought into each other, at some period of the revival of the faith, by an ambitious and zealous teacher—that there is an ancient and modern system of Buddhism, the ancient recognises the dogma of fate, the modern of free will." Fa Hian, a Chinese Buddhist Priest, who travelled through India at the beginning of the fourth century, mentions six different Buddhist sects existing in India, and that Buddha, their great lawgiver, died of dysentery from eating pork. The worship of the 24 Buddhist patriarchs, i. e. genii or deified men, is, in the opinion of various scholars, as much a corruption of *primitive* Buddhism, as saint worship is of ancient Christianity, or Hero worship of the patriarchal system. Monsieur Troyer states, " *primitive* Buddhism is lost." Even Sakya, the reputed founder of the Buddhists 10 centuries B. C. who was of the Khetrya caste, did not profess to preach a *new* religion. There were the Buddhist teachers Kakusando, Kassapo, previous to the advent of Sakya, who must be regarded chiefly as a *reformer.* The Nepalese and Chinese writings give a sketch of their lives. Hodgson is of opinion that the Buddhism of one age is not less different from that of another, than is the Brahmanism of the Vedas, from that of the Puranas and the Bhagavat—that the later Buddhist teachers, living in quieter times than those of the first doctors and instructors, in consequence of the taunts of their adversaries and because of adversity, have attempted to explain away what was objectionable as well as contradictory in the original system—that in Nepal there are *now* Buddhist priests, though original Buddhism recognised no *priesthood*—that Buddhism was different, " when it was a closet speculation, from what it was when it became the dominant creed of large states."

Ritter thinks that there was *an ancient and a modern Buddhism*, as distinct as Sabianism is from Pantheism. Colonel Sykes, in his "ancient India," states, that Sakya was a reformer of the *previous existing* Buddhism and that a qualified Buddhism existed in India *prior* to the 6th century B. C. and to an extremely remote period. The Rajaratnacari, an ancient compilation from the oldest Buddhist records of Ceylon, giving a history of the kings of Ceylon, from Vijaya B. C. 540 to the settlement of the Portuguese on the island, mentions that *heresies* occurred among the Buddhists at different times. The Mahavanso states that 18 heresies took place among the Buddhists, two centuries after the death of Buddha. Turner remarks that the differences between Kashmirian and Ceylonese Buddhism are " the conflicting doctrines of two antagonist sects professing the same faith." The progress of time,—the effect of persecution—and the want of the centralizing influence of an hierarchy must have produced various changes. Erskine is of opinion that there was a certain interchange of doctrine formerly between Brahmanism and Buddhism ; in Java and Bali we see a connection between the Sivite and Buddhist systems. Crawford, (in the opinion of Hodgson, who shows that the Sivites appropriated to their own faith Buddhist images not only in Java, but also in the caves of Western India), committed a gross mistake on this subject in his " Eastern Archipelago" in stating that all the images found in Java are Sivite. Many of them are Buddhist, but from their *similarity* to the Brahmanical they were *confounded* with them. In Mysore and the South of India the Jains admit certain of the Hindu deities into the courts of their temples, which they never do in the Mahratta country, or Marwara. The opinion of Erskine, " that Buddhism and Brahmanism had a common origin, and that Brahmanical Mythology is progressive, arising from a primitive simple system," will, if borne out fully by facts, clear up many difficulties in which this question is now involved. One point, however, is certain, that Buddhism flourished in India at an *early* period ; Prinsep states, " a century or two prior to the Christian era Buddhism flourished in the height of its glory from Kashmir to Ceylon." Sykes mentions, " at the time of Alexander's invasion, Buddhism must have been in the palmy days of its power, judging from the inscriptions, the coins, the topes, the temples, the monasteries, the obelisks, the multitudinous and gigantic cave excavations and other works of art, most of which are referable, not only by the internal evidence they afford, but by the testimony of the Mahavanso, to the period between the first and sixth centuries B. C. and more particularly to the period when Asoko reigned B.C. 319 to B.C. 282."

Klaproth, a great authority, styles Buddha a reformer of Brahmanism and this is the view of a numerous body of scholars. Hodgson gives a very strong argument in favour of this opinion: "Buddhism is monastic asceticism in morals; philosophical scepticism in religion; and whilst ecclesiastical history all over the world affords abundant instances of such a state of things resulting from gross abuse of the religious sanction, that ample chronicle gives us no one instance of it as a primitive system of belief." The existence of the laws of Manu at least twelve centuries B. C., implying a state of things in favour of Brahmanism preceding them for a considerable period, also supports this position. The strongest proof perhaps is, that Buddhism seems by *internal* evidence to be a reform of Brahmanism. But testimony adduced from China of late years throws considerable light in favour of the arguments advocating the claim of Buddhism in its *primitive* form to an equal antiquity with Brahmanism. The researches made in the cave temples of Western and Southern India, as well as the information drawn from Pali writings, cause modern scholars to pause and wait for fresh light ere they pronounce a decision on the rival claims of the "Scythism and Ionism" of Stanley Faber. Sykes in his "Notes" draws the conclusion, after a very strict examination of data, that the oldest inscriptions in India all relate to Buddhism and not to Brahmanism—are in the Pali and not in the Sanskrit language,—that of the oldest of the multitudinous coins so singularly brought to light within the last few years, all relate to Buddhism or Fire worship: "we have not any coins having reference to Hinduism before those of the Guptas, who were Sudras of Kanouj about the eighth century." Franklin states, "Buddhism is in many respects a creed *simple* and unformed, while Brahmanism is the very reverse; the presumption therefore is, that the latter is the more *finished* exhibition of the former; and consequently that Buddhism is more ancient than Brahmanism." Joinville writes on the question: "An uncreated world and mortal souls are ideas to be held only in an *infant* state of society, and as society advances, such ideas must vanish; *a fortiori* they cannot be established in opposition to a religion already prevailing in a country, the fundamental ideas of which are, the creation of the world and the immortality of the soul;" he also thinks that the Buddhists knew astronomy before the Brahmans and that as religion and astronomy are

I I

united, Buddhism was therefore the more ancient. Dr. Tytler states that, " the *simplicity* discernible in Buddhism, the genuine principles of disinterested humanity and piety which pervade the whole of the system, clearly demonstrate the originality of this admirable and unadorned fabric over the *complicated* structure, decorated under false notions of embellishment with meretricious ornaments of all kinds, which are visible in the multifarious tenets peculiar to modern Hindus." It would be easy to cite an array of authorities on both sides of this knotty question— but the safest decision to come to is that

Sub judice lis est.

Todd, Franklin, Faber and many others, thought that *Woden* the God of the Saxons and Buddha were the same personages. Much learned labour has been bestowed in tracing out this analogy by our old Mythologists, a class of men who will hunt up the etymology of every word to the tower of Babel and fix on its derivation with as much precision as some of the Welsh genealogists do, in pointing out the exact line in which a Welsh family descended from Adam. Happily the day of this knight errantry in ferreting out obscure derivations has nearly passed away, and though Woden may be twisted into Buddha by the change of a *w* into a *b ;* yet the voice of history declares that,— though the worship of Woden or Odin was probably introduced into Europe from Asia, about the period of the Christian era—and though there be many points in the adoration paid to Odin bearing a strong affinity to some Indian practices, such as the Scandinavian sacrifice of the horse, and the ancient rite of the Aswamedha,—yet *the genius of the two systems is widely different.* Buddhism has civilized the wild tribes of Central Asia, so as to render another Gothic invasion impossible. and has spread the arts of civilization over the sandy deserts of Tartary ; its offerings are flowers, incense, rice and fruit, and it holds the *life* not only of man, but also of beasts and insects as inviolable. But Woden is represented as the god of *battles,* and as slaughtering thousands at a blow, as living in the palace of Vallhalla along with heroes, who solace themselves with drinking mead out of the skulls of enemies whom they had *killed* in the days of nature. What a contrast to the *mild* and *pacific* spirit of Buddhism ! Sir W. Jones changed his opinion on this point a short time before his death ; he had long advocated the theory that Woden and Buddha were the same,—led astray by the *ignis fatuus* of endeavouring to ascertain a correspondence in minutiæ between the mythology of Europe and Asia. We find a writer of this class asserting that Stonehenge was a temple of Buddha !

Franklin, Joinville, Mahoney, Ward have thought Buddhism to be a system of *Atheism*—but the Buddhists in their creed believe in 130 hells and 18 heavens, which implies a belief in a future state of rewards and punishments, and consequently of a Supreme Being to reward and punish. The answers given by the Singhalese priests to a series of questions formerly submitted to them by the Dutch governor of Ceylon, shew that the old Buddhist philosophers were sceptics, but *not atheists*. Hodgson and Upham also concur in this view. The documents procured by Hodgson in Nepal have fully shewn Buddhism to be a system recognising a *Supreme Being*. Sir A. Johnston interrogated the Buddhist priests on this subject, and they distinctly acknowledged the *existence of a God*. Erskine states, " the Buddhists do not deny the existence of God, though they have no idea of him, as taking any active part in the creation of the world." There exist in Buddhism certain sects which have an atheistic tendency, like the Sankhya of Kapila, which taught the doctrine of a plastic principle or nature, the producer of all things. The Buddhists believe the dogma of the transmigration of souls, they offer yearly sacrifices to the manes of their ancestors, which implies their existence after death, and they also believe that by the exercise of virtue and knowledge an individual can obtain nibbuti or absorption into the deity.

The distinction between the Buddhists and Jains is very trivial, and in this article to prevent repetition, we shall include the latter under the name of the former. Colebrooke remarks, " The Buddhists and Jains are branches of one stock, hardly more difference exists between the two than between the diverse branches of the single sect of Buddha." Hodgson states " The Jains are sectarian Buddhists, who differ from their Buddhist brethren merely in carrying to a gross excess, and in promulgating publicly certain amorous dogmas, which the more prudent Buddhists choose to keep veiled from all but the initiated." Franklin mentions, " The worship of the Jains compared with that of the Buddhists, with very slight variations, is in fact one and the same thing." The Jains worship 24 deified heroes ; the Buddhists only 7. The Jains have caste, the Buddhists have none. The Jain images are naked, the Buddhist not. Professor Wilson writes, " The Jains are an emanation from the Buddhist stem, it is merely an expansion of that which the followers of Buddha devised." Sykes thinks the Jains were originally " a sect of Buddhists, a schismatical offset from the Buddhists." Taylor of Madras, the author of an analysis of the MacKenzie MSS. calls the Buddhists and Jains, " a people of one religion, under two modifications."

We come now to the province of BAHAR,—(the Kings of which formerly swayed the sceptre of North India, and were of the lunar race,)—the far famed and original seat of Buddhism in India—the holy land of Buddhism:—its very name (*Vihar*, a Monastery,) indicates its former connection with Buddhism.   The Burmese call it Makat; the Chinese, Moketo; and the Hindu writers, Magadh, or the country of the Magas, a tribe of Hindu colonists introduced into it from Sakadip.   Hodgson states that, "The philosophers of Ayodha and Magadh are the acknowledged founders of Buddhism."   The Buddhists admit the same.   The Chinese, the Mongols, the Tibetans, the Indo-Chinese, the Ceylonese, point to India as the cradle of their faith.   An interesting question connected with Bahar and Central India, is, Did Buddhism originate in it, or was it introduced from Persia?   It can be traced to no other two sources; for, as we shall show hereafter, Buddhism spread from Bahar to Tibet, Ceylon, China and the Eastern Archipelago.   In favour of the former opinion are,— Hodgson, "Buddhist literature is originally Indian:" Colebrooke, "The Buddhists were originally Hindus:" Klaproth, "The religion of Buddhism was originally from Hindustan, and spread over the greater part of Asia; its dominion extended from the sources of the Indus to the Pacific Ocean, and even to Japan; the fierce Nomades of Central Asia have been changed by it into men virtuous and mild, and its beneficial influence is felt as far as Central Siberia.   Buddhism spread from Bengal to Kashmir, North; and Ceylon, South:" Landresse, "Buddhism originated in North India."

In favour of Buddhism having an *ex-Indian origin* is Wilson, "It is not unlikely that a colony of Sacœ or Scythians settled in India, that they brought with them the faith of Buddha, and communicated it to India, whence it returned improved by the Scholarship of learned converts: Buddhism is still widely cultivated throughout Central Asia, and that part of Asia is most probably its ancient and original seat."   The Russians, in their incursions into Siberia in the beginning of the 18th century, found Buddhist monasteries and books, which have been since translated.   Prinsep has shewn that the coins of Kanauj were made on an Indo-Scythic model.   Todd thinks Buddhism in India is not indigenous, that it was brought into India by the Scythic tribes, that when they entered India they entered Europe also at the same time.   Sir W. Jones, was of opinion that from time immemorial Central Asia was the seat of the Hindu religion.   The Getes whose capital was on the banks of the Jaxartes, had, according to De Guignes, at an early period embraced Buddhism.

A close connection subsisted in former times *between India and Persia:* the Persian fire worshippers sought to propagate their faith in Bahar ten centuries before the Christian era. Ferishta attributes to Brahmanism a Persian origin. Whether we think with Klaproth that the Hindus came to India from the Caucasian mountains, or with Schlegel from the borders of the Caspian, we must at any rate assign to them an *ex-Indian* origin. A close correspondence exists in various points between the religions of India and Egypt; images were found in the temple of Ipsambul in Nubia, which bore the strongest likeness to Buddhist ones. Todd is of opinion that the lunar race was of equal antiquity with the solar race, who became idolaters and inhabited Assyria.

However, whether Buddhism originated in Bahar or not; one point is clear—that it existed there from a *remote* period and was the *dominant* religion of North India for a *long* time. J. Prinsep has shewn, by the evidence of coins and inscriptions, that at the time of Alexander's conquests India was under the rule of Buddhist kings and institutions, and that the *earliest* monarchs of India are not connected with a *Brahman* dynasty or creed. The annals of Ceylon lead us to conclude that in the 4th century B. C. Buddhism was the *predominant* religion of Bahar and South India; the testimony of Strabo and Megasthenes confirms this, who call the Indian priests Samaneans, the name given to Buddhist priests by the Siamese and many other nations. The final struggle of Buddhism for ascendancy in India took place in the 4th century B. C. when it became the religion of the state. The Vayu and Skanda Puranas admit the predominance of Buddhism over Brahmanism at an early period. Mahakýa, the 1st of the 33 Buddhist patriarchs was born in Magadh, so were the 2nd patriarch Ananda, the 5th Daitaka, and the 6th Michaka. The Mahavanso, an historical poem written in Ceylon in the Pali language, and translated into English by the Hon. Mr. Turner, throws a flood of light on the state of Bahar previous to the Christian era. It begins its details from 543 B. C. and gives an almost uninterrupted historical record for twenty-four centuries : both internal evidence and external testimony substantiate the veracity of its statements. The Foe Koue ki, giving an account of the travels of Fa Hian, a Chinese Buddhist priest, through India in the 4th century A. D., translated from the Chinese by Remusat with copious notes by Klaproth and Landresse, is also a valuable storehouse of facts. Bahar or Magadh was formerly the seat of a great empire in the time of Sandracottus or Chandragupta (the identity of these two is shewn by Dr.

Mill, and Prinsep) king of the Prasii,—Palibothra being the capital; he contracted an alliance with Seleucus Nicator, and Megasthenes was an ambassador at his court. Sir W. Jones mentions a Khetrya king of Magadh B. C. 2,000; the provinces situated on the Ganges were subject to him. Asoko reigned at Patna B. C. 319, he was the king of all India; his edicts, engraved on rocks from Kattak to Girner in Gujarat, and on the Delhi, Allahabad, and other columns, have been deciphered through the labours of J. Prinsep and Dr. Mill,—a detail of them is given in the Journal of the Asiatic Society of Bengal. Asoko was a great patron of Buddhism, and sent several Buddhist embassies to Ceylon; his son Mahindo went on a religious mission to Ceylon B. C. 306. Bahar is famous in all Buddhist countries for having been the scene of the life and labours of Buddha, the great teacher; he flourished according to the Chinese accounts and in the opinion of Klaproth and Wilson 1,000 B. C. and was born at Gaya: he was the son of Sudadan, king of Magadh, and of the family of Sakya; when grown up, he retired to the desert, where he spent six years in contemplation and ascetic practices; he then proceeded with a band of followers to Benares to propagate his doctrines, which were opposed by the advocates of fire worship who had come from Persia; he travelled as far as Ceylon and through Magadh diffusing his tenets.

Gaya has been a celebrated place for Buddhist pilgrims from China, Ceylon, Ava, &c. &c., who resorted to it as the spot where Buddha underwent sufferings for six years, having renounced all the pleasures and advantages attendant on his noble birth and his prospects as the son of a king. It is called Urawelaya or the abode of sand in the Mahavanso; Hamilton thinks "Gaya was once the centre of religion in India and the residence of a powerful king." An inscription in Pali, discovered there by the Burmese ambassadors in 1833, records that the Buddhist temple, originally built by Asoko and which had fallen into decay, was rebuilt A. D. 1305. These Burmese ambassadors worshipped there as in a sacred place of their religion: an inscription written about A. D. 1197 mentions Lakhman Sen and his invocation to Buddha. Fa Hian, when he visited Gaya, found three monasteries there with a numerous body of ecclesiastics: he states that the precepts of Buddha were strictly observed; he saw one of the towers of Asoko, erected in commemoration of the chief events of Buddha's life. The numerous rock caves and the many inscriptions in Pali deciphered by J. Prinsep, show that Gaya was famous for Buddhistical associations. In Gaya king Asoko held his court—but what is its present state?—there still exist the ruins of a Buddhist temple 108 feet high, the gate of which was so large that a man mounted on an elephant could enter : Buddhist images are scattered six or eight miles round ; the glory of Gaya has passed away and no remains are now to be seen but irregular heaps of bricks and stones and the traces of ancient buildings.   The Brahmans have changed Buddhist images into Brahmanical here as they have done in other parts of India ; they have even connected a Hindu legend with the origin of Gaya.   In Java, Crawford was deceived in thinking the images he saw in the ruins of temples were Sivite—they were Buddhist originally, but turned into Sivite by the Brahmans.

Rajgriha, i. e. the royal residence, called in the Mahavanso " the mountain girt city," was a celebrated metropolis, situated to the South of Gaya, long the seat of empire and a centre for Buddhism in Bahar, until the court was removed to Palibothra by king Asoko.   Buddha itinerated in the mountainous region to the south of it, preaching his doctrines. Jarasand king of India also resided here ; some ruins yet remaining are said to have been built by him : there are some Buddhist temples which have been repaired by the Jains of Patna.   There are sixty Brahman families, who perform the worship of the Buddhist temples ; they came 300 years ago from the Mahratta country.   The Mahavanso mentions Rajgriha as " a city perfect in every sacerdotal requisite," and that the first great Buddhist convocation was held in Rajgriha, near a cave, 500 priests being present, in the reign of Ajasattu, in order to suppress a schism which sprung up among the Buddhists ; the doctrines of Sakya were then reduced to writing.   Indagatto, a great Buddhist teacher, led a number of priests from Rajgriha to Ceylon to take part in laying the foundations of the great Thupo or temple at Anuradhpur ; temple caves have been found in the neighbourhood ; one of which could hold 500 persons.   Ananda, the 2nd Buddhist patriarch, of royal descent, was born in Rajgriha. The Ratnacari, a Buddhist historical book, written in Pali, records that king Ajasattu resided here in a most beautiful palace, in which he placed an image of Buddha of pure gold, with an establishment of 500 priests.   Basu Raja is said in the Vayu Purana to have lived here ; he was tributary to the Pal Rajahs, who were Buddhists, and as the Brahmans of Magadh were tinctured with Buddhist notions he introduced Brahmans from the south of India.   Kassapo also lived in Rajgriha.

Patna, in the opinion of the majority of Orientalists, now occupies the spot where Palibothra once stood. Col. Franklin thought Baglipur, and Wilford, Rajmahal to be the site.   The

Mahavanso calls it Pupphepura or the floral city. Asoko or Pyadas " sole sovereign of India" resided here and supported a great number of Buddhist priests and erected many monasteries; Fa Hian on his visit found many monasteries and colleges, where Buddhist students assembled from various parts of Asia to study philosophy, and particularly from the N. W. and W. of India; in his time the splendid palace of Asoko was still standing, built of stone and highly ornamented. B. C. 309 in the reign of Asoko, the 3rd great Buddhist convocation was held here in order to devise measures for the defence of Buddhism, as the Brahmans were then spreading their tenets. Between A. D. 650 and 683, according to Klaproth, the Chinese emperor Kaoteoung sent an ambassador to Patna, who erected a monument with an inscription on it in a Buddhist temple there. About A. D. 790, the emperor Tetsoung caused an inscription to be put on a bell which he presented to a temple in Patna. In A. D. 647, an embassy was sent from Patna to China. In A. D. 157, Mattino, the Buddhist priest, took with him to Ceylon, an immense member of Buddhist priests from Asoko's great monastery at Patna, to assist in laying the foundations of the great shrine in Ceylon, built by king Datthagamini. Patna was the capital of Sandracottus, the Chandragupta of Indian, and Bindusaro of Pali, history.

Parasnath hill, on the Ramgar frontier, 136 miles S. of Baglipur, is a celebrated place of Jain pilgrimage; the hill is so called from the temples on it being dedicated to Parasnath, the 23rd deified saint of the Jains; it bears also the name of Madhuvanam or the sweet grove, as in former times various kinds of fruits and flowers were preserved there. Todd thinks Parasnath appeared in India two centuries B. C., about the time when the Agniculas invaded it. A magnificent temple is erected to Parasnath on mount Abu, " the Sinai of the desert." The following description is given of Parasnath Hill and the temples, by Colonel Franklin, who visited them: " They consist of large square brick buildings with a dome in the centre and smaller domes at the corners, which are surmounted by cullises of copper gilt, which shine like burnished gold; in front of each temple is a Nabutkhana or gallery for music, from sun rise to sun set you hear nothing but the incessant din of their music. The ascent to the mountain commences by a narrow steep path surrounded by the thickest forest; as you ascend, the summit of the mountain presents a stupendous appearance; at intervals you perceive the summit of Parasnath appearing in bluff jagged peaks, eight in number, and towering to the clouds—from an opening in the forest the view is inexpressibly grand, the wide extent of the Jungle Terry appearing as if beneath your feet, and looking like the surface of a pictured landscape; the summit emphatically termed by the Jains Asmeed Sikur or the peak of bliss composes a table land, flanked by twenty small Jain temples, situate on the craggy peaks and in different parts of the mountain." On one of the hills are the twenty impressions of the feet of Jain Tirthakars, who obtained *mukh* or deliverance from matter and individual existence here; hence it was formerly a place of great pilgrimage for numbers of Jains from distant countries: a Jain king, who ruled at Rajgriha improved the place and built three Jain temples; the Mussulmans, when they invaded the country, placed obstructions in the way of the Jain pilgrims, and the petty chieftains of the district made them pay a heavy tax. In 1769, a rich Jain merchant from Murshedabad repaired the place and built a Jain Temple: the Sets of Murshedabad maintain an establishment of priests there. Two other Jain temples also have been built by the Jains of Murshedabad. Parasnath obtained his mukh or emancipation on the top of the hill: he was born at Benares.

Murshedabad, from having been the residence of the Sets, a wealthy Jain family, (they are now Vaishnavas), was a great place of resort for the Jains, who have (or had) six or seven temples there distinguished by their spires and gilt poles; the images were made of black or white marble brought from Jaypur. *Bagulpur* has three Jain temples built by King Srenika, and the print of Buddha's foot: Buddhist pilgrims go there. A Jain temple was built eighty years ago by the Jains of Murshedabad. In Fa Hian's time it had ten monasteries and two hundred ecclesiastics: its ancient name was Champa. *Benares* was " the scene of the preachings and labours of all the Buddhas, and particularly of the initiatory labours of Sakya"; when visited by Hiuan Thsang, a Chinese traveller in A. D. 630-40, it contained *thirty monasteries and* 4,000 *Buddhist priests and disciples*; Buddhism was then on the wane. A Mongolian book states that Benares was the seat of Buddhism from all antiquity. The late Mr. Duncan dug up an image of Buddha there. At Sarnath near Benares there is a Buddhist tope. *The Buddhists of Tibet refer the origin of their faith to Benares.* A Buddhist image has been found near *Mirzapur. Kesaria* in Tirhut has a Dahgope or hemispherical temple, situated about twenty miles North of Bakra on the banks of the Gandak river; a Buddhist image has been dug up near Bakra. *Tamluk* near the mouth of the Ganges, when visited by Fa Hian, had twenty-four Buddhist monasteries and a tower of Asoko's. Fa Hian spent two years there reading sacred books and painting images. He

K K

sailed from it to Ceylon. King Asoko sent an embassy to Ceylon, which embarked from Tamluk. The Hindus themselves have a tradition that Buddhism was dominant in *Purniya* before the time of Laksman, King of Gaur. A Jain image was found at *Joynagur* near Rangpur by Colonel Franklin. Many other Buddhist localities in *Bahar* might be pointed out, did the limits we have set to this subject allow us to notice them.

The testimony of pillars, inscriptions and coins, is very decisive as to the PREDOMINANCE OF BUDDHISM IN FORMER TIMES IN BAHAR. The *Bettiah* column has a Buddhist inscription precisely the same as that of Delhi and Allahabad, of the date B. C. 315, in the Pali language, mentioning Asoko. At *Sarnath*, images were found containing inscriptions giving a compendium of Buddhist doctrines ; near the same place copper plate inscriptions have been discovered, indicating that a Buddhist temple was erected by the sons of Bhupala, a Raja of Gaur, in the eleventh century. The mounds and ruins near Bakra in Tirhut testify to the existence of a former Buddhist city there. Numerous Buddhist inscriptions have been found in the Nagarjuna cave, Gaya, bearing the date of 1140, mentioning Dasaratha, a Buddhist King, and showing that the Buddhists had still a hold in India in the twelfth century. The columns of Delhi, Allahabad, Matteah, Radiah, all contain the same Pali Buddhist inscriptions, commemorative of Asoko, of the date B. C. 294. Of all the numerous coins found in different parts of India, the most ancient are those of the Guptas, who were sovereigns of Kanauj ; the coins from Gujarat and Affghanistan are chiefly Buddhist ; even the temple of Somnath was originally a Buddhist structure ; *coins dug up at Ougein have Buddhist emblems on them.* Sykes remarks, "We find the great majority of the coins from Affghanistan, Scind, Cutch, Gujarat, the Panjab, Ougein, Behat, Kanauj and other places, with Buddhist emblems upon them, indicating that they had issued from the Buddhist mints of Buddhist princes. We have also the foundation of the Rajput states, at the period of the decline of Buddhism : the non-appearance of Brahmanical inscriptions and coins, until the same period of the decline of Buddhism : the comparatively modern origin of all the present celebrated Hindu temples and tirthas, or places of pilgrims : the recent date at which Brahmanical literature flourished between the fifth and twelfth centuries of our era ;—the Puranas being invented or compiled in that interval—the history of Kashmir being written A. D. 1141." From these and many other data Colonel Sykes draws the conclusion that *Buddhism had prevailed uninterruptedly in India from the sixth century B. C. to the ninth century A. D.* The Pal Rajas, a powerful Buddhist dynasty, lived usually at Chunar. The most eminent of the Bahar Buddhist Kings were Bimbisaro B. C. 603, Ajatasattu B. C. 551, Kalasoko B. C. 443, Asoko B. C. 319, Dasaratha B. C. 250.

That the ORIGINAL RECORDS OF THE BUDDHISTS IN INDIA, WERE WRITTEN IN THE PALI OR MAGADH is shown by Prinsep, Turner, Ksoma de Koros—the Buddhists did not use Sanskrit in their writings before the seventh century A. D. Colebrooke pronouced the Pali to be " a jargon destitute of regular grammar." Burnouf and Lassen, however, in their admirable Essai sur le Pali refute this assertion, as does Wilson; and Turner, who was well read in the language, calls it " a rich, refined and poetical language of the land in which Buddhism, as promulgated by Sakya or Gautama, had its origin, at which period it was a *highly refined and classical language.*" The Indo Chinese and Ceylonese call the Pali—Magadhi or the language of Magadh. To J. Prinsep the literary world is indebted for the invaluable discovery of the means of reading the Pali inscriptions of India. Professor Lassen is of opinion that the legends upon the Bactrian coins are in Pali or Pracrit. Mr. Turner thinks that the Pali or Magadhi " had already attained the refinement it now possesses at the time of Gautama Buddha's advent," which, to take the latest date, was six centuries B. C. It was a language widely diffused; the Kavi or sacred language of Java bears a great affinity to the Pali, and most of the ancient inscriptions found in the temples there, are in the Pali. Fa Hian in his travels through India found no difficulty in communicating with the priests; and Pali was very probably the medium, the same as Latin was through Europe in the middle ages the common language of the clergy. Dr. Buchanan states that "the Pali, or sacred language of Ceylon and Ava, was introduced from Magadh."

What a contrast does Bahar present now! Buddhism throughout the length and breadth of that country is like "the tale of Troy"; few living representatives of it are to be found—the land of its glory and triumphs retains slight traces of the former state of things. Brahmanism is at present on the ascendant, destined ere long with all other false systems to be swept into the gulph of oblivion. HOW THIS CATASTROPHE OCCURRED, it is difficult to ascertain with precision: we can only get occasional glimpses of the mode. Wilson fixes the date of the Vishnu Purana's being composed to A. D. 954, and mentions that at that time Brahmans and even mountaineers were ruling in Bahar.   Upham states, " Buddhism might be traced back to a very early period in Hindustan, where for a long time it exercised supreme control : after *ages of sanguinary wars* it was finally expelled and turned out of India, and its vanquished followers fled in all directions from their relentless persecutors the Brahmans, many taking refuge in the North and East among the impervious recesses of the Himalaya mountains, while vast numbers emigrated to the fine and fertile island of Ceylon." Remusat writes, " Buddhism was proscribed in the country which gave it birth, this religious system insensibly lost the greater number of its partisans, and the feeble remains to which it is now reduced in India are still deprived of that unity of view and tradition produced long since by the presence of the supreme head."   Colebrooke mentions, " The persecutions instigated against the Buddhists by Sankara Acharya were enforced perhaps from political motives by persons of the Vaishnavite and Jain sects, who compelled the Buddhist monarchs to retire from Hindustan and to content themselves with their dominion of Lassa and Bhotan."   Bodidharma was the last Buddhist patriarch who lived in India, he quitted it for China in the 5th century.   Landresse writes, " *Buddhism originating in North India* 1000 *years B. C.* exercised its sway during many ages on a level with Brahmanism, which finally, gaining the ascendancy, annihilated its rival.   Then these Hindus, without caste, expelled from their native country, dispersed in all directions, carrying their contemplative idolatry among twenty nations, civilizing some, rendering others anti-warlike, altering the manners, institutions, languages of all, and arresting in some the full developement of the human faculties."   *The decline of Buddhism in Bahar, therefore, was the result of a persecution which amounted almost to extirpation : the date of it was contemporary with the arrival of Buddhist fugitives in different countries to the east and south of Hindustan ;* thus " vast numbers of Buddhists emigrated to the fine and fertile island of Ceylon from India after ages of sanguinary wars."   The period of the decay of Buddhism corresponds with the " rise of the *present popular forms* of the Hindu religion in the time of Sankara Acharya in the 8th *and* 9th *centuries.*"   The *Siva Rajputs,* who were at that time active agents in the extension of the worship of the Linga, were probably used by the crafty Brahmanical priesthood as the instruments of a persecution, *which lasted from the 7th century until the final overthrow of Buddhism in the 12th.   The opposition raised by Buddhism to caste and a lordly priesthood rendered it impossible that it could coexist with Brahmanism.*   Colonel Sykes, who has given considerable attention to this subject, remarks: "In the 7th century Buddhism, apparently crushed by the weight of its *gigantic monastic system* and rendered unpopular by the *rigid, self-denying* and *elevated character* of its practical doctrines, was fast disappearing from India, and Brahmanism as a system was about to take its place." The Mackenzie MSS. and the History of Kashmir mention the persecution of the Buddhists.

The persecutions and sufferings the Buddhists were exposed to in Bahar, in consequence of the gradual ascendancy of Brahman rulers and priests from the 5th to the 12th centuries, caused them either to forsake the country or to conform to the dominant religion; hence perhaps from this association of Buddhists with the Brahmans have sprung many of those *sects* among the Hindus, who received a leaven of *liberalism* from Buddhism. *Bahar was the fount of Buddhist propagandism to Ceylon, the Dekkan, Tibet, Nepal, China and the Eastern Archipelago;* all the Buddhists in those countries look to Bahar as the cradle of their faith. The Buddhists, like the followers of a purer system, when scattered abroad, went every where, preaching their faith. They forsook the fair fields of Bahar with all their endearing associations, rather than apostatise from their ancestral creed; their zeal for proselytism received an additional stimulus; like the pilgrim fathers of New England, they secured the foundations of their religion in lands far remote from the reach of their persecutors. We shall now notice the CHIEF COUNTRIES THAT OWE THEIR FAITH TO BAHAR.

CEYLON "THE ADOPTED COUNTRY OF THE PERSECUTED BUDDHISTS," is indebted for its Buddhist faith to missionaries of that persuasion, *who came from Bahar* and taught their creed without the aid of books which were not introduced until 300 years subsequently; Landresse however is of opinion that Buddhism was brought into Ceylon from *Kashmir.* The *Ratnacari,* one of the Pali Buddhist historical works of Ceylon, which is cited and appealed to as a document of undoubted veracity, represents Ceylon as having been the abode of devils before the time of Gautama who came and preached there; according to its authority, he was the 4th Buddha who arrived from *India,* having preached previously at Gaya and Benares. He planted his foot on Adam's peak, and after having published his tenets throughout the island, returned to India: he made two subsequent visits. *The period of Gautama's advent in Ceylon was probably about ten centuries B. C.;* he landed near Kandy, and was chiefly occupied in suppressing the Naga or *snake worship,* the aboriginal religion of Ceylon. The Puranas call the first inhabitants of Ceylon demons.

They apply the epithets *asuras, nagas, yachshas, rackshas,* to all tribes not of Hindu descent. "The turbulent and uncivilized state of Ceylon at Gautama's first visit is represented by a severe contest with the demons and nagas, most probably the *indigenous* and *savage* tribes of the island, who were worshippers of devils and serpents—the most ancient and most lasting of all the heathen superstitions." Even in the present day Kappuism or devil worship prevails extensively in Ceylon, and part of it has been incorporated into the Buddhist system there. The insular situation of Ceylon rendered it favourable as a retreat for the persecuted Buddhists, when driven from India. Upham, who has thrown much light on the condition of Buddhism in Ceylon, states, "vast numbers of Buddhists emigrated to the fine and fertile island of Ceylon from India after ages of sanguinary wars; protected by its position the fugitives there found security; they carried hither their arts and preserved with their sacred books the faith of which they formed the depository, and Buddhism seems to have struck deep root and to have flourished ever since in its insular retreat." Ceylon having been in the 6th century the emporium for the trade between China and the Arabian Gulph, and also having maintained extensive commercial relations with India, must have afforded great facilities for Buddhist emigrations. Fa Hian embarked for Ceylon from *Tamluk,* A. D. 412. *Tamluk then carried on great traffic both by sea and land.* The Mahavanso mentions that B. C. 157 a great number of Buddhist priests were sent from *Allahabad* to take part in laying the foundation stone of the great temple or thupa in the city of Anuradhpur in Ceylon; on the same occasion great numbers of Buddhist priests were also sent from *Benares,* and *Ougein.* B. C. 306, Mahindo, the son of Asoko, king of *Bahar,* was sent on a religious embassy to Ceylon by his father: he converted the King Dewanunpityatisso, who caused many monasteries to be founded in Ceylon: several members of his family were ordained priests: his prime minister built a college there.

After the close of the third great Buddhist convocation B. C. 309, held at Palibothra, in the reign of Asoko, a *dispersion of Buddhist missionaries* took place to foreign countries for the purpose of propagating their faith. Bijaya went from Bahar and settled in Ceylon, where he became King. When Fa Hian visited Ceylon A. D. 412, he saw a magnificent temple at Anuradhpur, which was ornamented with gold and silver, in laying the foundation of which B. C. 157, thousands of Buddhist priests assisted, *who came from Rajgriha,*

Ougein, Oude, Kashmir. Near it he saw a very large monastery in which were five thousand ecclesiastics, and which had been erected 87 B. C., in it was an image of Buddha, twenty-three feet high, of blue jasper, and set in precious stones; he mentions the introduction into Ceylon from Magadh of a branch of Sakya's tree, the Ficus Indica or banyan. The tooth of Buddha was seen by him in a temple: it had been obtained from the King of Kalinga or Orissa A. D. 275 by Mahasen, King of Ceylon; *this relic is now in the possession of the English.* The King and inhabitants of Ceylon were Buddhists in Fa Hian's time: he spent two years in Ceylon, and obtained several books there, written in the Fan or Pali language. The ruins of cities, temples and mausoleums, and the immense lakes for facilitating irrigation, bear witness to the former state of splendour that existed in Ceylon under Buddhist sway. The mountains of Ceylon have the finest Buddhist temples of the East, and its priests the highest character for their knowledge of the truths of pure Buddhism. The remains of former grandeur are to be seen in enormous blocks of stone and columns of marble as well as in inscriptions. On the *discrepancy between the Buddhism of Ceylon in some points and that of Nepal,* Upham remarks, " The metaphysics and cosmogony of the doctrine which the Singhalese received from Gautama, are as much in accordance with the Buddhism of Nepal as a system of ethics, founded on prescriptive doctrine and rules applicable to the relations of society, can agree with dogmas appealing only to the perceptions of the philosopher, and approachable alone by such subtle and intricate ratiocinations as few minds are able successfully to unravel and follow out to their extreme results."

BETWEEN THE DEKKAN OR SOUTH OF INDIA AND CEYLON a considerable amount of intercourse, political, religious and commercial, seems to have subsisted formerly. Geological data would lead us to conclude that Ceylon was at one period united with India; the Pamban Channel is very shallow and the shores on both sides correspond in their strata. The *Rajavali,* one of the historical books of Ceylon, translated by Upham under the patronage of Sir A. Johnstone, states that Ceylon was anciently joined to India and that there was no strait between. The *Ratnacari* another historical work, mentions that there was considerable intercourse between Ceylon and Malabar, that the Kings of Malabar often invaded Ceylon and destroyed the temples, and that the king of Kalinga i. e. the northern Circars, had a tooth of Buddha, which he restored to the king of Ceylon. In the 7th century A. D. Buddhist priests went from Ceylon to hold a discussion with Vasaka the prime minister of the Pandion king. According to Professor Wilson, " The Jain faith was

introduced into the Peninsula about the seventh century of the
Christian era ; its course South was stopped at an early period,
but it extended itself through the centre and in the West of
the Peninsula, and enjoyed some consideration in the tenth
and eleventh centuries ; it was mainly instrumental in its outset
to the declension of the Buddhas, and in the twelfth century the
joint attack of Saivas and Vaishnavas put a final term to its
career and enforced its decline.   There are still however many
Jain establishments in the Dekkan and the religion is not without numerous and affluent votaries.   The Buddhas according
to tradition came to the Peninsula only in the third century
after Christianity." Buddhism probably was introduced into the
Dekkan chiefly from Ceylon, with which it maintained a close
connection : the Rajavali however mentions that the Ceylon monarchy was founded by Vijaya B. C. 633, who came
from Kalinga, was of a royal family and brought with him
many persons from Madura ; *he became a convert to Buddhism.*   Remusat states that the Malabars conquered Ceylon,
B. C. 24 : In the tenth century of the Christian era, the natives
from the Dekkan multiplied so much in Ceylon, as to overthrow the power of the Ceylonese and to gain the ascendency
in the Government.   The oldest traditions however shew that
the *Southern part of the Dekkan was first colonised by a Hindu
race.* Ram's expedition to Ceylon was connected with the spread
of Hinduism : he brought Brahmans from the North of India
and civilized Kerala, i. e. Malabar.   Pandya, who went from
Oude, founded the Pandion Kingdom four centuries B. C.,
which in former days extended along the Malabar Coast, and
continued in a flourishing state until the 12th century A. D.
    THE DEKKAN OWES ITS RELIGION AS WELL AS CIVILIZA-
TION CHIEFLY TO BAHAR ; the country about the Kavery
river was cleared and cultivated *by settlers from Oude.*
Ram is said to have built the temple of Rameswar, which
drew numbers of pilgrims from the North of India, who
settled there and *first cultivated the country :* among them
was Pandion, who built the city of Madura.   The city of
Trinchinopoly was built by a colonist from Oude, named
Chola, *who gave his name to the Coromandel Coast* which is properly Cholomandal, i. e. the district of Chola. Agastya, the first
person who composed a Tamul grammar, came from North India,
and led the Brahmans across the Vindhya Mountains into the
Dekkan : he settled in the Dekkan, became " the father of Tamul
grammar and medicine," and introduced letters and religion
among the tribes of Dravira.   The Mackenzie MSS. lead us
to conclude that civilization was introduced into the Dekkan

from the North of India. Wilson writes, " All the traditions and records of the Peninsula recognise in every part of it a period when the natives were not Hindus, and that prior to the *introduction of civilization from the North* the inhabitants of the Peninsula were foresters and mountaineers or goblins and demons." Kumari, a goddess, the wife of Shiva, gave her name to Cape Comorin and was worshipped in the Dekkan at the commencement of the Christian era. The Tamul language began to emerge from its rude state in consequence of the intercourse maintained with North India ; the language of the mountaineers of Rajmahal abounds in terms common to the Telegu and Tamul. Places of note, mountains, temples have *Sanskrit* names ; *all the traditions of the Dekkan acknowledge an immigration of Brahmans from the North of India* ; the Tamul books are chiefly translations from the Sanskrit ; there was little Tamul literature before the introduction of the Sanskrit, and Tamul was the only literature cultivated in the Dekkan for a considerable period : the Telinga was reduced to fixed rules by the Brahmans : the Canarese language borrows largely from the Sanskrit.

BUDDHISM EXISTED IN THE DEKKAN BEFORE BRAHMANISM ; according to Sykes and Taylor the first inhabitants resembled the aborigines of other parts of India in religion and manners ; the Mackenzie MSS. show that the greater part of the Sanskrit inscriptions found there are not earlier than the 11th century, A. D. Buddhism was violently persecuted and the most cruel tortures were resorted to by the Shivites ; its overthrow was effected according to Mr. Chambers between *the 9th and 12th centuries, A. D.* Remusat shows from Fa Hian's travels " that Buddhism had penetrated into the Dekkan at a very remote period :" we find that Amara Singha, the author of the Amara Kosha, the best Sanskrit Vocabulary, and one of the nine gems at the Court of Vikramaditya, was a Buddhist. Nagardhuna, a celebrated Buddhist writer and preacher, the inventor of a Buddhist philosophical system, is said to have lived in Berar twelve centuries B. C. Dr. Buchanan in his " Journey through Mysore, Canara and Malabar" makes mention of numerous Buddhist and Jain remains scattered all over the country. The ruins of a magnificent Buddhist chaitya have been found at Amravati in Berar. The numerous cave temples of the Dekkan are chiefly Buddhist : those at Karli and Junir have Buddhist inscriptions in the Pali of the date of two centuries and a half B. C. Colonel Sykes, in analysing the ancient inscriptions, remarks " *that prior to the fourth century A. D. every inscription whatever is in the Pali language, and by*

L L

Buddhists; and subsequently to that period a rough Sanskrit makes its appearance, gradually refining into the polished Sanskrit of the tenth and eleventh centuries—affording ground for the presumption that the *Sanskrit gradually superseded and displaced the Pali.*" Much valuable information respecting the ancient state and religion of the Dekkan may be found in "Wilson's descriptive Catalogue of the Mackenzie MSS."

ORISSA, the Utkal of the Puranas, is also called Kalinga. Whether Buddhism spread to it from Central India or from Magadh or from the Dekkan is uncertain. No Brahmanical remains of ancient date are found in it. Mr. Stirling proves from the annals of Orissa that the temple of Jagarnath was not completed before 1198 A. D., that the temple of Shiva Bhobaneswar was finished A. D. 657, and the temple at Kanarak A. D. 1241. Colonel Sykes remarks that the Jagarnath worshipped in Orissa resembles closely the Buddha in the caves at Ellora, and that the temple of Jagarnath was probably founded *on the site of a great chaitya, or Buddhist temple, which contained Buddha's tooth;* this tooth was in 311 A. D. sent to Ceylon. *In the fourth and seventh centuries A. D. the princes of Orissa were Buddhists.* Hiuan Thsang, a Chinese Buddhist traveller, passed through it in the seventh century and saw several topes of Asoko; one of the eight great Buddhist chaityas was situated in Orissa. Turner states that Jagarnath is held in veneration by the Tibetans, who are Buddhists, and who make pilgrimages to his shrine and to Ganga Sagar; at his festival there is a *blending of all castes as if fragmentary remains of a period when caste did not exist:* thirty miles from Puri inland, the remains of a Jain establishment with numerous caverns cut in the rocks have been discovered and described by Colonel Mackenzie. At Udyagiri and Khandgiri caves in Cuttack, five miles west of Bhobaneswar, numerous Pali Buddhist inscriptions have been found of the date of three centuries B. C.; the caves are stated to have been excavated by Rajas of Kalinga. At Dhauli in Cuttack, a Pali Buddhist inscription of the date B. C. 330, has been found, mentioning Asoko or Pyadasi, the Greek King Antiochus, and one of the Ptolemies of Egypt: it contains local edicts, similar to those of Girnar in Gujarat, commanding the non-destruction of life. The Uriya language is chiefly of Sanskrit origin. Arrian and Ptolemy describe the coasts of Orissa as occupied by the Kirradœ, a savage race.

CENTRAL AND NORTH INDIA seem to have been the seats of Buddhism from a very remote period. Dr. Stevenson states that the universal tradition in the Mahratta country is, that

Brahmanism was introduced by Sankara Acharya into it in the 9th century. Todd shews the early advances made in civilization in Rajputana. Malcolm is of opinion that Buddhism existed in Central India nine centuries B. C. In *Western India* it has also prevailed for a long time; the specimens of architecture and sculpture taken from Somnath by Mahmud of Gizni in 1026 were of Buddhist origin; Fa Hian found in Scind Buddhists who had come from China; the caves of Western India, according to Mr. Erskine, who has investigated the subject very closely in the 3rd volume of the Bombay Transactions, indicate a Buddhist origin as the Cœnobite buildings are foreign to Brahmanical institutions; the caves of Kanari and Salsette offer the most genuine specimens to be found in India of Buddhist temple, caves and monasteries; of the caves at Ellora ten are Buddhist and nine Brahmanical; *the caves of Ajunta are Buddhist. The noblest remains of sacred architecture in western India are Buddhist or Jain;* the principal shrine of Buddha was at Dwaraka. " The number and magnitude of the caves in western India show that the wealth and power of established government and active power for years could only have produced them." The Jains were powerful in western India even in the tenth and eleventh centuries. *Cutch and Scind were Buddhist countries up to the seventh century A. D.:* Asoko built a stupa there: the Balabhi dynasty in Gujarat were Buddhists in the 2d century: the coins from Gujarat are chiefly Buddhist; the caves of Karli near Puna have Pali Buddhist inscriptions of the date 543 B. C. according to Dr. Wilson: the Ajunta caves have Pali Buddhist inscriptions of the date eight centuries A. D.; the inscriptions on the rock of Girnar on the coast of Gujarat are Pali Buddhist, of the date B. C. 325, mentioning Asoko; their chief object is to prohibit the slaughter of animals.

Wilson states that Buddhism did not enter CENTRAL INDIA—the Aryabhumi of Manu, until the 3rd century A. D.,—but modern discoveries overthrow this view and also show that Buddhism flourished from the sixth century B. C. to the sixth century A. D. on the banks of the Ganges and Jumna. *Ougein was eminent for its Buddhism in the third century A. D.;* it must therefore have taken root there a considerable time previously. The columns of Delhi and Allahabad bear Pali Buddhist inscriptions of the date 325 B. C.; Mount Abu and Rajputana are strewed with the remains of splendid Jain temples, as described by Todd in his " Annals of Rajasthan " *Kanau jin Fa Hian's time had a Buddhist tope:* the numerous coins and other Buddhist relics found there render it very probable that it was a

Buddhist town; Oude was Buddhist in Fa Hian's time : Allaha-bad in the seventh century had 100 *monasteries.* Benares, when visited by Hiuan Thsang, a Chinese traveller, in 638, had 30 *monasteries and* 3,000 *priests*, though Buddhism was then in a state of decay.   Fa Hian writes of Central India as "the seat of Buddhism for a number of centuries."   Fo preached in Kanauj, and towers were erected to his memory in the sur-rounding country.   The coins dug up at Ougein are supposed to be the most ancient coins in India, they have Buddhist emblems on them and Pali legends.

THE COUNTRIES TO THE NORTH OF INDIA have been long the strongholds of Buddhism.   Sakya Muni is said by some to have been born at Kapila near Oude.   In the countries to the east and north of the Indus, Buddhism was in a flourishing condition in the fourth century ; there *there were then* 1400 *monasteries:* as late as the seventh century Buddhism was the religion of the in-habitants, who maintained political relations with China.   Bud-dhism spread as far as *Kabul* and the neighbouring countries ten centuries B. C.   The introduction of the religion of Zoroaster into Bukhara however displaced Buddhism.   *It was in a palmy state in Affghanistan in the fourth century*, but was almost extinct in the seventh; the Scythians ruled Affghanistan from the second century B. C. until the third century A. D.; *they were Buddhists.*   Fa Hian found many Buddhist topes and temples near the Panjab, he crossed the Indus near Bukkur and all the surrounding country was then Buddhist.   He mentions, " all the kings of the different kingdoms to the east of the Jumna are firmly attached to the law of Buddha, and when they do honour to the ecclesiastics they take off their diadems.   They, and the princes of their families, and their officers, give them food with their own hands.   When this is done, a carpet is spread for the ecclesiastics, and they place themselves opposite."   Remusat points out the importance of Fa Hian's testimony, as shewing that *for a thousand years, from the sixth century B. C. nntil the fifth A. D., Buddhism had prevailed uninterruptedly in the very holiest places of Brahmanism, Oude, Mutra, Allahabad, Benares ; and that of the numerous coins and inscriptions found in India previous to the 5th century A. D. not one has any relation to Brahmanism.*   Fa Hian in his route from China through Tartary to Ceylon, with the exception of the deserts of Jessulmir and Bikanir, found *only* a Buddhist people and dynasty, with traditions of the *continuance* of the same state of things *for the preceding* 1000 *years.*

We proceed next to THE VALLEY OF NIPAL " once a lake." Hodgson has laid open its literature and that of Tibet to the gaze of the literati of Europe.   Two tides of emigration flowed to Nipal from Bahar; the one about the *second century A. D.* *composed of Buddhists flying from Brahmanical tyranny,* the other in the fourteenth century of Brahmans taking refuge from Moslem bigotry.   *The Buddhism of Nipal has been chiefly derived from Bahar;* Upham writes, "after ages of sanguinary wars Buddhism was finally expelled and routed from India, and its vanquished followers fled in all directions from their relentless persecutors the Hindu Brahmans, many taking refuge in Nipal and among the impervious recesses of the Himalaya mountains." The Nipal Buddhists attribute the destruction of a great portion of their literature to Sankara Acharya, who was a violent persecutor.   *The Nipal Buddhist writings are of India origin.* Hodgson states that, "the Buddhist works of Nipal were composed by the sages of Magadh, Kosalai, Oude, and Rajagriha, and were transferred to Nipal by Buddhist missionaries soon after their being composed."   The best of the Nipal Buddhist writings were composed in the *plains of India* before the dispersion of the Buddhists.   Tradition mentions that some of the earliest propagators of Buddhism in Nipal came to it *direct from India.*   Kashyap, Kanaka Muni, Sakya Sinha and many other Buddhists visited Nipal from India.   Sakya Sinha went with the Raja of Benares, 1350 bhikshus, and a crowd of peasantry on a pilgrimage from Oude to Nipal.   The *Bhutan* people, who are Buddhists, say their religion came from *Benares.*   In the opinion of Hodgson Buddhism was established in Nipal previous to the second century B. C.   Remusat thinks that the country between Nipal and the Jumna was the *birth place* of Buddhism,—it was the *chief scene* of Buddha's ministry.   Kapila, near the source of the Rapti, at the foot of the Nipal hills, was the birth place of one of the Buddhist patriarchs; but whether Nipal was peopled from China or from India is difficult to ascertain.   The Tao Zu, a Chinese sect, were seen by Fa Hian near the Nipal hills: they worshipped the relics of Buddha.   A. D. 428 and 466, ambassadors came from China to Kapila near Gorakpur.   The preponderance of arguments is perhaps in favour of the Indian origin of Nipal Buddhism—the Khas or Parbattia, the language of the Nipal mountaineers, an Indian Prakrit, spoken by the Garkhas, was introduced by colonies from India between the thirteenth and fifteenth centuries A. D.; four-fifths of it is Hindi; but the Nawar, or language of the valley of Nipal, is much like that of Tibet and the trans-Himalayan dialects; the character of the language however is Nagri.   The Brahman Newars who form the proportion of one-twentieth of the Newar population, say they came from *Tirhut* A. D. 1322, driven by the persecuting sword of the Mussalmans—*all the great Nipal writings are now composed in Sanskrit, which is the language of literature.* " The existing Buddha writings of Nipal are originally of Indian growth. The drawings of animals, implements, vehicles, dresses are alien to Nipal and proper to India." Inscriptions show the Indian origin of Nipal Buddhism and also the early existence of Buddhism on the borders of Nipal. The columns of Bettiah, Bakra and Radiah noticed by Mr. Hodgson, have precisely the same inscriptions with the Allahabad and Delhi columns : they are *Pali Buddhist* of the date 315 B. C., and mention Asoko: they were decyphered by Prinsep. Lauri, a village in Champaran near the Nipal tarai, has a pillar of Bhim Sing's, forty-one feet high: it is of Buddhist origin : a large city formerly stood in the neighbourhood of this pillar, some ruins of which have been found. In Fa Hian's time the Tarai jungle had *begun* to overwhelm the habitations of men. Fa Hian saw to the North of Gorakpur, a tower, built by a King of the country, and containing a relic of Buddha: near it were a monastery and ecclesiastics ; he describes the kingdom of Kapila, as " teeming with Buddhist monuments." Near Bettiah he saw numerous towers, columns and other monuments of Buddha. " In 1837, in confirmation of the locality being anciently devoted to Buddhism, Mr. Liston discovered in pergannah Sidowa, in the eastern division of Gorakpur, at a place called Kiusa, a colossal alto relievo figure of Buddha, surrounded by compartments in which were represented various actions of his life ; and in the neighbourhood were several heaps and mounds of rubbish, no doubt the remains of a Buddhist city." Bakra on the Gandak has a Buddhist pillar.

Colebrooke gives an account of Devapal Deva, who was a *Buddhist monarch and ruled over Bengal as well as Lassa and Bhutan ;* he successfully invaded Camboje, after traversing as a conqueror the Vindya range of mountains. Hodgson observes that " the Indian origin of Nipal Buddhism (whether it reached the valley direct or *via* Bhut or China) seems to be unquestionable from the fact, that all the great Sangata scriptures of Nipal are written in the Sanskrit language." He thinks that Nipal received some of the earliest propagators of Buddhism in the valley direct from India, but that the physiognomy, language, architecture and manners of the Newars shew that the greater part of them came to Nipal from the North. The Sambhu Purana records that a Buddhist teacher, Manjusri, led a colony - into Nipal from China, cleared Nipal of the *waters which then covered* it and erected the first

Buddhist temples. The primitive language was Chinese, which in the course of time became greatly altered in consequence of the emigration of people from Madhya Desa or Bahar. Dhermakar was a noted Chinese Prince of Nipal. Prachanda Deva, Rajah of Gaur, Kanaka Mani, Kashyapa, Sakya Singa are said at different periods to have made pilgrimages to Nipal with numerous trains of followers, the majority of whom remained behind and settled in the valley. Hodgson thinks—that Nipal Buddhism corresponds more with the original system than the Ceylonese does, inasmuch as the " written standard authorities of Buddhism in Magadha, in Kosala, in Rajagriha, in a word in the metropolis of Buddhism, were transferred directly and immediately to the proximate hills of Nipal," whereas the first book did not reach Ceylon until 300 years after the introduction of the creed,—that the medium for conveying Buddhist tenets to Nipal was the Sanskrit, which he thinks was used in North India and not the Pali—and that the Buddhist MSS. of Nipal are the only original treatises on Buddhism now extant and the only ones, through which we shall be enabled to elucidate the real nature of the religious doctrines of the Indo Chinese, Tibetans, and Mongolians.

TIBET differs in its Buddhist creed from Nipal in the following points,—*monastic* institutions are retained in Tibet, they have been abolished in Nipal; the Vajra Acharyas, however lead a conventual life—but they are married.—There is no *caste* in Tibet, but it exists *now* in Nipal, in a modified form, though formerly there was none—the Tibetan Buddhism retains less of the principle of *reserve*, it promulgates its faith by inscriptions and religious buildings, which exposure to the eyes of the vulgar would not be tolerated in Nipal. Georgi in his Alphabetum Tibetanum states that Buddhism was introduced into Tibet from China A. D. 60, but Sakya's Buddhism was not adopted until the seventh century; up to that time the doctrines of the Lao Tsen formed the faith of the people of Tibet. Remusat concurs in this view; other authors however consider Bahar as the source of Tibetan Buddhism. Landresse, in his very able introduction to the Foe Koue ki, gives the following opinion, " Between the seventh and tenth century A. D. the Tibetans left the limits of their country as conquerors, and carried on an almost uninterrupted war with China, and the rivers which flow from their valleys to the South East, affording them a passage to India; they extended their power so much in that direction as to give to the Bay of Bengal the name of the Tibetan sea. They formed then a powerful empire which included little Bukharia. At the commencement of this period of their glory Buddhism was introduced among them. Rejected at first by the mass of the nation, it finally gained the victory, and the Lamas assumed an authority, which increased progressively, until the period of the invasion of the Mongols, when it changed itself into a system of absolute power.   After that time they attempted no further conquests but those of proselytism, and the religion of which their country is become the centre, has perpetuated the influence that they had formerly acquired by their arms over the other Tartars. *Hindu missionaries were their first instructors.*" He is of opinion however that the Getae, who were Buddhists, and lived in the west of China, were dispersed on the ruin of their power, and sought refuge, partly in Tibet, and partly in other places, and that wherever they went they diffused their tenets.   Writers generally agree that *Buddhism was not established in Tibet until about the seventh century.*   The king of Tibet was married to a princess of China, who professed Buddhism.   Buddhism penetrated Central Asia a long time before it spread in Tibet, but the Tartar invasion gave it a shock and caused its followers to take refuge in Tibet.   Buddha is said when dying to have declared that his followers would be persecuted in India and would be obliged to fly to the high mountains of Tibet, which would become the residence of the true faith, from whence it would disperse itself among all people and through the world.   In A. D. 632, the king of Lassa sent his prime minister *to India* to study the doctrines of Buddhism; he built many temples and schools, and spent his life in propagating Buddhism; his wife was a native of India; he rendered Buddhism the dominant system; *civilization was introduced into Tibet from India;* the Tibetan alphabet is derived from the Indian.   The Kaligyur and Stangyur, the former of which consists of 100 vols., were written in Sanskrit about the ninth century, and give an account of the doctrines of Buddhism; an analysis of these works has been furnished by Professor Wilson.   Hodgson states, " *I have no doubt that Tibet is indebted for its literature to Buddha missionaries, and refugees from Hindustan.   These individuals carried with them and subsequently procured from India, many of the sacred and profane works of their sect, and as was their wont, they immediately began to instruct the people of Bhut in their own, that is, in the Sanskrit letters and language;* they subsequently translated all the Sanskrit works they had into the vernacular tongue of the country."

The *Newari, or language of Nipal* proper, bears a close affinity to the Tibetan language and is of trans-Himalayan origin.   "Bhutan literature is so widely diffused among the *humbler* classes of society as to reach persons covered with filth, and destitute of every one of these thousand luxuries which in our ideas precede the great luxury of books; printing is in general use; the invention of printing the Bhutiyas got from China, but the universal use they make of it is a merit of their own." Remusat founded the following conclusions on a close examination of the travels of Fa Hian—that at the beginning of the 5th century Buddhism was established in central Tartary to the west of the Great Desert; at Khotan and in all the parts North of the Himalaya where Fa Hian saw monasteries of religious persons —that Buddhism was then in a flourishing state in Kabul, and Kandahar,—and in all the states to the West of the Indus. In Affghanistan many Buddhist emblems and Pali inscriptions have been found on the coins. In A. D. 695, a Native of Khotan translated many Buddhist books from Sanskrit into Chinese. Buddhism flourished at Khotan before the Christian Era and was the religion of the country up to the period when the Mussalmans took all the cities of Little Bukharia. Fa Hian mentions that, in the country bordering on the lake Lob, the King was a Buddhist, and there were 400 priests who studied the books of India and the language of India. *Missionaries from Hindustan carried the doctrines of Buddhism to Khotan and communicated their literature to them:* Khotan was once a kind of metropolis of Buddhism and maintained *a close connexion with India.* We find that Buddhism exercised a considerable amount of influence even in Persia until the period of the Arab conquests. Fa Hian found the people of Khotan honouring the law of Buddha; he lodged in a monastery which contained 3000 ecclesiastics; he saw a procession of Buddhist priests with Buddhist images and a fine monastery near Khotan which took 80 years in building. The Chinese say that the people of Khotan are a *Hindu* colony. Buddhism was introduced among the Mongolians A. D. 1344. Concerning the Lao Tsen, or Doctors of Reason, whose tenets constituted the faith of the people of Tibet as late as the seventh century, Landresse remarks, "We cannot well deny the analogy which subsists between the Lao Tsen and those of the Buddhists, an analogy which extends to the very base of their doctrines as well as to the details of popular belief, and which could scarcely have sprung up in two countries independently of communication." This doctrine had extensive influence in China from the earliest times; mention is made of the followers of the Lao Tsen visiting Buddhist shrines near Gorakpur; they are not reckoned by the Buddhists in their list of heretics, but are called the followers of the mystic cross, which is a Buddhist emblem. Fa Hian states they came annually from all countries to adore Kasyapa, a Buddhist patriarch. Sykes is of opinion that documents show that 1400 years ago they were professors of a creed neither Buddhist nor Brahmanical, but referring to a remote antiquity, known both to India and China, and approximating rather to Buddhism than Brahmanism. The Lama of Tibet is a living representative of Buddha, a literal successor, or rather the same spirit, which according to the metempsychosis once animated the bodies of the Buddhist patriarchs in India, who, in the fifth century, emigrated into China and afterwards were continued in Tibet. The first Lama ruled in Tibet in the thirteenth century. The "Masters of the doctrine" were the hierarchs of Buddhism between the fifth and thirteenth century. Landresse terms Lamaism, "Buddhism reformed." When the first Romish Missionaries that entered Tibet saw the monasteries, processions, pilgrimages and festivals of the followers of the Lama, they thought that *Lamaism was a degenerate Christianity and a vestige of what the Nestorians had spread :* the same view was also taken by Thevenot, Renaudot and Georgi. Klaproth and Remusat however state that at the time the Buddhist patriarchs established themselves in Tibet, the neighbouring country of Tartary was filled with Nestorian Christians. Remusat remarks on the circumstances of pilgrims from India going to visit the Lama, " The credulous pilgrims departing from Benares to Ceylon, can climb the almost inaccessible mountains of Nipal, and delivering themselves to superstitious illusions, honour the person of the same Gautama, that their ancestors have banished from his native country, and that the succession of events has brought back by a thousand revolutions, to the place where the ancient mythology has placed his cradle."

In the fourth century A. D., according to the testimony of Chinese historians, Buddhism was predominant in *Tartary, Bactria, Khotan and Kashmir.* The lovely valley of KASHMIR, the Thessaly of India, once a lake, and said to have been drained by Kasyapa Muni, was in ancient times a stronghold of Buddhism. We cannot now enter on a discussion as to the origin of Buddhism in Kashmir, as it would involve the question of the *ancient religion of Central Asia.* The *Rajtarangini,* an historical work in Sanskrit, compiled A. D. 1148, first brought into notice by Abul Fazul, the learned minister of Akbar, analysed by Professor Wilson, and of which an excellent translation has lately been published with copious dissertations by Monsieur Troyer of Paris, throws a flood of light on the former condition of Buddhism in the regions bordering on the Hindu Kush. *The religious history of Kashmir deserves the deepest study of those interested in ascertaining the origin of Buddhism*—the Mahabharat mentions Kashmir as the residence of the Rishis of the north—the Himalaya mountains have been the scene of pilgrimages from the earliest times—Kashmir had religious relations with the Mongolians in the seventh century B. C.—in the eighth century A. D. an alliance was formed with Kashmir by the Chinese—in the time of Ptolemy, the geographer, the king of Kashmir held the Panjab in subjection—the Nagas or snake worshippers were the aborigines of Kashmir,—the land of Kashmir is considered holy by the Hindus—the Haravansa mentions that Gonard, king of Kashmir, was in alliance with Jarasanda king of Magadh and fought as his ally at the siege of Mathura—Kashmir was the native country of the Pandavas, who acted so conspicuous a part in the war of the Mahabharat—these and various other points show that the history of Kashmir is clearly identified with the history of religion in India. Fa Hian mentions that the country to the north of Kashmir was Buddhist; the king was a Buddhist, and there were 500 monasteries; there was a tower of Asoko's in Kashmir; during the reign of Asoko a Buddhist convocation was held in Kashmir; 1500 priests were present.

Dropping then any further consideration of the Buddhism of Kashmir, which seems to have been of an *ex-Indian* origin, though it derived much strength and system through the agency of missionaries from *Bahar*, we shall give a slight notice respecting THE DIFFUSION OF BUDDHISM TO CHINA AND THE EASTERN ARCHIPELAGO AND BURMA by means of the zeal of the Buddhists of Bahar, who entered on their system of propagandism about the third century B. C. sending out their missionaries to the Tibetans and Mongolians of the north, the Singhalese and Burmese of the South and the Chinese and Japanese of the East. The numerous monasteries scattered through the *Burman* empire shew the influence Buddhism exercises; in Rangoon alone there are 1500 priests. In the wars between the Burmese and Pegu, Buddhism was the common religion of both states; the *priests took no part in the dispute and were respected by both parties.* Pali is the sacred language of Burma. Major Moor in his Pantheon says, "in Ava, where Buddhism is orthodoxy, the idea is upheld that it was equally prevalent in the same form throughout India till about the second century before Christ, when the Brahmans are stated to have introduced themselves and their rites." The Burmese believe their religion was derived from Ceylon, from which it was brought to them via Arrakan. They derive their literature from Ceylon. Some authors state that the Burmese laws were introduced from Ceylon via Arrakan, others from Magadh via Arrakan.   Dr. Buchanan is of opinion that the Burmese received their religion and laws through the Mugs of Arrakan.   According to the Burmese tables of chronology the first Burmese King came from Magadh.   The opinion supported by the majority of writers is, that *Buddhism was introduced into Ava via Arrakan originally,* though it was afterwards recruited from Ceylon.   Tagung on the Irrawaddy was the ancient capital of Burma: the Burmese suppose it was founded by a Colony from Central India; Buddhist images with Pali inscriptions were found there in 1835.   Wilson shows that the topes of Central India are the same with the Dahgobs of Ava, Pegu and Ceylon.   Buddhagosa, who went from Ceylon to Burma B. C. 543, was a great propagator of Buddhism in Burma.   The Burmese state that 650 years after Buddha's death, a Brahman was deputed to Ceylon to copy works on the incarnation of Buddha.   In 1824 the King of Ava sent two learned men to Ceylon to procure the original books in which the Buddhist doctrines were recorded.

BUDDHISM WAS INTRODUCED INTO SIAM 529 B. C. according to Finlayson.   The traditions of Siam, Cambodia, Ava, Pegu, ascribe their civilization to *Ceylon.*   At different periods Buddhist Missions were sent from Siam to Ceylon to make enquiries on points of faith.   A. D. 1059 an embassy was sent from Ceylon to Siam to solicit pecuniary aid in order to re-establish the Buddhist dynasty in Ceylon, which had been overthrown by the Malabars: the aid was granted.   Siam was formerly famous for learning and political power.   The Siamese point to the trace of the steps of Buddha on the tops of one of their mountains.   *The country of Arrakan appears to have been the channel for transmitting Buddhist influences from Ceylon to Burma*—a communication was kept up, as in A. D. 1059 learned priests were sent to the Buddhist King of Ceylon by Anuradh, King of Arrakan.   Burnouf thinks that emigrants from India traversed the mountains of Sylhet, descended into Arrakan and from thence to Burma; in a cave near Islamabad an inscription has been found on a silver plate relating to the birth of Sakya.

Deguignes, in his "Histoire des Huns," shews that two centuries before the Christian era, the Chinese crossed the barrier of the Sandy Deserts on the West, and advanced their dominion as far as the Jaxartes and Oxus.   Remusat has proved that the Chinese traversed Asia long before the Europeans had doubled the Cape of Good Hope, and that two centuries prior to the Christian era they took an active part in the events and commerce of Western Asia, and formed political relations with those cities which extend from China through Tartary as far as Persia. The remaining members of the Sassanides, when driven from Persia by the arms of the Arabs, took refuge with the emperor of China. The zeal for proselytism led the Chinese very far from their own country. In the 6th century the sect of Lao Tsen, or the Doctors of Reason, were numerous in the regions to the west and south west of China as far as India. Georgi and Remusat mention that Ai, a Lao Tsen or Doctor of Reason, resided in the woods near Rajgriha at the time of Sakya's advent. The Lao Tsen sect were in India before the Chinese made their way to Hindustan and had influence in China from the earliest period. *They and the Buddhists were, in the opinion of Landresse, of the same religion* though differing in some points, " they are called followers of the mystic cross which is met with, initial and terminal, in so many descriptions of the Buddhist caves of India—and on so many of the Buddhist coins from all parts of India" B. C. 217. The first Buddhist Missionary Chelifang came from India, accompanied by eighteen fellow labourers, to spread his principles in China : he arrived at Chensi, which had been the seat of government of the first kings of China, and from which civilization was propagated through China. Two centuries later the Buddhists were in considerable numbers along the frontiers of China, and their doctrines were known, but not believed in China itself. A. D. 67 Mingti Emperor of China sent ambassadors to India to collect information respecting Buddhism and to take drawings of the temples and images ; they returned accompanied by two Buddhist priests. At this period Buddhism began to be professed publicly in the south of China. Before the close of the second century A. D. many Buddhist priests came from Bokhara, from the country of the Getæ and from India to China, where they founded religious establishments, in which they taught the languages of India and preached their doctrines. In the beginning of the 4th century A. D. Buddhism made the greatest progress in China, chiefly through the activity of Buddhist priests, who came from India and traversed the north and west of the empire. The wars which deprived the Chinese emperors of the western parts of their dominions, and divided them among petty princes of the Tartar and Tibetan race, proved almost fatal to Buddhism. At the close of the fourth century the sacred texts were found to be dispersed or mutilated, and the faith, wanting light and support, was almost extinct. Distressed at this state of things, Fa Hian, a Buddhist monk of Sian fou in China, accompanied by two priests, quitted China A.D. 399, traversed

Tartary and the mountains of Tibet and arrived in India, from whence he returned to China in 414,—having attained his object, the collecting Buddhist scriptures, in search of which he had travelled 36,000 miles by land and 6,000 by water, and had passed through thirty different kingdoms. Panjotolo the 27th Buddhist patriarch, was born in the East of India, the son of the king of Mawar.   He embarked on the Indian ocean, and went to China, where he died near Honan A. D. 495.   He said he went to China in order to extend the law and deliver men from their passions.   The 29th Buddhist patriarch was a native of China. Remusat, who gives an account of them, states that it is founded on accurate historical testimony, furnished by contemporaries.   *The departure to China of the Buddhists from the shores of Hindustan was the result of Brahmanical persecution and of the predominance of caste ; the immigration of the Buddhists to China and the rise of the Shivite system in India were contemporary events.*   In the years 428, 441, 455, 466, *embassies were sent from China to India.*   A. D. 642 the king of *Magadh* sent an embassy to China, and in 648 the emperor of China despatched one in return.   The first translation of Buddhist books into Chinese was made in 418 by a monk of Western India.   About A. D. 670 the emperor Kaotsoung sent an embassy to Patna. A. D. 650 Hiuanthsang, a Chinese Buddhist, who travelled through India, returned to China and has given a detailed account of his tour, which is analysed by Remusat : A. D. 964 the emperor of China sent 300 Buddhist priests into India to collect books and relics of Buddha.

FO IS CONSIDERED BY JONES, KLAPROTH AND REMUSAT TO BE THE SAME PERSON AS BUDDHA,—Fo being Buddha according to Chinese orthography.   The Chinese themselves refer to the country west of China as the birth-place of Fo.   Confucius told his followers that the most holy was to be found in the west. The Bonzes, Chinese priests, are Buddhists.   The Fan a dialect used by the Buddhists in China is similar to the Pali ; the books that came to China from the south are in the Fan language; those that came from the north are in Sanskrit, which renders it probable, that Buddhism was introduced into China from Ceylon as well as from India.   Chinese annals notice the immense influx of foreigners into China A. D. 527 and particularly from Ceylon.   Sir T. Raffles states that the 6th and 7th centuries are remarkable in the annals of the east for the surprising emigration of priests and people from the East bringing with them their idols.   Buddhism was introduced into Corea A. D. 530; from thence it was introduced into Japan.   The Indian form of Buddhism was brought into China only about the *commencement of the Christian era ;* but it is probable that the Tao Tsen, or doctors of reason, existed in China for a considerable period previously to Buddhists coming from India, and that they were a sect of Buddhists themselves. Chinese civilization came from Tartary and was in a very low state before the time of Confucius. Remusat has adduced very strong arguments to prove that the Chinese received from the west the Platonic dogma of reason, of a trinity, of the breath of harmony which unites spirit to matter—" The religion of China before Buddhism was monotheism."

IN THE EASTERN ARCHIPELAGO (as, according to Crawfurd, civilization has spread from west to east ;) it is probable that Buddhism is of Indian origin. Malacca maintained a close intercourse with Gujarat formerly: the Malays had frequent communications with Kalinga or the Northern Circars, whence much of their knowledge and literature was derived. The races in the Eastern Archipelago are fairer and more civilized as they approach the west. The island of JAVA is the most noted in the Archipelago for its ruins. Brambaban abounds with stupendous relics of Indian origin ; the vestiges of an extensive and splendid city are to be traced near it; prodigious monuments of the ancient Hindus appear in every direction. Dr. Tytler writes that the finest specimens of Buddhist statues in the world are to be met with in Java, that Boro Budho is the most magnificent relic of Buddhism remaining in any country—300 Buddhist images are there. The Javanese trace their origin to India with which they carried on trade in former times—most of the Buddhist temples there have been erected between the eleventh and fourteenth centuries: the most ancient coins of Java belong to the dynasty of the Buddhist kings, whose empire was at Mojopahit. Buddhist images are to be found in all the ruins of the island. Crawfurd states on this subject, " Hinduism in the form of genuine Buddhism flourished in Java from the middle of the thirteenth century of our time to that of the fourteenth, during which a considerable emigration from western India must have taken place ; from the middle of the fourteenth century to that of the fifteenth, no considerable body of emigrants arrived from India, and Buddhism languished in Java ; at the latter period a few emigrants arrived in India of the sect of Shiva and attempted to propagate their peculiar worship, but with every other description of Hindus were driven from the island by the triumph of the Mohammedan religion in the latter part of the fifteenth century. Buddhism was undoubtedly the prevailing religion of the ancient Javanese ; to Telinga the Javanese ascribe the origin of their Hinduism." Crawfurd is of opinion that as a commercial intercourse had subsisted between the Coromandel coast and Java from time immemorial, the Indian priests found by it a safe and easy conveyance,—that the emigration owed its origin probably to some political movement or religious persecution—that " the extensive influence of the Sanskrit language upon the Javanese is itself a prominent fact, which implies that the intercourse was of long continuance, and in fact we might safely believe that in the commercial intercourse with the Javanese, the beauty and fertility of the Indian islands, with the simplicity and credulity of their inhabitants would have brought to their shores a succession of adventurers and missionaries."

THE FIRST INTERCOURSE BETWEEN INDIA AND THE EASTERN ARCHIPELAGO began A. D. 63—180. This accords with the traditions of the Hindus respecting the dispersion of the Buddhists in the first and second centuries A. D. Crawfurd remarks on this, " it would be curious to trace the consequences of this emigration or dispersion ; it spread the worship of Buddha over the Indian islands, and contributed to civilise their inhabitants."   The trade of the Hindus extended in one direction to Arabia, until a religious schism induced them to undertake an enterprise to the Eastern Archipelago.   Bearing in mind the close affinity between the Sanskrit and Pali—though even Prinsep and the European orientalists for a long time thought the latter to be Sanskrit,—the references made by authors respecting the number of Sanskrit vocables incorporated in the languages of the Eastern Archipelago may apply to the Pali, " every language of the Eastern Archipalago will be found to have engrafted upon it a quantity of Sanskrit proportionate to the extent to which it has itself been cultivated."   Leyden thought the Javanese language was a corrupted dialect of the Sanskrit; the Kavi, a language of Java, is chiefly Sanskrit. *The Sanskrit language was spread through the Archipelago by Hindu missionaries who came from Telinga.*   The Javanese alphabet is confessedly formed on the principles of the Sanskrit. One-sixth of the Malay language is Sanskrit.   The people of Telinga introduced into Java their calendar, and eras, their zodiac and the names of the year. *From Java, civilization was propagated throughout the Archipelago*—but with the exception of a few mountaineers in the east end of Java and the people of Bali, the Hindu religion has been banished from every country of the Archipelago.   In Bali, the people are chiefly Shivites : Brahmanism was introduced about 400 years ago ; before that time Buddhism was the religion of the island.   Raffles remarks on it, " Bali is the only island of the eastern sea in which

Hinduism is the established and national religion of the country : the high spirit of enterprise which burst the bounds of the extensive confines of India, like the dove from the ark, rested its weary wing only for a while on Java, till driven from hence, it sought a refuge in Bali, where even among the rudest and most untutored of savages, it found an asylum."

The facts we have presented in this summary of Indian Buddhism, are supported by the testimony of scholars and eye witnesses of undoubted veracity : the rise and progress of Indian Buddhism can be traced out with as much accuracy as the history of any of the ancient systems of philosophy,—of course the judgment must often be exercised in separating fact from fables, poetic embellishment from reality.   Various lessons may be learned from the study of Buddhism,—the success that attended Buddhism was mainly owing to two causes—it resorted to *itinerant preaching* and *popular appeals* as means of diffusing its doctrines, " inscribing its most sacred texts (Sanskrit and Prakrit) on temple walls and pillars placed in *markets, high roads* and *cross roads.*"   Sakya and all the great apostles of Buddhism spent their time principally in *travelling* about diffusing their tenets.   By throwing open the priesthood to *all classes* and affording *scope* for talent, even in the *lowest* grades of life, to exert itself in its cause, it infused a spirit of the warmest zeal into the breasts of its votaries : it appealed to the *common sense* and judgment of the *mass :* " all the ancient inscriptions throughout India are in Pali, they are mostly for the instruction of the *people,* are addressed to the *people,* and must have been understood by the *people.*"   In opposition to Brahmanism, which inculcated the dogma of priestly mediators, it taught an " enthusiastic *self-reliance :*" it resorted to the *vernaculars* as the vehicles for its doctrines, instead of shrouding them within the veil of a learned language.   Buddhism is comparatively free from the endless mythologies and ontologies of Brahmanism, and its action upon Asiatic Society has probably exercised a less injurious influence.   Buddhism has been extinct for ages in Bahar, and the *Pali language, once in general use there, now unknown.*   The history of Buddhism shows in the clearest manner that the Hindus are not those *unchangeable* beings that some would represent them to be; it affords hope to the philanthropist as to the result of his plans, however discouraging may be the appearance of *present* prospects.

ART. II.—1. *The Cape of Good Hope Almanac and Annual Register for* 1845. *Compiled from the most authentic sources by B. J. Van de Sandt, Superintendent of the Government Printing Office. Cape Town,* 1845.

2. *The South African Commercial Advertiser,* 1835–45. *(Edited by J. Fairbairn.)*

THE CAPE.—There are not many of our readers, who will pause to ask, what Cape. To the Indian Resident, there is but one Cape, about which he concerns himself—the Cape of Good Hope—to some, a place to be " touched at" on the way to and from India—a pleasant, half-way house, as it were ;—to others, a sort of holiday-ground on which do congregate the servants of Government on sick furlough—the furthest point to which they are permitted to proceed, without incurring the penalty of a forfeiture of the greater part of their Indian allowances.

In either point of view the subject is one of some little interest—interest, indeed, sufficient to have warranted us in making it the text of an article, although it had possessed no other claim upon the attention of the Anglo-Indian public. But we hope, before we throw aside our pen, to be able to convince the reader, whether resident on one side of the Cape or the other, that it has further and more important claims to be considered in such a journal as this—that, as a *Colony,* it is entitled to far more extensive regard, than has hitherto been bestowed upon it by thinking men in the Eastern or the Western world.

The greater number of our Indian readers have, at some epoch or other of their lives, visited, or, in conventional language, " *touched at* "—the Cape of Good Hope. A considerable proportion of the home-ward bound and many of the outward-bound Indian ships, break in upon the monotony of their voyages, by putting in to this southern port, ere they turn their prows towards the place of their final destination. The voyage is thus protracted by some two or three weeks; but the advantages gained both by ship-owner and passenger, amply compensate, in most instances, for the detention. These vessels touch at the Cape, partly to convey passengers thither— the accommodation thus vacated being taken up by parties at the Cape, wishing to proceed to England or to India: partly, because the visit to the Cape, enables the vessel to proceed to sea, with a much smaller supply of water, live stock, cuddy stores, &c. than it is necessary to encumber the ship with when she makes the voyage direct from the English to the Indian port. Stock and stores are, for the most part, much cheaper at the Cape than in India or in England, and the risk of mortality among the former is of course diminished by thus dividing the voyage. The passenger finds his account, too, in the visit to the Cape. He may diminish the extent of his out-fit—repair any discovered omissions in it—and stretch his legs, to his own abundant contentment, for a week or so, on dry land.

And in truth we know no place, at which the sea-voyager,—weary of the constant monotony of the Ocean-view with which he has so long been surrounded, and impatient of the unceasing petty annoyances with which, under the most favorable circumstances, life on board-ship must ever be encompassed,—can more fully enjoy the delights of a temporary sojourn on *terra firma*—a brief period of quiescence after disturbance, of excitement after stagnation. The home-staying reader may start at the paradox; but few who have made the voyage between England and India will fail to recognise the truth which is embodied in this seeming contradiction. Life on board-ship is in reality a state of stagnation without rest—of perturbation without excitement. Of genuine repose there is none; and yet, in the midst of constant petty distractions there is, in truth, no excitement. A brief residence on shore, in the midst of the voyage, supplies both excitement and repose—pleasurable excitement after the wearisome monotony of board-ship life, and delightful repose after the unceasing noise and bustle and confusion—the endless small distractions and unavoidable publicity of daily life, in a floating boarding-house, where to escape from noise and to be at rest is a consummation not to be attained. After two months spent on board-ship, whether the time has galloped as " with a thief to the gallows," or stood still, as " with lawyers in the vacation;" whether it has been a season of actual pain or comparative enjoyment—of utter idleness or of profitable occupation—a week's residence on shore, be the resting place where it may, can scarcely be other than a period of enjoyment. It is possible, therefore, that passengers to and from India may carry away a more favorable impression of the delights of Cape Town and its environs, than a longer residence in the colony might confirm; and on this account it is not uncommon to hear such people, on these admitted grounds, qualify their expressions of approbation; but we are very much inclined to think that these qualifications, though the results of misgivings by no means unreasonable, are in reality somewhat unjust. Much of the enjoyment derivable from a visit to the Cape is to be laid to the account of the undeniable advantages possessed by the place itself; and there are many other advantages with which so brief a sojourn can not render the stranger familiar.   We would counsel such of our readers as have only seen the Cape, under these favorable circumstances, when the mind is apt to tinge everything with its own bright hues, not to take it for granted that the pleasurable emotions produced by surrounding objects were the offspring of nothing more real than the couleur de rose of the imagination—not to take it for granted that because they might have been, they must have been deceived into a too favorable estimate of their resting-place.   It is true that even muddy water may be relished in an arid desert ; but it is unjust to decide that the water, which appeared so pure and refreshing and still seems delicious in the restrospect, was nothing more than a muddy pool, because even that would have been a blessing under such circumstances.

With his shore-going toggery on—his blouse or rough shooting jacket thrown aside, and a bright Saxony frock coat donned in its stead, whilst his rude straw hat or blue cloth cap, which has covered his head on poop or quarter deck, gives place to a shining black beaver, and gloves of which during the last two months, his hands have been guiltless, perform in creaseless beauty, their appointed offices.   The passenger is all eagerness to escape over the side of the vessel.   For many days, speculation has been busy with conjectures as to the probable day and hour in which the ship will cast anchor in Table Bay ; bets have been made, lotteries have been drawn; and there has been, for topics of discourse are not very abundant on board-ship, an immense deal of discussion on this stirring subject with all the various incidentalities with which it is environed.   Land has been for some time in sight—at first it has been a moot point whether the dingy neutral-tint, undulating outline just above the horizon, in the direction where the shore ought to be,* is really land or only a cloud ; and certain it is that clouds are often much more like land and land much more like cloud than the actual thing which the appearance simulates.   To see land is a great matter, even though it, or something like it, be only visible through a telescope ; and every morning brings with it a fresh interest, for the land appears in a new aspect, or disappears altogether ; and so there are everywhere expressions of pleasure or mortification to be

* Passengers, by the way, often spy land just at the opposite point of the compass to that in which nature has planted and nautical men are wont to look out for it.   Ladies are very cunning in this respect.   They see land in the East—are quite certain of it—when it ought to lie in the west ; they see it, are quite positive and angry if contradicted, over the larboard quarter when, according to all modern geography, it ought to appear over the starboard bow.

interchanged, till at last the flat, cloud-girt summit of the table mount is distinctly visible; the rude peaks and jutting promontories of the bold high coast are to be clearly seen with the naked eye, and anon traces of human habitation are discernible, though at first in nothing more significant than a column of ascending smoke, blending itself with the light clouds which may be seen pouring down the sides of the many-colored, many-shadowed hills. Anon objects on shore become more prominently developed; houses are visible; and the masts of the shipping in Table Bay. Every one is on deck; all the glasses in the ship find employment; they who have never visited the Cape before ask questions, and those who have visited it, answer them; portmanteaus and carpet-bags are already stored, and money which has long lain idle, once again begins to discover the importance which is attached to it by mankind. Passenger-faces brighten up and do their best not to discredit the improved attire which sets them off. The stagnant pool is disturbed as by an angel's wing; and hearts flutter and lips smile, as they have not fluttered and smiled for months, whilst the vessel glides into Table Bay, takes up her position before the white cheerful-looking town, which lies at the foot of the huge Table mountain, and once more drops her anchor into the bed of the sea.

The passenger is all impatience to make his way over the side of the vessel; but is compelled to restrain his shore-going impulses, until the Port Captain has made his appearance on board, received assurances of a clean bill of health, and moved his boat from the gang-way. From this functionary the first news of the terrestrial world is received; the first question put to him generally is—" What ships have arrived?" " When did the *Prince of Wales* come in—when did she sail? Have you seen any thing of the *Hardwicke?*—Is the *Tudor* in yet?—Many people looking out for passages?" These are the interogatives which rapidly follow—put by the Captain of the ship, and responded to by the Captain of the Port. Soon other questions—the news from India or the news from England,[*] succeed each other in quick succession:—perhaps a newspaper or shipping list is ferreted out of the pocket of the visitor from shore. Every body wants to know something, if it be only whether the hotels are full—a matter of no small moment to those who are going on shore for a cruise and resolute to enjoy

---

[*] There is generally a month's or six-weeks' news from one point or the other to be picked up at the Cape—in spite of the steam communication between England and India. On one occasion, we believe, the Colony received English news viâ Bombay—but this was an extraordinary, we believe, a solitary instance.

it to the utmost.　It is something to see a new face, to hear a new voice—but in time all are satisfied; the Port Captain has done his duty and disappeared over the side of the vessel. The passenger is not slow in following him.　The bachelor goes off with his carpet-bag determined to find room or to make it.　The married man sets out unincumbered, on a voyage of discovery—eager to secure an asylum for his family at boarding-house or hotel, before he can venture to bring them on shore.　In less than an hour he has secured accomodation, ordered a dinner, and hired a carriage.　He has done much more than this.　Estimated by sensation and emotion, he has lived nearly a month on shore.　He has trodden, perhaps for the first time, another quarter of the globe.　He has looked upon a new race of men.　He has walked, with a more elastic step and more erect carriage than has characterised his movements, perhaps for many years,—through the streets of an apparently European continental town, located on a promontory of Africa.　He has seen hundreds of strange faces, English, Dutch, Hottentot, Indian, American— people from all quarters of the Globe.　He has admired the fine horses of the Cape, the stalwart oxen in the carts, the conical hats of the drivers, and the long whips warranted to reach the ears of the leading pair of a dozen-in-hand.　He has been wrapt in admiration at the sight of fresh healthy looking European ladies, walking briskly in the public streets.*　He has looked into several shop-windows; has perhaps made a few purchases; and the chances are that between the pier and the hotel, he has stumbled upon an old friend.　He has seen the once sallow cheek ruddy with health; the once wasted form swelling with flesh and muscle—he has paid, in his heart, a tribute to the glorious climate of the Cape, and built a castle—or rather should we say a farm-house, on the side of a hill, in one of the pastoral districts of the colony. His teeming fancy has carried him a long way into futurity; for a while he has forgotten England—he has forgotten India—he has forgotten his ship—almost has he forgotten his errand. But this obliviousness can not last long.　He has soon done what was required of him—has explored all the habitable portion of the George, and has vociferated *Waiter* a dozen times, in very wantonness—for the strangeness of the sound is delight to him.　There is scarcely anything it is possible to

---

* A very singular phœnomenon in the eyes of the old Indian.　A lady walking in the streets is a strange sight to him—one that has not been revealed to him for many a long year.

do, which he has not done, during the single hour of his first cruise on dry land.

And when he is comfortably settled on shore—oh! the strange joy of the week's holiday—the hotel is a very Paradise ; the dimensions of his sitting room, its height, its cheerfulness— the strange faces to be seen passing and repassing above the window blinds! Why what greater happiness can there be at such a time than to look out of the window—unless it be to walk out of the door? Yes ; the luxury of walking "right on end"—the extacy of unaccustomed freedom! To steer right on, without let or hindrance—no longer condemned, like a wild beast in a cage, to turn and return at the end of every ten yards. The very red dust which lies so thickly on the surface of the streets, and is, abstractedly considered, an abomination—inspires one with gratitude, for it is dry land ; and even, if it were not, the escaped prisoner would rather put his foot in a puddle than in a coil of ropes. Does one ever walk the streets with more elasticity of step—with more buoyancy of heart? It would take a great deal to discomfort a man at such a time as this. The invalid has left all his ailments behind him in his cabin. Inveterate dyspepsia stops on its way from the Pier, to eat mutton-pies at the pastry-cook's— chronic rheumatism bounds along the Heerengracht without the aid of a staff; whilst pale Consumption calls for the bill of fare with lungs which might be mistaken for a Stentor's. It is impossible to be in low spirits—to feel languid—to fatigue oneself even with exertion. There is so much to do, that one has no time to be poorly—scarcely time to think. The visitor's business is to do as much as he can, and to get rid of as much money as possible in a given time. The chances are that he is tolerably successful—at all events in the latter respect. It would be unreasonable, he thinks, to deny himself anything, when he is only on shore for a week, and two long months must elapse before he can throw away any more money. Enjoyment must not be sullied by any sordid thoughts of expense. Why then should he not spend his time in shopping and sightseeing? He buys a few things that he wants and a great many that he does not want. He orders a carriage-and-four, stows away a prog basket in a corner of the Britzka, and sets off with his party to Constantia or Camp Guys. There are no such drives as these in the world. The blue sky, the cheerful sun, the fresh air, the luxuriant greenery, the many-colored distant hills capped with light fleecy clouds—ay, even the Sea itself, *seen from land*—are so many joyous blessings. It is impossible not to be happy. He thinks that, throughout the wide world, there is not another such place as the Cape;—if it were only to gather the flowers, which grow wild in the jungles—to pick up the shells which cover the rock-girt coast. Here people suddenly discover a taste for rural pursuits, of which they had never suspected themselves, nor raised a suspicion in the breasts of their neighbours. They gather samples of heath and of gorgeous bulbous-rooted flowers—rave over simple flowrets, on which two months before they would not have bestowed a glance; and martyrs of science on a small scale, carry off on their fingers an incalculable number of the small spikelets, which cover the thick fleshy leaves of some of the huge cactuses, and so resent the injuries inflicted on them by that great foe of the vegetable world—man.

But time holds on its course, whether it brings to man sorrow or enjoyment, and even passengers on shore at the Cape are compelled to acknowledge the unerring certainty of the old man's footsteps. His ship is at last ready for sea—the sheep and poultry, and the supply of cape flour —the best in the known world—and the groceries and the baggage of the new passengers have been taken in, and the water is all on board. The passenger, therefore, must pack up his clean linen, call for his bill, and prepare with heavy heart to turn his face once more towards the quay. He has not in the least grown tired of the Cape; and he has yet something to see. He has tasted Constantia wine *at* Constantia; he has communed with Mr. Valette's Lions; he has botanized in Baron Indwick's garden; he has seen a horse with one eye, fixed like that of the Cyclops on its fore-head; he has risked his life on the edge of a precipice on the way to Camp ground, at the mercy of a team of four horses of whose dispositions he knows nothing; he has stuck in a quick-sand on the way to Simon's Town; he has eaten eggs and bacon at Farmer Peik's; he has bought ostrich feathers, and whips of rhinoceros hide, and carosses and porcupine-quills; he has sketched the Table Mountain and the adjoining hills in every possible position, and filled his sketch-book whilst emptying his purse.

And what of the happy man, who, at the end of his week on shore, enjoys the blissful satisfaction of knowing that—whilst his fellow-passengers are scrambling over the sides of the vessel, to plunge again into the depths of the old amalgam of abundant noise, scanty water, indigestible bread, and inclined plains,—to him it is permitted complacently to wish them a happy voyage and to order his dinner as usual at boarding house or hotel, without a nervous thought of the morrow? To him the Cape is something more than a place to be touched-at. To the Civilian, or the soldier, on sick-leave for two years from his Presidency, it is a Sanitarium, at which he is expected to shake off the maladies induced by exposure to the climate of India, by too much work, or by too much beer. The Government Gazettes teem with announcements that Mr. A., or Major B., or Captain C., are "permitted to proceed to the Cape for two years, for the benefit of their health." To a stranger these announcements would be somewhat incomprehensible. He would marvel, and not without reason, that, when England is—computing distance by time—much nearer to India than is the Cape of Good Hope, any one, requiring change of air and rest from his official duties, should prefer an African Colony to his own native land. A few words of explanation, however, will make the matter sufficiently clear to his understanding. The "Regulations" of the services, by which these things are governed, are framed, most innocently as regards intent, after a fashion peculiarly calculated to benefit the Cape Colony. An officer, able to obtain the necessary certificate, may proceed to the Cape for two years, retaining during the period of his absence, his full Indian pay and allowances. If he be on the staff, he is permitted still to hold his appointment; a temporary incumbent is nominated to "act" for him, and the absentee is allowed a moiety of the perquisites of office. The civilian too proceeds to the Cape under circumstances still more favorable; he retains his appointment and forfeits no more than a small fraction of the salary attached to it. Now the officer proceeding on medical certificate to England, *ipso facto*, vacates his appointment. He goes home on bare furlough allowance— the military officer drawing no more than the prescribed *pay* of his rank,* and the civilian nothing beyond the absentee allowance, to which he is entitled—and returns to India to seek anew for employment, which, in the case at least of the Military Officer, is rarely to be obtained, for years, beyond the limits of his own regiment. The inducements then to proceed to the Cape are manifest, and when it is added that medical certificates to visit the Cape are obtainable upon slighter pretexts, than are credentials enabling the invalid to proceed to England, it will no longer be matter of surprise that every Gazette dismisses one or more servants of the Company to Southern Africa in search of health. The Cape is a pleasant, salubrious place, at which a man may escape from the

* To render this intelligible to the European reader we must explain that an officer's "*pay*" is but a small portion of the salary he draws. The principal components of his income are called *allowances*, and are divided into *batta, tentage, house-rent, horse allowance, &c.* All these the officer forfeits when he sails for England.

scorching air and the pestiferous damps of India, without at once emerging into regions of ice and snow. It is possible even, that, *cæteris paribus*, many an old Indian would prefer the Cape, to Great Britain, as a dwelling place; but so long as the most important of all considerations—worldly interest—weighs so heavily in favor of the colony, we shall be sure to find a considerable portion of the accommodation of our passenger-ships taken up by the servants of Government proceeding to and returning from the Cape—sure to find in our Army Lists and Directories a greater number of " acting" appointments than the welfare of the public demands.

Whatever may be thought of the wisdom of the existing Furlough Regulations, it is undeniable that the Cape colony is greatly beholden to the framers of them. It has been computed that the annual expenditure of Indian officers at the Cape ranges between fifty and eighty thousand pounds. Even though the former sum be the maximum, the advantage to the colony from this influx of wealthy strangers is great; for the money thus expended is widely and often wisely distributed, and it is all clear gain to the colonists.* There is no doubt upon this point. So far as the Cape is concerned the existing regulations are truly beneficent, and we should be rejoiced to see them perpetuated. But it is no part of our system, theoretical or practical, to " rob Peter to pay Paul;" and anxious as we are for the advancement of the Cape Colony, and determined to do our best, conscientiously, to promote its interests, we do not wish to see it thrive at the expense of India. We must therefore look the present question boldly in the face; balance, with equal hand, conflicting interests; and fairly decide the case between them.

When it was first pretty well understood at the Cape, that India was on the eve of realising its splendid visions of a

---

* " Not to mention the advantage of having constantly in the bosom of our society so many educated and accomplished men, with their families and establishments, we have heard their annual expenditure here estimated at from *fifty* to *eighty* thousand pounds. Nor is this large sum wholly spent in supplying themselves with the necessaries or the luxuries of life. They contribute liberally to our charities and literary institutions, being in fact among the chief patrons and supporters of both."—*South African Commercial Advertiser, Nov.* 25. 1837.

We are happy to be able to add to this testimony in favour of our friends that of the Revd Mr. Shaw, who, in his *Memorials of South Africa*, observes, " This salubrity of the Cape climate attracts a great number of persons from India, who reside for a time in Cape Town or its vicinity, for the recovery of their health. It is calculated that those gentlemen benefit the colony to the annual amount of more than fifty thousand pounds The majority of invalids soon regain their strength in the use of air and exercise at the Cape and return with renewed vigour to their different appointments. Several of the visitors from India are gentlemen of decided piety, and both by their example and pecuniary influence make themselves extensively useful. "

regular steam communication with Great Britain, the Colonists began to take alarm. It appeared to them, and not unreasonably, that so soon as the Indian Presidencies were brought within a six weeks' journey from the shores of Great Britain, few men would undertake a voyage of two months to an African Colony, in search of health and relaxation. These expectations, we say, were not unreasonable in the abstract; but they were based upon a very imperfect acquaintance with the great propelling motive which had so long been stocking the Colony with decaying Indians. The arguments brought forward at the time, by the local press, in proof of the superior attractiveness and efficacy of the Cape were sufficiently sound in themselves, but viewed in connexion with the circumstances to which we have alluded, considerably wide of the mark : " It is admitted," says an ingenious writer in the *South African Commercial Advertiser*, " that what is called *seasoning*, or the ' removal of troops, for example, by stages, from one climate ' to another is injudicious, or at least useless—that soldiers ' removed in full health and vigor from Great Britain and ' set down at once on the burning plains of Hindustan, resist ' the climate as well, if not better, than men who have been ' seasoned at the Cape, or in the Mediterranean. Instead of ' being *acclimated* by such a process, their constitutions are ' softened, and let down as it were from their natural tone, and ' less able to rally and resist extremes, either of heat or cold, ' more especially of heat, if the atmosphere at the same time ' be charged with moisture, or infected with miasma. But ' the case is different with constitutions already broken down— ' the wheels shattered and the springs relaxed. Extremes to ' them are pernicious, whether it be of frost after fire or of ' fire after frost. An Anglo-Indian gasping for breath, in ' the thin, hot, unsatisfactory air of Calcutta or Madras, may ' for comfort, send his imagination to the 'frosty Caucasus'; ' but were his sickly frame transported thither, or even placed ' suddenly under the chilling winds and everlasting fogs of a *severe* ' *English* summer,—and there every summer to him would be ' severe,—he would soon acknowledge that congelation is no ' less intolerable than fusion—that death can wield the icicle ' as effectively as the fiery darts of the sun."

There is much of truth in all this. We believe that the climate of the Cape is peculiarly well adapted to the constitutions of Europeans weakened by long residence in India, or suffering under one of the many cruel diseases, which render life in that country a torment. It is, we believe, one of the finest climates in the world—equally pleasant and salubrious.

It is removed alike from the two extremes of heat and cold; and the plague of *damp*, so severely felt in India and in England, at the Cape is almost unknown. We are aware that in advancing these opinions, we have a high authority to contend against. Dr. James Johnson, whose work on the diseases of Tropical climates is in the hands of many Europeans in India, and ought to be in the hands of all, has given the Cape a worse character than in our estimation it deserves. "The Cape of Good Hope," says this eminent physician and agreeable writer, ' however well adapted to the refreshment of a crew after a ' long voyage, by its abundant supplies of animal and vegetable ' food, is by no means calculated, in regard to climate, for the ' recovery of hepatic or dysenteric individuals returning from ' the east. The daily atmospherical vicissitudes at this cele- ' brated promontory are very great indeed (25 or 30 degrees) ' and consequently injurious where the bowels are at all ' affected. I shall only mention one instance corroborative of ' this assertion. His Majesty's Ship *Albion* on her late return ' from India having touched at the Cape, sent a number of her ' people to the Hospital, afflicted with chronic bowel and liver ' complaints. By the time of her departure for England, how- ' ever, several of these had died, and all the others returned ' in a worse state than when they went on shore. This fact is ' worth attending to; and deserves to be kept in mind by the ' valetudinarian."

We always differ from Dr. Johnson with considerable reluc- tance. We esteem his authority so highly that we are wont to mistrust our own judgment when we find that our opi- nions are at variance with those of so able and experienced a writer. The men of the *Albion* may have died at the Cape, from other causes than an inherent badness of climate; and a solitary example proves nothing. In our own experience we have known many surprising cures of visceral disorders, the most grievous in character and degree,—the scrofulous form of dysentery among others—effected during a residence at the Cape, and that too, when the previous sea-voyage had rather aggravated, than diminished the original malady. That the daily atmospherical vicissitudes are considerable, as such, we readily admit. The fact is an unquestionable fact. But throughout the entire year the range of the thermometer is not very extensive, and whilst the heat is inconsiderable, when compared with that which scorches up the plains of India, the coldest weather to which the colony is exposed is not so severe- ly felt, by the Indian resident, as the cold seasons which he has left behind him in the east. The Cape would not so long have retained its character, as a santarium, if its salubrity had not been fully established by a long series of favourable results.

The most eminent physicians in India would not, year after year, send scores of patients to the Cape—nor would the Indian Government sanction the constant departure of their servants in this direction if the good effects of a residence in the Colony had not been evidenced in the most obvious and unmistakeable manner. Indeed, no homeward-bound passenger can touch, for a few days at the Cape, without perceiving with his own eyes, in the improved appearance of those, whom a few months before he had seen in India, sinking under the effects of its wasting climate, the strongest possible evidences of the salubrity of the Cape. We believe, that the air is not of a quality adapted to promote the recovery of consumptive patients. Though we have recently seen sufferers under this form of disease proceed confidently thither in search of health, we may, without being carried quite far enough to adopt Sir Francis Head's account of the properties of the Koch-brumnen of Wresbasden, that it "changes consumption into—death," recommend those who are afflicted with phthisis, not to bend their steps towards the Cape. We know no other disease, which demands a similar exception—no other disease, acute or chronic, which will not, if a fair trial be given to it, yield to the climate of the Cape. We make this condition, for many invalids, who have been suffering, for years, under obstinate chronic ailments are sometimes unreasonable enough to feel and to express disappointment—to return uncured to India, and to insist, all their lives, upon the absolute inefficacy of the Cape as a sanatarium, because a disease, which, for many years, has been eating into the constitution, has not been eradicated by the climate in a few months. That the fine air of the Cape can not literally work miracles, we admit: diseases of long standing never are cured in a short time. It is necessary, above all things, that the patient should not belie his name; he must really have patience. And in this view of the case, and this only, is it, that we may, in all candour, admit a question to be raised as to whether obstinate chronic complaints of long standing can be effectually cured by a residence of eighteen or twenty months at the Cape—the longest period, which the officer, absent on sick certificate, is permitted to spend in the colony. All the harrassing symptoms of his disorder may yield, within this time, to the revivifying influences of change of air and scene, the altered habits, the freedom from official care—the combination of mental indolence and physical activity, which generally characterise the holiday-life of the absentee; he will think himself restored to health, and he will enjoy, for a time, a delightful exemption from the pain and despondency of past years; but his constitution will, in all probability, not have had time to regain all that it has lost to raise itself to the standard from which it has slowly descended. It is not sufficient that the invalid should overcome the sensible part of his complaint, and then at once replace himself within the influence of all those deteriorating causes, the operation of which is certainly productive of disease, if there be not vigour of constitution sufficient to present a due amount of resistance. The cement must be allowed to become dry and indurated before the once broken vessel is again fit for use. The constitution must become settled. The exemption from all sensible disturbance of the system must be protracted, before the convalescent can safely expose himself again to the torrid blasts and reeking marsh-miasm of the sultry plains of Hindustan.

A large proportion of Indian invalids suffer under long-standing complaints—the neglected *sequelæ*, perhaps, of acute diseases. They have foolishly permitted their disorders to become almost parts of themselves. Avarice, or indolence, or a too sanguine temperament may have induced the sick man to hold on, until the periodical aggravations of his complaint have become so frequent, and his general prostration of strength and spirits so painful to endure, that he is almost weary of life. He has always clung to the belief that change of climate, which he can at any time obtain for himself, will fulfil all the requirements of his case; and when he at last betakes himself to a remedy, which ought to have been entered upon many years before, he is impatient and dissatisfied, restless and repining under protracted convalescence, and utterly forgetful of the fact that the period of recovery is generally in proportion to the age of the disease. Some of these impatient patients return to India before their leave has expired; others give the climate, to the utmost of their ability, a fair trial, and return greatly benefited by their sojourn at the Cape, but soon after their arrival in India, experience all the horrors of a relapse. In many instances, these relapses are the consequences of indiscretion. The invalid, on his return, allows himself indulgencies, which he would not, previous to his departure, have ventured upon, in his boldest moods. In this manner the sanative work of two years is often undone in a single day. But there are cases, we admit, in which, despite all precautions, the returned invalid is destined to a speedy relapse. But this in all probability indicates nothing more than that the invalid ought to have proceeded to the Cape at a much earlier stage of his disorder. He can not protract his time of suffering without also protracting the season of recovery. When a man has allowed his disorder to take such deep root in his constitution, the chances are that it is time for him to turn his back altogether upon the East, and to seek for the removal or mitigation of his sufferings in a continued residence beneath a milder sun. He has already been in India too long.

If a sojourn of nearly two years at the Cape is insufficient to enable the Indian invalid to resume his official duties at the expiration of his leave, it may be fairly assumed that a residence of equal duration in England would be equally inoperative. Our own opinion is, that, _cæteris paribus_, the climate of the Cape is more likely to produce the desired result than the climate of England; but we repeat that long-standing chronic disorders demand time for their removal, and the Regulations of the service limit absence on leave to the Cape to _two_ years, whilst it is permitted to the absentee, if necessary, to remain _five_ years in England. There are besides other considerations, of which in fair honest discussion, we ought not to lose sight. The advocates of the Colony have anticipated certain arguments, which are every where current, in support of the alleged advantages of a residence in the mother country. " _Native Air_," say they, " and the _scenes amidst which we were_ ' _young_ are indeed reviving recollections. They sooth and ' refresh whilst the hostile genius of stars, which knew not our ' birth shed malignant influence on our heads. But they are ' only recollections; or rather they are fancies merely spring- ' ing from regret, and nourished by a groundless hope. To ' him, who is no longer young, the scenes of infancy, the faces, ' the voices that charmed him when a boy, have perished for ' ever. They exist for other infants and other boys; they are ' visions vouchsafed to the soul but once, and for how short a ' space! To return to the regions where they are supposed to ' bloom, requires, to bear it without a bitter pang, a robust ' frame or an insensible heart. In maladies that involve de- ' spondency, as most diseases contracted from the climate of ' India do, he would be an unwise physician, who should pro- ' pose such an experiment."* This is sufficiently plausible; and to a certain extent, true. To revisit, after long absence on the shores of a strange and barbarous land, the scenes of our careless childhood—scenes, which have often risen up before us, in hours of sickness and solitude, disappointment

* _South African Commercial Advertiser._

and despondency, perhaps to charm with pleasant thoughts of by-gone happiness, perhaps to deepen the gloom of the present by contrasting it with the radiance of the past—is, we honestly admit, an experiment, which can not always be practically entered upon without suffering, in our heart of hearts, many a sharp pang of sorrow and regret. Happy is he who finds the old homestead—the old familiar faces, as he left them—happy is he who does not feel himself, in his native village, a stranger among strangers. But even this cup is not all bitterness; and if it were, it would be well to quaff it. It is well that the arid heart should be soothed and softened by such tender emotions as these. It is well that there should be something to break in upon the utter stagnation of feeling, which the isolated state of the Indian exile is but too well calculated to induce. The anguish of the hour is not too heavy a penalty to pay for the good it does us.

Admitting then that there is much to pain the heart, in a return to our "own old homes," after a protracted sojourn beneath an Indian sky—admitting, too, much more than the Cape Journalist calls upon us to admit—admitting that there is much, in the cold stateliness, the reserve, the suspicions of English Society, to repulse, to mortify, to dishearten the man who is accustomed to the greater openness and liberality of the east,—it must, in all fairness, be acknowledged that a residence in Europe has many compensating advantages, which the holder of the balance must suffer to weigh heavily on the other side. There is more amusement, more diversion for the mind to be derived from a residence in a country, overflowing with objects of interest, pregnant with historical associations, teeming with the treasures of science and art, presenting everywhere most cheering signs of the progress of civilization, than from a sojourn in a new country possessing no national institutions,—no monuments of antiquity—no rich store-houses of the produce of human genius—no wonderful evidences of the advancement of human science,—a country, whose resources, magnificent as is the promise of its youth, are as yet almost undeveloped. Now there is such benefit to be derived from *travelling* by the physical man—and at present we purposely confine ourselves to this branch of the subject—from a constant change of scene and climate—from the pleasant, but not too stimulating excitement, afforded by the constant succession of interesting objects presented to his senses—that we question whether there is any remedy so efficacious in diseases of long-standing—especially in those maladies, which, in the language of the Cape Convivialist, "involve despondency." Now, without undervaluing the benefits derivable from a mail coach journey to Graham's Town, or a rough ride from one district to another, claiming at every stage, the freely-granted hospitality of the resident farmers—many of them fine-hearted English gentlemen,—we must protest against the assumption that from such travelling—delightful though it be—the exhausted, enfeebled, hypochondriac Indian, can procure so certain an alleviation of his miseries, as from the circuit of his own island home—the country, which though often the last explored is the best worth exploring—or a tour through the continent of Europe. The constant succession of new objects presented to his senses effaces those painful impressions, which long familiarity with disease have stamped upon his mind, and which cling to him, from year to year, with fearful tenacity, so long as he is unable to emerge out of the old habits, the old localities with which they have so long been inseparably connected. There is a chain of morbid sympathies and associations to be broken asunder, before the morbid can hope to be restored to health ; and in order thoroughly to effect this disruption, it is necessary that the gentle excitement of frequent change should be kept up for some length of time—until, indeed, the hypochondriac has thoroughly shaken off the incubus, by which he has so long been painfully oppressed. Now a new country—however striking its natural advantages—does not possess those objects of attraction and interest, with which civilized Europe everywhere abounds. There is less to occupy the attention, less to fill the mind with a succession of gently exciting thoughts. Simple nature, however beautiful—however grand, does not suffice to fill the mind of the man, who has since the season of early youth, lived an artificial life, and who has never known what it is to derive pleasure from the contemplation of external nature. Fresh air, bright skies, active exercise, and fine scenery are, in many instances, wholly insufficient to emancipate the imprisoned spirit from the thraldom, which has so long possessed it. Art must come to the assistance of nature, for the natural man is lost in the artificial ; and we can only hope to effect a cure through the influence of those pleasurable sensations, which his previous habits and feelings have rendered him capable of receiving.

To the sufferer under the depressing affliction of a longstanding chronic disorder, we would recommend a visit to Europe—to be extended to four or five years, according to the length and severity of his previous sufferings ; and a considerable portion of the time to be consumed in travelling from one place to another. But where the disease is not of long-

r r

standing—where there is little more than atony resulting from acute disease, or where the object is to obtain temporary rest after long-continued and unbroken official labors in India, the invalid could scarcely betake himself to a better sanatarium than the Cape. The two years' absence allowed by the regulations of the service, will suffice to restore such patients to health and send them back, refreshed and re-invigorated, to follow their old avocations with new energy and new cheerfulness. This appears to us to be the *rationale* of the matter; but the truth is that the Cape advocates, in discussing the relative advantages of a visit to their colony and a visit to Europe, have lost sight, or written in ignorance of the circumstances, by which above all others, the present question is to be determined. It is not an abstract question of health alone— it is a question of rupees; and so long as the present Furlough regulations continue in force, the Cape Colony need not be under much apprehension that the progress of Steam-communication between India and Great Britain will draw away the wealth, which for many years the Cape Colony has derived from a never-failing supply of Indian invalidism. A Government servant, Civil or Military, as has already been shown, may visit the Cape for two years, retaining his especial appointment, during the time of his absence, and forfeiting but a very insignificant portion of his Indian allowances. Nor is this all; another very important consideration remains to be noticed. Whilst the officer proceeding to Europe on medical certificate feels that he is doing so to the detriment of his prospects, inasmuch as that the time spent at home is not calculated in his period of service, the one, who merely betakes himself to the Cape, enjoys his two years holidays, without any such drawback. The years spent on sick-leave at the Cape do not rise up against him reproachfully on a future day; they are not deducted from his time of service, when his title to the retiring pension comes to be determined. He is acknowledged by Government to have served at the Cape, whilst at home he would have been, as a servant of the Company, virtually defunct. These are important considerations, of which no man who visits the Cape on sick certificate, even for a moment, loses sight. So long as the present regulations are in force, that Colony need be under no apprehension that officers will cease to avail themselves of the privilege which such regulations accord.

Whether these regulations are worthy of a prolonged existence or whether they ought not immediately to be sentenced to death is another question—a question of no inconsiderable importance, but one which we are not called upon to discuss at any length in our present article. No one denies that they have ever been open to very serious objections ; and now that London has been brought nearer than the Cape to all the Presidencies of India, it is difficult to perceive even the shadow of a reason for the perpetuation of the present furlough-system. The services of absent officers are more available in England than at the Cape of Good Hope—a summons to return to India, in an emergency, can be more speedily presented, more promptly acted upon, when the absentee is within reach of the India-house, than when he is spending his furlough in an African or a more remote Australian Colony.* It is possible, we think, that before the present charter is much older, the Court of Directors will give their consent to a modification of the present system, allowing officers to proceed to England on more favourable terms than at present, and thus, we are afraid, realizing though after a different fashion the apprehensions which the Cape Colonists have so long entertained. We need not attempt to conceal the fact, that, if furloughs to Europe were granted to sick officers, on the same terms as they are now granted in favor of South Africa, a very large portion of the fifty or eighty thousand pounds now spent at the Cape will be diverted into other channels. The Colony must suffer by such a reform; but, being the advocates of no exclusive class interests, we can not allow any regret on this score to affect our judgment of the intrinsic propriety of the measure.†

We are hopeful, however, that before many years have elapsed the Cape Colony will derive something better from India than the annual thousands now spent by the flock of invalid visitors from the East. Where there is no especial object to be gained by a visit to England; where there are no family ties to renew—no peculiar train of morbid associations to be broken up, in the manner to which we have

---

* Officers Civil and Military are permitted to proceed to the Australian Colonies on the same advantageous terms as at the Cape. Many in the course of their time of absence, visit both settlements, and take the Mauritius in their way.

† We shall probably at no very distant period, have an opportunity of discussing more fully the subject of the furlough regulations in connexion with their influence on the prosperity of the country, as affected by the efficiency of the executive. We should be rejoiced to see the officer, civil or military, who has lost his health in the service of the Company, permitted to proceed both to England and the Colonies without any sacrifice of income, or any retardation of the long-looked for day, on which his claims to the retiring pension is to be acknowledged We believe that the well-being of the state, as well as of the individual would be promoted by such liberality ; but we can not add that we desire to see the perpetuation of that part of the system, which permits absent officers to retain their particular appointments ; a permission which we believe to be equally detrimental to the public and unjust to the " services'' at large.

already adverted; where the conditions to be fulfilled are
merely a withdrawal from the influence of the predisposing
causes of disease and the supervention of a season of rest and
relaxation after years of official labor,—the Cape will often be
preferred to England, as possessing a milder, a more salubrious,
a more exhilarating climate, and affording the means of living
in comfort—indeed in luxury—at far more reasonable cost, than
that for which he can purchase similar enjoyments at home.
Few visit the Cape, who do not on their return to India carry
with them pleasant recollections of their sojourn in the Colony,
and desire to return to the enjoyment of its bright skies and
genial weather. To men—especially to married men, whose
incomes are not very magnificent—the Cape offers a more
desirable because a more economical residence than England.
The necessaries of life are procurable at a rate, the lowness of
which would astonish the man habituated to the high price of
food in the over-taxed British Islands. Bread and meat of
the best quality are most encouragingly cheap. House-rent
in the town is moderate—in the delightful suburbs still more
moderate. Horses of an excellent breed are to be purchased
at an extremely low figure; and save in seasons of drought
(and such seasons are very rare) forage is plentiful and cheap.
Good servants are not procurable at the Cape, and every Indian
proceeding thither would do well to take with him two or
three good native servants. With these forming his household, he will be independent of colonial domestic servitude,
which it must be acknowledged is at present in a most miserable condition.

But it is not merely as a convenient resting-place, whereat to
spend a brief vacation after many years of toil beneath a tropical
sun, that we desire to recommend the Cape to the attention of
our Indian readers. When a man has worked himself out;
when he has lived long enough, perhaps, too long in India; when
the grey winter of life appears, by certain premonitory symptoms, to be not very far distant; and the pension, which renders the Indian services the finest services in the world, holds
out an inducement to him, weary and wasted, body and mind,
as he is, to seek for rest and relaxation, in a less exhausting
clime, we know no place under heaven, to which he could more
wisely take his shattered frame and drooping spirits. We have
already indicated those cases, in which we consider the Colony
would be insufficient to answer the required purpose; but,
these exceptions put aside, we honestly believe that every old
Indian officer, especially if he have a family, retiring on his
pension, or little beyond it, will end his days in far greater

happiness and comfort at the Cape, than his limited means could purchase for him in Europe.

The climate will be better suited to his constitution. More enjoyable in itself it will render him more capable of enjoyment, than he could ever hope to be beneath the drear and watery skies of England, wrapped in its dense yellow fogs or nipped by its cutting frosts. But a consideration, perhaps more important even than this remains yet to be noticed. There is no grievance more intolerable to the retired old Indian—nothing which more frequently makes him deplore his resolution, and exclaim bitterly against his folly in resolving to retire finally from the country in which his habits have been formed—than the cold formality, the stiff conventional decorum, the pride, the reserve, the suspicion, which characterise English society. He returns a stranger to his native land; he feels himself a stranger; and he is treated like a stranger. The manners of the people are even more freezing than the cold of his island home. The openness of his manners alarms his more formal brethren. Stiff bows, formal epistolary "*Sirs*," and an impenetrable incommunicativeness are given in exchange for the extended hands, the cordial "dears" and "my dears," and the general freedom from all mystery and restraint, which he has carried home with him from the East. He finds that in England it is the habit of almost every man to look askance at his neighbour; and that the openness, which he considers a virtue, is regarded as impertinent vulgarity. To use a not very elegant colloquialism, he "does not get on" at home; he is out of his proper element; and soon begins to sigh for the more genial society from which, in an evil hour, he has been induced, by illusive expectations, to withdraw himself. It is too late for him to put himself to school again in an academy of Etiquette; and the chances are, therefore, that he ends his days in isolation and discontent. Now at the Cape, he incurs the risk of no such disappointment as this. He finds in the Colony, society composed of the same elements, as in an Indian cantonment; he meets with old friends; he retains his old habits; he finds occupation in his garden, his daily rides, his visits to the Club, the reading room; there is no doubt of healthful recreation—of pleasurable excitement. Midway between England and India he is interested in the politics of both. Ships from both countries are constantly arriving, and every week sees an influx of passengers from the eastern or the western world, who can gossip with him of old friends and familiar scenes, and revive many pleasant remembrances and kindly thoughts of bygone years. This, and much more may be said in favor of the Cape, as a resting place—but there, some, who having enjoyed and profited by the opportunity of realising a little money in the East, are not dis-inclined to multiply their wealth, if they can see clearly the way to do it. There are children, perhaps, to be educated—to be provided for. English investments, however secure, are notoriously unprofitable. The retired Indian, therefore, naturally turns to some thriving Colony as the crucible, wherein with a little trouble he may turn his baser metal into gold. The thought is a happy thought; he does wisely and well.

And what if the Cape Colony should present itself as such a crucible. In this character do we desire to recommend it. We have shown what manner of place it is to be touched at by the Indian voyager, and to be dawdled at by the Indian invalid; let us now briefly consider it as a wide and valuable tract of country, under the Government of Great Britain—a Colony, which, though little appreciated in England and India, scarcely thought of in that character at all, is in truth a gem in the British Crown, which, albeit now dimmed by neglect, is worthy of more careful tending than many which are more highly esteemed and more vigilantly guarded.

The value of our possessions in Southern Africa has been hitherto thought to reside solely in their geographical position. It is necessary that England should hold the Cape, because she is the mistress of India. This is intelligible enough. "As a depot for the maintenance of a military force in India, the Cape is invaluable, and as a naval station it is still more important—" so wrote the Marquis of Wellesley, now nearly half a century ago. What he wrote is the truth in these days—but it is not the whole truth. The Cape can not only open her ports to the shipping, and furnish depots for the troops, but can send forth food and clothing of the best possible description to supply the wants of the people of Great Britain. She can do more than this. She offers a most advantageous asylum to the superabundant population of an over-taxed country, in which labor finds but a poor market, and corn demands a most exorbitant price. We feel that, in advancing this, we have some prejudices to contend against; for it is, and very naturally, almost inconceivable that thousands of emigrants should double the Cape in search of employment, at a distance only to be accomplished by a *five* months' voyage, when employment both for labor and for capital is to be found, under far more advantageous circumstances, at a more favored spot, to be reached by a two months' voyage from home.

The truth is that an immense amount of ignorance relative to the capacities of the Cape Colony almost universally prevails. It is as though knowledge on such a theme were not worth the trouble to be bestowed on obtaining it. A tract of country,—three sides of which are open to the sea, equalling Great Britain in extent, enjoying the advantages of an excellent climate and a luxurious soil,—lies under the charge of the British Government, on the great high-road between the western and the eastern worlds, at a distance which is ordinarily accomplished in seven or eight weeks.* This country is capable of producing, in any quantity, a great variety of important articles of consumption, all of the finest quality. It is often said that the Cape is not an exporting country ; and people ignorantly imagine that it is equal to nothing better than the supply of sour wines. They measure the capabilities of the Cape, in accordance with the estimate contained in that descriptive line of the late Thomas Hood's excellent *jeu d'esprit*

" Go to the *Cape, just capable of verjuice*—"

an estimate, which could not be much more soberly and serious-ly received into universal currency, if it had been promulgated on the authority of the most profound commercial statist in the world. The highly intelligent Editor of the *South-African Commercial Advertiser*, to whom the Colony is, on many accounts, greatly indebted, asked some emigrants, who touched at the Cape in 1837, on their way to the Australian Colonies, " why they preferred a voyage of twice the length—a perma-nent distance twice as great from their native land, to settling in a country in no respect inferior, and in many respects infinitely more promising than the settlements or wildernesses for which they were bound. " " They expressed surprise," continues this writer, " at the comparison implied in the question. One of ' them said bluntly, ' I never heard that the Cape was good ' for any thing from any body but yourself. What do you ' produce ? Will people leave England to grow Cape Wine ' at eight pence a gallon.' We then took up our parable ' and expounded to him the nature of our climate and soil and ' natural grasses, so well adapted to the constitutions of the ' best descriptions of sheep. We explained to him the great ' error that had been committed in filling our pastures with ' animals of this species that bear coarse hair instead of fine ' wool, while nearly all our labor and capital had been sunk ' in an attempt, under the most unfavorable circumstances, to ' rival the ancient wine-presses of Europe. Then we showed

---

* In 1837, the *True Briton* made the passage from Portsmouth to Table Bay in 48 days. Since this time, it has been made, we believe in a still shorter period, by the *Gloriana*, and one or two other ships.

' him how a better order of things had been commenced; how
' Biela and his compatriots in the West and Daniell and other
' men of sense in the East already exhibited flocks and fleeces
' not unworthy of their Spanish or Saxon origin: that
' some of the wools fetched from 1s. 6d. to 2s. a pound
' on the spot: that it was rapidly improving; and that the
' quantity exported had been *trebled* in four years—which was
' nearly true, for in 1830, we exported lbs. 33,407; in 1832,
' lbs. 83,257 and in 1833, lbs. 93,325, while the rate of increase
' in 1834-5-6 has been still higher"—" we spoke, moreover, of
' our wheat, the finest in the world, and to the production of
' which there, with us, is no limit, while the people of new
' South Wales have to import large quantities to feed their
' population. Of the excellence and abundance of our beef
' and mutton he was already satisfied by their flavor and their
' price; nor was he ignorant of our favorable position—by the
' side of the great highway between the eastern and the
' western hemispheres. When we had enlarged sufficiently on
' many things besides, and opened up to him the hopes and just
' expectations of the Colony, he very candidly said, " I never
' heard a word of this before: the Cape, as you describe it, is
' wholly unknown in England. What is the price of land
' here?" ' Land,' we replied, ' *on which you may in ten years rival*
' *the dt.ctor of Saxony, can be had in any quantity at from six*
' *pence to three shillings an acre.*"

It is to be lamented that there is not, in every village of
Great Britain, a person able and willing like the writer of the
above passages, to set forth, in a clear unmistakeable point of
view, truths which are so well worth knowing. That the Cape
is not an exporting country has long been generally believed.
Now the fact is that there is scarcely any natural product of
the animal and vegetable worlds which the Cape Colony might
not export, in a high state of perfection, and there are many
which it is *now* capable of exporting. Though for want of the
application of a due amount of labor and capital, they are not
yet fully developed, the resources of such a country are, indeed,
well nigh inexhaustible. The climate and the soil are
abundant sources of wealth if man will but stretch forth his
hand to receive the bounty which God vouchsafes to shower
into his lap. All that the Colony requires to prove its claim to
the high character, which we are bestowing upon it, is just what
the British islands possess in the greatest superabundance. It
requires labor—it requires capital. Whilst from one end of the
country to another, capitalists at home are seeking in vain for
investments and laboring men for work, the Cape languishes

for want of both, though the former may be doubled there in a few years, and the latter, in almost any department, may be supplied, at a rate of remuneration, which, with reference to the price of food in the Colony, may be considered highly encouraging. Wool and corn, both of the finest quality, may be produced to any extent. The chief difficulty, with which the colonists have to contend, resides in the absence of sufficient means for the conveyance of the produce, from the lands on which their corn has been grown, or their sheep have been reared, to the different sea-ports—an evil, which was long severely felt by the wine-growers—and this difficulty can not be surmounted without a large supply both of capital and of labor. The Colony, so blest in other respects, has no navigable rivers; and cultivators in the interior are therefore compelled to trust to land carriage alone for the conveyance of their goods from one part of the country to another. Thus the cost of every article is increased to an enormous extent, before it can be shipped at the nearest sea-port. It has been computed that wine in the course of transport from the Cape vineyard to the London market, incurs " travelling expenses" more than equal to the price of the wine, as purchased on the land which produced it. Wine is a heavy article, and labors, therefore, under greater disadvantages than wool ; but still the evil is felt severely even with regard to the latter staple, whilst it far more severely affects the interests of the corn-grower. When we know that British coal can be purchased in Cape Town, at almost as low a rate as in London, we can not be surprised to learn that at the former place American corn finds a ready market—the importer being able to undersell the proprietor of the indigenous grain, whose estates lie in the interior of the Colony, or, though not far remote from the sea-*coast*, at a long distance from any sea-*port*. Now, at present there are but four or five ports on the whole line of coast—indeed, as far as relates to commercial transactions, we might almost say that there are but three—Cape Town, (Table Bay) Port Elizabeth, and Port Beaufort. It is something to be able to say even as much as this ; for, a very few years ago, Cape Town monopolised all the trade of the Colony. The opening of the two Eastern Ports has conferred immense benefits upon the more remote districts, which are now enabled to ship their produce and to receive their supplies, at a much smaller expense for land carriage than they were formerly necessitated to incur. Port Elizabeth, indeed, is fast rivalling Cape Town in importance. It absorbs all the trade of the Eastern districts, including Albany, the

Q Q

most productive of all the divisions of the Colony. In the year ending January 5, 1844, the value of the Exports from Port Elizabeth was estimated at 1,10,952, whilst the Colonial produce exported from Cape Town did not exceed in value £1,54,297. Of the nature of these exports we shall presently speak more fully; but not until we have observed that private enterprise is now doing much to open new ports along the coast, and thus to abridge, as far as it is possible to do, the distance between the point of production and the point of exportation.*

Though bullocks and horses abound in the Colony, the roads are not as yet all that they ought to be; and though the farmer finds no difficulty in harnessing a yoke of strong oxen or a team of fine horses, and might contrive to overcome the impediment of bad roads, he looks about him in vain for men to drive his carts, to guard his produce, and to deliver it in safety. He has no superfluous hands to employ upon this work; there are no facilities for feeding the draught-cattle on the road;— and if these impediments did not exist the cost of conveyance by land to a distant port would press heavily upon him, or the consumer—or, as generally happens, on both. To obviate this difficulty some enterprising proprietors, whose estates lie at no great distance from the coast, have opened out ports of their own, and by employing or purchasing small coasting vessels have contrived considerably to lower the cost incurred prior to the ultimate debarkation of their produce.

We have no desire to exaggerate the natural advantages of the Cape. The zeal of the advocate, like vaulting ambition, often overleaps itself and falls on the other side. Men, not of

---

* We may quote, by way of illustration, a case with which we are familiar. The Klein River estate, which was the property of Major Parlby, formerly of the Bengal Artillery, but which has now passed into the hands of Captain Standford, an officer in the Queen's Service, who like many of his brethren, since the Peace, has turned his sword into a plough-share, lies in the Swellendam district contiguous to the Sea coast. It embraces a large and thriving tract of country adapted both to agricultural and pastoral purposes; and the value of the property has lately been considerably enhanced by the enterprise of the present owner, who has opened a port in a convenient and secure spot, and thus, in a great measure, has continued to supercede the necessity of land-carriage for the conveyance of his produce to the principal market. This port lies about sixty miles to the eastward of Simon's Bay; and we have chiefly selected the present illustration out of several, which might have been adduced; because it very aptly exemplifies the immense saving which consumers may derive from the purchase of produce conveyed to them entirely by water-carriage from the place of production. Simon's Bay is the naval station and all the vessels are supplied, at very exorbitant rates, from Swellendam and other districts to the Eastward, *through Cape Town*, to which place the goods are conveyed by land and subsequently re-despatched to Simon's Town—the Cape Town dealers of course making their profits on each article. Now, it is very easy to perceive that the navy might be supplied direct from one of the nearest districts on the coast (land-carriage being almost entirely avoided) at one half of the cost, at which the supplies are furnished through Cape Town.

the obtusest order, are apt to mistrust the laudations of those, who pour them forth without stint or qualification. The Cape Colony has, it must be acknowledged, never suffered, like its brethren of the Australian islands, from the reaction in the public mind, which is sure to follow the fastidious enthusiasm engendered by the indiscreet fervor of interested panegyrists. We hope that it will never suffer from such indiscretion, and should be the last ourselves to plant the blow.

There is no occasion in the present instance to overleap the boundaries of truth. No man, not utterly wanting in reason, will expect to find in any one spot, the natural advantages possessed by all the places of the earth. A perfect Colony is not to be looked for on this side of Utopia. The question to be decided is not, where shall we find *all* natural advantages, but, where shall we find the most. Now, judging by results, it would appear that, of all the Colonial dependencies of Great Britain, the Cape is considered to possess the fewest natural advantages. Let us take, even at some hazard of repetition, a comprehensive survey of the real state of the case. As regards *position*, the Cape is more remote from England than British North America. But its distance from the mother country is one half of that which lies between Great Britain and the Australian Colonies. It is situated, moreover, on the high-road to the Eastern worlds—half-way to India, half-way to Australia. The *climate* is highly salubrious. Contagious diseases are almost unknown; and there is nothing in the atmosphere injurious to the European constitution. The severe winters of the Canadas and the distressing arid heat of the Australian Colonies are alike unknown. It may be questioned whether there is a finer or more enjoyable climate in the world. The *soil* is by nature eminently productive. The finest fruits and the most beautiful flowers vegetate in profusest luxuriance. If nothing beyond production were required the Cape might become the granary of the civilized world. The corn grown in the Colony is the finest which has ever been produced in any quarter of the globe; whilst immense tracts of pasturage supply fodder to multitudinous flocks and herds, which furnish fleeces equal to any in the world, and provender for exportation, not inferior to any that Europe has supplied to her armies and navies. *Water*, though not so plentiful as in the Canadas, and, if we may believe its recent panegyrists, in New Zealand, is far more abundant than in the Australian colonies. Droughts are few and far between. There are heavy falls of rain during the winter season, and occasional down-falls at all seasons of the year. In many parts of the country, there are ever-living

springs, whilst but few spots are to be found in which water
may not be procured by digging for it. Were labor more
plentiful, the quantity of water would be sufficient for all pastoral and agricultural purposes. At present, the difficulty consists in turning the available supply to the best account. *Navigable rivers* there are none—a serious deficiency, we admit—and
one for which no remedy can be found. It is *the* deficiency of
the Colony, but one so over-balanced by the many advantages we
have detailed, that it is only to be regarded, as the one necessary
ingredient, the want of which mars the perfection of the whole.

We have thus, hazarding some repetition, briefly considered
the advantages of the Cape Colony, according to the admitted
standard by which colonial capabilities are to be determined.
We believe that in this recapitulation we have left no point of
importance unnoticed ; but it would be well to consider more
fully some of the matters, which we have thus summarily
touched upon, though we do not profess in this article, to do
more than to deal in a superficial way with such generalities,
as are likely to draw attention to the subject, and to induce men
to acquire for themselves more information than we can em-
body in a single paper. Of the *position* of the Cape, every one
with eyes to see, and faculties to comprehend, may satisfy himself
by opening out a map of the world. The voyage to the Cape,
as we have already said, is accomplished in seven or eight
weeks. Along the greater part of the track the perennial trade
winds are blowing. The passage is both safe and pleasant.
The finest vessels in the world, the East Indian passenger
ships, are constantly touching at the Cape. During the greater
part of the year the tall masts and capacious poops of these
splendid vessels enliven the harbour of Table Bay. In every
possible respect these Indiamen immeasurably surpass the
clumsy, ill-furnished craft, which sail for the Australian Colonies.
There must be then, something in these far-off lands, far more
attractive than anything presented by the South African Colony, to have induced so many emigrants year after year, to double
the Cape and the distance to be passed over, in incommodious,
ill-supplied, over-crowded vessels at a greater cost of money as
of patience. The last writer on the Australian Colonies,* whose
work has fallen into our hands, descants with much feeling, on
the misery of the voyage out, especially after the first moiety
of it had been accomplished. "Such was our dilapidated condition," she observes, "that two or three old powder canisters

* Since this article was written, several works on the Australian colonies have
appeared ; but we have not been able to give them the consideration which they
demand.

' or preserve-jars formed the entire drinking equipage of the
' cabin table, when the last wine glass, long the innocent cause
' of direct jealousy, was lamentably broken." They manage
these things differently on board the fine Indian passenger ships.
We ourselves have a vivid recollection of a party of emigrants,
from the better classes—fine, well-dressed young men and
women—gentlemen and ladies, we had almost written—radiant
with health and cheerfulness, who landed from a clumsy looking
barque in Simon's Bay, one fine bright morning in July.   The
vessel was " bound for Sydney and was touching at the Cape "
to take in water and stock, and the passengers had come on
shore for a cruise.   In those days we were among the number
of thoughtless ones, who looked upon the Cape only as a place
to be " touched at, " else it might have occurred to ask
some of the party, what earthly motive could have induced
them to travel so far beyond the Cape, in search of colonial employment.   Our speculations travelled in a different direction.   We saw the party enter the *Clarence* Hotel,
and some hours afterwards, we saw them emerge from
it.   It grieves us to add, that when they attempted to ascend
the hill on the Cape Town road, they followed but a devious
course,—the ladies to the full as erratic as the gentlemen—and
that many of them gave up the attempt in despair, and came
to anchor against the parapet-wall, as the only means of preserving even an approach to perpendicularity.   We learnt
afterwards that the whole party had been starved on board ;
that a meal at *discretion* had been a thing denied to them during
the last two months ; and that the out-break at which we were
so much scandalised, was a reaction after the compulsory abste-
miousness of the miserable voyage from the Thames—or rather
we believe from the Clyde.*   They manage these things better in our India-men ; the passengers from which are eager,
on landing, to regale themselves with nothing less innocent
than a pot of fresh butter—a luxury, however, which Cape
Town can very rarely supply.

Of the *climate* we have already written so much that we
need make but scanty additions to what has appeared in an
earlier part of this article.   We believe that in this respect the
Cape excels all our Colonial possessions.   In the Canadas,
during more than half the year, the cold is intensely severe.

* We have here only spoken of the better class of emigrants   It would be difficult to draw a true picture of the miseries and discomfort endured by the lower orders of emigrants—of the profligacy often abounding among them ; the dirt, the
indecency, the sickness, which must attend life on board an emigrant ship where
hundreds—male and female—are sometimes stowed in the narrow space between
decks of an indifferent vessel of five or six hundred tons burthen.

In the Australian Colonies, during three-fourths of the year, the heat is intolerable. A recent writer—one too of the most enthusiastic as well as the most intelligent of the advocates of the Canadian settlements—speaks of the "five months of summer's sun" and the "seven months reign of ice and snow which succeeds."* "I have heard," says Mrs. Meredith, "persons, who have lived for years in India, say, that they found the climate of Sydney by far the most oppressive; and I partly account for this by the better adaptation of Indian habitations to the heat, and their various contrivances for relief, which English people, choosing to build English houses in an un-English climate, never dream of providing. The only cool arrangement generally adopted is the substitution of an oil cloth or matting, for a carpet on sitting-room floors." And again the same writer observes, in another place, "After all my own grumblings at the climate of Sydney, which my impaired health and languid frame proved to be not without reason, I must give its *two months* of winter unqualified laudation, for then, existence is no longer a burthen, nor walking exercise absolutely unpleasant." We leave it to residents both in India and in England to determine whether either of these climates are enjoyable. Now at the Cape, neither heat nor cold, are experienced in an extreme degree. In the month of January, it is probable that the emigrant from the British Islands will be sensible of a more elevated temperature than he has ever experienced at home; but in many parts of Europe the heat is far more oppressive than at the Cape even in the hottest of the summer months. The editor of the Cape of Good Hope Almanac—a valuable compendium of useful information relating to the Colony—says, that in the Stellenbosch Division the thermometer "seldom rises to 80 in the hottest season"—and in other divisions, the temperature is not much more elevated. It appears to us that looking at the entire range of the thermometer throughout the year, there is not one of our many colonial possessions, whose climate is better suited to the requirements of the European constitution, and assuredly no climate so well adapted to the peculiar physical condition of those, who have spent the best portion of their lives under the wasting influences of a tropical sun.

Of the fertility of the Cape *soil* no doubt can be entertained. We have only to look at the luxuriance of the natural produce, where the labor and art of man have not been employed in the

* Dr. Ralph, in *Simmond's Colonial Magazine*, a very useful and well conducted Journal.

developement of the resources of the country. The full extent of the productiveness of the soil, under the most favorable adventitious circumstances, has not as yet been ascertained; for where land is more abundant than labor, there is little inducement to force the soil into any unnatural state of fecundity. Occasional experiments, however, have been made upon the productiveness of the soil, and these have fully established the fact, that, when it becomes an object of importance with the cultivator to raise a large amount of produce upon a small tract of country, the soil can be rendered, by proper culture, as prolific, as any in the world. In some places, artificial irrigation has been successfully employed; and as it is the usual custom to alternate, as far as possible, tracts of pasturage and of cultivation, on every estate, there is an abundance of available manure supplied by the flocks and herds. The proprietor, in the present state of affairs, would not find his account in purchasing even at the original cost, the guano deposited on the rocky islands, lying along the coast. *That* is left to be carried off to a country, where, as land is scanty and population superabundant, it is necessary to make every acre do the duty of half-a-dozen.

The value of land in the colony is of course dependent upon its position. As we have already shown, there is no difficulty in raising produce; but produce beyond what can be consumed upon the spot is only of value so long as there are the means of exporting it for consumption in other places. The land, which lies contiguous to the coast is necessarily of the highest value, whilst equally, nay more productive tracts of land lying in remote districts,* are, for want of the means of transport, comparatively valueless. We have little doubt that as time advances, ports will be opened along the whole line of coast, and thus an immense impetus will be given to the colonial trade. The more remote districts, however, must still to a great extent depend upon land carriage, and we are, therefore, well pleased to perceive that the Cape Government have recently addressed themselves, with much energy and perseverance, to the good work of improving old roads and making new ones, throughout the colony—a boon indeed to landed proprietors, which it would be difficult too highly to estimate. If labor were more abundant in the colony, these works would progress more expeditiously;†

* Indeed, the land in the interior of the Colony is often in itself more valuable than that in the littoral districts, for it is better adapted to the growth of corn. The wheat raised near the coast is inferior to that produced in the more remote regions.
† Convicts, as well as free laborers, are employed on the roads—the former working without chains.

still, much has been done ; and we may point, with no little satisfaction to the opening of the road over Cradock's Kloof to
Mossel Bay, which affords every facility for the conveyance of
the produce of the George, the Beaufort, and the eastern part
of Swellendam districts, which, in consequence of this work, is
fast rising into importance.   It lies between Port Beaufort and
Port Elizabeth and is likely ere long to attract to itself its
proper share of the commerce of the eastern districts.   We
have already incidentally mentioned that the trade of this
part of the colony has, within the last few years, increased to
a most encouraging extent.   The import and export lists, especially the latter—tell their own stories most intelligibly.

The estimated amount of exports from the Colony, for the
year ending July 5, 1843, was £302,838 : for the year ending
July 5, 1844 £384,217—showing an increase of more than
£81,000—above 25 per cent. in a single year ; and we have
no doubt that the returns of the present year, which we
have not yet had an opportunity of seeing, are equally satisfactory.   The increase in the value of the single article of wool
exported in the year 1844, is estimated at £33,000 ; in the article of wine, nearly £20,000.   These are at present, the
principal staples of the Colony.   Next to these in importance
are grain, skins, fish, aloes, tallow, &c.   From Port Elizabeth
alone, during the last year of which the returns are before us,
wool was exported to the extent of nearly a million and a quarter
of (lbs.) pounds.   This wool, now shorn from the backs of a
fine breed of merinos, which have almost entirely superseded
the old heavy-tailed Cape sheep, is of the finest quality and
successfully competes with the best produce of other countries
in the London market.   The shipments of grain are very
limited, when considered with reference to the capabilities of
the country ; but the causes of this lie on the surface. Scarcity
of labor, deficiency of land carriage, and the great incubus
of the British corn-tax are quite sufficient to deter the farmer.
under the present condition of affairs, from risking much in
the attempt to carry his grain into extra-colonial markets.
A quantity of Cape flour is annually exported, sufficient to
supply the confectioners and biscuit-bakers of India, the Mauritius, and many, we believe, in Europe, who have learnt that
it is the finest and whitest in the world; and every vessel,
which touches at the Cape, carries off a supply, for its own
consumption !   The amount shipped at Cape Town, in the year
ending January 5, 1844, was a little under lbs. 7,50,000.   Of
the entire grain the quantity exported annually is insignifi-
cantly small.

In the very important matter of a supply of *water*, without which no Colony, whatever may be its other endowments, can possibly thrive, we have said that the Cape, if not bountifully, is sufficiently provided. In this respect it enjoys a most decided advantage over the Australian settlements. In the latter, severe droughts are often experienced, and an abundance of water is a blessing with which the settlers are seldom or never familiar, for more than a few days together. Mrs. Meredith, whose interesting " Sketches of New South Wales," we have already quoted more than once, gives us an amusing picture of certain water-hunting and water-catching exploits to which she was a party, during her visit to that Colony :—

" Our whole and sole dependence," she writes, " whilst at Homebush for a supply of water on the estate, consisted of two or three holes, like old clay-pits, which were about half filled during heavy rains, and as no shade was ever near them, very rapidly evaporated in warm weather. At these the cattle and horses drank, and we had a water cart to convey the daily supply to the house ; but in the heats of summer these water-holes were completely dry, and then our unfortunate cattle and horses were driven three or four miles to another clay-pit, where we also sent the cart, with, of course, the constant fear, lest, with so many claimants on its bounty, (for all our neighbours were in as ill a plight as ourselves) even that source should fail us too. Some of our friends were at the same time sending five and eight miles for water, and *such* water ! I did indeed then bethink me of the English meadow *ditches* and how luxurious a draught their fair bright streamlets would afford .... I would have all discontented grumblers in England, who growl alike at November fogs and April showers, and who always carry umbrellas by way of an implied reproach to the seasons of their native land—I would have all such sent to New South Wales on a probation system ; let them enjoy sunshine, since they like it so much ; let them really luxuriate in a veritably " dry atmosphere" for a few years, and then see if their hydrophobia will not wonderfully abate. When a winter rainy fit does assail the sky in this land of extremes, it as certainly takes care to have no doubt of its intentions—for down comes such a thorough right-earnest deluge as not only washes away half your garden, but generally inundates the house, parched and warped as every part is by the previous baking process of the summer months. We enjoyed two visitations of this kind at Homebush, each of about a week's duration, and giving us the heartfelt advantage of an unexpected shower bath in nearly every room. Every imaginable vessel was enlisted in the water-catching service ; the tide in the clay-pits rose several feet, and our spirits in proportion; but the old dry exhausting weather soon returned."

The writer then describes, with much animation, the opening of an old well, " which had long been bricked over," under a very vague hope that it might contain fresh water—a scene which perhaps Wilkie might have painted, had he witnessed it : " Every one so ardently wished it fresh, that very daring anticipations were formed of the effect, which the air might have on it, and various other possibilities; but the experience of a week, fully proved that our labor had been in vain." She then adds, in a foot note :—

"Some years since, Mr. Meredith and an old servant, being out together on some expedition, were seeking fresh water near the coast, for themselves and their horses, and after vainly trying the qualities of many small pools, Godbold dismounted to taste another; but instantly began spitting out the water again with a sad wry face. "Is *that* fresh?" enquired my husband. "Fresh to me, Sir, for I never tasted anything so bad before."

In another place, the same agreeable writer, speaking of the Bathurst province, says :—

"We found it still suffering severely from the devastating and ruinous consequences of the terrible droughts; every article of food was extremely dear and nothing good could be procured at any price. Meat was lean to starvation; and flour literally adulterated with various cheaper ingredients; vegetables there were none; butter and milk had long been but a name; and all horse corn, hay, &c. so extremely scarce and exorbitantly dear that the neighbouring families had for some time ceased to use their carriage horses, the poor animals not having strength to perform any work. The cost of a horse, at livery, was then one pound per night and it had recently been two pounds."*

These distressing droughts are any thing but unusual occurrence in New South wales and Van Dieman's Land : now at the Cape there are sometimes droughts—there was one at the commencement of the present year, but the effects were very different from those represented in the above passages. Fodder was said to be scarce; and the stable-keepers were compelled to raise their prices; but the highest rates, which we can find quoted, are those contained in an advertisement, which appeared in the Cape Town papers of April last, and of which the following is a portion :—

"N. B.—In consequence of the high price of forage, the rate of livery will in future be as follow, viz. :—

For a horse, per month	£ 3 15 0
Ditto, per night	„ 0 3 0
Baits	„ 0 2 0"

So it would appear that a drought in New South Wales raises the price of horse-keep to *two pounds* a night; and at the Cape, to—*three shillings.*

Severe droughts are indeed never experienced at the Cape; and it very rarely happens that a month passes without a fall of rain. In January, according to the Cape Town Almanac, which we look upon as a very reliable authority, "rains occasionally;" in February "now and then a gentle rain

---

* From the VII Vol. of Murray's "Colonial and Home Library"—an excellent miscellany, which we cordialy hope will meet with all the encouragement it deserves.

refreshes the earth ;" in March, " smart showers of rain may be expected ;" in April, there is no entry in the Almanac but we know, by personal experience, that there are frequent smart down-falls; in May, " rain may be expected;" in June, there are frequent showers;" in July, " copious rains fall;" in August, "much rain falls ;" in September, " frequent showers of rain may be expected ;" in October, " rain falls now and then ;" in November, " there falls but little rain ;" and in December, "light rains may be expected." The greatest quantity of rain falls in the winter months of July and August, and it is to this season that the agriculturist mainly looks for the sufficient irrigation of his lands. He is rarely disappointed ; and never would be, if sufficient prudence were displayed in the preservation of water, at times when it is procurable in abundance. In the Colesberg Division, where water was at one time very deficient in quantity, and the farmers were sometimes driven to wander into other districts, with their flocks and herds, in search of the indispensable element, there are now few, if any farms on which it has not been found feasible, by the construction of dams, to save a sufficiency of water for all agricultural and pastoral purposes throughout the entire year.

We have said that the Colony is without navigable rivers, for we can scarcely admit that the Knsÿna is an exception of sufficient consequence to be noted in our estimate of the advantages of the Cape, as a settlement. This river, which runs through the George district to the Eastern Coast beyond Mossel Bay is navigable, by vessels of no great magnitude—but only to a distance of some ten miles. As there is a good supply of fine timber on the banks of the river, advantage has been taken of the stream to convey the wood to the Cape Markets; and we gather from the Cape Almanac that the " late Mr. Rex built two vessels at the river Knÿsna, one of 142, and one of 80 tons burden, of colonial wood." The Orange River, the most important stream in the Colony, though presenting, when swollen by the rains, a magnificent sheet of water, in some parts more than half-a-mile in breadth, is rendered unfit for purposes of navigation by the rocks, which in many places impede the current, and " confine the stream to a channel, not more than fifty feet wide." When thus pent up, we are told, " it rushes along with prodigious impetuosity, leaping over the masses of rock with the noise of thunder and here and there forming cataracts, in which the wild is blended with all that is magnificent and beautiful in nature." We may mention that hopes have been, for some time, entertained, that it would be practicable to turn the course of this river southwards, in such a manner as to render the stream available for purposes of navigation and irrigation, to an extent which will have a most important effect upon that part of the Colony. The great Fish River, the course of which, with all its sinuosities, is computed at some four hundred miles in length, is at some seasons, a swollen, rapid, impassible stream; at others, its current is almost totally dried up. These are serious, admitted drawbacks; but to some extent at least they may be obviated, or mitigated by human labor and ingenuity; for where God has given water, (in many places inexhaustible under any influences of season) man can make the channel, and apply the useless stream to every purpose of agriculture and commerce. But, as we have more than once emphatically remarked, the Cape Colony languishes for want of labor and for want of capital; and until the British Government will supply the one and the British public the other, the resources of the finest country in the world must remain almost undeveloped.

On these two important points, we had purposed to descant at some length, but our article has already exceded the limits which we originally assigned to it. Colonial mismanagement is only another name for Tory Government, and it would be unreasonable to expect that the Cape of Good Hope, should be spared; whilst so many other Colonies have been sacrificed by the mixture of impetuosity and incapacity, which fills the Colonial Office. The present regulations are assuredly not calculated to favor emigration to the Cape. It is not sufficient to grant a certain sum for the payment of the passage-money of emigrants; there must be such regulations established as will afford mutual protection to the laborer and to the master. We can advance nothing against a system which gives the utmost possible protection to the laborer; but the protection must not be extended only to the laborer. Whilst one party is placed above, the other must not be subjected to the influence of hostile contingencies. Security ought not to be granted to one party at the expense of the other. Much mischief we know has arisen from the improvident system of supplying before the demand has been created, and causing a glut in the labor-market. It is well that emigrants should not proceed, on mere barren speculation, to strange countries, there to suffer, in ignorance and uncertainty, many positive privations and the wearying apprehension of still worse calamities. But, at the same time, if we should encourage proprietors to import labor into the Colony, we must not subject them to almost certain loss, by inducing them to lay out capital, without conferring on them any power, to secure a return for the outlay on the arrival of the laborers in the Colony—laborers, whom perhaps the proprietor has collected at considerable trouble and expense, brought down from a midland county to the seaport, supported for some time previous to embarkation and again upon arrival at the Colony, besides defraying numerous incidental expenses, amounting in the aggregate to a considerable sum. We know parties, who have lost large sums of money, under the operation of the present system, and have been greatly disheartened by the failure of their attempts to import, *for their own use*, labor from Great Britain.* The difficulty, however, is not an insuperable difficulty, and, as the state and prospects of our Colonies become better understood in England, it will surely be overcome. Of the present supply of indigenous labor we had purposed to say something, but the subject, as one involving a question, not to be cursorily discussed, (we allude to the charges frequently brought, by landed proprietors, against resident Missionaries, who are accused of exercising undue influence over the emancipated slaves and other African laborers, and by raising the price of labor and increasing the difficulty of obtaining it, impeding the progress of improvement in the Colony), we shall do well to set aside for future consideration.

We conclude this article with the expression of a hope, that at least some of our Indian readers will be induced by the statements it contains, to obtain for themselves further information on a subject of so much interest, and, having done this, to consider well, whether the Cape of Good Hope be not a desirable place, to which to remove with their families and such capital as they may possess, at the end of their period of Indian servitude. We believe that the Colony possesses many advantages —especially to the man of limited income—not possessed by over-taxed, over-stocked England; and that the old Indian, retiring to such a place, will find that he lives in the enjoyment of better health and greater happiness,—that his means are more ample, his opportunities greater, and the prospects of his children far better, than of those of his old associates, who, under similar circumstances, have betaken themselves to their native land.

* We say nothing or the subject of emigration from India, as it is one scarcely thought of at the Cape, for reasons which will at once suggest themselves to the majority of our readers.

Hindi, Hindustani, Braj Bhakha, Dekhani, Rekhtus, Urdu, by whichever of these various appellations it sounds most familiar to the ear, the common language of Hindustan, has a claim on the attention of every English resident in our Empire of the East. We may know nothing and care as little about the learned languages of orientalism: Sanskrit may be to us as a sealed book, and Arabic a cabalistic charm of which we desire not to possess the key; but Urdu, to give it its own genuine appellation, is mixed up with our daily and ever recurring avocations. Manifold as are the shades of this comprehensive language, the amount of each European's knowledge is more varied still. How different is the same language when spoken by the purist of Delhi or the connoisseur of Lucknow, in the mouth of the Bengali Mussulman or in that of the Benares Pandit, who rigidly abstains from the use of foreign terms, or from degrading, by the mixture of the conqueror's language, the pure and unsullied vernacular of his fathers! Again, how different is the standard of proficiency which our English in India attain! Some, like those whom the good Bishop Heber would fain have urged on to greater exertions, can just muster sufficient to order bread to be placed on the table: some, bringing their Arabic and Persian lore to bear on the study of Urdu, will argue with a learned and bigoted Mussulman on the most intricate questions of his faith; and others, though unacquainted with the purest and most polished form, from their situation and habits of intercourse with the natives, are adepts at the harsh rustic dialects, the " thenth Hindi", which is in use with a few incidental fluctuations in the out villages of a large part of Upper India. But, whatever be our partnership, we all at least have a one-anna share. Like French on the continent, it is to a certain extent the medium of communication in every part of the British dominions; and like French, we find the acquisition of a certain amount a matter of small difficulty, but the complete mastery over root and branch to be a struggle too hard for our powers. Still, from the day we landed, we have never failed to employ it as the medium of intercourse with our immediate dependants, or with those of a higher class who visit us on occasions of ceremony: we may lawfully reckon it as one added to our previous stock : perhaps it was the language into which the undistinguished sounds of our childhood finally resolved themselves, and not unfrequently we hear it faltered forth in lisping accents from the lips of our children, whose first crude perceptions, whose earliest recognition of the father and the mother are expressed in the dialect which they have so constantly heard from the mouths of their native attendants !*

It is our intention in the following pages to glance at the Urdu language and literature, such as they are at present. Of the latter indeed we have formed no very high opinion, nor can we hold out to our readers any confident hopes of pleasure or profit to be derived from the perusal of its rather limited number of prose and poetical works: but, viewing it as a language, we hope to extract much that is worth consideration, whether we take it in its oldest form and rake up the past for inferences regarding the actual condition of India, or whether we regard it as one of the vehicles for the civilization of the mass of our subjects, and indulge, as we lawfully may, when the seed has been sown, in lively anticipations of a future harvest.

An impenetrable darkness hangs over the earliest ages of India. The scanty accounts of the Greeks, the results of a few occasional conversations with men who were nothing more or less than the pandits of the day, and the volumes of Manu and of the Mahabharata form the only sources from which we can hope to derive any information as to the state of men and things for a considerable period before the Christian era. The historian of India has managed to extract from the pages of the Hindu Howel Dha, a tolerable account of the great frame-work of society: but the filling up of the skeleton—the colouring of the vast outline with the bright and glowing hues of reality, is a work from

* The old custom of leaving all English children to the exclusive care of native servants, and making no attempt to teach them their own tongue until they were sent home at the age of five or six, has almost passed off, we are happy to say, with other equally edifying Anglo-Indian customs; and the nurseries of Chowringhi may now be heard to resound with the hymns of Watts and Keble instead of the low *gali* learnt from the native bearer or Ayah.

which even the most ardent must turn away in despair. We could have wished to know for instance something more of the internal relations of India than we can make out from even the advanced state of things which Manu has depicted. Whether Sanskrit was used by one particular caste or castes on all occasions, or even by them only on matters of importance or ceremony: how lands were held and transferred: whether the king recognised the proprietary right of men who cleared and tilled the jungle at their own expense, or whether he laid his embargo upon the enterprising spirit of individuals, and required them invariably to acknowledge him as the Lord paramount of the soil: what terms were used to designate land tenures before the inruption of Persian phrases and their almost universal adoption in matters of contract and sale: what was the amount of crime and of vice: whether dacoity was not a profession as popular as that of highwaymen in England two centuries ago, and far exceeding the utmost returns of the present day: whether a golden age, or more properly a Satya Yug, was not as ideal in India as the same beautiful fiction among the poets of the West:—these are a few of the questions with which we now perplex ourselves in vain, and to answer which—if indeed they can ever be answered —we must wait till the stores of knowledge within our reach have been thoroughly digested and combined. We might, however, were but a little allowance given to hypothesis, pourtray to ourselves the early state of Hindustan before *the time of Mahmud of Ghuzni.* The inhabitant of the sea coast could pursue his petty trade and barter with those adventurous spirits, who, tempting the open sea, made their annual trip from the Eastern coasts of Arabia to those of Malabar and Ceylon. The inland peasant would wring from the encroachments of the jungle his two or three roods of fertile soil, and enjoy in his own village a government as simple as that of the patriarchs, but whose influence was as widely acknowledged over India as that of Roman jurisprudence over the face of modern Europe. But the time had now come when the undivided authority of the old priestcraft, which, with a foresight we cannot help admiring, had raised for itself an unyielding bulwark on the foundations of prejudice and pride, was to bend before the advance of a power on which both Asia and Europe had gazed with awe. The sovereign, whose proudest boast it was to be a breaker of idols, armed with all the bigotry of his creed and the fiery temper of his race, and animated by the spirit of a restless borderer, rushed down in a series of forays on the wide provinces of Upper India. The riches of

Somnat and the holy temples of Mathura were alike profaned by the invader's touch : the ringing tones of Affghanistan's mountaineers were heard to sound in the sanctuaries of Gujarat : the Mamluk of Turkey roved in the lordly halls of Canouj ; and the wild cries of the Tartar horse disturbed those sacred shades, where Krishna, in the true spirit of an eastern Apollo, once had loved to sport with the Gopis!

We can have no doubt that the introduction of foreign words began with Mahmud's invasion, and kept steadily on the increase until the times of Akbar and his successors. In the preface to the well known story of the Bagh-o-Bahar there is an account of the formation of the Urdu language, which bears on its surface every convincing mark of probability. It is, as far as we can recollect, the only attempt at a critical disquisition— one indeed uncongenial to the native—in the whole range of the literature. The author, after launching out into the praises of Gilchrist and the Marquis of Wellesley with something more than the usual ground for an Oriental laudatory address, gives us a history of the formation of his native tongue as handed down by tradition.

" The following is the account of the Urdu language which
' I have heard from the mouths of old men. The metropolis of
' Delhi, with Hindus, is of the date of the four ages. Its kings
' and subjects were established there from early times, and
' were in the habit of speaking their own vernacular tongue
' (Bhakha). But Mussulman dynasties have now endured for a
' thousand years: first came Mahmud of Ghuzni, and then the
' princes of Ghori and Lodi. As intercourse increased the lan-
' guages of the Hindu and the Mussulman became to a certain
' extent mixed. Last of all came Timur, in whose family the
' royal descent remains up to this day, and he took Hindustan.
' After his arrival the camp of the army was fixed in the city,
' and the bazar itself received the name of *Urdu*. After this,
' Humayun, when harassed by the Pathans, became a sojourner
' away from India. On his return he punished the Pasmand and
' Pathan races, so that no turbulent spirits were left to foment
' strife and rebellion. When Akbar came to sit on the throne
' various races from all four quarters, on hearing the kind
' patronage and bounty of that incomparable family, came and
' presented themselves before him ; but the language and dialect
' of each individual were different ; when they came to live,
' traffic, buy and sell amongst each other, one single language,
' termed Urdu, became definitively fixed."

Slender as this account is, we owe its compiler considerable thanks for having thus treasured up a few of the sayings which had dropped from the mouths of old men.   It would have been too much to expect that he should dilate on each successive change—should point out to us the periods of stagnation and of rapid flow, the returning eddy or the quick rolling tide, by all of which in their turn the language was brought to its present state.   The mind,—which treasures up with avidity the grand-father's tale or the reminiscences of the old crone, which delights to hear from the lips of faltering age the customs of eighty years back, or the tale handed down from a generation entirely removed,—is not often to be met with among the unen-quiring sons of Bengal.   There is a void left in the history of the days of the Nawabs which we would fain fill up—a blank in our own earliest periods of conquest which we are most desir-ous of seeing supplied.*   A few vague and cursory hints regard-ing the days of Clive, or the still nearer period of Hastings, are all that can be hoped for: and to rely on the answers of natives, who too often convey the information which they imagine is sought for, would be to push our enquiries beyond the limits of prudence.   Nor, again, is the Eastern writer often found to com-bine and digest his knowledge—to bring points apparently far removed to illustrate each other with clearness and precision—or, having once raised an hypothesis, to discuss it without extra-vagance in all its mutual bearings.   It is for this reason that the above sketch is doubly valuable, as the spontaneous effusion of a native on a subject not often broached by his countrymen, but yet one to which he had directed his utmost attention. Still, the twelve invasions of Mahmud, though remarkable as the starting point, were transitory and never at any time of a wide extent.   It remained for the houses of Ghori and Lodi, to follow up the successes of the hero of Ghuzni, and to work, in the slow and sure progress of two hundred years, some decided change in the old Brahmanical institutions.   But a darker crisis was now at hand: and a fiercer spirit shed his baneful influence over the scene.   A scourge more dreadful than Attila and Chengiz had collected his myriad tribes, and no Œtius was forthcom-ing to stay the approach of the torrent.   With an indifference

---

* Occasionally however a happy exception is to be found.   A most respectable native informs us that one of his Ryots, an old man, by name Ram Prasad Rai, is still living, *above the age of one hundred years*, in the village of Lohagachi, thannah Hantara, in the district of Nuddea, who was a child of ten or twelve years old when the nawab marched down with his army to meet Clive at Plassey.   The villagers, hearing that "the Tilingas had come" (by which term they designated soldiers of every description, as the first regiments had been raised in the Madras Territory) went out to see the sight ; and he himself, concealed in a tree, saw the whole of the 50,000 men defile a few days before the decisive battle.   The *sons* of this veteran are dead, but the *grandsons*, men of about sixty-five years old, are living—old, and decrepid— while this relic of a former age is hale and hearty and may be met with any day at the place indicated above.

to shed blood which finds a parallel only in Napoleon, Tamerlane rolled down on the devoted metropolis of India. His followers, almost as numerons as the host of Xerxes, exhibited all the varieties of dress and speech which are to be found from the icy stream of the Trtish or the snows of Siberia, to the large steppes of Transoxiana or the walls of Shiraz. The grim brood of winter, enthusiastic as the Carthaginian soldiery, rushed down on sunny climes almost as fair and fertile as those watered by the Po. Dark Bulgaria had sent her tribute to swell the conqueror's march. Circassia's handsome race were conspicuous amid the renowned Tartar hordes; and the rugged form of the Cossack was seen to couch his lance against the shrinking and graceful bodies of the fairest daughters of the East.

It is very true that these inundations, although resistless in their might, were of short duration. The huge waves bore down every thing before them, but, when they passed away, the desolated territory soon recovered its peaceful and smiling aspect. It would seem unlikely that such visitations should ever have produced any material changes in the language; but still, when we consider that the fourteenth century was undoubtedly the epoch at which the great change commenced, we can hardly decide how far such repeated blows may have made a lasting impression. We know not how long the terror inspired by the conqueror's invasion may have dwelt on the minds of the inhabitants, and whether many terms from the strange dialects, vividly imprinted by fear and surviving the feelings of hatred entertained by the actual sufferers, may not have been frequently used at the time of the visitation, and thence, by a natural consequence, have passed permanently into the language.

After this, the victory might be said to be won. The reigns of Humayun and Baber, though unsettled and crossed alternately by victory and defeat, by advance and flight, must have seen the Hindi changing gradually into the Urdu. But the glorious epoch of Akbar, which first saw a regular revenue system established, and indulgence and the free use of their religion granted to the Hindus, was without doubt the period of the consolidation of the language. The free and unrestrained intercourse, which prevailed under the Hindu Charlemagne between Pandit and Maulavi, believer and infidel: the frequent interchange of sentiments, the meetings not for strife and blows but for the bloodless controversy of words: the more than oriental magnificence which glowed in the splendid train of the Emperor, and attracted thousands to gaze on a spectacle so congenial:—all these causes combined to centre, in the circle of an Agra and a Delhi, a language whose influence is felt as widely as the French, and whose latent capabilities are but a little less vast than the English. It was however reserved for a successor, whose splendour is still attested by the new city of Delhi, the Jama Masjid, and the never forgotten Taj Mahal, to establish, in the fort of the metropolis on which he bestowed his own name, a perpetual fountain whence should flow the living waters of Urdu,—pure, rapid and unceasing. The native author quoted above, mentions the reign of Shah Jahan as that in which the language was finally consolidated: after that date we have but comparatively immaterial changes, until we come to the time when European sources began to mingle with those of the East. The slight modifications introduced by the English and other adventurers will be noticed hereafter. At present, having described the succession of the Mohammedan invasions and their gradual establishment throughout the land, we must return to give a short sketch of the kind of changes which they naturally introduced.

The Mussulman, confident in his divine mission and in the hope of dispensing to those who fell under his sway the spirit of a civilization more enlightened than any they had yet enjoyed, came resolved to force on the conquered his arts, his sciences, and his language. It is with the latter alone that we have to deal. But here an innate horror of change presented against some of the attempted innovations a front stubborn and impassive. The terms of refined art, the qualities of the mind, the ritual of judicial proceedings, and the more complicated relations of society were indeed quickly amalgamated with the older Hindi; but it was vain to attempt to change the denominations of those great natural objects, which, as they attract more readily, remain fixed in the mind more deeply than the artificial distinctions of a more advanced state of civilization. The Moslem could engraft his law on the Hindu, and substitute for the heavy artillery of Manu and his regulations, the lighter and more effective ornament of the Persian Ayin: he might fill up the scanty vocabulary of the old dialect, and enrich with an inundation, fertilizing as the showers of Asharha, the barrenness of the aboriginal tongue. But beyond this was a barrier which he could not pass. The Hindu of course retained all the peculiar terms of his worship and his recurring round of duties unchanged—though he might in the course of time not disdain to mingle in his conversation many phrases introduced by his masters. And the Mussulman, though avowedly bringing with him the sentences of the Koran to replace the dogmas of Hindu

Sages, when descending to the intercourse of common life, was compelled to give up some part of his boasted pretensions. The vanquished asserted their rights over the victor, and, as in the case of conquering Rome, the mighty were again enslaved by the weak. The four cardinal points of the compass, the seasons, the months, and divisions of time, thunder and lightning, rain, water, fire, quadrupeds and birds in all their manifold variety, refuse to be uttered in any language but the old Hindi by either Hindu or Mussulman.* Let any one recall the Urdu terms for the above objects and he will acknowledge at once the truth of our observation. But, besides these familiar ones, there are one or two others which while they have no connection with any Persian or Arabic source, are equally irreferable to the more ancient Sanskrit. If the *mandal* or head man of a village may draw his origin from a Sanskrit word, no such source can be pleaded for the *mriddha*. We should be obliged to any one who would give us any solution of the latter term, or suggest what was the peculiar duty of that functionary whose name still survives in many parts of India, although his occupation is indeed gone for ever. And what again, we may ask, is the origin of the word *Cutcherry*, or when more properly spelt, *Kacheri* ? It is in use, we believe, in the three Presidencies of India, and its derivation seems totally unknown. Can it be the designation of some Indian Wittenagemote, as old as the Flood; or a nickname applied to courts established by the conquering Brahman ? Was it the *slang* term by which the cultivator indicated the new institutions of Mussulman lawgivers, or the primeval and primitive seat of a judge whose office was the large village tree and whose canopy was the sky ?

It has been said, that,—although we may safely refer nine-tenths of the Hindi to more lengthy Sanskrit originals, and philologists, without forcing the belief of the readers into a strained acquiescence with some fancied resemblance, may lawfully proclaim the Hindi, when denuded of its Sanskrit auxiliaries, to be unworthy the name even of a dialect,—still, there is a tenth part, the origin of which it is totally impossible to account for, according to a fair and straight comparison of the two. We understand that a considerable similarity has been discovered between words purely Hindi and the languages of the Dekhan, on which Sanskrit was engrafted at a later period, but in whose formation it did not claim to be an original element. It seems therefore probable that in the very remote times antecedent to

* The hare and the fowl are generally expressed by the Persian. Horse, ass, dog, cat, jackal, bear, rhinoceros, elephant and many others are Hindi.

the Mahabharat, a race, represented by the fables of the satyrs of Bacchus, and the apes of Hanuman, roamed over the unreclaimed hill and jungle of India. These children of nature, who in all likelihood had little claim to be ranked with the articulate speaking men of Homer, must have possessed few ideas beyond the merest wants of existence; and in a country where fishing and a fruitful soil supplied those wants as soon as formed, man's thoughts and ideas moved in a very limited sphere. The migration of that people,—whose written and perhaps whose speaking language was Sanskrit, in date possibly but little subsequent to the call of Abraham,—found in the aborigines of Hindustan, a race well calculated to take the first impression presented. The old nomad tribes of Persia, where society naturally divides itself into a priestly, a warrior, and a workman class, sent forth their thousands in search of warmer climes and a more abundant soil. These natural subdivisions were preserved in the countries to which they migrated; and the three first classes, with a politic, though an ungenerous spirit, incorporated the wild inhabitants of India into their own republic, but gave them a station in society deprived of all the privileges which could render life a blessing, and barely redeemed from slavery by a few concessions extorted by fear or prudence or time. The degradation of the Sudra is unaccountable on any other hypothesis; and that class, whose descendants perhaps live in the Gonds and other wild tribes of the present day, fell naturally into the position spread out before them, and made up the fourth estate in the republic of Manu. Such as retreated before the rolling tide of invasion took refuge in the Dekhan,—the country designated by Manu as " the abode of demons and evil spirits, without Brahmans," and far removed from the happy land of Aryavartta, where the presence of the favoured race conferred a perpetual blessing. Such as remained could have had but a feeble defence against change in either manners or language. Their barren vocabulary, when joined to the overflowings of the great Sanskrit river,—the fragments, so to speak, of a banquet spread with the utmost prodigality,—became in a moderate space of time the simple and articulate Hindi. What fluctuations it may have undergone in the period of nearly two thousand years which elapsed from the Sanskrit invasion to the first race of Mahmud; whether its course was not as slow and stagnant as one of those lateral creeks in the Sunderbunds, where the flow of the tide from two opposite directions renders the waters almost as motionless as the sluggish waves of the dead sea;—it is vain even for a moment to inquire. We believe that, in accordance with the unchanging spirit of the oriental, and the experience of times on which some light has been thrown, the Hindi, which drew more upon Sanskrit, was in use at great cities like those of Ayodhya and Ujayni, while the more rustic dialect maintained its position in the out districts, or to use a modern term, in the Mofussil. But we must pass over these periods of almost chaotic darkness, and return once more to the Mahommedan invasion. An historian—whose fragments, though less than we might expect from one of erudition and natural powers capable of aspiring to the highest dignity of history, have still found their place in the permanent literature of our age—has compared, in his usual lucid style, the fusion of Persian into Hindi, with that of the old Norman French into Saxon. The words of Sir James Macintosh, though not himself an oriental scholar, are at all times well worthy of our attention :—

" Though the natural tendency of an unwritten language
' be to break down both into dialects and afterwards into dis-
' tinct tongues, yet it happens sometimes in peculiar circum-
' stances that languages originally different run into each other.
' At the opposite extremities of the earth, the Hindustani and
' Anglo Norman were formed out of jargons used in inter-
' course between the conquerors and the conquered. The
' victors have sometimes imposed their language on the
' vanquished with little mixture, as in some provinces of the
' Western Empire. In India, it now seems to be the prevalent
' opinion that the Brahmans, either by the influence of reli-
' gion and learning, or by the power of arms, have deeply
' tinctured with Sanskrit all the varieties of Indian lan-
' guage which had sprung from entirely unlike and in-
' dependent roots."

If we make allowance for the Recorder of Bombay's unacquaintance with any eastern tongue, and pardon the contemptuous term of " Jargon" which he has applied to the Persian and the Hindi, we shall find in several other respects that the parallel is an exceedingly just one. We may even go a step further and discuss it in several of its bearings. William the conqueror came, proud and yet politic, with a host of greedy followers to war against old cherished institutions and the fixed hate of a brave and hardy race. Mahmud and his successors left Ghuzni to encounter in the Rajput, whose veins were still glowing with the unmixed blood of the Kshatriya, an opponent as stubborn as the Cedrics and the Athelstanes. But the barrier, at first maintained by haughtiness on the one hand, and stubbornness on the other, melted gradually away before the daily intercourse of the two races; and the language of the conquerors, while it engrafted itself in both instances on a masculine and hardy stock, produced in the end an offspring which surpassed the original parent. For a certain time both retained their provinces separate and free from mixture. The Norman French had been long established as the language of chivalry,—the tongue with whose flowing accents minstrels loved to celebrate the prowess of the knight or the true love of the Lady. Persian sent forth its laws and its sciences,—its lays devoted to wine, and the dark haired daughters of the East,—its historical page commemorative of great and stirring events and of the unrivalled magnificence of the Lord of the world. But when the two met on common ground, the Saxon refused to give up his old denominations of freeman and slave, and the quaint divisions of the land of his fore-fathers now no longer his own; and the Hindu kept unswerving to his religious institutions, and his ancient appellation for objects of nature over which art had not yet extended her sceptre. *Churl, tything,* and *hyde* were sounds which no master could change, and which have remained on the lips of a nation until the times in which we live. The *Mandal* or the *Patel* would not yield to the Kazi and the Darogah, although at times they might divide the dominion amongst each other. The Norman enriched the scanty fare of the Saxon with all the delicacies of the table; and though he could not give the *ox* and the *sheep,* the names they bore in Norman French, yet he so far gained his object, that the living animal now is known by the Saxon term, while the dead one is designated by the language of the conqueror. The Mahommedan in the same manner busied himself in household affairs, and arranged all the classes of domestics, so numerous in India, and public servants of almost every description, under titles of which the Hindi could have no previous conception. By the conquerors of England and India all the reforms of advanced civilization, the minute conveniences of existence, the wide appliances of art, were clearly defined and set forth. Nature alone in the one case, and religion in the other, which had become a second nature, were incorporated without change in the new world of the invaders. It would be dangerous to push to its utmost limit a comparison of which the broad features are so striking, but whose lighter shades may tempt us into fancifulness or extravagance. Here and there, however, the analogy on minor points is as complete; and our days of the week, derived from the old Saxon gods, may find a parallel in the months now generally received by Hindu and Mussulman alike, and derived in some instances from the old Heroes of the Mahabharat.*

We have before this described the successive blow of each Mussulman soldier of fortune to which India was forced to bow. We then showed what a Babel of tongues must have prevailed in the camp of the invader, and how repeated attacks, though marked by blood and not by civilization, must in all probability have filed, changed, and enriched the old vernacular dialect. But we will ask our readers to go a step beyond this and to visit that camp when pitched no longer for battle, but in accordance with the prevalent custom of Eastern monarchs, for the annual march throughout the subject's territory. We will request them to accompany us in the spirit of Roe or Tavernier, and, having made our obeisance in the *Huzur* of the great king, to take one stroll throughout the canvass walls of a city whose area is at least one half that of the modern Calcutta. It is a bright morning in the month of December, and the clear north breeze, whose bracing influence reminds the mountaineers of Affghanistan of the air of their native hills, is blowing straight out the endless forest of pennants and flags which glitter in the sun's unclouded blaze. Around the Pavilion of the monarch is spread another field of "the cloth of gold,"† while the steeds of Arabia and Kabul, and the elephants of India's jungles, are caparisoned with trappings of the most gorgeous profusion. The tents of the nobles and Amirs, who throng in the court, vie with each other in the attractions of elegance and novelty, and, stretching far and wide on the four sides of the spot honoured by the presence of the sovereign, a line of streets as regular as the brick walls of a permanent city, are thronged by the soldiery of almost every land of the East. The Rajput, military in his bearing by nature and education: the Brahman of Kanouj, who has so far forgotten his ancient prejudices as to bear the sword and the musket instead of the heavy tomes of his shastras: the independent mercenary from the North side of the Indus, who might have sat to Scott for a picture of the mercenaries in the Lay: the fierce and hardy Kurd, whose origin may have been drawn from the same dark source which Saladin could boast: the Scythian, little changed from those roving spirits who baffled the utmost efforts of the proud Persian conqueror: the Affghan, no unworthy ancestor of those warriors who inflicted on England one of the severest checks she has yet received: the Turk,

* It would be needless to repeat the old Saxon deities—as to the Hindu months, that of *Phalgun* is derived from Phalguna a name of Arjuna, and that of *Aswin* from the Aswini Kumaras, Nakula, and Sahadeva, the *dioscuri* of oriental mythology.

† History of England, Vol. I.

whose coarse but characteristic Tartar features have not as yet been changed by the introduction of pure Caucasian or Georgian blood, and whose masculine Tartar dialect is as yet unembellished by the foreign riches of the Persian, or Arabic: the Patan, betraying by his features a kindred origin with the branded race of Israel: the untameable Beluchi, and the wandering Bedowin :—these, and hundreds of other warlike tribes, distinguished by the one common appellation of *Hazari*, are mingled with an equally varied stream, where the merchants of Malwa, and the fair and comely Parsi, the rustic of Rohilcund, and the cunning Bengali mahajan, the Mahommedan Faquir, the Hindu Gosain, and the mystic performer of Indian legerdemain with his tangled locks and embrowned skin, are known by the equally comprehensive designation of *Bazari* or people of the *shop.* We hear the jest and the repartee, the interchange and the traffic, the laugh of the mansabdar as loud as that of the centurions of Persius,* who in his rough mirth applies the name of a dweller in paradise to the wretched drawer of water, terms the outcast sweeper a prince, and bestows on the farrier and the cloth-maker the well known appellation of the vice regent of Mahommed !†

The King's camp, which, after the fashion prevalent with us in India up to the present day but on a far humbler scale, was always pitched in the winter months, must undoubtedly have been the place where the Urdu language set up its main standard; and Urdu of the purest kind is now the speaking language of the large population of Mussulmans and the few Hindus interspersed among them in and about the Fort of Delhi. The real extent of the language as a speaking medium, though considerable, is far less than is generally supposed. Urdu of course is commonly spoken in the metropolis of each Presidency, where the natural indolence of Englishmen to learn anything beyond what is absolutely necessary, and the congregation of

---

* Vide the contempt in which the Greeks were held.

> Dixeris hæc inter varicosos centuriones,
> Continuo crassum ridet Palfenius ingens
> Et centum Græcos curto centusse licetur.

† The above may require some explanation. Every one must have heard the shouts of "Khalifa" when the services of the *darzi* or the blacksmith are in requisition, and most men are no doubt aware that *mahtar* or *matore* means *a prince*, and *bihishti* or *bheesti* a man of bihisht or Paradise. The reason for these high-sounding names being applied to individuals of such humble functions is not quite apparent. *Khalifa* is evidently a nickname; and the proper word for a water carrier in Arabia is *saka*, and for a sweeper *halal khor.* The interpretation we have given above, viz. that they were rude jests of the rough soldiery of the Great Mogul's camp is due to a talented member of the civil service, whose thorough acquaintance with the manners and customs of Upper India and the Arabic and Urdu languages, gives his opinion somewhat of the weight of judicial authority.

the inhabitants of so many parts of India, renders it convenient to have one general medium of intercourse. At Madras, where Telinga prevails to the north and Tamul toward the south of the Presidency, almost every servant can speak Urdu—though with less idiomatic precision than it would probably be spoken by men of the same class at Bombay or Calcutta. But if,—apart from all the local considerations and the almost compulsory process by which Urdu is always found to dog the steps of the European—we seek for the boundaries within which it is the speaking language of the cultivator, we shall find them to be somewhat as follows. Beginning from the district of Malda, where the conflux of Bengali and Urdu on a debateable ground, forms one of the most uncouth jargons ever heard or spoken, we mount upward in a north westerly direction till we arrive at the snows of the Himalaya, and the natural boundary of the Indus. With the Eastern part of the lower Provinces, Urdu has no connection ; and from Tirhut, in which zillah a rather peculiar form of Urdu is prevalent, in the direction of the East and South East, its place is usurped by an inferior sort of Bengali. But, in the whole of the North West, it is spoken with various modifications ; and many educated natives of the Behar Provinces are also found to speak it with precision little inferior to those nearer the fountain head itself. After taking the whole series of the North Western Provinces, we advance in a downward direction throughout Rajputana, where the older form of Hindi still lingers tenaciously, till we reach the countries on the Saugor and Narbudda, where a mongrel dialect prevails. Further on the Bombay side, and in the north of that Presidency, we are met by Gujarati ; and in the south, the Mahratta, which has a still closer affinity with Sanskrit than perhaps even Hindi itself, is the speaking language of the inhabitants of the Dekhan. On the west side of India, Urdu, as the vernacular of any particular district or as that of public business, is unknown. It is, however, spoken to a certain extent by all the Mussulman population, but differs in sundry provincialisms from the best court and camp language of Upper India. The real vernacular in use on that side of India is Dekhani or Mahratta. What we have seen of this dialect leads us to imagine a close affinity with the older Hindi, inasmuch as it was mainly dependent on Sanskrit for its foundation and structure, while it has now adopted a great many words of Persian and Arabic origin as Bengali has done with us. The best form of Urdu is equally out of date with our brothers of the Madras Presidency ; that called Dekhani is used by all Mussulmans, but is of a secondary kind. It is no where used in transacting business,

nor is it the language of any particular district.   In one respect,
however, it is put to a similar use in all the three Presidencies.
Those public servants, who, from indolence or inefficiency are
unwilling to master the dialects of peculiar districts, resort, in
order to solve the knot, to the universal interpreter Hindustani.
Which Presidency may be most given to this lame method
of carrying on business we cannot pretend to decide, but we
believe it to exist equally in all three; and the ryot, who would
naturally resort to Mahratta, Tamul, or Bengali as the means
of exposing his wrongs in the rude but impressive eloquence
of nature, is too often compelled to falter out his tale to the
Hakim in a dialect uncongenial, and incapable of conveying a
graphic picture of his feelings, or to have it filtered in interpretation through the ever useful medium of Urdu.   We
believe that a fine opening is left to linguists in the dialects
of the central part of India, and in that quarter generally
known by the name of the South Western frontier of Bengal.
There, still linger, if we mistake not, the aborigines of India,
and their equally aboriginal tongue.   But it would be the
work of a life-time to subdivide the hundred varieties of the
Urdu itself, which are to be found not only in different districts,
but in different villages of Upper India.   We are assured, that,
within the space of a few miles, pronunciation and even the
words themselves present differences more marked than the
dialect of Dartmoor and that of the plains of Somersetshire, or
the rough *burr* of the Cambrian peasant and the broad tones
of the Yorkshireman.   The quick ear of the wanderer Borrow,
who at times confessed himself fairly at a loss in the mountainous
districts of Gallicia, might be admirably exercised in the ever-
changing Hindi.

It will be found that, in accordance with the changes we
have described, this language, when spoken or written by an
educated native whom bigotry does not lead to cling to the
older Sanskrit words, or affectation to imbue his speech with
an overmixture of Persian phrases, generally consists of the following component parts.   The verbs are almost all pure Hindi
or Sanskrit.   Out of the immense number, which this language
can boast, but very few have been naturalized from the Persian.   It is this great command of what eastern grammarians

* Of the few for which Urdu is indebted to Persian the following are the most
essential:... *Goozree* and its causal *Guzranu*, *farmana* to order, *bakshna* to
bestow, *hairana* to tire as a gain, *wurghalana* to decoy, and others. Of the
rest many are closely connected with the Sanskrit, as *janna* to know, *chalna* to
move... *Achhna* and *lana* and even *hona* we think it would be hard to
trace to any Sanskrit root. An ingenious critic in *Blackwood's Magazine* represents the Sanskrit *bhu*, the Hindi *hona*, the Greek φύω and the Latin *fui* ∞

emphatically term the words of *action* (fal), which gives the Urdu such an undoubted superiority over the Bengali : every verb active or passive which we can possibly require is at hand in the rich stores spread out before us.   The substantives would at first be drawn from the older source; if the discourse rose in any degree, Persian would be summoned to supply the deficiency.   The same may be said of the adjectives.   For the commonest epithets, Hindi would be amply sufficient; for the finer shades of meaning, Persian must give its aid.   The composition of a house, the implements of husbandry, the furniture of the peasant's hut, would be the older form; and all connected with the great, with Oriental display, with increased civilization, would be expressed by the foreign source.   Hindi must have its natural abode in the cottage, and Persian in the palace. All the low terms of abuse, with which the Dictionary is laden to an extent as yet unacquired by the denizens of Billingsgate or Brixham, are, with *one or two exceptions*, Hindi.   All the terms of laudatory address, of compliment used by an inferior to his superior, and the subtle distinctions of mental qualities, are Persian or Arabic.   We protest, however, at the above being taken as a rule from which there is no exception.   Another instance of the vagaries of language in its formation may be admirably derived from the present condition of Urdu. We only know it as a fact, that, in many objects the commonest and most striking, the *Persian* or *Arabic* is the approved term, and the ancient one seems discarded or forgotten.   What peculiar insinuating power was possessed by the Mussulman, that his language should not only enrich the older one with new stores, but in some points entirely supplant it ;—why *things which must always have been in existence, and were once undoubtedly expressed by the Hindi, should now acknowledge no master but the Persian*—we cannot pretend to decide by one unfailing criterion.   Why *the house*, the *field* and the *jungle*, should be Hindi words, the *door* and the *plain*, Persian ; why *good* should be expressed by the older and *bad* by the new language ; why some things, trivial of themselves but of such general application as to have been of use long before foreign invasions, should have ceased to be known by any term but that of the invader,— are questions which may form matter for the speculation of the curious.   To go into the varieties of the Benares, and the Rohilcund and the Rajput districts, does not come within the province of this article.   Those who are fond of pondering over local terms, and the names and peculiarities of old Hindu

radicals distinct but yet similar, independent of each other and yet in reality one and the same.

tribes may consult in a glossary lately compiled by Mr. H. C. Elliott, of the N. W. provinces, the written results of long and sound experience in the subject therein so ably treated.*

As long as the Persian language continued to be the favoured medium of communication by writing, of official documents, and of the important province of History, there could be no inducement to Mussulmans, however well informed, to draw out the riches of their mother tongue. Though perhaps not as prodigal in offers of patronage as Mahmud, there would still be found many a Mæcenas among the Amirs of the Court, whose discriminating eye could raise from obscurity a humble Maro. But, after the glorious epoch of Akbar—who, with a comprehensive spirit worthy of the best sovereigns of Europe, extended his fostering influence alike to the fabulous twilight of the Mahabharat, and the genuine clear glow of the Mahommedan conquests—Persian literature began gradually to decline. In the troublous times of Aurangzib, more use was made of the sword than of the pen; and the sparkling lays of love or wine, to which Baber could listen with rapture, gave way to the dull realities of intrigues within the palace, and of hard fought battles with the Mahrattas. But there was an older literature —not indeed a very copious or polished one—but still remarkable as the national poetry of the cultivator of the soil. We allude to the old Hindi poems, such as the Ramayan of Tulsi Das, which bears about the same relation to the original of Valmiki as the Mahabharat of Kashi Ram to that of Krishna Vyasa. These books are but little sought after in the present day ; but there are besides a considerable quantity of songs, familiarly known to the sepoys, which exhibit in the same rude dialects some of the *disjecta membra*, well worthy of being collected into one. It were desirable that those of our officers whose bias is study, and who have access to opportunities closed against others, would collect the many scraps and snatches of old songs to be found within the precincts of a camp, and satisfy the public that some of the real poetic fire may lurk under an exterior rude and unpromising.

But our present subject is the later and not the earlier form of the dialect; and we therefore proceed to the time when the poets first began to introduce foreign words, and to break the harshness of the Hindi with the softer tones of the Persian.

---

* It would be foreign to the purpose to enumerate the many good Urdu Scholars to be found all over India. Our army contains many officers who from their abundance of leisure and natural talent, have made themselves complete masters of this and other oriental tongues ; and the cause of Eastern literature, we may say, the cause of Christianity, has lately sustained a loss which it could ill afford, in the death of that accomplished scholar, and excellent man, Dr. Yates.

The earliest of these is Wali, who flourished about the end of the seventeenth century: and a long line of successors have sprung up in his train. Of the poems of those worthies which are generally known by the appellation of *Dewan*, we do not profess to have seen one quarter; but from what we have read we think it possible that we can lay before our readers a tolerably just estimate of the present state of Urdu literature. Elphinstone has pronounced Souda to be the best of the poets, and he is reverenced by the learned Mussulmans as the Shakespeare of his age. In prose we have but few original works, as the greater parts, though not actually translations from, are little else than expanded versions of the original Persian. Amongst these, however, the series of tales,—so well known to every subaltern who has ever aspired to the post of interpreter of his corps, as the Bagh-o-Bahar, or the Char-Darvish—is perhaps the best specimen on which we can lay our hands. Its original— for even this favourite work is but a secondary version—exists in Persian, but, we believe, in an unprinted from. Its plot is as follows:—Azadbakht, the sovereign of Kustuntuniya, by which barbarous appellation is meant Constantinople, is surrounded by all the attributes of wealth which can add a charm to existence. His treasury is full, his soldiery—the Prætorian guards of an Eastern Rome—are peaceable, his subjects supremely happy under the just and kind rule of their sovereign. But one thing however is wanting in the midst of such splendour. Heaven has denied him the hope of a future life in posterity, and in the absence of this lamp—one indeed on which the oriental has ever set the greatest value—the brightness of his palace is as the darkness of midnight. A bitterness springs up out of the very fountain of his pleasures, and impregnates the cup of happiness with a deadly and blighting poison. In this state of mind his kingdom and its affairs became doubly distasteful; and regardless of the remonstrances of all his nobles, and the tears of a faithful vizier, whose voice had never before been lifted up in vain, he wanders forth one stormy night, unaccompanied, and soon reaches the dreary precincts of the burial ground. A light attracts his eyes, and despising the terrors of Ghoul or Afrit, he draws near to the spot. Four men, whose dress proclaim them to be the kalendars of the East, are sleeping near a taper whose flame never wavers in the strong night wind. A sneeze from one of the party awakes the rest, and in order to beguile the tedium of the night they agree to recount their adventures. Azadbakht from his hiding place hears two out of the four, and retires. The next day they are all four brought before him in open Darbar, and the king is forced to overcome the bashfulness of the two whose stories are yet untold, by first recounting his own personal history. The whole series smacks strongly of a close acquaintance with the Arabian Nights, both in the subject and in the introduction of episodes. One Prince—for the kalendars are all princes in disguise—is in love with a Princess to whom he is finally united after many vicissitudes. She is apparently carried away by the violence of a river and drowned. Another is separated from his beloved on the edge of a shoreless sea. A third is buried with his dead wife, like Sindbad in the mountain, but there finds a comforter in a widowed bride, who has been consigned to the same living tomb under the same stern law. A fourth, when ordered by the King of the Genii to bring a virtuous maiden to his presence, pure and unsullied, proves unequal to the task which was successfully performed by Prince Zeyn Alasnam, and falls a victim to his own blind and impetuous passions. The promise of future help has, however, been given to each afflicted lover by a veiled horseman who never fails to appear at the critical moment; and when the four shall meet a King equally unfortunate with themselves the curse shall be taken off and their ends will be obtained. The sequel may be imagined. One of Azadbakht's wives bears him a son: the horseman again comes forward, the strongholds of the genii again give up the Princesses who had been spirited away, and the four kalendars, restored to their Princely character, are finally united to the beloved of their hearts.

On the whole this book is deserving of the favour it has met with at the hands of native and European. The story of the third Prince, which contains the oft repeated tale of a king's son following a deer out of sight of all his attendants, and afterwards becoming attached to a beautiful girl, is perhaps the least interesting, and that of King Azadbakht himself introducing an episode of a Nishapur merchant and a dog who repeatedly saves his master's life, when exposed to the malice of two brothers, perhaps the most so.* Although the resemblance to the Arabian nights is sufficiently obvious, yet enough remains of originality to satisfy the critical reader; and many a novel has been read and sought after in England, whose claims are not of a nature to compete with the tale of "the garden and the spring."

We wish that the same meed of praise could be awarded to the Araish-i-Mahfil, a book compiled from older authorities

---

* An amusing incident occurs in the narration here. A *Farangi Elchi* or European ambassador ventures to smile in open Durbar at one of Azadbakht's orders and he is accordingly reproved by the King for *be-adabi* !!

on the ancient Kings, and the natural productions of India. After a notice of the various sects of Hindu Philosophers, which might perhaps be of some little use were we not possessed of the Sanskrit originals, and an enumeration of the domestic animals most in use with the natives, we come to what professes to be an account of each Zillah, taken from personal observation and from the Kholasat-alkind and other writers. We had here looked for some valuable information as to the relative merits of each district, and the physical difference of their inhabitants, with the varieties of their dialects; and, in spite of the frequent mention of the tombs of Mahommedan Saints, we might be thankful for notices of the various forts built by the Mogul Emperors in Upper India. But we are wearied beyond measure, when, in the enumeration of the Zillahs of Bengal, Behar, and the North West, we meet with statistical information of no greater importance than the fruits which each produces, and with comparisons of no higher kind than the respective merits of the water melons of Agra and Allahabad, and the plantains of Bengal, and those of Upper India. We then come to the historical part of the work which gives a history of the Kings of Hindustan from the renowned Yudhistira to Pithura. Here, however, we acknowledge with thanks a notice regarding the battle scene of the Pandus and Kurus. The ground of those Homeric wars is the modern Thannesar; and it was in front of the armies, when drawn up on that plain, that the Bhagavad Gita was recited by the Deity Krishna to the hero Arjuna. The Kings of Hindustan form a line of worthies almost as long as that with which the Egyptian priests of old astounded the enquiring Herodotus. But their virtues and vices are left to the imagination of posterity. They must be numbered with those brave men who lived before Agamemnon, and who died for want of a sacred bard. With the exception of a slight digression in the case of Vikramaditya and Salisahana, the record of these sovereigns is comprised in the simple announcement of their births and deaths. But the author, when mentioning the mere fact of their decease, is at times almost puzzled, even in the riches of his language, to find terms to vary the repeated announcement. It may amuse our readers to see the phrases, in which the Kings are made to die. They enter on the road of nonentity. They exchange the perishable home for that of permanency. They become dwellers in Vaikuntha. The lamp of their existence is quenched by the cold wind of annihilation. They pack up the chattles of life for the long journey of eternity. They are cut off by the sharp sword of Fate. Their breasts are smote with the stroke of necessity. They pass away, like smoke; and their places know them no more.

It is, however, rather hard to judge native authors by the test of European criticism, or to demand from the Oriental, whose eyes are yet hardly able to bear the blaze of day with which we would fain surround him, a glance as keen and comprehensive as that of his brethren of the West. We pass from the above to the ikhwani-sofa or brothers of Purity, a rather amusing translation from the older Arabic work. The classes of domestic animals are so wearied by the continual tyranny of their masters, mankind, that they implore the kings of the genii to hear the cause, and adjudicate between servant and lord. A day is appointed and the pleadings begin. This gives occasion to each to dilate upon his own utility and the ill return he has met with. The horse and ass, the camel and the sheep are all heard in turns, and plead their cause with an eagerness that reminds us of a similar contention of quadrupeds in one of the books of our childhood, which we have all read and admired a thousand times, the 'Evenings at home.' The book on the whole is not an unpleasing sample of eastern workmanship in this department, and the style, which is inundated with Arabic words, affords an excellent mode of gaining a knowledge of the varieties of dress which Urdu can assume in its almost unparalleled fertility.

The Khirad Afroz is an expanded form of the well known Hitopadesa; but though its tales are often amusingly told, yet no profuseness of incident or gayness of colouring can equal the quiet simplicity of the great original, or make us believe, as in the case of the Sanskrit work, that we stand on the ground where these, the nursery tales of every country, had birth. The Guli Bakawali lead us to the regions of fairy and jin, and show how the King Taj-Al-Muluk, after a wild series of adventures, attained the hand of the daughter of the King of Spirits, though guarded by eighteen thousand slaves. The publication of this work is connected like many others, with the time-honored name of Gilchrist: and if we may trust its preface, it was first translated from the old Hindi into Persian in the beginning of the eighteenth century. That language was then in almost undisputed possession of the field: and in order to advance his claims as a literary man with any hope of success, the author was compelled to clothe his offspring in that dress which alone could give it currency in the world. Such at least is the account given by the writer himself. But under the fostering care of the Marquis of Wellesley, the vernacular was encouraged, or rather brought out from obscurity, and the cunning hand of a native of Delhi, who though a Hindu, was acquainted with the purest form of the Camp language, gave it to the Oriental world in the shape it now bears. It would be vain to attempt a similar description of the poetical works to be met with in the language. We have taken the above prose authors because they are the established authorities to which learned natives appeal, and by which the language when tested must stand or fall. Even the whole catalogue can hardly be considered as a literature. The most learned Maulavi, partly from a lingering admiration of the Persian and Arabic writers, and partly from a consciousness of the weakness of his arms, founds no higher claim on the series than that they should be considered as comprehending all the riches and elegancies of a well formed language. It would be unfair to quit the purely literary part of the question without glancing at the general style of the writers and the topics they embrace. The devout feelings of a Mussulman and the consciousness that he is serving the one true God, whilst all around him are polytheists, invariably finds a vent in the preface to every work. The writer would fain be loud in the praise of the Creator, but that his tongue is dumb, as it were, in the vast ocean of His existence, and he himself is like a bubble on the surface of its waters. After this exposition of his devout feelings, the real business of the work commences; and if it is, as in nine cases out of ten, the account of a good king, we have the oriental amplification spun out even beyond the allowable limit. The glorious picture which Isaiah had drawn, and which Pope transferred to his own glowing lines, finds a transcript in the warm clime of the East, but is often in danger of being caricatured. The scriptural anticipation of that time when the most ferocious beasts should eat at the same crib with the domestic animals of the farm yard, and when the weapons of bloodshed should be moulded into those of husbandry and peace, is too faint for the over luxuriant imagination of the Eastern writer. He runs into the most extravagant conceptions, and the wildest comparisons. No flight can be too lofty, no domestic picture too humble to illus-trate the happy reign of a monarch with whom justice is the first quality. We may here observe that the constant praise of justice—a virtue so rare and so prized when met with,—speaks volumes against the general character of native officials in past times. "A minute of justice," says a Persian writer, "is of more weight in the scales than sixty years of devotion;" and we may be sure that the high price set on this jewel points at frequent venality and the selling of that prerogative of kings. It may be amusing if not actually instructive to cast one glance at the numerous figures employed to colour the pleasing landscape in which a monarch is ruling with more than the even-handedness of Nushirvan. In the rule of such a king all crimes cease by one accord. The shops remain open throughout the livelong night. The watchmen have no occasion to be at their posts, for the very thieves are now transformed into the protectors of property. Travellers pass along the high roads tossing up their purses, and the bait falls unheeded before the face of the reformed robber. An universal quiet reigns in the hearts of the ryot, and even the beasts of the field are not insensible to the blessing of such a government. The tiger and the goat come to one tank to drink. The shepherd surrenders his lambs to the care of the wolf, the lion when sick comes and reposes in the lap of the deer. The poor man, who stood for a moment at the door of the rich, is endowed with the means of being as generous as Hatim, and the ant which passed by the gate of the palace has suddenly found itself possessed of the strength of the wrestler. The hawk and the dove bring up their young in one nest, and the toad imbibes the mildness of the bird which is the emblem of peace. Nor is the universal bond of union confined merely to the animal kingdoms,—the mineral and the vegetable are also sharers in this inestimable blessing, and the power of the emperor extends to the dead as well as to the living. The skin of the slain wolf, when converted into a drum, refuses to utter the expected warlike sound, and will send forth nought but the softest tones of melody. Water and fire coalesce in amity. Sparks will not set the driest straw in a blaze, nor the flame of the candle burn a feather from the wing of the moth. If but the word is spoken, glass will bruise the mountain to mustard seed, and the smallest herb of the plain prove a match for the loftiest tree of the forest. The balls of justice are empty and the judge sits with folded hands. The bell is the only medium of giving utterance to any complaint. The destroying influence of time itself is suspended, and cankering rust may not imprint the smallest speck on the pure and spotless surface of the mirror !

The above is a theme which has exercised the pliant ingenuity of both poetical and prose writers. Several of the latter we have described at some length, but of the poets we know of none save Souda, who deserves to be noticed to any extent. In addition to the fact, that he is the most favourable specimen of the class and the authority oftenest quoted, we may glean from his works several hints which throw no inconsiderable light on the state of India in his time. Whether he rises in praise of the sovereign whose bounty he had no doubt

experienced, or descends in fierce invective against the "vitio-
sior progenies" of a degenerate age, his witness may not
be neglected by the historical enquirer. He lived in the reign
of Alamgir the second, who, we know, ended his days as
a pensioner of the British Government, after a life of disappointment and disaster in which he could hardly consider
himself securely master of the throne for a moment. The
outward symbols of royalty were, however, preserved by
the kingly puppet, and many will doubtless have seen the gold
mohar, coined about the 20th year of Alamgir the second, almost
as fresh as when it first issued from the coiner's hand. It is
to satirists like Juvenal that we look for striking touches regarding the general state of things in the decline of a great empire ;
and Souda, who was a satirist in a small way, can furnish many
a hint worthy the consideration of those who would pourtray
the last days of the Mogul Emperors and the first of the
English. An amusing episode, in which Souda describes himself as having taken a part with more bravery than Horace,
tells us of the daring inroad of the Mahratta cavalry up to
the very walls of Delhi : a long and querulous ode gives us a
vivid picture of the poverty of the age, and the fallen splendour of the Amirs and the nobles of the great Mogul : a lam-
poon against one Sidi Kafur, the Kotwali Darogah of the town
of Delhi, furnishes a likeness of the corrupt native official,
to which the most ardent reformer of the police could find no
parallel in any district of Bengal ; and a comical description
of the hardships endured by all who venture on the uncertain
prospect of a merchant's life, and encounter the duties and
demands of the custom house attendant, speaks volumes against
the harassing system of the *dastaks*, and the tyranny to which the
old trading license of the company's servants gave rise. But
Souda, who assumed that *cognomen* signifying the melancholy
one, in addition to his own name of Mirza Mahommed Rafi,
would rise up in judgment against us, were we to omit the
subject which he has handled with even more than the usual
warmth of Oriental poets. The passion of love has at all times
had a peculiar claim on the attention of the eastern songster ;
and Souda in this respect has not deviated from the path
so often trodden by his predecessors. The same similes and
tropes have attracted notice in the work of Persian authors, and
our poet, who was doubtless an excellent Persian and Arabic
scholar, has made free use of his learning to dress up in his
own idiom the extravagancies of older authorities on the subject.

If the monarch of the happy East was to be compared in his justice only to Nushirvan, or in his generosity to Hatim, the melancholy lover could know no type but Majnun, and the mistress of his affections resemble none but Leila in her harshness, or Zuleika *the wife of Potiphar*, in her charms. The beauty of opening manhood finds no parallel but in that of Joseph, "the moon of Canaan;" and the patient endurance of hard commands is represented by the indefatigable labours of Farhad who dug through a second Athos, in order to win the love of the peerless Shirin. The lover, the smoke of whose parched heart rises up in silent appeal to the skies, can do nought but extol the dark mole on the face of his beloved, which keeps watch over her beauty like a snake near a hidden treasure.* Worn out by the obduracy of his adored, he wanders disconsolate among the green shades of the garden. But, wherever he turns, he finds something to recall the image of what he can never hope to be his : something to remind him of the truth of that proverb which says that joy and grief are twins in the world. The breeze of the morning, which expands in graceful confusion the buds of the blooming rose, recalls his own heart entangled in the curling tresses of the hard-hearted : the thorn on the same flower can never pierce with a sting so sharp, or stab so unkindly, as the thorn of regret : the nightingale never complains in accents half so mournful as those of his own unguerdoned muse. The spring in all its opening charms,—blushing with roses, whose redness shall be pale by the lips of his mistress, and spreading a carpet of verdure over the gladdened face of nature, which once found a picture equally pleasing in the parterre of his mind,—cannot afford the slightest pleasure to one chilled by the piercing cold of winter; and should he wander, in his despair, in the same scenes, when the moaning gusts of autumn have despoiled them of their ornaments, where shall he find a parallel more complete, than in the ruined and desolate garden of his heart of hearts? The stream, in which the box wood was once reflected, is dried up and choked with weeds—so is the rivulet of joy which once watered his soul; but time, which has loosened the tenacious buds of the rose tree, has not been able to solve the twice tied knot of his sorrows; and the rising gale, which threatens to sweep with all the desolating influence of autumn, over regions lately blest by the presence of

---

* It may be new to some of our readers, that a dark coloured reptile is always supposed to be guarding the treasure deposited in the earth by the hand of the miser.

summer, shall spread no blight more deadly than that which has extended its universal sceptre over the gay and happy scenes of his fancy.

Serious criticism on the above would be superfluous. Lovers who burn their wings like the moth in the unsparing flame—mistresses with the stature of the cypress and the eye of the Narcissus—the *Bulbul* sighing for the union with the *gul*, and pouring forth incessantly its thousand tales—the Zephyr which drops pearls—the thin lace called *kutan* which is enamoured of the moon—all these are the offshoot of Persia and Hindustan; and with every allowance for the warm feelings of the Mussulman, we can hardly repress a smile at the exuberance of his fancy. Bishop Heber had imagined that considerable attractions must be concealed in the love sonnets of Persian poetry, but he would soon have turned away from the continual harping on the same subject, and the use of the same unchanging figures. That Sanskrit poetry, which, when viewed through the dull medium of translation he had too lightly estimated, must, in the opinion of every impartial observer, assume the first rank in the literature of the East. We intend no disrespect to the shade of Ferdusi or the manes of Hafiz: in fact we may have slightly digressed from our subject, to include the style of Persian poets likewise. But notorious as are the blots of Sanskrit poetry, it must rank the Hindu above his conqueror. Conquest and changing dynasties created writers which a long period of repose, but one step removed from lethargy, had been unable to supply; and the inferiority of Mussulmans in the poetical art, was more than compensated by their exclusive appropriation of the field of History.

In looking at the comparatively few specimens of the literature, we are again struck by a fondness for conceit and double entente which Eastern writers seem never to forego. In Urdu, however, such vagaries are not only pardoned, but welcomed; and an old Hindi couplet—for it belongs rather to the older form of the language—is a very good specimen of an ingenious play upon words. It is at least equal to most of those contained in the jest books of infancy :

Sarang ne Sarang gabyo, Sarang bolyo aie
Jo Sarang Sarang kahe, sarang munh ten jae.

Now the word *Sarang*, on which the whole couplet turns, has four different meanings ; a peacock, a snake, a cloud, and a peacock's cry. The Hindu poet imagines that peacocks utter a cry of joy, when they descry the first traces of the darkly frowning mass in the heavens, which is to pour forth its grateful streams on the thirsty earth. With this necessary explanation the whole, translated, will run thus: " A peacock seized a snake: a cloud uttered the cry, alas! If the peacock then utter his own cry, the snake will then drop from his mouth." It would seem as if the whole were a warning to the incautious bird who is destined, like the crow in the fable, to lose a rich prize already gained for an imagined one. The above is, at any rate, a clever and well contrived puzzle, and such may find a legal resting place in a language like Urdu.

We will now return once more to the language, and analyse a few of its component parts. We left off at the time when Persian had so far been amalgamated with the old Hindi as to form the speaking dialect of the men of both creeds, and we also then alluded to the Turkish horsemen who formed no inconsiderable portion of the armament of the Great Mogul. The share they had in the language, though minute and almost trifling, is too curious to escape notice altogether. The few words which the Turk left behind him as a memorial are indeed sufficiently professional and unique. The very title of the language—Urdu—signifies a camp in the Turkish tongue; and the remainder of the current expressions breathe every where a warlike tone. *Harawal*, the advance guard: *fiqan*, the division of an army: *top* its cannon: *Kuzzil-bashi* or red head, a set of soldiers descended from those given by Sheikh Haidar to Tamerlane, and conspicuous for their caps of that colour; *dah-bashi*, a commander of ten, from a barbarous conjunction of the Persian numeral and the Turkish noun: *kuli*, the porter or labourer whom we have naturally metamorphosed into the well known *cooley*; *karawal*, a picket: *talawa*, a forlorn hope: *kushun*, a large body of troops: *kash* the pommel of a saddle; *tamancha* a pistol: —these, and a few others, are the remnants of a people, whose trade was mercenary violence, and whose arguments were the sword and steel. There are of course other words of Turkish orgin, but mostly of rare occurrence, whilst some of the above are to be met with everywhere, and yet few are aware of the source whence they spring. Of contributions from other sources the Portuguese is now the first in order of seniority, although its solitary remnants cannot have the slightest claim to be considered as parts of the language. They are rather excrescences which have sprung up casually, and have attached themselves to the original trunk, than ingredients duly incorporated in the body. Such however as are deducible from extant Portuguese words are really curious. *Kamara*, a room, seems without any great degree of straining to claim affinity with camera: *martol* a hammer, with a Portuguese word of similar sound and meaning; the *nilam* of Messrs. Tulloh and Company with *leilam*, the *n* and *l* being changed according to a prevalent fashion with the natives; and *mascabar*—a term well known to every Indian official from the judge of the Sudder to the wearied Zillah Magistrate, or the greedy mohurrir on ten rupees a month—is said to be formed from two distinct Portuguese words *mes* a month, and *acabar* the end. The above are so unconnected that we can ascribe their permanency in the language to no cause but the chapter of accidents. We understand, however, that the strange dialect, in which Lascars and Dandies hold converse when on board, and that in which orders are given to the native crew regarding the working of the ship, is compounded of Portuguese words naturalized in their terminations and inflexions to suit the native tongue. One thing at least is certain—that the vocabulary is unintelligible to all but those whom it immediately concerns. Remains of the Frenchman and the Hollander,—except indeed in the mutilated fragments of their own names*—we have none; and the Englishman, for the time of his influence, advances but slowly, and only in the neighbourhood of great towns which cannot be taken as a criterion of universality. How far the free use of Anglicism will be adopted, as the language progresses, is another and a wider question. Among the few English words now generally used by the natives, the court term " appeal" recalls an age when judicial proceedings were of the most summary kind, and where the fiat of a Kazi or Kotwal, carried the order into execution from which there could be no release. It is obvious that the term has met with universal adoption, because such a power never existed in any definite shape in the time of " the Moguls."

It may now be asked, of what positive advantage is it, that attention should be directed to a language of which the literature is scanty, and, such as it is, claims no high place in the roll of nations? why have we brought our readers to the contemplation of a wide but unfruitful soil, from which no labour, though aided by the creative influence of stream and shower, can wring any produce beyond the barest pittance? It would indeed be a thankless office, had we indulged only in a dreary prospect whence no kind genius could hope to call forth the blooms of spring, and whose unvaried level should never acknowledge the power of verdure and cultivation. But the case is fortunately far different. Like Australia, with no past history to look back on, and with wonderful resources as yet

---

* Willandais is the term for Dutchman, and Farash-dunga, or the assembly of Frenchmen, denotes the town of Chandernagore.

w w

undeveloped, the Urdu may, in spite of the same blank void of the past, look forward to a better day when its powers shall be tested.   The English language, gradually fused into its present state from the union of Saxon and Norman, was chosen as a parallel to the formation of the language of Hindustan.   But we previously dwelt more on the resemblance between the obstacles encountered at the distance of so many thousand miles respectively, and the like changes to which they yielded, than on any actual similitude between the languages themselves in their complete and final state.   We shall now attempt to show what are the capabilities of our subject; and it may perhaps be thought rash to assert, that, out of the whole confusion of tongues, no two languages resemble each other so much as the Urdu and the English, not only in their conformation, but in their capabilities and prospects.   To panegyrise the English language may seem somewhat irrelevant here; but it is necessary to admit, to the fullest extent, all that the most ardent admirer of his own vernacular could express, before we can fairly compare it with the Urdu.   English, from the quaint and rugged, but ever racy and picturesque language of our old chroniclers, has gradually risen to be in the first rank, we would almost say, the *facile Princeps*, in the lists of Philology.   But its idioms have been purified by the masculine energy of sound and deep thinkers, and its beauties chastened and matured in the bright imaginations of poets.   All that the glowing warmth of the Orator, the progressive and stately march of the Historian, and the terse and comprehensive diction of the Philosopher could effect, with the best and purest materials at their command, has been done in a series of four hundred years.   There is, perhaps, but little to be wished for in the way of acquisition or conquest.   The question seems rather, how we should prevent the rush of waters from overflowing the banks,—how the river ever full and deep, but never straying beyond due bounds, should roll on its broad current to the ocean, with dignity inviolate, and purity undiminished. Southey anathemized the audacious writer who should venture to substitute a word of foreign origin for one drawn from the well of the pure old Saxon, where both are equally available; and Sir James Macintosh has shown in a very apt comparison the inferiority of a sentence composed of Latin derivatives to one shaped out of the materials of our Saxon ancestors.*   Yet, in spite of the authority of these distinguished names, the general practice of our best writers has gradually mixed the

---

* Felicity attends upon virtue.   Well-being follows upon well-doing !

two discordant elements. To use merely genuine Saxon vocables, when others are equally good as vehicles for thought,
would be to exclude that large portion of words, which come
to us originally from the Latin, but immediately from the
French ; and the general standard, as sanctioned by writers of
merit, seems rather to point to a careful mixture of all the component elements of our language, with an equally careful precaution against the over use of terms derived directly from the
classical tongues. · The same caution, in the admission and rejection of Arabic and Persian, is what we would inculcate in the
Urdu language. And it may here be not improper to glance
at the differences between the best languages of antiquity and
those of the present day. The most obvious difference
between the ancient and the modern, is, that the former
are complete in themselves, that is to say, they are made
up, of but one, or at most two elements, while the latter
are compounded of ingredients gathered, as it were, from the
four quarters of heaven. In Greek we see but one great
fountain from whence the stores were derived. All is plain,
simple and Greek. A stray old Homeric word, speaking
of bygone generations, here and there defies the utmost skill
of the grammarians, and at times a Persian or Phenician
term has crept in. It may be too that we catch a glimpse
of some still more ancient tongue antecedent to the Cyclopian
walls and their gigantic framers. But we can *clearly*
distinguish only one controuling influence, which is complete
in itself, and we ask no more. The Latin, though now and then
leaning for aid on its more perfect sister, and perhaps suggest-
ing a parent tongue, from which both were derived, presents in
the same manner, a picture, of which the whole is so pleasing
that we care not to analyse the parts even if we had the key
at our command. The Sanskrit evidently grew out of itself, or
was expanded from some remnant of the days before the
Deluge. The Arabic unfolds its marvellous copiousness of
terms from a series of roots which in themselves are plain and
unpretending.* We see but the state of things at the completion of a lengthy work and have no means of ascertaining the
process by which the edifice was gradually erected. But
widely different is the case with the most favoured of the

* We allude to the great variety of terms of which the original basis is so simple
From ركب we have ركاب a stirrup, راكب a rider, مركب a horse ;
from ساجد سيد an adorer, مسجد a mosque, سجاد adoring. Languages
so formed may well be content with their own stores and despise foreign aids. The
principal Arabic roots, however, must be regarded as essentially Hebrew.

modern languages. There we are introduced behind the curtain and can mark each successive transformation. The ingredients of the chalice are placed before our eyes, we can test each portion and determine its influence on the general result. Few are more diversified than the English, and yet few present a composition more exquisitely blended or more vigorous in its whole effect. The writers of the times of our Edwards, or those of the civil wars, might no doubt have thought it impossible that the language should ever be so enriched by foreign acquisitions, and yet so weeded from all false ornament, as to appear at once, rich, classical, and pliant ; and many may, in the same manner, doubt, if from the present state of Urdu, its stores could be digested and combined in a way which should satisfy the criticism of the purist, and the calls of the author. We will first then look at the languages mentioned above as vehicles for composition, and see how the Urdu gains or loses in the comparison. Now such as are principally drawn from one source, however pure and abundant that source may be, are in some respects unfortunate. They can command, it is true, a large variety of terms and a vocabulary rarely, if ever, at fault. But increasing knowledge and discoveries in science render the formation of new terms imperative, and the writer, though master of his own boasted wealth, is perhaps for a moment puzzled. He dreads infringing on the famed purity of his language, —as the barrier once broken, there would be no bounds to the inundation. He is thus driven to manufacture out of the materials at hand some strange combination by which the newly invented engine may be designated, and the term of art finds a resting place and a local habitation. The magic spell may not be broken, nor the uniform effect marred, to attain an immediate object of which the consequences can hardly be determined. Now the language, which is restrained by no such bonds, fears not to enlarge its vocabulary at the bidding of science or art. There is no dread of a jarring term which shall shock the old established sound : no hesitation at introducing a foreign expression where so many, previously introduced, are all blended into one. It is true that the range of the old language is so great, that difficulties of the kind enumerated, rarely, if ever, occur. We have ourselves almost unconsciously paid another tribute to the matchlessness of the classics when we returned to borrow from them all our scientific Dictionary ; but yet there is a point at which the fountain may fail and the rock no longer send forth its stream of running water. When this does happen, the pliancy of those tongues which welcome contributions from all sides, is seen to tenfold advantage. But we will take an example from the *classical* languages of the East as more apposite to illustrate the Urdu. Every one knows that Bengali, as spoken by the lower orders, is largely mixed up with Persian and old Hindi. Even in the districts, where it prevails with the greatest purity, and in the mouths of the most educated natives, the admission of foreign words is licensed to a large extent. But turn to a book,—original or translated—and the line is drawn as rigidly as in the case of the classics. It falls back immediately on its parent Sanskrit, and the further we go the more we are compelled to borrow from the great original store. Bountiful as is the hand which gives, and forcible the mode in which thought can be expressed, we are fettered by the impossibility of calling for aid from elsewhere, and at times we must have recourse to over ingenious or strained modes of expression. We are prisoners in a large and roomy park, it is true, but still we are prisoners. The sense of confinement, the want of intercourse with common and familiar terms, is one which can never fade. We are raised on a height from whence our glance is indeed keen and unobstructed, but we may not descend to the wished for level of daily life. The clouds are beneath us and our eyes are directed to the sun, but the valley, with its changing hues of light and shade, with the refreshing variety of pasture and stream, is removed from our tread by an impassable barrier.

The same difficulty which meets us in the case of the Bengali—the language in which we hope to impart at least some of the results of the master minds of Europe to the natives of Bengal—is no less to be feared in the case of the Arabic or Persian. Far be it from us to depreciate the powers or the utility of those noble languages; but we deem it necessary to show, that, if Urdu be a mixture of tongues as yet partially crude and undigested, it has escaped the great trial to which its parents are often exposed. The contrary danger, and one equally to be guarded against, is that of setting no bounds to the admission of foreigners. The commonwealth of words, like that of citizens, when free and unscrupulous in its choice, is in danger of being overwhelmed by the influx of other nations. Where the rule is exclusive, and the rights of citizenship are bestowed only on the genuine sons of the soil, the men of other tribes can have no incentive to settle in a land where they will meet with little sympathy. But once prostitute the freedom of the State to admit every claimant on the slightest pretence, and the result will be a crowding together of every tribe under the heavens. The traveller for amusement, and the merchant for gain, the fugitive from blood, and the fugitive from his own thoughts, flock eagerly to a city where they are sure of meeting with open arms. The Syrian Orontes pours its stream into the Tiber, and the latter shrinks not back from mingling with its waters. But time smooths away all discordancies and the mixture of races is in the end complete. This is exactly the case with the republics of languages. Some stand haughtily aloof, like the classical tongues, the Sanskrit and the Arabic, and refuse with scorn to alloy their proud blood by inter-marriage with those whose lineage is less pure. But others— as the Urdu—have no such fears and eagerly open their arms to receive the citizens of other states. There is no hesitation about admittance to the fullest privileges, and the new arrivals are soon domesticated, and partly change, or even entirely lose the rights, which they originally possessed in the land of their birth. But if the admission be free and unobstructed, care must be taken that the new citizens be assimilated in dress and speech, with those in whose society they have obtained an entrance. In other words, to carry out our metaphor still further, we must be careful that the Urdu should receive *words* alone and not *expressions* from the Arabic and other great stores. To explain this we have only to advert to the numerous Arabic terms which are interspersed so largely among the Urdu poets. These—the Gallicisms of the East—are as much to be depre-cated as the like failing at home. The Urdu is willing to draw perpetually on mines of such unfathomable depth, but it must fain assimilate the ore to its own peculiar idiom and dress. Nor can it be necessary, in the abundance of the inflections of the Urdu Grammar, that those of two other syntaxes should be added to increase the difficulties of beginners, or the confusion of the tongue. The natives, whose Urdu is the purest, and who would fain see the capabilities of the language brought out, invariably repudiate the use of Persian idioms, and require nothing more than the mere words of other languages which they arrange according to the genius of their own.* It seems undoubted that the constitution of the language should be as follows. The skeleton of the whole body, that is, the idiomatic turns of the sentences, must be essentially Hindí. The muscles and sinews by which we comprehend the verbs, are also the old dialect; nor is there any fear of their proving weak or ineffi-cient. But the filling up of the interstices, the flesh and blood, so to speak, may be left to the materials which we have deli-neated above, in their several proportions, as making up the

---

* To make this quite clear it is only necessary to allude to such terms as *min bad*, *bad as in*, instead of *bad is ke*, which are justly excluded from the best style.

bulk of the language. What we most stand in need of at present is some Hindu Addison, from whose pen shall flow a prose work of ease, nervousness, and purity; or a Johnson, whose research and critical power shall fix with certainty the boundaries of the language. The task is no longer that of enriching a dry tongue, but that of setting a bound to encroachments,—with a due reservation for those which growing circumstances and civilization shall license. And then, amalgamating the contributions of Arabic, Persian and Sanskrit, the whole body shall grow together, no longer a chaos of ill-arranged materials, but a kingdom whose limits are well and clearly defined, and whose internal arrangements bear the evidence of a guiding and masterly hand.

It has been urged with considerable reason that the genius of Oriental nations and their languages are so diametrically opposed to those of the Western Hemisphere that any attempt to translate the productions of European masters into the dialects of the East, must prove impracticable; and that if those great originals are not transfused into the minds of the natives of India, no copies, worthy of being admitted even as copies, can ever be looked for with definite certainty. Shakespeare and Bacon cannot give out their wisdom in Bengali: Persian can convey no adequate representation of the rolling eloquence of Burke; nor the harp of Milton utter its melodies at the bidding of Urdu. It is worse than folly not to admit the difficulty of the task, but almost as bad to set it down as wholly hopeless. How little can men,—who only know Urdu as the jargon in which natives abuse each other, or as that in which a few daily recurring words of command are uttered,—how little can they appreciate the range of its powers or the facilities of its idiom! Even as it is, and with the few works at our disposal, we may command several subjects on which its strength has been efficiently tested. The most difficult of the departments of literature would no doubt be sublime poetry like that of Milton, or deep sonnets—pregnant with meaning—like those of Wordsworth. We could not reasonably expect that Urdu would shine in either of these. But is there any other language in which perfect translations of the above authors could be looked for? Take any other field and the superiority is evident at a glance. Urdu is admirably fitted for scientific discussions. Its idiom is not so completely opposed to that of the English, as to render the transposition of each sentence absolutely necessary in translating: the narrative proceeds with a due regard for idiom, but without any violent distortion; and trifling and serious subjects are handled with equal readiness

and ease.   The minute details of art, the intricate wording
of philosophy, the most refined shades of meaning and the
technicalities which naturally occur in the departments of medicine, law and theology may with accuracy and precision be
transplanted into Urdu; and in History—should a second Ferishta arise—we have every thing which a writer could desire
most conscious of the dignity of such a subject and of the
image of power and beauty to be realized.   Turn to works of
a lighter kind, such as may allure the first awakened powers of
infancy.   Here again Urdu shall be found second to none.
The nursery tales of youth, which have *once* pleased, and those
which charm equally in after life—Jack the giant killer on his
stalk, Robinson Crusoe in his kingly solitude, and Gulliver in his
unrivalled travels, may put on an oriental dress and wander,
changed, but still easily recognized over the arid plains of Hindustan.   Gay and grave, severe and lively,—few European styles
may not become familiar to the ears of our Eastern subjects;
and were it conceivable that the works of Dickens should ever
flourish in scenes so totally opposed to those of the West,
Urdu alone might hope to monopolize some portion of that rich
vein of humour, and amaze the ears of the Hindustani with
specimens of the low life of England's metropolis.

In the hands of an able native writer who would carefully
shun the extravagancies of his predecessors, and seek to infuse
in his Urdu works, a genuine dash from the pure springs of
European literature, it is difficult to say what state of perfection, as a vehicle for thought, Urdu might not attain.   Fettered
by no idle fear of encroachments on a pure stock, harmonizing
all discordancies with a happy and correct judgment, joining
into unity the opposite elements of Persian and Sanskrit, and
yet conveying no shock to euphony and no harsh disruption of
the harmony of sounds, revelling without extravagance in the
riches of which he holds the key, and preserving in the exuberance of his treasures, a spirit of order and uniformity,—who
can tell whether some creative genius of Hindustan may not
worthily illustrate the combined and digested effusions of great
writers, or even strike out for himself and his countrymen a
new and unexplored path.   We have here given nothing but
the bright side of the picture, and whilst dilating on the excellencies of the language, we may have forgotten to enumerate manifold smaller difficulties—the ups and downs to be
found in a path generally smooth and uniform.   We at once
frankly acknowledge that Urdu is burdened with a considerable variety of inflections,—a confusion of genders and gramma-
tical rules, and various minute and fanciful distinctions which

have too often spoiled the best creations of the East. Perfect symmetry in the edifice of an oriental architect it is perhaps vain to expect. But with every allowance for the above failings it must be conceded, that the spectacle we have invited our readers to contemplate, is that of a speaking *tongue* so inviting as to be employed more or less in conversation over the whole of our Indian Empire, of a written *language* in which are united many of the best qualifications of those of the ancient and the modern world. The expressiveness of the verbs, the overflowing abundance of actives and neuters, and the additional aid of the comprehensive causal, the union of nouns and adjectives, or, to use the terms of oriental grammarians, of *names* and *qualities*, drawn from an old and a new source, the absence of all stiffness, and the clear but soft tones into which its sentences resolve themselves,—these are a few of the advantages which stamp the Urdu language as one to whose perfectibility there is no definite limit.

To speculate much farther on the powers of Urdu, or to imagine a set of subjects to which it shall be constantly applied, would lead us to the great question of the regeneration of India. At what hour the spark may be communicated and the train catch fire—when the ashes so long smouldering may again burst forth into life and heat—whether the process shall be gradual and imperceptible, or startling and electrical—is beyond the comprehension of man. Some may doubt whether a literary regeneration—a deep thirst for knowledge already stored up by others—or a new awakening of the creative faculties amidst a large body of Mussulmans, can ever be hoped for with reasonable chance of fulfilment. We may in time educate respectably a fair proportion and fit them for public offices by an English course of study, but we cannot excite a generous ardour for knowledge in itself, or a desire to extend its blessings to a large number of fellow-countrymen. We may prove clearly that a good education will make men useful members of society, but we cannot call forth the living fire of Firdusi or surround the British Durbar with spirits like the "nine gems." The most ardent must descend from the lofty heights of their aspiration, and calmly and dispassionately scan the means now at hand and the uses to which they can be put. It cannot be denied that from several incidental causes the want of knowledge is less keenly felt by the natives of the North West than by those of Bengal, and that the work seems likely to be one of much slower and more uncertain progress. Yet we cannot tell how soon the cry for education, now ringing in all the districts of lower Bengal, may produce higher and finer motives than have as yet actuated the students of the Calcutta Colleges; or whether the echo of that cry may not extend itself to the North West Provinces and stir into life the sluggish waters of the Mahommedan population. Should the Government hold out liberal rewards for any good translation of standard works in English literature into Bengali or Urdu, we shall then see who will press forward, to be first in the race: and, in spite of the great and acknowledged difficulties of the task, and here and there the utter deadness of all disinterested motives, we may coincide in the hope, confidently but not unreasonably expressed by the President of the Council of Education, that the students of the Hindu College might be the means of bettering and enlightening the unlettered portion of their countrymen. The same may be predicated of the Free Church and other institutions. And should such a hope ever be fulfilled in the lower provinces, and a corresponding state of things arise in the North West, we shall there have a finer field for our work with machinery of a more powerful and extensive kind: we shall have to infuse the learning of Europe into a population composed of better materials than the Bengali, by a language more perfect than the vernacular of Bengal. And we now rise from the contemplation of our subject with a settled conviction that, be the day late or early, Urdu will have its part to perform in the civilization of the great territory committed to our charge.

☞ *Urdu fukut alfaz ke waste* is a sentence which we have often heard from the mouths of well educated natives. Although we acquiesce in the notion that there are few books in the language worth reading, we are still no less deeply impressed with the idea that Urdu might be made a mighty engine in the civilization of India. It is for this reason that we have endeavoured in the above sketch to show its rise and progress, its present condition, and its future capabilities. Several parts of such a wide subject have of course been but slightly touched upon; and there is still plenty room left for disquisitions on the old Hindi, and the variety of dialects prevalent in Upper India. Besides the books enumerated in the above sketch, the poems of Mir Taki, Jurat and Tafish, are worthy of attention; and some of the Mahommedan religious tracts printed at Chinsurah deserve a perusal from their argumentative style. We are also informed on good authority that a translation of the Akhlaki Muhsini by the same hand which translated the Bagh-o-bahar, exists in the College Library of Fort William. Delhi is probably the place where the very best Urdu is spoken but beginning from Monghyr, educated Mussulmans are to be found in almost every large town, who speak the language *almost* as well as the inhabitants of the metropolis of Upper India.

Art. IV.—1. *Biographical Memoir of the late Rajah Rammohun Roy, with a series of illustrative extracts from his writings* Calcutta, 1834.

2. *Translation of the Abridgment of the Vedant or ˙Resolution of all the Vedas, &c. London* 1817.

3. *Apology for the Pursuit of Final Beatitude, independently of Brahmanical observances (in Sanskrit).* By Rammohun Roy. Calcutta, 1280. (*Hindu Era.*)

Viewed, in reference to native amelioration, the present is perhaps the most interesting and eventful period in the history of this country. It might be properly called the age of enquiry and investigation. The metropolis of British India is now undergoing a remarkable transition. Customs, consecrated by immemorial observance and interwoven with the fibres of Hindu society are unhesitatingly renounced as incompatible with the laws of God and man. Hinduism is arraigned before the bar of an enlightened reason, and will ere long be swept from the land which had so long groaned under its domination. But in reflecting on the change now being wrought by educational and other instrumentalities on the native mind, we are irresistibly reminded of the impetus originally communicated to it by Rammohun Roy. His name is inseparably connected with a great moral revolution. It is therefore peculiarly interesting to trace the history of this extraordinary man, for it is in a great measure the history of that revolution.

Rammohun Roy was born in 1774. He was descended from a long line of Brahmans of a high order, who were from time immemorial devoted to the duties proper to their race. Religion was their vocation. They led a purely monastic life down to his fifth progenitor, who, more than a century and a half ago, "gave up," to quote his own language, "spiritual exercises for worldly pursuits and aggrandizement." This change came over the spirit of his family in the reign of that able, energetic, but tyrannical Mogul emperor Arungzebe. Whether this change was voluntary, or the inevitable result of that bitter and fierce persecution to which the sacerdotal order had been subjected by that emperor is uncertain. The descendants of his fifth progenitor attached themselves to the Mogul Courts, held offices, acquired titles, and underwent the vicissitudes inseparable from a political life, especially under an absolute and arbitrary Government—"sometimes rich," as he himself assures us, "and sometimes poor, sometimes excelling in success, sometimes miserable through disappointment." The grandfather held situations of respectability and emolument at the Court of Murshedabad, the capital of the Soubah of Bengal, owing then nominally allegiance to, but being virtually independent of the Delhi throne. He served under Shurajadowla, who was the Nero of Bengal, and took a particular pleasure in burning and consuming to ashes the houses of his Hindu subjects, in causing boats full of men to be drowned in the middle of the Ganges, and in subjecting even pregnant women to atrocities which we dare not describe. The official career of Rammohun's grandfather was commensurate with that stirring epoch which

" Big with the fate of Cato and of Rome "

witnessed the struggles of a company of merchants with the Nabob—struggles which ultimately resulted in the establishment of a mighty and magnificent empire. Rammohun's father, Ramkunt Roy, experiencing some ill-treatment at the Murshedabad Court, and not being able to brook the disgrace as most of his countrymen would have done, retired from service, and took up his residence at Radahnagur, in the district of Burdwan, where he had taluks, the patrimony of the family. At Radhanagur Rammohun Roy was born.

Rammohun Roy's mother was a strict and orthodox woman. Though she was wedded to the superstitions of her country, yet her son succeeded in opening her eyes to its monstrous absurdities. She confessed to him a year before her death, that, notwithstanding she had been convinced of the folly of her faith, she had been too long accustomed to the strict observance of its ceremonies to give it up altogether. " Rammohun," said she to him, " you are right, but I am a weak woman, and am grown too old to give up these observances which are a comfort to me."* She was descended from Brahmans of the highest respectability who have, up to the present day, uniformly adhered to a religious life—a life of penance and devotion—a life of gloomy asceticism which aims at eternal beatitude through the literal mortifications of the flesh. The maternal ancestors of Rammohun were the prototypes of that class of Brahmans who are essentially and emphatically Brahmans—who conform, to the letter,

* This was said by her before she set out on her last pilgrimage to Juggernaut, where she died. With such self-denying devotion did she conform to the rites of the Hindu religion, that she would not allow a female servant to accompany her to Juggernaut or any other provision to be made for her comfort or support on her journey. When at Puri, she occupied herself in sweeping the temple of the uncouth idol. One-eighth of the infatuated pilgrims who crowd to Juggernaut at Dol and Rathjatras every year meet with untimely graves. They fall victims to the foetid air of the place and the extraordinary hardships of the journey.

to all the stringent rules of the *Ahnika Tattiua*—who conduct themselves in the same manner as the great-great grand-fathers of their great-great-grand-fathers had done.

Rammohun Roy received the first elements of native education at home in accordance with the system, which universally obtains among the upper classes of native society, of initiating the children in the mysteries of *Subankar* under the paternal roof before sending them to a public school. The initiation takes place under the auspices of that model of an educator, a guru-mahashay, who, instead of teaching "the young idea how to shoot," takes good care to cramp and check the development of all ideas except such as might be inspired by his example! It must not, however, be supposed that the boys acquire any mastery over the Bengali language. Far from it. They only pick up a few rules of arithmetic and letter-writing. They acquire enough of Bengali to enable them to conduct the duties of a sheristadar and a peshkar, but not enough of it to express their thoughts with correctness or elegance. They acquire enough of it to write a long rubakari, but not enough of it to pen a short decent letter. At the age of eight or nine, they are now generally sent to an English School. It is therefore obvious that the acquisition of the Bengali language—the language of their infancy—the language, in which their earliest associations are entwined, forms, properly speaking, no part of their education. Far different, however, was the case with Rammohun. Though he had received his elementary Bengali education from a gurumahashay, yet he not only attained, by dint of self-study, a knowledge of Bengali,—which, to say the least, was unrivalled by his contemporaries,—but afterwards brought the language itself to a very high state of improvement. We confess that it is, as yet, destitute of a literature ; that it may take generations, if not centuries, to bring it to the highest state of copiousness and refinement ; that, for elegance, flexibility and precision, it cannot be compared to the Sanskrit, which has been cultivated by a Vyasa, a Valmiki and a Manu ;—yet it must be admitted that it is far more adapted to be a living *national* language. Sanskrit—so called, because of its being a *finished* language —the language of the Gods, the Mohorshis, and the Rishis,— can never be the medium of imparting instruction to the great mass of the Hindus ; as the complexity of its grammar, which Panini and Vopadeva delighted to mystify, renders its acquisition an herculean achievement. All this was known to Rammohun Roy. He therefore undertook to create a Literature in Bengali, and his exertions were crowned with a success that exceeded the most sanguine expectation. The Bengali has

been so vastly improved by his careful cultivation, by his taste
and genius, that it can be now successfully devoted to the communication of western knowledge to the children of this great
country.   He was evidently the first who consecrated, so to
speak, the Bengali language by rendering it the medium of
moral and religious instruction.   But he experienced the
greatest difficulties in embodying in it his elevated ideas on the
nature and attributes of God.   He found it totally inadequate
to the expression of subtle metaphysical distinctions.   He
found here the same obstacles which Sir James Mackintosh
says "stood in the way of Lucretius and Cicero when they
began to translate the subtle philosophy of Greece into their narrow and barren tongue; and are always felt by the philosopher
when he struggles to express with the necessary discrimination
his abstruse reasoning in words, which, though those of his own
language, he must take from the mouths of persons to whom
his distinctions would be without a meaning."   But he obviated
these difficulties by the introduction into it of expressive Sanskrit words.   To his exertions, therefore, we are largely indebted
for the improvement of the Bengali language.   He was
evidently one of the best, if not the best Bengali writer ever
born.   He was second to none, except it might be to Varut
Chunder Roy,—who however prostituted his talents by enlisting
them in the cause of libertinism.   The court of Rajah Krishna
Chunder Roy, of which he was one of the brightest ornaments,
and which has been so graphically described by him, afforded
the most tempting premiums to such prostitution.   The Rajah,
who is said to have been the most accomplished gentleman of
his time, was a zealous patron of learning.*   He appreciated
the brilliant and caustic wit of Gopaul Bhar, the metaphysico-
theology of Buggonundun Srimony, as well as the poetry of
Varut Chunder.   But, though gifted with a keen appreciation
of intellectual excellence, his highness' taste was essentially
vicious.   A desire to pander to that taste was the cause of the
misdirection of the talents fostered by his patronage.   The
Vida-Sunder of Varut Chunder Roy, the most popular poem in
Bengal, and the words of which are as much household words
with its people as those of Hamlet and Othello among the people
of England, is nevertheless a filthy production.   Though it exhibits a rich fancy and almost Shakespearean knowledge of the
practical workings of the human heart, yet all its excellencies

* The great grandson of this Rajah, Srish Chunder Bahadur, seems to have
inherited his ancestor's liberality.   He has subscribed Co.'s Rs. 3,000, to the New
College at Kishnaghur.

are marred by that vicious tone which pervades it throughout. It's immoral tendency cannot be too strongly reprobated. But enough of this digression—into which the parallel we have endeavoured to draw between Varut Chunder Roy and Rammohun Roy has betrayed us. Rammohun Roy's Bengali was truly classical. All his vernacular writings are pre-eminently characterized by a chastity of diction, a suavity of style and a felicity of illustration, not to be met with in the writings of older Bengali writers. They are free from that meretricious orientalism which characterizes so often vernacular productions. But it must not be supposed that the Bengali language, though thus considerably improved by Rammohun, is yet entirely fitted for the use of the metaphysician or the theologian. It is destitute of a scientific nomenclature, which must be either created or borrowed to enable us to transfuse European science into it. We have no reason, however, to despair of the vernacularization of western knowledge. Since the time of Rammohun, the importance of this great work is fully recognized, and the establishment of the contemplated hundred and one vernacular schools in the Mofussil, with other collateral measures, will, we hope, tend to accelerate its accomplishment; since the demand, which it will create for vernacular books, must inevitably bring in a rich supply.

Having received the elements of Bengali education, Rammohun Roy was sent to Patna to study Arabic and Persian, the acquisition of which was then what the acquisition of English is now, a passport to wealth and distinction. The study of these foreign languages first opened his eyes to the absurdities of Hinduism. Struck with the simplicity of a faith of which the fundamental doctrine has been pronounced by its prophet to be " God is but *One*," he instinctively revolted from the unmeaning, frivolous, and disgusting ceremonies of Hindu idolatry. The Maulavis at Patna invited his attention to Arabic translations of the works of Aristotle and Euclid : and it must be easily perceived that the mental discipline, thus acquired by the perusal of these works, as well as his acquaintance with the doctrines of the Koran, contributed to cause that vigorous and searching scrutiny into his national faith which soon resulted in his emancipation from its chains, and ultimately led to the great and successful efforts he made to destroy its empire. Rammohun Roy, after finishing his course of study at Patna, went to Benares for the purpose of mastering the aristocratic language of his country. At Benares, the seat of the muses, the Oxford of India, he read the Sanskrit and Vedas. Here it was that, properly speaking, he laid the foundation of his greatness. The zeal and enthusiasm with which he devoted himself to the study of the Sanskrit, and the acquisition of the treasures locked up in it, can alone be conceived from the splendid results to which they afterwards led.

Young as he was, his clear and strong intellect could not fail to discern the absurdities of that superstition which has, from time immemorial, galled and manacled the great mass of his countrymen. Disciplined to the discovery of truth by the process of logical induction and mathematical demonstration, through the writings of Aristotle and Euclid, which he attentively studied in Arabic, it revolted from the detestable doctrines of the Puranic system. Saturated with comparatively pure and elevated ideas of God by the study of Mahommedan theology at Patna, it could not hold any fellowship with the puerilities of his national creed. Accordingly, at the age of sixteen, he composed a manuscript calling in question "the idolatrous system of the Hindus." Thus we see that,—at an age, hovering between boyhood and youth, which is seldom devoted to any graver pursuit in this country than playing *Kopoti* and attending school, and which we should deem too premature in any country for so important a decision,—he renounced Hinduism. His renunciation of it, however, to be duly appreciated, must be viewed in connection with the sacrifices inseparable from it. In casting off his allegiance to it, he braved the loss of caste, the loss of ancestral property (for the *Lex Loci* had not then been concocted) and what must have been perhaps more trying to the nerves of the young reformer, the enmity and persecution of his nearest relatives. His composition of the MSS. to which we have adverted, hastened, what could not be long retarded, an estrangement from his father, who was a bigoted Hindu, and could not brook the heresy of his son. It is cheering to contemplate Rammohun Roy at this time. Though literally a boy, and absolutely dependent upon his father for his support, he manfully asserted his principles, despite the obloquy which he knew their assertion must bring down upon him. The tenderness of youth, when associated with such moral courage and such energy and independence of character, challenges our admiration, and exhibits an interesting, we had almost said, a sublime spectacle. It were earnestly to be wished that the educated natives would follow the example of their illustrious countryman much oftener than they now appear to do. Their renunciation of Hinduism must not be lip-deep, but practical. It is not sufficient that they should *talk* of the folly of an observance of the rites and ceremonies enjoined by the shastras, while they conform to them in practice, by performing *shrads*, and marrying their children according to the Hindu mode. It is not sufficient, that, when taxed with their inconsistency, they should plead the necessity of bowing to public opinion. The habit of compromising with idolatry, they must know, is incompatible with a sincere and earnest love of God. It is high time, therefore, that they should try to wipe off the reproach so often cast upon them, that their actions clash with their professions.

The coldness which had been produced between Rammohun and his father by his secession from that religion, in which the latter had taken so much pains to instruct him, having rendered his home uncomfortable to him, he began to entertain the idea of travelling. Accordingly, at the age of sixteen, he left his paternal roof. He proposed to travel to different parts of the country in order to enlarge his acquaintance with the different systems of religion prevailing there—to watch their practical operation—and to ascertain their effects upon the character of their votaries. The enterprising spirit which led him to fulfil this design cannot be too much lauded, inasmuch as it so seldom characterizes the Hindus, who are religiously and constitutionally indisposed to all locomotion except in the cause of superstition. After visiting different parts of the country, he proceeded to Tibet, where he resided two or three years for the purpose of investigating the Buddha creed. The worship of Lama soon disgusted him, and he unhesitatingly ridiculed it before its disciples: the freedom of his remarks gave much offence to them. Prudence might have dictated a different line of conduct, but his frankness and sincerity at this early age gave utterance to his real sentiments. He travelled into other parts beyond the limits of Hindustan till the age of twenty, when his father consented to recall him, and restore him to favour probably through the intercession of his mother.

When he returned, he was met by a deputation from his father and received by him with great kindness. Being domiciled in his father's house, he appears to have devoted himself to the study of the Vedas and the Puranas. With what success he employed himself in these studies, it would be superfluous to inform our readers. From the undivided attention he paid to them, and the zeal and ardour with which he pursued his researches into Hindu theology as developed in the works of Vyas, Manu and Sankaracharya, we are disposed to believe that he had planned, even at this time, that moral revolution with which his name is identified. The evidence on this point is indeed, we confess, hardly sufficient to prove that any systematic scheme should have been so early formed even by so powerful and active a mind. But it is certain that he had been strongly convinced of the debasing and demoralizing tendency of Hinduism, and had seriously been thinking of making an attempt at its subversion.

At the age of twenty-two he commenced the study of the English language, but made no marked progress in it for the next six years. This was owing, we are firmly pursuaded, to his not having brought to bear upon its study that application and strength of mind which had enabled him to master so many languages. He afterwards addressed himself to it with his characteristic vigour and energy, and acquired so highly respectable a knowledge of it as to be enabled to write and speak it with accuracy. But we would have it distinctly understood that his English writings do not furnish a legitimate criterion of his English knowledge. They were, to a certain extent, the production of his European friends, though the thoughts and sentiments embodied in them owed their paternity to him alone. The matter was his, but not wholly the manner of expression; his acquaintance with the English language was, as we have said, highly respectable, and no more,—though, *for his time*, it might well be pronounced remarkable. In writing his religious and political pamphlets; in drawing up papers or even letters of any importance, he had constant assistance from an intelligent and highly educated friend. He did not send a line to the press without submitting it to his revision. The truth is that Rammohun Roy was exceedingly ambitious of literary fame.

It had been remarked by those who came into contact with him that he wrote English much better than he spoke it. The reason is obvious. What he spoke was really his own. What he wrote was not wholly his own *bonâ fide* production. In extenuation, if not in justification of this weakness,—for such, in part, we consider it to be,—we may observe that it was not wholly the result of vanity but of a solicitude to disseminate his sentiments among the European community, for which end it was absolutely necessary that they should be expressed with correctness and elegance. In his own English unquestionably they would not have found their way home to the business and bosoms of his friends; and thus a large proportion of the good, which he could alone effect through the co-operation of the intelligent and well disposed Europeans, would probably have remained undone.

To a man of Rammohun Roy's extensive and varied acquirements, it is however no disparagement to say that he was not an elegant English writer. One, who was decidedly the best Bengali writer, who was one of the most profound Sanskrit scholars, who had mastered Arabic, Persian, Urdu, and Hindustani, who had a tolerable knowledge of Hebrew, Greek and Latin, need not take any shame to himself for not having acquired a complete command over the English Language.

Rammohun Roy's father, Ramkant Roy, died in the Bengali year 1210, corresponding to A. D. 1803, leaving another son besides himself, viz. Jugomohun Roy. It has been roundly asserted by the writer of the memoir placed at the head of this article that Rammohun had been disinherited by his father. This is not true. The assertion owes its origin to the circumstance of his not having accepted any portion of his ancestral property, because of its having been in an encumbered state. As the succession to it would have involved, according to the Hindu Law, a liability to the payment of his father's debts, he thought it proper to have had nothing to do with it. The Maharajah of Burdwan, Tejchand, the father, by adoption, of the present Maharajah, instituted a plaint against Rammohun Roy in the Calcutta provincial Court in 1823, for a balance due from his father on a kist-bundy bond, when his defence was, that inheriting no part of his father's property, he was not legally responsible for his father's debts.

The death of his father having devolved upon his shoulders the management and maintenance of his family, he was led to seek official employment under the British Government. He was most desirous to obtain a provision which might enable him to devote himself to philosophy and literature. He had been favourably noticed by several civilians. His father and grandfather held responsible and lucrative offices under the Mogul Government. His own talents were such as the English Government might have been glad to enlist in the public service. But the road to official distinction had not then been rendered accessible to the natives. The system of making Hindus, Prime ministers and Generals, which constituted a redeeming feature of the Mahommedan administration, was swept away with that rule : and they had not yet been allowed to sit on the bench of justice. The enlightened policy of giving them a share in the administration of their country had not been recognized by the British Government. The narrow and mistaken Cornwallis policy of conducting the administration exclusively through European Agency, which has since proved such a miserable failure, was then in full operation.

The post of Dewan, since called *sheristadar*, was then the highest to which a native could aspire. Rammohun Roy,

wished to get it.   With this view he entered, as a clerk, the
office of Mr. John Digby, Collector of Rungpore.   Connected
with this subject, it is curious to observe that, on his entering
office, a written agreement was signed by Mr. Digby, stipulating that Rammohun should not be kept standing in " *the presence,*" or receive orders as a common Amla from the *Huzúr.*
This circumstance proves, beyond the possibility of contradiction, that the hauteur of the civilian toward the natives, which
has since grown into a proverb among them, and which precludes educated, respectable, and high-spirited men from seeking
employment in the Company's Courts, was, in Rammohun Roy's
time, appreciated as now.   What a reflection is it upon the official
character of the civilian ?   The sovereign contempt with which
many of our English Hukims look down upon the Amla is without a parallel in the annals of servitude, and has in a high
degree succeeded in alienating the better portion of the native
community.   The ranks of the Amlas, being for this reason
mainly supplied from the dregs of that community, their corruption should not be wondered at.   That they should sell their
official influence to the highest bidder, and convert the Mofussil
Courts into dens of iniquity and *Joachury,* is quite in the course
of things.   We would, therefore, strongly urge the desirableness
and importance of gradually levelling down that invidious line of
demarkation between the covenanted and uncovenanted service
which an imaginary necessity or a blind self-interest has up-reared.
We earnestly hope and trust that the discussion which the question of the renewal of the charter will give rise to in parliament, in 1854, will result in the abolition of a distinction,
which, in the opinion of the Bentincks, the Munros, and the
Metcalfes, is not only unjust in principle, but inefficient in
practice.

Free from that " insolence of office" against which the agreement entered into by him with the collector guarded him,
Rammohun Roy addressed himself to his duties with a zeal and
energy which elicited the approbation of his employer, and
soon earned for him the post of Dewan.   By serving in this
capacity, he is said to have realized as much money as enabled
him to become a Zemindar with an income of Rs. " ten thousand a year."   If this assertion be true, it must raise in the
mind a strong suspicion of the moral character of this extraordinary man.   But we are prepared neither to substantiate nor to
contradict it.   Whether his integrity was proof against those temptations, which are generally irresistible to the Amla, or whether,
like another Bacon, he exhibited a melancholy illustration of
the union of intellectual greatness with moral littleness, is a

problem the solution of which is beyond our power. Whether the apostle of Hindu reform, like the high priest of inductive philosophy, sold justice, is a question which, however interesting, we are not competent to decide. The evidence on this subject is too inconclusive to enable us to arrive at a decision. It is therefore impossible to ascertain, with any degree of certainty, whether there was any difference between Rammohun Roy the Reformer, and Rammohun Roy the Dewan—between Rammohun Roy, seated in his study, and discussing with his friends the means of ameliorating the moral and social condition of his countrymen, and Rammohun Roy, located in the collectorate of Rungpore and penning *foisallahs and rubakaries*—between Rammohun Roy, thundering against Hindu idolatry, and Rammohun Roy, conducting the fiscal duties of his office.

If Rammohun Roy did keep his hands clean, and abstain, as in the absence of all positive evidence to the contrary we are bound to suppose, from defeating the ends of justice for a—consideration,—he must have been a splendid exception. Constituted as human nature ordinarily is, it is preposterously absurd to calculate upon a faithful and conscientious discharge of duties by men who, while clothed with all but an irresponsible authority, are paid a pittance which hardly suffices to meet their pocket expenses. The same causes which led the European functionaries before the time of Cornwallis to be more true to their own interests than to those of their Honorable masters, must inevitably operate in producing the same results among the natives. For the system of small pay, and large responsibility, heretofore the pet-system of our Government, makes official corruption the rule, and official integrity the exception. Its inefficiency, however, has been recognized by Government in the late increase of the salaries of the Darogahs. While we rejoice in the adoption of that enlightened policy which has dictated this measure, we would urge its extension to other classes of ministerial officers. The emolument of the Dewan or Sheristadar, the first ministerial officer in the Mofussil Court, is totally inadequate to the responsibility and respectability of the office. We could name several districts and Zillahs where the Sheristadar is the *de facto* Magistrate, the *de facto* Collector, and the *de facto* Judge. It is absolutely necessary that the pay of this functionary should be at least doubled before we can have a right to reckon on his integrity.

The more Mr. Digby saw of Rammohun, the more he appreciated him. The esteem which they entertained for each other ripened into a warm friendship which only terminated with the death of the latter. They cultivated oriental and English

literature in conjunction—mutually aiding each other.   Mr.
Digby many years after, while in England, thus bears his
testimony to the acquirements and opinions of his quondam
Dewan :

"By perusing all my public correspondence with diligence and attention,
as well as by corresponding and conversing with European gentlemen, he
acquired so correct a knowledge of the English language, as to be enabled
to write and speak it with considerable accuracy.   He was also in the
constant habit of reading the English newspapers, of which the continental
politics chiefly interested him, and from them he formed a high opinion of
the talents and prowess of the late ruler of France, and was so dazzled with
the splendour of his achievements, as to become sceptical, as to the commission, if not blind to the atrocity, of his crimes, and could not help deeply
lamenting his downfall, notwithstanding the profound respect he ever professed for the English nation ; but when the first transports of his sorrow
had subsided, he considered that part of his political conduct which led to
his abdication to have been so weak, and so madly ambitious, that he
declared his future detestation of Buonaparte would be proportionate to his
former admiration of him."

Rammohun Roy resided alternately in the Zillahs of Rungpore, Bhagulpore, and Ramghur till the year 1814, when he
took up his residence in Calcutta.   He purchased a garden with
a house constructed in the European mode, and furnished in the
European style, in the upper Circular Road at the eastern
extremity of this city.   Thus we see that, at the age of fifty, he
carried into effect his long cherished plan of retiring from business, and consecrating the latter portion of his life to philosophy
and religion.   His love of literary retirement amounted almost
to a passion.   He used to say that a man, after acquiring a
competence, should spend his life in the enjoyment of philosophic ease.   "Old as I am," said he once to a friend, "I wish I
may retire to a solitary cave, and there apply myself to the
study of the Vedant and Mesnavi.*

To retire from the hurry and bustle of the world—to revel
in the luxuries of lettered leisure—to cultivate philosophy and
religion amidst the solitudes of jungles—to consecrate his
energies to the furtherance of the great work of his country's regeneration,—this was the *beau ideal* of his happiness.   Business,
which is the "be-all and the end-all" of the existence of the great
majority of mankind, whether located in civilized, demi-civilized,
or uncivilized countries, was considered by Rammohun Roy as
something too low to engross a whole life.   He not only knew but
felt the great truth, that man is created for higher ends than the

* The Mesnavi is a work of Maulano Rum, a celebrated Persian poet.   It treats
of religion, morality and politics.   " It is an astonishing work," says Sir W. Jones,
" and the highest flights of sublimity can be found in it."

acquisition of rupees—that being gifted with moral, and intellectual powers, nothing short of the cultivation of all these powers can promote his happiness—that there is that in man which the things of this world cannot altogether satisfy, which longs after eternity, and after Him of whom it hath been sublimely said that he "inhabiteth eternity."

Rammohun Roy, being permanently located in the City of Palaces, gathered around him many inquiring and intelligent Hindus. He soon become the centre of a circle composed of men in advance of their age. From this time forward his career as a reformer commenced. From this time forward to the last day of his existence he devoted himself, heart and soul, to the mighty work of his country's regeneration. He laboured day and night, right and left, to promote this great object. All his hopes and aspirations were centred in the prospect of its realization. It absorbed his energies. It engrossed the whole man.

So effectually has the cruel and demoralizing superstition of the Hindus extinguished the religious feelings of their nature, and perverted their ideas of the very fundamentals of divine worship, that they never think of worshipping their God except by means of unintelligible and unmeaning *montras*. These montras, which they have been taught to articulate without comprehending their import, are considered to be a passport to heaven. Such lip-deep and mechanical devotion is a mockery of worship, and a downright insult to Him who is *to be loved with all the heart, and with all the understanding, and with all the soul, and with all the strength.*

Rammohun Roy sought to reform the faith and worship of his countrymen. By teaching them to comtemplate the natural, intellectual, and moral attributes of God, he proposed to make them worship their Creator " in *spirit* and in *truth.*" The extermination of Hindu idolatry and the dissemination of sound and enlightened views of the Supreme Being—of the unseen and future world—of truth—of happiness—of final beatitude ;—this was the great object of his being. And to the furtherance of that object, he unhesitatingly devoted his talents, his time and his fortune. Endowed with an energy of character and strength of intellect of which his age furnished no model, he braved the most formidable obstacles which opposed themselves to the progress of the good cause he had espoused ; and the pecuniary sacrifices he made to promote that cause were indeed noble. Though his fortune was anything but princely, yet he gladly consecrated a large portion of it to its advancement. Never did a reformer labor more zealously, more sincerely, more indefatigably. Never did a reformer unite in himself more happily the urbanity of the gentleman, and the shrewdness of the man of the world, with the profundity of the philosopher, and the enthusiasm of the theologian. Of course, it will be understood, that we speak of him *relatively*, as a *Hindu reformer*, rising up, by self-effort, out of the chaos of Hinduism. It would be unfair to judge of him by the highest standard of Christian civilization.

It is impossible for us to estimate adequately the exertions he made to liberate the Hindu mind from spiritual bondage, and to indoctrinate it with the pure, elevated and living principles of veneration, justice, and benevolence. One of the means he adopted for the realization of this important end, was the publication and distribution of tracts, on moral and religious subjects. He published them all at his own expense, and distributed them gratuitously among his countrymen.

He first appeared before the public as an author by his translation into Bengali of the celebrated Vedant. It is a resolution of the Vedas, or a compendious digest of the Hindu Scriptures, accompanied with annotations on the more difficult passages. It owes it's paternity to that intellectual phenomenon of India, Krishna Dayapayana Vyas. Regarding this author and his system, enough has appeared in a previous article to render any additional statements necessary here.

Being written in the Sanskrit language, the Vedant is of course inaccessable to the great mass of the Hindus. By presenting to them a Bengali translation of it, Rammohun Roy did no small service to his cause. The Bengali translation was followed by a Hindustani one. In 1816, he published the English translation of the Vedant, " the most celebrated and revered work of Brahmanical theology." The preface, " addressed to the believers of the one true God," is so interesting and so much illustrative of the doctrines he endeavoured to inculcate, that we cannot resist the temptation of quoting it at length :—

" The greater part of Brahmans, as well as of other sects of Hindus, are quite incapable of justifying that idolatry, which they continue to practise. When questioned on the subject, in place of adducing reasonable arguments in support of their conduct, they conceive it fully sufficient to quote their ancestors as positive authorities ! And some of them are become very ill disposed towards me, because I have forsaken idolatry, for the worship of the true and eternal God ! In order, therefore, to vindicate my own faith and that of our early forefathers, I have been endeavouring, for some time past, to convince my countrymen of the true meaning of our sacred books ; and to prove, that my aberration deserves not the opprobrium, which some unreflecting persons have been so ready to throw upon me.

" The whole body of the Hindu Theology, Law, and Literature, is contained in the Veds, which are affirmed to be coeval with the creation ! These works are extremely voluminous ; and being written in the most elevated and metaphorical style, are as may be well supposed, in many passages, seemingly confused and contradictory. Upwards of two thousand years ago, the great Vyasa, reflecting on the perpetual difficulty arising from these sources, composed with great discrimination a complete and compendious abstract of the whole ; and also reconciled those texts, which appeared to stand at variance. This work he termed *the Vedant,* which, compounded of two Sanskrit words, signifies *the resolution of all the Veds.* It has continued to be most highly revered by all the Hindus ; and in place of the more diffuse arguments of the Veds, is always referred to as equal authority. But from its being concealed within the dark curtain of the Sanskrit language and the Brahmans permitting themselves alone to interpret, or even to touch any book of the kind, the Vedant, although perpetually quoted, is little known to the public : and the practice of few Hindus indeed bears the least accordance with its precepts !

" In pursuance of my vindication, I have to the best of my abilities translated this hitherto unknown work, as well as an abridgement thereof into the Hindustani and Bengali languages; and distributed them, free of cost, among my own countrymen, as widely as circumstances have possibly allowed. The present is an endeavour to render an abridgement of the same into English, by which I expect to prove to my European friends, that the superstitious practices, which deform the Hindu religion, have nothing to do with the pure spirit of its dictates !

" I have observed, that, both in their writings and conversation many Europeans feel a wish to palliate, and soften the features of Hindu idolatry ; and are inclined to inculcate, that all objects of worship are considered by their votaries, as emblematical representations of the Supreme Divinity. If this were indeed the case I might perhaps be led into some examination of the subject ; but the truth is, the Hindus of the present day have no such views of the subject, but firmly believe in the real existence of innumerable Gods and Goddesses, who possess, in their own departments, full and independent power ; and to propitiate them, and not the true God, are temples erected, and ceremonies performed. There can be no doubt, however, and it is my whole design to prove, that every rite has its derivation from the allegorical adoration of the true Deity ; but at the present day, all this is forgotten ; and among many it is even heresy to mention it. I hope it will not be presumed, that I intend to establish the preference of my faith, over that of other men. The result of controversy on such a subject, however multiplied must be ever unsatisfactory. For, the reasoning faculty, which leads men to certainty in things within its reach, produces no effect on questions beyond its comprehension. I do not more than assert, that, if correct reasoning, and the dictates of common sense, induce the belief of a wise, uncreated being, who is the supporter and ruler of the boundless universe ; we should also consider him the most powerful and supreme existence ;—far surpassing our powers of comprehension or description !—And although men of uncultivated minds, and even some learned individuals, (but in this one point blinded by prejudice,) readily choose, as the object of their adoration, any thing which they can always see, and which they pretend to feel, the absurdity of such conduct is not thereby in the least degree diminished.

" My constant reflections on the inconvenient, or rather injurious rites introduced by the peculiar practice of Hindu idolatry, which, more than any other Pagan worship, destroys the texture of society, together with compassion for my countrymen, have compelled me to use every possible effort, to awaken them from their dream of error : and by making them acquainted

z z

with their scriptures, enable them to contemplate, with true devotion, the unity and omnipresence of nature's God.

"By taking the path, which conscience and sincerity direct, I, born a Brahman, have exposed myself to the complainings and reproaches, even of some of my relations, whose prejudices are strong, and whose temporal advantage depends upon the present system. But these, however accumulated, I can tranquilly bear; trusting that a day will arrive, when my humble endeavours will be viewed with justice—perhaps acknowledged with gratitude. At any rate, whatever men may say I cannot be deprived of this consolation ; my motives are acceptable to that Being, who beholds in secret, and compensates openly."

After the publication of the Vedant, Rammohun printed, in Bengali and English, translations of the' Kena Upanishad, one of the chapters of the Sama Veda, according to the gloss of the celebrated Sankaracharya, "establishing the unity and the sole omnipotence of the Supreme Being and that He alone is the object of worship." The Upanishads constitute the least exceptionable portion of the Hindu scriptures. The Vedas consist of two portions, viz. : the *Karmakand* and *Gyankand.* The former inculcates the worship of the elements and the performance of rites and ceremonies. The latter, to which the Upanishads belong, treats of the existence and attributes of God. The one is the exoteric and the other the esoteric part of the Hindu religion. The object of his translating the Upanishad was to prove that the performance of the absurd rites and ceremonies, inculcated by the Karmakand, and the celebration of the Pujahs inculcated by the Purans, far from being sanctioned by, is seemingly repugnant to what appeared to be the real spirit, not of the Vedas themselves, but of *the better and more rational parts of the Vedas*, viz. the *Upanishads*.

He endeavoured to show that *Adwaita*, or unity of the Deity, as contradistinguished from that of *Dwaita*, or plurality of Gods, is the fundamental doctrine of the Vedantic system. How far he was correct in holding this opinion, or how far he succeeded in his object is a question which we mean not at present to handle. In the introduction to the Sama Upanishad he says, "this work will, I trust, by explaining to my countrymen the real spirit of the Hindu scriptures which is but the declaration of the unity of God, tend in a great measure to correct the erroneous conceptions which have prevailed with regard to the doctrines they inculcate. It will also I hope tend to discriminate those parts of the Vedas which are to be interpreted in an allegorical sense, and consequently to correct those exceptionable practices which not only deprive Hindus in general of the common comforts of society, but also lead them frequently to self destruction, or to the sacrifice of the lives of their friends and relatives."

In conformity with the plan he had proposed to himself of reasoning his countrymen out of their idolatry, by making them accquainted with the contents of the more rational parts of their own scriptures, he published a Bengali and afterwards an English translation of the Kuth Upanishad of the Yajur Ved, and Mundak Upanishad of the Atharva Ved, and distributed copies of them as widely as possible.

Intense was the sensation which these publications created among the Hindus. Opinions, entirely subversive of the popular and established tenets of Hinduism, had been pronounced by Rammohun Roy in broad daylight. Liberties in thought and action had been fearlessly assumed both by him and his followers, which shocked the bigoted pandits and the lazy ghee-fed Babus. The injurious effects of those customs and institutions, which had for ages marked the peculiar character of the Hindus, had been exposed to the wonderment of men taught to venerate them from their infancy. The Vedas and the Upanishads, which were sealed books to all but the privileged few, had been shewn to be decidedly opposed to the worship of the most popular deities, such as Kali and Durga, and Krishna and Shiva. The prerogative of the Brahmans to expound and study the scripture, had been set at nought. The great mass of the Hindus, whose belief in their creed was, so to speak, based on *hearsay*, had been called upon to examine, for themselves, nay, invited to pronounce the mysteries and pregnant monosyllable Om . Who could therefore assign any limits to the lengths Rammohun might go? The Hindus looked with trembling anxiety on the results of this terrible innovation. The Kali Yug was at hand. In the *Baito-khanahs* of the Babus, as well as in the Tols of the Pandits, the heresy of Rammohun Roy was the one great theme of conversation. Both the Brahman and the Sudra united in counteracting the efforts of the Reformer. The Nyayik, the Mimansik Yogi, and the Puranic, who agree in nothing else,—who wage a perpetual polemical warfare among themselves,—who, at a marriage rite, or a shrad shabha, are invariably to be seen seated on a carpet apart from the rest of the company, and engaged in wrangling on knotty points, relieved only by a dip now and then into their snuff boxes;—all agreed to enlist themselves under the banner of opposition.

The publication of the *Kuth Upanishad,* as well as the application of the term " Reformer" to him by the Editor of the *India Gazette* led to a controversy between him and Sankara Sastri, head English master in the College of Fort St. George, Madras. The Sastri, while he admitted the fact contended for by Rammohun, that the doctrine of unity, in a certain sense, was inculcated by the Puranic as well as the Vedantic systems, insisted that Rammohun had no claim to be considered as the "discoverer" of the doctrine. The controversialist, however, justified the idolatry of his countrymen and particularly the worship of the personified attributes of the Almighty, which he considered to have distinct and independent existence. "If a person," says he, reasoning from an analogy more plausible than correct, "be desirous to visit an earthly prince, he ought to be introduced in the first instance by his ministers, but not of himself to rush upon him at once, regardless of offending him. Should a man wish to ascend a flight of stairs, he ought to proceed, step by step, and not to leap up several at a time, so as to endanger the wounding of his legs. In like manner, the grace of God ought to be obtained by degrees, through the worship of his attributes." The indefatigable Rammohun soon published his reply. He disclaims in it the titles of "Reformer" and "Discoverer,"—justly observing that he was commonly stigmatized by his countrymen, as an innovator. With reference to the Divine Attributes, he shews, by ample quotations and excerpts from the Vedas, that the doctrine of their independent existence was obviously incompatible with the fundamental principles of the Vedantic system. Soon after, a Bhattachargjya of Calcutta appeared in the field. He published a letter in Bengali and English containing a fierce attack upon his opinions. It elicited a well penned tract from him entitled, "second defence of the monotheistical system of the Vedas."

But the opposition of his countrymen to his opinions was not confined to literary warfare. A degree of persecution had been excited against him which it required no ordinary moral courage to brave. His name was coupled with obloquy. So utterly incapable were his countrymen of appreciating his labours, or rather so utterly blinded were they by downright bigotry, that they nicknamed him a *nastik* (atheist.) That he was an ungodly man, and aimed at the destruction of all religion, was what they firmly believed. He had been several times threatened with personal violence,—so much so, that he made it a point, whenever he went out, to have a kind of guard accompanying his carriage. That he should be called an atheist by the bigoted Hindus is by no means to be wondered at. We know that the charge of atheism, the highest in our opinion which one man can prefer against another, usually proceeds from men who are apt to identify mere theism with atheism. The words *scepticism, atheism,* or *infidelity*, as *generally* applied, mean, when properly analysed, only a departure from national or popular religion. The Mahommedans call every body an infidel or an atheist who does not believe in the Alkoran. The educated native, who dares to disown the doctrines of Hinduism, is called by his idolatrous countrymen a *mlechha* and a *nastik*. Every nation on the face of the earth, and from the dawn of history to the present moment, has branded with the opprobrium of infidelity all those who, persuaded of the absurdities of the national and ancestral faith, embrace purer and more elevated views of religion.

That Rammohun Roy entertained the highest respect for the practical part of the Christian religion does not admit of dispute. No one could more thoroughly appreciate and venerate the code of morality inculcated in the Bible. That it was the purest, the most elevated, the most sublime code in the world, was cheerfully admitted by him. He had acquired the Hebrew and Greek languages in order to be able to read the scriptures of the Christians in the original. He had afterwards studied the Old Testament with a Jewish rabbi and the New Testament with some Christian divines. After having matured the fruits of his researches into the Christian and Hindu scriptures, he published in 1820, anonymously, his celebrated work, " The Precepts of Jesus the guide to Peace and Happiness." It consists principally of selections from the first three gospels. In the Preface to this work he says :—

" This simple code of religion and morality is so admirably calculated to elevate men's ideas, to high and liberal notions of one God, who has equally subjected all living creatures, without distinction of caste, rank, or wealth, to change, disappointment, pain, and death; and has equally admitted all to be partakers of the bountiful mercies which he has lavished over nature ; and is also so well fitted to regulate the conduct of the human race in the discharge of their various duties to God, to themselves, and Society, that I cannot but hope the best effects from its promulgation in the present form."

The publication of this work brought upon him an attack far more formidable than any he had encountered from his countrymen. In the first No. of the *Friend of India* (quarterly series) there appeared an elaborate and learned article, " Observations on certain ideas contained in the Introduction to the precepts of Jesus the guide to peace and happiness." This elicited a reply from Rammohun, under the signature of " A Friend to Truth," in " An Appeal to the Christian Public." The Appeal led to a reply from the *Friend of India*, and to a second Appeal in Rammohun Roy's own name, which again called forth an attack upon him from the same Journal. The first two appeals had been printed at the Serampore Press, but the proprietor having expressed some conscientious scruples about printing the " Final Appeal," Rammohun forthwith purchased types, and set up the " Unitarian Press, Dharmatollah." His " final appeal," as well as all his subsequent works were printed at this press.

It was amidst the sensation occasioned amongst the European and the enlightened portion of the native community, by the publication of the appeals of Rammohun, and the counter appeals of the " Friend," that Brojomohun Mujumdhar, a friend and disciple of the Hindu reformer, published an essay entitled, " Strictures on the present system of Hindu monotheism," in the Bengali language. We are inclined to believe, however, that it owed its paternity, at least in some degree, to an intellect superior to that of the apparent author; and our belief is strengthened by the fact of Rammohun's being in the habit of publishing his works either anonymously, or in the names of his friends. At all events it must have been published under the auspices of the Hindu reformer.

This brochure is evidently stamped with the impress of a strong mind. It is a clever and bold attack on Hinduism. It is " a masterly exposure," as Dr. Marshman in reviewing justly characterized it, " of the absurdities of the Hindu system." All the arguments brought in support of Hindu idolatry are unanswerably refuted. The tomfooleries of the Hindu mode of worship are held up to merited ridicule and contempt. It displays a profound acquaintance with the Hindu Shastras. In depth of argumentation, energy of diction, and keenness of satire it is surpassed by few Bengali works. But independently of it's merits, we hail it as the first production of the kind by a native in his own language. That in the heart of Calcutta, the very stronghold of wealthy bigotry, there should uprise a respectable Hindu to expose the absurdities of Hinduism, was a cheering illustration of the progress of improvement, and an auspicious omen of good things to come.

Though the exertions of Rammohun Roy to subvert Hinduism and disseminate purer and more elevated notions of religion and morality had alienated from him the great mass of his countrymen, and brought down upon him not only unmerited obloquy, but a large amount of persecution ;—yet it is comforting to know that they were appreciated by the thinking portion of the Natives. The seceders from the ranks of Hinduism daily increased and joined his standard.

Several intelligent, respectable, and opulent natives in whom we recognize some of the present leaders of the Native

Society, embraced his views. " The ground which I took," says he, in one of his letters before us, " in all my controversies was not of opposition to Brahmanism, but to a perversion of it ; and I endeavoured to show that the idolatry of the Brahmans was contrary to the practice of their ancestors and the principles of the ancient books and authorities which they profess to revere and obey. Notwithstanding the violence of the opposition and resistance to my opinions, several highly respectable persons, both among my own relations and others, began to adopt the same sentiments." He soon became the leader of a sect, the basis of whose creed was the unity of Deity in opposition to polytheism. It was composed of men who had been taught to think boldly, and who had been strongly persuaded of the evils of that idolatry which had dwarfed the national mind. They therefore readily joined him in establishing a Society for putting down that idolatry. The *Brahma Sumaj* was established in 1828. The Shabha holds weekly meetings on Wednesday evenings, when the Vedas are read and expounded, and discourses in Bengali are delivered. The subjects embraced by the discourses, relate to general principles in morals and religion. The meetings, " open to men of all persuasions," are now attended by considerable numbers. They always conclude with the singing of hymns composed by Rammohun Roy himself and his friends. The other means, adopted by the Society for the realization of it's object, are the preparation and publication of Bengali Tracts on moral and religious subjects, and the reprinting of Sanskrit works on Vedantism.

The excitement, created by this organization, was proportioned to the magnitude of the change aimed at by it's Founder. That the veil of mystery, which had enshrouded from time immemorial, the more sacred portion of the Hindu scriptures should be unceremoniously torn open, and its contents revealed to the irreverant gaze of those who had been studiously precluded, by interested priestcraft, from even a superficial acquaintance with them—that the Gáyatri should be pronounced before not only the sudra, but the *mlechha*—that the sudra, and the mlechha should be called upon to participate in the worship of Brahma ;—this could not fail to shock the feelings of the Hindus and impel them at last to adopt some strenuous measures for counteracting the efforts of the *Brahma Dol*. They established the Dharma Shabha, with the avowed object of upholding Hinduism in all its integrity. and preserving its laws and institutions from the inroads of the Brahma Shabha. This corporation soon increased in numbers and in strength. The success which had attended it's exertions showed that the national character of the Hindus—pre-eminently distinguished by a spirit of exclusiveness and disunion, and an apathetic indifference to all but the animal wants of life,—had changed for once. The noise of theological controversy reverberated throughout the country. The Hindu community became divided into two great parties, the Brahma Shabha party and the Dharma Shabha party. The principles of these Shabhas carried on their warfare in every part of Native Society, in every Tol, in every Baitokhana, in every Dalan, in every Chondimundub, in every Zenana. Sometimes the bigotry and fanaticism of the Dharma party, seemed to triumph over the Vedantism of the Brahma Shabha. Sometimes the Brahma Gyanis seemed to carry every thing before them.

Though the influence, exercised by the Dharma Shabha over the Hindus, was at one time all but omnipotent, yet we rejoice to know that it is now on the wane, and that the days of the Shabha itself are numbered. It has been rent in twain, and ceased to enlist the real sympathies of the Hindu public. Every educated and intelligent native would, we are sure, cordially participate in our wish for the immediate dissolution of a society, which preaches the doctrine of non-intercourse, and aims at the laceration of domestic and social ties. But the Shabha distinguished itself not only by its inquisitorial proceedings but by its opposition to every liberal measure. One of its first movements was, we believe, the presentation of a petition to Government *against* the abolition of the Suttee (Sati) rite, and one of its last movements has been the presentation of a similar petition against the Lexi Loci, in reference to the xi, xii and xiii clauses, emphatically called the *liberty of conscience clauses,*—abolishing that portion of the Hindu law which inflicts forfeiture of ancestral property on persons renouncing the Hindu or Mahommedan religion.

The Suttee rite, in the perpetuation of which the Dharma Shabha had been deeply interested, was one of the monster evils of this country. It had led thousands and tens of thousands of women to an untimely grave. Deluded by the hopes of perennial happiness, they performed the rite of *Shamaran*, i. e. burnt themselves alive with the bodies of their deceased husbands. The banks of the Bhagirathi exhibited for centuries the horrid spectacle of the *chulli* blazing fearfully, over the dead and the living! Rammohun Roy deeply felt for these infatuated victims of superstition. His heart bled at the horrors of Shamaran and Anamaran. He had always openly, and in no measured terms, denounced this inhuman and diabolical rite. He published in 1820, for general circulation, a tract both in Bengali and English languages entitled, "A conference between an advocate for, and an opponent of the practice of burning widows alive." This was followed by a second Conference which he dedicated to the Marchioness of Hastings. The object of these publications was to show that the rite of Suttee, though tolerated by Hariit, Ungira, and other inferior authorities, was by no means clearly sanctioned by Manu, and decidedly opposed to the tenets of the Vedas. By excerpts from the principal Shastras, he proved that these appeared to assign greater merit to a life of purity and austerity on the part of the widows than to the performance of the *Shahamaran*.

The unanswerable arguments, embodied in the "Conferences," silently paved the way for the abolition of this rite. Though the necessity of such abolition had been admitted by the Government as early as 1805, yet nothing was done towards it, because of the interference with the Hindu religion which it was supposed to involve.*

The "Conferences" contributed to dispel this error; and towards the close of 1829, Lord William Bentinck—a name enshrined in the hearts of the natives—at once abolished a rite not only horrid and revolting but fraught with incalculable mischief. When the Dharma Shabha got up the remonstrance we have alluded to, Rammohun Roy, in spite of personal outrage, led a deputation who presented an address to the Governor-General, embodying the grateful acknowledgments of the enlightened portion of the native community for this "everlasting boon" conferred on their country. His indefatigable exertions in putting lown this rite, as well as in elevating the females of this countiy from that state of intellectual abasement into which they are sunk, cannot be sufficiently lauded.

In the early part of 1830, an event occurred which signally illustrated his genuine liberality of sentiment. The Founder of the General Assembly, (now Free Church) institution, on his arrival in this country, was introduced to him, and propounded those educational views, which have since been so largely carried out in practice. Rammohun expressed his warmest approbation of them, declaring that all education ought to be based on religion, and that he saw no evil but much good likely to result to his countrymen from the teaching of the Christian

---

* Mr. Secretary Dodswell. in writing to the Register of the Nizamut Adawlut, of the Suttee rite, says, " *Should* this practice be not grounded on any precept of their law, the Governor General would hope that the custom, which at present prevails among Hindu women of burning themselves with the bodies of their deceased husbands, might gradually but not immediately be altogether abolished."

Bible as a class book in schools. More than this, he practically assited the Rev. Doctor, in every way in his power, in founding his proposed institution—reserved for the use of it the hall of the Brahma Shabha, then recently vacated for the one since occupied—attended daily for upwards of a month, and often afterwards, to encourage the boys, and reconcile them to the reading of the Bible. He approved of the institution's being daily opened with prayer, and recommended the use of " the Lord's Prayer," as being, in his view, the most compendious, and at the same time, the most compenhensive form of prayer in any book or language. For these and other services we have often heard the Rev. Founder of the institution speak of Rammohun Roy, with mingled emotions of affection, gratitude, and respect.

Rammohun Roy had cherished for some years a strong desire to visit Europe, and " obtain," as he says in one of his letters, " by personal observation a more thorough insight into its manners, customs, religion and political institutions." He longed especially to see the country to whose keeping the destinies of his own had been entrusted—the country, where philosophy, liberty, and science had achieved their proudest triumphs—the country of Lockes, of Bacons, of Newtons, of Hampdons, and of Watts.

The labors, in which he was engaged, tended to postpone for some time the fulfilment of this desire. The success, however, with which they were afterwards crowned, (as evidenced in the increase of his party and the spread of his views,) as well as the anticipated parliamentary discussion on the renewal of the Company's charter, induced him to make preparations for his visit. Another circumstance also favoured his design. The emperor of Delhi, considering himself entitled to the revenue of certain lands in the vicinity thereof, had applied to the Court of Directors. The subject had been considered by that body and afterward by the Board of Control; and it was determined that the Mogul received all that he originally agreed to accept, and all that he was entitled to, in law or equity. The emperor, resolved to try the experiment of an appeal to the king of England, had appointed Rammohun his ambassador, with full powers to manage the negotiation, and conferred on him by firman the title of " Rajah."

The announcement of Rammohun Roy's intention of visiting Europe—the land of the mlechas and beef-eaters—excited much speculation among his countrymen. Being incapable of understanding that enlightened curiosity, and that disinterested philanthropy which prompted him to undertake the voyage, they ascribed to him several unworthy motives. But the man who had braved their persecutions—who had triumphed over the formidable obstacles which threatened to neutralize his labors—who had set at defiance the thunders of the Dharma shabha, and the fulminations of the Brahmins, was not to be deterred, by the sneerings and howlings of his countrymen, from the performance of a resolution he had deliberately adopted. On the 15th November, 1830, the Rajah, accompanied by his adopted son Babu Rajaram Roy, and two Hindu servants, Ramrutten Mukerjya and Ramhori Mukerjya, left his native land in the *Albion*, bound for Liverpool. The particulars of the voyage have been thus graphically described by a fellow-traveller who is now among us, and who has been for many years connected with our periodical literature:—

" On ship-board Rammohun Roy took his meals in his own cabin, and at first suffered considerable inconvenience from the want of a separate fire place ; having nothing but a common earthern *chula* on board. His servants too, fell desperately sea-sick, (though, as if his ardour supported him against it, he himself never felt this malady at all) and took possession of his cabin, never moving from it, and making it as may be easily conceived, no enviable domicile ; in fact, they compelled him to retreat to the lockers ; but still the kindness of his nature would not allow him to remove them. The greater part of the day he read, chiefly, I believe, Sanskrit and Hebrew. In the forenoon and the evening he took an airing on deck, and always got involved in an animated discussion. After dinner, when the cloth was removed, and the desert on table, he would come out of his cabin also, and join in the conversation and take a glass of wine. He was always cheerful, and so won upon the esteem of all on board, that there was quite a competition who should pay him the most attention, and even the sailors seemed anxious to render him any little service in their power. In a gale of wind he would be upon deck, gazing at the foam-crested surges as they roared by the vessel, and admiring the sublimity of the scene. On one occasion I brought on deck the " Ocean Sketches,"[*] and read to him the first piece, entitled " The Breeze : "

" The distant haze, like clouds of silvery dust
Now sparkles in the sun. The freshening breeze
Whitens the liquid plain ; and like a steed
With proud impatience fired, the glorious ship,
Quick bounds exultant, and with rampant prow,
Off flings the glittering foam. Around her wake,
A radiant milky way, the sea-birds wave,
Their circling flight, or slowly sweeping wide,
O'er boundless ocean, graze with drooping wing
The brightly crested waves. Each sudden surge,
Up-dashed, appears a momentry tree,
Fringed with the hoar frost of a wintry morn ;
And then, like blossoms from a breeze-stirred bough,
The light spray strews the deep.
How fitfully the feeble day-beams pierce

[*] By D. L. R.,—a signature too well known in our Indian Literature to require any further explication here.

The veil of heaven !　On yon far line of light,
That like a range of breakers, streaks the main,
The ocean swan—the snow-white Albatross,
Gleams like a dazzling foam-flake in the sun !—
Gaze upward—and behold, where parted clouds
Disclose ethereal depths, its dark-hued mate
Hangs motionless on arch-resembling wings,
As though, 'twere painted on the sky's blue vault.
Sprinkling the air, the speck-like petrels form
A living shower !　A while their pinions gray
Mingle scarce-seen among the misty clouds,
Till suddenly their white breasts catch the light,
And flash like silver stars ! "

He recognized at once the fidelity of this picture ; although not much given to poetical reading."

The *Albion* arrived at her destination on the 8th April, 1831. The Rajah landed the same day at Liverpool and took up his lodging at one of the hotels there.　His arrival in England, which he had long wished to visit and where his fame had preceeded him, excited a considerable degree of interest.　His arrival too was at a period of extraordinary political fermentation.　The whole nation had been wrought up into a state of overpowering excitement.　Reform was then the one great subject which agitated the whole country.　Rammohun Roy became a zealous and enthusiastic advocate of it.　He saw at once the bearings of the great national measure which was calculated, in his opinion, to " promote the welfare of England and her dependencies, nay of the whole world."

No sooner was the advent of the great Brahmin philosopher known in Liverpool than almost every man of distinction in the place hastened to call upon him.　One of the first visits he received was from the three sons of the celebrated William Roscoe.　They came, not merely on their own account, but to convey to him the " affectionate greeting" of their distinguished parent.　Roscoe had not for years quitted his apartment—being troubled with a paralytic affection which incapacitated him from assuming any other than a recumbent posture.　When Rammohun arrived he was confined to his death-bed, and was not allowed to receive any visit.　He made an exception, however, in favour of Rammohun, with whom he had before corresponded.　The interview was deeply interesting and affecting ; interesting, because an event which was the theme of their conversation, viz. Reform, was one to which both had looked forward as a consummation devoutly to be wished for, but as one of those contingencies which was scarcely within the range of early probability ; and affecting, because they felt that this cheering interchange of sympathies, this delightful and unreserved expression of sentiments, must soon be terminated by the stern fiat of that dread tyrant under whose relentless grasp one of them seemed to be already writhing. This proved, as they had anticipated, their first and their last interview on this side of eternity. Rammohun Roy heard of Roscoe's death while residing in London.

This introduction to the historian of the Medici took place at the well-known house in Lodge-Lane; and though there were none present at the interview except the two great men, and one of Roscoe's sons, yet the room below was crowded with the gentility of Liverpool. Many and eager were the enquiries about the Stranger's political and religious opinions—his habits and his object in visiting England. They were hushed when he returned from the sick chamber, with agitated countenance and moistened eyes. As soon as he recovered from the effects of his interview, he reciprocated the cordial greetings of those around him, and got into a very interesting and animated discussion with some gentlemen. Thus it was that at Mr. Roscoe's house a Hindu was, for the first time in Great Britain, heard zealously and earnestly advocating civil and religious liberty throughout the world—and talking of the Edinburgh and the Quarterly—the Whigs and Tories—Lord Grey and Reform.

The first public place he attended at Liverpool was Dr. Grundy's Unitarian Chapel. The sermon was, *apropos* to the occasion, in exposition of the duty of unlimited charity in our judgments of the creeds of other men, and of their principles of belief. He listened to it with the utmost attention, and afterwards expressed himself very much pleased with it. When the sermon was over, the scene that ensued was curious enough. The congregation, instead of dispersing, thronged up every avenue to get a near view of the great Brahmin philosopher; and it was not till they had heard him address them in their own language and shaken hands with him that they could be prevailed upon to allow him to return.

At Liverpool, Rammohun Roy got acquainted with Dr. Spurzheim. Though the great phrenologist and the great reformer met often, and were good friends, yet the latter never hesitated to laugh at the science of the former. The bump of good nature being however largely developed in Spurzheim, he used simply to observe when thus attacked, that if his friend would only study the facts on which phrenology was based, he would change his opinions. Spurzheim was very anxious to get a cast of the head of Rammohun Roy; and though he was promised that he should be permitted to take one, yet the promise, we know not why, was not fulfilled. One of the visits which Rammohun received in Liverpool is described with great *naiveté* by one of his friends, who was, we believe, present on the occasion:—

" While he was at Liverpool he received a call from a gentleman with whom he was much amused ; his visitor, a retired Indian officer, of the old school, with a squat figure, a jolly face, and a conscious smile of self-satisfaction playing on his features, was much more gifted with good nature than good sense or good taste. As soon as he saw the Hindu philosopher, he began addressing him in that elegant dialect in which Europeans in this country make their coup d'essai in Eastern languages. *Ucha, toom Bengali, hum Bengali, toom Bengali*, well, *kysa hy Sahib ?* Then turning to the young Rajah, who was present, "Ah *Chuckera* (*Chokra*), well, *kitna burras ?* " (or rather *brass* as he made it) *kysa Mulk* (*Moolug*) *Utcha hy ?* and so on ; to all which Rammohun gracefully bowed. At length, the gallant officer was informed, that the gentleman he was addressing, spoke English as well as he did, (in truth he spoke it much more correctly.) It appeared, that he came as a delegate from no less a potentate than the mayor, who, fearful of compromising his dignity by calling himself, had deputed his friend to suggest the propriety of the distinguished stranger's calling upon this high civil functionary, and to hint that if he did, the honour would be acknowledged by an *invite* to a Lord Mayor's dinner ; and the intimation was delivered with an air of importance, which seemed to imply, " Think of that, Master Brooke. " It happened, however, that the party he addressed, had not formed exactly the same lofty estimate of its importance as his visitor, and therefore declined the invitation with cold ingratitude ; and when the Major was gone, he vowed, using an emphatic English expression, that if the mayor wanted to see him, he might call upon him, as his superiors had done, and as it seemed to me, that hospitality, propriety, and good feeling demanded ; but mayors are not always, it must be confessed, possessed of taste,—

—— " Unless it be
For calipash or calipee. "

And so our friend lost the opportunity of making his bow to the Mayor of Liverpool."

Rammohun Roy's stay in Liverpool was not long. As he travelled up to London he was delighted with observing the indubitable and living proofs of wealth, civilization and refinement which the country exhibited. The splendid villas, the smiling cottages with their well trimmed gardens, the magnificent prospects, the railroads, the canals and the bridges ; all afforded a rich banquet to his eyes, and were eagerly recognized by him as the triumphs of that knowledge, that industry, that energy, that public spirit which had given England her preeminence among the nations of the earth, and the lack of which had rendered his own country the abode of misery and destitution. He stopped at Manchester to visit the great factories. The machinery, which seemed to live, and breathe and move before him, attracted his attention and admiration ; but the scene that ensued at the great metropolis of manufacturing industry was curious and interesting. All the work people, men, women and children, left work and rushed in crowds to see the "*great King of Ingee.*" After shaking hands with many of the "great unwashed," he turned round and addressed them, "hoping they would all support the king and his ministers in obtaining reform." His appeal was cordially responded to with loud shouts of "the King and Reform for ever."

The Rajah arrived in London at night and was set down at a filthy Inn in a filthy part of the town. He had intended to remain there till morning, but the "abominable odours" that regaled his olfactory nerves in the bedroom allotted to him, necessitated him to leave. He ordered a coach and set off to the Adelphi Hotel where he arrived at 10 o'clock, P. M. When he had retired to rest, and it was nearly midnight, Bentham called at the Hotel, and left a laconic and characteristic note for him:—"Jeremy Bentham to his friend Rammohun Roy." The visit of the utilitarian Philosopher to the Hindu Reformer was a compliment which the latter fully appreciated. It was indeed a higher distinction than his subsequent lionization by the British people. That Bentham—who had secluded himself as it were from the world—who had made it a point to refuse all invitations to the convivial board, in order that he might "consecrate," to quote his very words, "every moment of his life to the service of mankind"—should have left his hermitage, for the purpose of seeing Rammohun Roy, was an unequivocal proof of his admiration for this enlightened and extraordinary Hindu. They afterward met each other, and it must have been a very interesting sight to have seen these two great men engaged in conversation on the greatest-happiness principle, in reference to politics and morals, on the condition of the natives, and on the administration of the East India Company. "Rammohun Roy," said the venerable founder of the utilitarian school, "has cast off three hundred and thirty millions of gods and has learnt from us to embrace reason in the all-important field of religion." He became so great an admirer of him that he addressed him as his "intensely admired and dearly-beloved collaborateur in the service of mankind."

No sooner was his arrival in London announced, than many of the most distinguished men crowded to see him. He had scarcely got into his lodgings in Regent-Street when his door was beseiged with carriages, from 11 in the morning till 4 in the afternoon. The urbanity of his manners and the suavity of his disposition, fascinated those with whom he came in contact; and the familiarity he discovered with every topic connected with the institutions, opinions, and religion of England, as well as his liberal views on all subjects, astonished even those who were prepared to find in him an enlightened and extraordinary man.

The recognition of his official relation and title by the ministers afforded an indubitable evidence of the estimation in which he was held by them. When we remember how much the people of England are ordinarily disposed to lionize distinguished foreigners, we should not at all be surprized at the splendid reception he met with from them. He mixed with the first circles. He was courted by the rich and the powerful. Not only the ex-Judges, and ex-Councillors, but ex-Governors sought his friendship. Many of the " nabobs," whose *huzurs* did not condescend to take any notice of him in this country, and who would not have allowed him to wait upon them at their kacharies without being slipshod, were all eager to claim the honor of his acquaintance. Though many of the Earls and Marquisses and Dukes wanted only to lionize him, and turn him to account as an attraction at their *soirees,* yet there were several men who appreciated him, and sought his company with a view to acquire information on India. Among these were Lord Brougham, Sir W. Horton, Sir Henry Strachy and Sir Charles Forbes. With Lord Brougham, or rather with Henry Brougham,—for then this great man was known only as the bold and uncompromising advocate of popular education and the abolition of slavery—Rammohun Roy lived on terms of the closest and most confidential intimacy.

Not only the greatest men in the kingdom, but royalty itself delighted to do him honor. He was presented to the King by Sir J. C. Hobhouse, the then president of the Board of Control, and his Majesty assigned him a place at the Coronation among the ambassadors. On the opening of the London Bridge, he was invited by his Majesty to the dinner which was given in celebration of that event. The Court of Directors, though they refused to recognize his embassy and his title, treated him with honor. They entertained him at a public dinner on the 6th July, in the name of the Company at the London Tavern.

In accordance with the avowed object of his visit to Europe, he frequented every kind of assemblage, religious, political, literary, or social. He was to be seen in the drawing-room of the nobleman, as well as in the study of the humble man of letters —in parliament, listening to the impassioned eloquence of the champions of the Reform bill, as well as in the church, following the preacher in his sublime flights to eternity.

The charms of enlightened Female Society were highly

appreciated by the Rajah. The amiability of his manners, and the orientalism and deferential respect of his address, rendered him in return an especial favourite with the Ladies. Though born in a country where the females, endungeoned in the Zenana, are sunk in the slough of ignorance and prejudice, yet he knew and felt that humanizing influence which is exercised by female society on European character. It is no wonder, therefore, that he was an ardent admirer of British females. " The particulars of my voyage," says he, " and travels will be found in a Journal which I intend to publish, together with whatever has appeared to me most worthy of remark and record, in regard to the intelligence, riches, power, manners, customs and especially the *female virtue and excellence existing in this country.*"

Besides the society of European females there was another society which he liked, viz. that of pious and enlightened clergymen. He had seen the generous and heroic sacrifices made by some of the Missionaries in his fatherland. He had witnessed their laudable exertions in promoting the moral and intellectual enlightenment of his countrymen. He had seen them take the lead in every thing that had a tendency to improve and elevate the native character. His intercourse with religious persons in Europe, increased therefore his esteem for a class of men who have done so much to benefit their fellow-beings. " If I were to settle with my family in Europe," he used to say, " I would never introduce them to any but religious persons, and from amongst them only would I select my friends; amongst them I find such kindness and friendship, that I feel as if surrounded by my own kindred."

It was not long before the discussion on the renewal of the charter came on in Parliament. Several individuals who had served under the Company, in their civil or military services, or resided in India as merchants or planters, were examined as witnesses. Rammohun Roy was also called upon to give his evidence before the select Committee of the House of Commons.

That his knowledge, experience, and patriotism entitled him to speak authoritatively on subjects connected with the government of his country, does not admit of a moment's question. His evidence has been since embodied in a volume entitled, " Exposition of the practical operation of the Judicial and Revenue systems of India and of the general character and condition of its native inhabitants." His replies to the queries of the Select Committee not only demonstrate an acquaintance with the evils of his country, but contain several valuable suggestions. They are not characterized by any unmeaning vituperation against the Indian Government, but breathe throughout a sincere and earnest wish to ameliorate the condition of his countrymen. They are distinguished, above all, by a deep and lively sympathy with the condition of those crushed and prostrate millions of India, known by the name of RYOTS.

The political creed of the Rajah was decidedly that of a liberal. But it did by no means border on ultra-radicalism. He was a reformer, but a moderate and judicious one. In his youth, he was violently opposed to the English Government. But as he saw more of it, and learnt to compare it with the Mahommedan Government, his strong aversion was converted into a warm admiration for its general character. He considered the conquest of this country by the English nation as a providential interposition, calculated to answer important ends in the economy of the moral world. Though he was fully cognizant of the complex organization of the Government, and of all the wrongs and grievances inseparable from it's operation, yet he cheerfully and gratefully admitted the manifold blessings it conferred on his country; and was strongly of opinion that the English were better fitted to govern it than the natives themselves, and that the withdrawal of the former, under existing circumstances, supposing it were to take place, would prove a curse rather than a blessing.

Rammohun Roy was a bold and enthusiastic advocate of civil and religious liberty. He watched with intense anxiety its progress in Europe, and tried his best to contribute to its advancement in his own country. When the Spanish Constitution was established, he and his friend Dwarkanath Tagore, to celebrate the event, gave a *Burra Khana* to their European friends. He was a great friend of Mr. Buckingham's, and when Governor Adam signed the death warrant of the " Calcutta Journal," and banished its spirited and philanthropic Editor, he got up, it is well known, the memorable appeal to the king in council for the liberty of free printing in India.

The influence which the Rajah obtained over the leaders of both the Whigs and Conservatives in England was extraordinary; and it was highly honorable to him that he rendered it subservient, not to his own aggrandisement, but to the political elevation of his country. We shall be able to judge of the extent of that influence, when we observe, that an urgent letter of his prevented the Conservatives from opposing one of the Indian Bills in the House of Lords; and we are sure that he would have carried many ameliorative measures with reference to this country, but for the influence of the Leadenhall magnates and the weakness of the ministry.

In the autumn of 1832, he paid a visit to France, where the reception he met with, was as splendid as in England. He was received by Louis Philippe with the highest consideration, and dined with his Majesty twice. Literary as well as political men vied with each other in testifying their regard for their extraordinary guest.

In the beginning of the year 1833, the Rajah returned to the hospitable mansion of Messrs. John and Joseph Hare, brothers of the late David Hare; but he returned with a dilapidated constitution. He had suffered before from bilious attacks. They were aggravated by the climate of Europe, and induced a slight pulmonary affection. In this state he went to Bristol, in the early part of September, to spend a few weeks with Miss Castles, at Stapleton Grove, intending to proceed thence to Devonshire, there to pass the winter.

Nine days after his arrival, he was attacked with a fever. Drs. Prichard and Carrick attended him. Medicine afforded him, however, only temporary relief. His fever returned with redoubled vigour, and swelled into what the native doctors would call *Bigar*. The delirium was succeeded by a stupor from which he never recovered, and he breathed his last at 25 minutes after 2 A. M. on the 27th September. He had a sort of consciousness that he was approaching his end. He conversed very little during his illness, but was observed to be often engaged in mental prayer. The intensity of his emotions, while thus occupied, was remarkably reflected by his expressive and transparent features.

Just before he had set out for Europe, the Rajah told his friends that, on his death, each sect, the Christian, the Hindu, and the Mahommedan would respectively claim him to be of their persuasion, but he expressly declared that he belonged to none of them. His prediction has been fully realized. No sooner did he depart this life, than the subject of his religious opinions became an apple of discord. A variety of speculations was hazarded by different parties. While some represented him to be a Hindu, others affirmed that he was a Christian. The church-of-England-party said, that he was attached to their church; while the Unitarians claimed him for their own. The Vedantists represented him as literally a believer in their professed revelation; while the Mussulmans contended that he was a follower of the son of Abdullah. We confess, however, that each of these sects had reason enough for wrenching him to its side. From his frequent attendance, while in England, at their chapels, and his known bias to their doctrines, the unitarians had some sort of right to claim him. The especial patronage which he thought it proper to bestow on Vedantism, made it more than probable that he was a Vedantist. The profuse, though not altogether unmerited laudation he was in the habit of lavishing on the Mahommedan creed, was calculated to produce an impression that he was a believer in the Alkoran. But that Rammohun Roy was not a Mussulman in his creed, it requires no lengthened demonstration to prove. Neither was he an unitarian. We would go further and say,—though it may startle some of our readers who have been accustomed to identify Rammohun Roy with Vedantism,—that he was *not* a Vedantist. What then was he? This is not merely a curious, but an interesting and important problem, of which we shall attempt to give a solution, as the religious opinions of the Hindu Reformer appear to be still enveloped in mystery.

All speculations, as to his belief in the abstract truth of any religion, founded on his advocacy of certain doctrines connected with it, or his attendance at it's place of worship, are obviously futile. For Rammohun Roy was a religious Benthamite, and estimated the different creeds existing in the world, not according to his notion of their truth, or falsehood, but his notion of their utility; according to their tendency, in his view, to promote the maximization of human happiness, and the minimization of human misery. His patronage, therefore, of any system of creed cannot be construed into a profession of it. He endeavoured to refine all gross and idolatrous systems into a system of pure monotheism. His works on Hindu Theology do not prove that he was a believer in the revelation of the Vedas, but that he aimed at engrafting a kind of universal unitarianism on it. But we have said that he was not an unitarian. To be sure not. At least, his unitarianism was essentially different from that of the Channings, the Carpenters, the Priestleys, and the Belshams. His was a sort of Catholic unitarianism. It was philosophical theism. It was Natural Religion. It was the religion of many of the ancient philosophers. His advocacy and support of the doctrines inculcated by religions which are in themselves diametrically opposed to each other, though it might apparently evidence his vacillation, was in fact the result of his religious utilitarianism; for we can confidently assert that, in reference to his religious belief, not the slightest change took place in his mind for the last fifty years of his life. From his first renunciation of Hindu idolatry, at the age of sixteen, to the last moment of his existence, he maintained his religious sentiments, whatever they were, nearly unaltered. The real religious sentiments of the Hindu Reformer are embodied in a pamphlet, written in the most choice Persian, with an Arabic preface. Though printed in his lifetime and seen by some of his friends, yet it was not published until his death; for he gave it as his last injunction, on leaving his country for Europe, that it should be published after his departure from this world. This work, which is entitled *Tohufut-ul Mowahedeen,* or a Present to Unitarians, discloses his belief in the unity of the Deity, his infinite power and infinite goodness, and in the immortality of the soul. It breathes an uncompromising and inveterate hostility to idolatry in all its forms. While due meed of applause is given to the Mahommedan creed, for being based on what he considered as the great doctrine of unity, the prophetical pretensions of the avatar of Mecca are treated with merited ridicule and contempt.

From what has been said, it is obvious, that Rammohun Roy was an eclectic philosopher. He was, according to our humble opinion, essentially a theo-philanthropist. To promote love to God, and love to man, agreeably to his own view of both, constituted the practical and most important part of his creed. He had a strong sentiment of natural religion. He was deeply impressed with the necessity and importance of religion to society. He had always cherished, and the longer he lived, became the more confirmed in the conviction, that religion was an ineradicable principle of our nature, and absolutely and indispensably necessary to the welfare of mankind. He had read history, and knew that a godless people could never be a great people. He knew that the social fabric would quake and be shattered to atoms, were the ideas of God, of immortality, of moral responsibility altogether obliterated from every mind. He knew that were men seriously to persuade themselves for a moment that there was no God—that their physical and mental organizations had been the work of chance—that the myriads of suns and planets, with which immensity is peopled, had all fortuitously leaped into existence—that, instead of being destined to survive those suns and planets, they were the creatures of a day, and that death was the dissolution of their being—that crimes, perpetrated by them in darkness, had no witness;—they would at once plunge into the slough of scepticism, and so relapse into primeval barbarism.

He deeply felt that the idea of God—the great first cause—the primitive and infinite intelligence—is the most sublime and comprehensive of all ideas. The development of this idea he considered to be the great end of education. He was strongly of opinion that the knowledge of God is superior to

every other.   All other knowledge dwindles into nothingness
before it.   It is the source and criterion of man's elevation.   It
is the foundation of his happiness here and hereafter.   To
disseminate, therefore, such knowledge among his benighted
countrymen, he considered as the object of his being here below.

Rammohun Roy, though he looked upon idolatry as a downright insult to the Supreme Being, and as necessarily and
eternally a sin, cherished a stronger aversion towards scepticism.
He loathed and abominated it as something worse than idolatry
—as something more unnatural—as something more incompatible with the constitution of man.

It has been observed by a writer, who is largely quoted in the
Biographical Memoir which we have placed at the head of this
article that,—

"As he advanced in age, he became more strongly impressed with the
importance of religion to the welfare of society, and the pernicious effects of
scepticism.   In his younger years, his mind had been deeply struck with
the evils of believing too much, and against that he directed all his energies:
but, in his latter days, he began to feel that there was as much, if not
greater danger in the tendency to believe too little.   He often deplored the
existence of a party which had sprung up in Calcutta, composed principally
of imprudent young men, some of them possessing talent, who had avowed
themselves sceptics in the widest sense of the term.   He described it as
partly composed of East Indians, partly of the Hindu youth who, from education, had learnt to reject their own faith without substituting any other.
These he thought more debased than the most bigoted Hindu, and their
principles the bane of all morality."

This passage, evidently penned by one who knew the Rajah
intimately, reads to us an awful lesson.   The progress of
circumstances, since his death, has clothed it with terrible import.
The party, alluded to by the Rajah, is now a large and increasing party.   The Hindu community is very much divided between
those who worship Durga and Kali, and those who worship
nothing—between those who believe in three hundred and
thirty three millions of gods, and those who believe in none—
those who think the world under the moral government of
multitudinous powers, and those who deny all moral government.
It is a humiliating but nevertheless an unquestionable fact, that
many of those who call themselves educated natives seldom
think of religion, and are known to manifest much indifference
to it.   We admit that they profess to believe in the existence
of one God; but their belief, in nine cases out of ten, is not a living conviction, but a passive acquiescence in a truth forced on
them.   They oscillate between the creed they have renounced,
and that which they profess.   In theoretically renouncing the superstition of their fathers, and disembarrassing their minds from

the fetters of that antiquated bigotry which still cleave to the great mass arround them, they have not, we deeply regret to observe, embraced a purer and nobler religion. We confess, therefore, that there is some truth in the assertion made by even the best friends of India, that several of the educated natives are practical atheists. This practical atheism, however much we may deplore it, is regarded by men whose judgment is entitled to respect in such matters, as one of the natural and inevitable results of that system of education hitherto pursued by the Government—a system, which, though pregnant with results of the last importance to this country, is not sufficiently calculated to realize the great objects of education, inasmuch as it addresses itself more to the *head* than to the *heart*—to the *intellectual* than to the *moral* man. But intellectual cultivation is not identical with moral and religious cultivation. The one does not necessarily imply the other. That the developement of our moral and religious feelings and affections cannot be effected by that of the mental faculties alone, is a truth which, though frequently repeated, does not appear to be sufficiently attended to by those, to whose keeping the interests of our youth are committed.

That Rammohun Roy should think the educated natives of his time, who had avowed themselves sceptics in the "widest sense of the term," as "more debased than the most bigoted Hindu, and their principles the bane of all morality," was quite natural and proper. He thought what Socrates and Plato,—what the sages of his own country, Vyas and Manu,—what, in later times, Bacon had thought—"I would rather believe," says the great apostle of inductive philosophy, "I would rather believe all the fables in the Legend and the Talmud and the Alkoran than that this universal frame is without a mind." It was, therefore, no wonder that the idolatry of the great mass of his countrymen was looked upon by him in a softer and more amiable light than the atheism of the *so-called* educated natives. Indeed, so alarming has been the progress of that atheism since his death, that a few Hindu Gentlemen, impressed with the necessity and importance of counteracting its pernicious effects, have established a society which has been noticed more than once in this Review. The *Hindu Theophilanthropic Society* owes its existence, as mentioned in the preface to the 1st volume of its published discourses, " to a conviction irresistibly forcing itself upon every reflective mind, that the great work of India's Regeneration cannot be achieved without due attention to her moral and religious improvement."

It is evident that Rammohun Roy had to battle with both

idolatry and atheism.   To wage a war of extermination against
the one, and to check the incipient progress of the other, was
the work, to the furtherance of which he devoted himself.   To
say that he had many endowments which eminently fitted him
for it would be redundant.   He was a man whose genius and
energy, under happier circumstances, might have achieved a
complete moral revolution among his countrymen.   He was
by nature one of those who lead, not one of those who follow—
one of those who are in advance, not one of those who are
behind their age.

Our opinion of Rammohun Roy has already been sufficiently
explained.   Rammohun Roy was emphatically a great man.
His talents were not only varied and brilliant but of an eminently useful kind.   He had a sound judgment, a large and
disciplined mind.   In variety of knowledge, in depth of reasoning, in correctness of taste, he was rivalled by none of his
countrymen.   Both intellectually and morally he would rank
very high among his species.   He had not only a strong intellect
but a generous heart.   No one was more strongly impressed with
the conviction, that to do good to man, was among the chiefest
of earthly duties and privileges.   The golden maxim of doing
to others as you would that they should do unto you was
frequently inculcated by him.   The exercise of benevolence was
associated by him with the greatest pleasure.   To relieve the
pains and to add to the pleasures of others was considered by
him as a source of purest enjoyment.   One winter day, as he
was returning from his morning walk, he saw a poor sunburnt
herb-seller—one of those men who daily cross the river with
their basket load of vegetables—who had alighted his burden
from his head to take a little rest.   Finding some difficulty in re-
placing it, as there was none to help him, Rammohun Roy generously gave his assistance and with his own hands helped the
man to lift his load.   We shall not surely be charged with
using the language of exaggeration, if we declare that, among
the philanthropists and reformers to whom alone the title of
"Great,"—too often lavished on tyrants, heroes and conquerors,
for building their aggrandisement on the prostration of their
species,—should be confined and kept sacred, and who alone
should monoplize all the places in the temple of fame,—
a high place must unquestionably be assigned to Rammohun
Roy.   With an energy which set at nought the formidable
resistance he encountered from the slaves of bigotry—with a
perseverence which was unwearying—with a moral courage
which triumphed over persecution—with a benevolence which
was not exclusive but catholic—with a religious aspiration,

which was fervid and impassioned but not impulsive and fanatical—he laboured, according to the light and knowledge which he enjoyed, to liberate the Hindu mind from the tyranny of superstition, and to inoculate it with the elevating principles of a more rational faith.

The life of Rammohun Roy was commensurate with one of the most important and stirring periods in the annals of this country. It embraces the commencement of that great social and moral revolution through which she is now silently but surely passing. When Rammohun Roy was born, darkness—even the darkness of ignorance and superstition—brooded over his fatherland. When he died, the spirit of enquiry was abroad in high places, and was triumphantly exploding antiquated errors. He lived to see a line of demarkation, which, since his death, has been considerably deepened, strongly drawn among the Hindus beween the enlightened few and the benighted many. Rammohun Roy was the author of a great religious schism, which is destined to spread and widen. He helped to break the crust of that rigid and unbroken superstition, which had braved the formidable attacks of the Buddhist, and the fierce persecution of the Mahommedan. No native had before been enlightened and bold enough to do any thing of the kind. He was the first who opened the eyes of his countrymen to the monstrous absurdities of their national creed. He was the first who thundered forth into their ears—which had been for ages accustomed to the invocation of *montras*, and hermetically sealed against all true religion—the great truth that, " *God is One and without a second.*" But, as yet, we have only seen the dawn of a better and more promising era. The number of those, upon whose taste and feelings, and sentiments, education has effectually told, is comparatively very limited. And even in their minds there is hitherto a strange mixture of light and darkness, truth and error. The great mass still grope in moral and intellectual night. But the light that is to travel eastward and westward, and northward and southward, has already begun to illumine the horizon. The days of Hinduism are therefore numbered. The time is coming, (and oh, may it approach with lightning speed!) when the millions of Hindustan, who now exhibit a heart-rending spectacle of the prostitution of all that is sublime in religion and divine in worship, shall,—liberated from the thraldom of ignorance, and bigotry, and superstition,—learn to love, and obey, and adore the one true and living God!

ART. V.—*Notes on Pondicherry ; or the French in India. To which is added a sketch of the Moguls, and the Mogul Empire in India. Also selected Essays on various subjects, by an officer of the Madras Artillery. Calcutta, W. Thacker & Co. 1845.*

IT is not with the view of furnishing a dissertation on the French in India that we have taken up these Notes. Such a theme merits and demands an ampler discussion than our time and space can at present permit us to afford to it. To do it full justice would require a combination of powers—historic, philosophic, and graphic—to the possession of which few men could venture to lay any claim. Even a good readable sketch, which, in recording the vicissitudes of war and civil policy, with their cruelties and crimes, glanced at the more agreeable and placid scenes and events of private and social life, would be a task of no ordinary magnitude and difficulty.

Our present aim, however, is altogether of a humbler and widely different description. In a previous article headed "English women in Hindustan," we were led cursorily to note some of the incidents of married life amongst us—more especially as regarded the lot of Missionaries and Military Officers. The subject, however, may be said to be inexhaustible. And, as we were musing upon it, the Notes on Pondicherry fell in our way. There we found some chapters on Society and customs—love and marriage—and women in the east. And as the fragmentary delineations therein contained, were the last which had issued from our local press, and happened at the same time to chime in with our own musings, we resolved to devote a few pages to some good humoured random *Notices of Married Life in India.*

First, however, we must in courtesy bestow a few words on the author of the Notes. He is evidently a gay, buoyant, light-hearted gentleman, with whom, however austerely or cynically disposed, we could not well be angry. He has a fund of good nature and kindly feeling and simple humour which carries his reader briskly and pleasantly along, without any undue racking of the mental powers or any excessive demand on the attention. His language is not always in accordance with the standard of refined taste ; and there is occasionally an incongruous blending of images. At the same time, passages do ever and anon occur, which evince considerable elevation of thought and elegance of expression. In his general sentiments respecting men and manners, he is, for the most part, liberal and candid. Living, as he evidently does, in the sunshine of our lighter literature, the eye of his mind is constantly ragaled with the tints and the hues of an ever active though not brilliant or powerful imagination. Pleased with himself, and happy in the contemplation of his own visions, he is naturally disposed to see all things in the fairest light—because, under the illusive influence of warm emotions which diffuse a portion of their own vividness all around, all things become so many mirrors that reflect the ever varying image of his own joyous mind. The only instance in which he is decidedly churlish and unjust, is, where he rates the Protestants as "illiberal" for "finding fault with every form of religion except their own." In matters of religion, he himself evidently cherishes loose, indefinite, and unsatisfactory views. He has yet to learn that there is a happy medium between the extreme of an all comprehending latitudinarianism and the extreme of an intolerant exclusive bigotry.

His literary ardour and energy cannot be better pourtrayed than in his own words:—

"The pursuit of literature in India, from the nature of the climate and society consequent upon it, must always be esteemed as the chief mode to exalt, instruct, and divert the mind. Its pleasures perhaps are never more strongly felt than when we are alone; for, with *its* aid, the miseries of solitude can never enter. The following pages were written during a march from Trichinopoly to Secunderabad in the months of May and June; and we do not think we could have written one whit the better, had we been comfortably caged in our own Bungalow, under the grateful influence of taties and a punkah. We mention this merely to show how usefully time may be employed, *even* on a long march, when, should the solitary not be a sportsman, the day is generally spent in *lying down and rising, dressing and undressing, feeding and waxing hungry, becoming weary, and then lying down again.*"

"Thus runs *his* world away."

"When, either by reading, or committing to paper what he knows or has seen, his time may be employed to eminent advantage. "It is not," says the author of Tremaine, "the monotony of employment, but the want of it altogether that occasions *ennui,* the mere love of reading, which Gibbon found out was a passion which derives fresh vigour from enjoyment, and supplies each day and each hour with perpetual pleasure, gives to the student an empire over himself which no emperor ever had."

A work, composed under such disadvantages, may be regarded as something more than a mere literary curiosity;—it is positively an achievement of literary heroism. Talk of its defects and short comings;—and do not the time and the place and the circumstances of its origin at once suggest a sufficient apology? But its information is exceedingly scanty and meagre. Very true. In judging, however, of its merits, in this respect, charity prompts and justice demands that we should apply the criterion proposed by the poet, and "regard

the writer's end." If he had undertaken what he failed to accomplish ; if his pretensions were of a soaring, lofty, ambitious
character, which, when tested by their fruits, disappointed all
reasonable expectation ; if he had assumed the air and port of a
giant, when the actual development of his powers proved him to
be a dwarf ;—then might there be room for stern criticism and
grave reproof. But, as the matter stands, there is really no
room for reprehension. The writer is altogether humble and
modest in his aims and object. His " end " has nothing in it of
the grand, the lofty, the soaring, or the presumptuous. As represented by himself it exhibits the very essence of moderation.
And judged with direct reference to it, as in fairness it ought to
be, the work is no failure. It realises all which it professes to
achieve. Respecting his historic sketch of the Moguls, the author says, that " it is drawn up for those who, with little study,
seek an acquaintance with some important facts in Indian history, the value of which is indisputable." And respecting the
entire miscellaneous contents of his work he writes in the following strain :—

" We wish these remarks to be considered apart from the comparative trifle
we now offer to the public, although fearless we launch our little craft into
the sea of public opinion. It is laden for the enjoyment of those who may
find an hour or so to hang heavy on their hands. As we are candid in all
things, we have used *plain* sailing, aud in the *Notes* we safely assert that
Truth has guided the helm. " No mercenary *writer* his homage pays."
Had we to support our existence by the pen in India, we are afraid the cases
of Butler starved to death, and Otway choked with a roll amid the agonies
of hunger, would be jokes in comparison with ours."

After such unpretending professions, on the part of our
author, it is even possible that some readers, on a perusal of the
work, may find their expectations exceeded rather than disappointed. At all events, the writer displays such occasional
touches of shrewdness and naiveté, such improveable powers of
observation, and such partially developed capabilities of literary
composition, that, with more patience, industry and perseverance, and under more auspicious circumstances, he might produce a greatly more complete, elaborate, and valuable work—
and one fitted to command more general attention. Wisely has
he done already in abandoning doggerel rhyme, and in making
his election of more tasteful prose. And if, with the enthusiasm
which manifestly glows in his ardent temperament, he can only
be persuaded patiently to persevere—ever remembering that
there is no royal road to literary accomplishment and renown
—he may yet attain to eminence in the walks of our indigenous
Indian literature.

Having thus, we trust, done justice to our author's general merits, we return to the subject, respecting which we proposed to furnish a few cursory notices, viz., *Married life in India.*

On this subject, as on all the rest of which he treats, our author's remarks are few and imperfect. They may be said, in substance at least, to be all contained in the following extracts :—

" Although marriage is universally allowed to be an extremely serious thing, and a philosopher has even gone the length of calling it a science,[*] still perhaps in India, there is no act in which men show so little judgment as regarding the present effects and future consequences. This evil is in a great measure brought on from the state of existing society : if a man should wish to marry, it does not allow him time to fathom the mind of his intended ; he must come to the point in a very short period, or he is set down as a trifler with the *poor dear girl's* affections ; thus he often becomes allied either to a Xantippe or a Lady Teazle, and in a few years exclaims, like Sir Peter, " *the crime has carried the punishment along with it.*"[†] Such need not be the case with the Englishman in India, should he wish to try his fortune in Pondicherry : there are always sufficient opportunities offered, bereft of all ceremony, to discover whether or not in one fate

Their hearts, their fortunes and their beings blend :

so, should an imprudent marriage take place, it is entirely attributable to the husband's folly or want of judgment.

Prudence in marriages is a *rara avis* of the first order, and we must just set it down as one of the miseries of our fallen nature, that we cannot use it more in that momentous event on which so much happiness depends. Marrying without means, may be called the bane of marriage in India, as in fact it is the same every where else, the husband being over confident of his abilities and perseverance, which are to make up the known deficiency. That admirable writer, Theodore Hook, says, in one of his novels " Where there is genius or talent, the very fact of having a fond and affectionate wife dependent upon him for existence, is an excitement to a man to exert his energies, baffle the waves of opposing ills, and ' by opposing, end them."[‡] We are confident that many marriages are effected, particularly among the Military in India, on the above speculative theory, and from its not being practised, proceeds many a doleful epitome of domestic misery.—" If to do," says the fair Portia, " were as easy as to know what were good to do, chapels had been churches and poor men's cottages princes' palaces."[§] It was man's general want of prudence that probably drew forth the sage's reply, who being asked when a young man should marry, said:— " a young man not yet, an elder man not at all."[||] From this we may deduce a maxim, love and ride away! but do not marry yet! The grand secret to know is *when* marriage ought to take place. We should say to the young subaltern, when you are not at all involved, when you can by dint of persuasion extract £300 from the pockets of your friends and relations, then like Benedick, " *tipp your staff with horn.*"

There can be no difference of opinion as to the seriousness and importance of the marriage tie. The memorable words of our great epic poet though possibly familiar to most of our readers, may fitly and seasonably be quoted here :——

> " Hail ! wedded love—mysterious law, true source
> Of human offspring, sole propriety,
> The paradise of all things common else ;
> By thee adulterous lust was driven from men,
> Among the bestial herds to range ; by thee
> Founded in reason, loyal, just, and pure,
> Relations dear, and all the charities,
> Of father, son, and brother first were known ;
> Perpetual fountain of domestic sweets !
>   Here love his golden shaft displays ; here lights
> His constant lamp, and waves his purple wings ;
> Reigns here and revels ; not in the bought smiles
> Of harlots, loveless, joyless, unendeared,
> Casual fruition ; nor in court amours,
> Mixed dance, or wanton mask, or midnight ball,
> Or seranade."

Neither can there be any difference of opinion as to the felicities which cluster around a marriage union, in which congenial tastes are happily blended, and the tokens of cheerful kindness and tender greeting are ever interchanged—a union which, agreeably to the portraiture of the poet of the seasons, is finely characterized by——

> " Perfect esteem, enlivened by desire
> Ineffable, and sympathy of soul ;
> Thought meeting thought, and will preventing will,
> With boundless confidence ; for nought but love
> Can conquer love, and render bliss secure.
>   *   *   *   *   *   *
> Till evening comes, at last, serene and mild,
> When, after the long vernal day of life,
> Enamoured more, as more remembrance swells
> With many a proof of recollected love,
> Together down they sink in social sleep ;
> Together freed, their gentle spirits fly,
> To scenes where love and bliss immortal reign."

But, in proportion to the seriousness and importance of the marriage tie, and the felicities which cluster around a well-matched union, must be the unhappiness and varied ills of rash, hasty, imprudent, ill-assorted alliances. While the great English moralist could gravely assert, that "marriage is the best state for a man in general, and every man is a worse man in proportion as he is unfit for the marriage state," he could not but sound the note of warning in these emphatic terms ;—— " What can be expected but disappointment and repentance from a choice made in the immaturity of youth, in the ardour of desire without judgment, without foresight, without inquiry after conformity of opinions, similarity of manners, rectitude of judgment, or purity of sentiment? surely many evils may be avoided by that deliberation and delay which prudence prescribes to irrevocable choice."

Now, that formerly European marriages in India were, to a great extent, of the description here reprobated, we are not prepared to dispute. Rather, yielding at once to the united phalanx of testimony on the subject, let us freely and fully admit that, in the majority of instances, many fell under this unhappy category. Accordingly, it is a simple matter of fact, that Indian marriages have long ere now acquired a celebrity of ill fame. And when any thing has once, not without reason, obtained a bad name, it usually cleaves to it with the tenacity of pitch—and that too in spite of subsequent amendment and reform. It is only by a process of attrition, slowly operating through periods of time, of greater or less duration, that the fast-cleaving stain can be finally wiped away. And thus it has fared with Indian marriages. From certain strange and unpleasant peculiarities which distinguished those contracted at an earlier stage of our social history, these had fallen into ill repute. And rumour, with her hundred tongues, did not tend to mitigate or abate the acknowledged evil. In this way, the prejudice against Indian marriages has been successively transmitted, until it has become hereditary. And it is our knowledge of the fact, that in Great Britain this inveterate prejudice continues in great measure unabated, that impels us to lend our aid towards its diminution or removal.

In England, it is still commonly supposed that Indian marriages are contracted, for the most part by mere boys, with artful and designing women, who have been shipped, as it has been said, for the Calcutta market, and who are at all times ready to sell their charms to the highest bidders. Marriage too in India is considered by many as the quickest and smoothest road to ruin, and is looked upon as the conclusion, rather than as it ought to be, and is, the commencement of real life.

To remove these prejudices and to give correct notions of married life in India by a calm and dispassionate discussion of the subject, (as dispassionate at least as it will admit of,) will be the object of the few following remarks. And if we succeed in removing such prejudices in a single instance, if we induce one more couple to join the ranks of those already happily and honourably married, we feel that we shall have earned the smiles of our fair country women, and the thanks of every honest Englishman.

Marriage is in all countries considered as a fair subject of banter, and has been treated of as a good joke from the earliest to the latest times, aye and will be so till time shall be no more;—and this too by men who profess to think for themselves, and who would be unwilling to allow that they depart from this character, when, on this subject, they follow the crowd implicitly, and "receive maxims without recalling them to a new examination." Many are the jokes we have ourselves indulged in on this subject, and probably shall indulge in, notwithstanding our assumed character as censurers of the custom: for so long as they contribute to the amusement of others and the satisfaction of ourselves, and are devoid of ill nature or mischief, so long they may be considered not only as innocent, but lawful. Who can read the sly sketches of Sir Walter Scott, or the true and amusing descriptions of Mr. Dickens on this subject, and not enter into the humour of them? Who can help smiling at the serio-comic hesitation of Mr. Lillyvick, on his wedding day, when he applies to Nicolas to remove his doubts, and yet not feel a share of his perplexity?

" Wont you take any thing to eat or drink?" said Nicolas. " No," said the collector, " I have'nt any appetite. I should think it was a pleasant life—the married one,—eh?"

" I have not the least doubt of it," rejoined Nicolas. " Yes," said the collector—" certainly, oh yes—no doubt of it—but—good night."

In India, to be sure, jokes are few and far between; for it is seldom that the privileged class of jokers—the impudent brothers and the mischief loving sisters, and the boisterous cousins—are to be seen at a wedding; or, if present, they are by age sobered down to the reality of the thing. They do not urge their claims to kiss and be kissed, or to scramble for the cake, which, having passed through the wedding ring, is endued with the magical power of giving husbands within the year to its fair possessors, provided it shall have been duly placed under the pillow for three successive nights. This experiment however—this sleeping on the cake—we have known tried by a few antiquated virgins, but without success; and to those of our friends who may be intending to try it, on the first opportunity which may present itself, we would earnestly give the advice given by Punch to the couple about to be married. ' Dont.' The noses of the ants will discover it sooner than the eyes of Cupid, whose presence it is supposed to ensure, (and who by the bye generally assumes the shape of some fancied brown one,) and who will, when they have eaten up the cake, rove about in search of more, and rapidly trace it, crumb by crumb, to the mouth of the beauteous sleeper. Stealthily at first will they, one by one, creep upon the chin; but emboldened by impunity, they will rush simultaneously to the attack. They will encourage one another with the old song—

Oh I scarcely ventured to take a kiss,
Though your lips they seemed to invite me,
But, fair one, I soon got over this
When I kiss'd and they did not bite me—

and by their numbers possibly cause suffocation.

And here we should like to offer a few remarks upon the custom of kissing, and of the use of a ring at weddings. The origin of kissing at a wedding we have been unable to trace; but we should not, we think, be contradicted, if we boldly asserted that it has been in fashion since the days of Adam and Eve. It is beyond all doubt of very ancient origin, and was originally a token of respect. We seriously think that the custom would be " more honoured in the breach than in the observance;" and we hold in especial reverence the practice of the Roman Fathers who never kissed their wives in the presence of their daughters. The origin of the custom most probably was derived from the parting of relations, at which of course friends were present, who were allowed to share in the ceremony, sometimes owing to the affection and sometimes to the nervousness of the bride, and it has been thence continued to the present day. It is however becoming obsolete, except among the lower orders, and is rarely indulged in by any except relations and the officiating Clergyman. The kiss of the Clergyman, though it sometimes to our ears sounds like a very worldly every day sort of kiss, is supposed to impart a preacher's benediction, and has thence been called the kiss of peace. It has been permitted in England from the earliest times, and was once considered of such especial sanctity, that the bridegroom was not allowed to see his bride till the next day, lest he should erase it by a less pious kiss. Happily, however, it is not now held in such veneration, and will, we hope, in the present generation, fall into disuse. Respecting the ring we are not left so much in the dark. The giving of a ring, at a wedding, is a very ancient custom, though not probably so ancient as the custom of kissing. A ring was originally a seal or pledge, and was affixed to the wedding contract as a pledge of its genuineness, in the same way as it is now affixed to the ordinary contracts of the civilized world. It was afterwards worn as an ornament of the hand, and thence became, by an easy transition, the visible and outward token of a married woman. It is made of gold, the most precious of all metals, to signify how noble and how durable is our affection—

to remind us that woman, though pure, is as soft and flexible as pure gold itself, yet when joined with man her alloy, is capable of great firmness and resolution. It is round, it has been said, to shew as that our affection shall have no end ; but to this we dissent, because, if true, it would equally shew that our affection had no beginning. It is round, we think, to remind us that woman is man's tether peg. He may rove at a greater or less distance according to the length of his string, but he must rove in a circle ; sooner or later, unless he break his string, he must, on the holding up of her finger, return to his wife. It is plain, to shew us how simple the ceremony of marriage is, and also to remind us of the unostentatiousness of that faith which is its best cement.*

It was used among the Jews, and is first mentioned as in use among the Christians, in the time of Clemens Alexandrinus, and was considered as a proof that the wife was deemed worthy of the government of the family. In this sense it is used, even among Mahommedans ; and we have occasionally heard it mentioned as a proof of affection, and trust that the wife was deemed worthy to use her husband's seal during his absence. It may be from this feeling of affection, that it is occasionally sent, among the same people, as a present from a bridegroom to a bride.

Marriages, however, among the English in India, as far as the ceremonies go, are very similar to marriages in England—favours and cake—smiles and tears—sobs and kisses—sorrow and joy are mixed up together in a strange medley, emblematic, as the wedding cake, of the sweets and bitters of life ; and like it, are equally partaken of, in a lesser or greater degree, by every one present at them. At the weddings we have witnessed, however, the happy, the dont-care sort of faces vastly predominated over the sorrowful ones, which are usually confined to parents ; —and theirs is an undefined sort of feeling, half sorrow and half joy,—and to a rejected lover or two ;—and who pities them ? Indeed, we should not mind, provided it were not our own, if we were called upon to take our share in one, once a week.—Not in Calcutta, however, for we must plead a fondness for wedding cake ; and the Doctors there have an opinion that there is cholera or dysentry in every mouthful of it, and prescribe some nauseous remedy to get rid of it, long before one has had time to decide whether it were ' *the thing* ' or not.

Three quarters of a century, nay even half a century ago, the charge against the Ship Captains of importing fair enslavers

* Those, who wish, to learn more on this subject, may consult Jeremy Taylor's sermon on the Marriage Ring.

for the Calcutta market, might have been sustained, even in the Supreme Court: but, in the present day, not the smallest suspicion attaches to any of them. The oldest English inhabitant will, if you ask him, deplore the decreased value of the cargoes which now arrive, and describe to you in glowing terms the anxiety evinced by every one for the arrival of the ships of other days. He will, too, if he has not worn them out by exhibiting them, or by comparing the article with the descriptive roll, shew you sundry little notes from his agents in Calcutta, urging his immediate presence, " as a girl of surpassing beauty and accomplishments had arrived in Calcutta, and had already rejected to his knowledge several very eligible elderly gentlemen,"—with a sly innuendo, " that she had heard of *his* matrimonial intentions," which, indeed, she had by her exceeding cleverness wormed out of his agent—the innocent fellow—who could not conceive why she had been induced to leave England: for, though there were rumours of a little indiscretion, still it must, if true, have been a very little one, as he could see no marks if it about her. He might, we say, be induced to shew a note or notes like these, if his vanity were aroused by the expression of a doubt as to whether such a bilious scarecrow could ever have been an eligible single gentleman; but we defy him to shew you one of a date later than 1800; or, if he do, we will proclaim it to be a forgery, and stake our reputation upon proving it to be one.

No; those days are gone for ever, never to return! And yet, though sneered at now, the women of that era deserved well of their country; deserved even the gratitude of the present generation. Every thing has a beginning, and their advent was the beginning of social happiness in India. Even such happiness as they could have to confer, (and we may believe that all were not bad, but that some were actuated by the love of their country to make a sacrifice of themselves) imparted a healthier tone to society. One by one, the native women were discarded; and the zenanas, which raised their unblushing heads in the compounds of almost every house in the Mofussil, were converted into modest godowns,—a purpose to which, with but few exceptions, they are still applied.

Bachelors, who envied the happiness of their old acquaintances, though afraid to take the step themselves, suddenly recollected kind good sisters in England, who were so fond of them, and so utterly forgetful of self, that they would, for their sakes, come out to India, and preside over their households. Many of them,—such was their kindness of heart,—did come; and a rivalry ensued among them, as to which could best maintain their brother's house in comfort and elegance. Thus it not seldom happened that a neighbour, who was sisterless, struck with the thousand little comforts of his friend, would inveigle the lady from her home to put his house in order too; and the bereaved brother was obliged, in self-defence, to retaliate upon some one else on the first opportunity.

Oh, woman, woman, thou hast much to answer for! Who that has had his house cheered by your enlivening presence does not, when you leave it, miss the soothing sound of your light footsteps, and, fretful, long for the exciting rustle of your silken gowns? Who does not feel that his house is melancholy, that his light is extinguished? And will you,—can you,—blame the man, who tries to rekindle his taper by the pure, the softened light of your own bright eyes? You know you do not, but with pity's welcome you hold forth the torch of love, and light a fire which yourselves alone, and not all the waters of the Ganges or the Megna, can extinguish.

From the marriages formed, as we have above related, and some few contracted in England, either by parties coming out to India or by those who have returned to England, have arisen the wives, the daughters of the present race—many of whom are descendants of the best families in Europe;—women, who, notwithstanding, or in spite of, the withering rays of our Indian sun, retain, like peaches, their bloom and down and dewy sweetness on them, and are in all early stages of tempting ripeness—women, of whom their country may well be proud, and from among whom the noblest of the nobles in England might with honour select a wife. The object in coming to India has long been changed; and instead of coming out to be married, women now came out to join the family circle of their own parents and relations:—they come in short to their home—"Home!"—yes—India is the home of every girl whose parents are in it; of every married woman. To all are applicable, with but a trifling alteration, the beautiful lines addressed by Michael to Eve when leaving Paradise—

Lament not Eve but patiently resign
What hardly thou hast lost, nor set thine heart
Thus ever fond on that which is not thine :
Thy going is not lonely : with thee goes thy husband,
Where he abides think there thy native land.

But, when is such a sentiment ever uttered? We all, both men and women, talk of home; but home, as we use it, means not India, but England, in which perhaps we have not a single relation or a single local tie. The phrase is pardonable, but yet we could wish it altered, especially among those who have both husband and parents in this land. It would conduce much to their contentment and happiness, if they would not only call, but learn to consider this country as home, and England but as England;—a country to which they may by possibility be driven to seek for the restoration of their health—in which they may possibly be buried.

From this often false notion of returning home, arise many of the ill-assorted marriages in India. With this view, girls, not out of their teens, are tempted to sell themselves to old and wrinkled men, who, with long purses and short leases of life, are about to take their pensions. Take their pensions!—the very name of pension brings before one the idea of a worn-out and jaded hack; of a man not clothed in purple and fine linen, but in calico and white ducks—a very never-sweat;—but still he is going home, and—he cannot last for ever!

With this exception we believe that marriages in India are not oftener than elsewhere made from sordid motives. We call the choice between a well paid civilian or a rich merchant, and an ill paid military man (cæteris paribus) but a praiseworthy prudence, and one productive, on the whole, of more heart-felt happiness than marriages in England. They are nearly always marriages of affection, though they are hastily made; for the Government or the cholera seldom allows a long time for courtship: and from the paucity of relations to share them, and of neighbours to divert or distract them, the affections are, as it were, more concentrated upon one another, and each becomes daily more necessary to the happiness of the other.

Such marriages cannot, in one sense, be characterised as imprudent, for the Services themselves, aided by their munificent masters, the Court of Directors, have established funds whereby a widow is endowed with a moderate competency, sufficient indeed to enable her to bring up her children, if she have any, and to maintain her as a lady as long as she lives.

So far from early marriages in India being the cause of ruin, they are, in the generality of cases, the salvation of the husbands, body and soul, and prove the foundation of that fortune for which all are, or are supposed to be, toiling. Many are the men that have been reclaimed by marriage from the vices peculiar to the climate—of smoking inordinately, of drinking brandy pani to excess—and of card playing in the middle of the day. Many are the men whom we have seen enter the married state as lean and long as bamboos—careworn from debt and haggard from irregular hours—who, at the end of a year, have appeared jovial and merry, and free from care, and stout and oily, as if like Mr. Wackford Squeers, they had been living during the whole time upon the richest pastry.

Nor is health only ruined by debauchery and idle hours; it is equally neglected by the slaves of business, by men who toil more than their duty requires of them, either in the sun, at drill, or in heated and over crowded offices, in the vain hope of raising for themselves a name. *The name* they frequently acquire; it is generally coupled with some epithet of pity or contempt; and never or but very rarely do they obtain that promotion and increase of salary which, in Services where promotion is gained by seniority, not by merit, it is foolish in them to expect, but to which their own cases, they fondly hope, will prove the triumphant exception. Here the quick eye of the fond wife will soon detect the almost imperceptible inroads of disease; and she will, either by the charm of her society, allure her husband from over exertion, or, by her persuasions, induce him to moderate his zeal. She will remind him that he has other and equally important duties to perform in the great drama of life. She will not induce or wish him to be idle, but teach him that his exertions should be restained within due bounds; and that he who labours to the injury of his own health, by forcing the body beyond its power, is not only the destroyer of his own happiness and of those dependent upon him, but the defrauder of the Public. This was the secret which induced the Athenian Lawgivers to render it imperative that every public officer should be a married man; and did the Court of Directors but understand their real interests, as well as the Athenians did theirs, they might perhaps make it as imperative that their officers should, on entering into their service, be provided with a wife, as they now do, that he should have a silver spoon and fork.

Nor is it only the bodily health of men that is improved by marriage. What is of more importance, their minds are regulated, their ideas and manners become softened, and their souls are cared for. The two first propositions are, we believe, generally admitted to be the effect of marriages in England, and the steps by which they are produced need not therefore be traced by us. The inducements to increased exertions is the same in both countries; and in both is the effect of women upon men's manners the same. But in India is an enhanced regard for religion more particularly the fruit of marriage.

That women are in general more religiously disposed than men is an almost indisputable fact; and their being so is their greatest charm, their greatest attraction: for religion is the only real security for their virtue. That they should be so, is not to be wondered at, for they are by nature gentler and more retiring than men, and their nature is strengthened by the barriers of their peculiar education. As married women, they are more intimately mixed up with those domestic trials and sorrows, which are naturally fitted to admonish them to "set their house in order" and be ready; and this preparation is not the work of a day or of an hour, but of years, of a life. The necessity of such a preparation, were any thing more forcible wanting to impress it on their minds, is in this country perpetually recurring to them, owing to the many instances of sudden death which they almost daily hear of; and as their fond hearts are ever ready to encompass those whom they love with imaginary changes, they picture to themselves the possibility that their husbands may be summoned next, and they are naturally rendered anxious about their future state. They remember that there are but few clergymen in India, and these scattered far and wide,—and they devote themselves with all the energetic warmth of their natures to supply their place, and endeavour to rescue the beloved one of their hearts from the pit of destruction. Sometimes their exertions are repaid by indifference, but oftener by success; and it is seldom that a thoroughly irreligious married man is to be met with. That there are such men we do not deny; for to deny it would be to deny that men are mortals.

In England, marriage is oftentimes considered as a signal for the reunion of families separated from political motives, and is the source of reconcilement after petty domestic quarrels; but in India it has become gradually and imperceptibly productive of greater benefits. In this country, where the English may be looked upon as a large family, there existed in bygone days a jealousy between the Civil and the Military servants of the Company—between, as it were, twin brothers. The Civilians were jealous of the honors earned and nobly earned by the Military, with the points of their bayonets, while the Military envied the salaries earned and honestly earned by the Civilians, with the points of their pens. In the seasons of war, the jealousy of the Civilians was paramount, in those of peace, the envy of the Military; and yet both were forgetful that each was slaving for the other—the Civilians, in collecting revenue—the Military, in securing the enjoyment of it to both.

By an unacknowledged arrangement each Service has, in the present day, obtained a share of the rewards of the other,—the Civilians, by obtaining Cadetships for their sons in the Army, the Military, by procuring Writerships for their sons in the Civil Service;—while the daughters of each have so intermarried with the sons of the other, that the honor and interests of both Services have become identified. The jealousy of each was discreditable to both, and both must rejoice that it is now virtually at an end.

One other benefit occurs to us as a peculiar result of marriage in India, which we will mention, though it may excite a smile, and that is—*good station roads*—the existence of which is of incalculable benefit both to the natives and the English. In Calcutta, the roads are kept in order chiefly for the purposes of traffic, but in the Mofussil principally for the accommodation of the English inhabitants; and, on entering a station, the practised eye will soon tell whether the Magistrate is a single or a married man. If the former, the station has generally a dirty and slovenly appearance; the roads are execrable and unrepaired—the very unevenness of them making the glass and bottle rattle against each other in the palanqueen as it enters. Herds of oxen are to be seen strolling on and defiling the roads at every step; the hedge rows are covered with shreds of old clothes; and if near the Kacherry, paper is to be seen blown about in all directions; the fences of the young trees, planted by some former married magistrate, are broken down, and a straight sapling, devoid of leaves, alone meets the eyes, destined, when big enough, to become a riding stick. Crowds of naked children are to be seen playing at Punchisi in every gutter, while Fakirs, clothed in nature's garb, alone are roaming at their leisure in all directions.

If, on the contrary, the magistrate is a married man, the roads are excellent; not a jolt is to be felt; the hedge rows are trimmed carefully, and the cornices of the bridges are white. Trees, planted with the view of shelter, are springing up in every direction with an eager growth; and an air of neatness and order pervades the whole station, which clearly speaks of woman's presence and of woman's influence. The inhabitants appear neatly and decently dressed, and move about with a light and jaunty step. Gardens, teeming with fruits and flowers, meet the eye in every direction, and the air is loaded with sweetness. The very crows caw joyously among their nests in the trees; and the doves moan forth their simple loves, secure of sympathy in woman's heart.

Having thus furnished subjects for reflection, by briefly shadowing forth the advantages of marriage, as peculiar to India, we must revert to some of the disadvantages—the separation of wife and husband, of parents and children. But as the causes and necessity of such separation were discussed in a former article, we shall, in this place, merely offer a few reflections on the subject. Let it, however, be borne in mind that we are writing only of those women who are really compelled by ill health to separate themselves for a season from their husbands, and not of those who are disgusted with India or tired of their husbands, or who are anxious to roseate a complexion which many rupees' worth of the far-puffed Rowland's Kalydor has failed to restore. Such women, we trust, are rare. Happy would it be if they never existed, but in the imagination.

The separation of a husband and wife really attached to each other, in consequence of ill health, is the most painful subject for reflection that we know of. It is as it were the temporary death of each, but it is armed with bitterness that death has not. In death, all anxiety for the departed one is at an end; we know that he is at rest, and that no exertions of our own can in any way alter the doom that has been passed. And though we may wish that the decree of the Almighty might be reversed, we wish that which we cannot really hope for; we know that the dead shall never return, that the past shall never be recalled.

In the temporary separation we are considering, the moment of departure is the commencement of anxiety, and of conflicting emotions. We know that the separation must be for years, and yet dread that it may be for ever. We know that we cannot ward off the unforeseen evils which may beset each other's path, and yet fruitlessly feel that they may be averted by our own exertions. We know that absence must produce some change in us, and yet we hope that we shall remain unchanged. We long for our reunion, and yet remember that unavailing longings should never be indulged in. " Our desires are not alone fixed upon the past, but look forward to the future, and we recollect that we have lost a possession which we hope to regain at some future time."

The pangs of separation are not perhaps so unendurable as they were in former days; the magical power of Steam has reduced distance, and enables us to receive letters from those we love with wonderful regularity. We are enabled thereby to render absence somewhat supportable, by mutually recalling to our recollection, with melancholy tenderness, the expressions of affection which have lately passed between us, and review again the many scenes, while fresh in our minds, which we have visited together. We can narrate and canvass the various transactions which are daily taking place around us, and fondly lay down plans of happiness for the future,—that future which perhaps we are destined never to arrive at. But these reflections ought not to make us melancholy or despondent; but should animate us to more than ordinary diligence and the exercise of virtue. We should live as if we were living in each other's presence; and we should thereby learn to practise a degree of charity and forbearance to one another when we meet again, of which we may now perhaps imagine ourselves incapable.

If there be any who, from the dread of separation, may be disposed to say, " we will never marry, we will never indulge in the luxury of fondness," we would address to them the words of the Rambler;—" an exact compliance with this rule might perhaps contribute to tranquillity, but surely it would never produce happiness. He that regards none so much as to be afraid of loving them, must live ever without the gentle pleasures of sympathy and confidence ; he must feel no melting fondness, no warmth of benevolence, nor any of those honest joys which nature annexes to the power of pleasing. And as no man can justly claim more tenderness than he pays, he must forfeit his share in that officious and watchful kindness which love only can dictate, and those lenient endearments by which love only can soften life. He may justly be overlooked and neglected by such as have more warmth in their hearts ; for who would be the friend of him, whom, with whatever assiduity he may be courted, and with whatever services obliged, his principles will not suffer to make equal returns, and who, when you have exhausted all the instances of good will, can only be prevailed not to be an enemy? If by excluding joy we could shut out grief, the scheme would deserve very serious attention ; but since, however we may debar ourselves from happiness, misery will find its way at many inlets, we may surely endeavour to raise life above the middle point of apathy at one time, since it will necessarily sink below it at another."

The real antidote against the sorrow of separation is employment, for " sorrow is a kind of rust of the soul which every new idea contributes in its passage to scour away. It is the putrefaction of stagnant life, and is remedied by exercise and motion." The separation of parents from their children is as painful, (only of shorter duration), as that of husband and wife ; nay more so, where, as is not unfrequently the case, the parents have no relations to watch over their offspring while in England. They are then consigned to the care of strangers ; and when they meet again, they meet as aliens, and are mutually ignorant of each other's dispositions. But this subject was fully discussed in a former paper.

We would now wish to say a few words to such of our countrywomen as have lately arrived in India, and may have taken on themselves, or may be about to take on themselves, the duties of Matrimony. Were they in our presence, we would address them somewhat as follows :—

" You will not, it is true, be able, as you would be in England
' to go about doing good,' but good may still be done by you ;
neither will you be able to pursue the same business, the same
occupations, but still both business and occupations are to be
found, which, if duly performed, may render you valuable members of society.   Indolence is the great enemy you will have to
contend with, and you must fight against him with undying
energy, or he will conquer you, as certainly as he has already
done many, who have but feebly resisted him.   By such you
will hear any plans you may form, laughed at,—any exertions you
may make, ridiculed. ' You will never be able to do that, for
I tried it myself.' ' In India no one thinks of doing so,' or
' it is not proper in India'—and a hundred other such phrases
will be cast in your teeth ; but disregard them all, and, with
becoming deference, judge, nay, try, for yourselves.   Try for
yourselves, and if you fail, be not discouraged, try again. There
is not one of your sex,—so it is said—who cannot gain whatever she has set her heart on ; and though this saying has arisen
from your perseverance in the pursuit of trivial or perhaps
unworthy objects, still it proves that the power of perseverence
is in you, and it may fairly be enlisted on the side of virtue.

Reading, music, drawing and working are occupations you
may employ yourselves on, in India, as well as in England; and
though the second and third are not, from the want of taste,
or defect of education, common to all, the first and last are,
and may very properly occupy a large portion of your time.

The History of India and the habits and manners of the
various nations and castes of men in it, may worthily engage
your attention ; and it is lamentable to know that many of us,—
not only women but men also,—live many years in India, and
leave it as ignorant of these subjects as if we had never been in
it.   The History of England and of her constitution, her manufactures, and her Courts of Justice may be as familiar to you
all as your mother tongue ; but what do you know of the policy
of the English in India? What of her manufactures? except that
muslins are made at Dacca, and scarfs at Delhi.   What of her
Courts of Justice ? but that Tom is the judge of one place, and
Dick the magistrate of another,—both of whom, if you are wives
of Civilians, you sincerely hope will soon return to England,
that your husband may obtain promotion.

The Natural History of India, her beasts, her birds, her fossils,
her plants, are but little known, and yet with these all around
you, almost unexplored ; you complain, perhaps, of ennui.
And though we would not, for the mere sake of procuring specimens, have you, with your own fair hands, destroy a single

creature, lest your sensibility be weakened or your hearts
hardened, we would gladly avail ourselves of your skill in
preserving them, and of the emulation you would excite among
your countrymen in procuring them."

We should like to see a museum established at every station
in India under the care of the ladies, which should contain not
only specimens of every bird, beast, insect, and other natural
productions of the district—but of its manufactures—plans of
its rivers—drawings of its remarkable buildings, or of its
scenery—sketches of the costume peculiar to its inhabitants,
with notices of their various castes and customs, and specimens
of their musical and warlike instruments—in a word, of every
thing. We should like to have duplicates, when procurable,
sent down at the end of every year, of every thing new, or supposed to be new, to the Asiatic Museum in Calcutta, the curators
of which should be requested to direct into proper channels
the exertions of the fair and useful laborers. And let it be
borne in mind that it is not the exertion of a single individual
that will develope the resources of India, but the cheerful aid
of many; and that each is bound to contribute his grain of knowledge as he finds it, though it be but small.

Though English Ladies cannot go out among the Natives,
and by their personal example shew how much good may be
done, their known wish to do good, and their conduct in their
own families, must have a great, though imperceptible, effect.
All natives, even the best educated among them, have the most
profound contempt for women, and regard them as formed alone
for their pleasure, or as necessary evils for the continuance of
mankind; and have not yet discovered the controlling influence
exercised by them over Europeans. Considering a woman,
among themselves, as virtuous only because she has not the
opportunity of being vicious, they regard the conduct of
English women with peculiar jealousy—her every look, word,
and gesture, is daily reported and canvassed in their Harems,
and every instance of depravity confirms them in the wisdom
of their own custom of seclusion. Did one-half of our country-
women reflect, that, upon their conduct depends possibly the
emancipation from imprisonment of thousands of their sex, they
would be doubly guarded in their behaviour. Alas! such is but
seldom the case: on the contrary they too often act as if those
Natives were not men. They look upon them (as an amusing
writer in the *Quarterly Review* has written on a somewhat different subject)—they look upon them as mere bundles of clothes, and
forget that there is a man in the midst of them. Instead of
which they should regard them as snakes in the grass, as imps

in petticoats; and the same precautions should be taken to avoid them as if they really were so. " It is only the tailor;" " It is only the bearer,"—is often remarked, as a lady stands before a man, in her dressing gown, or has admitted him into her private apartments,—those apartments, into which a man should never be admitted, at least as long as the lady is in them—and then only for the purpose of cleaning the furniture. What would be thought, nay said in England, if the footman or the groom were called in to make his mistress's bed, or were sent into her dressing-room, during her absence from it, to fetch her book or scissors or other little article ? And yet such things are daily done in India, the country of all others were they should be more particularly avoided.

It is not owing to an absence or a deficiency of delicacy in our country-women that this is so, but to the want of reflexion or to a careless indolence. If the female servant is not in attendance, the lady must go herself or send a man; and rather than give herself the trouble of moving, she prefers the alternative. We have sometimes seen a man sent into a bed-room for a trifling article, by women as modest and as sensitive as any in England, and whose innate sense of propriety, coupled with habit, prevented their engaging our services—and yet of the two, perhaps, we should have executed the commission with greater delicacy—but we are English, and he was only a black man.

There are but few out-door amusements for women in India, and even these are frequently neglected. Archery and Riding and Gardening are available to all, but the two first can only occupy a brief hour of time in the morning and the evening. The management of the flower garden, provided it be situated to the East of the house, or of some high and shady trees, may afford them exercise and amusement for at least two hours of every evening, and is peculiarly suited to many tender natures. A woman seems to us in her proper sphere when winding the "woodbine round the arbour," or directing "the clasping ivy where to climb," and is most attractive when officiating as Priestess,

> * * * * To the humid flowers that breathe
> Their morning incense, when all things that breathe,
> From th' earth's great altar send up silent praise
> To the Creator, and his nostrils fill
> With grateful smell.

Besides, horticulture is at a very low ebb in India, and is therefore worthy of our countrywomen's attention; and if they will not bestow it, to use a native phrase, who will ?

It is not our intention to enter into a discussion upon marriage among the Mussulmans and Hindus, for of their happiness or otherwise we know little for certain. We only know that, in many cases, the women and men never see each other till the marriage has taken place, and in others, that they are married when mere children, and may therefore form a guess that very frequently unsuitable marriages are made, and tempers associated which are little likely to produce happiness. Their parental feelings are however very strong, and we have often been called upon to admire,

> " His father's hope, his mother's joy,
> The darling little nigger boy."

And we sincerely hope that the diffusion of knowledge, which is now going on throughout the whole of India, may lead the descendants of the present generation to exalt their women to the same commanding eminence which we are proud to acknowledge is occupied by our own countrywomen.

The author of the Notes on Pondicherry appends to his work a series of " Selected Essays," which had previously appeared in a Madras Journal. One of these is entitled, " On women of the East." And as the subject, if not new, may be interesting to many, we shall here quote it as a fair specimen of the author's general style of treating the subjects which he handles:—

" If we peruse with attention some of the principal works relating to the various countries in the east, we cannot but feel for the state of the women contained in them. When beautiful, we find woman a slave to the passions of man, when not so, frequently little better than a beast of the field; the consequence is, we find none of that grand development of character which so distinguishes the women of most European countries. For many centuries they appear to have been in this degrading condition; the pure spirit of love seems seldom or never to have shed its influence o'er Eastern nations; the finest descriptions of their best poets, all are examples of this. How superior is the poor peasant girl in England, to the most lovely Sultana nature ever moulded, in the palace of the Sultan. What respect is paid to female beauty, even though it be worn by the most humble subjects! how different in the east, where we find the most lovely creatures even exposed for sale in the market place! This traffic has much decreased in Egypt. Lane, in his " Modern Egyptians," says, "latterly, from the impoverishment of the higher classes in this country, the demand for white slaves has been small. A few, some of whom undergo a kind of preparatory education (being instructed in music or other accomplishments at Constantinople), are brought from Circassia and Georgia. The white slaves, being often the only female companions, and sometimes the wives, of the Turkish grandees, and being generally preferred by them before the free ladies of Egypt, hold a higher rank than the latter in common opinion." Poverty, not increase of civilization, has decreased this traffic. Among the Turkmans, a wandering tribe who inhabit Turkestan, beautiful Persian women are made a source of traffic; the Turkmans sell them in the markets of Khiva and Bokhara. Conolly, in his " Overland Journey" gives the speech of a Turkman female, relative to the Persian girls. Do you call those thin-skinned daughters of the devil—women?" "The condition of these poor captives," continues Conolly, " must be very wretched, torn from their homes, and taken under every indignity and suffering through the desert." Respect for the fair sex in Persia has in a great measure vanished ; the beauty and virtue of women have shed no moral influence over that interesting land. " Sir John Malcolm," says Urquhart, " is of opinion, that women, in a former age, in Persia, occupied " an honourable station" in society ; since Quintus Curtius relates, that Alexander did not venture to sit down in the presence of the mother of Darius, until desired to do so." For a description of a Turkish Harem, perhaps none excels that of Lady Montague, in one of her letters to her sister from Adrianople, 1717. As I must give in this paper a description of Eastern beauty, I may as well take the clever Lady Montague's one of the lovely Fatima : " I was so struck with admiration," says she, " that I could not for some time speak to her, being wholly taken up in gazing. That surprising harmony of features ! that charming result of the whole ! that exact proportion of body ! that lovely bloom of complexion, unsullied by art ! the unutterable enchantment of her smile ! But her eyes ! —large and black, with all the soft languishment of the blue ! every turn of her face discovering some new grace. She was dressed in a *caftan* of gold brocade, flowered with silver, very well fitted on her shape, and showing to admiration the beauty of her bosom, only shaded by the thin gauze of her vest. The drawers were pale pink, her waistcoat green and silver, her slippers white satin, finely embroidered ; her lovely arms adorned with bracelets of diamonds, and her broad girdle set round with diamonds ; upon her head a rich Turkish handkerchief of pink and silver, her own fine black hair hanging a great length in various tresses, and on one side of her head some bodkins of jewels." This admirable picture of female loveliness may justly claim a place beside the Rebecca of Sir Walter Scott, in his famous romance of Ivanhoe. The Mahommedan *ladies* of India, as well as of other Eastern countries, are for the most part miserable specimens of seclusion ; no intercourse with any save their husbands, slaves and nearest relations, their life is one gilded scene of misery : by their religion, we are told, they are denied Paradise in the next state, or rather they are promised but half the blessings awarded to the lord of the creation. Cashmere has long been celebrated as an emporium of eastern beauty, and which has been so admirably sung by Moore in Lallah Rookh. The people of Cashmere are proverbial for their clear complexions and fine forms. " The women," says Bernier, " are very handsome," and later travellers have confirmed his opinion :—

> Who has not heard of the vale of Cashmere,
> With its roses, the brightest that earth ever gave ?
> Its temples and grottos, and fountains as clear
> As the *love-lighted eyes* that hang over their wave.

But, I believe on the whole that the Cashmerian women have been too much extolled for their beauty ; it is said that in Spain or the South of France, they would be called brunettes ; and Forster, a traveller, prepossessed with an opinion of their charms, was disappointed. I suppose now, if an Englishman, who had dreamt night and day of the beauty of the Cashmerian girls, from reading Lallah Rookh, were to visit the country through curiosity, he would not be a little astonished at finding such a scarcity of *Nourmahals*. It is a strange thing, when we search for beauty, we seldom find it ; it starts up before us unawares, and frequently through the appearance of one beauty or so, the *beautiful* character is given. But I do not say this is the case with Cashmere.

The Hindu and Persian women are almost totally devoid of delicacy.

They constantly even before men use the most indelicate expressions, and this exists even among the higher orders. When we consider the tenor of their lives, we cannot be much surprised at this behaviour, for a woman in the east is generally little better than a slave. In fact a woman in the east is looked upon as a most degraded being; a Hindu may beat his wife as often as he chooses, and they are much accustomed to this barbarous treatment. "The object," says the Abbé Dubois, "for which a Hindu marries, is not to gain a companion to aid him in enduring the evils of life, but a slave to bear children, and be subservient to his rule." This is also applicable to other eastern nations. Of all the women in the east, those of Hindustan, are by all accounts in the most wretched condition. "Nothing can exceed," says the historian, "the habitual contempt which the Hindus entertain for their women. Hardly are they ever mentioned in their laws, or other books, but as wretches of the most base and vicious inclinations, on whose nature no virtues or useful qualities can be engrafted." Even in their laws they ascribe every wickedness, that can possibly be conceived, to women, and the barbarians imagine it is almost impossible to find a woman without the bad qualities stated in their institutes. Is not this a shocking state of things? does it not prove what a poisonous darkness has surrounded Hindustan? the absurd religion of the natives, that disgraceful priestly influence, has caused an absolute prostration of every intellectual as well as moral good; how in such a country could the character of woman be expected to arrive at any state of perfection? The lascivious dispositions of the Indian rulers, I should suppose, has partly been the reason of the continued state of the low condition of women, and their filling their harems from such emporiums of beauty as Persia and Cashmere, and neglecting the darker beauties. Formerly at the Court of the Great Mogul nearly every individual, when first admitted to the Royal presence, selected beautiful girls with fair complexions, that their children might pass for genuine Moguls. The celebrated Runjeet Singh was famous for his collection of beauties. Sir Alexander Burnes, in his interesting Travels into Bokhara, mentions one of the Maharajah's regiments composed entirely of *Amazons*. "When the chiefs (the Seiks) had withdrawn, the Maharajah gave a signal, which brought a detachment of *his regiment of Amazons*, about seventy in number, richly attired in yellow silk, and uniformly dressed: they drew up in front of the Governor-General (Lord William Bentinck,) under the orders of a favourite Commandant, who controlled the division with a long cane. Some of the ladies were very beautiful; nor did they seem to regret that on such an occasion so many eyes were turned towards them. Many of them had stained their lips with roseate red; and *by accident* some had called in the aid of colour to increase the brilliancy of their complexions. The ladies succeeded in making an impression, and were desired to withdraw after chanting a few Persian odes on love and beauty." I should imagine one of the chief reasons for the effeminacy of the men of eastern nations is early marriage; what would they think in England to hear a rich Oriental eight-and-forty years old talking of his "Asherut Khanum," or as Conolly translates it, his "Lady of delight," that he had *long* wooed and at length won her, then but 13 years of age. It is a custom in the east among the moormen and others to marry while the wife is quite a child; frequently not more than 6 or 7 years old. The unfortunate victim is then kept in close confinement until she suits the fancy of her husband. In India it has always been the custom for parents to seek wives for their son: those who leave their homes in search of employment, always marry their children in their country, and among their acquaintance at home; never among the people with whom they reside. This, then, brings this slight sketch of women in the east to a conclusion; if it has not given much information, it will show on the whole, what a degraded being woman is, in lands where nature has poured forth her all, but where beauty and virtue have seldom gone hand in hand together."

We cannot now do better, in drawing our somewhat rambling and discursive remarks to a close, than gravely admonish all who have entered the married state, to cherish in lively remembrance one of the true secrets of happiness,—and that is, to manifest an habitual readiness to please, and an habitual disposition to be pleased—studiously to avoid occasions of offence and as studiously to repress the aptitude to be offended—carefully to cultivate the habit of proving oneself to be above trifles and of putting the mildest construction on all domestic occurrences, whether of a trivial or momentous character. " Do not expect," said Johnson, " more from life than life will afford. You may often find yourself out of humour, and you may often think your wife not studious enough to please you; and yet, you may have reason to consider yourself as, upon the whole, very happily married." " Two persons," remarks the Spectator, " who have chosen each other out of all the species, with design to be each other's mutual comfort and entertainment, have, in that action, bound themselves to be good humoured, affable, discreet, forgiving, patient, joyful, with respect to each other's frailties and imperfections, to the end of their lives." Or, if the substance of our admonition win its way more effectually to the conscience and the heart, when " wedded to immortal verse," let us listen to the soft sweet strain of the poet of Olney :—

> " The kindest and the happiest pair
> Will find occasion to forbear ;
> And something, every day they live,
> To pity, and, perhaps, forgive.
> The love that cheers life's latest stage,
> Proof against sickness and old age,
> Is gentle, delicate, and kind,
> To faults compassionate, or blind,
> And will, with sympathy, endure
> Those evils it would gladly cure."

ART. VI.—1. *Controversial Tracts on Christianity and Mahom-*
medanism, &c. by the Rev. S. Lee, A. M. Cambridge, 1824.

2. *Mahommedanism unveiled, by the Rev. Charles Forster, B. D.*
2 vols. London, 1829.

3. *Mizan-ul-Haqq, or a resolution of the controversy between*
Christians and Mahommedans; in Persian. By the Rev. C. G.
Pfander. Shúshy, 1835. *Ditto translated into Urdu, Mirza-*
púr, 1843.

4. *Miftáh-ul-Asrár : a Treatise on the Divinity of Christ, and the*
doctrine of the Holy Trinity, in Persian, by the same author.
Calcutta, 1839. *Ditto in Urdu. Agra*, 1843.

5. *Tarik-ul-Hyát ; a Treatise on Sin and Redemption, in Per-*
sian ; by the same author. Calcutta, 1840.

6. *Controversial Epistles between the Rev. C. G. Pfander and*
Syud Rehmat Ali and Mahommed Kazim Ali : Urdu ma-
nuscript.

7. *Controversy between the Rev. C. G. Pfander and Moulavi*
Syud Ali Hassun, in Urdu : published in the " Khair Khah
Hind," papers, from January to August, 1845.

8. *Khulása-i-Saulat-uz-Zaigham ; an Urdu Tract in refutation of*
Christianity. Lucknow, 1258 *Hegiri.*

9. *Answer to the above ; in Urdu. Allahabad*, 1845.

MAHOMMEDANISM is perhaps the only undisguised and formidable antagonist of Christianity. Popery on the one hand,
and Socinianism on the other, may pervert or neutralize her
principles, but they alike professedly bend to her sole authority.
From all the varieties of Heathen religions, Christianity has to
fear no aggression, for they are but the passive exhibitions of
gross darkness, which must vanish before the light of the
Gospel. But in the doctrines of Islam we have an active and
powerful enemy ;—a subtle usurper, who has climbed into the
throne under pretence of legitimate succession, and who has
seized upon the forces of the lawful sovereign to make war
against him. It is just because Mahommedanism acknowledges
the divine original, and has borrowed many of the weapons of
Christianity, that it is so dangerous an adversary. The length
too, of its reign, the rapidity of its early conquests, and the iron
grasp with which it has retained and extended them, the wonderful tenacity and permanent character of its creed,—all combine
to add strength to its claims, and authority to its arguments.

When the first tide of Mahommedan invasion set in towards the west, its irresistible flood seemed about to overwhelm the whole of Europe, and extinguish every trace of Christianity, just as its proud waves were repelled by the Pyrenees; but though different portions of Europe successfully resisted the attack, yet Mahommedan settlements continued for centuries to exist upon it. Again, during the twelfth and thirteenth centuries, when Europe poured her millions into the East, the invaders established, for a length of time, and in the midst of their foes, a succession of posts, which were gradually rolled back by the Turkish arms. And, finally, in the 15th century, the closing conquest of Constantinople and European Turkey, and the extended frontier towards Hungary and Italy, confirmed and perpetuated the last and most intimate connection which has taken place between Christian Europe and the Eastern infidels.

Here then we have a long period of twelve centuries, during which Christianity has been in contact with her mortal foe; and upon three marked occasions, that foe was the grand object of her hopes and fears. It would be natural, therefore, to expect that Christian Europe would have entered the lists not merely with the sword and with the shield,—we might have anticipated that her learned divines and casuists would have advanced to the combat clad in the celestial armour of the Gospel;—that the Popes, besides pouring forth the martial bands of their subjects, would have strenuously and unremittingly applied themselves and their hosts of learned monks and ecclesiastics, to overcome the adversary with those spiritual weapons which would better have suited their sacred character. The banners of Islam approached close to the Papal see, and the crescent, almost within sight of Imperial Rome, shone brightly upon Spain, Turkey and Sicily. Might we then have hoped that its inauspicious rays would have become dim and waned before the transcendent glory of the Sun of Righteousness? How fallacious were such expectations! We learn, indeed, that " in later times, when in the vicissitudes of military adventure, the arms of the Mahommedan were found to preponderate, some faint attempts were made, or meditated, to convince those whom it proved impossible to subdue;"—and still farther, that, " in 1285, Honorius IV. in order to convert the Saracens strove to establish at Paris, schools for Arabic and other oriental languages. The council of Vienna, in 1312, recommended the same method; and Oxford, Salamanca, Bologna, as well as Paris, were places selected for the establishment of the Professorships. But the decree appears to have remained without effect until Francis I. called it into life."* And where are the marks and effects of this feeble resolution so tardily executed? —as far as practical controversy is concerned, they are buried in obscurity : learned works upon the Arabic tongue, translations from its authors,—or at best, notes and commentaries, which too often fight with the air, and sometimes betray gross ignorance of the real views and tenets of Mahommedans, are all that remain. The dominion of the False Prophet needed to fear but little from such contemptible efforts, which even had they been known to his followers, would most probably have served only to confirm them in their belief. In truth, the spirit of the age was adverse to any spiritual success. Clogged and obscured by the errors of Popery, Christianity had abandoned her vantage ground, and what but defeat and dishonour were to be looked for ? We are not prepared, indeed, to say that the entire labours of the Christian world, from the time of Mahommed to the Reformation, were of this futile character. On the contrary, we believe that devoted Christians, during this interval, frequently and with zeal attempted the conversion of the Mussulmans ; but it is a melancholy reflection, that we have not a single account of their success, or of any beneficial effects resulting from their efforts. We find, it is true, in the twelfth century, the eastern Emperor erasing from his creed the anathema against the God of Mahommed, as likely to offend those Mahommedans who had embraced, or were disposed to embrace, Christianity ; but, except for such transient hints, we should hardly be aware that the controversy was going on ;—no *fruits* at least give token of its vitality.

How, then, are we to account for the want of success which characterized this period, in which neither party gained ground in this grand and momentous struggle ? There are four causes to which it may be attributed. And chief among these we place the errors among Christians, which, before the development of Mahommedanism, had already gained much ground in the time of Gregory, and which afterwards so rapidly increased, and sprang up so thickly ;—these crippled its exertions and stifled its efforts. The poison of tradition and superstition stagnated the circulation, and the blight of monachism and legality froze the current, which should have flowed unceasingly,—diffusing to the nations around the genial and healing streams of Christianity. Again, the want of any communication or interchange of sentiment, or even of the usual offices of courtesy, between the

* Waddington's History of the Church.

contending parties,—occasioned partly by their mutual intoler-
ance which absolutely separated them, and partly by political
circumstances,—not only stopped the mouth of the Christian
advocate by affording him no opportunity for discussion, but
debarred him from those scenes and intimacies of social life,
which, by rendering him conversant with the ideas and real tenets
of Mahommedans, would have enabled him to dispute with them
to advantage. Thirdly, the bigoted views of the Mussulmans,
and their worldly, sensual and ceremonial temperament—the
essence of the "natural man who understandeth not the things
of God"—acted then, even as they act now,—excluding light,
and rebutting conviction with contempt. Lastly, the actual
hostility of the Mahommedan Governments towards Christianity, checked all enquiry, prohibited all attempts at missionary
labours, and suppressed every approach to conversion by sanguinary measures and summary punishment.[*] The last three
causes extenuate, though they by no means wholly remove, the
guilt which the Christians of those ages incurred by indifference
towards this great controversy.

The fourth grand era of the connection of Christianity
with Mahommedanism arose with the dominion of Europeans
in India. And here every circumstance was in our favour.
The presence of Europeans was generally the effect of conquest, which, after the first feelings of irritation subside,
invests the conqueror's faith and opinions with the prestige of
power and authority : here, too, our foes are but a moiety of
the population; and the mixed character of the inhabitants
might be expected to have broken the bond of Mahommedan
union, so far at least as to weaken the thraldom of opinion
and custom, to diminish the intensity of bigotry, and to
exchange the narrow-mindedness of the Turk and the Persian,
for somewhat of enlightened liberality in the Mussulman of
India. *Now*, at least, we might have expected that Christian
Europe would early have improved her advantages for evange-
lizing the east ;—that Britain, the bulwark of religion in
Europe, would have stepped forth as its champion here, and
have displayed her faith and her zeal where they were most
urgently required. How different are the conclusions which
the 18th century forces us to draw ! England was then fearfully neglectful of her responsibility ; her religion was shown
only at home, and she was careless of the spiritual death of

---

[*] We recollect to have read some time ago, in the *Calcutta Christian Observer*, an
account of the ineffectual and dangerous labours of a Christian Missionary in the
middle ages, which, if we remember rightly, illustrated some of the hindrances which
were thrown in the way of the Evangelists of those days.

her benighted subjects abroad; while her sons, who adopted India as their country, so far from endeavouring to impart to its inhabitants the benefits of their religion, seemed to banish every trace and symptom of it from their own minds, and exhibited to Heathens and Mahommedans the awful spectacle of men without a faith. Were they then neutral and inactive in the contest? Alas, no! for they presented a practical and powerful, a constant and a living argument against the truth of our holy faith. The great controversy was thus silently advancing in favour of the Mahommedan, whose views, arguments and faith, were receiving so satisfactory and convincing a corroboration from the conduct and manners of their apparently infidel conquerors.

But the 19th century dawned with brighter prospects, and, as it advanced, the dark incubus of idolatry, superstition, and bigotry began gradually to be raised from the shores of this wretched land. Buchanan and Martyn, Brown and Thomason, are among the harbingers of this better era, in which Britain started from her lethargy, and, as if she had been treasuring up strength during her long inaction, came forth as a giant to the encounter. Her missionaries, with the venerable Carey at their head, led the van in a strong array; many of her exiled sons began to perceive their responsibility for India's regeneration, and their number has since steadily increased; and now— England plentifully pours forth her gold in the merciful and blessed work of enlightening the gross ignorance of her perishing subjects: and a great portion of the British Society in India has assumed a new aspect, and acknowledges by its deeds that its highest object is the happiness and the conversion of India. How, then, has the great argument between the Christian and the Mahommedean fared in this altered position: has it advanced as rapidly in the direction of *truth* as we might have anticipated: what have we done since the tone of society has thus improved?

In endeavouring to reply to this question, we propose to examine several works which have lately appeared and given rise to some important discussions;—which are remarkable signs of the times, if they do not indeed constitute a new epoch in the controversy. To give, however, as complete a view of the state of the argument as possible, we have been led to embrace in our review a previous treatise of great merit and interest, which was published twenty-one years ago by Dr. Lee, the learned professor of Arabic in the Cambridge University. It is entitled "Controversial Tracts on Christianity and Mahommedanism," and consists of three portions; a preface, embracing the previous state of the argument; translations of the controversy carried on in Persia, between Henry Martyn and the Mahommedan Doctors; and Dr. Lee's own continuation and conclusion of the argument. As this excellent work does not seem to have obtained that currency and circulation to which, at least in *this* country, its subject and worth entitle it, we propose, as far as our space admits, to give an account of its contents.

It is certainly not very flattering to our national pride, that the Portuguese should have so long preceded us in the earnest endeavour to christianize the Mahommedans. In the beginning of the 17th century, Hieronymo Xavier presented an apparently elaborate treatise on the truth of Christianity, to the Emperor Jahangir; the preface to Dr. Lee's work opens with an account of this composition, illustrated by a variety of extracts. Xavier, it would seem, visited Lahore during the reign of the great Akbar, and having finished his book in the year 1609, presented it to his successor. The table of contents and the specimens which are produced of his reasoning, appear to justify the author's remark that Xavier was a man of ability, and spared no pains to recommend his religion to the Mahommedan or Heathen reader, but that he trusted more to his own ingenuity than to the plain declarations of Holy Writ. Indeed, from the brief notices of the chapters and a few of the extracts, we cannot but perceive under what disadvantage the Roman Catholic labours in attempting to argue with a Mahommedan. He is compelled to leave his strongholds, and descend to the relief of his defenceless outworks; and his skill and subtlety are wasted in proving the reasonablness of relics and miracles, of prayers for the dead, and the worship of images. These arguments are not simply a loss of time and trouble. They actually throw discredit upon all the sound reasoning with which they are connected, and weaken the force of every other attack. We have space only for two short extracts:—

"The section closes with a panegyric on the advantages arising from observing the days of the Saints and of the Holy Virgin; and stating that Islamism can boast of no such ordinances. (?) In the sixth section of the last chapter we have a curious account of the elevation of the Pope, which is intended to show that he is the regular descendant of St. Peter, and Vicar of Jesus Christ on earth; and that he is both the spiritual and temporal ruler on earth: that it is in his power to dethrone or set up kings at his pleasure, and to bind or loose both in earth and heaven."—(*Preface, p.* xl.)

And again; "We have evident intimations that God

approves of the worship of these images, and this he has evinced
by miracles, which he has wrought in favour of those who have
paid particular reverence to them; as it may be seen from past
histories, and witnessed even now in Christian countries."
—(p. xxxiv.) Then follows a string of shrines, where the
Mahommedan is invited to go and witness such exhibitions for
himself. His opponent very quietly replies:—

"We need not now notice your worshipping wooden images
of the Virgin Mary and Jesus, whether such worship be intended as respectful to their persons, or for the purpose of paying them divine honours. And as a word is enough for the
wise, believing as we do that you are such, we shall content
ourselves with the mere hint." What a curse and a blight,
that idolatry and these miracles have cast upon our controversy
with the Mahommedans!

To this tract an answer was published about twelve years
afterwards, by a learned Mahommedan called Ahmed Ibn Zain-
al-Abidin; pretty copious extracts and translations from which,
comprising about sixty pages, are given in the preface. The
writer combats Xavier's objections against Mahommedanism,
occasionally with skill and sometimes with effect; but his direct
arguments against Christianity consist chiefly of the usual components of a Mahommedan attack,—groundless reasonings and
perverted interpretations of Scripture. These are, perhaps
however, more to be excused in this writer who had probably
but very slender means of acquiring any Christian knowledge.
The mode of reasoning does not seem to differ essentially from
that adopted in the present day, except that some of the positions taken up by the Roman Catholic afford the Mahommedan
a peculiar and advantageous line of argument. As a specimen
of the barefaced perversion which characterized almost every
Mahommedan polemical production, we may mention the manner in which Ps. IX. v. 20, is turned into a prophecy of Mahommed's advent. "'Oh God, send a lawgiver, that he may
come and teach men that he is a man.' Hence it is plain, that
God informed David of what the Christians would say respecting Christ. After which David is informed, that God would
send some one who would establish a law, and teach mankind
the right way; and that the Messiah would be a man. Hence
to worship him is inexcusable, much more to consider him as a
God." (p. xlix.) Mahommed Ruza, in his reply to H. Martyn,
still further corrupts the passage, thus; "David has also said,
send a lawgiver, Oh God, that men may know that Jesus is a
man and not a God."—(p. 231.)

The fact that Christ did not punish the woman taken in

adultery, is assumed as conclusive evidence that Christianity abrogated the Mosaical law. The following will serve as a good specimen of his reasoning :—" Moses was no prophet, because he opposed the law as given by Jacob. In the law of Jacob it was allowable to marry two sisters; for he married both Leah and Rachel; which is contrary to the law of Moses....You Christians are reduced, therefore, to this alternative, either you must deny the mission of Jesus; or must allow that he opposed Moses."—(p. lxv.) This is much the same style of reasoning as we have now a days. The greater part of the remaining arguments consist of attacks upon the credibility of the Scriptures, by showing that they contain discrepancies and unworthy sentiments, and that the apostles and evangelists were men of doubtful character. He gives the Catholics a sly hit about the Reformation:—" It appears that you Christians oppose all the prophets. You need not, therefore, reproach and reprobate the English as you do....You say that when some cursed persons came, who endeavoured to corrupt the Holy Scriptures, they were unable to succeed; but corrupted only those books, which their own reprobate Doctors had written out; and these are the English, some of whom are now at Isfahán."—(p. xciv.) What were our English ancestors then about; were the Reformers silent at Isfahán? There is a very curious account of the mode in which it is alleged the gospels were concocted, which is very properly replied to by Dr. Lee, at p. cii; but we have room for no more extracts from the preface, and must refer the interested reader to the original, which, we can assure him, will repay the trouble of a perusal.

Dr. Lee, having devoted a few pages to the refutation of Ahmed's more important objections, proceeds to give the contents of a Latin work, written in reply to the Mahommedan tract, and in defence of Xavier's, by Phillip Guadagnoli, a Professor in the College *de propag. fide.* The author's silence as to the merits of this work, confirms the opinion which the frequent reference, in the Latin Preface, to the authority of Popes, Councils, and Fathers, leads us to entertain. This preface is undoubtedly a curious and useful introduction to the controversy which follows; it might, however, with much advantage, be shortened : the *contents* of Xavier's work might be omitted, and all other extracts but those which bear upon the argument, as well as all the *Persian* originals, which are quite superfluous, as the translation is remarkably good and embodies all the meaning.* These suggestions, if attended to,

* The same remark applies to the extracts from Aga Akbar's treatise, and to

G l

would tend to lighten the work (which, with its 716 pages, is at present somewhat formidable,) as well as materially to reduce its cost.

The opening tract of Mirza Ibrahim, with Henry Martyn's three compositions in reply, possess for all the admirers of that devoted ecclesiastic an interest, which is quite independent of the subject;—which brings us back as it were to be personal witnesses of his exile in Persia; and which alone might have been supposed sufficient to render the volume a *popular* treatise. Mirza Ibrahim's production was the result of the sensation caused by Henry Martyn's visit to Shiraz, and his public disputations with the Mahommedan doctors; it bears the marks of coming from a man of talent and acuteness, and is remarkble for its freedom from violent and virulent remarks. His argument chiefly concerns the subject of miracles, which he accommodates to the Koran. He defines a miracle, as an effect exceeding common experience, accompanied by a prophetic claim and a challenge to produce the like; and he holds that it may be proved by *particular* experience, that is, it may be confined to any single art, but must be attested by the evidence and contession of those best skilled in that art. Thus he assumes the miracles of Moses and Jesus to belong respectively to the arts of magic and physic, which had severally reached perfection in the times of these prophets; the evidence of the magicians is hence deemed sufficient for the miracles of Moses, and that of the physicians for those of Jesus; but had these miracles occurred in any other age than that in which those arts flourished, their proof would have been imperfect, and the miracles consequently not binding. This extraordinay doctrine,—which Henry Martyn in the following tract shows to be founded upon an inadequate knowledge of history,—he proceeds to apply to the Koran, and proves entirely to his own satisfaction that it fulfils all the required conditions. This miracle belonged to the science of eloquence, and in that science the Arabs were perfect adepts; the Koran was accompanied by a challenge, and when *they* accordingly professed their inability to produce an equal, their evidence, like that of the magicians and physicians, became universally binding. He likewise dilates upon the superior and perpetual nature of the Koran, as an intellectual and a *lasting* miracle, which will remain unaltered when all others are forgotten. He touches slightly on Mahommed's other miracles, and asserts the insufficiency

many quotations in the notes, where (except for the elucidation of technical terms,) thereis not the slightest necessity for the Persian or Arabic originals.

of proof (except through the Koran,) for those of all former prophets.

Henry Martyn's first tract refers chiefly to the subject of miracles; he asserts that, to be conclusive, a miracle must exceed *universal* experience,—that the testimony and opinion of the Arabs is therefore insufficient, besides being that of a party concerned,—that, were the Koran allowed to be inimitable, that would not prove it a miracle,—and that its being an *intellectual* miracle is not a virtue, but by making it generally inappreciable, a defect. He concludes by denying the proof of Mahommed's other miracles, in which two requisites are wanting, viz., their being recorded at or near the time of their occurrence, and the narrators being under no constraint. The second tract directly attacks Mahommed's mission, by alleging the debasing nature of some of the precepts and contents of the Koran,—holds good works and repentance to be insufficient for salvation,—and opens the subject of the true atonement, as prefigured in types, fulfilled in Christ, and made public by the spread of Christianity which is mentioned as itself a convincing miracle. The last tract commences with an attack upon the absurdities of sufiism, and proceeds to show that the love of God and union with him can not be obtained by contemplation, but only by a practical manifestation of His goodness towards us, accompanied by an assurance of our safety ; and that this is fufilled in Christianity, not by the amalgamation of the soul with the Deity, but by the pouring out of God's Spirit upon His children, and by the obedience and atonement of Christ. Vicarious suffering is then defended by analogy, the truth of the Mosaic and Christian miracles is upheld, and the whole argument closes with proving the authenticity of the Christian annals by their coincidence with profane history.

It will be observed that the most important part of Henry Martyn's reply consists in refuting the assumptions of his opponent, and that mainly on his own ground ; he does not open any new principles of disputation, nor does he (except very briefly), touch upon the evidences proper to Christianity. His defence, therefore, paved the way for a lengthened reply from Mirza Mahommed Ruza; and in the end, to quote from Dr. Lee, " however the particular topics discussed by them might be vindicated or refuted, the general question at issue may nevertheless not be advanced by such a method ; and the reader, reduced perhaps to the mortifying consideration that time and pains had been thrown away, may at last ask, " to what purpose has been this waste ? " It must, however, be added that, " situated as Mr. Martyn was in Persia, with a short tract on the Mahommedan religion before him, and his health precarious, the course which he took was perhaps the only one practicable." In pursuing his argument, Henry Martyn has displayed great wisdom and skill, and his reasoning appears to be in general perfectly conclusive; in a few instances, however, he has perhaps not taken up the most advantageous ground.

And first, as to miracles, and the Koran as an intellectual miracle:—Henry Martyn has not denied that there might be an *intellectual miracle*, he merely depreciates it by stating that it would not be *generally* intelligible; (p. 93). Dr. Lee characterizes the Koran as a "miracle of the wrong sort," but he declines, in his argument, the subject of miracles altogether, stating that neither the Mahommedan nor Christian definitions are applicable to the question, and that, so great stress having been laid on magic, it was better to hold by the more certain guidance of prophecy (p. 535). He was probably right in so doing, considering the turn the argument had taken; but the weight of miracles is certainly not to be cast off by us in the general discussion. We would, therefore, reject the limitation of Mirza Ibrahim, and demand with Henry Martyn *universal* experience, as the test of a miracle, which must be a manifest interference of the Divine power suspending or exceeding the usual laws which He has established, and which have guided creation since the beginning. In accordance with this principle we would deny the name of miracle to any exhibition of *intellectual* power whatever; we hold that there is no such thing as an intellectual miracle, at least as far as man's faculties are capable of judging: a power might, indeed, be imparted of perceiving unseen or future events, but this would constitute properly, not an intellectual, but a prophetic miracle. We can easily ascertain the laws which govern matter, and therefore can perceive when those laws succumb to a superior power; but the laws, properly speaking, which govern the intellect, are more obscure, and we have no *standard* for measuring their limits. Thus we sometimes meet with unexampled, and almost incredible powers of memory and calculation; and those of eloquence and composition are equally irregular,* so that a surpassing instance in those sciences, though it might be unapproachably excellent, can not *possibly* bear any of the marks or requisites of a miracle. Mr. Pfander has treated the miracle of the Koran very ably,† but he has

---

* Had Lord Brougham forgotten the *Koran*, when, speaking of the wonderful composition of Rousseau's " Confessions," he says. "no triumph so great was ever won by diction; there hardly exists such another example of the miracles which composition can perform."—(Lives of men, letters, &c p. 183.)

† Mizan ul Haqq, pp. 216—220, and also in the controversy with Kazim Ali.

not exhibited it exactly in this light; he shows that the Mahommedan argument, admitted to its farthest extent, does not prove the Koran to be superior to works in *other* languages; but to this the Persian doctors reply, that *they* were not accompanied, as the Koran, with a challenge and claim to prophecy; and they impiously assert, that, when these are brought forward by *any* worker of wonders, it becomes *incumbent* upon the Deity, if the claim be false, to raise up an equal or superior!*

Again at p. 117, H. Martyn calls Christ the *word* and *spirit* of God, and proceeds to say, that these bear the same relation to God, as the word and spirit of man to man. This is combated by his opponent at p. 430, where Dr. Lee with propriety remarks, " It is certainly to be regretted that Mr. Martyn did not meet his opponent purely on his own ground. The title, *spirit of God,* seems here to have been adopted by way of accommodation, (it being the language of the Koran,) by which however nothing could be gained, but much lost in the further prosecution of this question." We have a curious illustration of the truth of this in Mr. Pfander's controversy. That writer, in the beginning of his treatise on the Divinity of Christ, very properly adduces the passage in the Koran alluded to above, along with others, not to prove Christ's divinity, but merely to show what illustrious attributes the Mahommedans should ascribe to him, and what concessions their prophet had made. Kazim Ali† denies the conclusion, and shows that Mahommed applied the very same expression to Adam: Mr. Pfander replies, that if the Koran makes Adam to share in the Divine nature, his opponent may believe the doctrine if he pleases. Kazim Ali of course rebuts the imputation, and holds, with a show of reason, that the application of the expression to Adam proves that it was not meant to imply divinity.‡—So much for the caution and wariness required in this great controversy.

Again, Henry Martyn's reference to Alchemy, (at p. 82) and to magic (at p. 85,) placed his argument upon a false position,

---

* Compare pp. 192, 204 and 210, of Mahommed Ruza's reply, where it is held, that a miracle does not necessarily exceed human power; but that *any* wonder or work brought forward with a challenge by a pretender to prophecy, and not surpassed, must be received as a miracle, otherwise the Deity would have interposed.

† MS. controversy.

‡ The author of the Saulat uz Zaigham, or " the Lion's onset," has a strange disquisition into the meaning of this phrase " Spirit of God ;" (pp. 85—88.) in which he endeavours to prove that the possessive case does not imply connexion (no more than to say, my meat is cooking, implies that it is yours and not the goat's flesh).—and that from this to argue Christ divine, would be to allow all other prophets divine upon whom God's Spirit descended ; that Gabriel and all other angels are styled " spirits of God," and that Christ was called a spirit *par excellence,* because his laws were pre-eminently spiritual, and he lived like the angels without marriage !

which his adversary did not fail to turn to advantage (pp. 203-5.) His reply too (at p. 93) is faulty where he says, that to suppose the evidence of miracles to diminish with the lapse of time, would be to imply that a person at sixty lost part of the conviction as to any fact, which he possessed at twenty: the Mirza replies that the cases are not parallel, one involving personal identity, the other a succession of individuals. He also takes up a weak position (at p. 104.), when he refutes the miracles of Mahommed by the circumstance that some of them are said to have been performed while he was yet an infidel, which at most would prove but little: Mirza Ruza resents the imputation and devotes fifteen pages (p. 253) to show that the passages produced by his opponent do not refer to infidelity;— " ' Thou wast in error, and I have directed thee,' that is to say, the religion of Jesus *was* with respect to him and his followers the true one; but may properly be termed *error*, with respect to the last prophet and his followers." Mahommed was, therefore, at first in error because he was a *Christian!* He also explains the verses where Mahommedan *sins* are mentioned as referring to the sins of his people. Our Indian antagonist Kazim Ali is a little more candid; for he does apply them to Mahommed, but alleges that they refer merely to omissions of prayer and other ceremonial observances, which even Prophets are sometimes guilty of, but which imply no *moral* stain. So easy is it by jesuitical reasoning to avoid the force of the clearest expressions!

But we must hasten to the reply which Mirza Ruza composed in answer to H. Martyn, and which appears to have been written in 1813, the year after his death; it is very prolix, occupying no less than 289 pages; but not being characterized by any peculiar exhibition of talent, and abounding with perversions of Scripture and unfair conclusions, it approaches nearer to the class of productions we meet with in India, and is not deserving of any lengthened notice. The Mirza treats many of his opponent's arguments with great injustice, brings forward a grand array of prophecies which he insists upon applying to Mahommed along with the foolish story of the Hebrew child, expatiates upon the wonderful superiority of the shía doctrines, and praises with the most fulsome panegyric the virtues of Mahommed and the Koran. About two thirds of this tract might easily be omitted without injuring its usefulness or affecting the argument. We shall not descend farther into particulars, but take leave of the Mirza with a few specimens of his style:—and first an instance of his proficiency in History :—

" It is told of Plato, that when he heard of Jesus having

restored one to life who had been three days dead, he said; I can do the same thing : which we suppose must be understood of a person in the longest possible fit of apoplexy. For it is an established principle with the Physicians, that the longest continuance of an apoplectic fit cannot exceed seventy-two hours. . . .And hence it is that when any one dies suddenly, he is not buried for three days; during which time every effort is made for his recovery, because there is still a possibility of his being restored." (p. 217.) And again, (p. 177.) when Plato wrote to Christ to know if any one could be saved with his intervention, the answer of Jesus was this; " Divine Physician ! without my mediation no one can be saved."—(p. 173.)

The reason assigned for Mahommed's having nine wives is very amusing, though we do not precisely comprehend its full meaning. He states, that women are in a very dependent state, that to have more than four wives would " superinduce oppression," and to observe justice with regard to nine would be " next to impossible ;" *therefore*, in conformity with the general mercies vouchsafed to the faithful, " none but the Prophet were allowed to have more than four. But *as he was the paragon of all justice he was allowed to have nine.*" This reasoning, he proceeds, " might be supposed to forbid a plurality of wives ;" but no, this would never suit the Mussulman; for " every sensible man must see that this reduction of the number of wives to *one*, would also reduce men to difficulties. For, it is the desire of most men to take women without any sort of restraint ; and it is well known that the object of Mohammed's law was to diminish difficulties. It has been our object, therefore, to show that Mahommed's allowing himself to take more wives than he allowed to others, was not founded on lust, but with the view of diminishing the difficulties above mentioned ;—*to point out the difficulty of other individuals preserving justice among four ;* and that this was not the case (with respect to Mohammed,) in a number exceeding five, six, or more." This is certainly the richest specimen of reasoning one could desire ; but let us see what he thinks of *our* law of marriage. :—

" The law, however, now in the hands of Christians, is, as every man of sense knows, of a very different description ; and, *therefore*, can never have come from God...... Their women too being allowed to take any man they may please, and whenever they please, cannot but superinduce great confusion in their tables of pedigrees, and must put an entire end to that chastity, which, every one knows, is both necessary and proper. In such a case no one can possibly know whose son he is."—(p. 380.) And then he reads a lecture to the Roman Catholics on the evils of monasticism and celibacy, which we recommend to their attention.

We shall quote but one passage more, and that because we think it deserves attention. The Mirza denies that Mohammed ever intended to say that he could not work miracles ;—" to say, therefore, that he pretended to nothing more than merely to be the messenger of a revelation from above : and then to argue, that a contrary supposition would involve a manifest contradiction to his own declarations, is evidently unfair ; and particularly so when applied to a period of time not less than three and twenty years."—(p. 255.)   This objection should be allowed due weight ;   and in order to answer it satisfactorily, it would be useful to find out at what different times the commentators suppose these expressions were used which disclaim the power of working miracles ; if they extended over the greater period of the prophet's ministry, it would render our attack unanswerable.

Dr. Lee now comes forward himself, and takes up the question discussed in the preceding pages, adopting however a different line of argument.   In his first chapter, he exposes the insufficiency of the evidence upon which the Mahommedans lean, and shows that the testimony of multitudes, if they are interested and but partially informed, is worth nothing; he then substitutes in the stead of these erroneous principles, the true laws of evidence, as enforced by Locke's six considerations. His second chapter is devoted to the integrity of the scriptures. The Mirza had asserted that the Old Testament was lost during the Babylonish captivity, and Dr. Lee's first section refutes this objection in a most satisfactory manner ; the second section refers to the period between the captivity and the time of Mahommed, during which the purity of the Bible is maintained by the most excellent and convincing arguments ; he here takes occasion to show the value of *versions,* which the Mirza foolishly imagined to have increased the corruption : a third section is employed in the consideration of Dr. Kennicott's notion of the Jews having altered their scriptures, which is shown to be most unfounded.   We have not time to dwell longer on this chapter, but it is recommended to the particular attention of our missionaries.   In the third chapter, Dr. Lee, as we have already stated, foregoes the proof by miracles, and lays down from Scripture that a true prophet must have the powers of prophesy ; and that even then, if he opposes a previous revelation, he is not to be credited : Mahommed of course is condemned by these premises.   The argument concludes with a brief explanation of the system of the Scriptures, in which, avoiding all metaphysical and abstruse subjects, he shows its adaptation to man, and refutes the objections of the Mahommedans.

Where all is excellent it is difficult to select; two short extracts, however, will give some idea of the Doctor's conclusive mode of treating his subject. The Mirza had discarded the doctrine of the atonement with a contemptuous sneer; " the statement," he says regarding H. Martyn's notice of it, " is perhaps more surprising than the foregoing, and calculated to provoke the smile even of a child. For all might have been obviated by one sentence, which the angel Gabriel might have delivered and explained to any one of the Prophets;"—and thus, too, he would have swept away the whole system of sacrifices: alas! the wisdom of God is foolishness with men. Dr. Lee calmly replies;—" However this *might have been done* concerns not us to know. Our question is not, as to what *might have been done*, but what has been done. If the Almighty had thought proper, he might have revealed his will in ways totally different from those which he has chosen; but as his will has been revealed, it is our duty to enquire what that is; and not to suggest what it might have been."—(p. 560.)

And, again, as to the miracles ascribed to Mahommed, "they are either said to have been performed in private, as his being saluted as a prophet by stocks and stones, when he was a child; or are false, such as his dividing the moon, causing the sun to stand still, &c. which would have been recorded by the Greeks and others, had any such thing actually taken place; or they were executed for no adequate purpose whatever, such as the poisoned shoulder of mutton speaking......Again, as to the number of the witnesses to these miracles, they may generally be reduced to one: Ali, for instance, or Ayesha, or Hasan, or Hosein, who delivered the account orally to some one who delivered it to another in the same way:—and so, after many generations, the account is committed to writing by Kuleini, or Bochari or some other respectable collector of traditions. These then, are copied by a number of compilers who follow; and then the number calculated to produce assurance is cited as worthy of all credit! "—(p. 567.)

This subject of the traditions, as evidence competent to prove miracles, or indeed fit for any thing, is very ably treated by Mr. Pfander in his Mizan-ul-Haqq, (pp. 255—263,*) where he shows that the original witnesses were interested, that their testimony never exceeded hearsay, and had already become

* The references are all made to the *Urdu* editions of Mr. Pfander's works.

traditionary before it was committed to paper; and that the traditions carry with them an internal self-refutation from the absurdity as well as discrepancy of their contents. This is a topic of extreme importance; and we should like to see a separate work devoted to its investigation. What we require, is a sifting analytical description of all the traditions, arranged according to the probable dates of their being recorded; an account of the individuals who registered them, of their general character for historical impartiality, and of the means and qualifications they possessed for arriving at a true knowledge of the facts; and a statement of the number of individuals through whom they successively descended, and how far they were parties concerned. Such a manual would prove exceedingly useful to the missionary, by enabling him to substitute specific arguments for general declarations; and, if written in a proper spirit, might tend to loosen the hold which the traditions have upon the Mahommedans, of whom the more intelligent portion are not slow in acknowledging the futility of hearsay, or in perceiving the insufficiency of interested evidence.

Besides the text of Dr. Lee's work, which we have thus briefly reviewed, there is a great deal of valuable matter in the appendices and notes; we refer especially to the extracts from Aga Akbar's tract* on Mahommed's miracles, to which are added some notes on the prophecies of the Koran, and to an important disquisition (p. 124—138) tracing Mahommed's scriptural knowledge to Syria, and many of his stories to Ephrem the Syrian. We should like to see this book in the hands of every missionary; in its present shape, indeed, it is bulky, and in some parts tedious and unprofitable; but if, as we previously suggested, the preface and the larger part of Mirza Ruza's tract were curtailed, the remainder might be printed in a cheap form fit for general circulation. But what have become of the *Persian originals and translation* of his own tract, which Dr. Lee promises at p. cxxiii. of the preface? We can assure him they would be highly prized in India. At

---

* At p. 109, this writer makes a very candid confession; in justifying Mahommed's religious wars; he says, that his prophet " was sent in mercy to mankind; but had he not put some to death, seized upon their property, and carried away the rest captives, the whole world must have remained in infidelity and discord, so that the light which he came to bestow would have fallen upon none. The Arabs, therefore, would have remained idolaters,—the Persians have rested in their doctrines or principles, * * * the Hindus have continued to worship cows and trees,—the Jews in their obstinacy,—and the Christians to dispute on the genealogies of persons who neither were nor are Father and Son."

From Martyn's memoir, however, as well as from the extracts given by Dr. Lee, it would appear that Aga Akbar was but a poor defender of the faith, and that he was advised by his brethren not to bring forward his discreditable production.

all events his *own* tract,* with so much of those which preceded,
as to render it intelligible, would prove most useful. The
portions which regard the *Shia* doctrines would not, however,
be so generally applicable here as in Persia ; for, excepting in
Oudh, and where our territory borders upon it, the Indian
Mahommedans belong to the Sunni faith.

We pass on to the consideration of Mr. Pfander's writings,
which consist of three separate treatises ;—the *Mizan ul Haqq,*
which embraces the general argument for Christianity and
against Islamism; the *Miftah ul Asrar,* in proof of the divinity
of Christ and the doctrine of the Trinity ; and the *Tarik ul
Hyat,* on the nature of sin, and the way of salvation. These
books were originally written in Persian, but they have also
been published in Urdu, excepting the last which is in progress
of translation. Mr. Pfander, from his residence and travels in
Persia possesses peculiar advantages, which fortunately qualify him in an unusual degree for the great controversy with
our Mahommedan population. He was attached for ten or
twelve years to the German Mission, at the Fort of Shushy,
on the confines of Georgia, from whence he made frequent and
protracted visits to Persia, penetrating as far as Bagdad, and
returning by a circuitous tour through Isfahan and Teheran.
In 1836, the Russian Government, which could not tolerate the
presence of any foreign ecclesiastics, put a stop to the mission,
and thus proved the means of providing us with labourers,
who, in the field of Persia, had acquired so valuable a knowledge of its language and so intimate an acquaintance with the
religion and tenets of the Mahommedans. Mr. Pfander joined
our Indian Missions in 1838.
Our author has not been backward in improving his peculiar
privileges, or in availing himself of the help which the previous
controversy and Dr. Lee's remarks afforded him. His first and
most important work is the *Mizan ul Haqq,* "a resolution of
the controversy between Christians and Mahommedans ;" and
as this is a book of extraordinary value, we shall endeavour to
present our readers with a complete account of it. The first
Persian edition was published at Shushy in 1835, and the
Urdu translation was lithographed at Mirzapore in 1843. The
argument is prefaced by asserting the insufficiency of the

---

* We have heard, that an Urdu translation of Dr. Lee's tract was published by the
American Missionaries at Ludhiana ; but it has not been circulated, nor had the
American Missionaries, at another station, from whom we procured the information,
ever seen it.

objects of sense for the soul, and that it can alone be satisfied with the knowledge and favour of God, to which, however, man in his present state is unable of himself to attain. A revelation being thus proved necessary, it is premised that a true one must fulfil the real desires, and satisfy the spiritual wants of man's soul ; coincide with the principles of right and wrong implanted in his heart ; exhibit the Deity as the just and holy, omniscient and unchangeable Creator ; entirely agree with itself in all its parts ; and not contradict, though it may transcend, human reason.

The choice is next shown to lie between the Bible and the Koran, and it is proved that the divine origin of the former is admitted by the latter. The notion that each revelation has successively abrogated its predecessor, is reprobrated as unfounded, and unworthy the Divine Government ; and the hypothesis that each advancing stage of society, requires a suitably advanced revelation, is refuted. The argument for the integrity of the Scriptures follows, and occupies a considerble space, but we have merely time to remark that it is sound, able, and satisfactory.

About half of the volume (chap. II.) is now devoted to the development of the doctrines of the Bible and the scheme of Christianity. In this are treated the attributes of God; man's condition; the nature of the great atonement, its proof from prophecy, and practical benefits; the influences of the Holy Spirit ; and the character of the true Christian ;—the truth of the whole system being enforced by a variety of proofs. It is difficult to say what is best done here, but the doctrine of the atonement and the spread of Christianity may be specified as remarkably well discussed. The quotations under the head of commands are, perhaps, too long ; it is, no doubt, necessary to show the Mahommedans that we have a code of morals fully developed in our Scriptures ; but when the extracts cover a very large space, and there is nothing to mark their beginning or their end, they become tedious and obstruct the flow of the argument.

The last chapter is reserved for the direct refutation of Mahommedanism. The first and second marks given for recognizing a true Prophet resemble those adopted by Dr. Lee, except that miracles are admitted : they are as follows,—his teaching must not oppose previous revelations ; it must be supported by proper evidence as miracles and prophecy ; his conduct must befit that of a prophet of God ; and his doctrines must not be enforced by violence. Several pages are now allotted to prove that Mahommed was not foretold, and a variety of prophecies advanced by the Mussulmans are shown to have no reference whatever to their prophet. This portion of the work is very ably executed; indeed the wonder is, that after its perusal any one could ever again have recourse to such absurd arguments, but unhappily a brazen face is not an article which a Mahommedan has far to search for. The contents of the Koran are next examined, and, while it is acknowledged that it inculcates some excellent precepts and correct doctrine, it is asserted that these are plagiarized from the Bible, while the grand and all important truths of the Sacred Scriptures are denied, omitted, or perverted. The mode of atonement through Mahommed and God's mercy is shown to be insufficient; and the sensual rewards, intolerant precepts and blind predestination set forth in the Koran are shown to be opposed to the dictates of reason, as well as to the express teaching of the Gospel. A few canons of correct interpretation are laid down, to obviate the far-fetched, absurd and cabalistic explanations, by means of which our opponents avoid the contradictory and unfavourable conclusion which may reasonably be drawn from the text of the Koran. Mahommed's own character is now brought under review; the claim advanced of his miraculous and prophetical powers is refuted, and the grossness with which he indulged his licentious passions is held up to deserved abhorrence. The measures of violence and other worldly means by which he spread his religion are vividly described. and the whole closes with a statement of the wonderful manner in which the Gospel is now being preached to all the world, preparatory to the glorious advent of Christ when he will take vengeance upon his enemies,—and with a solemn parting admonition to the Mahommedan reader. As an appendix, are added six stories, containing the histories of the conversion of several individuals of various nations, by way of exemplifying the practical working of Christianity.*

The Miftah ul Asrar, or "the key of secrets," is a short treatise devoted to the establishment of the divinity of our Saviour, and the doctrine of the Trinity. It sets out with showing the lofty dignity ascribed in the Koran to Christ, and the reverence with which Mahommedans ought, therefore, to regard him: the weakness and incapacity of the human intellect is then enforced, which can reason only upon the perceptions we

* These are very interesting. but perhaps they might be in parts curtailed without diminishing the effect. *Indian* stories will, in general, be more applicable and better understood than those of distant nations ; would it not be appropriate here to introduce a few instances of Hindu young men who have displayed, in their conversion, so noble a victory over the world, so complete a subjection to the love of Christ ?

receive, and is therefore incompetent to attempt the discovery of subjects regarding which we have no experience : and from this is deduced the necessity of bending to the revelation of God with humble and implicit faith. The first chapter takes up the proof of our Saviour's divinity, and a section is allotted to the evidence derived from his own words; this is a very suitable arrangement, as the Mahommedans always ask first for Christ's own assertions, pretending that no statements of another party are to be received towards the proof of that which our Saviour himself did not even affect to claim. But why is Gabriel's and the Angel's evidence admitted into this section? A maulavi remarked to us, that the Mussulmans would smile at this; " the Padre," they will say, " set out with proving Christ's divinity from his own words, and in the very first page, he is obliged to have recourse to foreign testimony :" this is in reality no great blemish, as the object appears to be to usher in the birth of that Saviour whose words are about to be brought forward : but it may be as well not to give any ground for the morbid hyper-criticism of our antagonists. The only other remark which appears to be called for upon this section, and upon the following, which is appropriated to the evidence of the apostles, is, that the expression " *only* begotten son " is not sufficiently insisted upon.' This was repeatedly referred by Christ to himself; and to have more prominently seized upon it would have strengthened the position assumed at p. 16. In other respects this portion of the work is full and satisfactory, as well as the third section, which continues the argument from the Old Testament.

The second chapter takes up the subject of the Trinity, and its first section contains copious selections from the Scriptures, which prove that sacred mystery and the personality of the Holy Ghost. There are one or two passages in the concluding paragraph which we doubt the propriety of introducing ; we refer especially to the threefold blessing which Aaron was directed to pronounce over the people of Israel : we are aware

* We learn from the author of the Saulat uz Zaigham (p. 89.) that " White and Williams, Padres," took their stand upon this expression, when pressed by him as to the ambiguous meaning of the word " son;" it is evident that he was hard put to in explaining away its meaning, for he has resorted to the convenient argument of *interpolation* ,—a subterfuge, which the fearless effrontery with which he forges interpretations and glosses to suit his purposes seldom renders necessary.

He fancies that he has discovered a famous argument against us in the expression " first begotten son," because it was applied by Moses to Israel, by Jeremiah to Ephraim, and in the Gospel to Jesus : but he argues, there can be but one first begotten," therefore the three authors contradict each other ; he then offers to extricate us from the difficulty by this interpretation ; viz. that Israel was termed " first begotten," in opposition to Ishmael, who did not inherit, and that the meaning therefore of Christ's being called God's first begotten son, is, that he was an Israelite ; and the word " only" was added as distinguishing and honouring him beyond all other Israelites. To what shifts the uncandid interpreter is driven!

that this is usually applied to the Trinity, and the tradition of the Jews regarding the mode in which the priest disposed his hand as he gave this beautiful benediction, may strengthen the idea: but, at the best, it is only an *accommodation*,—an *agreement*,—for there would be nothing unusual in imagining that the prayer might have been tripartite without any reference to the Trinity; and where there is any appearance of *forcing* an application, we had much rather see it entirely omitted. It is, at the same time, just to mention, that in the following page, Mr. Pfander clearly explains that the sacred mystery is referred to in the Old Testament by *allusions* alone, and that these can be interpreted only by the plain teaching of the New Testament.

The second part of this chapter contains a variety of arguments, which are intended to reconcile the mystery of trinity in unity with the conclusions of sound reason. We are not entirely satisfied with these arguments. At page 59 we are told that nature is the shadowing forth of the eternal principles, and to the pure mind is a "ladder," and a "school," whereby we may learn divine mysteries so completely, "that if man had not rebelled against God, and thus perverted and darkened his intellect, he would certainly have attained by the help of creation and the perceptions of his own heart, to a perfect knowledge of God and himself, so fully that no written revelation would have been necessary." To this we object: for it seems at least doubtful whether man, even in a perfect state, could, without any revelation, have discovered the doctrine of the Trinity; whereas the mode of expression here adopted intimates, that there are marks in creation which do plainly indicate the Trinity of the Creator. A number of explanatory instances or analogies are then given, after which, their force is summed up as follows:— " to conclude, it is clearly proved, from these examples, that *nature contains unequivocal marks of the existence of the Divine nature in Trinity;* and, in truth, whoever attentively considers them, will perceive that plurality in unity is possible," (p. 61.) There is no serious objection to bringing forward instances of plurality in unity, for the simple object of proving it not to be impossible: nay, if care be taken to make it known that they are not used as *direct* analogies, they may prove beneficial in displaying the inability of man to fathom mysteries infinitely short of the sublime doctrine of the Trinity: but the above expressions go beyond this and assert that nature directly *points out* the doctrine; and from this we dissent as unfounded, and as giving the adversary a needless advantage. We will not take upon ourselves to say which of the illustrations might safely be retained, but we think that of the *circle* to be decidedly reprehensible : that figure is stated to be an emblem of the Deity, having neither beginning nor end; and the fact that trigonometry is the key to its measurement and comprehension, is represented as an illustration of the Trinity, by which alone the Divine nature can be understood. Such exemplifications only pave the way for the blasphemy of our opponents. Thus the author of the *Saulat uz Zaigham*, in a passage which it would be painful to translate from the blasphemous nature of its expressions, draws the figure of a triangle, and, after some contemptuous remarks upon the inequality of its angles, adds this cutting scoff, " if this be the way of their arguing, why any body may join the Virgin Mary to the Deity, and drawing a square may assert that here is quaternity in unity;" and to complete the blasphemy he adds the diagram by way of illustration ! To display the species of reply which is given to one of Mr. Pfander's less objectionable analogies, that of the plurality in unity of man, we make a farther quotation from the same work,—" First, every composite subject is dependent upon parts, and to be dependent is not worthy of the Deity ; second, every such subject is liable to change, and cannot therefore be eternal ; third, if any one of man's component parts be taken away, the rest is no longer *man ;* if God, therefore, be composed of three persons, then when the Son came to this earth the Father and the Holy Spirit were no longer God ; and so with the Holy Ghost which descended upon earth after the Son's return : in that case the Almighty were imperfect and liable to change, which God forbid ! " He proceeds, " that illustrations prove nothing and if they did the Mahommedans might assert a quaternity from the creation consisting of *four* elements, and the Hindus from their *five* elements, a Deity of five in one." Many similar examples of the disadvantages and ridicule to which such a line of argument exposes us might be adduced,—but we forbear, and close the subject with an extract from Dr. Wardlaw's admirable lectures on the Socinian controversy, the sentiments of which we recommend to Mr. Pfander's consideration :—

" Of the precise import of the term *personality*, as applied to a distinction in the Divine essence, or of the peculiar nature and mode of that distinction, I shall not presume to attempt conveying to your minds any clear conception : I cannot impart to you what I do not possess myself :—and convinced as I am that such conception cannot be attained by any, it had been well, I think, if such attempts at explanation, by comparisons from nature, and otherwise, had never been made. They have afforded to the enemies of the doctrine, much unnecessary occasion for unhallowed burlesque and blasphemy. The Scriptures simply assure us of *the fact :*—of the *mode* of the fact they offer no explanation. And where the Bible has been silent, it becomes us to be silent also ; for when, in such cases, we venture to speak, we can only " darken counsel by words without knowledge." The fact, and not the manner of it, being that which is revealed, is the proper and only object of our faith. We believe that *it is so ;* but *how* it is so, we are not ashamed to say, we do not presume even to conjecture."

Mr. Pfander proceeds to prove, that no intelligent actor can exist in *absolute* unity, because rigid metaphysical unity implies mere existence ;—to which the superadditions of intelligence and will must be given, else the mere *being* remains passive and inactive ; hence the metaphysical speculations of the Hindu, Grecian, and Mahommedan philosophers, are shown to have all ended in proving the necessity of the Creator's existing in a species of trinity. As far as this argument and a display of the absurdities of Sufiism are resorted to, merely to unfold the opposite conclusions of trinity and unity to which man arrives when he reasons on the nature of his Creator, and even to prove that plurality in unity is not so inconsistent with sound reason as it at first appears, we do not object : but the greatest care must be observed lest this line of reasoning assume the appearance of an *a priori* argument,—as if, from the nature of things, the deity *must* exist in trinity ; and a few of Mr. Pfander's expressions seem calculated to give rise to such an impression. Again, in applying this reasoning to the Mahommedan, he argues thus :—" If you reject the doctrine of trinity, and hold to simple unity, you reduce your Creator to an inanimate exist-ence ; (pp. 75-76,) the Mahommedan will retort, " You confuse the terms of *personal metaphysical* unity ; the latter I do not hold : the former, viz., a Creator whose existence is endowed with the attributes of intelligence and will,—such is my God ;" and, we think, the reply would be just, because according to the supposed reasoning fully carried out, the Christian Trinity is not *one* but *three* trinities. It must not, however, be under-stood that Mr. Pfander in any degree intentionally employs the *a priori* argument ; on the contrary, his declared object is *simply* to show, that the doctrine of the Trinity as revealed does not oppose reason, and this he distinctly and repeatedly states ; at the same time, we trust that in a future edition the line of reasoning and cast of expression will be so far altered as to leave no possibility of misconception. The quotations from the Arabic and Persian metaphysical writings are, we think, unreasonably long.

The closing section proposes to shew that our knowledge of God, and hopes of salvation are bound up in the doctrine of the Trinity ; and, excepting some expressions of the nature just animadverted upon, its contents are most valuable. The

wonderful love of God in effecting man's salvation through his
eternal Son, and the blessedness of sanctification through the
Spirit, are shown to be so dependent on the Trinity, that he
who denies the Son, hath not the Father, and cannot obtain the
pardon of his sins.

The *Tarik ul Hyat*, or "the way of life," takes up a point
which was but briefly noticed in the *Mizan*,—the true nature
of sin,—to all a subject of extreme importance, but above all
to the Mahommedan, whose loose and imperfect ideas of sin
in general, and grossly perverted notions of *inward* sin, lull
him to sleep amid the outward ceremonies of his shallow faith,
and steel him against the attacks of conscience and the Gospel.
The true nature of sin, to which, in the introduction, are
ascribed all the unhappiness and misery of man, it is shown
must be sought for in God's word; the first portion of the
work is accordingly devoted to the Mosaical account of the fall,
the effects of which are traced in man's complete corruption.
A searching examination follows into the real evil of sin, and
its heniousness is found to consist in the *intention :* hence, and
from copious illustrations of Scripture, corrupt desires and lusts,
even though they do not break out into overt acts, are proved to
be offensive and deserving punishment in the sight of God.   The
erroneous notions of Mahommedans as to *venial* offences are
displayed as grounded upon false principles; and it is proved
that *all* sins, though they may differ in enormity, are alike
transgressions of the law;—nay, that what appears to us a
venial sin, may, from the *intention,* be in God's sight one of
the most aggravated nature.   The dreadful effects of sin are
next treated of: the pains of hell, it is asserted, will be chiefly
mental and spiritual, in opposition to the Mahommedan doctrine,
which depicts, with hideous and disgusting particularity, the
various species of bodily torments inflicted upon the damned.
The Mahommedan account of the fall of Satan is shown to
be without foundation ; the origin of evil is cautiously touched
upon ; and the reason of its permission prudently left with
Almighty wisdom.   The whole of this argument is conducted
with great ability.

In the next portion of the work, the various ways proposed
for procuring pardon are brought before the reader ; and first,—
the methods assigned by reason, as repentance and reformation,
are shown to be vain ; secondly, the means adopted by Pagan
religions, and among these the creeds of Zoroaster, the Hindu,*

* In the forthcoming Urdu edition, the remarks upon the Hindu religion might be
expanded so as to form a useful episode for the Hindus, who, we may hope, will
not be backward in reading the treatise.

and the Chinese, are considered,—opportunity being dexterously seized for describing the compulsory manner in which Islamism banished the first of these from Persia; thirdly, the Mahommedan religion is weighed in the balance, and, like its predecessors, found wanting; the ceremonies prescribed in it are classed in the same category with the heathen rites and practices just described; Mahommed is proved a sinner, and a mere man, incapable of being an atonement for the sins of others;—these and the other errors of Mahommedanism are shown to have originated in mistaken notions of the nature of sin; and a curious display is made of the doctrine which lays down that the intention to commit any *sin*, however rife or fondly cherished, is not counted by God against a Mussulman, while the mere intention to do a *good* action, is reckoned as one, and if it be carried out, as ten good deeds! Inward corruption and impurity are therefore ideas perfectly foreign to the Mahommedan creed. The Gospel mode of obtaining pardon is now introduced; expiation through Christ, and faith in it, which is stated to be the requisite and only acceptable accompaniment of repentance, and the wonderful splendour thrown upon the divine attributes by this exhibition of the love of God, are fully explained. But we hasten to the concluding division, which displays by copious extracts from Scripture, and with great power of language, the blessings conferred by participation in this salvation. The springs of the Christian's character and happiness, his restoration to God's favour, his delight in prayer, his love to all mankind, and his glorious prospects for eternity are described with a fascinating eloquence which cannot fail to captivate the reader. We have no space for details, but we cannot help drawing attention to the vivid parallel between the heaven of the Bible, and the paradise of Mahommed: this is a species of style which Mr. Pfander frequently adopts with great effect;—after dilating at length on the excellencies and the perfections of some Christian doctrine, he suddenly brings forward the corresponding tenets of the Mahommedan faith, when the comparison adds to their native deformity: thus, again (p. 146) after dwelling upon God's mercy and desire that all should be saved, the teaching of the Koran, that millions were *created* for damnation is held up in contrast. Such a course seems more effective, and likely to produce conviction, than successively to bring up each of the Mahommedan doctrines, as is sometimes done,* like culprits to the bar, and condemn them upon previously assumed positions.

* Such a mode is adopted in the *Din Haqks Jahqiq* " an investigation of the true

The *Tariq ul Hyat* stands unrivalled as an exposition of Christian doctrine in Persian. It is difficult to say whether greater ability is displayed in the conduct of the argumentative reasoning of the Mizan ul Haqq, or the moral discussions of the Tariq ul Hyat; the latter, perhaps, from the abstract nature of the subject, deserves the highest praise. Each, indeed, has its peculiar merit, and the *three* form a whole, proposing to the Mahommedan almost every point, which he is at present prepared to receive. To be interested or profited by the *Tariq ul Hyat*, requires, no doubt, a state of mind much in advance of that which the Mussulman now possesses, for the subject of inward corruption and impurity is one most foreign to his purposes and desires; but, the day is, we trust, approaching, when this will no longer be the case;—when the leaven of that knowledge which is even now pervading the country, will work a mighty change in their feelings and ideas; and then, by the blessing of God, will the Mahommedan heart respond with notes of conviction and repentance to the touches of truth contained in this volume. Mr. Pfander has indeed conferred, in these books, an inestimable boon upon this country; and we are much mistaken if they do not assume the place of standard treatises among the Mahommedan population who interest themselves in the great question, and indeed among all our native christians; for though they are *primarily* adapted to the professors of Islamism, their contents must always possess a general value and interest.

The *Tariq ul Hyat* displays an uncommon exuberance of language and richness of diction,—a perfect facility in the Persian idiom, and a degree of ease in adopting elegant and appropriate illustration, which astonishes the Mahommedans of this country, and perplexes them to account for the *Padre's* accomplishments.* Notwithstanding, therefore, the plainness with which their errors are laid bare, these treatises are viewed with great respect by learned Mahommedans; and that they have created a great sensation, is evident from the discussions,

religion," a prize essay published three years ago in "refutation of Hinduism and Mahommedanism and Establishment of Christianity." The principal and most important portion of this work is employed upon the Hindu religion,—the subject being elaborately treated, and the arguments in general conclusive. The part which applies to Mahommedanism, though it contains a deal of useful matter, is not, we think, composed in the style most likely to be beneficial; the imperative and peremptory tone assumed, can only excite opposition, and some of the arguments are weak,—such as the impossibility of keeping the fast of Ramzan, and observing the five daily prayers at the poles,—which, though to a certain extent true, is too strongly insisted upon. As this book has been translated and published in English, we have not thought any more lengthened notice of it necessary.

* If there is any fault in the style of the *Tariq*, it is, that some of the words are so difficult and uncommon as scarcely to be known even to the learned of this country; this must be avoided in the Urdu translation.

which will shortly be mentioned. Some of the learned Maula-vis of Tonk having seen a copy of the Mizan, addressed a note to its author, soliciting a further supply of what they term "a wonderful production," از معاہدات عجیبہ است ; and the *Muj-tahid*, or Royal Shia professor of Lucknow, in acknowledging the recept of Mr. Pfander's four books, confesses "that the style of these delightful treatises differs so completely from that hitherto adopted by Christian writers, that he strongly suspected some accomplished Persian of having, from worldly motives, assisted in their composition, for no such charms or merit had hereto-fore appeared in any writings of the *Padres*;" and his sense of their merit was proved by his threatening a refutation. The surmise of the celebrated professor, which we need not say is quite groundless, is sufficiently amusing; in correcting, indeed, and polishing the *style* of his books, Mr. Pfander did avail him-self of the services of a converted Mussulman, who, born an Ar-menian, was, when a boy, carried off by robbers and sold to a Persian nobleman, who educated and made him his Munshi. Mr. Pfander had to tutor both himself and his assistant in the work, and the marked superiority in the style of the *Tariq*, which was his latest composition, shows what rapid progress he was making in attaining the beauties of the Persian lan-guage. The *fourth* work referred to by the Professor of Luck-now, is "the tree of life," a small but useful Urdu tract containing a copious selection from Scripture, illustrative of the divine perfections and the Christian code of morals. Mr. Pfander has also composed a short treatise in English, on the "Nature of Mahommedanism," which is strongly recommended to the perusal of all who are interested in the controversy, especially to those who are unable to master the subject in the oriental languages.

The translation into Urdu of the *Mizan*, has been managed by Mr. Pfander with great success, considering it to be a first attempt; in a second edition, we hope that it will be im-proved, and a few of the Persicisms omitted; one of the most frequent of which is the phrase *malùm diláná*. The *Miftah* is by no means so well rendered into Urdu; the idiom is in some places defective, not to say inelegant, and occasionally the words ill chosen.

It is difficult to say how the *Mizan* was regarded in Persia: its distribution, in which great caution was required, was com-menced just as the Mission was called away; but there was reason to imagine that, notwithstanding the bigotry of the Per-sians, it was liked and perused by them with interest. When on his way to India, Mr. Pfander fell in with two respectable Persians, who made enquiries about the book and its author, and stated that the Governor of Casbin had received two copies, the contents of which had excited great attention; it was suspected by them to be the work of some renegade Mahommedan. That the countries about Kabul and Herat are prepared to peruse and receive benefit from it, is clear from the evidence of an officer who had ample opportunities of forming a correct judgment. He writes, that, during the period of four years' residence in that country:—

"He had several opportunities of proving the value of the work in question,* having found in it many arguments for the truth of Christianity, which the Mussulmans, with whom he conversed, were unable to refute." "It is written," continues he, "in a truly Christian spirit, and whenever shown to the followers of Islam, always excited much attention, so much so that I could,—had such a course not been at variance with the known wishes of the Government,—have distributed, with every prospect of a happy result, many copies among those who would use them.

Unable to give, I yet considered myself at liberty to show the work to those Afghans, who came to my house from time to time. The conversation, which generally turned on the subject of religion, afforded me opportunities for showing the Persian N. Testament, and Mizan ul Haqq, and often I have been entreated to lend this book for a more careful perusal. Next to the New Testament itself, it is the book most likely to be of use amongst Mahommedans. The contrast between Christianity and the religion of Islam is made so strong and in such moderate language, that it seemed to create an anxiety for future enquiry and investigation.

The Jews, too, of Kabul, were generally anxious to obtain copies, and as I considered the prohibition did not extend to them with such force, I on one occasion lent a copy of the work to the head of their tribe, but had considerable difficulty in recovering it, which I soon became anxious to do, on finding the deep interest it excited. To use their own expression, ' the Mizan-ul-Haqq put words into their mouth, and enabled them to speak out to Mahommedans, which before they had not been able to do.'" He adds, "in my humble opinion, the work is so valuable, that it should be translated into Urdu, Arabic, and every language in use with Mahommedans."

But it will be asked, and we proceed, therefore, to notice, what effect these productions have had upon the native mind in India? Mr. Pfander distributed copies very extensively with a solicitation that the arguments should be attentively considered, and if possible replied to. The gauntlet, thus thrown before the whole Mahommedan Society of the North Western Provinces, has been taken up by one or two distinguished opponents, who have hitherto treated with a smile of contempt the puny attacks made against their faith.† While we are writing this article, the

* The *Mizan ul Haqq*.

† The few tracts put forth by the Tract Society on the subject of Mahommedanism, which we have fallen in with, are of an inferior description: they contain, it is true, some useful matter, but mingled with inconclusive reasoning, and misconception of

promised refutation of the Royal Professor, Maulavi Syud Ali, has issued from the press of Lucknow, in the shape of an octavo volume of 232 pages; but as we have not seen its contents, we are not aware of the line of reasoning he has adopted.* A long and protracted controversy was carried on in Urdu by Mr. Pfander, with two Mahommedans, Syud Rahmat Ali, and Mohammad Kazim Ali,† of whom the latter appears to have been the leading writer. It began in 1842, and would seem to have lasted for two or three years; there are seven Epistles contained in it, which gradually increase in length, the last of Kazim Ali's being swelled out to 147 closely written pages. The Mahommedan sets out with the text, "I am not sent, but unto the lost sheep of the house of Israel;" he asserts that our Saviour here and elsewhere declared that his mission extended only to the Jews, challenges his opponent to prove its universality, and affects the most virtuous indignation at our missionaries practising so foul a deception as to attempt conversion to an obsolete religion intended only for the Jews. Mr. Pfander had here to argue at a disadvantage against the Mussulman's preconceived principle, that Christ's mission was, like any other prophet's, fully developed during his life; he had to concede that in one sense He was primarily sent to the Jews,—and did not proclaim the universality of his faith till his ascension; still a number of passages, which clearly establish the doctrine, are quoted from his own discourses, and the apostles' teaching is added as conclusive on the subject. Kazim Ali's objections display the perverse stubbornness, and (to human means,) incurable blindness of the followers of Islam. To all asseverations of Christ himself, made *before* his ascension, he objects that they contradict the verse from Matthew, and his own directions to the seventy. To the final command "Go ye, therefore and teach all nations," he objects that it is immediately preceded by a clause, which destroys all dependance on them,— "but some doubted." The apostle's declarations are treated as contradictory, and as insufficient to prove a doctrine which their Master himself is alleged not to have held: when particularly hard pressed an easy refuge is obtained behind the charge of

the Mahommedan doctrines; and the whole is ill composed; we are ashamed to say that we have been puzzled over several passages in the "comparison of Mahommedanism with Christianity," without being able to make any sense out of them. To complete these defects they are not free from unnecessary harshness.

* We hope to be able to give some account of this treatise in a note at the end of this article.

† These writers are, we believe, *vakeels* in the civil court at Agra; Kazim Ali seems to be possessed of some intelligence and sharpness, but his talents do not rise above mediocrity.

corruption, of which the smallest apparent discrepancy is regarded as full and satisfactory proof. The controversy then branches out into the general subject,—embracing the claim of the Apostles to inspiration; the Divinity of Christ; the prophecies applied by Mahommedans to their Prophet, &c. But Kazim Ali's perversity surpasses that of the most of his brethren: he assumes erroneous and fanciful interpretations, insists with consummate pride that his own explanation can be the only correct one, and holds to them with the most dogged obstinacy, however absurd and grossly perverted they may have been proved.* In the same spirit, the plainest and most faithful interpretations are constantly ascribed with irony to Mr. Pfander's extraordinary acuteness, and characterized as phantoms of his imagination. Mr. Pfander soon perceived what a *bully* he had to deal with, and in his second and third letters threatened to close the controversy, if more impartiality were not shown by his antagonists. Kazim Ali's fourth letter exceeded its predecessors in rabid bigotry, and its style began to descend to petulant if not to offensive remarks. Mr. Pfander accordingly carried his threat into execution, and refused to reply unless umpires were selected to decide whether certain points had been satisfactorily proved or not; to this Kazim Ali would not accede, and here the matter ended. The Mahommedan argument is conducted with some ability and much subtilty; and a surprising number of passages both from the Old and New Testaments are adduced; but the whole is guided by a determined wrongheadedness, which adopts the most fallacious weak and inconclusive reasoning merely because it ends favourably, and refuses to see its errors, however plainly pointed out. This controversy must have proved a severe trial to Mr. Pfander's temper; and if flippant contradictions, false insinuations and bitter scoffs may have occasionally led him to make some severe remarks,—it is not to be wondered at; on the contrary, we are surprised at the calm and candid manner which he preserved throughout. We should like to see the whole printed with appropriate remarks;

---

* For instance, " out of Zion shall go forth the law and the Word of the Lord from Jerusalem," the law *left* Jerusalem, and where else can it be pretended to have migrated but to Mecca? The passage, " he shall not cry, nor lift up, nor cause his voice to be heard in the street," refers to Mahommed, and it cannot apply to Christ who " cried" on the cross. In endeavouring to prove the corruption of the Scriptures, he says, " You ask, what object had the Christians in corrupting the notices of Mohammed? What! is it no object to eat pork and drink wine; to avoid praying five times a day, and fast for a month in the year"? Shortly after he says, " I do not mean to affirm that the Scriptures were corrupted in later ages when Christians were numerous and copies multiplied; no; it was in the early ages of the Apostles when there were but few to detect the change:" he forgets that the time he alludes to was to more than 500 years prior to the existence of the motives he had before supposed.

but Mr. Pfander is, perhaps, wise in keeping back any farther publication until he shall have seen all his adversaries' replies; then, we understand, he intends to come forward with a general and complete refutation.

Another discussion, contained in a series of twenty-two letters which passed between Mr. Plander and Maulavi Syud Ali Hassan,* of Agra, has gained greater celebrity, from its having been printed in the *Khair Kha Hind*.† As a translation of this controversy (though abounding with mistakes,) has appeared in the romanized version of that paper, our notice of its contents shall be very limited. After an amusing parley, in which the Maulavi bargains for the titles of respect by which his prophet and Koran are to be mentioned, he introduces his argument in the 9th letter, by defining two species of improbability,—logical and experimental; and then he puts this curious question, " If by rejecting an *experimental*, you are forced to believe a logical impossibility,—what course does reason recommend?"‡ Mr. Pfander, much against his will, is thus plunged among *impossibilities;* he acknowledges that where a logical impossibility is *really* established, it can under no circumstances be admitted, and must therefore cancel every supposition involved in it; but he denies the sovereignty of man's reason to determine *what* are absolute impossibilities; and he demurs to the argument altogether as being foreign to the subject in hand. The Maulavi however sticks manfully by his first position, asserting that if the doctrine of impossibilities be not within man's reason, and be not settled at the outset, all attempts at reasoning are absurd. After several futile endeavours on Mr. Pfander's part to draw off the Maulavi to the proofs of Christianity, and repeatedly challenging him to impugn the reasoning of his *Mizan*, the controversy falls to the ground. The Maulavi's closing letter afforded Mr. Pfander an opportunity of adding a long and valuable note upon the use and abuse of reason in matters of religion, and a sketch of his

* Syud Ali Hassan is evidently a man of very superior abilities; and we understand that he holds a high place in Mahommedan Society for attainments and learning. He is an officer of some standing in the the Sudder Dewany Adalut, N. W. P.

† This is a useful little monthly paper, published in Urdu by the Mission at Mirzapore: as it often languishes for want of matter, why do not the Missionaries of other stations contribute an occasional article? it is hard for the Editor to be reduced to the necessity of copying the Government Gazette into its columns :— much like printing the Acts of Parliament in a Missionary periodical or monthly Journal.

‡ In the 14th letter he illustrates his position by the following example : " If not to credit the fact of a bullock having spoken, imply belief in an infinite series or in the co-existence of contraries, which impossibility must be rejected?" Mr. Pfander's faculties must have been sadly puzzled to make out the learned Maulavi's meaning.

argument from the "Mizan ul Haqq." This controversy possesses a peculiar interest, because the line of reasoning taken
up by the Maulavi, is that which the most sensible and intelligent Mussulmans adopt; they erect blinded reason into a
sovereign judge, before which every thing must bow, and they
find that a very summary and convenient mode of despatching
the claims of Christianity. We must not, however, imagine
that this is any thing more than a skirmish on the part of Ali
Hassan,—the *attack* is yet to come; he is now printing a work
at Lucknow in refutation of Christianity and in defence of the
Koran, at which he has been labouring for 15 years, and which
is by the way to contain a full reply to the *Mizan* as well as to
the *Din Huqq.* We now leave Mr. Pfander's writings with
regret, and with admiration; let him not forget the singular
advantages and talents he possesses—nor abandon his post of
champion of Christianity against the Mahommedans; we are
sure, if God spare him, that he will soon be again in the field,
and we heartily wish him God speed in this most momentous
struggle.

The most popular work against Christianity in the North
West Provinces, appears to be the Saulat uz Zaigham, a rambling desultory attack, full of spite and animosity, and perfectly
unscrupulous as to the correctness and honesty of its premises,
but written in a vigorous and attractive style. An abridgement
of this treatise in Urdu has gained great currency among the
Mahommedans, and as a reply to it has just issued from the
press, our readers will probably be interested to know the
character and merits of both books. The *Khulasa i Saulat uz
Zaigham*, professes to have been written 13 years ago, but it
was only printed within the last three years. Its object, as
described in the concluding paragraph, is as follows; "In
former times when the Christians were not in power, and the
noisy violence of their abrogated religion was therefore concealed, our Professors seldom turned their thoughts towards its
refutation; but upon the learned of *this* age, it is incumbent
and their sacred duty to use every endeavour to overturn their
faith, otherwise these people by their insidious efforts will
gradually mislead whole multitudes. And be not discouraged
by the knowledge that such attempts will be thrown away upon
the infidels themselves; for when it became generally known
that I had written the *Saulat uz Zaigham*, people began to
dispute with the *Padres*, White and Williams, and with me, and
in the end, by God's assistance, I overcame them; and the effect
was that, of their friends, who had turned Christians, two came
to me and resumed the Mahommedan faith; then Praise be to

God, the Lord of both worlds!" The chief peculiarities of this treatise are the shameless audacity with which false assertions and dishonest proofs are resorted to, and the very lengthened extracts (including whole psalms and chapters,) taken from the Bible, which by an extraordinary facility of perverse application are turned into intimations of Mahommed. It is difficult, perhaps, impartially to determine, how far many of these may be the bona fide convictions of a sincere mind searching after the confirmation of what it deems the true faith, for we all know to what an extraordinary length the idol *prejudice* influences our conclusions; but some of the fancies are so conceited and puerile, some of them so extravagantly absurd, that the most extensive charity will not admit their sincerity. Thus, not only is every mention of armies, fear, terror, conquest, goodness, dominion,—construed as intended for Mahommed and for nobody else,—but the Prophet's very horses, swords and arrows were prefigured,—nay his love of perfumes and hatred of garlick and onions were not overlooked; the " white stone" of the Revelations *must* mean the famous stone given by Gabriel to Mahommed, or else it is the black stone of the Caaba, which *once* was white; and who could have been predicted to walk in " white garments," but our prophet who was so fond of them? The descendants of Ishmael, conveniently take up any prophecy which belong to the Israelites; " more are the children of the *desolate* (i. e. of Hagar,) than of the married wife," viz. Sarah. It is *Mecca* that was " forsaken," but is now "an eternal excellency, the joy of many generations." Again, in the parable of the sower, the three unfruitful species of seed are the Greeks, Jews, and Christians;—they that produced an hundred fold, the Mahommedans; the " tares" are the scoffing infidels who were slain in the battle of Bedr, and fell into the furnace of hell-fire; the " righteous," are of course the Mahommedans, " who shone forth as the sun."[*] In the parable of the vineyard, the husbandmen are the Jews, who are *said* [†] to have killed Christ, who was *called* the Son of God; the garden was therefore taken from them and given to the Arabs; on hearing our Saviour make this assertion, the

[*] In the parable of the talents, the king is Christ, the enemies the Jews, and the Christians who made good use of their talents, are those who doubled them by believing on Mahommed. The "morning star," of the Revelations, is the Koran, or perhaps Friday, (the Mahommedan sacred day,) which is *Sukbar*, or the day of *Venus* the morning star; or Christ may have called himself so, as being the harbinger of Mahommed his Sun!

[†] The mode in which he avoids the conclusion which might be drawn from this passage of Christ's having been *actually* crucified, and of his being the Son of God, is a beautiful specimen of sophistry.

Jews expressed their astonishment; when Christ replied, do
not be surprised, Isaiah told you this long ago, when he said,
"the stone which the builders rejected, i. e., the despised
Ishmaelites, will become the head of the corner, and thus in
Mahommed will be fulfilled the blessing promised to Abraham."
Such are the dishonest and gratuitous assumptions to which
the Mahommedans descend.   The disquisition on the *Fúrkalete*
and Holy Spirit, are perfect specimens of the Mahommedan's
blasphemous sophistry ;—a counterpart, in our imagination, of
the Jews who opposed Paul "contradicting and blaspheming."
Various other topics are taken up, but they are all treated in
the same insolent overpowering style.   Indeed, the abusive
and insulting language made use of in this treatise towards the
blessed Saviour, cannot but cut the Christian to the heart, and
occasion the most excruciating feelings.

The reply is written, we understand, by Mr. Rankin, of the
American Mission at Futtehgurh, and is in some respects a respectable performance ; it does not take up the whole of the
Mahommedan's positions in detail, but classes them under
several heads : it is good as far as it goes ; but the style is
lame,* monotonous and meagre, and the author wants the

* Mr. Rankin fails in the too frequent and inelegant use of the particle کہ, especially in conjunction with the relative ; and the style generally is defective. We strongly
recommend him to form his modes of diction more upon the model of his adversary,
and of the many Mahommedan religious works, which issue from the Lucknow press;
as the *Rah i Nijat, Nasihat ul Muslimin, &c.* the latter by the way contains many
nervous addresses and cogent reasonings against idolatry, the style and language of
which might be borrowed for our appeals to the Hindus.   And why not go farther in
the good work of learning from our enemies, and adopt the *form* in which they publish
their books.   There is nothing which could more tend to make Mr. Rankin's work
contemptible in the Mahommedan eye, than its English dress ; it is bad enough to ask
the Mahommedans to put up with our types, why give them our *notation* too ?   The
stops, commas, colons, semicolons, and notes of interrogation, which disfigure the
reply to the Saulat uz Zaigham must vastly amuse and sadly puzzle the Mahommedan reader, and probably raise a contemptuous smile : and what is the *use* of
them ? Good Urdu is perfectly intelligible without stops, and if the style be bad and
obscure, why then they only add to the native reader's difficulty and confusion.   The
star as a stop, is quite sufficient, and even that should be used sparingly.   Let us
consult the tastes and adapt our writings to the habits and ideas of our readers :
if we do not, we only defeat our own object ; for inconsiderable as such things may
appear to us, the unfavourable effect upon *their* minds is immense.   A late Quarterly
Review on "the French Lake," well described the feeling of repugnance entertained
by oriental nations towards foreign appearances ; a smart Frenchman (we quote
from memory,) is there stated to be the very quintessence of the aversion and contempt of the Mahommedan, who points to him in the streets, "Look, my child, to
what you would come, if you were to deny the prophet and become an infidel!"
Adopt, then, the native publications as your model : if you cannot afford to lithograph,
at all events consult the habits of your readers, and keep as close to their favourite
and long rooted customs as possible ; and above all, avoid with the utmost caution,
every thing foreign either in the construction of your style, or the appearance of
your book.   If you require *notes*, throw them into the lateral margin, and not to the
bottom of the page with distracting marks of reference as in the *Din Haqq.* Many
excellent and useful publications on this controversy have issued from the Allahabad
press, especially a series of valuable tracts by the Rev. Mr. Wilson, whose introduc-

vigorous, lucid, and attractive language of his opponent, to gain a favourable audience for his arguments, which are, however, in general sound. Nor does he sufficiently descend into particulars. However absurd many of the arguments in the Saulat uz Zaigham are, it is proper that they should *all* have a reply :— because the work is in the hands of so many, the ignorance of the vast majority of whom is so great, that they will not perceive the fallacies until they are plainly pointed out. We should like, therefore, to see the Saulat uz Zaigham, and a *full* reply, printed in alternate passages, or in parallel columns. The frequent and copious extracts from the Bible, which occur in almost every page, would afford the writer the most valuable arguments found ready to his hand ;—and the concessions made by the adversary in their explanation, would form when turned against him, materials for the most triumphant conclusions ; indeed, we have never seen so favourable an opportunity of closing upon an antagonist with an *argumentum ad hominem.* The passages which he has himself brought forward, cannot again be withdrawn by him on the plea of interpolation, and sufficient has been admitted in their interpretation, to overthrow him on his *own* ground.

In examining this controversy, we have gone sufficiently into details, to show that the three grand obstacles to our success are the *dishonesty,* the *prejudice,* and the *ignorance* of our opponents. The first of these it will be sufficient to expose, if we can only disseminate the exposition as widely as the original has spread : for the removal of the second, we must earnestly petition the Majesty on high ; and we must endeavour constantly to place before their view our mild but firm remonstrances, humbly trusting that divine truth will in the end overwhelm all vain opposition : the *last* can be vanquished by *knowledge* alone,— and that must therefore be imparted in an attractive form, accompanied with as little to offend the pride of our haughty adversaries as possible. The two latter,—prejudice and ignorance, are unfortunately almost always combined, and act and react upon each other. Henry Martyn's description of the Persian, is no less applicable to the Indian Mahommedan ; he is a compound of ignorance and bigotry ; and all access to the one is hedged up by the other.

That we may learn how best to treat this melancholy state of mind, there is no more useful means than the careful perusal of

tion to the Koran, was noticed in a former number : but most of them labour under the disadvantages we have been noticing. If our adversaries can afford to lithograph, why cannot we ? Mr. Pfander's publications are a model as to their *appearance,* as well as their contents.

these controversial tracts. Besides acquiring a knowledge of the subject in all its bearings, a thorough acquaintance with the Mahommedan ideas and tenets, an habitude and familiarity with their modes of polemical reasoning, there is a still more valuable attainment to be gained,—*experience to avoid their faults.* Arguments may reach to demonstration, and yet they may not force moral conviction : that depends upon a great variety of circumstances, many of which indeed are beyond our reach, while many may be materially modified by us. Cautious and unceasing endeavours, breathing kindness and love may lessen the prejudices of our opponents, but unguarded expressions and imprudent severity will certainly increase and perhaps render them insurmountable. Hence the paramount necessity for all those who are engaged in this work to be intimately acquainted, not merely with the rules of logic and the requirements of sound reason, but with the human heart,—with all those springs of feeling, of interest, of affection, of desire, which are so closely blended with conviction. This can only be fully acquired by the patient study of human nature in general, but much will be gained if each tries his own heart in such a crucible as the *Saulat uz Zaigham.* What effect does the haughty demeanour of the Mahommedan have upon you ; does it not raise an involuntary aversion and dislike of your opponent ? If his abuse does not excite hatred, is it not only because its risings are smothered by contempt ? And above all, his blasphemy against the Holy Ghost, his sneers at all that we hold sacred, the dishonour which he puts on the Divine founder of our faith, by derogatory insinuations and opprobrious epithets,—do they not cut us to the quick, lacerate our feelings, and make us cling still closer to those objects which are enshrined in our affections ? Now, all this, and probably a great deal more, does similar language stir up in the Mussulman bosom. We all know what a strong principle nationality is, and how easily it is wounded ; but the Mahommedan's is a *nationality of faith,* which is equally injured by any opprobrious imputation against his religion. Their prejudices are imbibed, as it were, with their mother's milk, nourished in childhood by the marvellous tales of their prophet and their saints, and welded into an impenetrable system by the constantly recurring ceremonies, which are interwoven with their very existence. We must also bear in mind the prescriptive hold which their religion has upon them. How many in our own country profess Christianity for no better reason than that it was the religion of their fore-fathers ; and if we examine our own hearts, we shall find that comfort and support are frequently derived from a reflection upon the numberless learned and illustrious characters who have adorned the Christian profession. Now, reverence for *their* cloud of witnesses and fathers is certainly no less an over-powering consideration with many, and a comfort and support to all, than it is with us. The fact that Islamism has not only stood for 13 centuries, but has expanded and progressed, and has seldom yet cowered before its present foe, must be a strong and satisfactory reflection even to the more sensible of our opponents. Again, we find with them a *religious nobility ;* the Syuds are the Peers of the Mussulmans; and we see even Mrs. Mir Hassan Ali, whose own religion should have shown her the futility of the title, pluming herself upon the supposed nobility of her foreign connexion : what then must it be, where Islam has been the pure and unbroken creed of their ancestors through a suc-cession of generations running up to the time of Mahommed! How deep rooted must be those feelings of pride, of high and ancient parentage inwrought with a faith deemed by them so noble, so unparalleled,—a faith which affords salvation to all mankind, and which reflects its glory and lustre upon *them !* If any where, we are to expect prejudice,—any where to make allowance for it,—surely it must be here. Let all our arguments, then, be framed, all our expressions selected with these feelings and prejudices prominently in our view; let there be no *unne-cessary* wounding of the national feeling, no harsh epithets, no irritating insinuations. We press this point with the greater earnestness, because the provoking insinuations, gratuitous seve-rity, and supercilious language, which we sometimes meet with are the most powerful adversaries of conviction. "If we wish the conversion of the infidel to the Christian faith, can we adopt a method more fitted, by fretting his temper, stirring his scorn, and rooting his prejudices, to steel him against conviction, and to frustrate the wish."* Let us not be mistaken ; we are boldly and unflinchingly to declare the message and truth of the Gospel, and the incompatibility of the Mahommedan faith with it, but it is to be done with prudence, with kindness, with love. The missionary of the cross will find it a difficult thing in the heat of controversy, when his own feelings are wounded in the ten-derest point, when his Saviour is afresh buffeted in his presence, to command his temper and his words ;—and yet it is absolutely necessary, as well for the exemplification of the Christian cha-racter, as for the success of his argument.

There are two more lessons we should learn from this

---

* These words were lately employed by an eloquent speaker (already quoted.) to describe the chafing effect of an establishment upon those without its pale. How much *more* strongly do they apply to the case before us.

controversy; the first is, never to employ a weak argument; for the effect generally is most disadvantageous to our position, and we may be certain that it will not escape the eagle eye of our adversary, who will leave all our stronger reasoning, to expose *its* fallacy or weakness. The second is, never to *force* a prophecy; fanciful and far-fetched interpretations must be studiously avoided by ourselves, if we wish with any consistency to deny those of the Mahommedans: let *our* conclusions be always the clear, unforced, unquestionable deductions of reason.

We cannot close the subject without referring to an argument, which is strongly urged by all the Mahommedan writers we have been reviewing, and which, if proved, would establish the divine origin of Mahommedanism; more especially as one of its most able supporters is,—will the reader credit us?—a clergyman of the Church of England. Mr. Forster, in his " Mahommedanism unveiled," proposes to explain the success of that creed, which he asserts has never been satisfactorily accounted for, by considering it as the fulfilment of the blessing promised to Abraham for Ishmael's seed.* How eagerly would our Maulavis welcome Mr. Forster! Ahmed,† Mohammed Ruza,‡ Kazim Ali,§ and the author of the *Saulat uz Zaigham*,‖ all adopt the very same line of reasoning,—that the blessing of Ishmael is fulfilled in Mahommed, that the twelve princes are the twelve Imams, and the "innumerable multitude,¶" Mussulman believers. Mr. Pfander, Mr. Rankin, and all our writers, *but* Mr. Forster, deny any *spiritual* accomplishment, and hold that the promise was fulfilled in the rapid increase of Ishmael's posterity and the twelve princes mentioned in Gen. xxv. Does Mr. Forster, then, acknowledge the *truth* of Mahommedanism? Oh no, he styles it a "false and spurious revelation," a "baleful superstition," and its author an "impostor, earthly, sensual, devilish, beyond even the license of his own licentious creed." Let us see then how he would make out this *imposture* to be the *blessing* promised by God to Abraham; we shall give Mr. Forster's views as far as possible in his own words, and beg of the reader to remark how he blends a spiritual with a temporal meaning,—the accomplishment of prophecy with the fulfilment of a promise :—

" The basis of the present argument is laid in the existence of a prophetic promise to Abraham, in behalf of his sons Isaac and Ishmael. By the terms of this promise, a blessing is annexed to the posterity of each, and on Ishmael as well as on Isaac, this blessing is pronounced, because he was

---

* Gen. xvii. 20.

† Lee's Controversial tracts, page xlviii.

‡ Ditto page 270-273.

§ Urdu M. S.

‖ Khu-Saul-Zaigh, page 10.

¶ Gen. xvi. 10.

Abraham's seed, and as a *special mark of the divine favour*. This last consideration is worth attending to ; since a promise to Ishmael, thus connected
by Jehovah himself with his descent from the father of the faithful, seems to
lead the mind naturally beyond the idea of a mere temporal fulfilment.
Some sufficient fulfilment, we are certainly authorized and bound to expect
for each branch of the original promise. The striking literal correspondence between the terms of its two parts appears to sanction the farther
expectation of an analogy equally strong between the respective fulfilments :
which expectation, moreover, receives fresh warrant from the fact, that the
promise in behalf of Ishmael was granted in *answer* to a prayer of Abraham,
in which he implored for Ishmael, the blessing reserved for Isaac."—(p. 87.)
The promises thus parallel are found actually to have had a parallel " fulfilment, as the facts of the case so strongly indicate, in the rise and success of
Mahommed, and in the temporal and spiritual establishment of the Mahommedan superstition..... The facts of the analogy are incontrovertible ;
they require to be solved ; and they admit of but the one satisfactory solution. We have only to receive the original promise to Abraham, according
to the terms of it, as germinant and parallel in both its parts ; and to
recognize in Christianity and Mahommedanism its twofold fulfilment, and
the whole doubts and difficulties of the question disappear."—(p. 89.)

In arguing the existence of a spiritual blessing for Ishmael,
great stress is laid on its being the answer to Abraham's
prayer. To this our plain objection is, that whatever the
nature of the petition was, God vouchsafed *only* a temporal blessing. Mr. Forster's reasoning hangs here upon
a very slender thread, and yet upon that is suspended the whole
of his argument! he says, the covenant of Ishmael, "would
seem, as well from the manner of its announcement, as from
the general analogy of character plainly intended by the parallel
terms of the two covenants, to contain a certain real, though
low and subordinate, spiritual application. Indeed that Abraham
should have offered up the petition that Ishmael might live in
the light of God's countenance, and under a divine blessing
and protection (a petition *certainly* implied by the prayer that
he might live before Jehovah, and inherit the promise granted
in favour of Isaac,) may be received as conclusive and moral
evidence on this point; for a blessing of a merely temporal
nature was little likely to be *thus* sought by ' the father of the
faithful ;' in whose eyes things temporal appear invariably to
have been held in little estimation."—(p. 119.) Assuming then
by this gratuitous reasoning, the whole point at issue, he
proceeds,

" In the case of Isaac, we know the precise manner and steps of the
accomplishment ; and in our knowledge of this detail, possess the clue for
investigating the analogous accomplishment, in the case of Ishmael. It is
requisite only, that the apparent historical fulfilments of the covenant of
Ishmael shall be found on examination to correspond with the ascertained
historical fulfilments of the covenant of Isaac, and if there be any force

in the scriptural analogy established between those brethren, the demonstration aimed at in these pages must be considered complete."—(p. 132.)

Mr. Forster's ideas, however, of a promised *blessing*, and its *fulfilment*, are very singular. He assumes that because Hagar was a *bondswoman*, and Ishmael *illegitimate*, the religion, therefore, of their descendants must partake of the qualities of both; in his own language,

"If from Isaac was to spring the true religion; from Ishmael there might be expected to arise as a counterpart, a *spurious* faith. If the true Messiah, the descendant of Isaac, and who, like him, came *by* promise, was to be the founder of the one creed; a counterfeit Messiah, the descendant of Ishmael, and who, like him, should come *without* promise, could be the only appropriate founder of the other." (p. 90.) And again, "Prophecy cannot be supposed to recognize in Ishmael, the child of the flesh, the son of the bond-woman, the illegitimate seed, any thing higher than the forefather of a false prophet, and the source of a spurious faith"—"the arch antitype of all preceding false Christs,"—"the spurious Messiah Mahommed."—(pp. 164 and 140.)

What! a *spurious faith*, a *false* prophet, a *counterfeit* Messiah, the fulfilment of a promised *blessing*! Is this the mode in which the true and covenant-keeping God fulfils his promises? Alas, for the perversions even of a Christian man's reason. To discover a parallel between Christianity and this "spurious revelation," is the object of the whole book, and it is effected in a very able and masterly manner by a succession of curious analogies in the prophetical anticipations,* morality, doctrine, ritual, scriptures, heresies, crusades, and civilization of Mohamedanism, Judaism and Christianity! These analogies prove nothing, because the foundation of the argument, as we have shown, is unsound,—there was no *spirituality* and therefore no analogy in the promise,—but they contain a vast fund of useful information, wrought up into a most interesting form, which will well repay the trouble of a perusal.

The nature of Mr. Forster's argument is such that upon approaching it, he is always led into confusion or inconsistency. Thus at page 102, he acknowledges that the lesser blessing of Ishmael was "manifestly of a temporal nature;" yet he hence deduces that, "through the Gospel and the *Koran*, the *promise* to Abraham, continually advanced towards its *fulfilment*, in the

* Some of the historical analogies are sufficiently far-fetched; for instance; Christianity rose in *Judea*, Mahommedanism numbered it among its earliest conquests. *Jerusalem* was the site of the Jewish temple, and it is that of the mosque of Omar. *Constantinople* was the imperial metropolis, and the cathedral of St. Sophia the central fane of eastern Christianity; but that city is now the metropolis of Mohammedans, and the Cathedral a mosque. "*Three* in company in flight to Egypt, Joseph, Mary, Jesus:—Gabriel their conductor: *Three* in company in flight to Medina, Mahommed, Abubeker, Amer Ebn Fohaira;— Gabriel their pretended conductor."

posterity of his sons, until of these two brethren was the whole earth overspread;" we have here the temporal confused with a spiritual blessing. Again he says, "the one was the covenant of the spirit; the other the covenant of the flesh,......the arm of flesh therefore was the natural and proper weapon for its enforcement." It is acknowledged to be "a covenant of the flesh," then why attempt to make it spiritual? Again, "the grand feature in the promise concerning Isaac was, *that in his seed all the nations of the earth should be blessed*; and the responding feature in the parallel promise respecting Ishmael, that *he should dwell in the presence of all his brethren;*" the former it is contended was fulfilled in Christianity, the latter in Mahommedanism. But we utterly deny that there is any "responding feature" at all here; Mahommedanism *may* be the accomplishment of a prophecy, but that is a very different thing from the fulfilment of a promise. Mr. Forster would make the sacrament of circumcision to "be equally at the root of both parts of the original covenant, and to be the common bond of a certain spiritual relation,—' to be a God unto thee and to thy seed after thee;'—and we can only tell the force of this application to Ishmael by an investigation of RESULTS," (page 130.) This argument, however, proves a great deal too much, as it would extend to the whole of Abraham's seed, including the children of Ketura.—to whom no special spiritual blessing was accorded. Mr. Forster sums up the whole of his argument thus, "Isaac becomes the father of the true faith; Ishmael,—of a spurious imitation of it;" but a "spurious imitation" is no fulfilment; and if Mahommedanism is actually the fulfilment of the promise it cannot be spurious, but must be acknowledged a divine faith. The whole fabric is based upon a contradiction and therefore falls to the ground.

It frequently falls in with Mr. Forster's views to prove Mahommedanism a blessing,—and then it is curious to observe how he avoids comparing it with the Gospel. At page 321, he decides that when we "submit Mahommedanism to a comparison with Christianity, exclusively of Judaism, we are not trying it by the proper and equitable standard,"—and that it is no more than the barest justice, that the parts of it derived from the law of Moses, should be tried by that law, instead of being condemned without reserve or discrimination, by another rule,—the infinitely perfect law of Christ." But, considering the age in which Mahommedanism arose, we can see no reason why his creed should not be tried and condemned by that faith which its founder supplanted, and in room of which he substituted his own. Again, "some of the most objectionable features of his moral law, instead of being, as heretofore, tried and condemned by the perfect rule of the Gospel, would seem entitled to be judged by reference to the *source whence it is derived*, and the *standard to which it appeals*." The source from whence he professes to derive his law is God himself: why then adopt a lower standard than His word?

Elsewhere he says, " the intrinsic merits of Mahommedanism, while utterly beneath comparison with the only true revelation, are yet confessedly superior to those of every other religious system which has obtained among men." (p. 103.)—" As opposed to the Gospel, indeed, Mahommedanism must be considered only as a curse; but as the pre-appointed scourge of heresy and heathenism, as cleansing the world from the gross pollutions of idolatry, and as preparing the way for the reception of a purer faith, it may well be regarded as a blessing." On a nearer inspection, we fear that Mr. Forster would have modified this praise: the God of the Mahommedans is not the true God; and their false worship opposes obstacles to conversion, greater perhaps than those of heathenism itself.

As to the *prospective* views of Mahommedanism, Mr. Forster's expectations are glowing in the extreme. After expatiating on the points *common* to both creeds, he proceeds,

" Suppose these, and similar positions, plainly deducible from the Koran and its commentators, once brought clearly and conclusively to *elucidate* the authoritative record of Scripture, by men whose zeal shall shine forth on the benighted east, sustained by extensive knowledge, and tempered by a wise discretion, while their walk among men forms that best of commentaries, a living one, on the truth and power of these doctrines;—suppose episcopal Christianity, in a word, one day taught and exemplified in Asia, as it was originally taught and exemplified in the Apostolic times, and who, that reflects on the whole providential history and relationship of the two religions, can doubt the eventual result throughout the Mahommedan world?" (vol. I. p. 400.) And thus, out of the most deadly and devastating apostacy with which the justice of Heaven ever visited the sins of men, does the mercy of God seem, all along, to have been secretly, but effectually, preparing the instrumental means for the glorious re-edification of our Eastern Sion, by the final bringing in of Jew, Mahommedan, and Gentile, to the church and kingdom of the Gospel."—(vol. II. p. 371.)

These are bright visions indeed; and may God of His infinite mercy grant them a speedy fulfilment: but we fear they are not borne out by the premises. Alas! No; there is nothing in Mohammedanism, which to *human* aspect and *present* appearance, warrants us in saying that it tends towards Christianity. At first sight, indeed, we appear to have many advantages in the contest; we have no infidel, and (in one sense,) no deistical views to oppose; the existence of sin, and its future punishment, are allowed; the necessity of a revelation, and even the facts of the Old and New Testament dispensations, are conceded ; the most of the attributes of God, the immaculate conception of Christ, and the miracles which attested his Mission are all admitted. But Mahommed well knew that he more than neutralized all these concessions, by the suspicions which he cast upon the genuineness of our Scriptures. The Mahommedans believe *a* Gospel, but it is not ours : they worship *a* God, but not the God and Father of our Lord Jesus Christ : they acknowledge *a* Jesus, but not Him who was so called, because he should save his people from their sins. Hear Mirza Ibrahim :—

" For we are not sure of the miracles of *that* Moses and Jesus, of whom the Jews and Christians speak ; and who as they say did not believe in the Mission of our prophet ; but we speak of the miracles of that Moses and Jesus, who have given their testimony to the mission of Mahommed : and how great is the difference between them when viewed in these different lights ? Let it not be said that the persons are the same in both cases. We believe in these prophets, in consequence of their being described in the Koran, and not as described by the Jews and Christians."—(Cont. tracts. p. 33.)

Yes,—it must be borne in mind, that it is *simply* as they are mentioned in the Koran, and only *because* they are mentioned there, that the Mohammedan believes in the prophets and the Bible ; and the misrepresentations of the Koran not merely destroy their identity, but substitute a false and noxious* system, which requires *exclusive* belief, cancels and overturns all preceding revelations, and by requiring its adherents to believe all former scriptures corrupted and interpolated, takes from us the only means we have of proving the imposture false. Could the infernal counsels of the Apostate angel have devised any more perfect and invincible plan for frustrating the Gospel and grace of God ?

It is true, indeed, that the Koran contains many plagiarisms from the Bible, and abounds therefore with approaches to the truth ; and it might have been hoped that these would prove as foundations upon which to build, as a *fulcrum* whereon to ply our arguments ; but it appears to be a melancholy truth, that in some stages of human nature, a certain amount of light and knowledge only renders it more difficult to drive the bigot from his prejudices. Thus the Mussulman is conscious of possessing truths, behind which he proudly entrenches himself, persuading himself that he has the *whole* truth, and that every thing else is absurd. The supposed advantages then,—the points common

* Mr. Forster, having quoted a verse from the Koran, says, be the matter asserted, true or false, this assuredly is none other than the voice of *Satan* speaking by the mouth of a " false apostle."—Strange Epithets for the promised blessing !

to both, are thus turned into a barrier against us,—into a thick, and, to human effort, impenetrable veil, which effectually excludes every glimmering of the true light. How delusive, therefore, are the anticipations quoted with approbation by Mr. Forster, (vol. I, p. 107.) " *Since we find among the followers of Mahommed, such favourable prepossessions, and established doctrines,* AS WILL RENDER EASY THE APPROACH TO THEIR CONVERSION, neither force of obligation, NOR PROSPECT OF SUCCESS,* is wanting to encourage our progress, and animate our zeal :" and again, he affirms, that the two religions "hold so many great fundamentals in common, that they contain a *natural and necessary tendency to convergence :*—the imperfect scheme, when its providential work shall have been accomplished, becoming absorbed in the perfect, and the moon of Mahommed resigning its borrowed rays, to melt in the undivided light of the everlasting Gospel." It is certainly a novel idea to speak of Mahommed or his Koran, under the simile of the moon ; his own people† style him the sun, and our Saviour the moon, and they would laugh to scorn any mention of " *borrowed* light" for their prophet. The radiancy of Judaism, indeed, bore testimony, like the moon, to the existence of an unseen but approaching luminary ; but that of Mahommedanism is a baleful vapour luring only to destruction.

These are melancholy reflections. Have we, then, no more encouraging thoughts with which to conclude this article ; have all our efforts been thrown away ; and after all this controversy, do we find our cause not in the least advanced? God forbid ! for, amid these discouragements, we think we can discern the pleasing tokens of actual progress. And first, the Mahommedans, it is evident, are closely and carefully examining our Scriptures ; this, the controversy we have been considering leaves without a doubt : the simple fact, therefore, of the perusal of the word of God is a step gained, and with His blessing will lead to favourable results. Again, as the controversy advances, and books on the subject are spread abroad, the mistaken views, which Mahommedans have hitherto entertained of most of our leading doctrines, will be removed, and correct and scriptural knowledge substituted in their stead ; this will of necessity sweep away many of their strongholds which were built on erroneous notions of Christianity ;—and if they continue faithless, it will be in the face of the clearest light. We trust, too, that *christian* character is now more generally exhibited to the view of our adversaries ; and its

---

* The *italics* are not ours.

† As in the Saulat uz Zaigham.

excellencies and graces cannot fail (if we are but true to our profession,) to aid their conviction of the truth of our holy faith. And, lastly, we look with anxious hope, to the society of *native* christians, which we earnestly expect will soon spring up from among our Orphan asylums and converts generally, and to the effect which appeals, thus sounding from among themselves, and addressing their feelings and reason with native *home-drawn* arguments (to which *we* have but little access,) will have throughout the country.

But of all human means we trust most to those exhibitions of *earnestness* and *anxiety*, which christian love is now prompting its professors to put into active motion.* Yes; it is a matter of joy and congratulation, that the attitude, which Protestant evangelical Europe and America are now assuming, is just that which is likely to strike conviction into the frozen heart of the Mahommedan. When he sees Christians so vitally alive to the infinite blessings their religion is calculated to impart;—so tenderly concerned for the perishing condition of his brother Mahommedans and Heathens,—and so filled with burning love and zeal to make them sharers of their own blessings, as cheerfully to undergo loss and suffer privation;—*this* is a practical argument, the most likely of any to convince him of the reality and divine nature of the Gospel. God be praised that Christianity is beginning gradually to assume her rightful position; and no sooner shall she have fully done so, than a light must break forth establishing, before the world, her truth and the unspeakable difference between her and every false religion.

In conclusion, we would earnestly press the necessity which lies upon *all* of removing, as far as their ability extends, the ignorance of the Mahommedans; and the responsibility those are under, who possess the requisite qualifications, of affording them access to those numerous subjects, a knowledge of which we are obliged to pre-suppose in most of our religious discussions. Let us attend to Dr. Lee:—" In ancient History and Scripture, the Persians are necessarily very ignorant,† the best means

---

* We recollect a simple anecdote in a late number of the " *Calcutta Free Churchman*," which vividly exemplifies what we mean : A person who had long sought in vain the conversion of an infidel neighbour, once burst into tears in his presence, and could say nothing more to his astonished friend than " Oh, I am concerned for your soul." This exhibition of feeling meletd the rigid scepticism which no arguments could affect. We do not mean to imply that untempered zeal should be employed or encouraged towards the conversion of *our* infidel neighbours ; but we do believe that concern *for their salvation*, appearing in all our conduct, would be the most cogent of all arguments we could resort to ; it would prove the steadfastness of our faith, and the value we put upon the blessings it carries with it.

† As an instance of the ignorance of our opponents in History. we may mention a passage in the *Saulat uz Zaigham*, where the author adduces the fall of Babylon,

they have of obtaining either being the fragments found in the Koran or the traditions ; nor is there much probability of their improving in this respect, until they shall possess a good translation of the whole Bible, with some such works as the connections of the Old and New Testaments by Prideaux, the connections of sacred and profane History by Shuckford, and some good commentary on the Text of Scripture."—(Pref. p. cxxii.)

And again : " It would be well to translate into the Persian some of our standard books on the apparent contradictions of the Scriptures, with Paley's evidences of Christianity, or the recent work of Mr. Sumner." Mere* translations, however, will seldom or ever do ; they must be adapted and remodelled, leaving out much that would be unsuitable to an oriental,—and supplying much that would be superfluous to a European reader. We would urge this sacred and paramount duty, as incumbent not upon our Indian Society alone, but upon the learned of England. Mahommedanism is not, like the religion of the Hindu, a subject *foreign* to the European ; for twelve centuries it has been his near neighbour ; it effected a footing in Spain and Italy, and it now reigns in Turkey ; from the stores of its learning was the darkness of the middle ages first enlightened ; and our libraries are full of learned and controversial works in defence and in defiance of both religions. Why then have we not more instances of our countrymen treading in the steps of Dr. Lee ? The stimulus of a *prize* is sufficient to entice the learned inmates of Oxford and Cambridge to combat the remote and dimly distinguished tenets of the *Hindu.* And shall not the interest and proximity of the subject, its close connection with Europe, and the ample resources near at hand for obtaining a knowledge of the principles of Islam, be sufficient to tempt our

as the accomplishment of ancient prophecies in favour of Mahommed. He says, plausibly enough. that Isaiah and Jeremiah successively predicted the destruction of this city, but had it fallen in their times, its overthrow would not again have been foretold by St. John in the Revelations. At last, he tells us, the priest *Sitih* predicted it to Noushirvan. as about to follow the establishment of Mahommed's creed. Our adversary here has evidently the best of the argument, in the eyes of his fellow Mussulmans ; and it will be difficult to disabuse them of the error. and of the idea that we are deceiving them in representing John's as a *spiritual* Babylon without a considerable knowledge of History on their part.

* A thousand such works are urgently required : when will our philanthropic spirit prompt us to supply our native fellow subjects with a theological library ? A running commentary on the whole Bible. but especially on the New Testament. is urgently needed. Brief notes taking up and satisfactorily explaining every difficulty, and lithographed in the margin of the text, would prove an invaluable book ; such a work should be executed so as to accommodate the native taste ; take the Lucknow Koran. with its running marginal Urdu notes as the model ; and a wide margin and smaller writing for the notes, will afford ample room for all that needs to be said. We do trust soon to see some such work of this description.

learned and pious countrymen to come forward in the Mahommedan contest; and thus without the labour or the banishment of a missionary life, to forward the Christian cause by aids more valuable than thousands of silver and gold?

We would also impress upon those who are unable to help by writing themselves, the duty which the more heavily devolves upon them of furnishing means for the printing, and forwarding the circulation, of the books which are already provided. We understand that Mr. Pfander's works are nearly out of print; and we would strongly recommend that *five*, or, if possible, *ten* thousand copies of Mizan ul Haqq, and two thousand of the other treatises, be struck off in Urdu, and a reasonable proportion in Persian; for this, we believe, extraordinary funds will be required, but we are greatly mistaken if the Christian public, when fully and intelligently awakened to a sense of the magnitude and urgency of the object, will be backward in furnishing them. At all events, we feel that, in thus prominently directing public attention to the subject, we have discharged a duty towards one of the worthiest of men and one of the noblest of causes. Of Mr. Pfander or his writings, many of our Indian residents may probably have never heard. And if what has been written shall prove the means of leading any of them so to esteem the author and so to appreciate the value of his works, as to stir them up to lend effective aid in circulating them throughout the Mahommedan world, one great object which we had in view shall have been gained. The Rev. Gentleman himself is an ordained minister of the Church of England; and it is by the multiplication of such agents, that that or any other branch of the Christian church can expect to obtain a secure footing and permanent ascendancy among the hitherto unreclaimed realms of heathenism.

Since writing the above article we have perused the treatise published by the Mujtahid of Lucknow, to which a reference was made at page 447. At the close of the volume are printed the letters which passed between the Mujtahid and Mr. Pfander, who appears to have forwarded his books to the

M l

Professor in the middle of 1842. The Professor replied, as we
have before stated, in a very courteous manner, complimented
Mr. Pfander on the uncommon merit of his productions, and
informed him that he had set one of his pupils to furnish a
reply.* The author of the book, therefore, is not the Shia
Professor, but Syud Mahommed Hadi, whose father, and the
present Mujtahid, are sons of the famous Syud Dildar Ali,
who we believe gained great celebrity by his travels in Arabia,
Persia, and other countries, and being a pillar of the Shia faith,
and a man famed for his attainments, became the spiritual guide
of the king, and the *Mujtahid* of Lucknow. The office would
appear to be in some measure hereditary, and the incumbent is
said to be enriched by the free will offerings of the Oude nobility,—so that the position is not only a dignified but a lucrative
one.

The work is entitled: فقرات بعض القسيسين والاحبار

بكشف الاستار لكسر مفتاح الا سرار ونقض that is, " The
curtain unveiled to display the *Miftah ul Asrar*, or key of
secrets broken, and the doctrines of a certain Christian minister
refuted." It is written in very high Persian, and abounds with
Arabic phrases ; the author, indeed, frequently breaks into whole
sentences and even pages of Arabic, especially where he reduces
his reasoning to a logical form : he may probably have found
that the technical and laconic language of the Arabians enabled
him at times to express his ideas with greater exactness and
precision, but the general effect is to give an appearance of pedantry and desire of display. The arrangement of the treatise
is much the same as we recommended for a reply to the *Saulat uz
Zaigham* ; a quotation is made from the *Miftah ul Asrar*, comprising generally a whole chapter or division, and headed with

the words, قال المسيحى " thus writes the Christian," in large

letters ; at the close follows his reply, begun in a similar man-

ner with the words, أقول وبه نستعين " I say in reply and

* At the same time he forwarded, for Mr. Pfander's perusal, five tracts in refutation of the Christian religion ; of these, one is a reply to the *Dalail Wafah*, a tract
which is noticed in *Saulat uz Zaigham*, but which we have not seen. Another is
an account of some controversies with the Rev. William Bowley, of Chunar,—who
we suspect is the same referred to in the *Saulat*, as " William Padre." A third is
a statement of disputation with " Padre Joseph Wolff," who is stated to have
visited Lucknow, and proclaimed the advent of our Saviour as about to take place
in 14 years ; this is a topic which is more than once mentioned with exultation as a
proof of the liability of Christians to err in the interpretation of their Scriptures.

from Him I seek assistance." After his general remarks, if he has occasion to notice any passage in particular, he introduces it with the title, قوله " His words," and proceeds to give his answer as above. This *mode* of reply we strongly recommend for imitation on similar occasions; the headings mark the alternations of text and commentary, as clearly as any division into chapters could, and the whole is a most convenient as well as strictly oriental mode of composition.

The line of attack shows the subtilty and skill of our adversaries. The Mujtahid, in his letter to Mr. Pfander, assumes that the turning point between us is the doctrine of the Trinity. Now this is quite a mistake. The turning point is the genuineness and integrity of our Scriptures; when that is proved, the truth of the Christian religion and falsity of Mahommedanism follow quite independently of the Trinity or any other Christian doctrines; these are, indeed, valuable subsidiary arguments, for they prove the Koran to oppose previous revelation, but they are all involved in the soundness of the Scriptures, and till that is proved on our side, or disproved on the part of the Mahommedans, the argument must remain incomplete and unsatisfactory. To have rendered the present attack, therefore, in any degree a fair one, the author was bound either to have acknowledged the genuineness of the Bible, or proved its corruption; but instead of this, he passes over the *Mizan ul Haqq*, with the sneer, that its arguments had been formerly refuted, and that it might more aptly have been called the *Mizan i Bátil*,* and proceeds to analyze and discuss the contents of the Miftah ul Asrar. The unfair position gives him this advantage that it enables him to take up at pleasure the whole range of objections usually brought against us; the object of attack is the most profound and mysterious doctrines of Revelation;—he appeals to reason to attest its absurdity and impossibility,—thence he insinuates the corruption of our Scriptures, and covertly advances other arguments towards the same point. He proceeds farther, denies that our Scriptures, even as they stand, contain the disputed tenets, and, by throwing into the shade the stronger passages adduced by Mr. Pfander, by describing others as metaphorical, by applying a few to Mahommed, and explaining away the remainder, he in

---

* He says, however, in the course of his book, that he meditates a reply to the *Mizán ul Haqq*, and we hope he will accomplish it. The integrity of the Scriptures is the ground upon which our closest struggle must take place, of which the Mussulmans are very shy; they hardly ever approach it fairly and openly, but delight in covert attacks.

appearance destroys the amount of cumulative evidence which before appeared irresistible: but the most unjust and gratuitous portion of his books is that which rejects *in toto*, the Acts and Epistles, and assumes that the four Gospels alone are to be regarded as inspired,—the rest being of no more value than the *Hyat ul Kulúb*, or other Mahommedan Histories.[*] Taking up such ground, and assuming to himself such unbounded license of dispensing with our evidence, it is not to be wondered that the Divinity of Christ and the Trinity are dogmatically rejected by the writer as unfounded and absurd, and pronounced to be the fabrications of a heated imagination. But we proceed to notice a few of his chief lines of reasoning and most remarkable arguments, which will probably prove interesting to many of the friends of native improvement.

The grand feature of his book, is, that he constitutes reason the supreme Judge, and that in the view of reason the Divinity of Christ and the Trinity are held to be *absolute impossibilities*. On both points he is directly at issue with Mr. Pfander, yet he regards his own positions as axiomatic, and proceeds quietly to draw his inferences from them. His work is therefore entirely beside the point ; it may be very profitable to those who accord in his axioms, but it cannot be regarded as any reply to the *Miftah*, until he strengthens his premises by argument and proof. The steps by which he advances to the supremacy of reason, are a mere frivolous quibble :—revelation cannot be proved without reason, because it must be communicated through a prophet, whose mission cannot be established until the existence and nature of the deity by whom he is commissioned be ascertained : and that can be done by reason alone ; therefore, reason is prior to revelation, and to imagine anything proved by revelation which is contrary to reason is to imagine a thing to be proved by itself, which is absurd : and hence he deduces that revelation must bend to reason, and that anything in the former which opposes the latter, must be explained as metaphorical or abandoned altogether. From such premises, we need not be astonished to hear him confess, that were the Trinity or any (so called) impossibility contained in an *acknowledged* revelation, it must be rejected as incapable of proof; and that therefore if it were shown to exist in our Scriptures, the fact would prove *their* corruption not the truth of the doctrine.

---

[*] When the Acts are adduced in support of a doctrine, he applies to us the proverb شاهد آلثعلب ذنبه " the fox saw his own tail," implying that they are a fabrication of the Christians, and therefore useless as evidence.

Our opponent thus enters the arena determined to resist the utmost possible amount of evidence; it was needless for him to have advanced farther; with a mind so prepared for the reception of truth, what advantage could be anticipated from discussion?

To the argument, that our reason is feeble, and that a thousand things about us are as incomprehensible as the divine mystery, he replies, that these things occur in *creation* and are therefore nothing to the point. Every thing that we can think of, he divides into three classes;*—the self-existent being from whose nature the very idea of change or imperfection is barred; the *impossible*, or what cannot be imagined to exist; and the *possible*, of which the existence and non-existence are equally likely. But all the mysteries of nature he contends, belong to the third class, and being liable to change and composition cannot be regarded as analogies of the Divine nature; and real trinity in unity is included in the *second* category, and, therefore, the mysteries of nature, however incomprehensible, cannot affect its impossibility. He thus asserts that the doctrine in dispute is not incomprehensible but clearly impossible; and he accuses Mr. Pfander of confounding that which it is impossible to comprehend, with what we comprehend to be impossible?† Thus by begging the question, he renders his reasoning inconclusive.

The Maulavi is fond of insinuating that Mr. Pfander has quite excluded reason from the argument, and feigns surprise that he should have recourse to that abstract reasoning which he has once renounced. Reason, he pretends, is abjured by us only for the occasion; in one sense indeed,—we do reject our own reason,—by taking up with that of the Devil. He taunts his opponent,--" at times you affect the extreme of piety, abandon your reason, and follow only *the word*; at others, you hold the most extravagant absurdities, which you have fabricated out of your own head, and even in opposition to the Scripture !" Thus (p. 42) he takes Mr. Pfander to task for having mentioned the planets as *hung in the air*; he proves from the Old Testament, the creation of a material *Heavens*, and accuses his adversary of substituting in their stead an empty

---

* viz. مُمْكَنُ الوجود and مُمْتَنِع الوجود واجبِ الوجود

† تفرقه بین علم الادراک وادراک العلم هنوز جانگرفته است ودر مدرکه او ادراک

space, upon the mere hypothesis of our star-gazing philosophers, and in direct contradiction to the general voice of Astronomy and Revelation.* The Maulavi's views on this subject are most unfounded, and show that he cannot distinguish between the *use* and the *abuse* of reason; he can not, or will not, see that we may employ reason to ascertain the existence of the Deity (without presuming to search out the mysteries of His nature,) and to guide us in recognizing His revelation; here reason must stop, and henceforth her only legitimate office is to search into the contents and discover the meaning of the Divine record. Until this principle be admitted we have little to hope from Mahommedan discussion: we do not, however, believe that the sovereignty of reason in divine mysteries is held by our opponents from *conviction*, but that it is in most cases assumed for the nonce, as the surest and most expeditious mode of refuting our arguments. The Mahommedans, indeed, are extremely superstitious; they dare not apply the rule to their own faith, and are more ready to incline towards credulity, than to exercise the unfettered license of reason.

In taking up the argument from Scripture, the Maulavi opposes to Christ's assumption of Divine attributes, his own express avowal of subordination; these attributes cannot be proved to exist in his nature *independently* and *absolutely* (which alone would imply Divinity,) for they are generally spoken of as derived from the Father, and this dependence is inadmissible in the idea of the Divine nature.

His union with the Father is stated to be a union of spirits, like that which subsists among believers, and the word "forsaken" pronounced upon the cross, is adduced as clearly proving the absence of any closer connection. He holds that there are two applications of the word *God*, one of which was, in the Old Testament, used towards prophets and princes, and in the New to Christ; and he dextrously adduces our Saviour's quotation, " I said ye are Gods," as perfectly conclusive upon this head. The argument of obeisance and adoration he treats in the same way, but does not explain how St. Thomas came to join them together in his act of worship. The "*word*" and "*spirit* of God," are explained in the usual manner, with nearly as much bigotry and quite as much absurdity, as the authors we have

---

* Not long after the publication of this book, Mr. Pfander received a note regarding it, from a learned Hindu resident of Lucknow, well versed apparently in Arabic philosophy: he discards the views of the Maulavi, and holds, that according to Grecian and Hindu Philosophy there is no material *Heavens*, and that a sect of Mahommedan Philosophers profess the same belief, though the remainder are bound to the opposite doctrine, as a part of their religious system.

already considered. The *word* means the particle "Be," by which all things were created, and specially Christ, who was born without a father; "the word *be* was in the beginning," before all creation, "and the word was God," that is, by an ellipse, "was the word of God;" and "the word became flesh," that is, was the cause of Christ's birth!* To the Catholic interpretation of this passage he opposes the dictates of reason regarding the impossibility of the incarnation of God; and he asserts that Mr. Pfander has mistranslated the words "dwelt among us,"—the Arabic version having in this place, حَلَّ فِى نا, "he entered into us," which involves the doctrine of migration or communication of the divine essence to another, حُلُول, a tenet regarded by orthodox Mussulmans with peculiar horror. Had the Maulavi consulted the *original*, he would have found that the words ἐσκήνωσεν ἐν ἡμῖν, were most aptly rendered by

و در ميان ماقرارگرفت. Indeed, the Maulavi is too much in the habit of throwing grave suspicions on the integrity of Mr. Pfander's views and translations, merely on the authority of Arabic translations; this may for a time acquire for him some credit with his unlearned brethren, but as soon as the untenableness of his positions become generally known, it will end only in his confusion: we would strongly recommend the Maulavi to become a student in Greek and Hebrew at the Lucknow Martinere, and to make himself thoroughly master of

* Of his frivolous perversions of the Sacred text, a few examples may be acceptable:—" No man hath ascended up to Heaven, but he that came down from heaven ;" this, and all similar passages as " I am from above," apply equally to Elijah, who also "ascended up" and must therefore have also "come down from heaven." The last clause, " even the son of man which is in heaven," is denied as an interpolation, and a curious tradition is mentioned (page 73) of Imam Riza having publicly stated before a Christian minister called *Hathuliq*, who could not deny the correctness of the quotation, that the verse originally ran thus ; " Verily verily, my disciples, I say unto you that no man shall ascend into heaven, but he that descended from heaven,—except the camel-mounted, the last of the Prophets,—he indeed will ascend to heaven, and again descend," referring to Mahommed's *mirage ;* and this tradition he says is a thousand times more deserving of credit than all your corrupted Gospels put together. Even admitting the present reading, he says. " who is in heaven," does not mean actual presence there, but alludes, by a common mode of speech, to his residence in heaven as being close at hand. The power of raising the dead, which Christ assumed as inherent in himself, he gratuitously describes as referring to the approaching miracle of Lazarus, and as implying no higher virtue than Elisha possessed. His presence, promised to his disciples to the end of the world, is explained metaphorically, " I shall be so aware of the state of each, that, as it were, I shall be always in the midst of you ;" or if it does mean spiritual presence, it is nothing more than what we believe of other angels, and extends at most to the Judgment day,—intimating that then like other men, he must die.

those languages, before he again ventures to call in question the renderings of competent persons.

The proofs from the Old Testament he treats with still less fairness; he passes over some of the most important passages, and under the pretext that many of them apply to Mahommed, he takes the opportunity of advancing a great many others;* and at last, quite forgetting the object of his book, produces what he considers two irrefragable arguments in substantiation of Mahommed's mission; the first is, the perfection of his religion as a code of morals and director of devotion: the second is, that Mahommed must have been either a true prophet or a mad man. He proves by his many virtues and talents that he was not the latter, and triumphantly asserts that he must have been the former.† He forgets that the same argument applies with incalculably greater weight to the apostles; for with them, we have many claimants to inspiration, instead of one,—we have pure morals,—and an utter absence of any worldly motive.

In taking up the chapter on the Trinity and Divinity of the Holy Ghost, he leaves almost unnoticed the strong passages and reasoning from the New Testament, and dwells upon the uncertain intimations, which Mr. Pfander himself acknowledged, were no more than allusions. He mistakes the *gift* and *influences* of the Holy Ghost, for that Divine spirit itself; and asserts that our doctrine would lead to the supposition that Christ was in the womb of Elizabeth and Mary at the same time; for " John was filled with the Holy Ghost from his

---

* Like Kazim Ali he applies the glorious promises of the XLII. of Isaiah to Mahommed ; though with greater candour. but less consistency, he allows that the introductory verses " he shall not cry, &c." refer to Jesus. With similar perversity, he holds that part of the second psalm applies to Jesus, and part to Mahommed; but he does not show us how to distinguish between the two. He denies that the 53rd of Isaiah can refer to Christ, because at V. 10, it is said, " He shall see his *seed;*" on the contrary, he holds, that V. 15, which contains promises of " a portion with the great and spoil with the strong," is an evident token of Mahommed, forgetting the remarkable words that follow, " because he hath poured out his soul unto death, &c." The commencement, too. of this chapter he insists could not designate Christ, because the Prophet speaks in the *past* tense, " he *was* despised, and we *esteemed* him not ;" it can therefore only mean that " we despised and rejected Ishmael," and, by a common figure of speech his descendant Mahommed in him : the " root out of a *dry* ground," is a reference to Hagar, who, to worldly appearance, was an unlikely source for a prophet ;—or more probably to the arid plains of Mecca, noted for their dryness and sterility. Truly, when the idea of his prophet gets into a Mussulman's head, it would appear as if all sense and reason got out of it!

† The learned Hindu of Lucknow, referred to in a former note, attacks the Maulavi on this point; he asserts that he has omitted a supposition which was much more likely than either of those he mentioned. viz. that of *fraud,*—which every body but the Mahommedans themselves attribute to their prophet. It is very pleasing to see the subject so soon attract the notice of the Hindus, and elicit so very pertinent a criticism.

mother's womb." He holds that it means the gift of repentance, or the spirit of faith, which was imparted by the apostles to those who believed. The Athanisian creed, turned into Arabic by Sabat, is brought forward, and by applying the attributes and nature of one person in the blessed Trinity to another, as he affirms he is warranted to do upon the supposition of real unity, he reduces the doctrine *ad absurdum*, and holds it up in a variety of lights, as involving contradictions and impossibilities. He wilfully omits, throughout his reply, the orthodox doctrine of the two natures of Christ, which—had he approached the subject in a proper spirit,—would have extricated him from many of his dilemmas.

The examples and analogies from nature are rejected, because, while the unity is that of figure or substance, the plurality is stated to consist in parts or qualities. He does not fail to take Mr. Pfander to task for the examples of the *circle*, &c.; but his language is perhaps less strong and improper than that of other Mahommedans upon similar occasions. Our opinion of the disadvantage of these illustrations, is, if possible, strengthened by the Maulavi's remarks, and we trust that they will find due consideration with Mr. Pfander.* The disadvantage of metaphysical reasoning on this vitally important subject is strikingly shown at pp. 153, 154, and 229, where it is assumed by our opponent that we consider the Son and the Holy Ghost to be *manifestations* of the divine essence; the former being the attribute of *wisdom* or *intelligence*, the latter, of *power* and *love*. Such views are far from scriptural, and however carefully the language may be chosen, are undoubtedly prone to denude the Blessed Persons of that individuality which the Bible attributes to them.

The Maulavi exults that his adversary has been driven for examples of the Trinity, to the tenets of idolatrous nations and heathen philosophers, and quotes the proverb الغريقُ يتشبثُ بكلّ حشيشٍ "the drowning man catches at every straw,"—to intimate that he could only have adopted so

---

* We apprehend that the verbal criticism upon the terms روح and جان *soul* and *life,* is correct : نفس ناطقه and روح حيواني are certainly more in accordance with the oriental idea, although the former, may not perfectly express the meaning of *soul :* the Maulavi is naturally surprised at the new nomenclature, and asks with wonder what that *life* is which stands " between " the soul and body ; and he requires whether *between* applies to *place* or *time* ; there may however be as much waggery as real surprise, in his remarks.

dangerous and fatal an expedient from the badness of his cause.[*] He warns him that religion is a serious and a delicate subject, and that we are not here as in worldly matters, to seek assistance from all by force or by fraud.[†] If these remarks be the genuine dictates of his mind, they show how totally he misunderstands Mr. Pfander's argument, which is to prove the consistency of a species of plurality in unity with human reason : now, the Grecian philosophers, for instance, had certainly by nature as strong and sound a faculty of reason as our adversaries or we possess; and since it is upon reason, *unaided by revelation*, that the Mahommedan hangs his cause, it is surely reasonable in us to adduce the evidence of impartial reasoners, whose minds, unwarped by any prejudices we may be supposed to contract, directed the intensest thought towards the discovery of the mode in which the Divine Being exists : such deductions, surely we may safely oppose to the simple *ipse dixit* of our adversaries, without being suspected of any intention to countenance the doctrines themselves. The *sufis* are abused by the Maulavi, as unbelievers, still more than ourselves, but he will not admit that their views in any degree assist us; because first, they hold a greater variety of manifestations than mere *intelligence* and *will*, and the analogy, therefore, proves too much ; and, secondly, their doctrines are not allowed by the orthodox Mussulmans. He likewise accuses Mr. Pfander of inconsistency, in first representing these sufi philosophers as believing in a trinity, and afterwards asserting that absolute metaphysical unity would land its professor in the sufi error of regarding the divinity as a mere existence, and all creation his attributes. He distinctly denies that they or any other Mussulmans look upon the deity as a rigid metaphysical unity,—but as a being endowed with attributes and perfections, although absolutely one in person and individuality.[‡]

---

* He throws the proverb in our teeth الكفرملة واحدة Idolatry and infidelity of every shade, are but one religion,—implying that we and the idolaters are much alike in error.

† He denies that the Hindus hold plurality in unity regarding their deity; asserting that Brahma, Vishnu, and Mahesh, represent the angels A-rafael, Michael, and Azra-l, and are in fact only the ministers of the Deity; and he makes large extracts upon this subject from a Persian writer. He, accordingly, denies that they hold the incarnation of the *Deity*.

‡ On this subject, we may mention that the Persian and English Dictionaries afford little facility for discovering the metaphysical or technical meaning of philosophical terms. If the learned editor of the last edition of Richardson's dictionary, would supply this deficiency, in the new edition which we understand is under preparation, he would confer a vast favour upon the Persian scholar. Such meanings would be of

Mr. Pfander's most important concluding chapter he treats with contempt, and allots but six pages to its reply. The knowledge of God, he says, can be obtained only in accordance with reason and revelation, and both he affirms point to unity and not to trinity. That the salvation of man is dependent upon this subject, he ridicules as the height of absurdity, because, he says, we hold that Christ actually descended into *Hell*, a shocking blasphemy which no other people ever dared to affirm of their prophet.* The all-important doctrine of Christ's vicarious suffering he treats with scorn, and applies to us this proverb,—

> " They flee for refuge from the rain,
> And stand for shelter 'neath the drain,† "—

that is, in seeking to escape from a *slight* misfortune, viz. the punishment of our sins, we run into the greater danger of charging God with extreme injustice, in inflicting the punishment of the guilty upon the innocent. Having thus abandoned the atonement, he satisfies himself with saying that faith in Christ, to which pardon is promised, is nothing more nor less than the faith and obedience which *every* prophet has insisted upon, and in return for which he has promised the same blessings.

Upon the whole, we see nothing to discourage us in this production. The fallacy of the greater part of the reasoning must approve itself to the majority of thinking Mussulmans, if they choose to reflect with impartiality ; and though it may for a time throw dust unto the eyes of the less candid and intelligent portion of the community, still, as Mr. Pfander's entire‡ work is quoted chapter by chapter, we cannot but rejoice that so great a portion of truth is placed before the Mahommedan reader (if he will but attend to it,) as an antidote to the poison. We understand that Mr. Pfander, at the close of the controversy with Ali Hussain, which he is about to publish, intends to add a few remarks in refutation of the volume we have been considering in this Note.

infinitely greater service than a multitude of indecent applications, which serve little practical purpose, but to disfigure the pages of that valuable Lexicon.

* This popular delusion the Mahommedans have probably picked up from the apostle's creed ; it certainly appears to be very generally promulgated among them.

† الغرار من العطر و الوقوف تحت الميزاب ;——the last word properly means *parnála* or *spout*.

‡ The eleventh page alone is omitted, we cannot see with what object.

ART. VII.—*Topographical Survey of the River Hooghly from Bandel to Garden Reach, exhibiting the Principal Buildings, Ghats, and Temples on both banks, executed in the year* 1841; *by Charles Joseph.*

WE now resume our brief notices of the places marked down in this map on the Right Bank of the Hooghly, which present any particular claim on the attention of the tourist. The first object which attracts notice is the large three story house, lying almost on the edge of the bank, which forms the residence of the Superintendent of the Honourable Company's Botanical Garden. This noble establishment originated in the enlightened views of Colonel Alexander Kyd, more than half a century ago, and was designed for the collection of plants indigenous in the country, and for the introduction and acclimation of plants from foreign parts. The Garden which is very extensive, is laid out with much taste; but those who have had opportunities of examining similar establishments in England are of opinion that it is susceptible of some improvement in the matter of scientific distribution. It combines the attraction of a Botanic Garden with that of a Park, and is therefore the great lounge of the citizens of Calcutta. The magnificent banian trees which adorn it are the scene of many a merry picnic party on the numerous holidays which the Hindu calendar bestows on the community of the Presidency. It possesses a noble botanical library which has been enriched, from time to time, by the liberality of Government, and the donations of botanists in Europe and America. The annals of the Garden embrace the successive labors of Dr. Roxburgh, Dr. Buchanon, Dr. Wallich, and last, but not least, of the original genius and thoroughly accomplished botanist, the late William Griffith, whose premature death, at the age of thirty-four, has been a source of such deep lamentation to the scientific world. A noble monument to the memory of the founder, who died in 1793, stands in a conspicuous part of the Garden, and arrangements formed in order to open it, from various directions, to public view, have contributed not a little to the improvement of the grounds. Monuments have also been erected in the Garden to commemorate the services of Dr. Roxburgh and Dr. Jack. It is not unworthy of remark, that the Committee assembled during Lord William Bentinck's administration, to curtail the expences of the public establishments, proposed that the salary of the superintendent should be reduced from 1500 Rupees a month to 500 Rupees, on the death of the existing incumbent ; but Dr. Wallich's constitutional stamina has hitherto baffled all financial calculations. Long may he live to enjoy the post with undiminished allowances, and whenever he is constrained to transfer the charge to a successor, may the Government be induced to reconsider a resolution which was adopted under the pressure of circumstances which have ceased to exist, and avoid the contempt of Europe, by endowing this pre-eminent scientific post with a salary not superior to that which crowns the wishes of a Deputy Collector. At the northern division of the Garden, there has long existed a Teak plantation, originally formed with the view of creating forest of that wood, so invaluble in ship-building, in this country, but it has proved an entire failure.   The trees present a puny and exotic appearance, and after the lapse of half a century, are still unfit to be used as timber.

At the north of the Garden lies Bishop's College.   The sudden appearance of its gothic turrets, and its green lawn, and its air of academical tranquillity, as the voyager ascends the Hooghly, rekindles in many a bosom those early associations which transport the mind back to the banks of the Cam or Isis. But the immediate succession of the port of Calcutta, with its forest of masts, and its tide of commercial life and animation, soon dispels these classical reflexions.   It is the metropolis of India, the great mart of Asia, which now bursts on the view. This College is a monument of the zeal and public spirit of Bishop Middleton, the first prelate of the English Episcopal Church after India had been erected into a see.   The object of the institution was " the education of Christian youth in sacred knowledge, in sound learning, and in the principal languages used in this country in habits of piety and devotion to their calling, that they may be qualified to preach among the heathen."   The importance of adopting this principle as the basis of missionary operations in India has not been practically exemplified or even fully recognized, by all the missionary bodies in the country ; by some it has been entirely repudiated. They have continued to import missionaries, year after year, from Europe, whom the climate periodically disables and sends back, to such an extent, that at the end of any given period, the actual number of labourers in the field, is found stationary, notwithstanding the constant accession of recruits from home. The sums of money expended by some of the missionary agencies of note in the outward and homeward voyages of missionaries, in ten years, would be found almost sufficient for the establishment of an institution, which should annually furnish treble the number of labourers in the country itself.   Bishop's

College, though never worked up to its full power, has furnished so constant a succession of ministers, missionaries and school
masters as to render the Society with which it is connected, to a
certain extent independent of European resources. Whatever
Society expects to produce a powerful and permanent impression
on the superstition of the East must adopt the same plan, and
make India rather than Europe its recruiting ground. The
same truth applies with equal force to the department of education. If Government desires to produce an impression on the
ignorance of India, instructors must be trained up in the
country, and the dependence on England must be proportionately diminished. With Bishop's College is associated the name
of one of the most profound scholars whose attention has ever
been devoted to the pursuit of Oriental literature. We allude
to its late Principal, Dr. Mill, whose attainments in the learned
language of the East were only exceeded by the extent of his
classical learning. His name is never mentioned by the native
literati except in conjunction with those of Wilford and Jones,
Colebrooke and Carey, Wilson and Yates.

Turning round the elbow of land which projects above
Bishop's College, we obtain a noble view of the City and port
of Calcutta; and find ourselves approaching an elegant country
residence, called Shalimar, where Sir John Royds, one of the
Judges of the Supreme Court thirty years ago enjoyed his
learned leisure, and the last tenant of which was Mr. Sutherland, the nephew of Mr. Colebrooke, from whom he imbibed that
partiality for Sanskrit lore, to which the public is indebted for
the translation of two learned treatises on law. Immediately above
it lies the island of Seebpore, thrown up within the present
century, which has so inconveniently narrowed the channel
of the river. Immediately before us lie Albion Ghat, Albion
Lodge, Albion Mills, all created by the energy of one of the
most enterprizing men in the annals of Indian improvement;
and one of the greatest benefactors of the country. We allude
to William Jones, who is deserving of the same distinguished
record as Watson, the father of shipbuilding, or Prinsep, the
first cultivator of Indigo. He came out to India in the year
1800. For the first ten years of his Indian career we find him
designated only as a mechanic, and we may therefore suppose
that he was struggling with difficulties during this period, of
monoply and stagnation without any opportunity for the
development of his abilities. In 1810, the Directory promotes
him to a Manufacturer, and the next year he is put down as
the proprietor of a Canvas manufactory at Howrah. It was
there that he first established himself to any advantage, and to

his energy and example may be in a great measure attributed the prosperity of that suburb.   For the canvas manufactory in India we are entirely indebted to his spirit of enterprize.   It continued for some time exclusively in the hands of Europeans, and at first yielded a considerable return, but like almost every other manufacture in this country, it has passed into the hands of natives, and, wanting the benefit of European superintendence and honesty, has lost its repute ; and the hopes which were once entertained of its superseding Europe canvas, have disappeared.   When the expedition was about to be despatched in 1811 for the capture of Java, its departure is understood to have been impeded by the want of cartridge paper, and Mr. Jones came to the assistance of Government.   His extraordinary mechanical skill enabled him to set up a little paper manufactory, from which he furnished all the paper that was requisite, and closed his new works as soon as the object of the expedition was accomplished.   He was not encouraged to continue his exertions, for the Court of Directors had not then become alive to the importance of calling forth and improving the resources of the country.   Down to that late period, India continued to be governed in a great measure upon the old colonial and selfish principle of the seventeenth and eighteenth centuries, of administering a colony solely for the benefit of the mother country, and fostering improvements only as far as they tended to promote that object.   The idea of governing the foreign possessions of Europe, and more especially those of England, on the enlarged principle of promoting their interest, though now reckoned among truisms, has been recognized and acted upon only within the present century.

Four or five years subsequently, Jones accidentally discovered the existence of coal in Burdwan, and with his characteristic ardor determined to open the mines.   From that new spirit of enterprize which had then begun to manifest itself, he foresaw that it could not be long before the powerful agency of steam was introduced into India, and he resolved to accelerate its progress by providing a supply of fuel.   It is chiefly in reference to our Indian coal, and in contemplating the vast benefit which Jones's labours have conferred on India, that his claim to the highest rank among her benefactors, rests.   At the end of less than thirty years, the coal fields which Jones was the first to work, produce *seventy thousand* tons annually, and supply fuel for 150 Steam Engines.   His last public engagement was the building of Bishop's College, which he undertook in some measure from his desire to promote every object of public utility, but also because he aspired to the honour of erecting the first Gothic edifice in India. That he should have ventured upon so difficult an undertaking and one so foreign to his previous pursuits, and that he should have so admirably succeeded in the execution of it, is of itself a sufficient demonstration of the lofty enterprize and genius of the man. His active and useful life was brought to an abrupt close in the month of September 1821, in consequence of a fever which he contracted while superintending the building : and which proved fatal in three days. Bishop Middleton, in his letters thus deeply lamented the loss of his invaluable assistance :

" In addition to other causes of solicitude, the Bishop at this time had a severe trial to endure in the loss of Mr. Jones, the gentleman with whom he had contracted for the building of the College, and who died towards the end of September, 1821, after an illness of two or three days. Any interruption to this noble work would have weighed most heavily on his spirit : but the loss of the able and zealous contractor, by whom it was begun, was felt by him almost as a personal calamity. In the first place, it threatened him with all the trouble and perplexities of a fresh contract ; and, what was still worse, with the probability of great additional expense. Besides, he anticipated the greatest difficulty in finding a person at all equal to the task of completing the work in the same admirable style in which it had been commenced. "The buildings," he observes to Archdeacon Barnes,* "are brought up to the level of the first floor of the second story : but more than half the masonry done, considering the vast mass of foundation. *It seems to be admitted that finer work was never seen in this country ;* and poor Jones was pleased with it himself. *He was all heart about his undertaking,* and was just beginning to see the effect produced. The grand entrance to the hall and chapel, a Gothic arch, seventeen feet high, and ten wide, is finished on the south side, and, very nearly so on the northern. I saw it a few evenings since, chiefly by flashes of lightning ; and, as unfinished buildings look like ruins, it reminded me of some ancient abbey gate. He has executed my idea admirably. But the chapel roof is the part in which he would have shewn himself to the best advantage; and here is my perplexity : but the plan cannot now be altered. The frames of the chapel windows are in, and the skeleton of the great eastern window, twenty-three feet high, is, I hear, completed. It is something, certainly, that Jones lived to do so much. It will still be his monument ! "

He was perfect master of the native language, which he spoke with as much facility and accuracy as if he had been born in the country. He was thoroughly acquainted with the habits, customs, and feelings of the natives, and was ever ready to assist those around him with his skill and advice, as well as with his purse. He came therefore at length to be known among the people as *Gooroo* Jones, or the teacher Jones. Like many other men of genius, he was incapable of saving a fortune out of the numerous lucrative schemes which he originated. They imparted a great impulse to national

* Dated October 5th, 1821.

improvement, and subsequently proved a source of no little wealth to others, but they brought little benefit to his family, to whom he bequeathed scarcely any thing beyond the high esteem and reputation which he had so richly earned.

There is little to notice in the villages of Seebpore, Howrah and Sulkea, the Southwark of Calcutta. The establishment of the Docks and a few manufactures, and of the Company's Salt Ware-houses, gives an air of life and activity to the place, but the number of European residents though not inconsiderable, is by no means proportioned to the vast population and wealth of Calcutta, of which it constitutes a suburb. Southwark enjoyed greater distinction as compared with the magnitude of London, three or four centuries ago, than Howrah does in this age of expansion and improvement, when viewed in connection with the commercial importance of Calcutta. But London had a bridge, and Calcutta has none; and some have ventured to affirm that nature never intended it should have one; that the engineering difficulties presented by the river are such as the skill of this age of engineering miracles is unable to overcome. The map before us has parallel lines dotted down below the Salt Golah for a Steam Ferry which was projected some years ago. But it has experienced the fate of too many of our metropolitan schemes. A Company was formed, and funds were raised, and boats ordered from England, but owing to the miscalculation and mismanagement of the Agents, the boats cost more than double the capital, and were eventually sold to pay the manufacturers at home, and the shareholders were stripped of all their donations, besides incurring the derision of society, for having begun a scheme in the hope of twenty-five per cent., which so speedily ended in total bankruptcy. When the apparatus which had been brought out from England for the bridge was for sale at half its original cost, it was expected that Government would have come forward and purchased it, and thus have given us the benefit of an invention, by which two hundred lives a year would have been saved. But an officer of the Engineers on whose judgment great reliance was placed, declared the plan impracticable, and the opportunity was allowed to be lost. A bridge over the river would fill our Borough with houses and residents, and prove of incalculable benefit to Calcutta; but, nearly a century after this city has become the metropolis of a mighty empire; in the middle of the nineteenth century, when scientific skill has reached the highest degree of perfection, and at a time when India yields a revenue of Twenty millions sterling a year, the City of Palaces enjoys no better means of conveyance to the opposite bank than the native ferry boat, as ricketty and unsafe as that which was in use in the country when the Ramayan was penned. As our Government in India is the greatest anomaly of modern times, so, as if to preserve the character of consistency, it presents a variety of minor anomalies, of which none is greater than the contrast between its imperial revenues, and the wretched means of conveyance still employed both by land and at the ferries. At what period of the present century Calcutta is destined to obtain the benefit of a bridge, it would be difficult to divine; there is, perhaps, little expectation of this blessing till some *one* man in a commanding official position, shall adopt it as his hobby, and combat all antagonist influences with that spirit of indomitable ardor, which appears so necessary to the accomplishment of all schemes of improvement. It would be a foul calumny on the age, to suppose that with our present perfection of means and appliances, a bridge over the Hooghly, capable of withstanding the ' freshes' of the river or the ' bore' from the sea, is an absolute impracticability. Meanwhile a greater and more formidable undertaking is to be immediately attempted, which will call into requisition all the resources of the Engineer's skill, to counteract inundations, and cross mountains and span rivers,—we allude to the Calcutta and Mirzapore Railway, the terminus of which it was originally proposed to fix at Howrah. It appears certain that the terminus will now be established in the heart of Calcutta; but if a bridge should be thrown over the river at or near Howrah, for this object, a new impulse of improvement will be given to our borough.

There are several extensive manufactories opposite Calcutta, but the prosperity of the town of Howrah depends chiefly on its dock-yards, and ship building establishments. In our notice of the left bank of the river we stated, that they were finally removed from Calcutta about twenty-five years ago, but a dock had been established at Sulkea, by Mr. Bacon, as early as the year 1796, and the *Orpheus* frigate was the first hauled into it. With the exception of the Government docks at Kidderpore, all such establishments are now very properly confined to the right bank of the river. In this brief notice of the docks, we must not omit to mention the establishment created by Mr. Reeves, the ship builder, a man of great enterprize, who has recently enlarged it so as to accommodate our magnificent steamers, the largest vessels which have ever come up to Calcutta. Recent experience has shewn that the convenience of docks sufficiently capacious for such vessels was quite as essential to the permanence and punctuality of a regular monthly communication with England, as the establishment of the vessels themselves. The Lower Orphan School was formerly located in Howrah, but the appearance of opthalmia among its wards induced Government to carry the establishment across the river to Allipore more than twenty years ago. Howrah has three Churches and Chapels, one of the Church of England, one connected with the Church of Rome, and one belonging to the Baptist denomination.

Above Howrah is the village of Ghoosory, without any thing to attract attention, but two or three manufactories, and a little Hindu shrine on the banks of the river in which, 'by no very lawful junction of the arts,' some Native architect has preposterously attached a Grecian portico to a Hindu temple of Shiva. The architectural anomalies of the native builders in the edifices entrusted to them by their wealthy fellow countrymen would fill a chapter. There is a constant endeavor among them to imitate the buildings erected in and about Calcutta by European architects; but as they have not the slightest idea of architectural proprieties, we see them constantly confounding the various orders, giving a rich freeze to a Doric pillar, inserting a large and highly elaborate window in low and narrow buildings, and disgracing the art of Palladio in every conceivable form. Although the buildings thus erected by them are a vast improvement on the miserable cabins in which the richest natives were formerly content to hive, and the large window of three feet and a half by seven is a most agreeable exchange in this sultry climate for the little opening in the shape of a cow's mouth,—called from that circumstance the *Gomukhi*,—which formerly disfigured their baronial residences, yet they offend the eye by the total absence of all taste and simplicity, and by the vicious exuberance of ornament. The whole reach of the river from the point of Ghoosory to the village of Bali is singularly uninteresting, and offers no ancient associations or modern improvements to attract attention. While the opposite bank of the river, comprizing Cossipore and Barnagore, presents a lively scene of manufacturing and engineering industry, and is gradually becoming studded with elegant villas, the right bank does not contain a single European or civilized residence. It has a wild and almost jungly appearance, which is diversified only by stacks of timber and brick, or tile kilns, quite unworthy of the approach to a great metropolis. The erection of a bridge at Calcutta would soon correct this appearance, and adorn the bank with country houses, and green sloping banks, and render it the counterpart of its neighbour on the opposite side of the river.

We pause at the village of Bali, which was a place of note long before a European vessel had ascended the Hooghly. We have evidence of its existence three centuries ago in the old poem of Kobi Kunkun, one of the earliest productions now extant in the Bengali language. It was one of the eight places which furnished Bengal with an almanack before the art of printing was introduced into the country. These almanacks were much fuller, and of far greater interest and importance than the old almanacks in England, which originated in the days of judicial astrology, and have been continued from Partridge to More, till cast into the shade by the light of modern improvement. An almanack, is indispensible to a Hindu. He is obliged to refer to one in almost every transaction of life, because it is so entirely regulated by astronomical conjunctions and the " influ- ence of the heavenly intelligencies." It teaches him how to time the innumerable affairs of ordinary life so as not only to avoid inauspicious conjunctures, but to seize upon the precise moment when the aspect of the stars and planets is most propitious. If any man would learn how Hinduism interferes with every movement in life, however trivial—constantly re- minding its votary of something to be done or something to be forborne—let him consult the almanack. These annuals are drawn up by the brahmans who have some smattering of Indian astronomy ; and are deeply versed in the mysteries of astrology. In addition to the superstitious notices which formed the staple of the old almanacks, those of the present day give a variety of useful information of a secular character, such as the schedule of stamp duties, the rates of postage, and the like. The almanacks of Bali have lost their credit, and that which is now published at a native press in Serampore, has risen into vogue, and commands a circulation of more than four thousand copies a year.

Bali, however, is still one of the most orthodox and holy towns in the neighbourhood of Calcutta. It is said to contain no fewer than a thousand families of brahmans, many of whom prefer living in a state of primitive simplicity, like the sages of Hindu hagiography, on the scanty produce of their fields and orchards, to attending the feasts and festivals of their wealthy fellow countrymen, and accepting the wages of men- dicancy. It used to be affirmed that some of the most exclusive and sanctified brahmans of Bali who stood around the scaffold on which Nundkumar was judicially murdered by Sir Elijah

Impey, were so struck with horror at the sight, that they ran down to the river, and having washed out the pollution of this spectacle in the sacred stream, embarked for their own village, and vowed never again to set foot in a city which had witnessed the execution of one of the twice born. On the northern extremity of the village, stand two small temples, the singular architecture of which attracted the notice of Bishop Heber. It is at this place that the Bali Khal or creek, turns off from the river and runs up into the country. Over this creek one of the largest and most beautiful suspension bridges was erected during the course of the present year by Captain Goodwyn of the Engineers, but an untoward accident, originating in some error or misapprehension of the subordinates, prostrated it into the water, just as it had been completed. The confidence of the Engineer in the soundness of the principle on which it was erected has induced him to adopt the same principle in its reconstruction, and it is expected to be opened to the public at the beginning of the present year. There is no bridge in Bengal of so bold and magnificent a character, or which stands in a more picturesque situation. The traffic which crosses this little creek, on the high road between Howrah and Benares, is so great that the produce of the ferry exceeds 3000 Rupees a year. Within the last six years very extensive sugar factories have been built on its southern bank, which give it a pleasing air of manufacturing activity. Indeed no place for twenty miles above Calcutta exhibits so much bustle and animation. The anchorage at the mouth of the creek and a little way farther up is particularly safe, and the great, unwieldy, and heavily laden vessels from the Upper Provinces which are unable to make Calcutta with the tide, generally anchor here. The vessels with valuable freight which leave Calcutta for the Upper Provinces with every tide, usually make this their first stage, after having cleared the port.

Passing by the two next uninteresting hamlets we come to Connugur, a populous and wealthy village, the family residence of many natives who have amassed, or are amassing, wealth in Calcutta. The most prominent object in it is the series of twelve temples and the noble landing stairs on the banks of the river erected at the expense of Baboo Hurusoonder Dutt. A stone's throw to the north of them a careful observer will perceive the remains of an ancient but now dilapidated dock. The only vestige which remains of it is the solid pillars of the gates, which continue to resist the ravages of the current; but the excavation of the dock may be distinctly traced within.

The premises are surrounded with a wall, and the title deeds are of a date anterior to the establishment of British authority in Bengal. Just above this spot, along the village of Rishera, the bank describes a curve, and the anchorage is sheltered from storms. It was here that the Danish vessels sometimes anchored instead of coming up to Serampore, and there is some reason to believe, that the dock which we have alluded to, had some reference to this anchorage, though no mention of it appears in the records of Serampore. A few brick-built houses are to be seen in the village of Rishera, which is evidently losing the wealth and importance it once enjoyed. At the northern extremity of this village stands a factory which has existed for half a century, and passed successively through the hands of various European houses of business into those of its late possessor, Bissumbhur Sen. It was one of the oldest and most profitable Chintz manufactories in the country, having been established not long after Mr. Prinsep had introduced the art. With the decay, or rather the extinction, of our trade in piece goods, which the produce of English looms has so entirely superseded, the manufacture of chintz cloths has dwindled almost to nothing. None but the coarsest and cheapest chintz are now prepared, and only for the most indigent class of society. But in its stead a very extensive business in the printing of silk handkerchiefs has grown up, and those who were formerly employed on our cotton cloths, now find remunerating employment in printing bandannos. The house and grounds now belong to the family of Bissumbhur Sen, who affords an example of the large fortunes which the vast traffic of the country and especially of Calcutta, combined with the confidence our institutions inspire, enables natives to accumulate in the space of a single life. This man began his career upon eight or ten Rupees a month, and before his death had created a large fortune of some two hundred thousand pounds, out of nothing, by dint of economy, skill and perseverance. A dozen such instances of prosperity within the last twenty-five years might be pointed out, and they may be regarded as an index of the prosperity of the country, of which the accumulation of capital is one of the most unequivocal tokens. It is not unworthy of remark, that all the colossal fortunes which were made before the close of the last century, were of official origin, and grew out of the oriental process of converting power into money. In that period, more than half a dozen natives are known to have amassed a million sterling by the plunder of the state and the oppression of its subjects. Those days of official peculation have happily ceased. Within the last quarter of a century, we believe, not more than two or three natives are admitted to have accumulated a sum above ten lakhs,—or a whole plumb—in the public service. A lakh or two is at present the utmost limit to which a native, who enjoys and abuses the confidence of an easy Judge, Magistrate or Collector, can expect to attain.   On the other hand, the fortunes made by commercial enterprize in Calcutta, and the larger towns at this Presidency, and which are brought into notice year after year, are continuous, as well as magnificent.

Adjoining the factory, we have Rishera House.   Perhaps no place presents more of the appearance of an English country seat than this mansion, as it is viewed on coming down the river, with its green velvet lawn and venerable trees, which may almost be mistaken for the oaks of a park, it has always been a favorite retreat with Calcutta residents.   It is surrounded by a brick wall, the western portion of which is lined with a row of ancient mango trees, one of which excites great admiration for the boldness and grandeur of its branches.   The tradition runs that the trees were planted by Mrs. Hastings, when she and Warren Hastings made this villa their temporary residence.   A little higher up is the village of Muhesh, written by Mr. Joseph, Moyse.   It extends from the upper creek at Rishera to Bullubpore on the confines of Seramporc and is one of the most ancient villages in this part of the country.   There is evidence that it was in existence three centuries ago, and that it stood, where it now does, on the banks of the river.   Indeed, in this brief notice of the banks of the river from Calcutta to Hooghly, it would be improper to overlook the fact that while villages above that town which are known to have lain on the banks of the river at the commencement of the Mogul dynasty, are now in some cases four or five miles distant from it, every village within the tract embraced by the map, appears from the itinerary on which we have drawn for our information, to stand precisely where it stood three centuries ago, on the immediate bank of the river.   This leads us to the conclusion that there has been scarcely any material change in its current within these limits during this long period.   The village of Muhesh has nothing to distinguish it in appearance from any other village. All its houses are buried amid the foliage of trees, many of them of great antiquity ; and its very existence is revealed to the tourist only as he wanders through it.   But it has a peculiar attraction to the natives throughout Bengal on account of its Temple of Jugunnath, which enjoys greater celebrity than any other abode of the ' lord of the world,' after the parent shrine at Poori.   It may fairly claim an antiquity of three hundred years.   The present proprietors have been in possession of the image for seven generations. The popular legend, which is universally believed by a people as much given to credulity as the most superstitious nation in Europe, is, that the god Jugunnath stopped and bathed at Muhesh, on his way to Poori, where he dined. To commemorate this event, a grand festival is held on the full moon in the month Joisti, which falls in May, and occasionally in June. On that high occasion the image is brought out of the temple, wrapped in broadcloth, and hoisted up on a brick-built stage raised about seven feet from the ground. Just at the time when the conjunction of the planets indicates the most auspicious moment, the officiating priest pours the water of the sacred Ganges on its head from a silver *kulsi*, or water pot. The ground before the stage is a large open era which is densely crowded with devotees at this festival, a hundred and fifty thousand of whom have been known to assemble at one time in front of the image. As the water descends upon the head of the consecrated log, one long and deafening shout arises from that vast multitude, making the welkin ring; the hands of the worshippers are at the same moment lifted up and clapped together,—and the density of the crowd, the forest of hands, the shouts and the clapping, combine to give an idea of superstitious enthusiasm which is rarely presented in any other scene.

About fifteen years ago, this bathing festival was rendered memorable by a singular event. If the reader turns to Joseph's map, he will discover a little village noted down to the north of Serampore, of the name of Sharafully. It is distinguished from other villages only by the residence of the Zemindar or Rajah, who is usually called after its name. The Rajah, who is of the writer caste, is descended from one of the most ancient and respected families in Bengal, the well known designation of which is *Sudra muni,* or the jewel of Sudras. The original seat of the family was at Patoolee, a few miles distant from Cutwa, and we find the Zemindary of Patoolee marked down in the rent roll of the Mogul viceroys as paying a revenue of 52,000 Rupees a year. We may therefore conclude that this was one of the Zemindary families which arose into note about the close of the seventeenth century. The principle which had been established a century before by the emperor Akbar, of admitting no middle men between the cultivator and the state, began at that period to be relaxed, and those who had been appointed to collect the land tax aimed at making the office hereditary in their families, and were in a state of transition from collectors of revenue to landholders. The Zemindary system appears to have been brought to maturity by Moorshed

Kooly Khan, the greatest of the Mahommedan viceroys of Bengal,—Aly Verdi Khan, perhaps, excepted.   Moorshed Kooly found it more convenient to apply the revenue screw to a limited number of large landholders than to a million of tenants.   The modes in which he exacted the public revenue from unwilling Zemindars are too well known to need recounting.   On some occasions he caused them to be dragged through a pond filled with ordure ; and this contrivance for obtaining the Government dues, however inodorous, was generally found successful in unlocking their hoards.   It happened that a brahman Zemindar had thus fallen into arrears and was about to be consigned to this paradise, as the pond was called in derision, when Munohur Roy, the Zemindar of Patoolee, stepped forward and paid off the whole debt.   The Nabob was so much gratified with this act of generosity, that he conferred on him the title of *Sudra muni,* or the "jewel of Sudras," a name which the family has retained for nearly a century and a half.   For several generations they vindicated their claim to this distinction by their liberal donations to various shrines, an l it is said that few temples of any note can be found in the country which have not received some tokens of their devotion and bounty.   They were great benefactors to the establishment of Jugunnath, which owes its most productive endowments to their munificence.   Partly from this cause, and partly because the ground on which the temple is erected is within the estate of the Rajah, the annual ceremony of bathing the image was invariably postponed till the principal member of the family arrived, and issued orders for its performance.   The late Rajah Hurrischunder, who was fully alive to the honor which this distinction conferred on his family, in the midst of a hundred thousand of his fellow countrymen assembled from all parts of the country, usually rode to the shrine on horseback, with half a dozen outriders, and a long array of followers.

Within the last thirty or forty years, a family in Serampore of the Telee cast has arisen from utter insignificance to great wealth, by establishing one of the under monopolies of Salt, which have grown out of the great monopoly of the Company.   There are still living one or two of the ancient residents of the town who can remember the time when the grand father proceeded to market with a basket of thread on his head, and was happy to earn four or five Rupees a month by the sale of it.   Although on one or two occasions they have exhibited the arrogance of upstarts, yet it is but just to acknowledge that, generally speaking, they have endeavored to weaken the feeling of envy which their elevation could not fail to create, by peaceful, just, and moderate conduct. In the course of time, the large estates of the Sharafully Rajah were subjected to a partition, and a portion of them was allotted to a branch of the family now seated at Bali. Of this division a part had been mortgaged to this Telee family. In this country, as well as in England, the possessions of ancient families who are strangers to the principles of economy, are constantly passing into the hands of new men who have risen to wealth in the course of trade. The mortgage was duly foreclosed, and the *parvenu* family became landholders, and entered on possession of a portion of the land which forms the endowment of Jugunnath. It will of course be understood, that in spite of all the consideration which their wealth confers on them, they are regarded by the community as infinitely inferior in distinction to the time-honoured family of Sharafully. In fact, the difference between the two families may be compared to that which subsisted in popular estimation between Glossen, the purchaser of Ellangowan, and the historical Bertrams. In an evil hour, the Telees determined to arrogate to themselves the honor of giving orders for the bathing of Jugunnath ; and, having obtained the concurrence of the priests by offers which were irresistible, the head of the family proceeded with due pomp to the stage, and the image was bathed at his command, and the crowd began to disperse. The late Rajah Hurrischunder, as he advanced with his cavalcade, met the retiring multitude, and his indignation may be more easily conceived than described when he learned that the son of the hawker of thread had thus invaded the ancient prerogatives of his family. He rode up in haste to the temple, caused the chief priests to be bound and conveyed a distance of five miles to his own residence and there subjected them, for three days, to every possible indignity, short of actual violence. The intercession of the neighbouring Zemindars and of the most wealthy men in Serampore, succeeded at length in softening his resentment, and they were liberated on the promise of never repeating the transgression, or paying the slightest attention to the new men; a promise which they have since held sacred.

The present temple of Jugunnath was built by the family of the Mulliks of Calcutta. The car, one of the largest in Bengal, was the gift of the Boses. About eight or ten years ago, the old car was found to be unsafe by reason of decay and the ravages of the white ants. These tiny and yet most formidable enemies seem to be utterly destitute of all respect for things sacred, for in the last few years they have attacked with equal presumption the organ of St. Andrew's Church, and the carriage of Jugunnath. The head of this family—of the Boses, not of the white ants—accordingly, caused a new car to be constructed at his own expense. And here we must not forget to notice the token[1] of improved feeling which was exhibited on this occasion. The old car was covered with figures, not only of an indecent but of a most infamous character, such as the Police even in England, where we have neither moral nor medical police, would not tolerate for an instant. This had always been a source of great regret to all the Europeans in the neighbourhood. For the festival of Jugunnath, which lasts eight days, and presents the attraction of a fair, is also the period of a general jail delivery for all the respectable females in a circle of more than thirty miles. On this occasion they are allowed to come abroad and see life; to visit the shrine, and present their offering. They usually make a few purchases at the fair, and seldom neglect to walk round the car, and examine its pictures. It was distressing to see females of respectability, on one of the very few occasions when they were allowed to move beyond the walls of their own prisons, gazing on representations of so detestable a character. But although the pictures with which the new car is covered have little pretension to modesty, and are calculated, if not designed, like every other Hindu exhibtion, to minister to a prurient imagination, they are not so revolting to the feelings as those which made the old car a public nuisance.

Two or three weeks after the bathing festival, the image of Jugunnath is placed upon his car, three or four hours before sunset, and drawn by means of hawsers by the crowd of worshippers a distance of about a mile to the vicinity of the temple of Radhabullub, on the confines of Serampore, to which the image is conveyed. During the eight days in which the two gods reside together, the shrine is crowded, day and night with devotees, chiefly of the female sex, who come from a considerable distance to see them in each other's company. This visit of Jugunnath to his fellow god is a mere conventional arrangement, originating in the avarice of the priests. The rule in reference to his journey is simply that he shall be lodged in some house near the car, and if possible, in the temple of some brother divinity. It was supposed that the presence of both images under the same roof would form a great attraction to the public, and fill the purses of the brahmans; and the respective proprietors came to an understanding to divide the profits. About fifteen years ago, the priesthood of Radhabullub's temple manifested a desire to withhold a due share of the offerings from their brethren of Jugunnath's temple, and they, in their turn, retaliated by conveying their idol to a private lodging. But the offerings at Radhabullub's shrine were found to suffer so considerably by the loss of this attraction, that the priesthood of both temples, after a good deal of huckstering, agreed to renew the old arrangement, and it has continued in force ever since. It is generally supposed that the offerings during the eight days of the festival amount to about 2000 Rupees, but they are not equally distributed over this period, for some days are found to be more profitable than others. The gifts of each day are separately farmed out to some one connected with the temple, in the mercenary spirit which pervades every Hindu institution. The farmer appoints his own officials to collect them, and he is sometimes a gainer, but always a loser on a day of unexpected rain.

Immediately above the village of Muhesh stands that of Bullubpore, which grew up around the image and temple of Radhabullub, to which we have already alluded. Every shrine of any note in India has some miraculous legend attached to it with the design of attracting the confidence of the people. It is believed that about eight generations ago, Roodru Pundit, who was related to a family of distinction at Chatra, a mile to the west of Serampore, was reproved by his uncle for having presumed to scour the sacrificial vessels of the domestic idol, on which he forsook the family mansion, and retired to Bullubpore, which was then a *forest*, where he began a series of religious austerities, in the hope of one day being able to possess an image and temple of his own. The gods are never indifferent to such acts of devotedness, and Radhabullub himself is said to have appeared to him in the form of a religious mendicant, and given him instructions to proceed to Gour, the capital of Bengal, and obtain a slab of stone which adorned the door way of the Viceroy's private room, and construct an image out of it. He proceeded to that city and found that the prime minister and favorite of the Viceroy was a devoted Hindu. To him he announced the revelation he had received, and was assured, that no effort should be spared to obey the commands of the god. Soon after, the stone began to emit drops of water, and by a singular coincidence, the Viceroy himself happened to pass by at the time. The minister pointed out the circumstance, and asserted that the drops thus distilled were the tears of the stone, and that no time should be lost in delivering the palace from so inauspicious an omen, by the removal of this object. Permission was immediately given to this effect, and Roodru was blessed with the gratification of his wishes.   But he was greatly perplexed about the means of removing this treasure, when the god again appeared, and directed him to return forthwith to Bullubpore, and there await in patience the arrival of the stone. Soon after he had reached his village, it was miraculously conveyed to the river side, and floated down the stream of its own accord to the landing stairs at Bullubpore, where the devotee was in the habit of bathing.   Superstition presents the same aspect in all ages, and in all countries, and not only makes the same demand on the credulity of its victims, but adopts nearly the same mode of securing it.   The legend of the image which fell down from Jupiter ; of the Santa Casa, which was carried by supernatural power from Palestine to Dalmatia, and from Dalmatia to Loretto, and of the stone which floated from Gour to Bullubpore, belong to three different and independent systems of superstition, yet we find the contrivances employed in each case to give a miraculous sanctity to a shrine, and draw forth the homage and gifts of devotees, precisely the same.

Roodru set to work immediately on the stone, and by the aid of the sculptor obtained an image which is much celebrated for its beauty.   The mysterious origin of the image soon attached worshippers, and the proprietor was enabled from their gifts to construct the temple which forms one of the most prominent objects at the entrance of Scrampore from the south.   In process of time, the encroachments of the river brought the temple within the limits of three hundred feet of the edge of the water, and it became necessary to seek some other abode for the god, because no brahman is allowed to receive a professional gift or meal within that distance of the sacred stream.   It is in reference to this injunction of the Shastras that wealthy natives guard against erecting their houses on the immediate banks of the river.   The forsaken temple was subsequently purchased by the Reverend David Brown, and the image was removed to another spot, a quarter of a mile inland, where a more magnificent temple was built at the expense of the wealthy family of the Mulliks of Calcutta, whose religious liberality has almost obliterated the remembrance of the low caste to which they belong.   The splendor of Radhabullub's establishment is, however, of more recent origin than the celebrity of the image.   The Raja Nubukissen of Calcutta, the Munshi of Clive, and the first native who rose to wealth and distinction after the birth of the British empire in India, took a great fancy to this god.   When he was called to perform the funeral obsequies of his mother, he employed the great influence he enjoyed in the country, to convey to his own residence in the metropolis, the three images to which Ugrudeep, Churdah and Bullubpore owe their distinction.   They were carried down to the river on a stage, on the shoulders of brahmans—for it would be an act of sacrilege for any but the twice born to touch an image, inhabited by the spirit of the gods;—and were conveyed from the ghat in Calcutta to the Rajah's residence on the same sacerdotal shoulders.   Soon after, he dismissed two of the images, but retained that of Radhabullub for a twelvemonth, and exhibited a strong indisposition to part with it.   He offered large sums of money to the priests— according to popular report, to the extent of 10, or 12,000 Rupees—for permission to keep it ; but they refused to part with the heirloom of their family.   They importuned him for its restoration, time after time, but without success.   An appeal to the Courts of Law would at once have secured its return, but such a proceeding would have reflected dishonour on them throughout the country.   At length, they threatened the Rajah and his family with a more fearful calamity than a law suit in the Supreme Court,—with the curse of the brahmans.   These menaces are said to have reached the Rajah's wife, who besought him to send away an image which was likely to prove so inauspicious to the family, and he was persuaded to relinquish it.   At the same time, he gave the most substantial proofs of his generosity to its proprietors by endowing them with the village of Bullubpore, which is supposed to yield them an annual income of about 800 Rupees a year.   The patronage of so distinguished a character as Rajah Nubukissen tended greatly to increase the popularity of the shrine, and it is now one of the most wealthy in this part of the country.

We now enter the town of Serampore, which, after having been in the hands of the Danes for ninety years, has just been transferred to the English.   Within this brief period, is comprised the history of the rise, progress and consolidation of the greatest colonial empire the world has ever seen.   Within nine months after the Danish Agent had erected his flag in Serampore, the factory of the English in Calcutta was plundered by the Nabob ; their establishments throughout the country were broken up, and every hope of their regaining a footing in Bengal, was apparently extinguished.   In the last year in which the Danish flag floats over Serampore, the British Government is engaged in hostilities with the Government of Lahore, which will probably end in the annexation of the Punjab and Cashmere to its empire, and give us a postal road from one extremity of it to the other, of not less than Two thousand Three hundred miles in length.   The Danes originally established their trade in Bengal in the year 1698, and paid 30,000 Rs. in ten annual instalments for their firman, which was granted them by the Prince Azim-ud-din, the grandson of the Emperor Arung-zebe. In 1753, we find Mr. Soetman, the chief of the Danish establishment, residing at Chandernagore, where the vessels consigned to him unloaded their cargoes. The return cargo was shipped from that town, as the property of the Governor, M. de Lejrit, though not without many disputes with the Nabob's custom house officers, who doubtless had some suspicions of the ownership of the goods. The Danish factors therefore felt the necessity of obtaining a settlement which they might call their own in Bengal, and they opened a negotiation with the Nabob, through the well known Monsr. Law, the French Agent at Cossimbazar, who enjoyed pre-eminent influence at the Moorshedabad durbar. The letters which he wrote in April and the two succeeding months of 1755, were lately in existence at Tranquebar, and would doubtless throw much light on the politics of the Moorshedabad Court at this interesting period. There were no public posts in Bengal at that time; and Mr. Law's letter of the 30th July announcing that he had succeeded in obtaining a *perwanna* for the erection of a factory at Serampore, was twelve days in reaching Chandernagore.

Mr. Law himself arrived with that document on the 6th of September, together with an order on the Fouzdar of Hooghly to deliver possession, but a month elapsed before the arrangements with this important personage could be completed. Old Soetman's records say, " we went to Ackna and Serampore on the 7th October, 1755, to take possession of our ground with the necessary ceremonies, but the whole day passed in disputes, and we were obliged to go there again." They were entitled by the Viceregal firman to the occupation of sixty bigahs of ground. They preferred taking three bigahs in Serampore and fifty-seven in Ackna; because " no ship could lay at Ackna, though a good factory might be built there on a large open spot of ground." They discovered that if they took the whole quantity in Serampore, they would have been obliged to purchase all the houses which stood in it, of the value of 10, or 12,000 Rupees. This shows that the village was of some mark even before a European settlement was established in it. Soetman, therefore, contented himself with the river frontage, and the secure anchorage before it. On the 8th of October 1755, the Danish flag was hoisted at Serampore and four peons were appointed to guard it. The expenses incurred at the Durbar in obtaining the firman, in presents to the three Nabobs, and in the purchase of the ground from the proprietors, had amounted to a Lakh and sixty thousand Rupees, £16,000. The factory however, advanced slowly.   It was seven weeks before the factor appointed a Gomasta, " in which he followed the example of the other nations in Bengal," and he was a person of the *Catmah*, or weaver caste.   On the 15th of December, Ziegenbalk, the second in command, remeasured the ground, and it was resolved to surround the factory with a mud fence and a straw roof, to protect it during the rains.   Most opportunely, some one at this time offered to enter the Danish service on 40 Rs. a month, to superintend the building of the factory and the fencing of the ground, if he was honored with the rank and title of Lieutenant; whereupon Soetman and Ziegenbalk passed an order in Council, that " if he could not be prevailed on to serve for less, he should have 40 Rs., but without a free house or lights."   It was just at this juncture that the young Nabob, Seraj-ud-dowlah passed down with 50,000 men on the opposite bank, breathing vengeance on the English for having fortified Calcutta and given protection to Kissendass.   He sent across the water to order Soetman to join the army with all his troops, cavalry, infantry and artillery ; to which the Governor replied, that he had neither horse, foot, or guns, but was living in a miserable mud hut, with only two or three servants.

The settlement grew and flourished under the predominance of European influence in Bengal, and participated in that security for property which the establishment of the English Government had introduced.   It was also greatly assisted by the Capital of the servants of the English East India Company. They had formerly been permitted to remit their fortunes to England by bills from the local authorities on the Court of Directors ; but this permission was found to afford such great facilities to the Government of Bengal for borrowing money. the payment of which the Court was expected to provide for at home, that it was very wisely withdrawn.   The British officers were therefore constrained to make their remittances through the foreign factories, and this accession of capital gave a new impulse to their commercial enterprizes.   At the close of the American war, England was involved in hostilities with the three maritime nations of North America, France and Holland, and English vessels were exposed to the attacks of privateers, and English trade subjected to very heavy insurances.   These were the golden days of Serampore commerce.   Before the close of that war, no fewer than Twenty-two ships, mostly of three masts, and amounting in the aggregate to more than Ten thousand tons, cleared out from the port, in the short space of nine months.   This trade, though eminently profitable to the

Danish East India Company, was perhaps still more advantageous to their factors, who, while in the receipt of salaries not exceeding Two Hundred Rupees a month, drank champaign at 80 Rupees a dozen, and in a few years returned to Denmark with large fortunes. The late John Palmer, of Calcutta, usually styled the prince of merchants, was the Agent of the Danish Company, and has repeatedly assured us, that he has sat, day after day, in the godowns at Serampore, counting and weighing out goods, and that he seldom realized less than a lakh of Rupees a year.

The first interruption which the trade of Serampore received after a course of uninterrupted prosperity for forty-five years, was in the year 1801, when, in consequence of hostilities between England and Danmark, it was sequestered by the English authorities. But it was restored almost immediately after, at the peace of Amiens, and the loss was rapidly repaired. For five years after it throve beyond all former example. As the Bay swarmed with French privateers, and insurances had risen almost to a prohibitory rate, the merchants of Calcutta eagerly availed themselves of the neutral flag of Denmark, and obtained Danish papers and a Danish commander for their vessels as a protection against the privateers which infested the Sand Heads. English vessels fell into the hands of the French by the dozen, and were carried to the Isle of France and confiscated. It was currently reported, and never contradicted, that some of the Calcutta merchants despatched vessels under Danish colors to that island, and purchased their own cargoes at a reduced rate, and brought them back to be sold in Calcutta. In 1808, the sun of Danish prosperity set for ever in Bengal, after it had shone for a little more than half a century. England robbed Denmark of her fleet at Copenhagen, and a detachment of British troops crossed over from Barrackpore and took possession of the town, and of the well filled store houses of Serampore, while the Hon. Captain George Elliot, the son of the Governor-General, Lord Minto, sent up the boats of the *Modeste* frigate, which he commanded, and seized on three rich vessels lying in the harbour. From the blow thus inflicted, the Danish East India Company never recovered. Serampore was restored after the pacification of Europe in 1815, but the Company was on the verge of bankruptcy. The traffic in country piece goods, which had been the staple of Danish commerce, had begun to yield to the rivalry of English manufactures, and, a short time after the restoration of the town, the products of English power looms, completely extinguished the trade in Indian goods. Since 1815, one vessel, and one vessel alone, has visited the port.

For the last thirty years the settlement has been maintained only by draining the home treasury. The King of Denmark has at length yielded to the wishes of his people and disposed of possessions which entailed a heavy expense; and Serampore and Tranquebar were at the beginning of the last year transferred to the British Government, for the sum of Twelve lakhs of Rupees, 120,000*l.*, and on the 11th of October 1845, just ninety years and three days after Soetman had first hoisted the Danish flag in this town, it was taken down, and the English colors hoisted in its stead.

The celebrity of the town through the Christian world, arises from its having been the residence of the Serampore Missionaries. It appears that about the year 1796 or '97, two Moravian Missionaries settled in it, and acquired a knowledge of the native language, and gave Christian instruction to all who resorted to them; but they never went out among the people, and their labours soon ceased. On the 13th of October 1799 four Baptist Missionaries, who had arrived in the *Criterion*, an American vessel, and had neither friend nor acquaintance to receive them in Calcutta, proceeded to Serampore by the advice of their kind commander, Capt. Wickes, and took lodgings at the hotel, which was then in a very flourishing state. Their intention was to join Dr. Carey in the district of Malda, and pursue their Missionary labours in that neighbourhood. The Editors of the Calcutta journals, at that period, had probably never heard of the existence of such a denomination as the Baptist, and therefore announced that four *Papist* Missionaries had arrived in Bengal. Just at this period the emissaries of Buonaparte were known to be in the country in the guise of Roman Catholic priests, collecting political and military information. It used to be affirmed at the time, that Mr. Pitt, having discovered the intention of the French to send an engineer officer on this errand to India, had contrived to obtain his portrait, and transmitted it to Lord Wellesley, who on the arrival of the agent in Calcutta sent for him, and enquired whether he recognized the likeness, and on his confessing the object which had brought him out immediately ordered him to quit the country. We cannot vouch for the truth of this anecdote, but it was generally believed at the time, and may serve to explain the vigilance which the British Government was obliged to exercise at this season of political danger.

When Lord Wellesley's eye caught the announcement that four Papist missionaries had arrived in a foreign vessel, and had proceeded direct to the foreign settlement of Serampore without so much as landing in Calcutta, he concluded that their mission was connected with the machinations of the French Government. The Commander of the vessel in which they had arrived was therefore summoned to the Police, and ordered to enter without delay into an engagement to take them back, on pain of not being allowed to discharge his cargo. In this dilemma, the Missionaries applied to the Rev. David Brown, who enjoyed the confidence of the Governor-General, and who explained the error to his Lordship, and assured him that Dr. Marshman and Mr. Ward, and their two colleagues were not French spies, but Dissenting Missionaries; and the embargo on the vessel was immediately removed. But their journey into the country to join Dr. Carey was effectually arrested. At that period, no European was permitted to proceed into the interior without a pass. The rule was not rigidly enforced, and many resided in various parts of the country, under what used to be termed the " tacit permission" of Government, being liable, however, at any moment to deportation when they began to give trouble. The mistrust which the Government servants entertained of all Missionary efforts, and the notoriety which the arrival of the Missionaries had obtained in official circles, convinced them that their movements would be watched, and that it would be unsafe for them to leave Serampore for Mudnabatty without a pass; and Lord Wellesley refused to grant this, or to permit the establishment of a Press beyond the limits of the metropolis. This was in strict conformity with the spirit of the age, and the instructions of the Directors, and did not, we believe, originate in any personal feeling of hostility to Missionary efforts. Perhaps Lord Wellesley, knowing, as he well did, the dread with which the authorities at home regarded the establishment of Missions in India, was not altogether displeased to find the Missionaries settled under the safeguard of a foreign flag, and beyond the reach of British interference. During the remaining five years of his administration, though they were known to be in the habit of preaching and distributing tracts and Scriptures in the British territories, he offered no interruption to their labors, and was not deterred from conferring on the senior Missionary, Dr. Carey, an important post under Government, from the fact of his being a Missionary.

A few weeks after they had thus been constrained to take up their abode in Serampore, they were joined by Dr. Carey, when he and Dr. Marshman and Mr. Ward commenced the establishment known throughout the Christian world as the " Serampore Mission," and which subsisted as a separate and independent agency for the diffusion of Christian truth in India till the death of the last of the number, Dr. Marshman, in 1837. As soon as they had determined to make Serampore the scene of their labours, the local authorities offered them every encouragement, and reported the establishment of the Mission to the Court of Denmark, which had for more than a century enjoyed the distinction of fostering Christian Missions in the east. His Majesty, Frederick the VI. was pleased to take the institution under his own especial protection, and to direct the public functionaries to afford the Missionaries every support.   While Lord Wellesley continued at the head of the Indian adminstration, no opportunity was afforded them of appreciating the value of this protection; but no sooner had he quitted India than the British Government began to take umbrage at the labours of the Missionaries, which on the arrival of Lord Minto was increased into the most active hostility. The Governor of Serampore was ordered to withdraw his protection from them, and to send them and their Press to Calcutta, that they might be within reach of the British authorities. He informed Lord Minto that they were under the immediate patronage of the Danish Crown, and that it was impossible for him to disregard the positive orders of his own sovereign.   The most strenuous efforts were made by the British Government to shake his resolution ; but he continued manfully to resist all importunity, and was at length gratified with the information that the surrender of the Missionaries and of the Press was dispensed with. It is due to the memory of Lord Minto to state that he became gradually reconciled to the prosecution of Missionary labours in Bengal, and endeavoured by personal kindness to obliterate the remembrance of the official severity he had manifested when he was new to his office, and listened to the advice of those in India who were anxious to persuade him that the salvation of the British empire around him depended on the banishment of the Serampore Missionaries.

It would be foreign to the design of this article, to enter into any detail of the labours, the devotion, the liberality and the sufferings of the Three men, whose remains now repose in the same hallowed ground in the Mission cemetry at Serampore, together with those of their highly gifted and affectionate associate, Mr. Mack.   No burying ground in India is consecrated with four such tombs.   But as we have touched on the singular circumstances connected with the origin of their establishment, we shall be forgiven for making a slight allusion to the scarcely less remarkable circumstances which marked its close.   The three illustrious men, who had thus devoted the energies of their life to the work of envangelizing the Heathen, devoted to this object also the pecuniary result of their labor, instead of enriching their families. We speak greatly within the mark when we state that they were enabled, by the blessing of God on their labors, to devote more than Fifty thousand Pounds Sterling to the Mission which they had established. Next to the success of their labors, the object which they held most dear was the independent prosecution of them. A gradual change of circumstances, however, at length curtailed their incomes, and they found themselves constrained to solicit the assistance of friends in England for the support of their Missions. For other departments of labor they had always received support from home. Mr. Ward died in 1823; Dr. Carey in 1834. In 1837, Dr. Marshman's iron constitution began to break up, and the gloomy prospects of the Mission weighed heavily on his spirits. The stations which he and his colleague had been instrumental in planting, required an outlay of more than 2000 Rupees a month; the laborers stationed in them were three months in arrears, and their missonary utility was crippled by their pecuniary embarrassments. At the beginning of 1837, the late Mr. Mack was deputed to England to endeavor to recruit the finances of the Mission. He found its warmest friends disheartened and lukewarm. Its firmest and most wealthy supporter, Mr. Samuel Hope, of Liverpool, was removed by death in that year, and the sums which, out of a fortune of between Two and Three hundred thousand Pounds Sterling, he had generously advanced to the good cause at Serampore in that spirit of affectionate confidence which subsisted between him and the Missionaries, were rigidly demanded by his representatives. Despairing of success in the object of his mission, Mr. Mack was constrained to open a negotiation with the Baptist Missionary Society, on the basis of transferring the whole missionary establishment to their management. While these arrangements were under discussion, Dr. Marshman was gradually sinking into his grave. Day after day did he anxiously enquire whether the mail had arrived, with tidings of Mr. Mack's success; but no mail came. It happened that the mails of July and August of that year, were unaccountably delayed, and arrived in conjunction with those of September, The intelligence, therefore, of the commencement, progress and conclusion of Mr. Mack's negotiations reached Calcutta just twelve hours after Dr. Marshman's spirit had been joined to those of his beloved colleagues, who had preceded him to their eternal reward; and he was thus happily spared the anguish of hearing, in the last moments of his earthly existence, that the Mission to which for thirty-seven years he had consecrated health, strength, time and fortune, had passed from Serampore. It was buried in his sepulchre.

There is a peculiar interest attached to the place which was the scene of their holy and disinterested labours. A feeling of solemnity pervades the mind in contemplating the spot where the first Missionary press was established; the first version of the Scriptures in the languages of this Presidency, and the first tract in the language of Bengal was printed, and the first vernacular school opened; the first converted Hindu baptized; —and the first Steam Engine, ever seen in India, set up, in order to manufacture paper for the printing of the Sacred Scriptures. The Botanic garden in which Dr. Cary took such delight, and which he stocked with plants collected from all parts of the world, is kept up with the most affectionate veneration for his memory. The Chapel, consecrated by the ministrations of the Serampore Missionaries, has been recently repaired and improved, and the plain, simple old pulpit, in which they and their associate, Mr. Mack, preached for forty-five years, is still preserved in the place where it so long stood. The College which they erected from the proceeds of their own labour at an expence of a Lakh and a half of Rupees, after having fallen into abeyance through the failure of the houses of business in Calcutta, in which its funds had been unhappily deposited, and from the removal by death of its chief supporters both in England and in India, is now undergoing repair, and arrangements are in progress in connection with the Baptist Missionary Society, which it is hoped will result in carrying out to the fullest extent the comprehensive views of its founders.

We must not forget in this brief reference to Serampore, to notice that the Revd. David Brown, the Senior Chaplain on the Bengal establishment, made it his favorite residence soon after he was appointed Provost of the College of Fort William in Calcutta. He purchased a house on the banks of the river at the southern extremity of the town, and gradually acquired possession of a large extent of ground, to which he gave the appearance of a park. Here, at Aldeen House, he spent all the time he could spare from his official avocations in Calcutta. The deep interest which he took in the spiritual improvement of India, combined with a conformity of religious views and feelings, produced a close intimacy between him and the Serampore Missionaries. For many years, the plans which they devised for the spread of general knowledge and evangelical truth through the country were discussed with the utmost frankness and confidence at Aldeen House, and scarcely any important measure was adopted, in the severe trials which the Missionaries were called to undergo during the first twelve years of their settlement, without the valuable advice of Mr. Brown. A few years after he had taken up his abode in Serampore, Mr. Martyn and Mr. Corrie arrived from England as Chaplains on the establishment, and came up to reside with him, and took a lively interest in the various conferences which were held at his house in the spirit of a total oblivion of all denominational differences. The Rev. Dr. Buchanan was also a frequent visitor at Aldeen, and it was there that the rough sketch of an Ecclesiastical Establishment for British India, which he embodied and published in a separate pamphlet on his arrival in England, was repeatedly brought under discussion, It was at one of these friendly meetings that Dr. Marshman asked him where he expected to obtain funds for the endowment of the Establishment, on which he replied, that the Temple lands would eventually answer for the Churches, and the Brahman's lands for the Ministers, to which Dr. Marshman replied with deep emphasis: " You will never, never obtain them, Dr. Buchanan." The Temple of Radhabullub, which we have alluded to as having been abandoned when the river had approached too near to allow brahmans to receive gifts with a safe conscience, was purchased by Mr. Brown and fitted up for a dwelling. In the centre compartment where the image once stood, an organ was placed, and the dome which once resounded with the songs of idolatry, echoed with the praises of the living and true God, and his son Jesus Christ. As yet, Puseyism was not born. The feeling which animated Brown and Martyn and Corrie, was that enlarged spirit of Christian liberality which imparted such lustre to the character of Newton and Scott. They rejoiced in holding fellowship with Carey, and Marshman and Ward; and often did the three ministers of the Established Church meet their three Dissenting brethren around the same altar, and their mingled prayers and praises ascended in unison to Him, whose most earnest and repeated command when on earth, was, that his disciples should love one another.— But the place consecrated by these holy associations was but lately turned into a Rum manufactory, and the brand which its casks bore was that of the " Pagoda Distillery !"

Serampore contains three places of Christian worship. The Mission Chapel, to which we have already alluded, was part of the building purchased in 1800 by Dr. Carey and his associates, and was till lately surrounded with private rooms. It was subsequently repaired, and covered with an iron roof, which has given it a light and elegant appearance. A Roman Catholic Chapel was originally erected in 1764, but it was found too small for the increasing community. It was therefore taken down in 1776, when the present handsome edifice was erected in its stead at an expense of 13,386 Rupees, from subscriptions raised partly in Serampore but chiefly in Calcutta, under the auspices of a family which stood foremost in wealth and liberality half a century ago, but had apparently become extinct,— we allude to that of the Barettos. Adjoining the Catholic Church, a Convent has been erected within the last three or four years. The establishment consists of two nuns and two assistants. The Lutheran Church was built by public subscriptions through the exertions of Colonel Bie, and completed in 1805, at an expense of 18,500 Rupees. Of this sum 1,000 Rupees was contributed by the Marquis of Wellesley, who is said to have remarked at the time, that nothing was wanting to Barrackpore Park, but the distant view of a steeple. The sum of 8,000 Rupees was collected in Calcutta, and the remainder in Serampore and Denmark. No service has ever been performed in it by a Danish clergyman, in consequence of the capture of the town by the English soon after its erection, and the small body of Danes resident in it subsequently to the restoration of the town. The services have been gratuitously conducted by the Serampore Missionaries and their colleague, Mr. Mack, during the long period of thirty-seven years. The Church has a lofty steeple, which is surmounted by a globe and cross; but this circumstance did not prevent Dr. Carey and his associates preaching in it for years, though they would doubtless have objected to the erection of such a symbol in any edifice built under their own immediate direction. It has also the rudiments of an altar,—but it was orientation. The only property belonging to the Church consists of a pair of large silver candlesticks presented in 1803 by Mrs. Schow. According to the usual custom, these candles were placed on the altar, for six months, when the Church was covered with the insignia of mourning on the death of the late King, and regularly lighted up during the hours of divine service; but as this exhibition of lighted candles in the day on such an occasion, was in comformity with national usage, and not connected with superstitious associations, the late Mr. Mack raised no manner of objection to their introduction, nor were they found to weaken the effect of his admirable discourses.

Immediately above the town of Serampore lies the village of Chatra, which presents no object of interest. A little to the west of it is the village of Shawrafully, remarkable only as the family residence of the Rajah of whom we have already spoken. The late head of the family, Hurrishchunder, was greatly distinguished by the spirit of his enterprizes, and his religious liberality.   For nearly a century there had been a large and flourishing market at the neighbouring village of Buddybati, which yielded a considerable revenue to its proprietors.   He determined to erect a rival market in its vicinity on his own ground, and to draw off its traffic.   He commenced with establishing an image of the goddess of Kali, under the name of Nistarini, or 'Kali the deliverer.'   He set the pundits to search the Shastras for the precise form of the idol, and collected the most renowned sculptors from all parts of the conntry, and by the united labours of the pundits and sculptors, obtained an image which is celebrated among the natives for its symmetry and beauty.   So large was the sum expended in the preparation of the image and the construction of its temple, that it is popularly estimated at more that 10,000 Rupees.   After the completion of the shrine, he spared no expence to establish the market, in which he at length succeeded.   It has become a source of great emolument to his family, for he himself died soon after, leaving two widows with directions for each of them to adopt a son.   This has been done and the two minor Rajahs will soon attain their majority, and succeed to an estate, which, during their nonage, has been cleared of the encumbrances with which the uncalculating expenditure of Hurishchunder had saddled it.   Ashootosh Deb, the son of the well known Ramdoolol Deb, the millionaire of his day, and himself a wealthy and influential citizen of Calcutta, lately endeavoured to break up this new market and establish one on his own property, but his efforts have proved entirely abortive.

Adjoining the village of Shawrafully, lies Buddybati, or the residence of the Mediciners, so called from the number of families of the medical caste which it formerly contained.   The present native head of the Calcutta Medical College, comes from this village.   Until it was supplanted by the rival market to which we have just reverted, the market of Buddybati was the largest in the vicinity of Calcutta, to the establishment of which city, indeed, it may be said to owe its chief importance.   There are two market days in the week; and as it adjoins the great road leading to Singoor and Dwarhatta, and which was till lately the great thoroughfare to Benares, the produce of the numerous gardens and orchards with which each side of that high road is adorned for miles inland, are poured into these markets, and conveyed by more than a hundred boats to Calcutta, which depends on them for a very large portion of its vegetable supplies.   The map notices a temple of Bhudra Kali, which, though an ancient establishment, is not much in vogue.   There is, however, another sacred place in its neighbourhood, which is held in great veneration, especially by Hindus who reside at a distance from it.   It is called Nimaitirth's Ghat.   In popular estimation, whatever place a Muhapurush, or man renowned for his religious merit, has honored with his presence, is deemed a tirth, or holy place.   Chitunya, the great modern heresiarch as he is considered by the orthodox, though revered as an incarnation of the deity by his own followers, rested at this ghat on his journey to Jugunnath, Poori in Orissa, and reposed under a Nim tree, which produces no flowers fit to be offered to the gods.   He performed an act of mental devotion in which he expressed a desire for some sacrificial flower, when the tree instantly presented him with a *vilva* flower.   We may here observe that if we were to proceed from shrine to shrine in this land of superstition, we should invariably find that every place of sanctity or renown, has its local legend of some miraculous occurrence, and that the superstitions of Europe and of the East, present in this respect, likewise, a very palpable coincidence.   The ghat, notwithstanding its supernatural myth, has no peculiar attraction for those who live on the banks of the holy Ganges, the great stream of sanctity, which affords the means of religious merit to all who may dip themselves in it, through the whole course of its current ; but the people of Orissa, who come up in large numbers to the great festival at Tribeny, about thirty miles higher up the river, never fail to pay their devotions at this shrine.

The next stage brings us to the village and heath of Champdani, once as much dreaded for scenes of robbery and murder as Hounslow or Bagshot, but which the traveller may now cross with perfect confidence.   The place is marked down as Mr. W. Storm's factory.   The estate was conferred as rent free tenure on Sir Eyre Coote by the Nabob of Moorshedabad, and the title deeds are still in the possession of the native family, to whom the lands have come by purchase.   It lies exactly opposite the village of Pultah, where Regiments proceeding from Barrackpore and Calcutta to the Upper Provinces, or from them to the neighbourhood of the Presidency, cross the river.   It may serve to demonstrate the snail like pace of internal improvements in Bengal, to state, that this is the only horse ferry within thirty miles of Calcutta.   On the ghat stand three or four monuments erected to the memory of travellers who have here completed the journey of life ; but their names and connections have long since perished in this land of pilgrimage and change.

Immediately to the north of this ghat is the French Garden of Giretty, about one-third the extent of the Barrackpore

Park.   If there be any one place in Bengal, after Gour with its ruined palaces and mosqes, which presents an air of the most melancholy desolation, heightened by the remembrance of its former beauty and cheerfulness, it is this country house of the French Governors of Chandernagore.   Whether we pass it from the river side, or look upon it from the road, it wears the appearance of the thickest jungle of the Soonderbuns, where the imagination pictures to itself the foot marks of the tyger and the wild deer.   At the northern extremity of the grounds are the remains of its once splendid mansion, which has become so entirely dilapidated as to be scarcely even picturesque.   In this house, seventy years ago, were assembled the beauty and fashion of Chinsurah, Chandernagore, Serampore and Calcutta. The walls of the saloon, which was thirty-six feet in height and of proportionate width and length, were adorned with paintings, and when in all its splendor, and filled with company, must have carried back the mind to some of the public rooms in the Chateau of Versailles.   Here the Governor of Chandernagore entertained Clive and Verelst and Hastings and Sir W. Jones, with a degree of magnificence little inferior to that exhibited in the old Government House in Calcutta.   The long alley of magnificent trees to the north of the house was formerly filled with the carriages of guests to the number it is said of more than fifty.   Captain Stavorinus tells us, that on the 22d of February 1770, the Dutch paid a national visit to the French Governor, and as these visits were accompanied with much ceremony, when the guest was received at the chief factory, the Dutch Director preferred paying it at the country seat of Giretty.   The party set off from Chinsurah at four o'clock, in six carriages, and reached the chateau at six, where they were received at the bottom of the steps and conducted into a large saloon, in which the principal ladies and gentlemen of Chandernagore were assembled.   At seven, the Dutch guests were invited to witness a play in a slight building, which had been erected for the purpose.   The play was over at ten, when they were led into a large room, in which a hundred ladies and gentlemen sat down to an elegant supper.   The party broke up at one, and returned to Chinsurah.

The next town on the map, is Bhuddeshur, the greatest mart between Culna and Calcutta.   The numerous brick built dwellings and warehouses with which it is filled, have been erected within the present century, and there are many who can remember the time, when it was a place of no commercial importance and contained only a few thatched store rooms. It is the great granary of the metropolis, and of the country for twenty miles round it.   It derives its name from a celebrated image of Shiva, the origin of which lies in unfathomable antiquity. All the shrines throughout the country, such as Tarukeshur, Bhubuneshur, Bydenath, with many others, the establisment of which is beyond the memory of man, and of which no record is known to exist, are styled *Swayumbhu,* or the self existent. They are believed to have come into existence without human instrumentality; and they possess this peculiarity, that they may be touched by the hands of Sudras without being polluted, and without the necessity of re-consecration. The image at Bhuddeshur is of this number. It is chiefly popular with the female sex, and is visited by Hindu ladies of the first respectability in a circle of ten or a dozen miles. It is an act of great religious merit to refre_h the head of the image in the burning month of May with an effusion of cold-water; and women may be seen day after day at the shrine, pouring water on it, from a silver or earthen water pot. This act of devotion is accompanied with offerings to the temple, and a gift to the officiating priest, which varies from four annas to two Rupees, according to the means of the devotee. Vows are also made to the god at Bhuddeshur, for the attainment of every variety of object; for deliverance from present difficulties, impending distress, for the acquisition of husband, wives, children, wealth or honor; and the vow is paid by offering a hundred thousand leaves of Shiva's favorite tree, the *vilvu* to his stone representative. Ten millions of leaves would always be more grateful to the deity, and more advantageous to the interests of the devotee; but where can this number of leaves be obtained? The vows of the faithful are therefore in general limited to the more moderate figure.

Chandernagore stands next on the map. At what precise period it was first established, we have not been able to ascertain; but we find it mentioned as a French settlement in 1700. It appears to have made little progress for more than a quarter of a century after that year. Its prosperity dates from the arrival of Mons. Dupleix, the most enlightened and energetic administrator the French have ever had in India. The boldness and vigour with which he prosecuted his commercial enterprizes in this country gave an extraordinary impulse to the prosperity of Chandernagore; and during his incumbency more than two thousand brick houses were erected in it. In 1740, while Calcutta was in a state of comparative insignificance, Chandernagore had risen to great opulence and splendor under his influence. It was in the mansion on the banks of the river, on the site of which stands the present Government House, that he contemplated the establishment of a French power in this country, and determined himself to lay the foundation of it;

but Providence had otherwise determined the destiny of India. In the year 1742, upon the first irruption of the Mahrattas into Bengal, tacit permission was given to surround the European factories on the banks of the Hooghly with fortifications. Both the French and the English availed themselves of this permission, and put their settlements in a state of defence : but it was done by the English in the little spirit of counting house economy ; by the French in the spirit of political ambition ; in the one case to protect the godowns from plunder ; in the other, to repel the most formidable attack that might be made by the native powers. Hence, while Calcutta was found unable to stand for two days the assault of so contemptible a rabble as the Viceroy's army, it required all the resources of European strategy, and the assistance of three men of war, besides a large land force to reduce Chandernagore. It is certain that if the infuriated Nabob had turned his arms against the French settlement, he would have been obliged ignominiously to raise the siege, and would probably have been pursued by the French to his own capital ; and the foundation might then have been laid of a French monarchy in Bengal.

The capture of Chandernagore by Lord Clive, who was resolved to extinguish all European influence in Bengal except that which he himself directed, inflicted a blow on the prosperity of the French from which they never recovered. The palmy days of Chandernagore extended only from the arrival of Dulpeix to its capture by the English during a period of little more than thirty years. As the star of England rose on the horizon of India, that of the French declined. We have had no means of access to the records of Chandernagore, but from the reports of travellers who visited it between the peace of 1763, and the commencement of the French revolution in 1793, it would appear that every effort to restore its former splendor proved unsuccessful. The aim of the French was the establishment of a political power in India, and when that object was defeated by the genius of Clive, and all their dreams of ambition were destroyed, they sunk into comparative insignificance, and were far outstripped in the race of commercial enterprize by their plodding neighbours, the Dutch. In 1793, Chandernagore was captured by the English, and though it was restored twenty-two years after, it has since that time existed as a French establishment without any object, political or commercial, and the only advantage it confers on the parent state consists in the patronage of an overgrown establishment. While the affairs of Serampore have been managed with great ease by two Danish civilians, the administration of Chandernagore embraces no fewer than ten European officers.

The same anomaly is visible on the Coast, in the settlement of Pondicherry, which contains an establishment of officers altogether disproportioned to the size of the territory, or the requisitions of public duty. The settlement of Chandernagore is now supported from the Three hundred chests of Opium, which the French receive from the British Government on the condition of not engaging in the manufacture of that article—for which they enjoy no facilities. This privilege was restored to them at the Congress of Vienna through the forethought of Talleyrand; but a privilege of the same nature, though not to the same extent, which the Danes had enjoyed before the war, was lost through the ignorance or supineness of their Minister.

Chandernagore has two Catholic Churches. The fine old Church of St. Louis, on which four pieces of cannon were mounted in the siege of the town in 1757, was demolished during its progress. A magazine in the rear of it was afterwards fitted up for a Church, and in it, we believe, divine service is still performed. In the year 1726, the Italians who had long before established a Mission at Agra, built a Church on the banks of the river at Chandernagore, with a dome for the roof; and it continues to this day in a state of complete preservation, demonstrating how easy it would be to construct public edifices, which should resist the effects of the climate, and the depredations of white ants, by simply avoiding the use of wood on which both time and the ants make so rapid and fatal an impression in India.

Of the history of Chandernagore during the eventful period of the French Revolution of 1792 and 1793 we have never been able to obtain any consistent account, and there may, therefore, be some little discrepancy in the reports which have been handed down. But it is generally understood that the infection of revolutionary principles extended even to this distant possession of France. The French populace of Chandernagore determined to enact on a small scale the proceedings of Paris, and revolutionize the Goverument. When they had succeeded in obtaining possession of the public authority, the Governor fled to his country house at Giretty. When it was announced that the mob of Paris had proceeded to Versailles and conducted the King as a prisoner to the capital, the mob of Chandernagore are said to have gone to Giretty, and brought back the Governer in triumph to the town, where he was subjected to much indignity. He was at length released from his dangerous position by the aid of the English Government, who sent a party of soldiers and put down the revolution. Soon after, the town was taken formal possession of, on the declaration of hostilities in Europe.

The Dutch settlement of Chinsurah lies within three miles of Chandernagore.   There is no intermediate object of interest except the field on which Col. Forde defeated the troops of the Dutch, and nipped in the bud the projects of ambition in which they had begun to indulge.   The circumstances are so well known, that a very brief reference to them will serve the object of this sketch.   The Nabob, Meer Jaffir, who owed the enjoyment of his master's throne to the English, became anxious to throw off their yoke, and encouraged the Dutch to import troops, and to attempt the establishment of a counter influence in Bengal. A large fleet arrived from Batavia, consisting of seven ships, three of thirty-six guns, three of twenty-six, and one of sixteen, with 1100 troops, European and Malay.   It was given out that the armament was intended for the Dutch settlements on the Coromandal Coast, but had been *obliged* to run up the Hooghly. It was impossible for a man of Clive's penetration to mistake its object.   He was not ignorant of the feeling or the intrigues of the Nabob.   The Dutch had hitherto confined themselves strictly to mercantile undertakings.   Their commercial privileges were not curtailed by the establishment of British authority in Bengal; on the contrary, the transfer of political influence to a European nation of approved good faith, with whom the Dutch were on terms of amity, was likely to prove beneficial to their trade.   It was clear to the mind of Clive that their object was to take advantage of the breaking up of the Mahommedan power, and endeavour to supplant the English in Bengal.   Although he had no such absolute proof of these designs as to justify him in the bold measure he determined to pursue, yet we, at this time of day, have the clearest evidence of the fact, in the journal of one of their own officers, Stavorinus, who writes, " The Dutch began to trade in Bengal as early as the commencement of the last century; they were always the first in opulence and importance, till the English became the rulers of the country, in the last revolution; and perhaps they would still have been so, had the well planned, but badly executed attempt, made as before-mentioned, during the administration of the Governor General Mossel in 1759, succeeded to our wishes."   The two nations were at peace, and Clive clearly had no right to prevent the progress of Dutch ships and Dutch troops to their own settlement.   But he did not fail to perceive that the presence of a large foreign force, in the vicinity of Calcutta, composed in a great measure of European soldiers, and commanded by European officers, would not fail to disturb the dependence of the Nabob on the English, and kindle hopes of ambition which would have been to him a source of great embarrassment.   He determined to defeat the projects of the

Dutch at the risk of his own commission. He was accustomed to affirm that an Indian Governor must always act with a halter about his neck, and in this instance, he exemplified his own assertion. During a period of profound peace, he captured the Dutch vessels proceeding up the river, and sent Col. Forde to attack the Dutch army, and prevent its reaching Chinsurah. Forde, who seemed to feel the halter already chaffing his neck, demanded the Governor's written authority for an act so inconsistent with the law of nations. Clive, to whom the note of demand was addressed, received it when playing at cards. Without quitting the table he wrote an answer in pencil—" Dear Forde, fight them immediately. I will send you the Order of Council to-morrow." There is nothing greater than this in all Livy. Forde met and discomfited the Dutch, and Dutch ambition was quenched by the daring genius of Clive, as that of the French had previously been.

Of the origin of Chinsurah we have been able to obtain no account, but one of the escutcheons in the Church, refers to a Governor who died in 1665. Fort Gustavus, before it was entirely demolished eighteen years ago, bore the date of 1687 on its northern, and 1692 on its southern gate. It must therefore have been a century and a half old when it was levelled with the ground. The beams of this edifice, which were of the largest scantling and equal in size to two of our modern beams, were found to be as sound as the day they were inserted into the building. They were of Java teak, and had been sent up from Batavia. It may not be unimportant thus to place on record the fact that teak has been found to resist the humidity of the climate, and the attacks of white ants for a hundred and fifty years. The garden of the Government House was tastefully laid out, and adorned with statuary. The statues have long since disappeared, and the walk in the alley of trees, is now trod only by British soldiers.

The Dutch grew and flourished in India, as they had done in Europe, by their steady perseverance in mercantile pursuits, from which they appear to have been diverted on only one occasion, when in 1757, the successes of Clive revealed the weakness of the Mahommedan government, which they had been accustomed to regard with feelings of awe, and to conciliate with humiliating gifts, and gave them hopes of being able to establish a political power. But Col. Forde cured them of all such ambition. We think the period between 1770 and 1780 may be regarded as that in which their trade had attained its most palmy state. At an earlier period, the charge of the Dutch settlements in Bengal appears to have greatly exceeded the profits. A large and useless military force was entertained, and the agents of the Company, plundered them in the most flagrant manner. Their conduct is thus described in a letter from the superior authorities at Batavia : : " For a series of years, a succession of Directors in Bengal have been guilty of the greatest enormities, and the foulest dishonesty; they have looked upon the Company's effects confided to them, as a booty thrown open to their depredations ; they have most shamefully and arbitrarily falsified the invoice-prices ; they have violated, in the most disgraceful manner, all our orders and regulations, with regard to the purchase of goods, without paying the least attention to their oaths and duty."

At a subsequent period the Military and Naval establishments in Bengal were reduced to ten artillery men, sixty-nine seamen and marines and forty-eight soldiers, including officers, and seven surgeons and assistants. At the same time, we find that there were sixty-four civilians, and two ecclesiastical functionaries. Great and successful efforts were made to repress the spirit of peculation which had grown up in the administration. It appears that the chief profit of the Company was derived, not so much from its exports to Europe, as from the trade in Opium to Java. Eight hundred chests of the drug were annually obtained at the Patna Agency and shipped to Batavia, from whence it was distributed through the Archipelago and possibly sent on to China. Each chest contained 125 lbs. and cost the Company between 7 and 800 Rupees, including freight, insurance and other charges. The chest sold at Batavia for about 1250 Rs. ; and the clear profit on the investment of the year was about Four lakhs of Rupees.

The settlement of Chinsurah was subordinate to that of Batavia, and all vacancies were filled up by the public authorities of that place, the local Council being permitted only to nominate to officiating appointments. The Government consisted of a Governor or Director, and seven members of Council, five of whom had a right to vote, as well as to advise, while two had no other privilege than that of advising. The chief was obliged to submit all matters of importance to the consideration of his Council, and to be guided by the voice of the majority ; but as its members were dependent on him for their emoluments, the check of the Council was more nominal than real. Although the official salary of the Chief Director was exceedingly small, his perquisites were very extensive. Mr. Vernet stated the annual expences of his household at 36,000 Rs. which was considered moderate, in comparison with those of his predecessors, some of whom expended not less than a Lakh of Rupees a year, a sum equal to that which the English President at Calcutta was supposed to disburse in his domestic establishment. Though only the head of a commercial factory he maintained no little

s 1

state. He was the only person in the settlement who enjoyed the privilege of being carried " in a palankeen, sitting on a chair"—this kind of vehicle is now completely extinct. When he rode through the town, the natives were obliged in some places to play on their instruments of music. He was preceded by *chobdars*, or attendants armed with a staff entirely covered with silver, while the inferior members of Council were allowed chobdars with only half mounted staves. The members of Council were styled senior merchants, as in the English service ; and each one had some distinct department of business entrusted to him. The fiscal, or sheriff, who was also the mayor of the town, had the rank of a senior, with the pay of a junior merchant ; but in those days, the emoluments of one who united in his person the powers of Judge and Magistrate, made his mere pay a matter of indifference. He had authority to punish by flogging at a stake, or by fines, and the fines appear to have been appropriated to his own use. We are even told that he sometimes fined wealthy banians 20,000 Rs. for the most trifling offence, and tied them up to a post and whipped them till it was paid. It will be readily supposed that the fiscal was the most important person in the town. " The Indians," says Stavorinus, " stand more in awe of him on account of his office than of the Director," just as in our own administration the Magistrate is more regarded by the people than the Commissioner.

Chinsurah is described in 1770 as requiring three quarters of an hour to walk around it. The houses were built, like all other houses of the period, without flues, and the lower floor was almost level with the ground, and of course so completely saturated with humidity that we cease to wonder at the extraordinary mortality of the times. Glass windows were unknown ; frames of twisted cane were used in their stead. " Glass," says our authority," would be very uncomfortable in the great heats which prevail for nine months of the year." This was before Punkas had been invented,—and for them we are indebted to the ingenuity of a Dutch Governor, who first brought them into use, at the close of the last century. Glass windows are now essential, not so much to Indian comfort, as to Indian existence. Without them we should be unable to exclude the cold air in winter, or the hot wind in the summer. In this age of modern luxury, the only mode of keeping a house cool, is to close all the glass windows, darken the rooms, and set the punkas in motion. The Church at Chinsurah which stands immediately above the ghat at the entrance of the town from the south, was the joint gift of Mr. Sichterman and Mr. Vernet. Sichterman erected the steeple, with a chime clock in 1744, and Vernet added the Church twenty-four years afterwards ; thus reminding us of the popular remark that the Frenchman invented the frill, and the Englishman added the shirt. But the Dutch appear to have been very indifferent in matters of religion. For many years after the Church was erected, there was no clergyman ; service was performed by a *Ziekentrooster* or " comforter of the sick," who was not in holy orders. When children were to be christened, the Dutch were obliged to send for a clergyman from Calcutta, " who was liberally paid for his trouble."

The earliest Christian Church in Chinsurah was built by the Armenians in the year 1695, and it was also the first Church ever erected in Bengal, by that once powerful body who united political negotiations with their mercantile enterprizes, and enjoyed such extensive influence throughout the east. In the Church at Chinsurah, there is or there was an epitaph over the tomb of Johannes Marcar, the son of the founder, in which this influence is proudly commemorated. " Here lies interred the famous Kharib—or foreigner Coja Johannes, the son of Marcar, an Armenian, from Julpha, of the country of Shosh. He was a great merchant, honored with the favor of kings and viceroys. He travelled north, south, east and west, and died at Hooghly, in Hindustan, 7th November 1697." The Catholic chapel was completed in 1740, chiefly from funds bequeathed to that object by Mrs. Sebastian Shaw.

The most interesting object at present in Chinsurah is the College, usually denominated the Hooghly College, one of the largest and most efficient educational establishments under the patronage of the state in India. It owes its origin to the munificence of a Mahommedan gentleman, Mahommed Moshin, who left large funds for an embara, or place of Mussulman worship, and an institution of public instruction. Of the sum annually derived from the estates, and the public securities which he left for these objects, more than fifty thousand rupees are devoted to the expences of the College, the average attendance of students in which is about five hundred, while the number borne on the list is about six hundred. This institution in which education is carried to as high a pitch as in any public College in India has contributed to diffuse a thirst for knowledge, not only throughout the Hooghly district, but greatly beyond its limits, and has thus paved the way for the establishment of other institutions at a greater distance from the metropolis. It is held in a splendid mansion, originally erected by one of the French generals who accumulated large fortunes in the Mahratta service, but which was purchased by the Committee of Public Instruction sometime back for a sum greatly inferior to the original cost.

Chinsurah derives considerable interest from its having been the residence of two distinguished characters in the history of

Indian benevolence, Kiernander and Weston.   Kiernander, who arrived in Calcutta soon after its re-capture and re-establishment, was received with the highest distinction by Col. Clive, and the other members of government.   Though he had been stripped of every thing at Cuddalore by Lally, and landed in Calcutta with scarcely a farthing, he soon rose to affluence through the undertakings on which he entered for his own support, in the days in which every thing which a man of spirit touched, turned to gold.   From the proceeds of his own labor, he erected the Old Church, at an expence of 60,000 Rupees, and founded a Mission School for two hundred and fifty children on his own ground.   He was overtaken, by misfortune in 1786. His liberality had exceeded his means, and the sheriff's seal was affixed to his property, and even on the Church he had erected. Strange to say, it was appraised at only 10,000 Rupees and an auctioneering establishment, possibly that of Tulloh and Co., which has been in its vicinity for more than half a century— already contemplated the purchase of it, when one gentleman, either Mr. W. Chambers or Mr. Charles Grant,—stepped forward, and paid down the money.   After his misfortunes, Kiernander retired to Chinsurah, and offered his services to the Dutch, and was appointed Chaplain to the settlement by Mr. Titsing, the Director.   In July 1795, Chinsurah was captured by the English, and Kiernander became a Dutch prisoner of war, and, as such, received a small pittance of Fifty Rupees a month, which was all he now possessed for his subsistence, though not equal to a fifth of the interest of the money he had expended on pious and charitable objects. He closed his chequered career at Calcutta in April, 1799, at the age of eighty-eight, after a residence of more than sixty years in India.   The other individual to whom we allude was Charles Weston, an East Indian gentleman, the son of the Recorder of the Mayor's Court, who was born in Calcutta in 1731, and was the friend and associate of Holwell, and carried arms under him, as a militia man, at the seige of the Old Fort in 1756.   He amassed a large fortune by his commercial speculations, and eventually retired to Chinsurah, where, on the first day of each month, he distributed the sum of sixteen hundred Rupees, " with his own venerable hand," to a large body of the poor and the unfortunate, whom his liberality had attracted to him.

We obtain an interesting view of the state of the Dutch factory of Chinsurah, and the footing on which it stood in reference to the English Government of Bengal, as well as of the manners of the times, from Stavorinus's narrative of the official visit paid by the Dutch Director to the English President in 1770.

Though that writer is by no means an authority in matters beyond the sphere of his knowledge,—as, for instance, when he tells us that the Vedas were originally written in Persian, and that Patna was ninety miles above Chinsurah,—yet there is no reason to question his credibility relative to transactions in which he himself bore a part.   The visit he describes was intended as a compliment to Mr. Cartier, who had just assumed the Government of Calcutta.   The Dutch Director embarked at four o'clock in the afternoon at Chinsurah in company with eight persons.   The garrison was drawn up on the occasion in two lines, and a detachment consisting of an officer and twenty-four privates, accompanied the Director, to serve as his body-guard.   He embarked in the " Company's great budgerow," in the large room of which thirty-six people could sit down to table.   A salute of twenty-one guns announced his departure from his own settlement.   Each individual in his suite had his own private budgerow; there were also two vessels used as kitchens, or cook boats, and two as " storeships," to carry the provisions, for this long voyage from Chinsurah to Calcutta, besides those in which the body guard was embarked. The whole fleet consisted of no fewer than *thirty-three* vessels. It reached Chitpore at seven the next morning, where the party awaited the arrival of the deputation sent from the English Government to receive the Director, and which consisted of Mr. Russel, the second in command, and several other functionaries.   On his arrival, the Dutch gentlemen went on shore, and, after breakfasting at his garden house, proceeded to town in five carriages sent by the Governor, and at ten o'clock alighted at the house prepared for their reception.   It stood next to the old Government House, and had recently been purchased by Mahommed Reza Khan, for a lakh and twenty thousand Rupees. It contained many roomy apartments, and was hung with damask silk, and fitted up in the European style.   In the area before the house stood a company of eighty sepoys commanded by a European officer, and they continued to act as guard of honor as long as the Dutch Director continued in the settlement. As soon as Mr. Cartier heard of his arrival, he proceeded to pay his respects, accompanied by all the members of Council.   The Director said that the object of his visit was to congratulate the Governor on his appointment, and added, as " a particular compliment, that he hoped Mr. Cartier would so well manage matters as to be able to return to Europe in a few years ; to which that gentleman replied with a smile."   This visit of ceremony lasted an hour.   The Governor and Council then departed, and, within half an hour, the Dutch Director proceeded to return the visit, and remained three quarters of an hour.   *At half past twelve* he again went to Government House to dinner, where he found a table of sixty or seventy covers laid out in a large and airy saloon. Half the guests consisted of military officers for whom we are told the Government kept open house every day. When the cloth was removed, a Hookah was placed *on the table* before each one of the company, which they smoked for half an hour: they then rose from table and retired to their respective dwellings.

At six in the evening, Mr Cartier waited on the Dutch Director and conducted him to his country seat at Belvidere, about two Dutch miles from Calcutta, where he was entertained with an excellent concert performed by amateurs, and an elegant supper. At midnight he returned to his residence in town. The next morning at nine, Mr. Cartier again waited on him with an invitation to a grand ball which was to be given that evening at the Court House. The ball was opened by Mrs. Cartier and the Dutch Director. The company was very numerous, and " all were magnificently attired, especially the ladies, who were decked with a profusion of jewels." A collation was served in an adjoining room, and the assembly did not break up before the following morning. The next afternoon, at half past three, the Dutch Director took his leave of the Governor of Calcutta and returned with his suite to the fleet at Chitpore in the Governor's coaches, accompanied by the same gentlemen who had been deputed to welcome him, and escorted by six of the Governor's life guards. The Director was saluted on his departure from Calcutta, as he had been on his arrival, with nineteen guns from the ramparts of Fort William. The visit cost him a thousand Rupees in *buxis*, or vails to the Governor's servants. The fleet weighed anchor with the flood tide, and reached Giretty early the next morning, where the party were received by Mr. Chevalier and breakfasted with him. At nine o'clock—the breakfast in those days of formality and etiquette seems to have been rather early—they rode from Giretty to Chandernagore, and after paying some visits, proceeded to Chinsurah, where all the members of Council were in attendance to honor the return of their chief, and a salute of twenty-one guns was fired from Fort Gustavus.

The Fort, from which these salutes were fired has ceased to exist. The Dutch, finding their settlements in India, a mere burden on their finances, after they had ceased to be valuable as factories, very wisely resolved to dispose of them; and the British Government was not displeased with an opportunity of being relieved from the extravagant and profligate expenditure incurred by their servants on the island of Sumatra. An exchange accordingly took place twenty years ago;

the Dutch were left in undivided possession of the island, and the English received Malacca and Chinsurah, together with the subordinate factories, in lieu of Fort Marlborough and its costly dependencies. The old Fort and Government House at Chinsurah were soon after demolished to make room for a splendid range of barracks capable of accommodating a thousand men, and no token remains to tell that the settlement once belonged to the Dutch, but the escutcheons of the Governors which still continue to adorn the walls of the Church.

Immediately above Chinsurah, and closely adjoining it, we have the town of Hooghly. In a note attached to the 6th Section of Stewart's History of Bengal, we find it stated, " as a circumstance worthy of remark, that the name of Hooghly is never mentioned in Faria de Souza's History of the Portuguese, although he acknowledges that they lost a large town in Bengal in the year 1633, but which he calls Golin." But the identity of Golin and Hooghly is settled beyond controversy by an inscription in the Church at Bandel in which the neighbouring convent of Ugolym, is distinctly mentioned. Hooghly owed its celebrety to the Portuguese, before whose time it was probably an inconsiderable village. They are stated to have established a factory and built a fort there in 1599 ; and in the same year, the Missionaries of the order of St. Augustin founded the Cathedral Church of St. Paul, and the Church of Miserecordia. The Portuguese settlement appears to have risen rapidly to great magnificence. In 1631, it was beseiged by the whole Mogul army of Bengal, which, however, the governor Michael Rodrigues was enabled to repel for three months and a half, and the town is said to have eventually fallen into the hands of the Mahommedans through the treachery of a deserter. The fortifications were undermined, and the Mogul troops rushed in as soon as the mine was sprung, and subjected the place to indiscriminate plunder. It appears that, at the time, there were no fewer than sixty-four large vessels, fifty-seven grabs, and two hundred sloops anchored off the town, of which it is said that only three escaped. All the property afloat or ashore was of course confiscated. The pictures and images which adorned the Churches and had given such great offence to the Mahommedan emperor, were taken down and destroyed. A thousand Portuguese fell in the seige, and four thousand were made prisoners, of whom all the priests, and five hundred of the handsomest boys and girls are stated to have been sent to the Imperial Court of Agra. The extent of the calamity may serve to shew the extent of power and prosperity which the Portuguese had once attained in Bengal. But we are much disposed to doubt the accuracy of the date given of the origin of the settlement. It appears scarcely credible that an establishment could have grown up to such extraordinary magnitude, in so short a period as thirty years. Neither does it appear probable that the foundation of a great Cathedral should be laid in the very first year of a new settlement. It appears safer to assign an earlier date than 1599 for its commencement, and there is reason to infer that it must have been formed soon after the first expedition of the Portuguese to Bengal in 1537, when nine vessels entered the Ganges.

Hooghly, having thus come into the possession of the Mahommedans, was established as the royal Port of Bengal; and Satgong, after fifteen hundred years of commercial splendor, was abandoned. The public offices were removed from it; the importance which it had enjoyed from the time when the Romans ruled the world, was extinguished; and it gradually sunk down into an insignificant village, and is now known only as the residence of a few native paper-makers. It was soon after Hooghly had become the Port of Western Bengal, and the residence of the Mogul officers, that the other European nations began to establish factories in it. The Dutch, the French and the English continued to trade to it, till they were enabled to obtain settlements of their own; after which it began rapidly to decline. It was however of sufficient import-ance in the days of Clive to enduce him to attack it after the re-capture of Calcutta; and he obtained much booty there. This calamity gave the death-blow to its prosperity and con-sequence. On the establishment of Calcutta as the seat of Government, all the public offices of Hooghly were withdrawn, and since that period, only one circumstance has occurred to rescue its name from oblivion. It was at Hooghly that the first press ever established at this presidency was set up; and there in 1778, the first book was printed in Bengal,—the Bengali Grammar of Halhed, from Bengali types,—the punches of which were cut with his own hands by Mr. afterwards Sir Charles Wilkins. But such an event, the harbinger of civilization and improvement, is of itself enough to immortalize any place, even though all its political and commercial greatness should be entirely forgotten. We bring these rambling notices to a close, by stating that the last place mentioned in Joseph's map is Ban-del,—known at present only by its Convent, in which there are no nuns, but which is the oldest Christian Church in existence in Bengal. It was erected in the year in which Queen Eliza-beth sanctioned the establishment of that East India Company which now occupies the throne of the Great Mogul—in 1599.

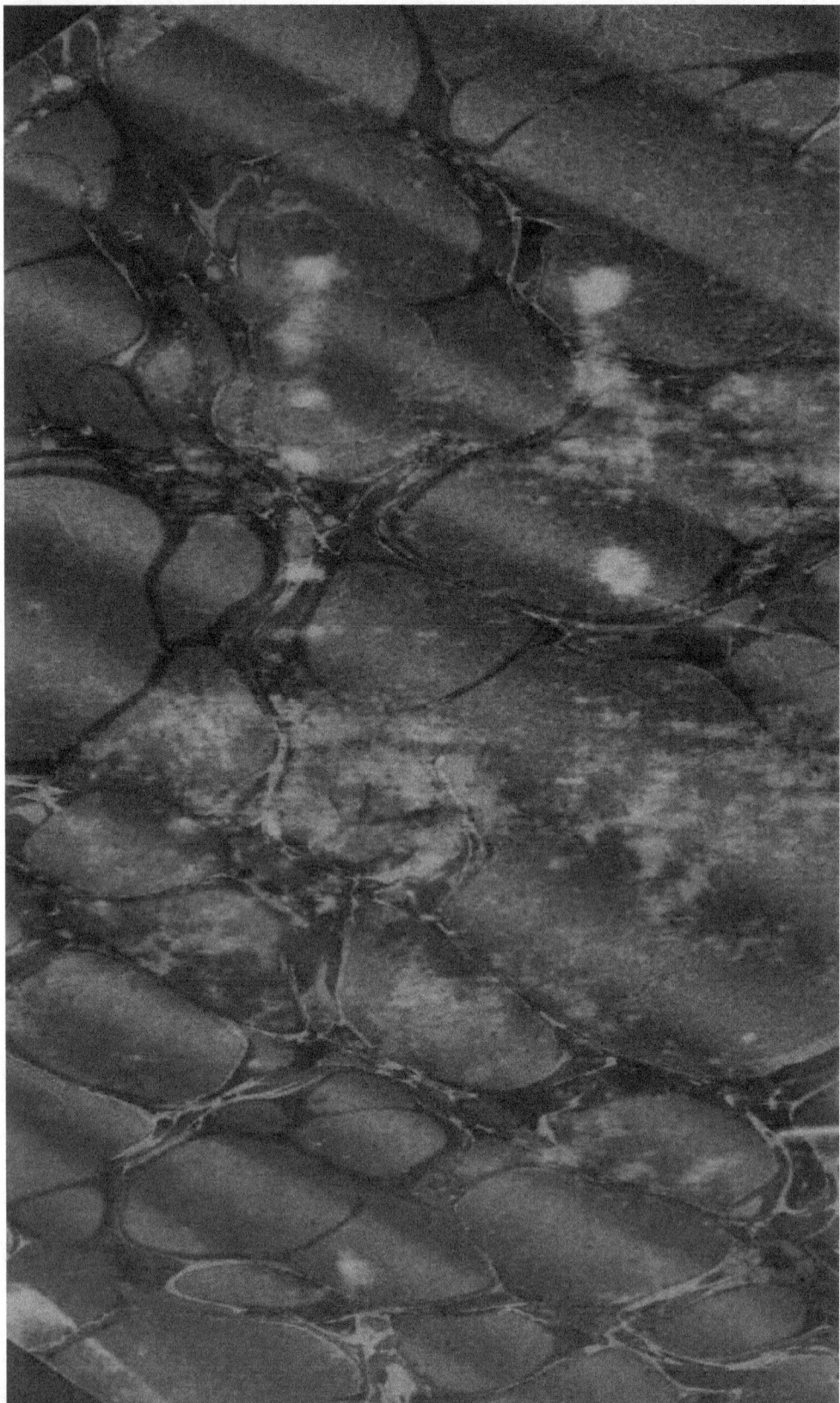

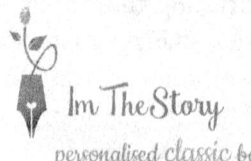

CPSIA information can be obtained
at www.ICGtesting.com
Printed in the USA
BVHW040620130819
555626BV00023B/694/P

9 781318 665112